MEDICINAL PLANTS OF THE WORLD

MEDICINAL PLANTS
OF THE WORLD

An illustrated scientific guide to
important medicinal plants and their uses

Ben-Erik van Wyk

Michael Wink

Timber Press
Portland, Oregon

Published in North America in 2004 by
Timber Press, Inc.
The Haseltine Building
133 S.W. Second Avenue, Suite 450
Portland, Oregon 97204, U.S.A.
www.timberpress.com

First edition, first impression, 2004

ISBN 0-88192-602-7

Note that some of the terms used in this book may refer to registered trade names even if they are not
indicated as such.

IMPORTANT WARNING

This book contains general information about medicinal plants and their uses. It is intended as a
scientific overview and not as a medical handbook for self-treatment. Several medicinal plants described in this book have toxic ingredients and may cause severe allergic reactions or serious poisoning.
Neither the authors nor the publishers can be held responsible for claims arising from the mistaken
identity of plants or their inappropriate use. **Do not attempt self-diagnosis or self-treatment.** Always
consult a medical professional or qualified practitioner.

Cover photograph: *Nelumbo nucifera*, Ben-Erik van Wyk

Managing editor: Reneé Ferreira
Proofreader: David Pearson
Cover: Sally Whines, The Departure Lounge
Typesetting: Melinda Stark, Lebone Publishing Services
Reproduction: Unifoto, Cape Town
Printed and bound by Tien Wah Press (Pte.) Ltd, Singapore

CONTENTS

PREFACE

The aim of this book is to give the reader a bird's eye view of more than 320 of the best-known medicinal plants of the world and their uses, in a compact, colourful and scientifically accurate reference text. A comprehensive review of each species was not our aim (this would have required several thousand pages) but rather a user-friendly guide to quickly find accurate answers to the most obvious questions: Where does this plant originate? What does it look like? In which culture is it traditionally used? What is it used for? Which chemical compounds does it contain? How safe is it? What is known about its pharmacological activity? What evidence is there that it is effective? We also provide short overviews of the various health conditions for which medicinal plants are used and the active compounds (secondary metabolites) found in the plants and their modes of actions.

Since maximum user-friendliness was our aim, species are arranged alphabetically by their scientific names (not by their family or drug names). The most commonly used vernacular names are given in several languages, together with well-known botanical synonyms. The regulatory status of each plant is also given – whether it is listed in one or more pharmacopoeias (abbreviated as "pharm."), including the German Commission E monographs, the new ESCOP monographs of the European Community and the World Health Organisation's series of monographs (all species treated in the last-mentioned three works will be found in this book). If efficacy has been proven in human clinical trials, this is also indicated. In order to have as wide a coverage as possible, a summary table of more than 900 species was added, and a few plants have been treated as main species despite a lack of good photographs of flowers or fruits. We also thought it would be useful to cover those plants that are sources of medically important chemical compounds – they are not really used as plant drugs and are therefore often excluded from books on medicinal plants.

The subject of medicinal plants is a highly active field of scientific study all over the world. Ongoing research, including name changes, makes it virtually impossible to keep up to date with all aspects of this vast topic. Furthermore, some species may actually have become more important than we are aware of, while others are now merely of historical interest. Corrections, criticism, additions and offers of high quality original photographs would therefore be highly appreciated and can be sent to any of the authors.

Medicinal plants are an important part of human history, culture and tradition. Let us not be too sceptical about seemingly outrageous claims that are sometimes made about particular plants. Several centuries ago, lime fruits were given to British seamen who miraculously recovered from the symptoms of scurvy. It took science about 200 years to find out why (the discovery of vitamin C). It is likely that some traditional medicinal plants included here hold the key to new advances of great importance to human health. We hope that this book will be found useful as a quick reference guide to medicinal plants of the world and that it will stimulate and inspire health care practitioners, students and anyone else interested in medicinal plants to find out more about this fascinating subject.

The authors
August 2003

INTRODUCTION

Medicinal plants and plant-derived medicine are widely used in traditional cultures all over the world and they are becoming increasingly popular in modern society as natural alternatives to synthetic chemicals. As more and more natural remedies are being commercialised, there is a need for a user-friendly but scientifically accurate reference guide to the plants and their products. This book is a **photographic guide to the most commonly used and best known medicinal plants of the world,** including their botany, main traditional uses, active ingredients, pharmacological effects and evidence of efficacy (if known). The biological activity of many medicinal plants has become known through scientific research and any literature search (via the Internet, for example), would reveal that numerous new publications are added to the scientific literature every day. There is simply no space to allow for a comprehensive literature list for the more than 320 plants and their relatives treated and illustrated in this book. The reader can consult the list of Further Reading (p. 442) for further information.

Natural products and their derivatives (including antibiotics) represent more than 50% of all drugs in clinical use in the world. Higher plants contribute no less than 25% to the total. Well-known examples of plant-derived medicines include quinine, morphine, codeine, colchicine, atropine, reserpine and digoxin. Recently, important new anticancer drugs such as taxol and vincristine have been developed from plants. Health shops and pharmacies all over the world are experiencing a rapidly growing interest in healthy living, self-medication and natural remedies. The international consumer market for herbs and botanicals alone is estimated at about US$ 18 billion, which is just under half of the total market for supplements (including vitamins, minerals, homoeopathic products and sports supplements), estimated at more than US$ 50 billion.

How do medicinal plants work? An overview of the various active ingredients (secondary metabolites, p. 371) is provided in an attempt to clarify the complexity of metabolic effects caused by medicinal plants. Phytomedicines often contain a mixture of substances that have additive or even synergistic effects, so that the health benefits are difficult to test and verify. Plant medicine or phytomedicine may have subtle effects on several different biochemical pathways and receptors in the body-mind continuum that may all contribute directly and indirectly to restore equilibrium and balance. It is hard to dismiss medical claims of safety and efficacy when a plant medicine has been used in traditional cultures for centuries without evidence of serious side effects. Research results generated over the last few decades have given us a much better understanding of the scientific rationale behind many natural remedies.

A section is also included on the various health conditions (p. 351) that are treated with medicinal plants. In traditional cultures, plant products are used in combination with psychological treatments in an integrated, holistic approach to primary health care. The psychological part of the treatment often takes the form of magical, ritual, spiritual or symbolic practices that are difficult to understand when taken out of their cultural contexts. Our modern formulations, too, can deviate quite often from the traditional form. The use of alcoholic extracts (tinctures) instead of traditional watery extracts (infusions) for example, may result in ineffective treatment or even harmful side effects. As with all medicine, the correct dosage form and desirable level(s) of active ingredients are key elements in treating ailments or disorders and maintaining health.

A checklist of commercial medicinal plants is provided (p. 395), giving the correct scientific name, common name(s), family, origin, main compounds, main actions and main uses of more than 900 medicinal plants. To further enhance the general utility of the book, a glossary of medical terms (p. 433) is provided.

MEDICINE SYSTEMS OF THE WORLD

Rational herb use in antiquity

The vast majority of people on earth still rely on their traditional *materia medica* (medicinal plants and other materials) for everyday health care needs. It is likely that the profound knowledge of herbal remedies in traditional cultures developed through trial and error over many centuries, and that the most important cures were carefully passed on verbally from one generation to the next. Modern allopathic medicine has its roots in ancient medicine, and it is likely that many important new remedies will be discovered and commercialised in future, by following the leads provided by traditional knowledge and experience.

The use of medicinal plants is often associated with witchcraft and superstition, because people did not have the scientific insight to explain or predict the curative action of plants. One example of such an irrational concept is the Doctrine of Signatures, elements of which are found in many of the healing cultures of the world. It is based on the assumption that the appearance of plants may give clues to their medicinal properties – it is interpreted as God's signature on the plant. Red juice or sap, for example, is associated with blood and menstrual ailments, yellow flowers with bile and jaundice, the human shape of certain roots with the female form and fertility, and so on. Sometimes this concept apparently worked: *Chelidonium majus* contains yellow flowers and a yellow, alkaloid containing latex, and has successfully being used to treat jaundice.

People who use traditional remedies may not understand the scientific rationale behind their medicines, but they know from personal experience that some medicinal plants can be highly effective if used at therapeutic doses. Since we have a better understanding today how the human body functions (with all its intricate biochemical details) we are also in a better position to fully appreciate the healing power of plants and their potential as multi-functional chemical entities for treating complicated health conditions. Medicinal plants typically contain mixtures of different chemical compounds that may act individually, additively or in synergy to improve health. A single plant may, for example, contain bitter substances that stimulate digestion, anti-inflammatory compounds that reduce swelling and pain, phenolic compounds that act as antioxidants and venotonics, antibacterial and antifungal tannins that act as natural antibiotics, diuretic substances that enhance the elimination of waste product and toxins and alkaloids that enhance mood and give a sense of well-being. While modern allopathic medicine usually aims to develop a patentable single compound or "magic bullet" to treat a specific condition, traditional medicine often aims to restore balance by using chemically complex plants, or by mixing together several different plants in order to maximise a synergistic effect or to improve the likelihood of an interaction with a relevant molecular target.

In most societies today, the allopathic and traditional systems of medicine occur side by side in a complimentary way – allopathic medicine (sometimes originating from plants!) to treat serious, acute health conditions, and medicinal plants for self-terminating or chronic illnesses – to reduce symptoms, maintain health and improve quality of life in a cost-effective way.

European medicine

The European healing system is said to have originated with Hippocrates (460-377 BC) and Aristotle (384-322 BC), whose own ideas were rooted in ancient beliefs from India and Egypt. The principles were first defined by Galen (AD131-199) and the healing system thus became known as "Galenic medicine". Greek and Roman medicine was based on the belief that the world is composed of four elements – earth, air, fire and water. Each of these has its corresponding humour, linked to the four vital fluids in the body. The four humours – blood, phlegm, black bile and yellow bile, influence both health and temperament (respectively sanguine, phlegmatic, melancholic and choleric). In order to restore balance, drastic measures such as bloodletting (to reduce excess blood) and purging (to remove excess black bile) were used. The four humours were also associated with cold, heat, dampness and dryness, and each of these had a correspond-

Conium maculatum, used to kill Socrates

An Assyrian clay tablet with cuneiform text on medicinal plants, written in the 7th century BC.

Mandragoro officinarum, a medieval medicinal plant

ing range of cold, hot, damp or dry herbs that were supposedly able to restore imbalances. European tradition also had many regional influences based on local folk practices and traditions.

One of the most powerful influences was the famous book *De Materia Medica*, written by the Greek physician Dioscorides in the first century AD. It is generally accepted to be the first European herbal and was the standard reference in Europe for more than 1 000 years, providing the base for most of the later herbals. As early as AD 800, medicinal plants were cultivated according to a standardised layout in monasteries in central Europe. One of the famous healers of this era was Hildegard of Bingen (1098-1179). In later years a Swiss alchemist known as Paracelsus (1493-1541) emphasised the importance of the correct dose for medical treatments. Famous herbals (often beautifully illustrated) that brought medicinal plant knowledge to ordinary people include the *Historia Stirpium* (1542) and *New Kreuterbuch* (1543) by the German physician Leonhart Fuchs, the *Kruydtboeck* (1581) by the Flemish botanist Matthias de Lobel, the *Herball* (1597) by the English horticulturalist John Gerard and *The English Physitian* (1652) by the English pharmacist Nicholas Culpeper.

Herbal medicine is part of everyday life in many countries in Europe and to this day has remained popular as a sophisticated and rational method of treating ailments, often considered to be supportive rather than curative. The use of herbal teas and herbal mixtures is particularly popular in Germany, Austria, France, Italy, Great Britain and Switzerland. In addition to these "natural" products that are mostly taken in their crude (unprocessed) form as teas or decoctions, sophisticated phytomedicines (standardised and formulated extracts of plants, often subjected to rigorous testing in humans) remain a popular alternative to medicinal products derived from pure synthetic chemicals. New remedies from all over the world are continuously being added to the European medicinal repertoire, while others are being "rediscovered" as a result of modern scientific investigation. Emphasis seems to be shifting towards a more and more rational approach, where serious medical claims have to be properly backed up by clinical studies that clearly prove safety and efficacy.

A large number of traditional herbal remedies in Europe have become widely known as a result of commercialisation, including *Arnica montana* (arnica), *Atropa belladonna* (deadly nightshade), *Foeniculum vulgare* (fennel), *Matricaria recutita* (chamomile), *Silybum marianum* (milk thistle), *Urginea maritima* (squill), *Urtica dioica* (nettle) and *Valeriana officinalis*, to name only a few. In addition, a number of active compounds have been isolated from medicinal plants that are used today as single chemical entities, such as atropine, reserpine, morphine, quinidine, ajmaline, digoxin, taxol or vinblastine.

Traditional Chinese medicine

This ancient system of medicine, believed to be more than 5 000 years old, is based on two separate theories about the natural laws that govern good health and longevity, namely *yin* and *yang*, and the five elements (*wu xing*). Among the earliest records of ancient Chinese herbalism is a text by the Chinese emperor and scholar Shen Nong of the Sung Dynasty entitled *Shen Nong Ben Cao Jing* or *The Great Native Herbal* (ca. 2800 BC). This was later translated by Tao Hung Jing and became well known as *Comment on The Divine Husbandman's Classic of the Materia Medica*. Other important texts include *Formulas for the 52 Ailments* by Wu Shi Er Bing Fang (403 BC) and the *Classic of the Mountains and the Seas* by Shan Hai Jing (between 403 and 221 BC). Traditional Chinese Medicine was systematised mainly by the *Huang Di Nei Jing* (*Yellow Emperor's Inner Classic*) written between 100 and 200 BC and also the more recent classic *Ben Cao Gang Mu*, compiled by the famous Li Shizhen in AD 1590. The most complete reference to Chinese herbal prescriptions is the *Modern Day Encyclopaedia of Chinese Materia Medica* published in 1977. It lists nearly 6 000 drugs, of which 4 800 are of plant origin.

Yin and *yang* denotes opposites that complement each other, such as dark and light, soft and hard, female and male, wet and dry, cold and hot. The five-element theory is similar to the four humours and elements of the Greeks or the three humours of Ayurvedic medicine. The five elements are earth, metal, water, wood and fire, each of which are linked to the main organ systems of the body (respectively the spleen, lungs, kidneys, liver and heart), the emotions (reflection, grief, fear, anger, joy), the climates (damp, dry, cold, windy, hot), the seasons (late summer, autumn, winter, spring, summer) and tastes (sweet, pungent, salty, sour, bitter), and so on. Medicine is used to restore or maintain balance between these elements and to grant vital energy (*qi*), which has both *yin* and *yang* aspects. Treatment is therefore based not only on symptoms but also on patterns of imbalances, often detected by taking the pulse or observing the patient's tongue. Warming or hot herbs such as ginger and cinnamon, for example, are used to treat ailments associated with cold symptoms such as cold hands, abdominal pain and indigestion.

In common with Western herbal teas and African traditional medicine, Chinese herbs are usually given in fixed mixtures or formulas of up to 20 herbs, carefully prepared according to traditional recipes contained in ancient compendia. There are hundreds of these formulas that are commonly used in hospitals and pharmacies alongside conventional Western medicine. As in other healing cultures, herbal remedies are usually favoured for chronic or self-terminating conditions, while acute or serious illnesses are treated by Western medicine. Korean traditional medicine is closely related to traditional Chinese medicine, both of which influenced traditional Japanese medicine (known as *kampo*). The spread of traditional Chinese medicine to most continents has undoubtedly contributed to the current popularity of herbal medicine throughout the world.

Examples of famous Chinese medicinal plants are *Angelica polymorpha* var. *sinensis* (*dang gui*), *Artemisia annua* (*qing hao*), *Ephedra sinica* (*ma huang*), *Paeonia lactiflora* (*bai shao yao*), *Panax ginseng* (*ren shen*) and *Rheum palmatum* (*da huang*).

Ayurvedic medicine

This ancient system of medicine, possibly older than traditional Chinese medicine, is actually a practical and holistic set of guidelines to maintain balance and harmony and to ensure a long and happy life. *Ayurveda* is derived from the Indian words *ayur* (life) and *veda* (knowledge or science) and therefore means "the science of life". Following the system would help to ensure a long life, which is considered to be the instrument for achieving righteousness (*dharma*), wealth (*artha*) and happiness (*sukha*).

Statue of Li Shizen

Santalum album from Köhler's Medizinalpflanzen (1887–1888)

Cultivated ginseng

In India, knowledge and wisdom were passed from one generation to the next through songs and poems, which scholars and physicians had to learn by heart and recite. The *Veda* is an ancient text in four parts (*Rig Veda*, *Sama Veda*, *Yajur Veda* and *Atharva Veda*), the earliest of which dates back to around 2000 BC. The principles of Ayurvedic medicine and the medicinal uses of herbs are contained in thousands of poetic hymns in the *Rig Veda*. Knowledge about herbs is also found in the *Atharva Veda* and in later works such as *The Charaka Samhita* and *The Sunshrita Samhita*. One of the most popular texts is the *Astangahrdaya*, a shortened, user-friendly version, entirely in poetry (7120 verses), of the *Astangasangraha*, a classical text in which the so-called eight branches of Ayurveda were collected into a single treatise for the first time. The *Astangahrdaya* (and perhaps also the original *Astangasangraha*) was written by Vagbhata, son of Simhagupta (who lived around AD 550 to 600).

Ayurveda is similar to Galenical medicine in that it is based on bodily humours (*dosas*) and the inner life force (*prana*) that is believed to maintain digestion and mental activity. Good digestion and all aspects of health are linked to the six tastes (*rasas*) that are important in Ayurvedic herbalism – sweet (*madhura*), sour (*amla*), salt (*lavana*), bitter (*tikta*), pungent (*katu*) and astringent (*kasaya*). Herbal remedies are formulated to balance these tastes, each of which has beneficial properties but also negative side effects (resulting in abnormalities and disease) when used in excess.

The *dosas* may be classified as somatic (*vata*, *pitta* and *kapha*) and psychic (*rajas* and *tamas*). Health manifests when each of the *dosas* is in perfect balance. *Vata* is associated with bodily wind and air – in its normal state it protects the body and gives enthusiasm, inspiration and ensures the proper execution of all bodily urges and sense organs. *Pitta* is associated with bile and fire – in its normal state it regulates digestion, temperature, vision, hunger, thirst, complexion, intelligence, courage and suppleness of the body. *Kapha* is associated with phlegm or dampness – in its normal state it ensures stability, lubrication, firmness of joints, the ability to withhold emotions and to withstand physical and emotional stress. Specified physical and psychological disorders are thought to result from the abnormal increase or decrease of each of these three *dosas*.

Famous Ayurvedic medicinal plants include *Azadirachta indica* (neem), *Centella asiatica* (gotu kola), *Cinnamomum verum* (cinnamon), *Elettaria cardamomum* (ela or cardamom), *Rauvolfia serpentina* (Indian snakeroot), *Santalum album* (sandalwood), *Terminalia* species (myrobalan) and *Withania somnifera* (ashwagandha).

African traditional medicine

African traditional medicine is the oldest and perhaps the most diverse of all medicine systems. The biological and cultural diversity of Africa that constitutes the cradle of mankind (there are more than 2 000 languages in sub-Saharan Africa!) is reflected in the marked regional differences in healing practices. Unfortunately, the various systems are poorly recorded and remain so to this day.

African traditional medicine in its varied forms is a holistic system involving both body and mind. The healer typically diagnoses and treats the psychological basic of an illness before prescribing medicines to treat the symptoms. The Khoi-San people of southern Africa, nowadays considered to be the most ancient of all cultures, have a remarkably diverse *materia medica* which typically includes general tonics, fever remedies, sedatives, stomachics, diuretics, laxatives and numerous wound healing plants.

Famous African medicinal plants include *Acacia senegal* (gum arabic), *Agathosma betulina* (buchu), *Aloe ferox* (Cape aloes), *Aloe vera* (of North African origin), *Artemisia afra* (African wormwood), *Aspalathus linearis* (rooibos tea), *Boswellia sacra* (frankincense), *Catha edulis* (khat), *Commiphora myrrha* (myrrh), *Harpagophytum procumbens* (devil's claw), *Hibiscus sabdariffa* (hibiscus or roselle), *Hypoxis hemerocallidea* (African potato) and *Prunus africana* (African cherry or red stinkwood).

North African and Middle Eastern traditional medicine

The Middle East is known as the cradle of civilization and many of the plants we grow as crops today were domesticated in this region. The Babylonians, Assyrians and Sumerians recorded herbal remedies in cuneiform writing on numerous clay tablets that date from 2600 to 4000 BC or even earlier (see figure on page 9). Of special interest is the Code of Hammurabi (ca. 1700 BC), a comprehensive set of civil laws carved in stone and commissioned by the King of Babylon. It lists several medicinal herbs. Sumerian clay tablets from near the ancient Sumerian city of Nippur are thought to be the oldest known prescription pads (ca. 2 000 BC). Several herbs are also recorded in the Bible, dating back to at least 1500 BC. The Assyrian King Ashurbanipal of Nineveh recorded 250 herbs on over a hundred cuneiform marble tablets around 668–626 BC.

Many early records of medicinal plants are found in wall-paintings of tombs in Egypt, dating from the Old Kingdom (3rd to 6th Dynasties), about 2700–2200 BC. The Codex Ebers or Ebers Papyrus dates from about 1500 BC but is said to contain ancient medicinal knowledge from before 3000 BC. This famous document is a papyrus scroll of about 20 m long, inscribed in Egyptian hieroglyphics. It is named after Prof George Ebers, who discovered it in a tomb at Thebes in 1872. More than 700 of the 800 medicinal recipes given in the Codex Ebers contain medicinal plants.

Arabian herbalism was well established in the Middle Ages, mainly as a result of the famous physician Avicenna (AD 980–1037). His *Canon Medicinae* included elements of other healing cultures and forms the basis for a distinct Islamic healing system known as *Unani-Tibb*.

Amongst the many famous medicine plants of the Middle East and Egypt are *Allium cepa* (onion), *Astracantha gummifera* (tragacanth), *Carthamus tinctorius* (safflower), *Carum carvi* (caraway), *Ferula assafoetida* (asafoetida), *Lawsonia inermis* (henna), *Papaver somniferum* (opium poppy), *Peganum harmala* (Syrian rue), *Prunus dulcis* (almond), *Punica granatum* (pomegranate), *Rosa* x *damascena* (Damask rose), *Ricinus communis* (castor oil plant), *Salvadora persica* (toothbrush tree), *Senna alexandrina* (senna), *Sesamum indicum* (sesame), *Trachyspermum ammi* (ajowan), *Trigonella foenum-graecum* (fenugreek) and *Vitis vinifera* (grape).

North American traditional medicine

As in other cultures, the indigenous healer or shaman approaches illness by addressing both the physical and spiritual dimensions of disease. Shamanistic ceremonies involve chanting, dancing and other rituals aimed at expelling evil forces so that the patient or the community as a whole can be healed. Early pioneers learnt from native practices and adopted many of the herbal remedies, which later formed the basis of the

Gum of mastic (*Pistacia lentiscus*) is used in dentistry

Devil's claw (*Harpagophytum procumbens*) in the Kalahari desert

Sassafras (*Sassafras albidum*) is a traditional North America herbal tea

Pharmacopoeia of the United States. An example is Samuel Thompson (1794–1868), who relied on traditional remedies such as *Capsicum frutescens* (cayenne) and *Lobelia inflata* (Indian tobacco). Another system combining the best of Native American and European herbal medicine was Eclecticism, proposed by Wooster Beech around 1830. At the turn of the 19th century, several thousand health care professionals were following the eclectic approach. Between 1850 and 1900 a boom period developed, marked by the Physiomedicalists movement and the popularisation of now famous plants such as echinacea (*Echinacea purpurea*) and goldenseal (*Hydrastis canadensis*). The influence of this period is still evident in Britain, where many North American plants are popular to this day.

During most of the 20th century, herbs (or *botanicals* as they are referred to in the USA) have been regarded with scepticism and the practise of herbal medicine went into decline. Plants were viewed mainly as a potential source of pure chemical compounds for medicine development. In recent years, however, herbs and botanicals have become very popular in the USA and Canada but are still regarded by many as nutritional supplements rather than medicines in their own right.

Central and South American traditional medicine

In common with Africa, the rich but diverse healing cultures of this region are poorly recorded but will undoubtedly be a source of many new herbal remedies in the years to come. South and Central America is one of the most important cradles of agriculture and a large number of crop plants (including maize, potatoes, tomatoes, pumpkins, cassava, peanuts and sweet potato) originated here. Rural people in countries like Mexico, Cuba, Chile, Guyana, Peru, Ecuador, Bolivia, Venezuela, Brazil and Argentina still use traditional Indian herbal medicine but Spanish, European, Indian and African influences are evident. Examples of famous medicinal plants are *Cinchona pubescens* (Peruvian bark), *Erythroxylon coca* (coca), *Ilex paraguariensis* (maté), *Myroxylon balsamum* (Tolu balsam), *Paullinia cupana* (guaraná), *Peumus boldus* (boldo), *Psidium guajava* (guava), *Spilanthes acmella* (Brazilian cress), *Tabebuia impetiginosa* (lapacho) and *Uncaria tomentosa* (cat's claw).

Australian and Southeast Asian traditional medicine

All over this region there is a resurgence of interest in traditional medicine and many countries now promote research into medicinal plants as a potential source of new remedies. The Aborigines undoubtedly had a complex healing system but much of the traditional knowledge in Australia was lost before it could be systematically recorded. In contrast, many healing cultures in places like Malaysia, Thailand, Vietnam, New Zealand, Borneo and the Polynesian islands remained intact and are being recorded and developed. A strong Chinese influence is seen in most countries – some of it ancient, as in Thailand and Malaysia; some more recent, as in Australia. Amongst the well-known medicinal products originating from this region are *Croton tiglium* (purging croton), *Duboisia hopwoodii* (pituri), *Eucalyptus globulus* (bluegum), *Melaleuca alternifolia* (tea tree), *Myristica fragrans* (nutmeg and mace), *Piper methysticum* (kava kava), *Strychnos nux-vomica* (strychnine), *Styrax benzoin* (benzoin) and *Syzygium aromaticum* (cloves).

Aromatherapy

Aromatherapy is a healing system that uses essential oils in the form of inhalations, massages, baths and perfumes to treat disease and maintain health. The healing power of aromatic substances has been known since ancient times and aromatic medicinal plants are found in all healing cultures around the world. An interesting example is the San people of southern Africa, who were allegedly called *San* or *Bushmen* because they continually massaged themselves with powdered aromatic bushes mixed with fat or oil. Perfumes and aromatic products were well known to the Egyptians (consider frankincense and myrrh). Aromatherapy appears to be an ancient African practice even though the term was first used by the French chemist René Gattefossé in 1928.

Essential oils are known to have various health benefits when absorbed through the mucous membranes of the nose or lungs (some argue the term aromatherapy should be reserved for this route of administration) or through the skin (by massaging the skin or adding oils to the bath). Some aromatic compounds are known to act directly on the central nervous system, others are spasmolytic and antiseptic; it is likely that some of them help restore health through a positive effect on the mind and mood of patients.

Homoeopathy

Homoeopathy (or *homeopathy*) is a system developed by Samuel Hahnemann in Leipzig between 1811 and 1820. The theory is based on the assumption that plants can be used in very dilute form to treat illnesses associated with the symptoms produced by high doses of the same plants. For example, if a high dose is emetic, then a dilute dose can be used as anti-emetic. The word is derived from the Greek *homoios* (like) and "-pathy", a suffix denoting curative treatment – from the Greek *patheia* (suffering). The number of times the mother tincture has been diluted ten-fold ("potentised") is given after the name of the medicine. *Amika* D3 (three times a ten-fold dilution, i.e. a 1 000-fold dilution) is still fairly concentrated and therefore considered less potent than *Amika* D30, which is assumed to be highly potent. The idea is that potentiation sets free immaterial forces from the extracts. In addition to plants, minerals (e.g. sulphur) and animal products (e.g. bee venom) are popular in homoeopathy. In most cases the medicine is so dilute that no molecules of the original product are left but it is claimed by protagonists of this theory that active molecules leave behind a "fingerprint" or "curative power" that is not yet properly investigated or understood by modern science. Plant-derived products with therapeutic quantities of active ingredients (e.g., D1 to D6) are often incorrectly referred to as homoeopathic remedies, perhaps to benefit from the less stringent safety regulations applied to these products. If highly diluted preparations are used, the therapy is no longer part of phytotherapy.

Ageratum conyzoides, from Central America

Noni fruit (*Morinda citrifolia*), a medicinal plant from Southeast Asia and the Pacific

Stevia rebaudiana, a South American sweetener

Anthroposophical medicine

The concept of anthroposophical medicine (founded by Rudolf Steiner in the early 20th century) also had an influence in Europe and other parts of the Western world. It is a holistic approach that contains elements of Galenical theories and homoeopathy, aimed at stimulating the body's natural healing powers and taking into account the important role of soul and spirit in maintaining good health. Although anthroposophical medicine uses medicinal plants, it is not considered part of phytotherapy.

Bach flower remedies

Bach Flower Remedies is a system similar to homoeopathy devised by Edward Bach in the 1930s in which the healing power of flowers is supposedly transferred to water by sunlight. There were originally 38 different Flower Remedies but similar systems have been developed in other parts of the world. It is not considered part of phytotherapy even though plants are used.

PLANT PARTS USED

Different parts of a plant (leaves, roots, bark, fruit or seeds) often contain quite different active ingredients, so that one part may be toxic and another one quite harmless. The fruit capsules of the opium poppy (*Papaver somniferum*) produce powerful drugs, while the seeds are almost alkaloid-free. In phytotherapy, the whole plant may be used (*herba tota*) or often only a specified part of the plant. In official documents and on product labels, the pharmaceutical names of plants and plant parts are given in Latin to avoid confusion.

Root (*rad.* or *radix*). The fleshy or woody roots (or outer root bark) of many species are used medicinally. Roots may be fibrous (stinging nettle, *Urtica dioica*; *Urticae radix*), solid (licorice, (*Glycyrrhiza glabra*; *Liquiritiae radix*), or fleshy (devil's claw, *Harpagophytum procumbens*; *Harpagophyti radix*).

Rhizome (*rhiz.* or *rhizoma*). A rhizome is a woody or fleshy elongated stem that usually grows horizontally below the ground, forming leaves above the ground and roots into the ground. One should distinguish between true root (*radix*) and rhizomes. There are several examples of medicinal plants that are used primarily for their rhizomes, including kava kava (*Piper methysticum*; *Kava-kava rhizoma*) and ginger (*Zingiber officinale*; *Zingiberis rhizoma*).

Bulb (*bulbus*). A bulb is a fleshy structure made up of numerous layers of bulb scales, which are actually leaf bases. Bulbs popular for medicinal use include onion (*Allium cepa*; *Cepae bulbus*), garlic (*Allium sativum*; *Allii sativi bulbus*) and the European squill (*Urginea maritima*; *Scillae bulbus*).

Tuber (*tub.* or *tuber*). A tuber is a swollen, fleshy structure below the ground, usually of stem origin but often partly stem and partly root. Hypoxis (*Hypoxis hemerocallidea*; *Hypoxidis tuber*) and tubers of autumn crocus (*Colchicum autumnale*; *Colchici tuber*) are well-known examples.

Bark (*cort.* or *cortex*). Bark is the outer protective layer of a tree trunk, formed by layers of living cells just above the wood itself. High concentrations of active ingredients are found in bark, hence its frequent medicinal use. There are numerous examples, including quinine bark (*Cichona* species; *Chinae cortex*), pepperbark (*Warburgia salutaris*), oak bark (*Quercus* species; *Quercus cortex*) and willow bark (*Salix* species; *Salicis cortex*).

Wood (*lig.* or *lignum*). Thick stems or the wood itself is used. Examples include sandalwood (*Santalum album*; *Santali album lignum*) and quassia wood (*Quassia amara*; *Quassiae lignum*).

Leaf (*fol.* or *folium*). Leaves alone may be used (*folium*), or leaves may occur in a mixture with petioles and twigs (*herba*). Stems (**stip.**, **stipes** or **stipites**) and even stems tips (**summ.** or **summitates**) are sometimes specified. An example is the maidenhair tree (*Ginkgo biloba*; *Ginkgo folium*), where only the leaves are used.

Aerial parts (*herba*). All aboveground parts are harvested and used, often while the plants are in flowers. An example is St. John's wort (*Hypericum perforatum*; *Hyperici herba*).

Flowers (*flos*). Flowers are popular in traditional medicine. Examples are cloves (the flower buds of *Syzygium aromaticum*; *Caryophylli flos*), chamomile flowers (*Matricaria recutita*; *Matricariae flos*) and Roman chamomile flowers (*Chamaemelum nobile*; *Chamomillae romanae flos*). Flower parts are sometimes used, such as hibiscus calyces (*Hibiscus sabdariffa*; *Hibisci flos*), the stamens of saffron (*Crocus sativus*; *Croci stigma*), the stigmas ("beard") of maize (*Zea mays*; *Maidis stigma*) or even pollen (*pollinae*). The whole inflorescence is sometimes used, such as the "cones" of hops (*Humulus lupulus*; *Lupuli strobulus*).

Fruit (*fr.* or *fructus*). Amongst the most commonly used ones are the small dry fruits (often wrongly referred to as seeds) of members of the carrot family (Apiaceae). These include fennel fruit (*Foeniculum vulgare*; *Foeniculi fructus*) and anis (*Pimpinella anisum*; *Anisi frutus*). Dried, whole fruits may be used, such as juniper berries (*Juniperus communis*; *Juniperi fructus*) or milk thistle achenes (*Silybum marianum*; *Cardui mariae fructus*). In some cases, only specified parts are used, such as pomegranate peel (*Punica granatum*; *Granati pericarpium*) or bitter-orange peel (*Citrus aurantium*; *Aurantii pericarpium*).

Seed (*sem.* or *semen*). Seeds are contained within a fruit and are sometimes used on their own. This means that the fruit rind or peel is discarded. Examples are the true seeds (nuts) of the castor oil plant (*Ricinus communis*; *Ricini semen*) and fenugreek seed (*Trigonella foenum-graecum*; *Foenugraeci semen*).

Honduras sarsaparilla root (*Smilax regelii*)

Rhatany root (*Krameria lappacea*)

Cape gum (*Acacia karroo*)

Ammoniacum (*Dorema ammoniacum*)

Gum (*gummi*). Gums are solids consisting of mixtures of polysaccharides. They are water-soluble and partially digested by humans. Gum sometimes flows from a damaged stem, as a defence mechanism of the plant to stop wood-boring insects and to seal off wounds so that wood-rotting fungi and bacteria are kept out. An example of such an exudate gum is gum arabic (from *Acacia senegal; Gummi acaciae*) that is used in the pharmaceutical industry. Gums mixed with water are known as gels. An example is the gel present in the inner leaf pulp of *Aloe vera*.

Resins (*resina*). Resins are excreted by specialised cells or ducts in plants. They consist of a mixture of essential oils and polymerised terpenes, usually insoluble in water. Examples are frankincense (from *Boswellia sacra; Olibanum*), myrrh (from *Commiphora myrrha; Myrrha*) and mastic (*Pistacia lentiscus; Resina mastix* – used as an adhesive for dental caps). Balsams (or balsamic resins) are resins with a high content of benzoic acid, cinnamic acid or their esters. Well-known examples include tolu balsam (from *Myroxylon balsamum* var. *balsamum*), Siam benzoin (from *Styrax tonkinensis*), and Sumatra benzoin (*Styrax benzoin*). Storax balsam is collected from *Liquidambar* species and should not be confused with balsams from *Styrax* species – Levant storax ("balm of Gilead" in Bible) comes from *L. orientalis*, and common storax from the sweet gum tree (*L. styraciflua*).

Fatty oil (*oleum*). These are non-volatile vegetable oils pressed from the seeds or fruits of plants that are insoluble in water. Oils are described as acylglycerides because they are made up from a glycerol molecule attached to various types of fatty acids. Castor oil (from *Ricinus communis* seeds) is an example with direct medicinal properties. Others (olive oil, safflower oil) are used as carriers in liquid formulations and ointments (e.g. in aromatherapy).

Essential oil (*aetheroleum*). These are volatile oils, usually extracted from plants through a process of steam distillation. They consist mainly of monoterpenoids, sesquiterpenoids, phenylpropanoids and coumarins, and are of considerable importance as active ingredients of medicinal plants. Examples are camphor (from the wood of *Cinnamomum camphora; Camphorae aetheroleum*) and peppermint oil (from leaves of *Mentha* x *piperita; Menthae piperitae aetheroleum*).

DOSAGE FORMS

Extracts are liquid, powdered or viscous crude mixtures of chemical compounds, extracted from plant material using water or organic solvents such as alcohol (ethanol). As a result, the extract contains only the soluble fraction of the plant material (usually about 20% of the total weight) and the non-soluble (fibrous) residues (about 80%) are discarded. Volatile oils are extracted by steam distillation or less often by solvent extraction. The herb to extract ratio (HER) is typically 5:1 for normal extracts, or say 100:1 for a herb with 1% essential oil. The extract (*extractum*) has its origin in tradition but is still commonly used today.

Special extracts are extracts in which the conditions of extraction are modified and manipulated (by using liquid CO_2, for example) so that desirable chemical compounds are extracted in high yield, while undesirable ones are reduced to low concentrations or are completely excluded.

Monopreparations are medicinal products that contain only a single plant or herb (or an extract thereof) as active ingredient.

Mixtures are medicinal products containing two or more plants or herbs that act individually, additively or even synergistically to restore or maintain health. In traditional Chinese medicine and African traditional medicine, medicinal plants are typically used in mixtures, rarely on their own.

Teas are infusions (see below) prepared by steeping herbs in boiling water. The word "tea" is derived from *t'e*, the name of black tea (*Camellia sinensis*) in the southern Chinese Amoy dialect. In many parts of the world, the product is known as *chai* (after the Cantonese and Mandarin name). Other infusions are often referred to as "tea" but then the raw material has to be specified, such as hibiscus tea (*Hibiscus sabdariffa*) or rooibos tea (*Aspalathus linearis*). Terms such as "mint tea" or "ginger tea" are ambiguous as it may imply infusions of these herbs alone or (more often) black tea simply flavoured with them. The distinction between non-medicinal teas (used merely as pleasant hot drinks) and medicinal teas (used for some therapeutic benefit) is not always clear.

Tea mixtures (*species*) are fixed mixtures of herbs (usually 4-7) containing active components (herbs of major importance for the indication), supplementary components (supportive of the stated indication) and adjunct components (components added to improve the taste, smell or colour of the mixture). Examples are *species anticystiticae* (= bladder tea), *species amaricantes* (= bitter tea), *species carminativae* (= carminative tea), *species sedativae* (= sedative tea or nerve tea), *species laxantes* (= laxative tea).

Decoction (*decoctum*) refers to a preparation that is made by adding cold water to the required amount of drug. It is then heated to boiling and allowed to simmer for five to ten minutes, after which it is strained.

Infusion (*infusum*) refers to a preparation that is made by adding boiling water to the required amount of drug, which is allowed to steep for five to ten minutes before it is strained. Such a preparation is often loosely referred to as "tea".

Maceration (*maceratio*) refers to a preparation made by adding cold water to the required amount of drug, which is allowed to soak at room temperature for six to eight hours before it is strained.

Juice (*succus*) is prepared by crushing freshly harvested plant parts in water and then expressing the juice. The product has to be pasteurised or treated with ultra-high temperature to extend shelf life.

Syrup (*sirupus*) is a viscous preparation containing about 66% sucrose (not less than 50%). Saturated sugar solutions are free of microorganisms because no free water necessary for microbial growth is available. Syrups are mainly used as flavouring agents, to mask an unpleasant taste of other ingredients. When used as cough remedies, they are slowly sipped to allow maximum contact with inflamed mucous membranes.

Tincture (*tinctura*) refers to an alcoholic solution (usually containing 30 to 70% water) prepared from medicinal plant material. The herbal mixture is extracted for a specified period, after which it is pressed and/or strained to separate the liquid and solid materials. A mother tincture is often prepared by using 70% ethanol, and the solution is then diluted with clean water to a predetermined herb to extract ratio. Glycerides may be prepared by using glycerol as the solvent instead of alcohol.

Medicinal spirits or medicinal essences are volatile compounds (usually essentials oils) dissolved in alcohol or alcohol-water mixtures. Medicinal spirits are often produced by mixing aromatic herbs with alcohol and then recovering the alcohol and volatile components by steam distillation.

Medicinal oils are fatty oils or liquid waxes mixed with medicinal extracts and intended for internal or external use. Garlic oils are often prepared in this way. In aromatherapy, it is customary to dilute essential oils in some carrier oil, such as olive oil, almond oil or jojoba oil (the last-mentioned is actually not an oil but a liquid wax).

Instant teas are dry (powdered) herbal extracts that are usually mixed with carrier substances such as sucrose, lactose or maltodextrin to add bulk, reduce viscosity and to improve solubility. The carrier substance or filler is often introduced during spray-drying, when a concentrated infusion of the herb is sprayed into a heated column in such a way that the filler particles become coated with the dry herbal extract.

Tea bags are filter bags used to pack a predetermined quantity (dose) of herbal material or herbal mixture. They are convenient to use but have a relatively short shelf life, because the finely chopped material provides a large surface area that is subject to oxidation by air and evaporation of volatile compounds.

Granules are produced by binding powders or powdered extracts into small units, using suitable excipients such as solutions of gelatin, lactose or sucrose. Granules may be used as such or are more often compressed into tablets or included in capsules.

Capsules are small containers, usually made from gelatin, that contain medicinal products or extracts in a predetermined dose and protect them from air, light and moisture. Hard gelatin capsules have two halves that fit together closely after being filled with powdered or granulated product. In addition to gelatin, the capsule shell contains a softening agent (glycerol or sorbitol), water, colouring agents and antimicrobial compounds. Since gelatin is an animal product, special capsules known as Vcaps™ or vegecaps are now made for vegetarians. Soft gelatin capsules are variously shaped (often spherical or ovoid) and contain liquid or semisolid products that must be free of water, such as oily extracts.

Tablets. Uncoated tablets are made by compression of powdered active material after addition of a suitable inert excipient or binder (to provide the bulk) and sometimes also other additives to improve colour and flavour, or disintegrators to ensure that the tablet rapidly dissolves when placed in water. Coated tablets are similar but they are covered in a thin layer of sugar, colouring agent, fat, wax or special film-forming agents, such as cellulose acetate phthalate. In the latter case, film-coated tablets (FCT) are produced, that are designed to protect the drug from gastric juices or to protect the stomach lining, so that the active substances are only released after the tablet has reached the bowel. Coated tablets have a longer shelf life, and are easier to swallow because of the smooth coating that may also mask an unpleasant taste.

Pills are made by cutting semisolid preparations into small portions of predetermined size or weight, shaping or rolling the portions before allowing them to harden. The manufacture of pills is nowadays fully mechanised, but in former times pill-making was part of the practical training of a pharmacist.

Lozenges or pastilles are variously shaped tablet-like products that are intended for sucking or chewing, so that the active substances are slowly released in the mouth. These products are not made by compression but are cut or moulded from semisolid, usually sugary masses. Sucrose is often the main constituent, together with smaller quantities of gum (e.g. gum arabic or gum tragacanth), flavouring agents and water.

Suppositories are oblong, tablet-like products that are intended for inserting into the rectum, vagina or urethra and left there to melt. Herbal products are rarely used in this form.

Ointments, pastes and gels are semisolid preparations intended for external application that contain medicinal substances in a suitable carrier substance (watery or oily solvents).

Note: Although modern galenic forms, such as tablets or pills, look respectable and are easy to swallow, it can be difficult to provide an adequate dose of an extract, especially if an extract contains several compounds that need a higher dosage for optimal efficacy. The old-fashioned tea might be a more appropriate dosage form in such a case.

USE OF MEDICINAL PLANT PRODUCTS

Route of administration

The chemical compounds in medicinal plants need to be resorbed in sufficient quantity for the product to be effective. The ease with which active ingredients can enter human cells or the bloodstream (bioavailability) depends on the polarity, stability and other chemical characteristics of the compounds involved, as well as the route of administration. Some active compounds, for example, pass through the digestive tract without being resorbed, but are highly active when injected directly into the bloodstream. Volatile compounds may be effective when inhaled (as in aromatherapy) but practically inactive when taken orally.

Medicinal plant products can be administered in the following ways:

Oral. Infusions, tinctures, decoctions, syrups and tablets are most often taken orally (by mouth), or sometimes sublingually (under the tongue).

Nasal. Powdered material (or suspensions) may be snuffed – drawn up into the nasal passages, where the active compounds are resorbed through the mucosa.

Topical. Lotions, oils or creams containing medicinal plants and their extracts are applied directly to the skin, where the active compounds are resorbed.

Rectal. Liquid preparations may be administered as enemas. The active compounds are effectively resorbed by the mucus membranes of the rectum. It is sometimes desirable or necessary to bypass the stomach, because the active compounds may be inactivated or modified by stomach acid and other gastric juices.

Smoking and steaming. Smoke from burning material is inhaled, and the active compounds resorbed through the lungs (in the same way as nicotine is resorbed while smoking). Volatile oils of medicinal plants are inhaled in the same way by steaming them in boiling water.

Bathing. Herbs or herbal extracts may be added to bath water.

Subcutaneous or intramuscular injection. Some phytomedicines (often pure chemical entities derived from medicinal plants) are injected directly into the bloodstream. It is interesting to note that some compounds may be totally inactive when taken by mouth, yet highly active when injected. For example, the Menispermaceae alkaloids are traditionally used as muscle-relaxant dart poisons; however, the meat from the killed animal is harmless when eaten.

Appropriate dose and realistic expectations

Herbal drugs or so-called botanicals generally have a wide therapeutic window (i.e. the effective dose differs markedly from the toxic dose). With most medicinal plant products sold today, it is almost impossible to ingest sufficient material to reach dangerous or life-threatening levels of toxicity. In contrast, pure chemical compounds are highly concentrated and the desirable dose is easily exceeded. When a new herbal product is developed, the traditional dosage form and route of administration are carefully considered. A plant that is safely consumed as a tea may be totally unsuitable for human use as a tincture. The alcohol (ethanol) may dissolve poisonous substances that would not be present in tea.

Most phytomedicines are used for short periods (up to three weeks) against self-terminating illnesses (conditions that will generally clear up even without treatment). The value of medication is simply to alleviate the symptoms or to shorten the recovery time. There are notable exceptions, where a period of several weeks is required for the remedy to become effective. This is true where products are used in supportive treatment of chronic conditions, such as mild depression, poor blood circulation, mild asthma and some forms of diabetes. An example is *Hypericum* preparations, used in supportive treatment of mild depression. Crude herbal drugs are rarely used for serious health conditions (except in some Third World countries where people have limited access to modern medicine) but rather carefully tested and standardised modern phytomedicines (or isolated compounds extracted from crude drugs). It is important to note that the treatment of any chronic or serious ailments should only be done within the safeguards of the traditional health care system and/or under the supervision of a qualified heath care professional.

Replica of an old-style pharmacy with herbal drugs   Modern pharmacy with ready-to-use products

Replica of a medieval medicinal garden

Modern mass-cultivation; seedlings of rooibos
(*Aspalathus linearis*)

Medicinal plants provide a cost-effective means of primary health care to millions of people around the world. In former times, the treatment of intestinal parasites and the frequent use of purgative medicines were necessary to maintain health. As standards of hygiene improved, the emphasis has shifted to preventative rather than curative medicine, and many people nowadays take responsibility for their own health by emphasising a balanced diet and sufficient exercise. As a result, the modern trend in product development is towards functional foods and dietary supplements. An estimate of the size of the global nutritional supplements industry is given in the table below.

Size of the global nutritional supplements industry: consumer sales (million US$) for the year 2000 (source: *Nutrition Business Journal*)

	Vitamins & minerals	Sports, homoeo-pathy & specialist products	Functional foods	Herbs & botanicals
Africa	160	70	120	80
Australia	300	90	540	190
Canada	510	250	1 500	380
Europe	5 670	2 510	15 390	4 070
Japan	3 200	1 280	11 830	2 340
Latin America	690	250	360	260
Middle East	180	60	140	90
Russia	350	250	260	220
United States	7 070	4 230	16 080	4 070
TOTAL	19 620	9 960	47 670	17 490

ACTIVE INGREDIENTS

Plant drugs (also called **phytomedicines** or **phytopharmaceuticals**) are plant-derived medicines that contain a chemical compound or more usually mixtures of chemical compounds that act individually or in combination on the human body to prevent disorders and to restore or maintain health. **Chemical entities** are pure chemical compounds (isolated from natural sources such as plants, or produced by chemical synthesis) that are used for medicinal purposes (usually with a clearly defined and tested mode of action). Some phytopharmaceuticals may contain a single chemical compound extracted from a plant. Although they derive from plants, they are legally not considered as phytopharmaceuticals in a strict sense. The active chemical compounds in medicinal plants and phytomedicines are known as **secondary metabolites** (see page 371 for a detailed review of these compounds and their modes of action).

How do plant medicines work? Modes of action of secondary metabolites

Several secondary metabolites have been used by mankind for thousands of years as dyes (e.g. indigo, shikonine), flavours (e.g. vanillin, capsaicin, mustard oils), fragrances (e.g. rose oil, lavender oil and other essential oils), stimulants (e.g. caffeine, nicotine, ephedrine), hallucinogens (e.g. morphine, cocaine, scopolamine, tetrahydrocannabinol), insecticides (e.g. nicotine, piperine, pyrethrin), vertebrate and human poisons (e.g. coniine, strychnine, aconitine) and most importantly as therapeutic agents (e.g. atropine, quinine, cardenolides, codeine).

In order to be effective as a therapeutic agent, a secondary metabolite must interfere with an organ, tissue, cell and ultimately with a molecular target in the human body. Secondary metabolites usually are multifunctional compounds because most of them carry more than one pharmacologically active chemical group. In addition, secondary metabolites usually occur in complex mixtures. In consequence, the extract of a medicinal plant affects more than one molecular target and it is likely that several targets are affected concomitantly when taking phytomedicines. In complex disorders the application of such extracts increases the chances of "hitting" one or several relevant targets.

In general, we find a series of related compounds in a given plant species; often a few major metabolites and several minor components, which differ in the position of their chemical groups. The profile usually varies between plant organs, within developmental periods and sometimes even diurnally. Also marked differences can usually be seen between individual plants of a single population, even more so between members of different populations. Even small changes in chemistry can be the basis for a new pharmacological activity. This aspect is important for quality control in phytotherapeutics.

On the opposite page a human cell is shown together with an overview of all the main molecular targets that are modulated by plant medicines. Structures of allelochemicals appear to have been shaped during evolution in such a way that they can mimic the structures of endogenous substrates, hormones, neurotransmitters or other ligands; this process can be termed "evolutionary molecular modelling". Other metabolites intercalate or alkylate DNA, inhibit DNA and RNA related enzymes, protein biosynthesis, modulate metabolically active enzymes or they disturb membrane stability. As a consequence of such interactions, plant medicines can interfere with organ malfunctions (heart and circulation, stomach and intestines, lung, liver, kidney, CNS disorders, gonads), inflammation and infections. In conclusion, phytotherapy is a traditional approach to use the right plants in the right concentrations to restore health or to relieve symptoms of disorders and disturbances.

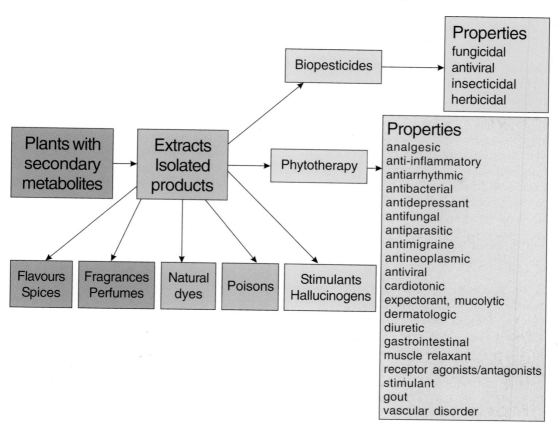

The diversity of natural products and their biological properties

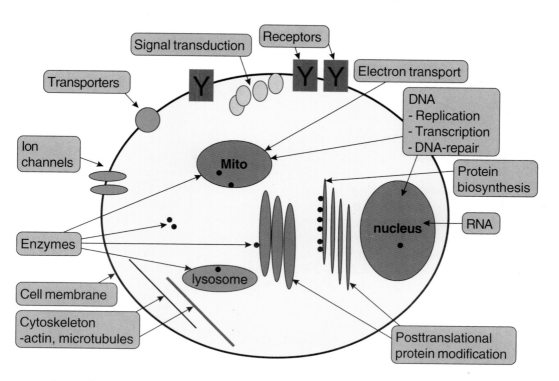

Overview of the main molecular targets that are modulated by plant medicines

QUALITY AND SAFETY

Quality control is the procedure that ensures safety and efficacy of phytomedicines by carefully checking (1) the correct identity of active ingredients – herbs or extracts (2) the correct (therapeutic) concentrations or doses of the active ingredients (3) the purity and hygiene (to ensure that no adulterants, undesirable chemicals or biological contaminants – e.g. bacteria – are present in the product).

Pharmacognosy is the science that deals with the identification of medicinal plants and drugs. The correct identity of the plant or product is important because a toxic plant may have been mistaken for the desired one. Positive identification requires botanical knowledge (identifying the plant or its parts), anatomical knowledge (identifying characteristic tissues or cells, such as glands) and phytochemical knowledge (identifying the main compounds in the plant or comparing a chromatographic fingerprint of the main constituents with that of an authentic reference sample).

Purity. High quality raw materials or finished product have to be free from adulterants, because these may have safety implications or they may dilute the product so that it becomes ineffective. Foreign organic matter is usually limited to 2%. The presence of soil and inorganic materials can be monitored by determining the ash value of the material (total ash value is often fixed at 3 or 5% of dry weight, and acid-soluble ash at no more than 1%, depending on the product). Heavy metals, organic pesticides, radioactive residues and bacterial contaminants have obvious safety implications. Lead and cadmium levels are usually set at 10 and 0.3 mg/kg respectively in the finished product. International guidelines are followed for pesticide residues. In the case of aldrin and dieldrin for example, the upper limit is usually 0.05 mg/kg. International guidelines also apply to the analysis of radioactive residues, including strontium-90, iodine-131, caesium-134, caesium-137 and plutonium-239 in medicinal raw materials. Microbiological tests are performed as a matter of routine to test for various microbial contaminants. Maximum acceptable levels differ between products, depending on their intended use (topical or internal, for example). In the case of the latter, *Salmonella* species and *Escherichia coli* must be negative, while fungi and aerobic bacteria may usually not exceed 10^4 and 10^5/g or ml respectively.

Standardisation of phytomedicine is done to ensure that all batches contain the same specified concentration of the active chemical compounds or marker compounds. Concentrations or dosages are important because herbal medicines (in common with conventional medicine) contain biologically active substances that may produce non-trivial side effects when taken in excessive doses. Very low doses, on the other hand, may have no therapeutic value. In practice, plant material is often highly variable, so that a minimum concentration or a concentration range is often used rather than an exact level. An upper limit is only necessary with highly active or potentially harmful ingredients, as most plants have a wide therapeutic window (i.e. the toxic dose is considerably higher than the therapeutic dose). In the case of compounds with a narrow therapeutic window, chemical entities are often used instead of extracts (e.g. cardiac glycosides, alkaloids).

Safety studies. These usually form part of a strict protocol that is required by regulatory authorities before a new phytomedicine can be registered (see notes on clinical trials). Animal studies have become less popular, so that tissue culture systems are now often used. However, in the case of traditional medicine, safety is generally accepted on the basis of a long history of safe use, without any serious side-effects reported in the literature. It should be noted that the incidence of serious toxicity due to traditional medicine is extremely rare when compared to accidental deaths resulting from the inappropriate use of conventional medicine.

EFFICACY OF MEDICINAL PLANT PRODUCTS

An important question is often asked about medicinal plants – do they actually work? If one considers the long history of herbal medicines in all cultures of the world, and the miracle cures for serious diseases such as leukaemia and malaria that were derived from medicinal plants, then the obvious answer is yes. However, in many cases, the scepticism about efficacy is justified, and is the result of unrealistic claims made by producers of herbal products. But how can we prove that a product is actually effective and that the claim on the label is valid? While no one would question the efficacy of a laxative medicine for example (easy enough to test!), the situation becomes more complicated when we deal with more complex health conditions.

There are several levels of evidence that can be taken into account:

1. **Traditional use** of a medicinal plant for a particular indication over a long period. The chemical compounds in the plant may provide a scientific rationale for the efficacy of the remedy that has been determined empirically through many generations.

2. **Plausible anecdotes** are clinical observations by health care practitioners that may support the claimed efficacy of a medicinal product. The more anecdotes that are reported by independent observers, the more plausible the claims become, especially if there is some physical evidence (e.g. blood tests or pathology reports).

3. **Pharmacological studies** are done to demonstrate pharmacological activity using *in vitro*, *in vivo* and *ex vivo* techniques. Isolated cells rarely behave in the same way as when they are part of a complicated system (the human body). Complex mixtures of chemical compounds (as is typically found in medicinal plants) may have numerous, synergistic effects on various organ systems. A single herb may, for example, have bitter tonic, diuretic, laxative, sedative, analgesic, anti-inflammatory and antioxidant effects. Extracts or compounds applied directly to cells in culture may show activity, but their pharmacokinetics (are they actually absorbed into the bloodstream or are they perhaps hydrolysed or broken down in the digestive tract?) may prove them to be ineffective.

4. **Observational studies** are appropriate in cases where many people have already been using the medicine out of their own free will (e.g. when it has been available on the market for some time). By studying a large number of patients and a control group, it may be possible to show statistically significant benefit.

5. **Clinical studies** are the most convincing scientific method of proving safety and efficacy. A serious obstacle to this approach is the fact that herbal preparations are seldom patentable, so that a company is unlikely to invest in expensive clinical trials when its competitors will benefit at no cost to themselves. The development of pharmaceuticals is done in four phases. Starting with a preclinical phase, clinical trials follow in three phases. **Phase I trials** are done in relatively few healthy people (as few as 12) to determine the best dosage form, as well as the safe dose. **Phase II trials** are done in a larger number of patients to evaluate how well the new drug works (test of efficacy) and to further evaluate safety. **Phase III trials** are done on a relatively large number of patients to test the new drug against the current standard treatment. A person will be assigned to the treatment group (new drug group) or control group (standard treatment group) at random (called randomisation). In some cases, a placebo (inactive product that closely resembles the treatment) is used as control. A double-blind design is often chosen, in which neither the patients nor the doctor or principal investigator know which persons are receiving the treatment and which ones the placebo. The aim is to show statistically significant differences between the treatment and the control group. In future product development, scientific proof of efficacy will undoubtedly become more important, even for traditional medicinal plants.

REGULATION OF HERBAL REMEDIES AND PHYTOMEDICINES

Regulation is mostly concerned with the safety, quality and efficacy of medicinal plants. Claims are limited to protect the public from being exploited. The traditional approach is to compile a pharmacopoeia of traditional medicinal plants that are considered to be safe and effective on the basis of a long history of use. A positive monograph in a recognised pharmacopoeia can then be viewed as an "official approval" for the use of the plant or plant part for specified indications.

In the United States of America, medicinal herbs ("botanicals") are sold as "dietary supplements". This is a legislative anomaly unique to the USA – in all other parts of the world, medicinal plants are regulated and sold as medicine. According to the *Dietary Supplement, Health and Education Act* of 1994 (DSHEA), dietary supplements include vitamins, minerals, herbs or botanicals, amino acids and other dietary substances not intended as food but to affect the structure and function of the body. Depending on the intended use, medicinal plants may therefore be marketed as dietary supplements – no medical claims allowed – or as medicine – then it is regulated as any other medicine, either as over-the-counter (OTC) drugs or as prescription drugs.

In Germany and Europe, the marketing of medicinal plant products is legally regulated. If plant products fulfil the requirements which would apply to synthetic drugs they are registered as medicines in their own right. In contrast to this group there are many plant products which are essentially used traditionally. They can be registered as traditional phytomedicines with soft indications if their use can be plausibly explained by pharmacopoeas or monographs. The monographs of the German Commission E and the new ESCOP monographs play an important role in this context.

In Japan, herbal products are classified according to how they are regulated, either as prescription drugs, generics or over-the-counter drugs (*Pharmaceutical Affairs Act*) or as functional foods (*Nutritional Improvement Act*). They are also classified according to how they are marketed. *Kampo* drugs are mixtures of between two and 32 different species, formulated strictly according to ancient Chinese compendiums. These are legally considered to be both prescription drugs and generic drugs – 130 such formulas are listed in the National Health Insurance Drug List. Herbs in Japanese pharmacopoeia are excluded because they are used alone and not in mixtures. Over-the-counter herbal drugs are based on traditional family formulas or old Chinese compendia. There are 210 such formulas (dosage and therapeutic claims are limited). New drugs include any new synthetic or plant-derived product (an expensive route). Functional foods are regulated in much the same way as generic drugs, and limited claims are allowed. Health foods are becoming very popular, but no therapeutic claims are allowed.

In Australia, herbal medicine is regulated by the *Therapeutic Goods Act* of 1989, which is aimed at controlling the quality, safety, efficacy and timely availability of therapeutic goods. Unless specifically exempted, all therapeutic goods must be entered on the *Australian Register of Therapeutic Goods* (ARTG) before they can be marketed, imported or exported. Herbal medicine may either be registered (as prescription drug or as over-the-counter drug) or more often listed (through a relatively simple procedure – the so-called *listing system*).

In China, safety or clinical data are required for new medicines, while traditional herbal medicines are listed in the *Pharmacopoeia of the People's Republic of China* (the latest English edition was published in 2000).

In India, any herbal medicine can be registered as long as it appears in standard texts, as part of the Ayurvedic or Unani medicine systems.

THE PLANTS
IN ALPHABETICAL ORDER

Abbreviations used in species treatments
Comm.E+ = positive monograph by the German Commission E.
ESCOP = new monograph series of the European Scientific Cooperative on Phytotherapy (plus volume number)
Pharm. = treated in pharmacopoeia(s)
WHO = monograph series of the World Health Organisation (plus volume number)

Acacia catechu
catechu acacia • black catechu

Acacia catechu

DESCRIPTION Catechu acacia is a small, thorny tree of up to 12 m high, with a crooked stem, straggling stems, compound, feathery leaves and pale yellow, fluffy flowers in dense heads. This multipurpose tree is used in forestation schemes in dry parts of India and in addition to its medicinal uses, it is also a source of fodder, fuel wood, charcoal, strong poles and timber.

ORIGIN India, Burma and Thailand to China. The product is mainly wild-harvested, but plantations of the tree have been established in parts of India.

PARTS USED Heartwood; sometimes leaves, young twigs or bark. An aqueous extract of the heartwood is concentrated by boiling. Upon cooling, it yields crystals (known as *katha* or *kath*) and the supernatant is concentrated and dried to form *cutch*, a dark brown solid mass.

THERAPEUTIC CATEGORY Anti-diarrhoeal; haemostyptic; antibiotic.

USES AND PROPERTIES Catechu or black catechu extracts are used to a limited extent against diarrhoea, dysentery, chronic catarrh, haemorrhage and mouth inflammation. It is employed in diluted form as a gargle for sore throat and mouth and gum infections. Externally it is applied to boils and ulcers. The extracts are produced on a large scale in Southeast Asia for tanning and dyeing.

PREPARATION AND DOSAGE The product is used in mixtures, tinctures and tablets.

ACTIVE INGREDIENTS Black catechu contains monomeric and polymeric flavanoid derivates, as well as flavonoids and a gum. The monomeric phenolics (mainly catechin and epicatechin) are concentrated in crystalline material (*katha* or *kath*), which has more than 55% catechin.

PHARMACOLOGICAL EFFECTS Tannins and other phenolic compounds have astringent qualities and make the product useful in the treatment of diarrhoea. They stop bleeding and may be used as an antibiotic to treat mucosal inflammations of the mouth and gum.

NOTES *Cutch* is particularly well known for its use in the colouring and shrinking of traditional khaki cloth. Pale catechu is a different product, derived from *Uncaria gambir*, a member of the family Rubiaceae.

STATUS Traditional medicine; Pharm.

Acacia catechu (L.f.) Willd.   family: Fabaceae

katha (Hindi); *cachou* (French); *Gerberakazie* (German); *catechu* (Italian)

Acacia senegal

gum acacia • gum arabic tree • gum Senegal tree

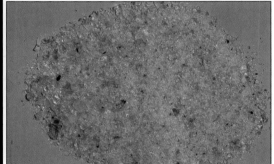

Acacia senegal fruits

Acacia senegal flowers

Gum arabic

DESCRIPTION This is a small, thorny tree (up to 6 m) with a rounded to spreading crown, compound leaves and elongated spikes of pale yellow to cream-coloured, fluffy flowers. Thorns are arranged in groups of three.

ORIGIN Africa. The tree occurs naturally in the arid parts of tropical regions, from southern to northern Africa; production of the gum occurs mainly in North Africa (Mali, Mauritania, Senegal and especially the Sudan; tree is known as *hashab*).

PARTS USED Gum, "gum arabic" (true gum arabic). This is the air-dried exudate that may flow naturally from the trees (after infection and under stress condition) and is simply collected, or the trees may be tapped (by the careful removal of strips of bark without injury to the cambium). The raw product comprises rounded, brittle, yellowish or pale brown masses or irregular glassy fragments. It is tasteless and odourless. Gum is also obtained, albeit to a minor degree, from other *Acacia* species in Africa (*A. nilotica*, *A. karroo*, *A. seyal*, *A. abyssinica*, *A. horrida*, *A. kirkii*, *A. erioloba*), Australia (*A. dealbata*, *A. decurrens*, *A. homalophylla*, *A. pycnantha*), Asia (*A. arabica A. ferruginea*, *A. leucophloea*) and America (*A. angico*, *A. farnesiana*).

THERAPEUTIC CATEGORY Protective of skin and mucosa.

USES AND PROPERTIES Medicinally, gum arabic and Cape gum have been used as emollient and skin protective agents and as pharmaceutical aids: as emulsifiers, stabilisers of suspensions and additives for solid formulations. It is sometimes used to treat bacterial and fungal infections of the skin and mouth.

PREPARATION AND DOSAGE The product is applied to the skin or is included in formulations and tablets.

ACTIVE INGREDIENTS Gum arabic is a complex polysaccharide (MW 270000) comprising mainly arabinose, galactose, D-glucuronic acid and L-rhamnose subunits.

PHARMACOLOGICAL EFFECTS Gum arabic softens and soothes the skin and mucosa, and has a moisturising, antibiotic and protective action that promotes healing.

NOTES The gum has numerous industrial applications (adhesives, inks and paints). Gums from various species of *Acacia* are important food items in rural areas and are used commercially as additive in the food industry (as tasteless and non-toxic stabilisers and emulsifiers).

STATUS Pharm.

Acacia senegal (L.) Willd.

family: Fabaceae

acacie gomme arabique (French); *Verek-Akazie* (German); *acacia del Senegal* (Italian)

Achillea millefolium

yarrow • milfoil • woundwort

Achillea millefolium (white form)

Achillea millefolium cultivar

DESCRIPTION A perennial herb with several erect stems arising from multiple rhizomes below the ground. The compound leaves are bright green and feathery. Numerous small, white to pink flower heads are borne in flat-topped clusters. *A. moschata* occurs in the Alps, has similar secondary metabolites as *A. millefolium* and has been traditionally used for similar indications.

ORIGIN Yarrow represents a species complex with many forms and grows naturally in Europe and western Asia but is cultivated as an ornamental and medicinal herb in many parts of the world.

PARTS USED Whole plant (*Millefolii herba*) or the flowers (*Millefolii flos*); sometimes the essential oil.

THERAPEUTIC CATEGORY Anti-arthritic, anti-pyretic, anti-inflammatory, diuretic.

USES AND PROPERTIES The herb is traditionally used to treat arthritis, fever, the common cold and hypertension. It is nowadays mainly recommended for lack of appetite and minor dyspeptic complaints. For external use, it is added to bath water to treat pelvic autonomic dysfunction (painful cramp-like conditions of the lower pelvis in women).

PREPARATION AND DOSAGE Infusions or tinctures are used and the herb (with or without the flowers) may be included in mixtures. For internal use, Commission E recommends a daily dose of 4.5 g of yarrow herb (or 3 g of yarrow flowers and three teaspoons of fresh juice). For external use in a so-called sitz-bath ("Sitzbad"), use 100 g of the herb in 20 liters of water.

ACTIVE INGREDIENTS Pyrrolidine alkaloids (betonicine and stachydrine), flavonoids and volatiles (including β-pinene, camphor, 1,8-cineole, caryophyllene and azulenic compounds – in the form of sesquiterpene lactones such as achillicin – and numerous others). The bright blue azulenes are not present in the fresh herb, but are formed as artefacts from "proazulenes" during steam distillation of the oil.

PHARMACOLOGICAL EFFECTS Antibacterial and anti-inflammatory activities have been documented, and are mainly ascribed to the sesquiterpene lactones and azulenic compounds. The flavonoids are thought to be antispasmodic, while the alkaloids are said to have antipyretic and hypotensive effects.

WARNING Fresh plants may cause dermatitis in sensitive people.

STATUS Pharm.; Comm.E+.

Achillea millefolium L.

family: Asteraceae

millefeuille (French); *Schafgarbe* (German); *achillea millefoglio* (Italian); *milenrama* (Spanish)

Aconitum napellus

aconite • monkshood • wolfsbane

Aconitum napellus

Aconitum napellus flowers and fruit

DESCRIPTION Aconite is a perennial herb with erect flowering stems that grow from a tuberous rootstock. The stems bear deeply dissected, toothed leaves and clusters of purple to blue flowers. Enlarged sepals (calyx lobes) form the conspicuous part of the flower – the upper one is characteristically hood-shaped and gives the flowers their distinctive appearance.

ORIGIN A. napellus occurs in mountainous parts of western and central Europe. Several species are commonly cultivated as ornamentals. Tubers are also harvested from wild plants. A. anthora, A. ferox, A. vulparia and A. lycoctonum have been used in traditional European medicine (today in homoeopathy). Species such as A. carmichaelii and A. kusnezoffii are important in Chinese medicine (chuan wu and chao wu).

PARTS USED Tincture of the fleshy tubers (rarely leaves).

THERAPEUTIC CATEGORY Externally, sometimes as anti-rheumatic, analgesic and anti-neuralgic.

USES AND PROPERTIES Aconite tincture is commonly used as one of many ingredients in cough syrups. The main alkaloid, aconitine, can be used in pure form (in 0.1 mg granules) to treat facial neuralgia. In traditional medicine in India and China, the tuber has been used topically as analgesic, anti-neuralgic, anti-inflammatory and antipyretic.

PREPARATION AND DOSAGE Dilute tinctures are widely used with galenicals and in homoeopathy. The product may also be applied topically in higher concentrations to treat rheumatism and neuralgia.

ACTIVE INGREDIENTS Aconitum contains numerous diterpenoid alkaloids in concentrations of 0.5 to 1.5% of dry weight. Aconitine is the main compound.

PHARMACOLOGICAL EFFECTS At toxic concentration, aconitum causes numbness, abnormal cardiac rhythm and death through respiratory arrest. Aconitine stimulates Na^+-channels; it first activates and then paralyses the peripheral nerve endings. The compound is highly lipophilic and can be resorbed through the skin.

WARNING The tubers are extremely toxic when ingested – the lethal dose in adults is only about 10 g. Several human intoxications due to Aconitum (including the two Chinese species) have been reported.

NOTES Aconite was formerly used as arrow poison, to kill vermin and enemies.

STATUS Pharm. (formerly), but discontinued in recent years due to the risk of intoxication.

Aconitum napellus L.

family: Ranunculaceae

aconit napel (French); Blauer Eisenhut (German); aconito (Italian); acónito (Spanish)

Acorus calamus

calamus • sweet flag • flag root

Acorus calamus flower spike

Acorus calamus rhizome

Acorus calamus

DESCRIPTION A reed-like, perennial, aquatic plant with bright green, sword-shaped leaves growing from creeping rhizomes. The leaves are aromatic, relatively broad (more than 15 mm wide), with a distinct midrib. Minute flowers are grouped together in small oblong spikes. Grassy-leaved sweet flag (*A. gramineus*), is well known as *shi chang pu* in Chinese medicine. It is easily recognised by the non-aromatic, narrow leaves (less than 10 mm wide) which are without a distinct midrib.

ORIGIN The plant is indigenous to northern temperate zones (Europe, Asia, North America); in Asian tropics it occurs from India to New Guinea. *A. gramineus* occurs naturally in China, Japan and Southeast Asia.

PARTS USED Rhizomes (fresh, dried or powdered).

THERAPEUTIC CATEGORY Bitter tonic (*amarum*), stimulant.

USES AND PROPERTIES The aromatic, bitter rhizomes are used to treat indigestion and flatulence or to stimulate appetite. Traditional uses are mainly as a digestive and carminative, but sometimes as an emetic, anti-spasmodic, stimulant and anthelmintic. It appears to relieve stomach cramps, chronic dysentery and asthma. It is believed to have a strengthening effect on the nervous system and has been used in Ayurvedic and Chinese medicine. The plant was found in Tutankhamen's tomb in Egypt, and is mentioned in the Old Testament (Exodus XXX).

PREPARATION AND DOSAGE Tinctures are generally used but dried or candied rhizomes may be directly chewed or taken as an infusion in boiling water.

ACTIVE INGREDIENTS The essential oil contains monoterpenoids (farnesene, geranylacetate, camphene, *p*-cymene, linalool) and sesquiterpenoids (acorenone), especially phenylpropanoids (β-asarone =cis-isoasarone) in the Indian variety.

PHARMACOLOGICAL EFFECTS The spasmolytic properties of the essential oil and the sedative effects of the main component of the Indian variety, β-asarone, have been demonstrated. Asarone and the monoterpenes show antimicrobial properties.

WARNING The use of *Acorus* in digestive medicines has been discontinued in most countries due to possible harmful effects (mutagenic and embryotoxic properties). The European variety contains only trace amounts of β-asarone and is sometimes allowed in food products.

STATUS Pharm.

Acorus calamus L.

family: Acoraceae

acore vrai (French); *bacc* (Hindi); *Kalmus* (German); *calamo aromatico* (Italian); *cálamo aromático* (Spanish)

Adonis vernalis
yellow pheasant's eye • spring adonis

Adonis vernalis

DESCRIPTION A small perennial herb with divided, feathery leaves and large, bright yellow flowers produced in early spring.

ORIGIN Europe (excluding the British Isles), West and East Siberia.

PARTS USED Aerial flowering parts (*Adonidis herba*). Raw material comes mainly from Eastern Europe and Russia.

THERAPEUTIC CATEGORY Heart stimulant.

USES AND PROPERTIES The product is sometimes used as a heart stimulant, in the same way as more familiar sources of heart glycosides such as digitalis. It is considered particularly useful when cardiac conditions are accompanied by nervous symptoms. Several traditional uses are known, including the treatment of bladder and kidney stones.

PREPARATION AND DOSAGE Standardised powder is used (more rarely weak tinctures), but the dosage has to be carefully controlled to avoid negative side-effects. The powdered drug contains about 0.25 % cardiac glycosides, standardised to have the same activity as 0.2% cymarin (see below). The average daily dose of adonis powder is 0.6 g. According to the Commission E, the maximum single dose and maximum daily dose should not exceed 1 g and 3 g respectively.

ACTIVE INGREDIENTS Several heart glycosides (cardenolides) are present, in concentrations of 0.2 to 0.5%. Cymarin is the main active compound (hydrolysis gives k-strophantidin and *D*-cymarose), with smaller amounts of adonitoxin (hydrolysis gives adonitoxigenin and *L*-rhamnose) and 26 additional cardenolides. Also present are flavonoids (flavone-C-glycosides).

PHARMACOLOGICAL EFFECTS The drug shows positive inotropic and venotonic effects. Cardenolides inhibit Na^+, K^+-ATPase and indirectly increase the concentrations of cellular Ca^{++} ions that trigger muscle contraction. Cardenolides are known to increase the strength of contraction of the heart muscle without increasing the pulse.

WARNING The plant or products derived thereof are potentially dangerous and should not be used without the supervision of a qualified health care professional.

NOTES *Adonis vernalis* is not used in its pure form in OTC herbal medicine (except in mixtures with other cardenolide-containing plants and in some highly diluted homoeopathic remedies).

STATUS Pharm.; Comm.E+.

Adonis vernalis L.   family: Ranunculaceae

Frühlings-Adonisröschen (German); *adonide de printemps* (French); *adonide* (Italian); *botón de oro* (Spanish)

Aesculus hippocastanum

horse chestnut

Aesculus hippocastanum flowers

Aesculus hippocastanum tree with fruit

Horse chestnut seeds

DESCRIPTION Horse chestnut is a deciduous tree of up to 30 m high with large, compound leaves and attractive white flowers spotted with pink. The large, brown, nut-like seeds have a shiny surface and are borne in spiny capsules. Other *Aesculus* species are used in homoeopathy, such as *A. glabra, A. octandra, A. pavia* and *A.* x *rubicunda.*

ORIGIN Horse chestnut occurs naturally from Eastern Europe (the Balkans) to central Asia (the Himalayas). The original species is widely cultivated but several hybrids are also found in gardens and parks.

PARTS USED Mainly the seeds (*Hippocastani semen*); less often the leaves (*Hippocastani folium*) or bark.

THERAPEUTIC CATEGORY Anti-inflammatory, venotonic and anti-oedema.

USES AND PROPERTIES Seed extracts are commonly used to treat varicose veins, ulcerations and piles, as well as other symptoms of venous and lymphatic vessel insufficiency, especially of the legs. It is sometimes employed to treat rheumatism and fever. Seeds were formerly used as washing powder.

PREPARATION AND DOSAGE Special extracts of dried seeds are mainly used in modern phytotherapy.

The daily oral dose is 250 to 750 mg dry extract (equivalent to 30 to 150 mg aescin); taken twice per day. Tinctures (of the seeds, leaves or bark) are also used both internally (to be drunk, or gargled in the case of mouth ulcers) and components of skin creams.

ACTIVE INGREDIENTS Seeds contain a mixture of triterpene saponins (collectively known as aescin) in concentrations of up to 5% of the dry weight. Extracts are used to adjust the level of aescin to the required level (16-21%). The main saponins are glycosides of two triterpenoids, protoaescigenin and barringtogenol C. The seed coat contains proanthocyanidins (oligomers of epicatechol and catechol) of which procyanidin B2 is a main component.

PHARMACOLOGICAL EFFECTS Aescin, as well as the dry seed extract, have proven anti-exudate and venotonic (vascular-tightening) activity. The saponins and possibly the tannins of horse chestnut have anti-inflammatory and anti-oedema activities. They increase vascular tone and increase the stability of capillary veins.

STATUS Pharm.; Comm.E+; ESCOP 6; clinical studies+ (seed extract).

Aesculus hippocastanum L.

family: Hippocastanaceae

Rosskastanie (German); *châtaignier de cheval, marronnier d'Inde* (French); *castagna amare* (Italian); *castaño de Indias* (Spanish)

Agathosma betulina
buchu • round leaf buchu

Agathosma betulina

Agathosma crenulata

DESCRIPTION Buchu is a gland-dotted shrub of up to 2 m in height, with small, characteristically rounded leaves of which the tips curve backwards. The white or pale purple flowers are small and star-shaped. This species is sometimes confused with oval leaf buchu, *A. crenulata* (synon. *Barosma crenulata*), but in the latter the leaves are more than twice as long as they are broad. Several other species have rarely been used as a source of "buchu".

ORIGIN *A. betulina* occurs only in South Africa and has a restricted natural distribution area in the mountains of the Western Cape Province. It is cultivated on a small but increasing scale.

PARTS USED Dry or fresh leaves (*Barosmae folium; synon. Folia Bucco*).

THERAPEUTIC CATEGORY Diuretic, diaphoretic and stimulant tonic.

USES AND PROPERTIES Buchu is widely used and has a great reputation for treating kidney and urinary tract diseases, for the symptomatic relief of rheumatism, and also for external application on wounds and bruises (in folk medicine as "buchu vinegar"). Buchu is an excellent tonic and is used to treat minor digestive distur-bances. Buchu leaf and buchu oil are important flavour components in herbal teas and food products.

PREPARATION AND DOSAGE A dose of 1-2 g of dry leaf (or equivalent quantities in the form of tinctures) are taken three times per day.

ACTIVE INGREDIENTS Buchu contains essential oil (2.5%) with limonene, isomenthone, diosphenol (buchu camphor) and terpinen-4-ol as the main compounds. Sulphur-containing minor compounds (such as 8-mercapto-p-methane-3-one) are partly responsible for the characteristic blackcurrant smell and flavour. Oil from oval leaf buchu (*A. crenulata*) is less desirable because it contains little or no diosphenol and high levels of pulegone, a potentially toxic compound. Mucilage, resins and flavonoids (mainly diosmin) are present.

PHARMACOLOGICAL EFFECTS Buchu and buchu oil are considered to have urinary antiseptic, diuretic and anti-inflammatory properties. However, there is as yet no published scientific evidence to justify any of the traditional indications, including the use as urinary tract disinfectant.

STATUS Traditional medicine; Comm.E+; Pharm.

Agathosma betulina (Berg.) Pillans [= *Barosma betulina* (Berg.) Bartl. & H.L. Wendl.]   family: Rutaceae

buchu (French); *Bucco* (German); *buchu* (Italian)

Agrimonia eupatoria

common agrimony

Agrimonia eupatoria

Agrimonia procera

DESCRIPTION An erect, perennial herb (up to 1 m high), with compound, toothed, hairy leaves and small yellow flowers borne in slender spikes. A closely related species, the fragrant agrimony, *A. procera* is sometimes also used and is considered an acceptable alternative source of raw material. It is similar to *A. eupatoria* but can easily be distinguished by its fragrant smell. In traditional Chinese medicine, *A. pilosa* is used.

ORIGIN Europe and Near East (*A. eupatoria*); Asia Minor (*A. procera*, often cultivated) and Asia (*A. pilosa*). The herb is gathered while flowering – commercial sources originate mainly from eastern Europe.

PARTS USED Dried, aboveground parts of *A. eupatoria* (*Agrimoniae herba*).

THERAPEUTIC CATEGORY Anti-diarrhoeal, astringent, mild diuretic.

USES AND PROPERTIES The plant is historically important as an astringent in the treatment of external wounds, especially to stop bleeding. Nowadays it is mostly used to treat mucosal inflammations of the throat and acute diarrhoea, but also for piles, cystitis and urinary incontinence. It is claimed (without scientific evidence) to have benefits in rheumatism, arthritis and gall-bladder disorders.

PREPARATION AND DOSAGE The herb is used in tablets and tinctures. It is an ingredient of numerous commercial preparations, mainly liver, bile and stomach remedies. A tea can be prepared from 1.5 g of the herb (taken two or three times a day).

ACTIVE INGREDIENTS Agrimonia (like other herbs from the Rosaceae), is rich in tannins, particularly catechol tannins and gallotannins. One of the main compounds is agrimoniin. The herb also contains 20% polysaccharides, triterpenoids and flavonoids (glucosides of luteolin and apigenin). Small amounts of essential oil may be present if *A. procera* was included in the material. *A. pilosa*, rich in agrimophol (a polymer of gallic acid), also shows anthelmintic properties.

PHARMACOLOGICAL EFFECTS Gallotannins are astringent; they have the ability to form hydrogen and ionic bonds with macromolecules such as proteins. Extracts show antiviral and marked antibacterial activities. Agrimony is considered to have diuretic effects but there is limited scientific evidence to support the traditional use in ailments of the urinary tract.

STATUS Pharm.; Comm.E+.

Agrimonia eupatoria L.   family: Rosaceae

aigremoine gariot (French); *Kleiner Odermennig* (German); *agrimonia* (Italian); *agrimonia* (Spanish)

Alchemilla vulgaris

lady's mantle

Alchemilla vulgaris

Alchemilla alpina

DESCRIPTION A perennial herb with rosettes of lobed leaves and sparse clusters of small yellow flowers. The leaves are somewhat funnel-shaped and shallowly lobed, with conspicuous teeth along the margins. *A. vulgaris* is a species complex (formerly named as *A. xanthochlora*). The Alpine lady's mantle (*A. alpina* and *A. conjuncta*) is sometimes also used for medicine. It has palmately compound leaves with oblong, free lobes. These plants should not be confused with parsley piert (*Aphanes arvensis*, previously known as *Alchemilla arvensis*), a related, tannin-rich plant used in traditional medicine.

ORIGIN Europe, North America and Asia (*A. vulgaris*) or central, western and northern Europe (*A. alpina*). *A. vulgaris* is mainly used, and raw material is imported from eastern Europe.

PARTS USED Dried aerial parts, collected while the plants are in flower (*Alchemillae herba*).

THERAPEUTIC CATEGORY Astringent, anti-haemorrhagic.

USES AND PROPERTIES The plant is considered useful in treating minor cases of diarrhoea, sore throat and externally for sores and septic wounds. Traditional uses include gynaecological ailments, especially dysmenorrhoea.

PREPARATION AND DOSAGE For the main indication (diarrhoea), a daily dose of 5-10 g is used. The dried herb and extracts thereof is included in mixtures, ointments, mouthwashes and throat lozenges.

ACTIVE INGREDIENTS High concentrations of ellagitannins (6-8%) are present, including agrimoniin, laevigatin F and pedunculagin. Flavonoids (including a quercetin glucuronide) have also been found.

PHARMACOLOGICAL EFFECTS In common with several other tannin-containing herbs of the Rosaceae, lady's mantle is highly astringent and thus useful to treat mild diarrhoea and sore throat. It may also be of some value as a venotonic to treat vascular disorders.

WARNING Severe or persistent diarrhoea is potentially dangerous (especially in infants and children) and should receive medical attention.

NOTES *Alchemilla alpina* has been used to treat menstrual disorders, and as diuretic and antispasmodic medicine, while *Aphanes arvensis* is used mainly to dissolve kidney stones. None of these uses have been substantiated by scientific studies.

STATUS Pharm.; Comm.E+ (*A. vulgaris* only).

Alchemilla vulgaris auct. non L. (= *A. xanthochlora* Rothm.)　　　　　　　　family: Rosaceae

alchimille, manteau de Notre-Dame (French); *Gewöhnlicher Frauenmantel* (German); *alchemilla* (Italian); *pie de leon* (Spanish)

Allium cepa

onion

Allium cepa flowers and fruits

Allium cepa

Onions

DESCRIPTION A bulbous perennial with hollow green leaves arising from a bulb formed by dense layers of fleshy leaf bases. The hollow flowering stem bears a rounded cluster of white or purple flowers. Related plants such as scallion (*A. ascalonium*), Chinese shallot (*A. chinense*) and leek (*A. porrum*) are used as culinary herbs.

ORIGIN *Allium cepa* is a cultigen of uncertain origin, probably originating from wild plants in the Eastern Mediterranean or the Middle East. Known from ancient archaeological sites, it is nowadays widely cultivated on a large scale as an important culinary herb and vegetable.

PARTS USED Fresh or dried bulb (*Allii cepae bulbus*).

THERAPEUTIC CATEGORY Antibiotic; cholesterol lowering.

USES AND PROPERTIES Treatment of appetite loss and prevention of age-related changes in blood vessels (arteriosclerosis). Onions and its juice may be used to treat minor digestive disturbances and is used to overcome the immediate effects of insect stings. Juice mixed with honey or sugar is a traditional treatment for colds and cough. The treatment of dysentery, wounds, scars, keloids, asthma and diabetes are amongst the many traditional uses.

PREPARATION AND DOSAGE An effective daily dose is considered to be 50 g of fresh onion or 20 g of dried product (or equivalent amounts in preparations). The raw bulb may be applied externally or fresh juice is taken on its own or mixed with honey or sugar.

ACTIVE INGREDIENTS The activity (and pungent smell) is due to several sulphur-containing compounds – mainly sulfoxides, but also cepaenes (α-sulfinyl-disulfides). Sulfoxides (such as trans-S-(1-propenyl)-L-(+)-cysteinesulfoxide, an isomer of alliin) are present in the intact bulb, but they are converted by enzymatic action (i.e. by alliinase) into various sulfides that spontaneously form disulfides. These compounds can easily form disulfide bonds with SH-groups of proteins and thus alter their biological activities.

PHARMACOLOGICAL EFFECTS Onions are known to have antimicrobial, hypoglycaemic, anti-platelet aggregation, anti-asthmatic, antiallergic, lipid- and blood pressure-lowering effects. Clinical trials hitherto focused mainly on garlic (see *Allium sativum*) but there is good clinical evidence of efficacy of onions in treating appetite loss and preventing arteriosclerosis.

STATUS Pharm.; Comm.E+; WHO 1; clinical trials+.

Allium cepa L.   family: Alliaceae

oignon (French); *Küchenzwiebel* (German); *cipolla* (Italian); *cebolla* (Spanish)

Allium sativum

garlic

Allium sativum

Allium sativum bulbs

DESCRIPTION Garlic is a perennial herb with fleshy and slightly greyish leaves, rounded flower heads and numerous small bulbs (bulbules, cloves) borne in a group and surrounded by a white papery sheath. Bear's garlic (*Allium ursinum*) is common in Europe and Asia and its leaves are used as a garlic substitute.

ORIGIN Middle East or central Asia. The exact origin is uncertain – garlic is known only in its cultivated form. It has been used as a food, spice and medicinal crop since antiquity.

PARTS USED The fresh bulbs or cloves (*Allii sativi bulbus*), garlic powder (*Allii sativi pulvis*) and garlic oil.

THERAPEUTIC CATEGORY Lipid lowering activities; antibacterial, antiviral.

USES AND PROPERTIES The main medicinal uses are supportive dietary treatment of high blood lipids and the prevention of age-related vascular changes (e.g. triglyceride and cholesterol lowering activities). Garlic has become a popular remedy against the common cold, with claimed diaphoretic, expectorant, antiviral, antispasmodic and antiseptic properties.

PREPARATION AND DOSAGE The average daily dose is 4 g fresh garlic (or equivalent amounts in preparations). Garlic is best used fresh, but carefully dried garlic (as powder) and the essential oil are included in tinctures and syrups.

ACTIVE INGREDIENTS Various sulphur-containing compounds in garlic or garlic oil are known to have biological effects. The main compound in intact garlic is alliin, which is degraded by an enzyme, alliinase, first to an unstable intermediate and then to allicin (often the main component in processed material). Another metabolite, known as ajoene (Z and E forms), also inhibits the aggregation of platelets. These sulfides can form disulfides with SH-groups of proteins and thus modulate a wide range of proteins and enzymes.

PHARMACOLOGICAL EFFECTS Numerous studies in animals and humans have demonstrated antimicrobial, antiviral and lipid lowering effects. Allicin and ajoene are thought to act as platelet aggregation inhibitors, leading to prolonged bleeding and clotting time. Antimycotic activity is ascribed to inhibition of lipid synthesis in yeasts.

WARNING Garlic may interact with standard anticoagulant agents such as warfarin.

STATUS Pharm.; Comm.E+; ESCOP 3; WHO 1; clinical trials+.

Allium sativum L.

family: Alliaceae

ail blanc (French); *Knoblauch* (German); *aglio* (Italian); *ajo* (Spanish)

Aloe ferox

bitter aloe • Cape aloe

Aloe ferox

Tapping of *Aloe ferox*

Aloe lump (Cape aloes)

DESCRIPTION The bitter aloe or Cape aloe is a robust, single-stemmed succulent with broad, spiny leaves and usually bright red or orange flowers in erect, candle-shaped clusters.

ORIGIN Southeastern parts of South Africa. The products are wild-crafted on a sustainable basis.

PARTS USED The bitter, yellow leaf juice is dried to form a dark brown resinous solid, known commercially as aloe lump or Cape aloes (=*Aloe capensis*). The gel (non-bitter, inner fleshy part of the leaf) is used in tonics and cosmetics.

THERAPEUTIC CATEGORY Bitters: laxative, tonic; Gel: tonic, wound healing.

USES AND PROPERTIES Cape aloes is an important laxative and is included in bitter tonics. The gel has become popular as a health drink. Minor uses include the treatment of arthritis, eczema and conjunctivitis. Extracted and spray-dried leaf gel is used in skin care products.

PREPARATION AND DOSAGE A small crystal of the drug (0.05-0.2 g), is taken orally as a laxative. Half the laxative dose is taken for arthritis. Fresh bitter sap is instilled directly against conjunctivitis and sinusitis.

ACTIVE INGREDIENTS The main purgative principle (15-30% of aloe lump) is the anthrone C-glucoside aloin (=barbaloin). Aloin occurs as an equal mixture of two stereoisomers, aloin A and aloin B. The wound-healing properties of the gel are ascribed to polysaccharides and glycoproteins and to hydrating, insulating and protective effects.

PHARMACOLOGICAL EFFECTS Aloin is converted in the colon by bacteria into aloe-emodin anthrone. Anthrones are responsible for a stimulant laxative action. Molecular targets include a chloride channel and less importantly the Na^+, K^+-ATPase. Anthranoids enhance peristalsis and the secretion of water and inhibit its resorption in the colon. Aloe extracts have antimicrobial, antiviral and cytotoxic properties.

WARNING The product has a griping and abortifacient effect and should therefore not be used during pregnancy. Laboratory studies indicate that anthraquinones may be carcinogenic. Anthraquinone-containing laxatives should not be taken for prolonged periods, since K^+ homoeostasis will be changed.

STATUS Pharm.; Comm.E+; ESCOP 5; WHO 1.

Aloe ferox Mill.   family: Asphodelaceae

aloès féroce (French); *Kap-Aloe, Gefährliche Aloe* (German); *aloe del Capo* (Italian)

Aloe vera

aloe vera • Curaçao aloe

Aloe vera

Aloe vera plantation in Texas

Aloe vera leaves

DESCRIPTION This aloe is a stemless plant with one to several rosettes of thick, fleshy, non-thorny leaves and erect, yellow or red flower clusters.

ORIGIN North Africa. *Aloe vera* is an ancient cultigen and forms the basis of a very large industry, mainly in Central America and the southern USA.

PARTS USED The gel is the non-bitter, slimy inner leaf pulp, nowadays the main product. This should not be confused with the extremely bitter, yellow leaf exudate, which is dried to a crystalline substance known as Curaçao aloes or Barbados aloes. Pure gel is obtained by cutting away the outer aloin-containing layers of the leaf. Known as "filleting", the process can be done by hand (the best quality) or mechanically. Alternatively the whole leaf is pulped and the aloin removed by filtration (so-called "whole leaf extract").

THERAPEUTIC CATEGORY Gel: wound-healing, skin care, tonic drink; Bitters: stimulant laxative, bitter tonic (*amarum*).

USES AND PROPERTIES Curaçao aloes is still used to some extent to treat constipation and as a bitter tonic. Millions of litres of gel are used annually for health drinks and dietary supplements. It is assumed to be beneficial in treating burns and other skin disorders, infections and inflammations, the immune system, diabetes, high cholesterol, and even cancer.

PREPARATION AND DOSAGE The minimum dose to maintain a soft stool is used (20-30 mg aloin per day), while 50-100 ml of the gel may be taken three times a day as a tonic.

ACTIVE INGREDIENTS Curaçao aloes has aloin (an anthrone C-glucoside) as main laxative compound (up to 38%). The gel contains 0.5-2% solids, including complex polysaccharides (glucomannans), glycoproteins, amino acids, minerals, salicylic acid and enzymes. An acetylated mannan (acemannan, Carrisyn™) is used in wound therapy. Gel used for health drinks is often bitter and mildly laxative, with aloin present at levels of 10 ppm or more.

PHARMACOLOGICAL EFFECTS Apart from the laxative bitters (see *A. ferox*), the gel has anti-inflammatory, wound-healing and immune stimulatory properties (though not scientifically established in detail).

WARNING Chronic laxative use is potentially dangerous (see *A. ferox*).

STATUS Pharm.; Comm.E+; WHO 1 (gel).

Aloe vera (L.) Burm.f. (= *Aloe barbadensis* Mill.)

family: Asphodelaceae

aloès vrai, laloi (French); *Echte Aloe, Aloe vera* (German); *aloe vera* (Italian); *sábila, zábila* (Spanish)

Aloysia triphylla

lemon verbena • vervain

Aloysia triphylla

Lippia javanica

DESCRIPTION Lemon verbena is a perennial shrub of up to 1 m high. The unifoliolate leaves are oblong, more or less hairless and have a strong lemony smell when crushed. They characteristically occur in whorls of three at each node. Tiny white or pale purple flowers are borne in slender clusters, and can be quite attractive when they are present in large numbers.

ORIGIN South America (Argentine and Chile); a popular garden plant in warm and temperate regions.

PARTS USED Fresh or dried leaves (*Lippiae triphyllae folium*) and essential oil (*Lippiae triphyllae aetheroleum*).

THERAPEUTIC CATEGORY Digestive, sedative (aromatherapy).

USES AND PROPERTIES Dried leaves are sold for use as a relaxing health tea (especially in France) and are included in commercial herbal teas. It is considered to be antispasmodic, antipyretic, sedative and stomachic, so that it is used to treat nervous disturbances, colds, fever, asthma, as well as for minor digestive disorders, such as indigestion, colic, flatulence and diarrhoea.

PREPARATION AND DOSAGE A tea can be prepared from 1-2 g of dried herb and taken three times per day.

ACTIVE INGREDIENTS The plant contains an essential oil, with neral and geranial (the mixture is known as citral) and photocitral A (formed by light from citral) as characteristic compounds. Also present are other monoterpenes (borneol, limonene, geraniol, nerol and terpineol) as well as some sesquiterpenoids (caryophyllene, curcumene, myrcenene and isovalerianic acid). Flavonoids include apigenin, luteolin and 6-hydroxylated flavones, together with their methyl esters (eupafolin, hispidulin, eupatorin, and salvigenin).

PHARMACOLOGICAL EFFECTS The traditional uses of lemon verbena may be partly explained by the presence of essential oil and flavonoids. The claimed sedative and anxiolytic effects of the tea need to be demonstrated in clinical trials.

NOTES Lemon verbena was previously included in *Lippia*. Species of this closely related genus are used as herbal teas in Africa, including *L. javanica* and *L. scaberrima* and in South and Central America *L. dulcis*, *L. graveolens* and *L. lycioides*.

STATUS Traditional medicine.

Aloysia triphylla (L'Hérit.) Britton [= *Lippia citriodora* H.B.K.; *L. triphylla* (L'Hérit.) Kuntze]   family: Verbenaceae

verveine odorante (French); *Zitronenstrauch* (German); *limoncina, erba luigia, cedrina* (Italian); *verbena olorosa, hierba luisa* (Spanish)

Alpinia officinarum
galangal • Siamese ginger • lesser galangal

Alpinia officinarum flowers

Alpinia officinarum rhizome

Alpinia officinarum dried rhizomes

DESCRIPTION A robust, leafy perennial herb of more than 1 m high that grows from thick, fleshy rhizomes below the ground. Clusters of attractive, white and purplish flowers are infrequently borne on the stem tips. The plant resembles ginger (*Zingiber officinale*).

ORIGIN Galangal is indigenous to eastern and southeastern Asia and is widely cultivated, mainly in China, Malaysia, Thailand and India.

PARTS USED Fresh or dried rhizomes (*Galangae rhizoma*).

THERAPEUTIC CATEGORY Carminative, digestive tonic, anti-emetic.

USES AND PROPERTIES The main medicinal use of galangal is as a stomachic to treat dyspepsia and appetite loss. Galangal is a popular ingredient in Chinese cooking and is traditionally used in China as a medicine against indigestion, stomach pain, nausea and hiccups. It is also used in traditional Indian and European medicine.

PREPARATION AND DOSAGE Tea made from about 0.5-1 g of dried rhizome is taken half an hour before meals. A daily dose of 2-4 g of the dry product (or its equivalent in fresh form) can be taken. It is also used as

a tincture, decoction or in powder form.

ACTIVE INGREDIENTS Galangal is highly aromatic and contains essential oil (0.5-1%). The main ingredients are monoterpenoids (α-pinene, cineole, linalool), methylcinnamate and eugenol. The pungent principles are various non-volatile diarylheptanoids (formerly known as galangol), together with phenyl alkyl ketones (known as gingerols). Flavonoids (mainly quercetin and kaempferol glycosides) are also present.

PHARMACOLOGICAL EFFECTS Galangal has proven antispasmodic, anti-inflammatory, antibacterial and antimycotic properties. The diarylheptanoids (and also the phenyl alkyl ketones) are known to inhibit prostaglandin biosynthesis.

NOTES Other *Alpinia* species that are used in traditional medicine include greater galangal (*A. galanga*) in Southeast Asia, *A. oxyphylla* (fruit; *yi zhi ren*) and *A. katsumadai* (*cao dou cou*) in China, and *A. calcarata* (*rasna*) in India. Seeds of the West African *Aframomum melegueta* (Zingiberaceae) are known as "grains of paradise" and are used medicinally for the same indications as galangal rhizome.

STATUS Pharm.; Comm.E+.

Alpinia officinarum Hance   family: Zingiberaceae

gao liang jiang (Chinese); *galanga* (French); *Echter Galgant* (German); galanga (Italian); *galanga* (Spanish)

Althaea officinalis
marshmallow • white mallow

Althaea officinalis flowers

Althaea officinalis

Alcea rosea flowers

DESCRIPTION An erect perennial herb of about 2 m in height, with hairy leaves and attractive pink flowers.

ORIGIN The plant is indigenous to Asia, but has been distributed from Europe to China and became naturalised in America. It is cultivated for medicinal purposes and as ornamental in Europe.

PARTS USED Mainly the roots (*Althaeae radix*); also the leaves (*Althaeae folium*) and flowers (*Althaeae flos*).

THERAPEUTIC CATEGORY Anti-irritant, expectorant.

USES AND PROPERTIES Marshmallow root infusions or extracts are traditionally taken orally as a soothing medicine for cough, peptic ulcers and inflammation of the mucosa of mouth, throat and stomach. Leaf infusions or marshmallow syrup (*Sirupus Althaeae*) are used specifically for dry cough associated with irritation and inflammation of the respiratory tract. Externally, preparations are applied to burns, sores and ulcers. Commercially, only the roots are used, while leaves and flowers are popular for self-medication.

PREPARATION AND DOSAGE A daily dose of 6 g of the root, 5 g of the leaf (or 10 g marshmallow syrup, in a single dose) is recommended. The herb is extracted in cold or lukewarm water, or in alcohol (but not in hot water). It may be sipped or gargled. For external application, powdered leaves are mixed into ointments.

ACTIVE INGREDIENTS All parts of the plant contain mucilages (polysaccharides), mainly composed of galacturonic acid, glucuronic acid, galactose, arabinose, and rhamnose, located in special mucilage cells. Roots harvested late in the autumn give the highest yield of mucilage (about 15%), while leaves and flowers usually have less than 10%.

PHARMACOLOGICAL EFFECTS The polysaccharides form a protective film over inflamed mucosal tissues and thus reduce irritation. The presence of mucilage leaves no doubt that the herb has anti-irritant properties, but there is some evidence for anti-inflammatory or other beneficial effects. A hypoglycaemic activity has been observed in mice after injection of A. *officinalis* polysaccharides.

NOTES The well-known marshmallow sweets were once made from root extracts of this plant. Hollyhock flowers, from *Alcea rosea* (=*Althaea rosea*), seem to be useful for respiratory and inflammatory ailments and as colourant and brightener in herbal teas.

STATUS Pharm.; Comm.E+; ESCOP 1; WHO 2

Althaea officinalis L.

family: Malvaceae

guimauve (French); *Eibisch* (German); *bismalva, altea* (Italian); *malvavisco* (Spanish)

Ammi visnaga

visnaga • khella • bishop's weed

Ammi visnaga

Ammi majus

DESCRIPTION The plant is an erect annual herb with divided, feathery leaves and large, compound umbels of tiny white flowers. The small, dry fruits, often referred to as seeds, are about 2 mm long and have a very bitter taste.

ORIGIN Mediterranean region, from the Canary Islands and Morocco, eastwards to Egypt and Iran. It has become naturalised in South and North America. Commercial cultivation is centred mainly in Egypt, Morocco and Tunisia.

PARTS USED Ripe fruits (*Ammi visnagae fructus*) are used, or more usually standardised extracts thereof.

THERAPEUTIC CATEGORY Antispasmodic, vasodilator, anti-asthmatic.

USES AND PROPERTIES Compounds from the plant, or synthetic derivatives are used as muscle relaxants in the preventive treatment of asthma, spastic bronchitis and *angina pectoris* (sudden chest pain resulting from a lack of oxygen to the heart muscle). Fruits are traditionally used to clean teeth and to treat numerous other ailments, including intestinal colic, the pain of kidney stones (symptomatic relief) and as diuretic.

PREPARATION AND DOSAGE Visnaga fruits are rarely used in the form of tea (0.5 g in a cup of boiling water).

Preparations standardised to the level of active compounds in the fruits (khellin or visnadin) are included as ingredients of various commercial formulations (spasmolytics, as well as cardiac, coronary and urological remedies).

ACTIVE INGREDIENTS The main active ingredients are furanocoumarins (khellin, visnagin, khellol) and angular pyranocoumarins (visnadin, samidin, dihydrosamidin).

PHARMACOLOGICAL EFFECTS Visnadin is a powerful vasodilator that acts by blocking calcium channels. Both visnagin and khellin (and synthetic derivatives) have antispasmodic effects.

WARNING Visnaga extracts are no longer considered safe for the treatment of mild *angina pectoris*. New evidence of negative side effects (including pseudo-allergic reactions, insomnia, and reversible liver ailments) prompted the German Commission E to withdraw their positive monograph.

NOTES Fruits of a related species, *Ammi majus*, are a commercial source of phototoxic furanocoumarins that are used in photochemotherapy (so-called PUVA) to treat skin disorders (psoriasis, vitiligo). However, this treatment may increase the risk of skin and lung cancer.

STATUS Pharm.; Comm.E+ (withdrawn in 1994).

Ammi visnaga (L.) Lam.

family: Apiaceae

khella (Arabian); *herbe aux cure-dents* (French); *Khellakraut, Bischofskraut* (German); *visnaga, kella* (Italian); *viznaga* (Spanish)

Ananas comosus
pineapple

Plants of *Ananas comosus*

DESCRIPTION Pineapple is a distinctive perennial herb with rosettes of firm-textured leaves, each of which are sharply toothed along the edges. The purplish flower cluster, including the axis and the bracts, all become fleshy to form the well-known pineapple fruit.

ORIGIN Central America. The plant is now widely cultivated in tropical regions of Africa and Asia.

PARTS USED Ripe fruit and stems. They are used commercially to extract a mixture of proteolytic enzymes known as bromelain (*Bromelainum crudum*).

THERAPEUTIC CATEGORY Digestive, anti-inflammatory, anti-oedema.

USES AND PROPERTIES Bromelain is used to treat post-traumatic and post-operative oedemas (particularly of the nasal passages and sinuses), as well as inflammation. It may be taken for digestive complaints. Pineapple juice is traditionally used as a digestive tonic and diuretic. Plant proteases such as bromelain and papain (obtained from the latex of the unripe fruit of papaya – see *Carica papaya*) are sometimes added to products made from animal pancreatic tissue, aimed at relieving the symptoms of pancreatic insufficiency through replacement therapy. However, there appears to be no strong rationale for the inclusion of proteases in such preparations.

PREPARATION AND DOSAGE Bromelain is administered in the form of tablets. The daily amount of 80-240 mg is taken in two or three doses. The maximum duration of treatment is generally limited to eight or 10 days.

ACTIVE INGREDIENTS Pineapple contains at least five enzymes collectively known as bromelains. The main compounds are two proteolytic enzymes known as bromelin A and B. Ripe fruits also contain 20 mg per 100 g vitamin C and up to 15% sucrose; esters of caffeic and *p*-coumaric acid with glycerol have been described.

PHARMACOLOGICAL EFFECTS Available studies show that bromelain has anti-inflammatory, anti-oedemic, anti-platelet aggregation and fibrinolytic activities. There is evidence that a small percentage of orally administered bromelain may be absorbed into the bloodstream and lymph system. There appears to be sufficient clinical evidence that bromelain is effective in the treatment of post-operative and post-traumatic swelling.

WARNING Side effects of bromelain use include an upset stomach, diarrhoea and allergic reactions.

STATUS Comm.E+ (bromelain).

Ananas comosus (L.) Merr. (= *A. sativa*)   family: Bromeliaceae

ananas (French); *Ananas* (German); *ananasso* (Italian); *piña* (Spanish)

Anethum graveolens

dill

Anethum graveolens fruits

Anethum graveolens

Apium graveolens flowers

DESCRIPTION Dill is a slender annual herb with bright green leaves that are pinnately divided into numerous thin segments, giving them a feathery appearance. The typical flower heads are borne at the tips of hollow stems and the small, dry fruits (mericarps) are flattened, with pale brown, narrow marginal wings.

ORIGIN Unclear (perhaps South-western Asia); the plant has been cultivated since ancient times in Egypt, Asia and Europe.

PARTS USED Mainly the small, dry fruits (*Anethi fructus*) – usually referred to as seeds, also the aerial parts (*Anethi herba*) and volatile oil (*Anethi aetheroleum*).

THERAPEUTIC CATEGORY Stomachic, carminative, diuretic.

USES AND PROPERTIES Dill fruits are traditionally used to treat dyspepsia, flatulence, other digestive disorders and as a diuretic. Dill "seeds" are particularly well known as an ingredient of baby's gripe water, used to treat colic and flatulence. The plant has a very long history of medicinal use (mentioned already in Ebers papyrus, about 1 500 BC) and was usually considered to be soothing and calming (hence the name dill, derived from the Norse word *dylla* – to soothe). Dill is also well known as a culinary herb and the fresh leaves are traditionally used to flavour fish.

PREPARATION AND DOSAGE A daily dose of about 3 g of the whole fruits ("seeds"), taken as an infusion or tincture, is recommended for dyspeptic complaints. In the case of the essential oil, 0.1-0.3 g is considered an appropriate daily dose.

ACTIVE INGREDIENTS Dill contains volatile oil in the fruit, of which carvone is the main constituent. Flavonoids, furanocoumarins and coumarins may also contribute to the beneficial effects of the herb.

PHARMACOLOGICAL EFFECTS Dill fruits are known to have antispasmodic and bacteriostatic effects. Volatile oils in general are well known for their carminative and diuretic properties.

NOTE Several other well known culinary herbs of the Apiaceae, such as *Apium graveolens* (celery), *Carum carvi* (caraway), *Coriandrum sativum* (coriander), *Foeniculum vulgare* (fennel) and *Petroselinum crispum* (parsley) also have volatile oils and furanocoumarins. They are typically used as stomachics, carminatives, diuretics and emmenagogues.

STATUS Pharm.; Comm.E+ (fruits only).

Anethum graveolens L.

family: Apiaceae

aneth (French); *Dill* (German); *aneto* (Italian); *eneldo* (Spanish)

Angelica archangelica
garden angelica • archangel

Angelica archangelica

Angelica archangelica flowers

Angelica archangelica fruits

DESCRIPTION Angelica is a robust biennial herb with large, compound leaves, sheathing leaf bases and thick, ridged, hollow flowering stems. Small, greenish white flowers are borne in rounded clusters and the fruits (mericarps) are relatively large, flattened and winged.

ORIGIN Eurasia. It is commonly cultivated.

PARTS USED Mainly the roots (*Angelicae radix*), sometimes the whole herb (*Angelicae herba*), fruits or essential oil (*Oleum angelicae*).

THERAPEUTIC CATEGORY Appetite stimulant, stomachic, spasmolytic.

USES AND PROPERTIES Angelica root is nowadays specifically recommended for the treatment of appetite loss, stomach cramps and flatulence. Dried roots and root extracts are of commercial importance in alcoholic beverages (e.g. benedictine) and in the flavour industry.

PREPARATION AND DOSAGE Infusions or tinctures of the dried root are taken. The daily dose is 4.5 g of dry root (or an equivalent dose), or 10-20 drops of the essential oil. Root extracts are used as ingredients of various commercial preparations to treat digestive ailments.

ACTIVE INGREDIENTS The plant is rich in furanocoumarins, including xanthotoxin, imperatorin, ang-

elicin, archangelin and coumarins such as umbelliferone, osthol, osthenol, and others. Osthol is the major compound in roots, imperatorin in fruit. The essential oil of the roots and fruits have α-phellandrene, β-phellandrene and α-pinene as main ingredients.

PHARMACOLOGICAL EFFECTS The pharmacology appears to be poorly known but the plant stimulates the flow of gastric juices and has definite antispasmodic and cholagogue activities.

WARNING Furanocoumarins are phototoxic (they form DNA adducts) and may cause skin irritation and allergic reactions when taken in large amounts. As a result, the levels of these compounds in skin tan lotions are controlled.

NOTES The roots of *Angelica polymorpha* var. *sinensis* (= *A. sinensis*) (*dang gui*; Chinese angelica) and *A. dahurica* (*bai zhi*) are very important in traditional Chinese medicine. Chinese angelica is considered to be second only to ginseng in terms of its value as a tonic. It is used for some types of anaemia, constipation, irregular menstruation, pain and numerous other ailments.

STATUS Pharm.; Comm.E+ (root only); WHO 2 (Chinese angelica).

Angelica archangelica L.

family: Apiaceae

archangélique (French); *Engelwurz* (German); *archangelica* (Italian); *angélica* (Spanish)

Arctium lappa

burdock • greater burdock

Arctium lappa

Arctium lappa flower heads

DESCRIPTION Great burdock is a robust biennial weed with large leaves and rounded purple flower heads surrounded by bristly, hooked bracts. Three other species are sometimes used as a source of raw material: *A. minus*, *A. tomentosum* and *A. nemorosum*.

ORIGIN *Arctium lappa* is indigenous to Europe, and introduced to northern Asia and North America. It is sometimes cultivated for its edible roots and leaves. Supplies of raw material come mainly from eastern Europe.

PARTS USED Mainly the dried roots (*Bardanae radix*), sometimes also the leaves and fruits.

THERAPEUTIC CATEGORY Diuretic, skin disorders.

USES AND PROPERTIES The roots are traditionally used to treat gastrointestinal ailments but the herb has become almost obsolete recently. Externally, root or leaf extracts are used specifically for eczema and psoriasis, but also for acne, skin infection, slow-healing wounds, dermatosis, furunculosis, itches, insect bites and other ailments. Claims have been made that it stimulates hair growth, but this appears to be based on the doctrine of signatures (that the herb will somehow transfer its powers of hairiness to humans).

PREPARATION AND DOSAGE A cold infusion of the root is made for internal use, while the root oil or powdered leaves are applied externally as emollient. Burdock root is an ingredient of powders, tablets and tinctures sold for skin complaints and rheumatism.

ACTIVE INGREDIENTS Various types of polyacetylenes are present in roots: sulphur-containing heterocyclic acetylenic compounds such as arctinal and lappaphens and several sulphur-free compounds. Roots also contain essential oil (with benzaldehyde, acetaldehyde and pyrazine derivatives), large quantities of inulin, triterpenes and numerous other minor constituents. Leaves contain a bitter germacranolide type sesquiterpenoid lactone, arctiopicrin. Fruits are rich in lignans.

PHARMACOLOGICAL EFFECTS The roots and leaves are thought to have hypoglycaemic and diuretic activities. A wide range of biochemical activities has been reported including PAF antagonism, inhibition of cAMP phosphodiesterase, and antimicrobial and anti-inflammatory properties. Some of these activities can be explained by the presence of lignans and polyacetylenes.

NOTES The fibrous roots are eaten in Japan (*gobo*). Young leaves are eaten as salad.

STATUS Traditional medicine; Pharm.

Arctium lappa L. (= *A. majus* Bernh.)   family: Asteraceae

gouteron, grateron (French); *Große Klette* (German); *bardana* (Italian); *bardana* (Spanish)

Arctostaphylos uva-ursi

bearberry • uva-ursi • upland cranberry

Arctostaphylos uva-ursi

DESCRIPTION Bearberry is a variable evergreen shrub with small bright green leaves. The branches grow flat along the ground and are smooth, with reddish brown, flaking bark. Delicate, white or pinkish urn-shaped flowers are followed by bright red berries.

ORIGIN The plant is widely distributed in the arctic region and is common in Europe, Asia and North America. Leaves are wild-harvested.

PARTS USED Leaves (*Uvae ursi folium*).

THERAPEUTIC CATEGORY Urinary antiseptic.

USES AND PROPERTIES Bearberry is traditionally used as a urinary antiseptic, mainly to treat infections and inflammatory disorders of the lower urinary tract. Specific indications are given as cystitis, dysuria, pyelitis and lithuria.

PREPARATION AND DOSAGE The dried leaves are taken as infusions and are commonly included in commercial herbal teas marketed for kidney and bladder health. The maximum single dose is 3 g of the dry herb (or preparations containing 100-210 mg hydroquinone equivalents), while the maximum daily dose is 3 g of herb taken up to four times per day (or 400-840 mg of hydroquinones).

ACTIVE INGREDIENTS The leaves contain a phenolic glycoside known as arbutin, together with other hydroquinone derivatives. Arbutin is not in itself active, but is metabolically modified to hydroquinone derivatives (such as hydroquinone glucuronide and hydroquinone sulphate). It has been assumed (but not shown experimentally) that these compounds are hydrolysed in alkaline urine to the active hydroquinone, so that sodium bicarbonate may be prescribed as part of the treatment. The leaves also contain large amounts of tannins (gallotannins and ellagitannins), a well as hyperoside (a flavone), monotropeine (an iridoidglucoside) and triterpenes.

PHARMACOLOGICAL EFFECTS Hydroquinone is active against bacteria and fungi and has an antiseptic and astringent effect on the mucous membranes of the urinary tract. The maximum activity is seen after 3-4 hours but the concentration in urine must exceed 60 μg per ml. The effects of hydroquinone have been demonstrated in animal studies.

WARNING Arbutin-containing medication should not be used for prolonged periods (a maximum of one week at a time and no more than five times per year).

STATUS Pharm.; Comm.E+; ESCOP 5; WHO 2.

Arctostaphylos uva-ursi (L.) Spreng.   family: Ericaceae

raisin d'ours, busserole officinale (French); *Echte Bärentraube* (German); *uva ursina* (Italian); *gayuba del pays* (Spanish)

Aristolochia clematitis

birthwort

Aristolochia clematitis

Aristolochia clematitis flowers

Asarum europaeum

DESCRIPTION Birthwort is a perennial herb and has erect stems arising from spreading rhizomes and heart-shaped leaves. All parts of the plant have an unpleasant smell. The flowers are yellow and have a peculiar shape, reminiscent of the shape and orientation of a human foetus prior to birth, hence the Greek *aristos* = best, *lochia* = childbirth. This is another example of the doctrine of signatures, where a distinctive feature of the plant supposedly gives a clue about potential uses.

ORIGIN Central and southern Europe. It is widely cultivated as an ornamental plant.

PARTS USED Whole herb (*Aristolochia herba*), root.

THERAPEUTIC CATEGORY Child birth, abortifacient, wound-healing.

USES AND PROPERTIES The plant is traditionally used to induce labour and to treat sores and wounds. Also used in the past to induce menstruation and abortion.

PREPARATION AND DOSAGE Internal use is no longer considered safe.

ACTIVE INGREDIENTS The plant and many other species of the genus *Aristolochia* contain aristolochic acids I-IV, highly toxic substances with substantial mutagenic and carcinogenic activities.

PHARMACOLOGICAL EFFECTS Aristolochic acids form DNA-adducts, resulting in tumours and kidney damage. Nevertheless, the compounds are claimed to have wound-healing and immune-stimulating properties.

WARNING The medicinal use of *Aristolochia* species has been banned in Germany since 1981 because of their toxicity. Chinese birthroot (see below), for example, has been held responsible for several cases of kidney damage (renal interstitial fibrosis) in Belgium.

NOTES *Aristolochia* species are sources of traditional medicine in many parts of the world. *A. fangchi* (Chinese birthroot; *guang fang ji* in Chinese) and *A. kaempferi* for example, are used in traditional Chinese medicine. Other examples are *A. indica* (acts as contraceptive), *A. rotunda* (used in Iran as tonic), *A. cymbifera* and *A. ringens* (used in South America to treat snake bites, fever, ulcers and colic), *A. serpentaria* (Virginian snake root) traditionally used as snake bite remedy and for dyspepsia in North America. Another member of the family is *Asarum europaeum* (asarabacca) formerly an emetic and still used in homoeopathy (<D3!).

STATUS Traditional medicine (today obsolete, because of toxicity; except in homoeopathy).

Aristolochia clematitis L   family: Aristolochiaceae

sarrasine (French); *Gewöhnliche Osterluzei* (German); *aristolochia* (Italian); *aristoloquia* (Spanish)

Armoracia rusticana

horseradish

Armoracia rusticana flowers

Armoracia rusticana

Raphanus sativus

DESCRIPTION Horseradish is a leafy perennial herb with large, dark green leaves arising directly from a thick taproot. Small white flowers are borne on long flowering stalks of up to 1 m high.

ORIGIN Possibly from the Volga-Don area in eastern Europe. The fruits do not form viable seeds and it is therefore possible that the plant is a sterile hybrid. It has been cultivated since ancient times from root cuttings and is today found on all continents.

PARTS USED Root (*Armoraciae radix*).

THERAPEUTIC CATEGORY Disorders of respiratory and urinary tract; skin irritant.

USES AND PROPERTIES Traditionally used to treat bronchial conditions and urinary tract infections and externally applied as a counter-irritant to treat rheumatism and inflammation. It is best known as a spice.

PREPARATION AND DOSAGE Fresh root (20 g per day) are taken or preparations containing 2% mustard oil are applied externally. Freeze-dried root or extracts are sometimes used.

ACTIVE INGREDIENTS The fresh root is rich in glucosinolates (mustard oil glycosides) of which gluconasturtin and sinigrin are the main compounds. During the drying process the glucosinolates are hydrolysed by myrosinase to yield phenylethyl isothiocyanate and allyl isothiocyanate respectively, that are present in the volatile oil. The root is a commercial source of the enzyme peroxidase, and contains coumarins, phenolic acids, ascorbic acid, and others.

PHARMACOLOGICAL EFFECTS Isothiocyanates can form covalent bonds with proteins and thus alter their activity. They have antimicrobial, spasmolytic, cytotoxic and skin irritant (hyperaemic) properties.

WARNING Allyl isothiocyanate is toxic and may cause allergic reactions and irritation to mucous membranes. Even as a spice, horseradish should be taken sparingly. The pure essential oil is considered a hazardous substance.

NOTES Horseradish should not be confused with the edible common radish (*Raphanus sativus*), which also contains mustard oil glycosides. According to the German Commission E, fresh radish juice (50-100 ml) is effective against "peptic disorders, dyskinesia of bile ducts and catarrhs of the upper respiratory tract". For medicinal use, black radish (*R. sativus* var. *niger*) is preferred.

STATUS Pharm.; Comm.E+ (horseradish and radish).

Armoracia rusticana P. Gaertn., Mey. & Scherb. (=*Armoracia lapathifolia* Gilib.; =*Cochlearia armoracia* L.) family: Brassicaceae
grand raifort (French); *Meerrettich, Kren* (German); *cren* (Italian); *rábano picante* (Spanish)

Arnica montana

arnica

Arnica montana flower heads

Arnica montana

Arnica chamissonis subsp. foliosa

DESCRIPTION A perennial herb with hairy leaves and large, deep yellow flower heads. A. *chamissonis* differs from A. *montana* in the more erect habit and smaller flower heads.

ORIGIN A. *chamissonis* is a North American species that has become an important commercial (cultivated) source, together with A. *fulgens* and others. The well-known A. *montana* occurs naturally in central and northern Europe. Material from the wild has become limited.

PARTS USED Mainly flower heads (*Arnicae flos*) or tinctures and volatile oil thereof, rarely roots or whole plant.

THERAPEUTIC CATEGORY Anti-inflammatory, counter-irritant, wound-healing.

USES AND PROPERTIES Arnica is traditionally used to treat bruises, haematomas, sprains, burns (including sunburn), diaper rashes and as a counter-irritant to treat rheumatism. It should only be applied externally or used as mouth wash (when treating inflammation of the mucous membranes). Ingestion of the herb is no longer recommended.

PREPARATION AND DOSAGE Extracts or tinctures are used as ointments and liniments, often applied as a compress. An infusion of 2 g of herb in 100 ml water

can be used, or tinctures (10 times dilution for mouth rinses, somewhat more concentrated –3:1 to 10:1 dilution – for external application). Ointments should contain 20-25% tincture. "Arnica oil" is prepared from an extract of 1 part herb to 5 parts fatty oil.

ACTIVE INGREDIENTS The main active principles (0.2-0.5%) are helenalin and related sesquiterpene lactones, to which the bitterness of the herb is ascribed. Also present are flavones and flavonols, a volatile oil (with thymol, thymolmethylether and azulene), triterpenoids, phenolic acids and polysaccharides.

PHARMACOLOGICAL EFFECTS Sesquiterpene lactones, such as helenalin, can form covalent bonds with proteins and thus alter their properties. These and the other arnica compounds have mutagenic, antimicrobial and anti-inflammatory properties. Topically applied they show analgesic, antiseptic, hyperaemic and wound-healing effects.

WARNING Internal use can cause abortion and even death. Internal and external application may cause severe allergic reactions. Avoid contact with eyes and open wounds.

STATUS Pharm.; Comm.E+; ESCOP 4.

Arnica montana L.   family: Asteraceae

arnica (French); *Arnika, Bergwohlverleih* (German); *arnica* (Italian); *arnica* (Spanish)

Artemisia absinthium

wormwood • absinthe

Artemisia absinthium

Artemisia abrotanum

DESCRIPTION A perennial herb of up to 1 m high. The leaves are pinnately compound and silvery in colour, with deeply dissected leaflets. Numerous small, pale yellow flower heads are borne along the branch ends.

ORIGIN Europe and western Asia; presently also in parts of Asia, North and South America. The main commercial source is eastern Europe.

PARTS USED Whole herb – mainly the upper leafy parts – (*Absinthii herba*).

THERAPEUTIC CATEGORY Bitter tonic, dyspepsia, bile tract disorders.

USES AND PROPERTIES Wormwood is traditionally used to stimulate appetite and to treat dyspeptic complaints, including gastritis and gall bladder ailments (biliary dyskinesia). It is topically used to treat skin disorders.

PREPARATION AND DOSAGE A hot water infusion (up to 3 g of dry herb per day) is taken before a meal (or as a cholagogue after a meal). Also used for oral applications are extracts, tinctures and solid preparations.

ACTIVE INGREDIENTS The bitter taste and activity of the herb is ascribed to several sesquiterpene lactones, of which absinthin and artabsin are the main compounds. The essential oil is rich in mono- and sesquiterpenoids, especially α-thujone, but also β-thujone and chrysanthenyl acetate.

PHARMACOLOGICAL EFFECTS The bitter compounds and volatile oil are responsible for the effectiveness of the herb as an aromatic bitter and for its antimicrobial properties. Thujone enhances the effects of alcohol but is a convulsant poison at high doses. Chronic thujone poisoning causes delirium, hallucinations and seizures. The painter Van Gogh produced some of his masterpieces under the influence of absinthe.

WARNING Since thujone is known to be a CNS toxin, the traditional use of wormwood to flavour absinthe, vermouth and other alcoholic beverages has been banned in most countries. However, sporadic ingestion of small quantities of thujone in medicinal preparations and in food products is probably not a health risk.

NOTES Several species of *Artemisia* are used in traditional medicine (see A. *afra* and A. *annua*). The European A. *abrotanum* (southernwood) has frequently been used in the past as a bitter tonic, to treat menstrual disorders and as an anthelmintic to rid children of threadworm.

STATUS Pharm; Comm.E+; ESCOP 4.

Artemisia absinthium L.   family: Asteraceae

grande absinthe, herbe d´absinthe (French); *Wermut, Absinth* (German); *assenzio* (Italian); *ajenjo* (Spanish)

Artemisia afra

African wormwood

Artemisia afra

Artemisia afra flower heads

DESCRIPTION African wormwood is an aromatic, multi-stemmed perennial herb of up to 2 m in height, with silver, feathery leaves and inconspicuous, cream-coloured flower heads produced at the end of summer.

ORIGIN Eastern parts of Africa, from Ethiopia southwards to South Africa. Most material is wild-crafted, as the plant is exceptionally common, but selected clones are cultivated on a small scale.

PARTS USED Fresh or dried leaves and stems (*Artemisiae africanae herba*) are used.

THERAPEUTIC CATEGORY Bitter tonic (*amarum*), analgesic, anthelmintic.

USES AND PROPERTIES In many parts of Africa, this plant is traditionally used for a wide variety of ailments, including coughs, colds, sore throat, influenza, asthma, headache, indigestion, flatulence, colic, constipation, gout and intestinal worms. Powdered leaf has been used as snuff to treat headache.

PREPARATION AND DOSAGE Fresh or dried leaves and stems are used to prepare infusions, decoctions or tinctures. Leaves may be boiled in water as a steam bath and the fumes inhaled, or fresh leaves may be inserted in the nostrils to treat a blocked nose. In view of potential harmful effects (see *A. absinthium*), the daily dose should not exceed 3 g of dry herb.

ACTIVE INGREDIENTS The volatile oil of African wormwood is remarkably variable and a large number of monoterpenes (1,8-cineole, α-thujone, β-thujone, borneol, camphor and others) and sesquiterpenes (e.g. davanone, chrysanthenyl acetate) are present in different amounts, depending on the provenance. Sesquiterpenoid lactones, coumarins and polyacetylenes have also been reported.

PHARMACOLOGICAL EFFECTS Preliminary tests have demonstrated analgesic and antihistaminic activity. The volatile oil has definite antimicrobial and antioxidative properties. Benefits in digestive complaints may be linked to the presence of bitter sesquiterpene lactones. The plant is remarkably similar to *A. absinthium* and may have similar pharmacological properties.

WARNING High doses and chronic use should be avoided due to the potential harmful effects of thujone (addiction and cerebral dysfunction).

STATUS Traditional medicine.

Artemisia afra Jacq. ex Willd.   family: Asteraceae

umhlonyane (Zulu); *lengana* (Sotho); *wildeals* (Afrikaans); *armoise d'Afrique* (French); *Afrikanischer Wermut* (German)

Artemisia annua

Chinese wormwood • sweet wormwood

Artemisia annua leaves

Artemisia annua

Artemisia annua flower heads

DESCRIPTION Chinese wormwood is an erect, annual herb of up to 2 m in height, with bright green feathery leaves and minute, cream-coloured flower heads.

ORIGIN The plant is a common weed over large parts of eastern Europe and Asia, and has become naturalised in North America. It is cultivated on a commercial scale in eastern China, in the Balkans and more recently in India and Africa.

PARTS USED Whole herb.

THERAPEUTIC CATEGORY Anti-malarial; also a tonic, febrifuge, antibiotic.

USES AND PROPERTIES Qing hao is considered to be a "cooling" herb in Chinese tradition and is used for a wide variety of ailments. It is taken as a useful tonic for dyspeptic conditions and since ancient times, against fever. Recent studies have shown that it is highly effective against malaria, both as preventative medicine and for treatment of the disease. It is effective even against drug-resistant strains of malaria. As a result, the plant has become an important source of raw material for the production of modern, cost-effective anti-malaria products.

PREPARATION AND DOSAGE Infusions and tinctures of the dry herb are traditionally used, but for ma-

laria treatment, standardised extracts in the form of tablets and suppositories are nowadays available. Recovery from malaria is often rapid (within 24 hours) after a single dose.

ACTIVE INGREDIENTS The main active compound is artemisinin (previously referred to as arteannuin), a sesquiterpene lactone with an endoperoxide bridge. Selected clones of the plant may produce up to 1% artemisinine. Artemisinic acid can be used as a starting material, as it occurs in the plant at much higher levels than artemisinin. A semisynthetic drug based on artemisinin (artemether) has been registered in Africa.

PHARMACOLOGICAL EFFECTS Artemisinin (and synthetic or semisynthetic derivates) have significant antimalarial and antibiotic activity. Numerous clinical studies all suggest that various artemisinin drugs are effective and safe for treating uncomplicated malaria. Artemether is recommended by WHO for resistant and cerebral malaria.

WARNING The use of the plant or its products should be under the supervision of a health care professional.

STATUS Traditional and modern medicine: artemisinin; clinical studies +.

Artemisia annua L.

family: Asteraceae

qing hao (Chinese); *absinthe chinoise* (French); *Einjähriger Beifuß* (German)

Artemisia vulgaris

mugwort

Artemisia vulgaris

Artemisia vulgaris flower heads

DESCRIPTION Mugwort is an erect perennial herb of up to 1 m in height. The leaves are pinnately dissected, with a feathery appearance – they are dark green above and markedly silvery below. Inconspicuous yellowish or reddish-brown flower heads are borne in terminal clusters.

ORIGIN Widely distributed in the temperate regions of Europe and Asia, (introduced to North America) where it is a weed of disturbed places.

PARTS USED Dried leaves or aboveground parts (*Artemisiae herba*), sometimes also the roots.

THERAPEUTIC CATEGORY Stomachic, emmenagogue, cholagogue, anthelmintic.

USES AND PROPERTIES Since ancient times, mugwort has been used for numerous medicinal and magical purposes (e.g. as anthelmintic to expel threadworm and roundworm). The main modern use is as an aromatic bitter to treat dyspepsia and lack of appetite. It is traditionally considered to be a useful medicine for the treatment of neuroses, depression, restlessness, insomnia, anxiety and irregular or painful menstruation.

PREPARATION AND DOSAGE Hot water extracts of 0.5-2 g of the dried herb are taken two or three times per day. It is an ingredient of herbal teas and diet tablets.

ACTIVE INGREDIENTS The plant contains a very variable volatile oil (up to 0.3%) with 1,8-cineole, camphor, linalool, thujone and numerous other monoterpenenes and sesquiterpenes (depending on the source). Also present are sesquiterpene lactones (including vulgarin and psilostachyin), flavonol glycosides and coumarins.

PHARMACOLOGICAL EFFECTS The uses and effects correspond to those of wormwood (*A. absinthium*) but the therapeutic value has not yet been substantiated by modern studies.

NOTES Tarragon or estragon (*A. dracunculus*) is used as a culinary herb – to flavour vinegar – but it is also considered to have appetite-stimulant and mild sedative properties. The wormwood mentioned in the Bible is *A. herba-alba*. In addition to the species treated here, several others are used in traditional medicine: Levant wormseed (*A. cina*) used mainly as a vermifuge in classical times, Japanese wormwood or *yin chen hao* (*A. capillaris*), used for centuries in China to treat liver and intestinal disorders, and *A. scoparia*.

STATUS Traditional medicine; Pharm.

Artemisia vulgaris L.

family: Asteraceae

armoise (French); *Gemeiner Beifuß* (German); *amarella* (Italian); *artemisia* (Spanish)

Asclepias tuberosa

pleurisy root • butterfly-weed

Asclepias tuberosa

Asclepias tuberosa flowers and fruit

DESCRIPTION The plant is a sparse, single-stemmed perennial herb of up to 0.6 m high with narrowly oblong leaves and attractive orange flowers that are arranged in clusters at the branch tips. The seeds are borne in pointed capsules and are dispersed by means of silky seed hairs.

ORIGIN North America; mainly wild-harvested.

PARTS USED Roots.

THERAPEUTIC CATEGORY Expectorant, diaphoretic, antispasmodic.

USES AND PROPERTIES The dried roots have traditionally been used specifically for pleurisy, but also for bronchitis, pneumonia and influenza. The plant is still commonly used for these ailments in the United Kingdom but is less popular in mainland Europe and other parts of the world.

PREPARATION AND DOSAGE A dose of 1-4 g of dried root is taken three times per day by infusion. Tinctures of 1:10 in 45% alcohol are taken in 1-5 ml quantities three times per day.

ACTIVE INGREDIENTS The chemical compounds of *A. tuberosa* are poorly recorded but it shares with other *Asclepias* species the presence of cardiac glycosides of the cardenolide type, such as glucofrugoside, frugoside and coroglaucigenin, and others. Flavonols, flavonol glycosides, phytosterols and triterpenes are also present.

PHARMACOLOGICAL EFFECTS Pleurisy root stimulates the heart and circulation. The cardiac glycosides are known to cause nausea and vomiting in larger doses. Animal studies showed uterotonic and oestrogenic effects but efficacy for the traditional indications has yet to be proven scientifically. Since cardenolides can also act as saponins, a positive secretolytic effect appears plausible.

WARNING Excessive use is not recommended, as high doses are known to be toxic. It may interfere with cardiac drug therapy and antidepressant and hormonal therapies.

NOTES Three other American species, milkweed (*Asclepias syriaca*), swamp milkweed (*A. incarnata*), and Curassavican swallow-wort (*A. curassavica*) have been used as expectorants and to treat asthma. In Africa, *A. crispa*, *A. fruticosa* and *A. physocarpa* are popular in traditional medicine to treat various ailments, ranging from stomach complaints to tuberculosis and headache.

STATUS Traditional medicine; Pharm.

Asclepias tuberosa L.

family: Asclepiadaceae

asclépiade tubéreuse (French); *Knollige Schwalbenwurz* (German); *esculapia* (Italian)

Aspalathus linearis

rooibos tea plant

Aspalathus linearis leaves and flowers

Aspalathus linearis

Rooibos tea

DESCRIPTION Rooibos is an erect, much-branched shrub of up to 2 m in height with reddish brown stems and dark green, needle-shaped leaves. The flowers are small, yellow and typical pea-flowers.

ORIGIN South Africa. The plant is restricted to the western parts of the Western Cape Province, and commercial cultivation is still centred in this region.

PARTS USED Leaves and twigs (*Aspalathi linearis herba*). Processing involves cutting or chopping the leaves and stems into very short pieces, followed by bruising, "fermenting" (more accurately enzymatic oxidation) and finally drying. A modern development is to prevent oxidation by a short heat treatment, resulting in green tea with enhanced levels of antioxidants.

THERAPEUTIC CATEGORY Antispasmodic, general health tea.

USES AND PROPERTIES The main medicinal use of rooibos tea is as a milk substitute for babies who are prone to cholic. Rooibos tea has become a very popular health drink because it is totally devoid of potentially harmful stimulants such as caffeine. The antioxidant effects of flavonoids (especially that of the green tea) are considered to delay the onset of ailments associated with ageing. Extracts have been included in cosmetic products and are said to be beneficial against eczema.

PREPARATION AND DOSAGE Rooibos tea is made and enjoyed in much the same way as ordinary tea. It makes an excellent ice tea.

ACTIVE INGREDIENTS Several flavonoid glycosides are known from the plant (including orientin, isoorientin, quercitrin), of which the dihydrochalcones aspalathin and nothofagin are the main constituents. These compounds are altered during the oxidation process, so that green tea is now preferred because of its enhanced flavonoid levels and thus antioxidant effects.

PHARMACOLOGICAL EFFECTS The health properties have been ascribed to the absence of stimulants, the low tannin content, the presence of minerals and the antioxidant (free-radical capturing) effects of the phenolic compounds.

NOTES Rooibos tea is nowadays used as ingredient of herbal and medicinal teas – as filler to provide bulk but also to improve the taste and colour of the products.

STATUS Traditional medicine (herbal tea).

Aspalathus linearis (Burm. F.) Dahlg.   family: Fabaceae

rooibos (Afrikaans); *aspalathus* (French); *Rotbusch, Rooibos* (German); *aspalathus* (Italian)

Asparagus officinalis

asparagus

Asparagus officinalis

Asparagus officinalis flowers and fruits

DESCRIPTION A perennial herb (up to 1 m high), with wispy, leafless, green stems and minute white or yellowish flowers. The small green berries turn bright red when they ripen. Young stems are white (when grown underground) or green (above ground) and are a popular vegetable.

ORIGIN Europe, Asia and North Africa. The plant is cultivated in many temperate regions of the world.

PARTS USED Dried rhizomes, known as asparagus root (*Asparagi radix*).

THERAPEUTIC CATEGORY Diuretic.

USES AND PROPERTIES Asparagus root has been used since ancient times as a diuretic to increase urine flow and to treat urinary tract infections through irrigation therapy. It is also thought to be effective in preventing the formation of kidney stones.

PREPARATION AND DOSAGE The dried rhizome is taken in the form of a hot water infusion. A daily dose of 45-60 g of the rhizome (or equivalent preparations) is recommended by the German Commission E. It is important to drink sufficient fluids while under treatment. Although the stems are generally accepted to also have a diuretic effect, their efficacy is not considered to be adequately documented.

ACTIVE INGREDIENTS Asparagus rhizomes and roots contain numerous steroidal saponins (derivatives of sarsasapogenin and diosgenin), together with flavonolglycosides (rutin and others) and unusual sugars (inulin-like fructans). The shoots contain high levels of the amino acid asparagine, together with tyrosine, arginine and a methylsulfonium derivative of methionine. Ingestion of asparagus leads to a characteristic strong odour in the urine of some people due to metabolic transformation of S-methyl-3-(methylthio) thiopropionate to methylmercaptane.

PHARMACOLOGICAL EFFECTS The roots and rhizomes of asparagus have a distinct diuretic effect that has been confirmed in animal experiments. Asparagine is thought to be at least partly responsible for this effect.

NOTES The tuberous root of *Asparagus racemosus* is an important traditional remedy in Ayurvedic medicine. It is known as *shatavari* in Sanskrit and is used as a coolant, aphrodisiac, nervine tonic, antispasmodic and for several other medicinal purposes. Also used are rhizomes of *A. falcatus* and *A. ascendens*.

STATUS Traditional medicine; Pharm.; Comm.E+ (rhizomes).

Asparagus officinalis L. family: Asparagaceae

asperge (French); *Spargel* (German); *asparago* (Italian); *esparrago* (Spanish)

Astragalus membranaceus

astragalus • membranous milk vetch

Astragalus mongholicus

Astracantha gummifera

DESCRIPTION *Astragalus membranaceus* is a perennial herb of up to 0.4 m tall. It has pinnately compound leaves and 10 to 15 yellowish flowers arranged in short, oblong clusters. The closely related *A. mongholicus* (sometimes called *A. membranaceus var. mongholicus*) is a slightly taller plant with smaller flowers and is also used commercially. The roots are fibrous and yellowish brown.

ORIGIN China, Korea, Mongolia and Siberia (both species). They are cultivated in China and Korea.

PARTS USED Dried roots (*Astragali radix*) or extracts thereof.

THERAPEUTIC CATEGORY Traditional tonic (adaptogen), immune stimulant.

USES AND PROPERTIES This is one of the most important tonic herbs in traditional and modern Chinese medicine. It stimulates the immune system and is therefore thought to be valuable in decreasing the duration and severity of the common cold, as well as recurrent infections, slow healing wounds and general debility (see similarity with *Sutherlandia*). Astragalus is also used to treat diabetes and kidney disorders.

PREPARATION AND DOSAGE Crude plant material and hot or cold aqueous extracts are taken orally, in doses of 9-30 g of dry root per day.

ACTIVE INGREDIENTS Numerous triterpene saponins (astragalosides I-X, isoastragalosides I-IV, soyasaponin I) occur in the roots, together with polysaccharides (astragalan, astraglucan AMem-P) and isoflavones (calycosin, formononetin).

PHARMACOLOGICAL EFFECTS Pronounced immuno-stimulant and possible antimutagenic effects have been reported. Studies on antiviral activity showed the involvement, amongst others, of interferon induction. None of the traditional uses are supported by clinical trials, although several human studies have been conducted. Furthermore, the drug shows liver protectant, hypotensive and diuretic properties. The medicinal activities have not yet been directly linked to any particular chemical compounds.

NOTES *A. microcephalus* from Asia Minor, Syria and Iran is the main commercial source of tragant or gum tragant, an important hydrophilic and colloidal agent used in pharmaceutical products, creams and jellies. Gum tragant has also been tapped from *Astracantha gummifera* (previously known as *Astragalus gummifer*) and other species.

STATUS Traditional medicine; WHO 1.

Astragalus membranaceus Bunge

family: Fabaceae

huang qi, huang-chi (Chinese); *astragale* (French); *Chinesischer Tragant* (German); *astragalo* (Italian); *astragálo* (Spanish)

Atropa belladonna

deadly nightshade • belladonna

Atropa belladonna

Atropa belladonna flowers and fruits

DESCRIPTION A perennial herb with soft stems, large simple leaves and brown or yellowish brown tubular flowers; typical are the attractive, shiny black berries.

ORIGIN Europe, Asia and the Mediterranean part of North Africa; cultivated in many parts of the world.

PARTS USED Leaves (*Belladonnae folium*) and roots (*Belladonnae radix*).

THERAPEUTIC CATEGORY Narcotic, spasmolytic, hallucinogenic.

USES AND PROPERTIES Leaves or roots are traditionally used as sedatives to relieve asthma and to treat pain (and nowadays especially abdominal spasms and pain in the area of the bile ducts). The isolated alkaloids are used as tranquilisers, spasmolytics and in eye drops (to dilate the pupil of the eye). *A. belladonna* has a long history of medicinal applications, but is infamous for its aphrodisiac and hallucinogenic properties.

PREPARATION AND DOSAGE Belladonna is used as standardised powders, extracts or tinctures. Belladonna leaf powder (*Belladonnae pulvis normatus*) is standardised to contain 0.28-0.32% alkaloids – the maximum daily dose is 0.6 g (equivalent to 1.8 mg total alkaloids). The corresponding doses for belladonna extract, containing 1.3-1.45% total alkaloids, are 0.15 g (maximum daily dose; equivalent to 2.2 mg hyoscyamine). Pure atropine is widely used in modern medicine.

ACTIVE INGREDIENTS Dry leaves contain 0.3-1 % tropane alkaloids, of which L-hyoscyamine (forms a racemic mixture in dried material =atropine) is the main compound. The roots have somewhat higher concentrations of alkaloids (up to 2%); since the alkaloids are formed in the roots, the pattern is more complex than that of the aerial parts.

PHARMACOLOGICAL EFFECTS Hyoscyamine inhibits the muscarinic acetylcholine receptor and is thus a parasympatholytic. At low concentrations, the alkaloids have a depressant and sedative effect, but high doses lead to analgesia, hallucinations, confusion, insomnia and death. At therapeutic doses, atropine increases the heart rate and relaxes smooth muscles. As a result, the secretion of saliva and sweat is decreased, while gastrointestinal and bile duct spasms are relieved.

WARNING The alkaloids are very toxic so that any treatment needs to be professionally supervised.

STATUS Pharm.; Comm.E+; modern medicine: atropine

Atropa belladonna L.   family: Solanaceae

belladonne, morelle furieuse (French); *Tollkirsche* (German); *belladonna* (Italian); *belladonna* (Spanish)

Avena sativa

oats

Avena sativa ripe fruits

Avena sativa

Oats grain

DESCRIPTION Oats is an annual grass of up to 1 m in height with hollow stems and characteristically nodding spikelets, each protected by two large, leafy, persistent glumes.

ORIGIN Mediterranean region (southern parts of Europe and North Africa to Ethiopia); nowadays cultivated in many parts of the world.

PARTS USED The aerial parts, harvested just before full flowering are a traditional product known as oats (green tops) or *Avenae herba recens*. Oats straw (*Avenae stramentum*) and the ripe, dried oats fruits (*Avenae fructus*) are also used.

THERAPEUTIC CATEGORY Antipruritic – oats straw; dietary aid – oats grain.

USES AND PROPERTIES Oats straw (added to a bath) is considered effective for the relief of inflammatory and seborrhoeic skin disease. Oats grain is a useful dietary supplement in cases of general weakness, and dietary disturbances. Oat bran in daily doses of 100 g is thought to lower cholesterol levels. Green oats is claimed to have a sedative effect (reduced craving in smoking cessation).

PREPARATION AND DOSAGE 100 g of oats straw is added to one full bath. The grain is used as part of the diet or infusions and tinctures are prepared from fresh or dried plant material.

ACTIVE INGREDIENTS Oats herb and straw contains high levels of soluble silica and minerals (iron, manganese and zinc). The presence of amino acids, vitamins (especially of the B-group), minerals, trace elements and polysaccharides are important in nutrition. Of interest is the presence of triterpene saponins (avenacin A and B; avenacosides A, B), scopoletin and a simple indole alkaloid (gramine).

PHARMACOLOGICAL EFFECTS The therapeutic value of oats straw may be due to the silica and mineral content. Dietary benefits are clearly derived from the nutritional value of oats. Other claimed health benefits are not yet supported by scientific evidence. It is speculated that the sedative (calming) effect is due to gramine, while the anti-atherosclerotic activity may be linked to the gel-forming dietary fibre in oat bran. Human studies involving oat bran have shown possible cholesterol lowering activity.

STATUS Traditional medicine; dietary supplement; Comm.E+ (oat straw only).

Avena sativa L.

family: Poaceae

avoine (French); *Hafer* (German); *avena* (Italian); *avena* (Spanish)

Azadirachta indica

neem tree • neem • nim

Azadirachta indica leaves and flowers

DESCRIPTION Neem is an evergreen tree of 10 m or more in height with large, pinnately compound leaves. The leaflets are somewhat sickle-shaped and have serrate margins. Inconspicuous white flowers are borne in summer.

ORIGIN The tree is thought to be indigenous to Sri Lanka, India and Burma. It is now widely cultivated in many parts of the Old World tropics, including Indonesia and Africa.

PARTS USED Bark, leaves, twigs, seeds.

THERAPEUTIC CATEGORY Skin healing (possibly anti-malarial, contraceptive, anti-arthritic).

USES AND PROPERTIES Neem is widely used in Ayurvedic medicine, mainly to treat skin infections and wounds. Numerous other ailments are traditionally treated, including stomach problems, haemorrhoids, malaria and intestinal parasites. It is also used in soaps, lotions and toothpastes.

PREPARATION AND DOSAGE Infusions are generally used but the exact dosages are poorly recorded.

ACTIVE INGREDIENTS The medicinal activity of neem is due mainly to bitter triterpenoids (limonoids) of which azadirachtin is one of the main compounds; also tannins and flavonoids are present.

PHARMACOLOGICAL EFFECTS Azadirachtin is a powerful insect antifeedant that disrupts metamorphosis in moth larvae at extremely low concentrations. The main focus of research on neem has been on the insecticidal properties but in recent years investigations have expanded to the medicinal utilisations. Several papers have shown antifungal and antibacterial activity in extracts of neem leaves and seeds, likely to be due to the limonoids. A volatile fraction of neem seed oil (coded as NIM-76) was shown to have potent *in vitro* spermicidal activity. The activity has been linked to various free fatty acids and their methyl esters. A large number of studies have been published on the medicinal properties of neem and neem extracts, covering a wide range of indications and ailments.

NOTES Few cultivated trees are more hardy, useful and versatile than the neem tree – in addition to medicine, it provides shade, firewood, fodder, oil (from the seeds), natural insecticide and ingredients for toothpaste and soap.

STATUS Traditional medicine.

Azadirachta indica A. Juss.   family: Meliaceae

margousier, neem (French); *Nimbaum, Neembaum* (German); *nem* (Italian); *margosa* (Spanish)

Ballota nigra

black horehound

Ballota nigra

Ballota africana

Prunella vulgaris

DESCRIPTION Black horehound is an erect, perennial herb (up to 1 m high) with bright green, opposite leaves and purple flowers arranged in dense, multi-flowered groups along the stem. Mature plants take on a characteristic purplish or blackish colour and a strong smell. Several subspecies are known. *Ballota nigra* subsp. *foetida*, previously considered to be a distinct species (*B. foetida*), is the most popular form used in traditional medicine.

ORIGIN The plant is indigenous to Europe and Asia and has become naturalised in North America. Material is mainly wild-harvested.

PARTS USED Flowering tops (*Ballotae nigrae herba*).

THERAPEUTIC CATEGORY Spasmolytic, sedative.

USES AND PROPERTIES Black horehound is reputed to be a calming herb and is traditionally used for the symptomatic treatment of cough and nervous disorders (especially minor sleeplessness) in adults and children. It is also used to treat stomach spasms, nausea and nervous dyspepsia.

PREPARATION AND DOSAGE Dried herb (2-4 g) is taken by infusion three times daily, or as liquid extracts (1:1 in 25% alcohol, 1-3 ml three times daily) or tinctures (1:10 in 45% alcohol, 1-2 ml three times daily).

ACTIVE INGREDIENTS The plant contains diterpenoid lactones of the labdane type such as ballotenol (main compound), ballotinone, 7α-acetoxymarrubiin and preleosibirin (a prefuranoid). Also present are flavonoid glycosides, phenylpropanoids (chlorogenic acid) and traces of volatile oil.

PHARMACOLOGICAL EFFECTS Experimental or clinical studies that would support the traditional indications have not been carried out.

WARNING Since the biological activity is poorly known, high doses and use over prolonged periods should be avoided.

NOTES Ballotenol is similar to hispanolone (found in African horehound, *B. africana*) and marrubiin (found in white horehound, *Marrubium vulgare*). African horehound has a wide range of traditional uses. Selfheal (*Prunella vulgaris*, also Lamiaceae) is a traditional wound-healing plant in Europe and is still used in China for liver and gall problems.

STATUS Pharm.; traditional medicine.

Ballota nigra L.-(= *B. foetida* Hayek)   family: Lamiaceae

ballote (French); *Schwarznessel, Schwarzer Andorn* (German); *ballota nera* (Italian); *balota* (Spanish)

Berberis vulgaris

common barberry • European barberry

Berberis vulgaris fruit

Berberis vulgaris flowers

Mahonia aquifolium

DESCRIPTION Barberry is a thorny shrub of up to 3 m high with small leathery leaves in clusters along the stem, small yellow flowers and edible, bright red berries.

ORIGIN Barberry is indigenous to Europe and Asia. *Berberis* species (e.g. *B. thunbergii*, similar to *B. vulgaris*) are popular garden shrubs.

PARTS USED Fresh or dried fruits (*Berberidis fructus*), stem bark (*Berberidis cortex*), root bark (*Berberidis radicis cortex*) or root (*Berberidis radix*).

THERAPEUTIC CATEGORY Digestive tonic, antibiotic, liver stimulant.

USES AND PROPERTIES Bark and roots are traditionally used for digestive complaints, liver ailments, and disorders of the kidneys and urinary tract. Berberis is used to treat hepatitis, cholecystitis (inflammation of the gall bladder), jaundice and gallstones. Pure berberine has been included in eye drops to treat conjunctivitis.

PREPARATION AND DOSAGE Tea made from 2 g of the dried bark or root can be taken up to twice a day.

ACTIVE INGREDIENTS Several isoquinoline and protoberberine alkaloids (up to 13 %) are present, including berberine (the main compound), colum-

bamine, jatrorrhizine and palmatine. The ripe berries are almost free of alkaloids.

PHARMACOLOGICAL EFFECTS Protoberberine alkaloids intercalate DNA and inhibit various enzymes and neuroreceptors. They show broad anti-bacterial, anti-fungal, amoebicidal and cytotoxic activities. Pure berberine is toxic above a level of 0.5 g. Berberis alkaloids exhibit hypotensive and cholekinetic properties.

NOTE All *Berberis* species contain bioactive alkaloids and several have been used in medicine in much the same way as *B. vulgaris*; e.g., several Chinese species, including *B. soulieana* and *B. wilsoniae*. The related garden plant, *Mahonia aquifolium*, the Oregon grape of North America is chemically similar to *Berberis* species and is traditionally also used as bitter tonic and liver stimulant. In addition, it is employed to treat psoriasis and other skin conditions. Yet another member of the family is blue cohosh or squaw root, *Caulophyllum thalictroides*, a traditional North American Indian remedy for gynaecological ailments and rheumatism (rich in *N*-methylcytisine and other quinolizidine alkaloids).

STATUS Traditional medicine; Pharm.; modern medicine: berberine.

Berberis vulgaris L.

family: Berberidaceae

épine-vinette, berbéris commun (French); *Gewöhnliche Berberitze, Sauerdorn* (German); *crespino* (Italian); *bérbero, agracejo* (Spanish)

Betula pendula

birch • silver birch • common birch

Betula pendula leaves and catkins

Betula pendula tree

Betula pendula bark

DESCRIPTION Birch is an erect tree (up to 30 m in height), with a characteristic white papery bark. Flowers appear in the form of slender, inconspicuous catkins. *Betula pubescens* (downy birch or white birch) and *B. pendula* commonly hybridise. Downy birch has coarsely toothed leaves with short, soft hairs on both surfaces, while silver birch has doubly dentate, hairless leaves. Both species and their hybrids are used medicinally.

PARTS USED Leaves (*Betulae folium*), bark (*Betulae cortex*), leaf buds (*Betulae gemmae*), tar oil from bark (*Betulae pix*).

ORIGIN Both species occur naturally in the northern parts of Europe and Asia and have become popular garden trees in many countries.

THERAPEUTIC CATEGORY Diuretic (leaf), antipruritic (tar oil).

USES AND PROPERTIES Birch leaves are mainly used in irrigation therapy against various inflammatory disorders of the urinary tract, including urethritis and cystitis. The increased urine flow prevents the formation of kidney and bladder stones. The leaves are also traditionally used as a diuretic in cases of rheumatism, gout and oedema (dropsy). Birch tar oil is applied topically against itching, in cases of eczema, psoriasis and other skin disorders.

PREPARATION AND DOSAGE Infusions, tinctures and extracts made from 2-3 g of dry leaves (or equivalent doses) are taken orally several times per day.

ACTIVE INGREDIENTS The activity of birch leaves is ascribed mainly to flavonoid glycosides (2-3 % of dry weight). Hyperoside and quercitrin are the main compounds. Also present are flavone methyl esters, phenylpropanoids, steroidal saponins, methylsalicylate and resins. Tar is rich in phenolics (6%), such as guajacol, kresol, and pyrogallol.

PHARMACOLOGICAL EFFECTS The diuretic effect of birch leaves is ascribed to the flavonoids and has been confirmed in animal experiments. Possible saluretic effects (increased secretion of salts) have been disputed.

NOTES The leaves, bark, sap, essential oil and tar of *Betula* species have numerous practical uses (e.g. in cosmetics) in Europe, Asia and North America. Stripped bark has many traditional uses (e.g. as paper, roof tiles).

STATUS Pharm.; Comm.E+; ESCOP 1.

Betula pendula Roth

family: Betulaceae

bouleau blanc (French); *Hängebirke* (German); *betulla bianca* (Italian); *abedul* (Spanish)

Borago officinalis

borage

Borago officinalis

Borago officinalis flowers

Cynoglossum officinale

DESCRIPTION Borage is a robust annual herb of about 0.5 m in height with large hairy leaves and attractive blue flowers.

ORIGIN Southern Europe and the Mediterranean region; cultivated worldwide as a culinary herb.

PARTS USED Flowers (*Boraginis flos*), flowering tops (*Boraginis herba*) or the seed oil.

THERAPEUTIC CATEGORY General tonic, anti-irritant.

USES AND PROPERTIES Borage flowers or borage herb are traditionally used as diuretic, diaphoretic, expectorant, anti-inflammatory, and emulcent, and also as mild sedative and anti-depressant. The seed oil is known commercially as "starflower oil"; it is similar to evening primrose oil (see below).

PREPARATION AND DOSAGE About 2 g of dried herb in a cup of boiling water is taken three times a day.

ACTIVE INGREDIENTS Borage contains mucilages (about 11%) and trace amounts (0.004%) of several unsaturated pyrrolizidine alkaloids (PAs) (including amabiline, supinidine, lycopsamine, and intermedine). The seed oil contains high levels of unsaturated γ-linolenic acid (abbreviated as GLA), an essential fatty acid.

The oil contains about 21% GLA (compared to the 9% in evening primrose oil; see *Oenothera biennis*), together with linoleic acid (30-40%) and oleic acid (about 15 %). The oil appears to be alkaloid free.

PHARMACOLOGICAL EFFECTS Unsaturated dietary fatty acids have been shown to influence stress reactivity and performance. In a trial of 10 individuals, a dose of 1.3 g of seed oil (taken daily for 28 days) increased cardiovascular reactivity. GLA is used to treat eczema and neurodermitis (see *Oenothera*). The soothing properties can be ascribed to the mucilage content. PAs alkylate DNA and are known to be hepatotoxic and carcinogenic.

WARNING PA intake should not exceed 1 μg per day. Since borage has much higher levels in leaves and flowers, a prolonged use of borage (as in herbal teas or spice) is not recommended. Borage seed oil should be used with caution in epileptic and schizophrenic patients.

NOTES Another member of the family Boraginaceae is *Cynoglossum officinale* (hound's tongue), which contains PAs and allantoin. It is traditionally used in much the same way as comfrey (see *Symphytum officinale*).

STATUS Traditional medicine; Pharm.

Borago officinalis L.   family: Boraginaceae

bourrache (French); *Boretsch* (German); *boragine* (Italian); *borraja* (Spanish)

Boswellia sacra

frankincense tree

Boswellia sacra tree

Ethiopean frankincence (from Boswellia papyrifera)

Boswellia papyrifera tree

Olibanum (from Boswellia frereana)

DESCRIPTION Frankincense is a small, much-branched tree with thick stems and a smooth, papery bark. Compound leaves, each with about 11 dentate leaflets, are clustered towards the branch ends. The small, pale yellow, star-shaped flowers are borne in slender clusters. Other sources of incense or olibanum, produced mainly in Kenya, Ethiopia and Somalia, include B. frereana, B. papyrifera and B. neglecta.

ORIGIN Northeastern Africa and southern Arabia.

PARTS USED Resin (Olibanum). Tapped resin is inferior to that which flows spontaneously from the bark.

THERAPEUTIC CATEGORY Antiseptic, expectorant, sedative.

USES AND PROPERTIES The aromatic resin, known as frankincense or olibanum, has been used since ancient times for religious and medicinal purposes. It stimulates circulation and is antiseptic, analgesic, expectorant and sedative. It is applied as plasters to treat rheumatic conditions and is sometimes taken internally for respiratory and urinary ailments. Volatile oil distilled from the resin is used in aromatherapy against anxiety and tension.

PREPARATION AND DOSAGE The resin is usually applied topically or is included in inhalants.

ACTIVE INGREDIENTS Frankincense contains 5-9 % volatile oil (α-pinene, phellandrene, 1-octylacetate, and various other monoterpenes and diterpenes), together with about 60 % resinous material (mainly pentacyclic triterpenoids, such as boswellic acids and their acetates). It also contains other triterpenes and mucilage.

PHARMACOLOGICAL EFFECTS Beneficial effects in the treatment of arthritis are thought to be due to the inhibition of 5-lipoxygenase, thus preventing the formation of leucotrienes. The essential oil has decongestant and antibiotic properties. Several clinical studies have been done on boswellin (an oleoresin from Boswellia serrata – Indian frankincense) in the treatment of arthritis. Boswellic acids have definite anti-inflammatory properties in animals but the results of human studies have not yet been conclusive.

NOTES Frankincense has a bitter taste and is practically odourless. The characteristic smell is released only when the granules of resin are placed on glowing coals. Frankincense (gum olibanum) should not be confused with myrrh, scented myrrh or gum opopanax derived from Commiphora species (see C. myrrha).

STATUS Traditional medicine.

Boswellia sacra Flueckiger (=B. carteri Birdw.)   family: Burseraceae

arbre-à-encens (French); Weihrauchbaum (German); incenso (Italian); incienso (Spanish)

Brassica nigra

mustard • black mustard

Brassica nigra flowers and fruit

Brassica nigra

Sinapis alba flowers and fruit

DESCRIPTION An erect leafy annual herb of up to 1 m in height with lobed leaves, yellow flowers and oblong, smooth seeds capsules. White mustard (*Sinapis alba*) is quite similar but has distinctive hairy fruit capsules. *B. juncea* (Indian mustard) is not a medicinal herb.

ORIGIN Europe and Asia (black mustard); Europe (white mustard); southern and eastern Asia (Indian mustard). The plants are all grown as seed crops.

PARTS USED Ripe seeds (*Sinapis nigrae semen*) or seed oil (*Sinapis aetheroleum*), and sometimes as tincture (*Spiritus sinapis*). Black mustard is the source of pungent mustard oil and is mentioned in the Bible.

THERAPEUTIC CATEGORY Antibacterial, counter-irritant.

USES AND PROPERTIES Mustard seeds are considered effective in stimulating the circulation and digestive system. Mustard oil is traditionally applied to the skin as counter-irritant to treat rheumatic pain. Internal application of the oil against bronchitis, influenza and urinary tract infections is no longer recommended.

PREPARATION AND DOSAGE Used in the form of mustard spirits (*Spiritus sinapis*) or mustard plasters (made from crushed seeds soaked in lukewarm water). Diluted oils may be rubbed into the skin in case of stiff or painful muscles.

ACTIVE INGREDIENTS Plants accumulate glucosinolates (mustard-oil glycosides) – sinigrin in black mustard and sinalbin in white mustard. Hydrolysis by the enzyme myrosinase (=thioglucosidase), gives volatile allylisothiocyanate (from sinigrin) and non-volatile *p*-hydroxybenzoyl isothiocyanate (from sinalbin).

PHARMACOLOGICAL EFFECTS The isothiocyanates of mustard oil can form covalent bonds with proteins and thus alter their properties. They have proven antibacterial effects against both gram-positive and gram-negative bacteria. The oil acts as skin irritant to increase peripheral blood flow. It causes rapid reddening of the skin and sharp pain lasting up to 48 hours.

WARNING Mustard plasters cause blistering, ulceration and necrosis if not removed within 15-30 minutes.

NOTES Several other plants of the order Capparales contain mustard oils (see horseradish – *Armoracia rustica* and nasturtium – *Tropaeolum majus*).

STATUS Traditional medicine; Pharm.

Brassica nigra (L.) Koch   family: Brassicaceae

moutarde noire (French); *Schwarzer Senf* (German); *senapa vera* (Italian): *mostaza negra* (Spanish)

Brucea javanica

Java brucea

Brucea javanica

Ailanthus altissima

Ailanthus altissima fruits

DESCRIPTION Java brucea is a shrub or small tree with hairy, compound leaves, clusters of small purple flowers and small, black, egg-shaped fruits (drupes), each containing a single flat seed.

ORIGIN Asia to Australia, including India, Vietnam, China and Indonesia. The product is mainly wild-harvested.

PARTS USED Dried, ripe fruit (*Bruceae fructus*) or seed (sometimes just the seed with the fruit pulp removed – known as *ya dan zi* in Chinese medicine).

THERAPEUTIC CATEGORY Anti-dysenteric, anti-malaria.

USES AND PROPERTIES Extracts are used against malaria and amoebic dysentery. Fruits and seeds are traditionally used as poultices in the treatment of boils, ringworm, and various intestinal worms, including whipworm, roundworm and tapeworm.

PREPARATION AND DOSAGE Seeds or seed capsules are dried, powdered and used in decoctions. A decoction or powder is given three times a day for three to seven days to treat amoebiasis (total daily dose of 4-16 g). For malaria, 1-2 g are given three times a day after meals, for four or five-days (total daily dose of 3-6 g).

ACTIVE INGREDIENTS The plant contains numerous bitter triterpenoids (bruceosides and related quassinoids – bruceosides A-C, bruceins A-D, dehydro-brucein A, bruceantin, bruceantinol, yadanzigan, yadanziolides A-D and others). Tannins are also present.

PHARMACOLOGICAL EFFECTS The amoebicidal activity is ascribed to quassinoids (bruceantin, brucein C). It is thought that *Brucea* fruits are less effective in treating amoebic dysentery than emetine, but they are nevertheless important as traditional medicine, especially to rural people without access to sophisticated health care systems. Several quassinoids have also shown significant cytotoxic activity against malaria parasites (*Plasmodium falciparum*). Compounds such as bruceolide, bruceins A-D and brusatol have activity comparable to or better than chloroquine.

NOTES *Ailanthus altissima* (also Simaroubaceae) is important in traditional Chinese medicine. The bark contains quassinoids and alkaloids and has antitumour activity. The class of bitter triterpenoids known as quassinoids are named after quassia wood, obtained from another medicinally important member of the Simaroubaceae family (see *Quassia amara*).

STATUS Traditional medicine; WHO 1.

Brucea javanica (L.) Merr. (=B. *amarissima* Desv.)   family: Simaroubaceae

ya dan zi (Chinese); *brucea* (French); *Javanische Brucea* (German); *brucea* (Italian)

Bryonia dioica

red bryony

Bryonia alba

Bryonia dioica

Citrullus colocynthis

DESCRIPTION Perennial plants with creeping branches growing from a large, tuberous rootstock. *B. dioica*, also known as *B. cretica* or *B. cretica* subsp. *dioica*, is dioecious (the male and female flowers occur on separate plants). Because it is sometimes also called white bryony, it may be confused with the true white bryony, *B. alba*. The latter is monoecious, i.e. with male and female flowers on the same plant. The two are easily distinguished by the colour of the ripe berries: bright red in *B. dioica*, black in *B. alba*.

ORIGIN Central Europe and the Mediterranean region (*B. dioica*); eastern Europe (*B. alba*).

PARTS USED The dried tuberous taproot, harvested in early summer before the plants flower (bryonia root – *Bryoniae radix*).

THERAPEUTIC CATEGORY Anti-rheumatic, cathartic, expectorant, emetic.

USES AND PROPERTIES The plant is extremely poisonous and is nowadays only used orally in diluted form (D3 to D6) in homoeopathic medicine to treat fever, bronchitis, rheumatism and gout. The purgative and emetic uses can no longer be justified in view of the risk of serious side effects. For topical use it is included in creams and ointments to treat rheumatism and muscle pain.

PREPARATION AND DOSAGE Dilute tinctures of the fresh or dried tubers are taken orally or extracts are included in creams for external application.

ACTIVE INGREDIENTS Mixtures of bitter triterpenoids, so-called cucurbitacins, which occur in free and glycosidic form (cucurbitacins B, D, E, I, J, K and L, together with di- and tetrahydro-cucurbitacins).

PHARMACOLOGICAL EFFECTS Cucurbitacins have emetic, strong laxative and cytotoxic properties. Exposure to skin may cause blistering. Renewed interest in bryony resulted from reports that the bitter cucubitacins may have adaptogenic properties.

WARNING *Bryonia* species should under no circumstances be used for self-medication.

NOTES Colocynth – *Citrullus colocynthis* – from North Africa, Arabia and southern India is another traditional purgative medicine of the pumpkin family containing cucurbitacins. The fruit (*Colocynthidis fructus*) is no longer used because of its toxicity and undesirable side effects.

STATUS Traditional medicine.

Bryonia dioica Jacq.

family: Cucurbitaceae

bryone dioïque (French); *Zweihäusige Zaunrübe* (German); *brionia, vite bianca* (Italian); *alfesira* (Spanish)

Bupleurum falcatum

bupleurum • sickle-leaved hare's-ear • Chinese thorowax

Bupleurum falcatum leaves

Bupleurum falcatum flowers

DESCRIPTION This is a perennial herb of up to 1 m in height, with simple lance-shaped leaves and small flowers arranged in umbels, followed by small, dry fruits of about 4 mm long. The plant is somewhat woody at the base and arises from a permanent, branching rhizome. *Bupleurum chinense* and *B. scorzonerifolium* are no longer considered to be distinct from *B. falcatum*.

ORIGIN Northern Asia, northern China and Europe.

PARTS USED Dried roots (Chinese *Bupleuri radix*).

THERAPEUTIC CATEGORY Tonic, anti-inflammatory, antipyretic.

USES AND PROPERTIES The root is traditionally used as a tonic for influenza and the common cold (to treat the associated fever, inflammation and pain). It is also used specifically to treat liver ailments, hepatitis and amenorrhoea. It appears to protect the liver and is believed to create balance between various organs in the body.

PREPARATION AND DOSAGE Decoctions of about 3-9 g of roots are taken three times per day.

ACTIVE INGREDIENTS The major compounds are triterpenoid saponins ("saikosides"), including saikosaponins A-F and and saikogenins A-G. Also present are fatty acids, polyacetylenic compounds and polysaccharides.

PHARMACOLOGICAL EFFECTS The activity of the medicine is ascribed mainly to the saponins. Saikogenin A and saikosaponin A have been used in various studies showing analgesic, antipyretic and sedative effects. Some evidence also exists for anti-ulcer and hepatoprotectant activity. The saikosaponins are known to be responsible for the anti-inflammatory effects. Immune regulation effects are ascribed to a biologically active polysaccharide known as bupleuran 2IIb, which enhances the binding of immune-complexes to macrophages, and also to saikosaponin D, which is thought to modify T lymphocyte function. Most of the traditional uses of *Bupleurum* have been studied but no formal clinical trials seem to have been done. Antipyretic (fever-reducing) effects were shown in patients with fever caused by the common cold, influenza, malaria and pneumonia.

WARNING *Bupleurum* should not be used with alcohol or with sedatives or depressants of the central nervous system.

STATUS Traditional medicine; WHO 1.

Bupleurum falcatum L. (=*B. chinense* DC., =*B. scorzonerifolium* Willd.) family: Apiaceae

chai hu, saiko (Chinese); *buplèvre en faux* (French); *Sichelblättriges Hasenohr, Chinesisches Hasenohr* (German)

73

Calendula officinalis

marigold • pot marigold

Calendula officinalis flower head and fruits

Calendula officinalis (wild form)

Calendula officinalis (garden cultivar)

DESCRIPTION Marigold is an annual or biennial aromatic herb with soft glandular leaves and attractive yellow or orange flower heads.

ORIGIN Central, eastern and southern Europe; a popular garden plant and cut flower. Raw material comes from eastern Europe and North Africa (Egypt).

PARTS USED Flower heads (*Calendulae flos*) or volatile oil. The product is sometimes specified as petals only (*Calendulae flos sine calyce*) or flower heads (*Calendulae flos cum calyce*).

THERAPEUTIC CATEGORY Anti-inflammatory, antispasmodic.

USES AND PROPERTIES The product is mainly used for external and local application to treat slow healing wounds, burns, dry skin, eczema, oral thrush and haemorrhoids. Taken internally, it has anti-inflammatory and spasmolytic effects and is effective against inflammation of the mouth and throat. It is also thought to improve digestion, stimulate bile production, heal gastric ulcers and regulate menstrual disorders. The dried flowers are included in herbal teas to improve their appearance.

PREPARATION AND DOSAGE For topical use, in-fusions, tinctures, creams, lotions and ointments containing 2-5 g of crude herb per 100 g are suitable. About 1-2 g of dried flowers in a cup of boiling water may be taken two or three times per day.

ACTIVE INGREDIENTS The main compounds are up to 0.8% flavonoids (*O*-glycosides of quercetin, kaempferol and isorhamnetin), together with several bisdesmosidic and monodesmosidic saponins (up to 10%) and hydroxylated and esterified triterpenes (taraxasterol, faradiol, helianthriol). The essential oil contains mainly sesquiterpenoids (cadinol, α-ionone, β-ionone and many others). Also present are coumarins (scopoletin), carotenoids, and polysaccharides.

PHARMACOLOGICAL EFFECTS The saponins, triterpenes and flavonoids appear to be responsible for the wound-healing effects as they show anti-inflammatory and antimicrobial properties. Extracts are also known to stimulate the development of granulation tissue, and show immune stimulant and estrogenic properties.

NOTES The leaves and petals are edible but marigold extracts should not be taken at high doses or for prolonged periods.

STATUS Pharm.; Comm.E+; ESCOP 1; WHO 2.

Calendula officinalis L.

family: Asteraceae

souci des jardins (French); *Ringelblume* (German); *calendola* (Italian); *caléndula* (Spanish)

Camellia sinensis

tea plant

Tea plantations

Camellia sinensis

Green tea, oolong tea and black tea

DESCRIPTION A large shrub (clipped to 1.5 m to facilitate harvesting) with glossy leaves and attractive white flowers. The ornamental plant *C. japonica* is a close relative.

ORIGIN Indigenous to southern and eastern Asia; grown in China since ancient times; commercial cultivation spread to India, Sri Lanka, Malaysia, Indonesia and Africa.

PARTS USED Young leaves (*Theae folium*), usually with the unopened apical bud (pekoe). Three main tea types can be distinguished: black tea (rolled, fermented; dried), green tea (heat-treated and rapidly dried; rolled) and oolong tea (semi-fermented). Fermentation (i.e. enzymatic oxidation) changes the colour from yellowish green (green tea) to reddish brown (black tea) and also the chemical composition (formation of flavour constituents and oxidation of the polyphenols).

THERAPEUTIC CATEGORY Stimulant, antioxidant, possible antimutagen.

USES AND PROPERTIES Tea is mainly a beverage but is medicinally used to treat mild acute diarrhoea and functional asthenia. Today, tea leaf products are applied externally as supportive treatment in weight loss programmes and for symptomatic relief of skin disorders. Green tea is taken as antioxidant and diuretic, and is thought to be antimutagenic and anticarcinogenic.

PREPARATION AND DOSAGE Infusions are taken as tea or extracts are included in commercial preparations and mixtures.

ACTIVE INGREDIENTS Tea contains 2-4% caffeine; theobromine and theophylline are below 0.05%. Up to 30% phenolics are composed of a complex mixture of phenolic acids, gallotannins, flavonol glycosides and especially numerous flavan-type phenolics (including epigallocatechin gallate, epicatechin gallate and proanthocyanidins). Also present are triterpene saponins, carotenoids and non-protein amino acids (theanine, 2-amino-6-ethylamidoadipinic acid).

PHARMACOLOGICAL EFFECTS Tannins interact with proteins and are astringent; they are responsible for the anti-diarrhoeal activity of tea. Antioxidant, antimutagenic and diuretic effects are also ascribed to the tannins and other phenolic compounds. It is claimed that tea inhibits the absorption of cholesterol. The stimulating effect is due to caffeine – it affects adenosine receptors and blocks phosphodiesterase.

STATUS Traditional medicine; Pharm.

Camellia sinensis (L.) O. Kuntze (= *Thea sinensis* L.)   family: Theaceae

théier (French); *Teestrauch* (German); *tè* (Italian); *té* (Spanish)

Camptotheca acuminata

camptotheca • cancer tree • happy tree

Camptotheca acuminata flowers

Camptotheca acuminata leaves

Camptotheca acuminata flowers

DESCRIPTION Camptotheca is a large tree of up to 25 m in height, with glossy green, leathery leaves and rounded heads of small, whitish flowers. Cultivars with higher yields of active compounds are being developed.

ORIGIN Indigenous to China; it is nowadays grown as ornamental tree and crop plant in India, Japan and the USA. The tree has been placed on the endangered list in China, so that exports from China are now regulated.

PARTS USED Originally the stem wood, bark or seeds, but now mainly the young leaves. Trees are clipped to facilitate repeated harvests.

THERAPEUTIC CATEGORY Cancer treatment.

USES AND PROPERTIES Extracted alkaloids or semisynthetic derivatives are used against various forms of cancers, including ovarian, colorectal and pancreatic cancers. In China, the plant is known as *xi shu* ("happy tree") and has been used for centuries to treat colds, psoriasis and diseases of the stomach, spleen, liver and gall bladder.

PREPARATION AND DOSAGE Pure alkaloids are administered by intravenous drip (in the case of irinotecan – see below– 100 mg per m^2 of body surface in a weekly treatment repeated six or more times). Weak infusions are used in folk medicine.

ACTIVE INGREDIENTS Camptothecine, a pentacyclic quinoline alkaloid, is the major compound (about 0.01% in stem bark, 0.02% in root bark and 0.03% in fruits). Camptothecine is poorly soluble in water and causes severe side effects such as diarrhoea and haemorrhagic cystitis. As a result, various semisynthetic analogues have been developed (approved by the American FDA), including 9-amino-20S-camptothecine, irinotecan (also known as irinotecan hydrochloride trihydrate, CPT-11 or Camptosar™) and topotecan (Hyacamptin™).

PHARMACOLOGICAL EFFECTS Camptothecine has proven cytostatic and antitumour activity but is also quite toxic. The anticancer effect is due to the unique ability of camptothecine and related compounds to inhibit the nuclear DNA topoisomerase I enzyme so that replication and transcription are interrupted.

NOTES Camptothecine is also produced by *Ophiorrhiza mungo* (Rubiaceae), *Mostuea brunonis* (Gelsemiaceae) and *Nothopodytes (Mappia) foetida* (Icacinaceae).

STATUS Traditional medicine (plant); modern medicine: camptothecine; clinical trials +.

Camptotheca acuminata Decne   family: Cornaceae (formerly Nyssaceae)

xi shu (Chinese); *camptotheca* (French); *Glücksbaum* (German); *camptotheca* (Italian)

Cannabis sativa

marijuana • Indian hemp

Cannabis sativa subsp. *indica* flowers

Cannabis sativa subsp. *indica*

Cannabis sativa subsp. *sativa*

DESCRIPTION An erect annual herb (up to 4 m in height), with characteristic serrate leaflets and small male and female flowers borne on different plants. Two subspecies are cultivated – subsp. *sativa* for its fibre and seed oil; subsp. *indica* as intoxicant and medicinal plant.

ORIGIN Asia; widely cultivated (often illegally) in most temperate regions.

PARTS USED Female flowers and associated leaves (=marijuana; *Cannabis indicae herba*), resin of female plants (=hashish) and seeds (the *huo ma ren* of traditional Chinese medicine).

THERAPEUTIC CATEGORY Intoxicant, sedative, analgesic, anti-emetic.

USES AND PROPERTIES Traditional uses include the treatment of pain, rheumatism and asthma. The herb has been used medicinally in Ayurvedic medicine and traditional Chinese medicine since ancient times. In the 19th century, marijuana was popularly used as a painkiller, especially for menstrual pains. Nowadays it is also used for the nausea caused by chemotherapy, depression and lack of appetite in AIDS patients and to lower intra-ocular pressure in cases of glaucoma. Seeds are still used in Chinese medicine as a mild treatment of constipation in elderly people.

PREPARATION AND DOSAGE Tinctures and extracts have been used medicinally to some extent (medicinal dose: 0.1 g of *Cannabis indicae herba*).

ACTIVE INGREDIENTS Numerous phenolic terpenoids (cannabinoids); the hallucinogenic effect is ascribed only to Δ^9 tetrahydrocannabinol (THC). Marijuana contains about 1%, hashish c. 5%. Furthermore, flavonoids, alkaloids and a volatile oil with mono- and sesquiterpenes.

PHARMACOLOGICAL EFFECTS THC has a powerful effect on the central nervous system, including euphoria, relaxation, loss of coordination and slurred speech. THC has analgesic, anti-emetic, bronchodilatory, spasmolytic, and hypotensive effects.

WARNING Cannabis smoking is illegal in most countries. Chronic use may result in personality problems and a lack of motivation. As so-called "gateway drug", cannabis may apparently lead to the use of other, more harmful intoxicants.

NOTES Low THC hemp is a versatile fibre and seed oil crop.

STATUS Traditional medicine.

Cannabis sativa L.   family Cannabaceae

chanvre (French); *Hanf* (German), *canapa indiana* (Italian); *cánamo* (Spanish)

Capsella bursa-pastoris
shepherd's purse • capsella

Capsella bursa-pastoris

Capsella bursa-pastoris flowers and fruits

DESCRIPTION This well-known weed is a small annual or biennial herb with a rosette of oblong, deeply lobed leaves directly on the ground. Small, white flowers are borne on a single central stalk that may be up to 0.4 m in height. The characteristic heart-shaped fruit resembles a traditional shepherd´s purse (hence the common name).

ORIGIN Europe; now a cosmopolitan weed. Raw material for medicinal use is wild-harvested in eastern Europe and Asia.

PARTS USED Whole herb (*Bursae pastoris herba*).

THERAPEUTIC CATEGORY Antihaemorrhagic, urinary antiseptic.

USES AND PROPERTIES The herb is traditionally used to stop bleeding and to treat heavy periods (menorrhagia), diarrhoea and cystitis. In Chinese medicine it is used for unspecified eye diseases and dysentery.

PREPARATION AND DOSAGE The herb is traditionally taken as a tea (mostly in combination with other herbs). For internal and external use, about 3-5 g of finely chopped material is added to a cup of boiling water. As a styptic, it is applied to bleeding injuries of the skin and instilled in the nose to treat nosebleeds.

The daily dose is about 10-15 g. Commercial tinctures and tablets are available.

ACTIVE INGREDIENTS The plant contains numerous flavonoids (rutin, diosmin, hesperidin), amino acids (proline), monoterpenoids (camphor) and glucosinolates (sinigrin). The presence of various amines (acetylcholine, choline, tyramine) and saponins has been reported and details need to be verified.

PHARMACOLOGICAL EFFECTS Despite animal studies showing anti-inflammatory, anti-ulcer, diuretic, hypotensive and other effects, the traditional uses of shepherd´s purse are not well explained. It is thought that a peptide with oxytocin-like activity is responsible for the antihaemorrhagic action. When injected, extracts show muscarine-like effects (dose-dependent decreases and increases in blood pressure), positive inotropic and chronotropic effects on the heart and increased contraction of the uterus.

WARNING Excessive or prolonged use is not recommended.

NOTES The archaeological record shows that *Capsella* seeds have been used by man since ancient times.

STATUS Pharm.; Comm.E+.

Capsella bursa-pastoris L.

family: Brassicaceae

bourse-à-pasteur (French); *Hirtentäschel* (German); *borsa del pastore* (Italian); *bolsa de pastor* (Spanish)

Capsicum frutescens
chilli pepper • Tabasco pepper

Capsicum frutescens

Capsicum annuum

DESCRIPTION Chilli pepper is a perennial herb (up to 0.5 m) with dark green, stalked leaves, white flowers and oblong, green or red fruit that are carried upright. It is often confused with pungent forms of *C. annuum* (paprika, hot pepper, Spanish pepper), an annual plant with drooping fruit.

ORIGIN Both species are indigenous to tropical America and have become important crop plants in most parts of the world.

PARTS USED Dried, ripe fruit and seeds (*Capsici fructus acer*); *C. annuum* is used as *Capsici fructus*.

THERAPEUTIC CATEGORY Topical analgesic, carminative, counter-irritant.

USES AND PROPERTIES Capsicum is used for local pain relief in a number of complaints, including rheumatism, arthritis, neuralgia, itching, lumbago and spasms (especially spasms of the arm, shoulder and spine). Internal uses are traditional - against dyspepsia, colic, flatulence and chronic laryngitis (as a gargle).

PREPARATION AND DOSAGE For topical use, extracts are included in skin creams and other preparations. These should contain 0.02-0.05% capsaicinoids in semi-liquid preparations, 0.005-0.01% in liquid preparations and 10-40 mg per cm² in poultices.

ACTIVE INGREDIENTS Pungent capsaicinoids are present at levels of 0.4-0.9% in *C. frutescens* and 0.1-0.5% in *C. annuum*. The main capsaicinoid is capsaicin (63-77%). Capsaicinoids are mainly found in the seeds and placentas (the fruit tissue where seeds are attached). Furthermore, vitamin C, saponins, and pyrazines; the colour of the fruit is due to carotenoids.

PHARMACOLOGICAL EFFECTS When applied to the skin, capsaicin causes redness and gives a sensation of pain and warmth. This is followed by an extended period (hours or even weeks) of insensitivity (the nerve ends are reversibly desensitised, apparently with no lasting injury). Several clinical trials have shown that capsaicin in skin creams is effective in treating various kinds of pain.

WARNING Chilli and and paprika may cause painful irritation of mucous membranes, especially of the mouth, throat and eye. Excessive use could be dangerous (even lethal in infants) but amounts normally ingested in foods are considered safe.

STATUS Pharm.; Comm.E+ (capsaicin-rich species, for external use); clinical trials+.

Capsicum frutescens L.   family: Solanaceae

piment (French); *Tabasco, Chili* (German); *peperoncino arbustivo* (Italian)

Carica papaya

papaya tree • paw paw

Carica papaya

Papaya plantation

Carica papaya fruits

DESCRIPTION A single-stemmed small tree with a thick, somewhat fleshy trunk and very large, palmately lobed leaves clustered at the top. Male and female flowers are borne on separate trees. The fruits are large and fleshy, initially green but bright orange upon ripening.

ORIGIN Tropical America (cultivated throughout the tropics for its edible fruit).

PARTS USED Unripe fruits (*Caricae papayae fructus*), rarely the young leaves (*Caricae papayae folium*). The fruits are processed to obtain a latex (papaya-latex, *Caricae papayae succus*, *Papainum crudum*, *papayotin*) from which papain is extracted.

THERAPEUTIC CATEGORY Digestive, wound-healing, anthelmintic.

USES AND PROPERTIES The crude latex (*papayotin*) or the purified proteolytic enzyme (papain) is included in digestive preparations. It is also applied to the skin to clean wounds and in injection therapy in cases of damaged intervertebral cartilage. In the past, the latex has been used to treat intestinal parasites. Raw or purified papain has been employed to treat post-traumatic inflammation, traumatic and post-surgical oedema, swelling and numerous other conditions. High

doses (1500 mg papain per day) seem to work in the treatment of oedemas and swellings.

PREPARATION AND DOSAGE Papain is used in standardised preparations only; 0.1-0.3 g of pulverised latex is given per day.

ACTIVE INGREDIENTS Papain is a proteolytic enzyme, which is extracted in crystalline form from the latex papayotin. Papain is 15 times more active than the crude product. In addition to papain, other enzymes are also present in the latex: chymopapain A and B and papaya peptidase A. Roots, leaves and seeds contain glucosinolates; leaves alkaloids and saponins.

PHARMACOLOGICAL EFFECTS Papain has antibacterial properties but is mainly used for its enzymatic activity. It has proven oedema-reducing effects, but analgesic, anti-inflammatory and numerous other activities have not yet been sufficiently demonstrated. There is some doubt about the efficacy of raw papaya latex or papain in the treatment of intestinal worms.

NOTES Papain is best known as a meat tenderiser and is used to shrinkproof wool and silk and to reduce cloudiness in beer.

STATUS Traditional medicine.

Carica papaya L. family: Caricaceae

papayer (French); *Papaya, Melonenbaum* (German); *papaia* (Italian); *higo de mastuero* (Spanish)

Carthamus tinctorius

safflower • saffron thistle

Carthamus tinctorius

Carthamus tinctorius seeds

Saffron (left) and safflower (right)

DESCRIPTION Safflower is an erect annual herb with toothed, prickly leaves and attractive yellow flower heads surrounded by bristly bracts. The fruits are small, white, one-seeded nuts (achenes).

ORIGIN Unknown. The earliest archaeological records are from Mesopotamia. The plant is cultivated for medicinal use mainly in China, while production of seed oil is centred in India, the USA, Mexico and Ethiopia.

PARTS USED Flowers (*Carthami flos*), also the seeds and seed oil (*Carthami oleum*).

THERAPEUTIC CATEGORY Emmenagogue, anti-inflammatory.

USES AND PROPERTIES Flowers are important in Chinese medicine for treating gynaecological ailments, inflammation, heart disorders, and fever. Also used to relieve lower abdominal pain and to clean and treat wounds, scars, swellings, and sprains. The unpurified oil is slightly purgative; used against Crohn´s disease.

PREPARATION AND DOSAGE Infusions and tinctures of the flowers are used, or the crude or purified seed oil. A tea made from one teaspoon of the dried flowers in a cup of boiling water is taken twice a day.

ACTIVE INGREDIENTS The yellow pigments in the flowers are glucosylated dichalcones (such as carthamin, safflor yellow B, safflomin C, hydroxysafflor yellow A and tinctormine). Also present are numerous flavonoids (mainly glycosides of quercetin and luteolin), α-tocopherol, triterpene alcohols (mainly helianol) and polysaccharides.

PHARMACOLOGICAL EFFECTS Both the flowers and the oil have cholesterol lowering effects, while the polysaccharides are reported to act as immune stimulants. Uterotonic activity has been demonstrated in animal studies. Tinctormine has strong calcium antagonistic action, the flavonoids show antioxidant effects, α-tocopherol has vitamin E activity and the triterpene alcohols are anti-inflammatory.

NOTES Flowers are a source of yellow or red dye and are used as an adulterant of saffron and to colour butter, liqueurs, confectionery and cosmetics. The oil has the highest linoleic acid content of any known seed oil and is used as a source of this acid in the health food industry.

STATUS Traditional medicine; Pharm.

Carthamus tinctorius L.   family: Asteraceae

hong hua (Chinese); *carthame* (French); *Färberdistel, Saflor* (German); *cartamo* (Italian); *cártamo* (Spanish)

Carum carvi

caraway

Carum carvi

Carum carvi leaves and fruit

DESCRIPTION Caraway is a sparse biennial herb with compound, feathery leaves and small white flowers arranged in umbels. The small dry fruits are dark brown and somewhat sickle-shaped.

ORIGIN The herb is indigenous to Central Europe, the Mediterranean region and Asia. It is cultivated in many parts of the world.

PARTS USED Dried ripe fruits, known as "caraway seed" (*Carvi fructus*) and the essential oil (*Carvi aetheroleum*).

THERAPEUTIC CATEGORY Carminative, stomachic, spasmolytic, expectorant.

USES AND PROPERTIES The main use is to treat dyspepsia, spasms of the gastrointestinal tract and flatulence in adults and children (including babies). Caraway is added to laxatives (to prevent griping) and included in cough mixtures. Numerous other beneficial effects are claimed: appetite stimulant, breath deodorant, expectorant and tonic.

PREPARATION AND DOSAGE The fruits or the volatile oil are included in mixtures or taken on their own (the fruits may be chewed). A daily dose of 3-6 drops of the essential oil is recommended (taken with some sugar), or 1.5-6 g of freshly crushed fruits (taken internally in the form of infusions or other preparations). Fruits are often included in tea mixtures.

ACTIVE INGREDIENTS The activity of caraway is ascribed to the volatile oil, of which (+)-carvone is the main constituent (45-65%), together with smaller quantities of limonene, dihydrocarvone, carveol, and others. Fruits contain 2-7% essential oil, up to 20% fatty oil, 13% polysaccharides, phenylpropanoids (caffeic acid, chlorogenic acid), flavonoids and flavonolglycosides (quercetin, isoquercitrin) and traces of furanocoumarins (bergapten).

PHARMACOLOGICAL EFFECTS The fruit and the essential oil have proven spasmolytic and antimicrobial activity. The stomachic and carminative effects are ascribed to the essential oil. Caraway is considered to be one of the most effective of all carminative herbs (including aniseed, coriander and fennel).

NOTES Caraway fruits have been a popular spice since ancient times. They are still widely used to flavour bread, cake, cheese, sauerkraut and liqueur (Kümmel).

STATUS Pharm.; Comm.E+ (fruit and oil); ESCOP 3 (fruit).

Carum carvi L.

family: Apiaceae

carvi (French); *Kümmel* (German); *carvi, cumino tedesco* (Italian); *alcaravea* (Spanish)

Castanea sativa

sweet chestnut • common or Spanish chestnut

Castanea sativa leaves and flowers

Castanea sativa flowering tree

Chestnuts

DESCRIPTION A large, deciduous tree of up to 30 m in height. The simple, oblong leaves are distinctly serrate along the margins. Male and female flowers are arranged in long thin catkins, followed by large, brown, edible nuts enveloped in spiny capsules. Sweet chestnut should not be confused with horse chestnut (see *Aesculus hippocastanum*), which is also an important medicinal plant.

ORIGIN The tree occurs naturally from the Mediterranean region to the Caucasus. It has been an early introduction into many countries on account of the edible nuts and has become a popular ornamental tree. The medicinal product is collected in plantations in eastern Europe and western Asia.

PARTS USED Leaves (*Castaneae folium*) or rarely bark.

THERAPEUTIC CATEGORY Astringent, antitussive.

USES AND PROPERTIES Leaves and bark extracts are a traditional remedy for diarrhoea. Leaves have also been used in folk medicine to treat cough, whooping cough, bronchitis and asthma. Extracts are used as a gargle to treat mucosal inflammations.

PREPARATION AND DOSAGE A tea is made from 2-4 g of chopped dried leaves or a decoction can be made from the same amount of leaves by briefly boiling them. Leaf extracts are widely used in commercial preparations and in homoeopathic remedies.

ACTIVE INGREDIENTS The leaves and bark contains tannins at a level of about 9 %, mainly ellagitannins (including tellimagrandin II). Quercetin, myricetin and the glycosides rutin, quercitrin and myricitrin are present in the leaves, together with triterpenoids such as ursolic acid.

PHARMACOLOGICAL EFFECTS Tannins strongly interact with proteins and alter their properties. The use of tannins to treat diarrhoea, infections and inflammations can therefore be plausibly explained. However, there appears to be no solid evidence for the efficacy of chestnut leaves as a traditional antitussive medicine.

NOTES Chestnuts are commonly roasted and sold along the streets in Europe. The seed flour is used in Italian cooking. North American species such as *Castanea dentata* also yield edible nuts. Valuable timber is obtained from *C. sativa* and other species, and the bark has been used in tanning.

STATUS Traditional medicine; Pharm.

Castanea sativa L.   family: Fagaceae

châtaignier (French); *Esskastanie, Edelkastanie* (German); *castagno* (Italian); *castaño* (Spanish)

Catha edulis

khat tree

Catha edulis leaves

Catha edulis tree

Catha edulis flowers

DESCRIPTION Khat is a small, erect tree (up to 15 m in height), with reddish stems, shiny green, dentate leaves and inconspicuous white flowers.

ORIGIN Southern and eastern Africa, the Arabian Peninsula and eastwards to Afghanistan. The main commercial sources are Ethiopia, Somalia and Yemen.

PARTS USED Fresh leaves. Bundles of leafy twigs are wrapped in banana leaves to keep them fresh.

THERAPEUTIC CATEGORY Stimulant, appetite suppressant.

USES AND PROPERTIES Khat chewing is an ancient, socially accepted tradition in the Afro-Arabian culture. The fresh leaves relieve fatigue, hunger and sleepiness. These effects are accompanied by stimulating and euphoric sensations. Khat has numerous traditional uses in Africa, including treatment of malaria, fever, cough and asthma. In European countries it has recently been used as an appetite suppressant (not recommended; severe side effects!).

PREPARATION AND DOSAGE Fresh leaves are chewed within 24 hours of harvesting. Stimulating and euphoric effects usually become evident only after a handful of leaves have been chewed in a single session.

ACTIVE INGREDIENTS The stimulating effects are due to several phenylethylamines (=khatamines) such as cathinone (the main consituent), norpseudoephedrine and norephedrine. Also present: sesquiterpene polyester alkaloids, flavonoids, catechol tannins and triterpenes.

PHARMACOLOGICAL EFFECTS Cathinone is chemically related to ephedrine and amphetamine and acts in a similar way. These compounds enhance the release of neurotransmitters, such as noradrenaline from catecholic presynapses ("indirect sympathomimetics"). This effect stimulates the mind and increases mental power, sociability and produces euphoric sensations. Feelings of fatigue, hunger and thirst are suppressed. Khat apparently suppresses the sexual drive, evidenced by a high degree of bachelors among khat chewers.

WARNING Excessive or prolonged use is not recommended, as it may lead to hypertension, dependency, aggressive behaviour and personality disorders.

NOTES Khat became known as a recreational drug in the USA after American soldiers were exposed to its use in Somalia. Khat is subject to legal restrictions in many countries.

STATUS Traditional medicine.

Catha edulis (Vahl) Endl.

family: Celastraceae

qat (French); *Kathstrauch, Khatstrauch* (German); *catha* (Italian)

Catharanthus roseus
Madagascar periwinkle

Catharanthus roseus (wild form)

Catharanthus roseus (cultivar)

DESCRIPTION Madagascar periwinkle is a short-lived perennial of up to 0.4 m in height, with dark green, glossy leaves and attractive pink or white flowers.

ORIGIN Madagascar; it has become naturalised in tropical regions.

PARTS USED Roots or leaves (traditional medicine); pure alkaloids extracted from aerial parts (modern medicine).

THERAPEUTIC CATEGORY Anti-diabetic, anticancer.

USES AND PROPERTIES The leaves and roots are traditionally used to treat diabetes and rheumatism. In modern medicine, isolated alkaloids are used to treat various cancers, including breast and lung cancer, uterine cancer, melanomas, and Hodgkin´s and non-Hodgkin´s lymphoma.

PREPARATION AND DOSAGE Dilute infusions, mainly of roots, are used to treat diabetes. Small doses of two purified alkaloids, vinblastine and vincristine, are administered intravenously in combined chemotherapy to treat cancer. The alkaloids are injected about once a month at doses of 5 mg (vinblastine sulphate) or 1.4 mg (vincristine sulphate) per square meter of body surface in adults. Semisynthetic derivatives of these alkaloids are used in a similar way.

ACTIVE INGREDIENTS Madagascar periwinkle contains more than 95 alkaloids, mostly monoterpene indole alkaloids. The hypoglycaemic effects are due to indole alkaloids such as catharanthine and vindoline. The two dimeric indole alkaloids, vincristine and vinblastine (or semisynthetic derivatives, such as vindesine and vinorelbine) are used in cancer therapy. Vinblastine and vincristine occur at very low levels in the plant (less than 3 g per ton in the case of the latter).

PHARMACOLOGICAL EFFECTS The dimeric alkaloids are antimitotics (spindle poisons) – they block cell division by binding to tubulin, the protein that forms the microtubules (spindle) during metaphase. They are extremely poisonous, even in dilute mixtures and may cause gastrointestinal and neurological disorders because the alkaloids also inhibit axonal microtubules of neurons and stop cell division of normal cells.

WARNING Do not attempt self-medication!

NOTE *Catharanthus* alkaloids are said to be 10 times as active as colchicine in blocking mitotic cell division.

STATUS Traditional and modern medicine: vinblastine, vincristine; Pharm; clinical trials+.

Catharanthus roseus (L.) G. Don (= *Vinca rosea* L.)　　　　family: Apocynaceae

pervenche de Madagascar (French); *Madagaskar-Immergrün* (German); *vinca* (Italian)

Ceanothus americanus

red root • New Jersey tea

Ceanothus americanus shrub

Ceanothus americanus flowers

DESCRIPTION Red root is a robust shrub of up to 1.5 m in height with bright green, oval leaves and clusters of small, white flowers.

ORIGIN Eastern parts of North America. The plant is easy to cultivate and is commonly grown as an attractive garden shrub.

PARTS USED Roots, root bark and leaves (*Ceanothi folium, Ceanothi radicis cortex*).

THERAPEUTIC CATEGORY Haemostyptic, astringent.

USES AND PROPERTIES The roots and root bark is a traditional North American Indian remedy for sore throat, fever and to stop bleeding of the lungs. They also used root extracts to treat skin infections, and the leaves as a herbal tea. During the American civil wars, the leaves were used as a substitute for black tea, known as "New Jersey Tea". It is said to be used as a mouthwash and gargle. The roots are thought to be effective in relieving spasms, clearing mucous from the lungs and are used in the supportive treatment of swollen lymph nodes and ailments of the spleen.

PREPARATION AND DOSAGE A tea is prepared from one teaspoon of root bark in a cup of boiling water. The daily dose is one or two cups. Extracts and tinctures are also used.

ACTIVE INGREDIENTS The plant contains unusual macrocyclic peptide alkaloids composed of five amino acids (ceanothin B-E, adouetin X,Y), together with several flavonoid glycosides (including quercitrin, rutin). Also present are tannins and triterpenes (mainly ceanothic acid, 27-hydroxy ceanothic acid and ceanothenic acid).

PHARMACOLOGICAL EFFECTS Ceanothic acid and ceanothenic acid have demonstrated anti-microbial activity against oral pathogens. The anti-spasmodic properties have been linked to the alkaloids, while the astringent effects are due to tannins. With the exception of the anti-microbial properties, there is as yet no convincing scientific evidence to support the varied uses in traditional medicine and modern herbal medicine.

WARNING Since the safety of the plant has not yet been established, excessive use should be avoided.

NOTES *Ceanothus* species are an important component of chaparral vegetation in California and are widely used as garden shrubs.

STATUS Traditional medicine.

Ceanothus americanus L.   family: Rhamnaceae

céanothe d'Amérique (French); *Amerikanische Säckelblume* (German); *tè del New Jersey* (Italian)

Centaurea benedicta

holy thistle • blessed thistle

Centaurea benedicta flower head

Centaurea benedicta (previously *Cnicus benedictus*)

Carlina acaulis

DESCRIPTION Holy thistle is an erect annual herb (up to 0.7 m), with lobed hairy leaves and characteristic yellow flower heads surrounded by spine-tipped bracts.

ORIGIN Mediterranean region; introduced in most parts of Europe, Asia, South Africa and Central and South America. Commercial product comes from eastern and southern Europe.

PARTS USED Whole herb (*Cnici benedicti herba*).

THERAPEUTIC CATEGORY Appetite stimulant, dyspepsia.

USES AND PROPERTIES Used mainly as a bitter tonic and stomachic to treat dyspepsia and loss of appetite. It is a component of various herbal teas, including cholagogues and remedies for gastrointestinal ailments. The herb has been taken to treat internal cancers, diabetes, gout and rheumatism and applied topically for wounds and ulcers.

PREPARATION AND DOSAGE Half the daily dose of 4-6 g dried herb or equivalent preparations are taken as tea twice a day, an hour before meals.

ACTIVE INGREDIENTS The plant contains volatile oil (*p*-cymene, citronellol, cuminal; also cinnamaldehyde, benzaldehyde) but the biological activity is ascribed mainly to the bitter substances – sesquiterpene lactones of the germacrane type. The main constituent is cnicin, with smaller quantities of artemisiifolin and solonitenolide. The bitterness is partly due to trachelogenin and arctigenin, lignan lactones. Also present are polyacetylenes, triterpenes and flavonoids.

PHARMACOLOGICAL EFFECTS Bitter terpenoid lactones with an α-methylen-γ-lactone structure can form covalent bonds with proteins and are known to have antiphlogistic and antibacterial activities. Cnicin shows cytotoxicity in cell cultures and some antitumour activity in mice. As an aromatic bitter, the herb stimulates the secretion of gastric juice and saliva, and thus increases appetite.

NOTES Extracts are traditionally used in Europe in herbal liqueurs. Another traditional European stomachic is the stemless carlina, *Carlina acaulis*. It is wild-harvested in eastern Europe (collection has been prohibited in Germany). Roots are considered to have diaphoretic, diuretic, anti-inflammatory and antiseptic properties. The essential oil contains up to 80% carlina oxide and other polyacetylenes with strong antibacterial activity.

STATUS Traditional medicine; Pharm.; Comm.E+.

Centaurea benedicta (L.) L. (=*Cnicus benedictus* L.)

family: Asteraceae

Benediktenkraut (German); *chardon bénit* (French); *cardo santo* (Italian); *cardo santo* (Spanish)

Centaurea cyanus
blue cornflower

Centaurea cyanus amongst wheat

Centaurea cyanus flower head

DESCRIPTION An annual, widely branched herb of up to 0.5 m in height and width. The lower leaves are lobed and stalked; the upper ones simple, oblong to linear and sessile. The attractive flower heads are usually bright blue, but white, purple or pink forms (mainly ornamental varieties) also occur.

ORIGIN Europe and the Near East. It is well known as a weed of cornfields (introduced with cereal seeds around the world) but is no longer common as a result of modern weed control methods. Plants are collected in the wild.

PARTS USED The flowers; the pharmacopoeas distinguish between drugs prepared from ligulate flowers and those with complete flowers (*Cyani flos*), rarely the leaves. When produced for use as a natural colorant, the flower heads should be dried in the dark to prevent fading.

THERAPEUTIC CATEGORY General tonic, stomachic, diuretic.

USES AND PROPERTIES The main uses of cornflower flowers are as a colouring ingredient in herbal teas and traditionally as a lotion to soothe irritation of the eyes. A wide range of traditional uses have been recorded, including the use of infusions to improve digestion, regulate the gall bladder, liver and kidneys, menstrual disorders, and to increase resistance to infections. Externally, it has been used to clean infected wounds and as a hair wash. Leaf decoctions were once used to treat rheumatism.

PREPARATION AND DOSAGE Infusions of one or two teaspoons (1 g) in a cup of boiling water are taken or applied externally. Dried flowers are incorporated in herbal teas.

ACTIVE INGREDIENTS The active ingredients are thought to be anthocyanins (anthocyanidin glycosides), and sesquiterpene lactones, including cnicin – see *Centaurea benedicta*. Also present are polyacetylenes and flavonoids.

PHARMACOLOGICAL EFFECTS The anthocyanins are mainly used as natural colorants but are known to have some antibacterial and antioxidant effects. There is no documented scientific support for the various traditional uses. See also *Centaurea benedicta*.

NOTES One of the most common purple pigments in flowers is called cyanidin because it was first extracted from the flowers of *Centaurea cyanus*.

STATUS Traditional medicine.

Centaurea cyanus L.   family: Asteraceae

bleuet (French); *Kornblume* (German); *fioraliso* (Italian); *azulejo* (Spanish)

Centaurium erythraea

common centaury

Centaurium erythraea

Centaurium erythraea flowers

DESCRIPTION *Centaurium* represents a complex of at least 12 subspecies. It is a sparse, erect biennial of about 0.5 m high. A basal rosette of oblong leaves is formed in the first year and a slender, much-branched flowering stalk bearing small pink flowers emerges in the second year.

ORIGIN Europe and the Mediterranean; products mainly from eastern Europe and North Africa.

PARTS USED Dried aerial parts, collected while the plant is in flower (*Centaurii herba*).

THERAPEUTIC CATEGORY Bitter tonic (dyspepsia).

USES AND PROPERTIES A bitter tonic to treat digestive disturbances, chronic dyspepsia, and lack of appetite. Traditionally thought to be helpful to treat fever and gastrointestinal, liver, bile, bladder and urological complaints. Externally used for wound treatment.

PREPARATION AND DOSAGE The crude herb, tinctures or extracts are included in remedies and supplements. In Europe, a bitter tonic tea is prepared by steeping one heaped teaspoon of the dried herb in a cup of cold water for several hours and then heating it to drinking temperature. The recommended daily dose is 6 g of the crude herb or 1-2 g of extract.

ACTIVE INGREDIENTS The plant contains bitter iridoid glycosides, so-called secoiridoids – mainly swertiamarin but also gentiopicrin, deacetylcentapicrin and sweroside. Small amounts of dimeric secoiridoids, such as centauroside, occur with flavonoids, xanthone derivatives (such as methylbellidifolin), other phenolics (phenylpropanoids), triterpenes, sterols and trace amounts of secoiridoid alkaloids.

PHARMACOLOGICAL EFFECTS The bitter iridoids are known to act as appetite stimulants by reflectorily increasing the flow of saliva and gastric juices. Some anti-inflammatory and antipyretic (fever reducing) activity has been shown in animal studies.

WARNING Do not use when suffering from ulcers of the stomach or duodenum.

NOTES Small quantities of centaury are added as a bitter food flavouring to foodstuffs and to alcoholic and non-alcoholic beverages. *Centaurium* species all have bitter iridoid glycosides; several of them are used medicinally, e.g. the Chilean *C. chilense* is an ingredient of homoeopathic medicine.

STATUS Traditional medicine; Pharm.; Comm.E+; ESCOP 6.

Centaurium erythraea Rafin.

family: Gentianaceae

petite centaurée (French); *Echtes Tausendgüldenkraut* (German); *centaurea minore* (Italian); *centaura menor* (Spanish)

Centella asiatica

Indian pennywort • hydrocotyle

Centella asiatica leaves

Centella asiatica flowers and fruit

Dried product in Madagascar

DESCRIPTION A trailing herb of moist places with slender stems, rounded, simple leaves and inconspicuous flowers in short clusters. The small fruits are laterally compressed schizocarps, each comprising two mericarps that split apart at maturity.

ORIGIN Pantropical, found over large parts of Africa, Madagascar, North America, South America, Asia and Australia.

PARTS USED Dried whole plant (*Centellae herba*).

THERAPEUTIC CATEGORY Venous insufficiency, wound-healing, general tonic.

USES AND PROPERTIES The main use is for treating wounds, burns and ulcers, to accelerate healing and to prevent the formation of scar tissue following surgery. It is traditionally used for leprous ulcers and also for stomach and duodenal ulcers. A wide range of other traditional uses have been recorded, indicating that the plant acts as a multifunctional general tonic or so-called adaptogen.

PREPARATION AND DOSAGE A dose of 0.6 g dry weight can be taken three times a day. As a vegetable and dietary supplement, larger amounts of fresh leaves are sometimes ingested. For skin treatment (including varicose veins), a wide range of extracts, creams and ointments is available.

ACTIVE INGREDIENTS The main compounds are the triterpenes asiatic acid and madecassic acid, together with triterpenoid ester glycosides, known as asiaticoside and brahminoside. Also present is a volatile oil (with *p*-cymol, β-caryophyllene and farnesene).

PHARMACOLOGICAL EFFECTS In terms of wound healing, the triterpenoids are thought to stimulate the production of human collagen I, a protein associated with wound healing. Several trials are available that have shown efficacy in the treatment of wounds, burns, ulcers and the prevention of scars. Animal experiments also show sedative, anti-inflammatory and antimicrobial activities. Small clinical studies indicate a positive action on patients with venous insufficiency. Asiaticoside and related triterpenoids are selectively toxic to the tubulin (which forms the spindle during cell division) and as a result prevents or slows down cell division.

NOTES Madecassol™ might have tumour-promoting activities.

STATUS Traditional medicine; Pharm.; WHO 1; clinical studies+.

Centella asiatica (L.) Urban

family: Apiaceae

gotu kola (Sanskrit); *brahmi* (Hindi); *hydrocotyle asiatique* (French); *Asiatischer Wassernabel* (German); *idrocotile* (Italian)

Cetraria islandica

Iceland moss

Usnea barbata

Cetraria islandica thallus (plant body)

Parmelia species

DESCRIPTION Iceland moss is neither a seed plant nor a moss, but a lichen (an association between a fungus and an algae) that grows on the ground and on rocks. The short, finely divided branches of the thallus are up to 0.1 m long, olive brown above and greyish below. Two species are harvested for commercial use, namely *C. islandica* and *C. ericetorum*. Hanging lichens of the genus *Usnea*, such as *U. barbata* are also used. In South Africa, *Parmelia* species growing on rocks are used in Khoi-San traditional medicine.

ORIGIN Iceland moss occurs naturally in Arctic regions and cold northern parts of the Northern Hemisphere, where it is wild-harvested.

PARTS USED Whole herb (thallus), known as Iceland moss (*Lichen islandicus; =Cetrariae lichen*).

THERAPEUTIC CATEGORY Antitussive, anti-irritant, bitter tonic.

USES AND PROPERTIES The main use of Iceland moss and of *Usnea* is as an emmolient and expectorant against cough and throat irritation. It is known to be effective in treating loss of appetite.

PREPARATION AND DOSAGE Infusions (4-6 g per day) are taken for cough and gastroenteritis, while bit-ter-tasting cold water macerates are used to treat appetite loss. The herb is included in cough remedies (mainly tablets and lozenges) and applied topically to slow healing wounds.

ACTIVE INGREDIENTS More than 50% of the drug is represented by water-soluble polysaccharides, comprising mainly lichenin (=lichenan) (60 to 200 glucose units) and isolichenin (about 44 glucose units). Also present are alkali-soluble galactomannans and glucans. Characteristic for lichens is the presence of bitter-tasting lichenolic acids, the so-called depsidones, of which fumaroprotocetraric acid and cetraric acid are the main components in the fresh product. With storage, they are thought to break down to protocetraric acid and fumaric acid. Also present are aliphatic lichen acids, such as protolichesterin acid with a reactive exocyclic methylene group. Lichenic acid and usnic acid occur in *Usnea* species.

PHARMACOLOGICAL EFFECTS The anti-irritant, antitussive effects and immune stimulating properties are ascribed to the polysaccharides. The acids have proven antibacterial activity. Lichenin has shown anti-tumour activities in mice.

STATUS Traditional medicine; Pharm.

Cetraria islandica (L.) Ach.   family: Parmeliaceae

lichen d'Islande (French); *Isländisches Moos* (German); *lichene islandico* (Italian); *liquen islandico* (Spanish)

Chamaemelum nobile

Roman chamomile

Chamaemelum nobile

DESCRIPTION A perennial herb with feathery leaves and relatively large, often double flower heads bearing mainly ray florets. The base of the flower head is solid (hollow in German chamomile, *Matricaria recutica*).

ORIGIN Southern and Western Europe, and the Mediterranean region. The herb is cultivated in parts of Europe, the USA and Argentina.

PARTS USED Dried flower heads of a variety with mainly ray florets (*Chamomillae romanae flos*) and volatile oil (*Chamomillae romanae aetheroleum*).

THERAPEUTIC CATEGORY Sedative, antispasmodic, anti-inflammatory.

USES AND PROPERTIES The herb is mainly used for stress-related flatulent dyspepsia, nausea (also the nausea of pregnancy), vomiting and dysmenorrhoea. It is also used to treat mucosal inflammations of mouth. The essential oil is used for flavouring liqueurs and especially for shampoos and other cosmetic products.

PREPARATION AND DOSAGE Infusions of one to two teaspoons of the drug in a cup of boiling water are taken three times per day. Small amounts (1 %) may be added to herbal tea mixtures as a brightening agent. Liquid extracts (1:1 extracts in 70% ethanol) may be used at a dose of 1-4 ml three times per day. The pale blue essential oil is used in aromatherapy.

ACTIVE INGREDIENTS Volatile oil rich in esters of angelic-, tiglic-, methacrylic- and isobuturic acids with C_3 to C_6 alcohols, in addition to the normal azulenic compounds (see *Matricaria recutica*). Sesquiterpenoids of the germacranolide type (mainly nobilin) are present, together with triterpenes, flavone glycosides (apigenine-, luteolin- and opatuletin-7-glycosides), esters of caffeic and ferulic acid, and polyacetylenes.

PHARMACOLOGICAL EFFECTS Animal studies have shown anti-allergic, anti-inflammatory, antidiuretic, sedative (ascribed to the volatile components) and even some antitumour effects (resulting from the sesquiterpenoids). The volatile oil has antimicrobial properties.

WARNING Allergic and anaphylactic reactions have been documented and are ascribed to the sesquiterpene lactones. Large doses may have an emetic effect but the toxicity of the herb is relatively low.

NOTES Roman chamomile is very similar to German chamomile which is thought to have more marked anti-inflammatory and analgesic properties.

STATUS Traditional medicine; Pharm.

Chamaemelum nobile (L.) All. (= *Anthemis nobilis* L.)   family: Asteraceae

camomille romaine (French); *Römische Kamille* (German); *camomilla romana* (Italian); *manzanilla romana* (Spanish)

Chelidonium majus

greater celandine

Chelidonium majus flower

Chelidonium majus

Chelidonium majus fruiting plant

DESCRIPTION A perennial herb with yellow-green, deeply lobed leaves and orange-yellow flowers. It closely resembles plants of the family Brassicaceae (Cruciferae) but may be recognised by the bright yellow or orange latex that exudes from broken stems.

ORIGIN Europe, Asia and North Africa; naturalised in North America.

PARTS USED Whole herb (*Chelidonii herba*) – usually as extracts, rarely the roots.

THERAPEUTIC CATEGORY Cholagogue, antimicrobial, spasmolytic.

USES AND PROPERTIES Extracts are used to treat spasms of the gastrointestinal tract and bile duct. It is said to clean the gall bladder and stimulate bile flow in cases of hepatitis, jaundice and gall stones. The yellow sap is traditionally applied to warts (alkaloids are virucidal!) and employed for other skin disorders, e.g. tinea (ringworm) and eczema; treatment of eye complaints.

PREPARATION AND DOSAGE Extracts of the alkaloids are nowadays used as standardised medicines. A daily dose of 2-5 g of the dried herb (containing 12-30 mg of alkaloids) may be taken as an infusion. About 0.5-1 g (half to one teaspoon) is steeped in 150 ml water for 10 minutes and taken three times per day between meals.

ACTIVE INGREDIENTS More than 20 protopine, protoberberine and benzophenanthridine alkaloids are present (up to 1% of dry weight). The main compounds are protopine, berberine, coptisine, chelidonine, sanguinarine and chelerythrine. The alkaloids are complexed by chelidonic acid.

PHARMACOLOGICAL EFFECTS Berberine and sanguinarine are strong DNA intercalating agents and therefore antimicrobial and antiviral. Most alkaloids can interfere with neuroreceptors and other proteins, which explains their antispasmodic, analgesic, and anti-inflammatory properties. The herb seems to directly stimulate bile secretion rather than just bile flow. Animal studies have indicated choleretic activity.

WARNING Overdoses can cause stomach cramps, colic and dizziness. The use of the herb as a tea is potentially harmful because it is difficult to regulate the dose of alkaloids in infusions of crude material. Furthermore, there have been claims of potential liver toxicity.

NOTES The yellow flowers and sap were formerly used to treat jaundice (Doctrine of Signatures).

STATUS Traditional medicine, Pharm.; Comm.E+.

Chelidonium majus L.   family: Papaveraceae

chélidoine, grande-éclaire (French); *Schöllkraut* (German); *celidonia, cinerognola* (Italian); *celidonia* (Spanish)

Chenopodium ambrosioides

wormseed goosefoot

Chenopodium ambrosioides var. *anthelminticum*

C. ambrosioides var. *anthelminticum* flowers

C. ambrosioides var. *ambrosioides*

DESCRIPTION Wormseed goosefoot is a weedy annual or perennial herb of up to 1 m in height with oblong leaves and inconspicuous flowers. The medicinal plant was previously known as *C. anthelminticum* but it is now considered to be merely a variety of *C. ambrosioides*. The variety *ambrosioides* (*Chenopodii herba*) also contains ascaridol and has been used in a similar way as the variety *anthelminticum*.

ORIGIN South and Central America (especially Mexico). Cultivated throughout temperate and tropical America.

PARTS USED Mainly the essential oil (*Chenopodii aetheroleum*). 1 g oil dissolved in castor oil (2.5% solution) has the best anthelmintic effect.

THERAPEUTIC CATEGORY Anthelmintic.

USES AND PROPERTIES The plant and its essential oil have a long history of use to treat intestinal parasites, particularly ascaris (maw worm) and hookworm in adults and children. Wormseed appears to have been used against snake bite, stomach ache and as a tonic; externally against ectoparasites.

PREPARATION AND DOSAGE The essential oil was once very popular as vermifuge but it is nowadays rarely used. Since it is known to be quite toxic, the dose should be carefully controlled. For children, as many drops of the oil as they are old are given orally, up to a maximum of 10 drops. The adult dose is typically 8 drops every three hours (repeated up to three times), with a maximum daily dose of 1 g.

ACTIVE INGREDIENTS The plant contains up to 0.6% essential oil, of which ascaridol comprises 45-70%. Also present are *p*-cymol (20-40%), α-terpinene, limonene and camphor.

PHARMACOLOGICAL EFFECTS Ascaridol is a known anthelmintic agent that immobilises and kills parasites. In veterinary medicine it is used to treat infections by trematodes.

WARNING Both the plant and the essential oil are poisonous to humans. Symptoms: ringing in the ears, spasms and coma.

NOTES Jesuits introduced the dried herb to Europe in the 18th century. Since then the so-called *Tinctura botryos mexicanae* or "Jesuit tea" has been used for abortion. Several other species of *Chenopodium* are utilised in medicine, as green vegetables or grains.

STATUS Traditional medicine

Chenopodium ambrosioides L. var. *anthelminticum* (L.) A. Gray family: Chenopodiaceae

chénopode anthelmintique (French); *Wurmtreibender Gänsefuß* (German); *chenopodio* (Italian); *quenopodio* (Spanish)

Chionanthus virginicus
fringe tree • old man´s beard

Chionanthus virginicus tree

Chionanthus virginicus flowers

DESCRIPTION The fringe tree is a large shrub or small tree of up to 10 m in height with bright green leaves and clusters of small, slender white flowers, followed by dark blue berries.

ORIGIN Southeastern part of North America. The tree is commonly cultivated in many parts of the world for the attractive mass display of flowers.

PARTS USED Dried root bark (*Chionanthi virginici radicis cortex*).

THERAPEUTIC CATEGORY Cholagogue, liver tonic (also bitter tonic, anti-emetic, laxative).

USES AND PROPERTIES Nowadays the root bark is used mainly to treat liver and gall bladder ailments (gall stones, hepatitis, jaundice and other ailments related to poor liver function). It is also considered to be a useful general tonic, diuretic and febrifuge. Externally it can be applied to minor wounds, sores and bruises and to wash inflamed or infected wounds. Original traditional uses by American Indians include malaria and wound healing. The root bark is used in homoeopathy to treat migraine, headache, liver and gall bladder disorders and depressive symptoms.

PREPARATION AND DOSAGE Decoctions, infusions and extracts of the root bark are used. A cup of boiling water is poured over 1-2 teaspoons of chopped root bark and left to steep for 10-15 minutes. This infusion is drunk three times a day. In the case of a tincture, an equivalent amount (about 1-2 ml) is taken three times a day. Fresh root bark, with attached minor roots are used in homoeopathic medicine for the treatment of liver and gall ailments.

ACTIVE INGREDIENTS The bark contains saponins, a lignan glycoside (phyllirin; =chionanthin) and the secoiridoid glucoside ligustrolide.

PHARMACOLOGICAL EFFECTS The product appears to act as a cholagogue (increases the flow of bile) and a mild laxative but the exact biological activity appears to be poorly known. Anecdotal evidence suggests a hypoglycaemic effect. Traditional uses have not been validated experimentally.

NOTES Directly translated, the scientific name means snowflower – it is derived from the Greek words *chion* (snow) and *anthos* (flower).

STATUS Traditional medicine.

Chionanthus virginicus L.   family Oleaceae

arbre de neige (French);*Virginischer Schneeflockenstrauch* (German); *albero della neve* (Italian)

Chondrus crispus

Irish moss • carragheen

Chondrus crispus

Ascophyllum nodosum

Chondrus crispus

Fucus vesiculosus

DESCRIPTION This is a small seaweed (red algae) that grows on rocks just below the water surface.

ORIGIN North Atlantic coast (Europe and North America). Commercial aquacultures in USA, Canada, and Japan.

PARTS USED Whole plant (it is harvested at low tide and dried in the sun).

THERAPEUTIC CATEGORY Anti-irritant.

USES AND PROPERTIES Mainly to treat cough and bronchitis. It is mucilaginous and therefore sedates dry coughs and also gastric inflammation. It is considered to have mild expectorant and mild laxative properties. Extracted polysaccharides, known as carrageenans, may be used as bulk-forming laxatives for the symptomatic treatment of constipation and as non-digestible and non-toxic adjuncts in weight loss diets. They are also used as fillers, stabilisers and emulsifiers in the pharmaceutical and cosmetics industries, in the formulation of gels, ointments, creams, lotions, toothpastes and shampoos.

PREPARATION AND DOSAGE Isolated carrageenans are most often used. The dried, powdered product may be included in mixtures.

ACTIVE INGREDIENTS Carrageenans occur in high yields in Irish moss and several other red algae, together with proteins, amino acids, iodine and bromine salts. Carrageenans are galactans (polymers of sulphated galactose). They form viscous solutions in water but unique gels when K^+ or NH_4^+ ions are added.

PHARMACOLOGICAL EFFECTS The polysaccharides have a soothing effect on mucous membranes.

NOTES Seaweeds are important sources of commercial polysaccharides (used mainly as industrial thickening and gelling agents (such as agar-agar), especially in the food industry. *Fucus vesiculosus*, a brown algae known as bladderwrack and *Ascophyllum nodosum* (knotted wrack) have been used for iodine therapy and as ingredient in slimming teas. The air bladders on the thallus are paired in *Fucus* and single in *Ascophyllum*. Iodine, present as inorganic salts, is supposed to stimulate thyroid activity, increase the metabolism and thereby reduce fat deposits. Note that there is a risk of hyperthyroidism and thyrotoxicosis. Tablets made from kelp (*Laminaria* species) are used in the same way but are also considered to be highly nutritious and helpful in treating general debility.

STATUS Traditional medicine.

Chondrus crispus (L.) Stackh. family: Gigartinaceae

mousse d'Irlande, crépue (French); *Carrageen, Irländische Alge* (German); *muschio d'Irlandica, fuco carageo* (Italian); *musgo de irlanda* (Spanish)

Chrysanthemum x *morifolium*

chrysanthemum • common chrysanthemum

Chrysanthemum x *morifolium* dried flower heads

Chrysanthemum x *morifolium*

Chrysanthemum balsamita leaves

DESCRIPTION The common or garden chrysanthemum is an erect perennial herb with aromatic, lobed leaves and attractive flower heads in a wide range of shapes and colours. Numerous cultivars, all considered of hybrid origin and thought to be derived from *C. indicum*, have been developed in China over centuries. The form mainly used for medicinal purposes has small, double, yellow or white flower heads. Another well-known species with medicinal properties is *C. balsamita*, known as alecost, costmary or camphor plant. It is a robust, erect, aromatic herb with distinctive lobed leaves and relatively large flower heads with yellow disc florets and a single row of white ligulate florets around the edge. It was formerly used as a vermifuge and to give a bitter flavour to ale (long before hops became popular).

ORIGIN Eastern Asia (*C. indicum* and *C.* x *morifolium*); Europe to central Asia (*C. balsamita*). Flower heads of *C.* x *morifolium* are produced in plantations in China.

PARTS USED Dried flower heads of *C.* x *morifolium* (*Chrysanthemi flos*) or leaves (*C. balsamita*).

THERAPEUTIC CATEGORY General tonic, anti-inflammatory.

USES AND PROPERTIES In China, the dried flower heads have been used as a tea or as an ingredient of herbal tea for centuries. It is thought to be effective in treating sore eyes, high blood pressure, fevers and microbial infections. External application of poultices or powdered herb is for sore eyes, skin infections, sores, boils and acne.

PREPARATION AND DOSAGE A few flower heads are steeped in boiling water and drunk as a tea. In China, commercial tea mixtures, based on traditional recipes and including particular mixtures of herbs, have become popular.

ACTIVE INGREDIENTS The flower heads contain at least 15 triterpene alcohols, including helianol, β-dictyopterol, chrysanthediol A and chrysanthediacetate B, to name a few.

PHARMACOLOGICAL EFFECTS The triterpenes have anti-inflammatory activity and are cytotoxic against human cancer cells. Extracts of the herb were shown to have antimicrobial activity. Clinical trials indicated that the herb may lower blood pressure.

STATUS Traditional medicine.

Chrysanthemum x *morifolium* Ramat. (= *Dendranthema* x *grandiflorum* Kitam.)　　　　　family: Asteraceae

ju hua (Chinese); *chrysanthème des fleuristes* (French); *Garten-Chrysantheme* (German); *chrysantemo* (Italian)

Chrysanthemum parthenium

feverfew

Chrysanthemum parthenium flower heads

Chrysanthemum parthenium plant

Chrysanthemum parthenium garden cultivar

DESCRIPTION A perennial herb of about 0.5 m in height with erect stems bearing lobed, aromatic leaves and attractive flower heads. The heads are borne at the branch tips and have yellow tubular florets and white ray florets. In most books, feverfew will be found under it old name, *Tanacetum parthenium*. It has been suggested that the common name, feverfew, was derived from the feathery leaves of the plant ("featherfew") and not from fever.

ORIGIN Southeastern Europe and Asia Minor. It is commonly cultivated in many parts of the world and is often grown in herb gardens.

PARTS USED Whole plant or aboveground parts (*Tanaceti parthenii herba*; synon.: *Matricariae herba*).

THERAPEUTIC CATEGORY Migraine prophylactic, anti-inflammatory.

USES AND PROPERTIES The main uses of the herb are to treat migraine, fever, rheumatic and skin conditions, and gynaecological disorders.

PREPARATION AND DOSAGE Daily dose of 50-200 mg of dried leaves; alternatively, 2½ fresh leaves or tinctures (1:5; 25% ethanol).

ACTIVE INGREDIENTS Feverfew contains a large number of sesquiterpene lactones of the germacranolide, guaianolide and eudesmanolide type, of which parthenolide is the main compound. The strong smell is due to volatile oil containing camphor, chrysanthenyl acetate, camphene, germacrene D, *p*-cymene, terpinen-4-ol, borneol and other compounds.

PHARMACOLOGICAL EFFECTS Parthenolide and the other sesquiterpene lactones have a lactone moiety with a reactive exocyclic methylene group, that can form covalent bonds with thiol groups of proteins. Fewerfew extracts inhibit platelet aggregation and the formation of prostaglandins and leucotrienes; they are anti-inflammatory, spasmolytic, antimicrobial and cytotoxic. Clinical trials have shown a reduction in the number of migraine attacks in people using feverfew capsules (one per day) containing about 100 mg feverfew equivalent to about 0.5 mg of parthenolide. Animal experiments suggest that the herb may be useful to treat arthritis, but a clinical trial failed to show any significant benefits.

WARNING Possible side effects include mouth ulcers, abdominal pain, digestive upsets and skin rashes.

STATUS Traditional medicine; Pharm.; ESCOP 2; WHO 2; clinical studies+

Chrysanthemum parthenium (L.) Bernh. [=*Tanacetum parthenium* (L.) Schultz-Bip.]   family: Asteraceae

grande camomille (French); *Mutterkraut* (German); *partenio* (Italian); *matricaria* (Spanish)

Chrysanthemum vulgare

tansy

Chrysanthemum vulgare plants

Chrysanthemum vulgare

Chrysanthemum cinerariifolium

DESCRIPTION Tansy is a perennial herb (up to 1.5 m in height), with erect, mostly unbranched stems bearing compound, feathery leaves. The clusters of small, bright yellow flower heads without ray florets are characteristic.

ORIGIN Europe and Asia.

PARTS USED Dried flower heads (*Tanaceti flos* = *Chrysanthemi vulgaris flos*), the dried aboveground parts (*Tanaceti herba*) and essential oil (*Tanaceti aetheroleum*).

THERAPEUTIC CATEGORY Traditional vermifuge.

USES AND PROPERTIES Tansy is traditionally used as an anthelmintic against tapeworms, roundworms and threadworms. It also has a reputation as a carminative, antispasmodic and stimulant medicine. It has been used to treat migraine, digestive and liver disorders, loss of appetite and externally for neuralgia, rheumatism (as counter-irritant), and various skin conditions.

PREPARATION AND DOSAGE The normal daily dose is about 1-2 g of dry herb, taken as an infusion on an empty stomach in the morning. Tinctures are sometimes used (1-2 ml, three times per day).

ACTIVE INGREDIENTS Several chemotypes of tansy exist, differing in the composition of their volatile oil (α-thujone-, β-thujone-, camphor-type etc.). The ac-tivity is ascribed to the essential oil, which contains β-thujone (up to 95%), together with smaller quantities of camphor and other mono- and sesquiterpenes. Also present are sterols (mainly β-sitosterol), triterpenoids (α-amyrin, β-amyrin), polysaccharides, thiophens, and sesquiterpenoid lactones of the germacranolide, eusdesmanolide and guaianolide types (crispolide, tatridin, armefolin, tanacetin, germacrene D, tanacetol A, chrysanthemin and others).

PHARMACOLOGICAL EFFECTS Tansy has proven anthelmintic, antimicrobial and choleretic activities that were confirmed in human studies. The sesquiterpene lactones may cause allergic reactions, while thujone is a known neurotoxin. The oil (and thujone) may cause abortion, vomiting, abdominal pain, rapid breathing, rapid heart beat, loss of consciousness and death.

NOTES Also of interest is the pyrethrum plant, *C. cinerariifolium* (= *Tanacetum cinerariifolium*) cultivated in eastern Europe and in East Africa. The flower heads contain pyrethrins and are traditionally used against lice. Nowadays, pyrethrin-containing extracts are included in commercial and household insecticides.

STATUS Traditional medicine; Pharm.

Chrysanthemum vulgare (L.) Bernh. (= *Tanacetum vulgare* L.) family: Asteraceae

tanaisie (French); *Rainfarn* (German); *tanaceto* (Italian); *tanaceto, atanasia* (Spanish)

Cichorium intybus

chicory

Cichorium intybus plant

Cichorium intybus flower heads

DESCRIPTION An erect perennial herb (up to 1 m in height) with a thick root, large dentate leaves and attractive, pale blue, sessile flower heads.

ORIGIN Europe and Asia. Chicory is cultivated in many parts of the world and has become a weed.

PARTS USED Mainly the root (*Cichori radix*), some-times the whole herb (*Cichorii folia et radix*).

THERAPEUTIC CATEGORY Bitter tonic, laxative, diuretic.

USES AND PROPERTIES The dried, whole herb is used mainly as a digestive tonic for loss of appetite and dyspepsia. It is a traditional choleretic, cholagogue, carminative, diuretic and "blood purifier" in both European and Ayurvedic medicine. Chicory syrup is a traditional tonic for infants, and a cleansing medicine for those suffering from rheumatism and gout.

PREPARATION AND DOSAGE An infusion is made by adding about 40 g of dried herb to one litre of boiling water. About half a cup or less is taken three times a day for three days.

ACTIVE INGREDIENTS The bitterness of chicory is due to the presence of sesquiterpene lactones, of which

lactucin and lactuprikrin are the major compounds. Also present are coumarins (umbelliferon, cichoriin), phenolic acids (caffeic, ferulic acids and esters with quinic acid) and various flavonoids. The root contains high levels of inulin (50-60 %) as a storage compound.

PHARMACOLOGICAL EFFECTS Extracts show choleretic and anti-inflammatory effects in rats. The therapeutic value of chicory is not clear, but it is generally accepted to have mild choleretic effects in man, so that the traditional treatment of liver and gall bladder complaints seems justified. Bitter lactones are likely to contribute to the tonic effects; however, the medicinal role (if any) of inulin and the potential benefits of the herb in treating rheumatism and gout are less obvious. Inulin is used as sucrose substitute for diabetics. Allergic skin reactions may rarely occur in sensitive people.

NOTES Chicory and its close relative, endive (*C. endivia*), are grown as bitter leaf vegetables. Chicory root is commercially dried and roasted as a coffee additive or coffee substitute.

STATUS Traditional medicine; Pharm.; Comm.E+.

Cichorium intybus L.   family: Asteraceae

chicorée sauvage (French); *Wegwarte* (German); *cicoria* (Italian)

Cimicifuga racemosa

black cohosh • black snakeroot

Cimicifuga racemosa plant

Cimicifuga racemosa flowers

DESCRIPTION An erect, perennial herb (up to 2 m in height) with large, compound leaves and long, slender clusters of small white flowers. It is an attractive garden subject but is often confused with the more common C. simplex from East Asia. This species and three others from Asia (C. dahurica, C. heracleifolia, C. foetida) are also used medicinally.

ORIGIN Canada and the northeastern parts of the USA. The plant is easily cultivated but most of the raw material comes from wild-harvesting.

PARTS USED Dried rhizome and roots (Cimicifugae racemosae rhizoma).

THERAPEUTIC CATEGORY Treatment of menstrual disorders; sedative.

USES AND PROPERTIES Treatment of premenstrual and menopause problems associated with neurovegetative complaints. Also included in tonics and cough mixtures, and used to treat rheumatism, chorea (Saint Vitus's dance – a nervous disorder characterised by lack of coordination), dizziness, and tinnitus.

PREPARATION AND DOSAGE 0.5-1 g of the drug is taken up to three times per day, but in several studies only 40 mg of the crude drug was used per day.

ACTIVE INGREDIENTS The drug contains several tetracyclic triterpenoid glycosides (actaein and cimicifugoside) and their aglycones (cimigenol, acetylacteol). Also present is an isoflavonoid, formononetin. Other compounds are isoferulic acid, salicylic acid, gallotannins and possibly cytisine and other quinolizidine alkaloids.

PHARMACOLOGICAL EFFECTS Black cohosh has an oestrogen-like action, usually ascribed to the isoflavonoids and triterpenoids. It appears to act as a selective oestrogen-receptor modulator and is said to suppress the activity of the luteinizing hormone. Extracts containing actaein are known to be spasmolytic, vasodilatory and hypotensive. Controlled studies (but without a double-blind design) have indicated efficacy in the treatment of menopausal symptoms in women. A recent study failed to show efficacy in treating "hot flushes".

WARNING Black cohosh should be avoided by patients suffering from hormone-dependent cancer. It should not be used continuously for more than three months. More than 5 g can cause toxic symptoms.

STATUS Traditional medicine; Pharm.; Comm.E+; WHO 2; clinical studies+.

Cimicifuga racemosa (L.) Nutt. (=*Actaea racemosa* L.)   family: Ranunculaceae

actée à grappet (French); *Amerikanisches Wanzenkraut* (German); *cimicifuga* (Italian); *cimicifuga* (Spanish)

Cinchona pubescens

red cinchona

Cinchona pubescens

Cinchona pubescens leaves

DESCRIPTION *C. pubescens* (=*C. succirubra*) is a large forest tree with tall stems and bright green, simple leaves. The second main source of *Cinchona* bark is a species alternatively known as *C. officinalis* or *C. calisaya* (=*C. ledgeriana*). In commerce, *C. pubescens* is known as the source of reddish bark (much used in pharmacies in Europe), while cultivated *C. calisaya* yields a yellowish bark which is an industrial source of alkaloids. Brown or grey bark is obtained from wild forms of *C. officinalis*.

ORIGIN Colombia, western Ecuador and northern Peru (*C. pubescens* and *C. calisaya/C. officinalis*). Commercial cultivation occurs mainly in India, Indonesia and Africa (DRC, formerly Zaïre).

PARTS USED Bark (twigs, stems) (*Cinchonae cortex*).

THERAPEUTIC CATEGORY Antimalarial, bitter tonic, anti-arrhythmic (quinidine).

USES AND PROPERTIES The bark contains quinine, formerly a most important antimalarial drug. As a bitter tonic, it is used to stimulate appetite (e.g. gin and tonic before a meal). Bark is sometimes included in herbal teas to treat flatulence and loss of appetite. Isolated pure alkaloids, such as quinine and quinidine are used to treat malaria and heart rhythm complaints.

PREPARATION AND DOSAGE For malaria treatment, a minimum daily dose of 1 g fluid extract (4-5% alkaloids) is necessary (not more than 0.5 g at a time, and up to no more than 3 g per day), while lower doses (ca. 0.2 g) are used for other applications. In tonic water, about 67 mg quinine per litre is the usual concentration.

ACTIVE INGREDIENTS Quinoline alkaloids (5-15%), such as quinine, quinidine, cinchonine, cinchonidine and others. Furthermore, triterpene saponins, epicatechins (cinchonain) and proanthocyanidins (cinchonain IIa), catechol tannins and red phlobaphens are present in the bark.

PHARMACOLOGICAL EFFECTS Quinine interferes with the metabolism of blood forms of various *Plasmodium* parasites. Another molecular target is their DNA, which is intercalated by quinine. Several synthetic and more powerful anti-malaria drugs have been developed as a substitute for quinine. Unfortunately, a number of *Plasmodium* strains have become resistant to chemotherapy. Quinidine inhibits Na^+ channels and is employed as an antiarrhythmic drug.

STATUS Pharm.; Comm.E+ (tonic use only); modern medicine: quinine, quinidine.

Cinchona pubescens Vahl-(=*Cinchona succirubra* Pavon ex Klotsch)　　　　　family: Rubiaceae

Roter Chinarindenbaum (German); *quina, quinquina* (French); *china rossa* (Italian); *quina* (Spanish)

Cinnamomum aromaticum

Chinese cinnamon • cassia bark tree

Cinnamomum aromaticum leaves

DESCRIPTION C. *aromaticum* is a large evergreen tree of up to 10 m in height with simple, alternate leaves that are three-nerved from the base. The inconspicuous flowers are yellowish white and are followed by round drupes of about 8 mm in diameter. It may be distinguished from true cinnamon (C. *verum*) by the alternate leaves (opposite or subopposite in C. *verum*) and by the smaller, rounded fruit (larger – ca. 15 mm, and oblong in C. *verum*).

ORIGIN Myanmar, formerly Burma. The tree has a long history of commercial cultivation in China, Indonesia and Vietnam.

PARTS USED Bark from the tree trunk, but with the outer cork layers removed (*Cinnamomi chinensis cortex*); the dried flowers (*Cinnamomi flos = Cassiae flos*) and essential oil (*Cinnamomum cassiae aetheroleum*)

THERAPEUTIC CATEGORY Appetite stimulant, dyspeptic disorders.

USES AND PROPERTIES Bark or oil is used to treat appetite loss, dyspepsia and spasms associated with bloating, flatulence, nausea and diarrhoea. It has also been used to treat the common cold and exhaustion. The flowers are a traditional "blood purifier".

PREPARATION AND DOSAGE 0.5-1 g of bark (or infusions thereof) is taken three times per day (total daily dose of 2-4 g). The average daily dose for cassia oil should be about 0.05-0.2 ml.

ACTIVE INGREDIENTS Bark contains volatile oil with cinnamaldehyde as the main constituent (about 90%) and other derivatives of cinnamate. It is easily distinguished from real cinnamon (C. *verum*) by the presence of 0.45% coumarin and the almost complete absence of eugenol (except for a provenance from Nigeria). Bark is rich in procyanidins, phenylpropanoids and mucilage.

PHARMACOLOGICAL EFFECTS Anti-ulcer, antispasmodic, choleretic, hypotensive and antiseptic properties, amongst many others, have been documented for mostly the oil. Anti-spasmodic activity has been linked to cinnamaldehyde.

WARNING Cassia bark is generally regarded as safe, even during pregnancy (GRAS status in the USA) provided that the daily intake of cinnamaldehyde, through spices or medicine, not exceed 0.7 mg per kg body weight. The oil (probably the cinnamaldehyde), may cause allergic reactions in some people, so that topical use is not recommended.

STATUS Pharm.; Comm.E+; WHO 1.

Cinnamomum aromaticum Nees (= C. *cassia* Blume)   family: Lauraceae

canelle de Chine (French); *Chin. Zimtbaum* (German); *cassia lignea* (Italian)

Cinnamomum camphora

camphor tree

Cinnamomum camphora tree

Cinnamomum camphora leaves and berries

DESCRIPTION This very large tree of more than 50 m in height has a massive trunk and spreading crown. The characteristic leaves are glossy green, with three main veins arising from near the base and a strong camphor smell when crushed.

ORIGIN Japan, Taiwan and China. It is an ornamental tree in most parts of the world. Commercial production in Japan and Taiwan.

PARTS USED Timber is distilled to give an essential oil. Further fractionation gives a camphor fraction, known as camphor or gum camphor and a white, cineol-rich oil which is used medicinally (*Cinnamoni camphorae aetheroleum;* =*Oleum camphorae*).

THERAPEUTIC CATEGORY Circulatory and respiratory stimulant (internal); counter-irritant (topical).

USES AND PROPERTIES Traditional uses of camphor are varied, but relate mainly to colds, influenza, fever, pneumonia, inflammation and diarrhoea. Externally the oil is specifically used to treat rheumatic conditions of the muscles; internally for circulatory disorders. It is used both internally and externally against inflammation and congestion of the respiratory tract.

PREPARATION AND DOSAGE Semisolid prepara-tions intended for external application (nasal ointments, inhalant solutions and chest rubs) should contain 10-20% camphor, while camphor spirits should contain 1-10 %. For internal use, an average daily dose of 30-300 mg is proposed by the German Commision E.

ACTIVE INGREDIENTS The biological activity is linked to natural camphor (*d*-camphor). Commercial gum camphor should contain at least 50% camphor. The white oil fraction contains cineol as main com-ponent, and also borneol, carvacrol, eugenol and li-monene.

PHARMACOLOGICAL EFFECTS Camphor and the essential oil have definite antiseptic, spasmolytic (e.g. in bronchia), counter-irritant, carminative, circulatory stimulant and analeptic properties. The pleasant, cool-ing sensation in the nose and lungs is due to stimula-tion of the cold receptors in the mucous membranes and not to any direct decongestant effect.

WARNING Camphor is toxic in large doses and should not be taken orally without professional supervision. High doses applied to the face or nose may cause respi-ratory arrest in children under two years of age.

STATUS Pharm.; Comm.E+.

Cinnamomum camphora (L.) J. Presl   family: Lauraceae

camphrier du Japon (French); *Kampferbaum* (German); *camfora* (Italian); *alcanfor* (Spanish)

Cinnamomum verum

cinnamon bark tree • Ceylon cinnamon

Cinnamomum verum leaves

Cinnamomum verum tree

cinnamon bark

DESCRIPTION A medium-sized, evergreen tree with leathery, opposite or subopposite leaves. The small flowers are followed by oblong, dark purple fruits, 10 to 15 mm long. The old name for the tree is *C. zeylanicum*.

ORIGIN Sri Lanka (formerly Ceylon) and parts of India. It is cultivated commercially in many tropical parts of the world, including eastern India, Africa, the Seychelles, South America, the West Indies and Indonesia.

PARTS USED Inner bark of branches and coppice shoots (cinnamon or cinnamon bark; *Cinnamomi ceylanici cortex*); essential oil (*Cinnamomi aetheroleum*).

THERAPEUTIC CATEGORY Dyspeptic disorders, astringent.

USES AND PROPERTIES Cinnamon is a traditional remedy for dyspeptic conditions (flatulence, gastrointestinal spasms, loss of appetite and diarrhoea). It is also used in folk medicine to treat inflammation, rheumatism, colds, nausea and vomiting and menstrual disorders. Cinnamon is used to improve the taste and aroma of some medicinal products. Non-medicinal uses are well known – it is a popular spice in cooking and the essential oil is used in perfumery.

PREPARATION AND DOSAGE The bark is used in its crude form or as powder or extract. A dose of up to 1.2 g of dry bark may be used (daily dose of 2-4 g – in the case of the essential oil, 0.05-0.2 g).

ACTIVE INGREDIENTS Cinnamon bark contains essential oil, with cinnamaldehyde as the main constituent (65-80 %) and smaller amounts of trans-cinnamic acid, *o*-methoxycinnamaldehyde, about 10% eugenol and monoterpenoids. Also present are procyanidins, diterpenes, phenylpropanoids, and polysaccharides. Oil from leaves contains 70-90% eugenol.

PHARMACOLOGICAL EFFECTS The oil has documented carminative, antispasmodic and antimicrobial properties. Antispasmodic activity is due to cinnamaldehyde, while antifungal and antibacterial effects are attributed to the presence of *o*-methoxycinnamaldehyde and eugenol.

WARNING Medicinal use is best avoided during pregnancy (high doses can induce abortion). It should not be used by persons with a cinnamon allergy, or those with stomach and duodenal ulcers.

NOTES Cinnamon is often adulterated with the less desirable *C. aromaticum*.

STATUS Pharm.; Comm.E+; WHO 1.

Cinnamomum verum J. Presl (=*C. zeylanicum* Nees)   family: Lauraceae

canellier, canelle de Ceylan (French); *Ceylon-Zimtbaum* (German); *cannella* (Italian); *canelo de Ceilán* (Spanish)

Citrus aurantium

bitter orange • Seville orange

Citrus aurantium subsp. *aurantium*

Citrus aurantium subsp. *aurantium* fruit

Citrus aurantium subsp. *bergamia* flower

DESCRIPTION Bitter orange is an evergreen tree (up to 10 m), with gland-dotted leaves and fragrant, white flowers. The short leaf stalk is conspicuously winged in the upper part. The form used for bergamot oil is known as *C. bergamia* (or *C. aurantium* subsp. *bergamia*). It is a smaller tree – up to 5 m.

ORIGIN *Citrus* species originally came from southern and southeastern Asia and have a long and complicated history in cultivation. Bitter orange is grown in the Mediterranean and in many other warm parts of the world, while bergamot is cultivated mainly in Calabria (Italy) and France.

PARTS USED Green fruits, peels of ripe fruits, flowers and oil are used. Most of the inner, spongy, white part of the peel (*albedo*) is removed and the glandular outer part (*flavedo*) yields bitter orange peel (*Aurantii pericarpium*). Note that orange peel (*Citri sinensis pericarpium*) is obtained from the sweet orange (*C. sinensis*). Unripe fruit (*Aurantii fructus immaturi*) is the *zhi shi* of Chinese medicine.

THERAPEUTIC CATEGORY Appetite stimulant, aromatic, stomachic.

USES AND PROPERTIES Bitter orange peel is mainly used to enhance appetite and to treat dyspeptic complaints. There are numerous traditional uses for both sweet and bitter peel, such as the treatment of minor sleeplessness. *Zhi shi* is used for flatulence and bloating.

PREPARATION AND DOSAGE The daily dose is 4-6 g of dried peel, usually taken as a tea.

ACTIVE INGREDIENTS The peel contains essential oil (mainly limonene, linalool, terpineol), bitter flavanone glycosides (naringin and neohesperidin) and bitter triterpenes (limonin).

PHARMACOLOGICAL EFFECTS Bitter compounds are known to stimulate appetite by increasing the secretion of gastric juices. The non-bitter flavonoids in sweet orange peel are thought to act as venotonics.

WARNING Bergamot oil may cause photosensitisation in fair-skinned people due to the presence of bergapten (a phototoxic coumarin) so that a maximum of 2% of the oil is allowed in perfumes and tanning lotions. Pure oil should not be taken internally.

NOTES Marmalade is made from bitter oranges. Neroli oil (30% linalool; used in perfumes, such as eau-de-cologne) is distilled from the flowers.

STATUS Pharm.; Comm.E+.

Citrus aurantium L. subsp. *aurantium* (=*C. aurantium* subsp. *amara*)   family: Rutaceae

orange amère (French); *Pomeranze, Bitterorange* (German); *arancio amaro* (Italian); *naranjo amargo* (Spanish)

Citrus limon

lemon tree

Citrus limon flowers and fruit

DESCRIPTION Lemon is a small, evergreen tree (up to 6 m), easily recognised by the scarcely winged leaf stalks and the flowers, which are not pure white but tinged purple.

ORIGIN Southern and southeastern Asia; cultivated in warm climates (notably southern Europe, southern USA, India and China).

PARTS USED Dried peels of unripe but fully mature fruits (*Citri pericarpium*); also fresh juice and oil pressed from the outer layer of the fruit wall (lemon oil).

THERAPEUTIC CATEGORY Aromatic, stomachic, against scurvy.

USES AND PROPERTIES Lemon juice (sometimes loosely referred to as "limejuice") was once an important remedy for scurvy (long before vitamin C was discovered), hence the name "limer" or "limey" given to British seamen. Nowadays, the peel and oil are used to improve digestion and circulation.

PREPARATION AND DOSAGE Lemon peel is sometimes included in stomachic medicines or in fruit tea mixtures. Fresh juice may be gargled for sore throat, or applied to the skin to treat acne, sunburn or fungal infections.

ACTIVE INGREDIENTS Essential oil contains monoter-penoids of which limonene (up to 75%), α-pinene and β-pinene are the main compounds. Small amounts of citral (a mixture of geranial and neral) give the characteristic lemon smell. Numerous bitter flavonoids are present, mainly naringenin and hesperidin, and citric acid.

PHARMACOLOGICAL EFFECTS The oil is aromatic and is thought to have antiseptic, diuretic, anti-inflammatory and decongestant properties. Bioflavonoids are known to be antioxidants and to reduce the permeability of blood vessels and capillaries.

NOTES Oil pressed from the fresh pericarp is called lemon oil. Bergamot oil (the flavour in Earl Grey tea) is similarly cold-pressed from *C. aurantium* subsp. *bergamia*, bitter orange oil from subsp. *aurantium*, sweet orange oil from *C. sinensis*, grapefruit oil from *C. x paradisi*, mandarin orange oil from the tangerine (*C. reticulata*), lime oil from *C. aurantiifolia* and citron oil from *C. medica*. Dried or candied peels are produced, especially from citron. Oil distilled from the stems and leaves of various *Citrus* species, often used in aromatherapy, is known as petitgrain oils (bergamot petitgrain, lemon petitgrain, etc.).

STATUS Traditional medicine; Pharm.

Citrus limon (L.) Burm.f.   family: Rutaceae

citron (French); *Zitrone, Limone* (German); *limone* (Italian); *limón* (Spanish)

Coffea arabica
coffee tree • Arabian coffee

Coffea arabica flower

Coffea arabica fruit

Coffee trees

DESCRIPTION Coffee is a shrub or small tree (4-7 m) with dark green, lustrous leaves, clusters of small, white, fragrant flowers and small, rounded berries that turn yellow, red or purple when they ripen.

ORIGIN Ethiopia. Large-scale cultivation occurs in countries such as Brazil, Colombia, Indonesia, Ivory Coast, Mexico and Kenya.

PARTS USED Seeds (green or fermented, sundried, roasted and ground, as coffee; *Coffeae semen*) or carbonised, "coffee charcoal" (*Coffeae tostae carbo*; *Coffeae carbo*).

THERAPEUTIC CATEGORY Stimulant, diuretic.

USES AND PROPERTIES Coffee is used as a stimulant beverage and forms the basis of a very large industry. Caffeine, the main active compound, however, is incorporated into numerous formulations used against fever, pain, and flu symptoms. It has a specific function in the mixture, for example to counteract drowsiness. Coffee carbon is taken orally to treat diarrhoea and mild inflammation of the mouth and throat.

PREPARATION AND DOSAGE The recommended daily dose of coffee carbon is 9 g per day. As a beverage, coffee is rarely used for medicinal purposes other than to increase alertness, promote concentration and reduce fatigue.

ACTIVE INGREDIENTS Mainly caffeine, with other minor purine alkaloids (theobromine, theophylline, theacrine). Coffee seeds contain about 1-2% caffeine (about 150 mg per cup). Also present are chlorogenic acid, various diterpenes, and trigonelline.

PHARMACOLOGICAL EFFECTS Caffeine binds to adenosine receptors and inhibits phosphodiesterase. Caffeine is a central stimulant, affects the cardiovascular system and has a positive inotropic action, resulting in tachycardia and an enhanced output (good for patients with hypotonia). Coffee enhances gastric secretions and gut motility.

WARNING Excessive amounts of coffee may lead to nervousness, palpitations, high blood pressure, insomnia and indigestion. Caffeine is known to be addictive.

NOTES Of lesser commercial importance are *C. canephora* (robusta or Congo coffee, often used in instant coffee) and *C. liberica* (Liberian or Abeokuta coffee, added to blends because of its bitter flavour).

STATUS Traditional medicine and modern medicine: caffeine; Comm.E+ (coffee charcoal).

Coffea arabica L.

family: Rubiaceae

caféier d'Arabie (French); *Kaffeestrauch* (German); *caffè* (Italian); *cafeto* (Spanish)

Cola acuminata

cola nut tree

Cola acuminata fruit

Cola acuminata leaves

Cola nitida seeds

DESCRIPTION Cola is a medium-sized tree (up to 15 m), with large leaves and yellow flowers in clusters. The nuts are borne in large, multi-seeded follicles. Another important commercial species is *Cola nitida* (previously known as *C. vera*). It differs from *C. acuminata* in having narrower leaves and larger flowers, which are pale yellow streaked with purple. The seeds of *C. acuminata* are split into about four irregular pieces of endosperm when the seed coat is removed, while those of *C. nitida* split in two.

ORIGIN West Africa (Nigeria and Sierra Leone to Gabon); cultivation in tropical America and Asia

PARTS USED Seeds or nuts (*Colae semen*), with the seed coat or testa removed.

THERAPEUTIC CATEGORY Stimulant.

USES AND PROPERTIES Cola seeds are used to treat mental and physical fatigue. Extracts or tinctures are included in various energy drinks and give the user a short-term energy boost. The fresh seeds are traditionally chewed for their stimulating and tonic effects. They are also astringent and said to be useful in treating diarrhoea, wounds and inflammations.

PREPARATION AND DOSAGE The daily dose is 2-6 g of cola nut, taken as extract or tincture. It has been traditionally used in cola drinks but artificial flavours are currently used.

ACTIVE INGREDIENTS The main compound is the purine alkaloid caffeine (1.5-3 %) that co-occurs with much smaller amounts of theobromine. Also present are phenolics (4-6%) such as catechin, epicatechin and procyanidins, that can complex the purine alkaloids.

PHARMACOLOGICAL EFFECTS Cola nuts are similar in their effect to other caffeine-containing products such as coffee, tea, guarana and maté. They have a stimulant effect of the central nervous system and the heart. Animal experiments indicate, too, that cola nuts have analeptic and lipolytic properties, and that they stimulate the secretion of gastric juices. In human studies, cola nuts have shown positive chronotropic and weak diuretic effects.

WARNING People suffering from stomach and duodenal ulcers or hypertension and heart disorders should restrict their intake of cola products.

STATUS Traditional medicine; Comm.E+.

Cola acuminata (Pal.) Schott & Endl.   family: Sterculiaceae

colatier (French); *Kolabaum* (German); *cola* (Italian); *cola* (Spanish)

Colchicum autumnale

autumn crocus • meadow saffron

Colchicum autumnale flowers

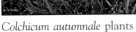
Colchicum autumnale plants

Colchicum autumnale fruit and seeds

DESCRIPTION *Colchicum* is a perennial with strap-shaped leaves that emerge from a fleshy corm in spring, together with the fertilised young fruit that was produced in the previous flowering period. In autumn, several long, tubular pink flowers are produced from the now leafless plant. The ovary remains underground in winter and matures during spring and early summer into a three-locular capsule that contains numerous small, hard, black seeds.

ORIGIN Europe and North Africa. Most of the material is still wild-harvested.

PARTS USED Cut and dried corms (*Colchici tuber*), dry seeds (*Colchici semen*) or fresh flowers.

THERAPEUTIC CATEGORY Treatment of acute gout attack.

USES AND PROPERTIES Extracted alkaloids are used in carefully measured dosages to treat acute attacks of gout. It is also used for the therapeutic treatment of familial Mediterranean fever.

PREPARATION AND DOSAGE The total daily dose of alkaloid (corresponding mostly to colchicine) should not exceed 8 mg. An initial dose of 1 mg colchicine may be administered orally, followed by 0.5–1.5 mg doses at 2-3-hourly intervals as necessary. The latter dose is also suitable for treating familial Mediterranean fever.

ACTIVE INGREDIENTS Mainly colchicine (0.3-1.2% of dry weight of the corm, flower or seeds). It occurs with other minor phenethylisoquinoline alkaloids.

PHARMACOLOGICAL EFFECTS Colchicine binds to tubuline and inhibits the formation of microtubules. At therapeutic dose, colchicine is an extremely effective anti-inflammatory agent and painkiller, as it prevents the migration of macrophages to the inflamed joints, associated with an acute attack of gout (caused by precipitation of urate crystals). It often causes diarrhoea (so that anti-diarrhoeal ingredients are usually included in the formulation). The toxic dose in humans is about 10 mg, while 40 mg would always be fatal (respiratory and cardiovascular disruption within a few days).

WARNING Self-medication should not be attempted. Colchicine is contra-indicated during pregnancy and in cases of kidney, liver and heart disorders.

NOTE Colchicine is no longer used in cancer therapy, but in cytodiagnostics (to halt cells in the metaphase) and in plant breeding (creation of polyploid plants).

STATUS Modern medicine; Comm.E+.

Colchicum autumnale L.

family: Colchicaceae

colchique d'automne (French); *Herbstzeitlose* (German); *colchico* (Italian); *cólquico* (Spanish)

Commiphora myrrha

myrrh tree • African myrrh

Commiphora abyssinica

Commiphora species

Myrrh (left) and scented myrrh (right)

DESCRIPTION True myrrh is a thorny shrub or small tree of about 3 m in height. The hairless, toothed leaves each has a large terminal leaflet and two lateral leaflets which are much smaller or sometimes absent. Pink and yellow flowers are followed by beaked fruit of about 12 mm long.

ORIGIN Somalia, Ethiopia and parts of Kenya; wild-harvested for centuries.

PARTS USED Bitter tasting oleo-resin that exudes naturally from the bark (myrrh; *Myrrha*). Damaging the stems to increase the exudation gives an inferior product.

THERAPEUTIC CATEGORY Astringent, antiseptic, anti-inflammatory.

USES AND PROPERTIES Myrrh is mainly used as an antiseptic and anti-inflammatory for the topical treatment of mouth and throat infections (gingivitis and other gum diseases, tonsillitis, mouth ulcers). It is bitter tasting and astringent, and is used traditionally for a wide range of other conditions, including the common cold (relief of nasal congestion and cough), wounds and ulcers and particularly for infections in the mouth, gums and throat.

PREPARATION AND DOSAGE For topical use, undiluted myrrh tincture is dabbed onto the affected area two or three times a day. For a mouth rinse or gargle, up to 60 drops of tincture are added to a glass of warm water, while dental powders contain 10% of dried, powdered resin.

ACTIVE INGREDIENTS Myrrh contains complex polysaccharides, triterpenoids, triterpene acids and an essential oil (3-6%) rich in sesquiterpenes (β-elemen, δ-elemen) and furanosesquiterpenes of the elemen-, eudesmen-, guaien- and germacren-types. Furanoeudesma-1,3-diene (about 50%) is the main compound.

PHARMACOLOGICAL EFFECTS Animal studies have shown anti-inflammatory, antipyretic and astringent activities.

NOTES The myrrh of the Bible originates from Ethiopian and Somalian *Commiphora guidottii* and is today referred to as scented myrrh. *Commiphora abyssinica* yields Arabian or *Fadhlî* myrrh, while *C. gileadensis* is the source of balm of Gilead (Mecca myrrh). Gum opopanax is collected from *C. kataf* and other species. Another type of myrrh, gugulon, originates from Indian *C. mukul*. It is an important anti-inflammatory in Ayurvedic medicine and lowers blood cholesterol levels.

STATUS Pharm.; Comm.E+; ESCOP 6.

Commiphora myrrha (Nees) Engl. (= *C. molmol* Engl.)

myrrhe (French); *Myrrhe* (German); *mirra* (Italian); *mirra* (Spanish)

family: Burseraceae

Convallaria majalis
lily-of-the-valley

Convallaria majalis flowers

Convallaria majalis fruit

DESCRIPTION An attractive perennial herb with a pair of broad leaves arising from the ground that grows in large clumps. It produces an elegant cluster of small, bell-shaped, white, fragrant flowers, all arranged on one side of the stalk. The fruits are small red berries.

ORIGIN Europe, NortheastAsia; naturalised in North America; wild-harvested in eastern Europe. It is cultivated as a garden plant.

PARTS USED The aboveground parts (*Convallariae herba*; *Convallariae flos*) are harvested during the flowering season and are then dried and cut.

THERAPEUTIC CATEGORY Heart stimulant.

USES AND PROPERTIES The herb is used against mild cardiac insufficiency associated with old age and chronic *cor pulmonale*.

PREPARATION AND DOSAGE Standardised powder containing 0.2% of convallatoxin is used in three doses of 0.2 g (total daily dose of 0.6 g); tinctures and extracts are also employed.

ACTIVE INGREDIENTS Lily-of-the-valley contains numerous cardiac glycosides in yields of about 0.1-0.5% of dry weight, together with saponins. The level of cardiac glycosides is highest in the flowering period.

Convallatoxin is the main constituent (about 40% of the total heart glycosides) and occurs with the structurally similar convalloside, convallatoxol, locundjoside and numerous others. Roots contain the toxic non-protein amino acid acetidine-2-carboxylic acid.

PHARMACOLOGICAL EFFECTS Convallatoxin is similar to other cardiac glycosides. It inhibits Na^+, K^+-ATPase and indirectly increases the intracellular Ca^{++} concentration. This strengthens the contraction of the heart muscle, lowers the internal heart pressure and thereby increases the efficiency of the heart. It also has venotonic effects and promotes the excretion of sodium and potassium salts in the urine.

WARNING The herb is very toxic and must only be administered under the supervision of a qualified practitioner. It may cause nausea, vomiting and gastrointestinal symptoms when taken in large amounts. *Convallaria* cardenolides are fortunately poorly absorbed in the stomach and intestines and therefore rarely deadly.

NOTES Lily-of-the-valley is sometimes preferred to *Digitalis* as it is thought to be tolerated better, with fewer side effects.

STATUS Traditional medicine; Pharm.; Comm.E+.

Convallaria majalis L.   family: Convallariaceae

muguet (French); *Maiglöckchen* (German); *mughetto* (Italian); *lirio de los valles* (Spanish)

Coptis chinensis
Chinese goldthread

Coptis japonica flowers

Coptis japonica plant

Coptis chinensis dried rhizomes

DESCRIPTION Coptis species are perennial herbs with long leaf stalks that arise directly from the ground, lobed and finely dissected leaves and small, greenish-white flowers. The brownish rhizomes are yellow or orange inside. In addition to C. chinensis, several other species are used in Oriental and in North American traditional medicine. These include C. trifolia (North America), C. japonica (Japan), C. teeta (India) and C. deltoides (China).

ORIGIN China. The plant is cultivated in China.

PARTS USED Dried rhizomes (Coptidis rhizoma).

THERAPEUTIC CATEGORY Antidysenteric, antimicrobial.

USES AND PROPERTIES In traditional Chinese medicine, huang lian is mainly used to treat bacterial diarrhoea, but it is also used against gastroenteritis, conjunctivitis and external sores. Other Coptis species are used mainly as bitter tonics and remedies for stomach ailments and infections (including ulcers and inflammations of the mouth and tongue). These plants are similar to the related goldenseal (Hydrastis canadensis) in their chemical composition and medicinal properties.

PREPARATION AND DOSAGE The recommended daily dose of the crude product is 1.5-6 g.

ACTIVE INGREDIENTS Berberine, an isoquinoline alkaloid, is present in the dried rhizomes at a level of about 5-7 %, together with other so-called protoberberine alkaloids (including palmatine, coptisine and berberastine). The other species listed above also contain these alkaloids and they seem to differ quantitatively only.

PHARMACOLOGICAL EFFECTS Berberine and other protoberberine alkaloids intercalate DNA, inhibit various receptors, proteins and enzymes. These properties explain the documented antimicrobial activities against a wide range of organisms. A recent study of C. chinensis rhizome showed that extracts at a concentration of only 1.7 µg/ml (with little evidence of cytotoxicity) are highly effective as trypanocides against Trypanosoma cruzi (a protozoan that causes serious infections in humans). Studies on both berberine and Coptis rhizomes have failed to show convincing anti-diarrhoeal effects.

WARNING Berberine and Coptis rhizomes might be mutagenic, so these products should be avoided during pregnancy and used with caution.

STATUS Traditional medicine; WHO 1.

Coptis chinensis Franch. family: Ranunculaceae

huang lian (Chinese); huánglián, coptide chinois (French); Chinesischer Goldfaden (German); cottide (Italian)

Coriandrum sativum

coriander

Coriandrum sativum leaves and flowers

Coriandrum sativum

Coriandrum sativum fruit

DESCRIPTION An annual herb with aromatic leaves and pale pink flowers arranged in umbels. Upper leaves are much dissected and feathery in appearance; the lower ones are undivided and quite different in shape. The peripheral flowers in each umbel have the outer petal enlarged, so that the clusters superficially resemble the flower heads found in Asteraceae. The small, dry, spherical fruit (schizocarp) split into two mericarps at maturity.

ORIGIN Coriander orginates from the eastern Mediterranean region and western Asia, but has been cultivated as a spice in other parts of the world for centuries.

PARTS USED Ripe, dry fruits (*Coriandri fructus*), usually referred to as seeds and the essential oil (*Coriandri aetheroleum*).

THERAPEUTIC CATEGORY Stomachic, spasmolytic, carminative.

USES AND PROPERTIES The main medicinal use is to treat loss of appetite and dyspeptic complaints. It may be added to laxative medicines to ease griping. Since ancient times, the fruits have been used topically to treat wounds and burns and the oil is sometimes included in lotions used as counter-irritant to treat painful joints, rheumatism and menstrual disor-

ders. Fruits may be chewed as breath deodorant after eating garlic.

PREPARATION AND DOSAGE For internal use, the equivalent of about 3 g of dry fruit is considered an appropriate daily dose.

ACTIVE INGREDIENTS The essential oil is considered to be responsible for the therapeutic actions of the fruit. It is present in a concentration of about 1% of dry weight, and contains linalool as the main ingredient (about 60-70%). Also present are coumarins, phenylpropanoids, and triterpenes (coriandrinondiol). Unripe fruits and leaves have a peculiar "bedbug" smell, which is due to minor components (decanal and tricen-2-al).

PHARMACOLOGICAL EFFECTS Coriander has documented spasmolytic, carminative and antimicrobial properties which would be plausible for essential oils.

WARNING When applied to skin, the oil may cause allergic reactions in sensitive people, due to the presence of phototoxic furanocoumarins (coriandrine, dihydrocoriandrine).

NOTES Coriander is an important ingredient of curry powders and liqueurs.

STATUS Traditional medicine; Pharm.; Comm.E+.

Coriandrum sativum L.

family: Apiaceae

coriandre (French); *Koriander* (German); *coriandolo* (Italian); *cilantro* (Spanish)

Crataegus monogyna

hawthorn

Crataegus monogyna

Crataegus laevigata

DESCRIPTION *Crataegus* species are shrubs or small trees (up to 10 m), with lobed leaves, thorny branches and white flowers, that emanate amines to attract pollinating insects, followed by red fruit. Two species (that readily hybridise) are mostly used for medicine, namely C. *monogyna* (deeply lobed leaves, single-seeded fruit) and C. *laevigata* (=C. *oxyacantha*) (shallowly lobed leaves, 2-3-seeded fruit). Furthermore, C. *azarolus* and C. *pentagyna* are used in European phytotherapy; C. *cuneata* and C. *pinnatifolia* in Chinese medicine.

ORIGIN C. *laevigata*: Europe; C. *monogyna*: Europe and Asia.

PARTS USED Dried leaves with flowers (*Crataegi folium cum flore*); flowers and fruits are sometimes used on their own.

THERAPEUTIC CATEGORY Cardiotonic.

USES AND PROPERTIES Hawthorn products are used to treat cardiac insufficiency (NYHA stages I and II) and bradycard rhythm disorders.

PREPARATION AND DOSAGE In modern phytotherapy defined special extracts are used. The German Commission E recommends a daily dose of 160-900 mg of hawthorn extract containing 4-30 mg total flavonoids and 30-160 mg of oligomeric procyanidins. More recently, a dose of 600-900 mg of extract per day was recommended. Hawthorn products are taken orally and are only effective if used for a minimum period of six weeks.

ACTIVE INGREDIENTS The drug contains 1-3% oligomeric procyanidins, together with about 1-2% flavonoids, such as vitexin-rhamnoside, hyperoside and rutin as the main flavonoids. Also present are chlorogenic acid, caffeic acid, and triterpenes.

PHARMACOLOGICAL EFFECTS Procyanidins and flavonoids represent the medicinally important compounds because of their phenolic hydroxyl groups they can interfere with various enzymes and receptors, among them Na^+,K^+-ATPase, and ACE (angiotensin converting enzyme). Numerous studies have shown an increase in the strength of contraction and the stroke volume of the heart. Anti-arrhythmic effects and increases in coronary blood flow have been documented. Controlled, double-blind clinical studies have shown the efficacy of treating patients with NYHA II; some evidence suggests that it might also work for NYHA III.

STATUS Pharm.; Comm.E+; ESCOP 6; WHO 2; clinical studies+.

Crataegus monogyna Jacq.
family: Rosaceae

aubépine (French); *Eingriffeliger Weißdorn* (German); *bianco spino* (Italian); *espino albar* (Spanish)

Crocus sativus

saffron • saffron crocus

Crocus sativus

Crocus sativus dried styles and stigmas

DESCRIPTION Crocus sativus is a bulbous plant with narrow, strap-shaped leaves and tubular purple flowers with three bright red style-branches. It is very similar to Colchicum, but the ovary and fruit are borne below the ground (the stalk does not lengthen during maturation of the fruit). Furthermore, Crocus has only three stamens, while Colchicum has six.

ORIGIN Southern Europe and southwestern Asia. Saffron is a sterile cultigen that probably originated in the eastern Mediterranean region. It is grown commercially on a large scale in Spain.

PARTS USED Only the stigmas (actually the stigmas and style branches; Croci stigma).

THERAPEUTIC CATEGORY Sedative, antispasmodic, stomachic.

USES AND PROPERTIES Saffron is traditionally used to treat spasms and asthma (and numerous other ailments) but there is no scientific evidence to support these uses. It is an ingredient of "Swedish bitters" but is no longer of much importance as a medicinal product. Saffron is mainly used as a spice for its distinctive aroma and taste and as colouring agent.

PREPARATION AND DOSAGE The maximum safe dose is considered to be 1.0 g per day.

ACTIVE INGREDIENTS The yellow, water-soluble pigment in the stigmas is derived from a glycosylated linear diterpene known as crocetin. The bitter taste is due to a glycoside, picrocrocin. The characteristic aroma results from safranal, which is the main compound in the essential oil (up to 1% of dry weight). Safranal is the aglycone of picrocrocin and is formed during the drying process.

PHARMACOLOGICAL EFFECTS It is generally accepted that saffron has sedative and spasmolytic effects, while crocetin has lipid lowering properties. Extracts show anti-tumour properties (cell cultures, mice) and uterus contractant activity. Saffron is also known to be very poisonous- even 5 g may cause severe symptoms (vomiting, bleeding). 10 g per day will cause abortion and uterine bleeding, while 5-20 g can be lethal.

WARNING Saffron is safe only at the low doses that are typically used in food.

NOTES Powdered saffron is often adulterated with safflower, turmeric, paprika or various other yellow pigments.

STATUS Pharm.

Crocus sativus L.

family: Iridaceae

safran (French); Safran (German); zafferano (Italian); azafrán (Spanish)

Cucurbita pepo

pumpkin

Cucurbita pepo leaves and flowers

Cucurbita pepo fruit

Pumpkin seeds

DESCRIPTION Pumpkin is a robust, creeping annual herb with large hairy leaves, coiled tendrils and large, funnel-shaped, yellow flowers. The enormous fruit is technically a berry, and has numerous flat seeds embedded within the spongy fruit flesh. The seeds are oval in shape, flat, pointed at the one end and usually green to white or pale brown in colour. Seeds of various other species generally known as winter squashes or pumpkins (including *C. maxima*, *C. mixta* and *C. moschata*) are used to some extent.

ORIGIN South and Central America, cultivated in most parts of the world. Nowadays, cultivars are used that produce seeds with soft shells or even without a seed coat (testa) to eliminate the need for shelling.

PARTS USED Ripe, dried seeds (*Cucurbitae peponis semen*) or seed oil.

THERAPEUTIC CATEGORY Prostate hyperplasia; diuretic.

USES AND PROPERTIES Pumpkin seeds or seed oil have become popular in recent years for the symptomatic relief of benign prostatic hyperplasia (a traditional practice in central Europe) and irritated bladder. Seed extracts have been employed as a vermifuge (especially against tapeworms and roundworms) and externally for wound-healing.

PREPARATION AND DOSAGE An average dose of 10 g seeds per day (or its equivalent) is recommended. To be effective, the treatment should be maintained for several weeks or months.

ACTIVE INGREDIENTS The seed oil contains fatty acids, of which linoleic acid (about 60%) is the main compound. Of interest are various plant sterols and sterol glycosides (about 1%) (especially Δ^7-sterols) and tocopherols. Also present is cucurbitine (3-amino-3-carboxypyrrolidine), a cyclic non-protein amino acid.

PHARMACOLOGICAL EFFECTS Beneficial effects against benign prostatic hypertrophy is associated with the presence of Δ^7-sterols. Clinical studies suggest that they may inhibit the binding of dihydrotestosterone within the prostate, or perhaps work through inhibition of 5α-reductase and aromatase. The activity against tapeworm is attributed to cucurbitine.

WARNING The treatment of an enlarged prostate should be supervised by a health care professional, as pumpkin seeds and other products only provide symptomatic relief.

STATUS Traditional medicine; Pharm.; Comm.E+.

Cucurbita pepo L.   family: Cucurbitaceae

pépon, citrouille (French); *Gartenkürbis* (German); *zucca* (Italian); *calabaza* (Spanish)

Curcuma longa

turmeric

Curcuma longa flowers

Curcuma longa plants

Curcuma zedoaria plants

DESCRIPTION Turmeric is a stemless, leafy perennial herb closely resembling ginger (*Zingiber*), with broad, hairless leaves arising from near ground level. Attractive yellow and white flowers are borne in oblong spikes. The fleshy, smooth rhizomes are bright orange inside.

ORIGIN The plant is an ancient cultigen thought to have originated in India. It is cultivated in most tropical parts of the world, including China, India, Malaysia, Indonesia, Africa and Madagascar.

PARTS USED Rhizomes (*Curcumae longae rhizoma*). For medicinal purposes, they are sliced and dried (sometimes dried without cutting) or used fresh.

THERAPEUTIC CATEGORY Choleretic, anti-inflammatory.

USES AND PROPERTIES *Curcuma* species are widely used for their benefits in peptic complaints, including the stimulation of bile secretion, the healing of peptic ulcers and the carminative effects. Turmeric is best known for its varied uses as a spice (an ingredient of curry powders, for example) and vegetable dye.

PREPARATION AND DOSAGE A daily dose of 2 g of the dried rhizome is recommended (up to 9 g of fresh rhizome per day).

ACTIVE INGREDIENTS The yellow, non-volatile pigments (3-5% of dry weight) are known as curcuminoids (comprising curcumin, monodesmethoxycurcumin and bisdesmethoxycurcumin). The essential oil (2-7% dry weight) is rich in bisabolane-(characteristically high levels in *C. longa*), guaiane- and several germacrane-type sesquiterpenes. The latter includes α- and β-turmerone, curlone and zingiberene. Also present is a polysaccharide (arabino-galactan) known as ukonan A.

PHARMACOLOGICAL EFFECTS Curcumin and related compounds are known to be anti-inflammatory, antioxidative, antimicrobial and cytotoxic towards tumour cells; they are thought to be at least partly responsible for the choleretic and cholecystokinetic properties of turmeric. Ukonan A stimulates phagocytic activity.

WARNING Turmeric is contraindicated in cases of obstruction of the bile duct, or gallstones.

NOTES Various *Curcuma* species are used against dyspeptic complaints, as stomachics and carminatives, including wild turmeric (*C. aromatica*), Javanese turmeric (*C. xanthorrhiza*) and zedoary (*C. zedoaria*).

STATUS Traditional medicine; Pharm.; Comm.E+; WHO 1.

Curcuma longa L. (= *C. domestica* Valeton)

family: Zingiberaceae

curcuma (French); *Kurkuma, Gelbwurzel* (German); *curcuma* (Italian); *turmérico* (Spanish)

Cyclopia intermedia

honeybush tea

Cyclopia intermedia leaves and flowers

Cyclopia intermedia plant

Cyclopia subternata plant

DESCRIPTION Honeybush tea is a woody shrub with yellowish green trifoliolate leaves and attractive bright yellow flowers. Several species can be used, but the broad-leaved *C. intermedia* (a multi-stemmed, resprouting plant that survives fire) and *C. subternata* (a single-stemmed plant that regenerates from seed after fire) have become the main commercial sources.

ORIGIN The fynbos region of the Cape, South Africa. In recent years, *C. intermedia*, *C. subternata*, *C. genistoides* and *C. sessilifolia* have been developed as crops.

PARTS USED Leaves and twigs, sometimes with the flowers. The leafy branches are cut into short sections, dampened with water and allowed to "ferment" (actually an enzymatic oxidation process) in a warm place until a sweet smell is generated. The product is then air dried.

THERAPEUTIC CATEGORY Antioxidant (health beverage).

USES AND PROPERTIES Honeybush tea is free from any stimulants or harmful substances and has therefore become a popular herbal drink, mostly enjoyed simply as a hot beverage or as iced tea.

PREPARATION AND DOSAGE Honeybush tea is made and enjoyed in much the same way as ordinary tea, except that the flavour improves if it is boiled for a short while.

ACTIVE INGREDIENTS The processed herb (all four crop species) contains mangiferin as one of the major constituents, together with smaller amounts of isomangiferin. Other phenolic compounds include 4-hydroxycinnamic acid, flavones (naringenin, eriodictyol, hesperitin, isosakuranetin, hesperidin), isoflavanones (formononetin, afrormosin, calycosin, pseudobaptigen, fujikinetin) and coumestans (medicagol, flemichapparin, sophora-coumestan B). Small amounts of inositol, also known as (+)-pinitol, are present.

PHARMACOLOGICAL EFFECTS The beneficial effects of honeybush tea are generally accepted to be linked to the antioxidant effects of the phenolic compounds and the absence of stimulants, but the pharmacological effects are poorly known. A recent study of the processed and unprocessed ("green") tea has shown antimutagenic effects. Pinitol has documented anti-diabetic effects. Isoflavones often show phyto-estrogenic activities.

STATUS Traditional medicine (health tea).

Cyclopia intermedia E. Mey.

family: Fabaceae

cyclopia (French); *Honigbusch* (German)

Cymbopogon citratus

lemongrass

Cymbopogon citratus plant

Cymbopogon citratus stems

DESCRIPTION A perennial tuft with sturdy stems and rather broad, aromatic leaves. The species grown commercially for oil distillation are mostly distinguished by their characteristic smell and chemical composition of the oil. In addition to *C. citratus*, the main ones are *C. nardus* (Ceylon citronella grass, the source of citronella oil), *C. martinii* (ginger grass, palma-rosa, rusha) and *C. winterianus* (Java citronella oil).

ORIGIN Unknown (thought to have originated in southern India and Sri Lanka). It is now grown as a crop plant in many parts of the world. *C. nardus* occurs naturally in tropical Asia, *C. martinii* originated in India but is cultivated in Malaysia and *C. winterianus* is a cultigen of unknown origin grown commercially in India and Indonesia.

PARTS USED Dried aboveground parts (*Cymbopogonis citrati herba*) or the essential oil (*Cymbopogonis citrati aetheroleum*).

THERAPEUTIC CATEGORY Weak sedative, stomachic.

USES AND PROPERTIES The leaves and essential oil are used to treat dyspeptic disorders, colds, nervous conditions and exhaustion. Some massage oils and aromatherapy oils contain lemongrass oil.

PREPARATION AND DOSAGE Leaf infusions or dilute oil may be taken orally; oil is also applied topically.

ACTIVE INGREDIENTS Lemongrass oil contains large amounts of citral (geranial, neral) and numerous other monoterpenoids. Citronella oil has geraniol, citronellol and citronellal as main ingredients.

PHARMACOLOGICAL EFFECTS Lipophilic monoterpenes interact with biomembranes of cells and can modulate the activity of membrane proteins, especially ion channels and receptors. These properties might explain the antimicrobial, sedative, spasmolytic and carminative effects of the oil. Oils containing high levels of citronellal are used in insect repellents.

WARNING Much diluted lemongrass oil and citronella oil are flavourants of food or drinks. In their pure form however, they may be toxic or even lethal if taken orally in large amounts.

NOTES Lemongrass is an important ingredient in Oriental cooking. The oils of *Cymbopogon* species are mainly used in the perfume industry and have limited medicinal applications.

STATUS Traditional medicine; Pharm.

Cymbopogon citratus (DC.) Stapf   family: Poaceae

verveine des Indes (French); *Lemongras, Zitronengras* (German); *citronella* (Italian); *sontol* (Spanish)

Cynara scolymus

globe artichoke • garden artichoke

Cynara scolymus plant

Cynara scolymus flower head

DESCRIPTION Globe artichoke is a robust perennial herb of up to 2 m in height with sturdy flowering stems arising each year. The large, compound leaves are silvery-grey in colour and the conspicuous flower heads have green bracts and purple florets.

ORIGIN Europe (thought to be an old cultigen); now widely cultivated.

PARTS USED Fresh or dried leaves (*Cynarae folium*).

THERAPEUTIC CATEGORY Choleretic, liver protectant, lipid lowering.

USES AND PROPERTIES Artichoke leaves and extracts thereof are mainly used for dyspeptic problems. It is known to increase the flow of bile and to detoxify and protect the liver. Observations and human studies have shown that the herb lowers triglyceride and cholesterol levels.

PREPARATION AND DOSAGE A daily dose of 6 g of the drug (or an equivalent dose in preparations) is recommended.

ACTIVE INGREDIENTS Artichoke leaves contain numerous phenolic acids, including caffeic acid, monocaffeoylquinic acid derivatives (such as chlorogenic and neochlorogenic acid) and dicaffeoylquinic acid derivatives such as cynarin (1,5-di-O-caffeoylquinic acid). They also contain a bitter sesquiterpene lactone (up to 4%), cynaropicrin. In addition, various flavonoids (rutin, luteolin) and sesquiterpenes (especially caryophyllene and β-selinene) are present.

PHARMACOLOGICAL EFFECTS Hepatoprotective properties were demonstrated in isolated liver cells. The choleretic and hepatoprotective properties are attributed to cynarin, to chlorogenic and neochlorogenic acid. Cynarin is thought to be responsible for lowering the levels of triglycerides and cholesterol in blood. Clinical studies have shown definite choleretic and lipid lowering effects of leaf extracts (it could therefore play a role in the treatment of arteriosclerosis). Cyanopicrin, as bitter substance and tonic, may be involved in the improvement of appetite and digestion.

NOTES The involucre bracts and receptacle of the young flower heads are eaten as a popular vegetable. It is interesting to note that the bitter substance cyanopicrin is found in the leaves and not in the fully mature flower heads.

STATUS Traditional medicine; Pharm.; Comm.E+ (dyspeptic problems only).

Cynara scolymus L.

family: Asteraceae

artichaut (French); *Artischocke* (German); *carciofo* (Italian); *alearrhofa, alcachofera* (Spanish)

Cytisus scoparius

common broom • Scotch broom

Cytisus scoparius

Cytisus scoparius flower and fruit

DESCRIPTION The common broom is a branched shrub of up to 2 m in height, with ridged stems, small trifoliolate leaves, bright yellow flowers borne towards the branch ends and oblong, flat, slightly sickle-shaped pods that turn black when they ripen.

ORIGIN Central, southern and eastern Europe. The plant is naturalised in North and South America, South Africa and other countries.

PARTS USED Aboveground parts or flowers, but most often the flowering tops (*Cytisi scoparii herba;* synon. *Scoparii herba*).

THERAPEUTIC CATEGORY Heart and circulatory disorders; diuretic.

USES AND PROPERTIES The herb is mainly used to regulate the circulation. It decreases the excitability of the heart muscle, thereby slowing and regulating the heart beat. It may improve low blood pressure. In traditional medicine, common broom was used mainly as a diuretic and to treat snakebite. It is an ingredient of a large number of traditional combination products.

PREPARATION AND DOSAGE A tea is made from 1-2 g of the dried herb and taken up to four times per day. Preparations should not contain more than 10 mg/ml sparteine, equivalent to 1.5 g of the drug.

ACTIVE INGREDIENTS The activity is ascribed mainly to tetracyclic quinolizidine alkaloids, of which sparteine is the main compound in the stems. Also present, especially in the flowers, are amines (tyramine, dopamine and epinine) and flavonoids (mainly isoflavones, such as sarothamnoside and genistein; also flavone C-glycosides of apigenin and luteolin).

PHARMACOLOGICAL EFFECTS Sparteine stimulates muscarinergic acetylcholine receptors and blocks Na^+ and K^+ channels. It is known to act as an anti-arrhythmic, similar to quinidine and ajmalicine, by decreasing the stimulation of the nerve impulses in the heart. It extends diastole and at the same time has a positive inotropic effect. Tyramine has vasoconstrictive and hypertensive effects. The herb is known to be oxytocic, stops uterine bleeding and increases the tone and strength of uterine contraction.

WARNING Broom is not suitable for self-medication. It should not be used in cases of hypertension or in combination with MAO-inhibitors. The herb has abortive properties and should be avoided during pregnancy.

STATUS Traditional medicine; Pharm.; Comm.E+.

Cytisus scoparius (L.) Link [= *Sarothamnus scoparius* (L.) Wimmer ex Koch]   family: Fabaceae

genêt à balai (French); *Besenginster* (German); *ginestra scopareccia* (Italian)

Datura stramonium

thorn-apple • Jimson weed • Jamestown weed

Datura stramonium var. *stramonium*

Datura stramonium var. *tatula*

Datura stramonium var. *stramonium* seeds

DESCRIPTION A robust annual of up to 1.5 m in height, with unpleasantly scented leaves, large, white or purplish tubular flowers and characteristic fruit capsules containing blackish, kidney-shaped seeds.

ORIGIN Tropical North America (now a cosmopolitan weed). Two varieties, the smooth-fruited var. *inermis* and the purple-flowered var. *tatula* are cultivated.

PARTS USED Mainly leaves (*Stramonii folium*), sometimes the seeds (*Stramonii semen*).

THERAPEUTIC CATEGORY Anti-asthmatic, sedative, analgesic (also an intoxicant).

USES AND PROPERTIES Stramonium has been used as an analgesic, as an ingredient of cough syrup and cigarettes to treat asthma and other respiratory disorders. Pure atropine/hyoscyamine is used as a spasmolytic, and mydriatic to aid eye examinations. Scopolamine is employed in skin patches to treat motion sickness and may also be injected as a treatment for Parkinson's disease and painful visceral spasms.

PREPARATION AND DOSAGE The maximum daily dose of atropine in injections must not exceed 2 mg (a single dose is 0.25-0.5 mg). It is used in eye drops at a concentration of 0.5-3%. Skin patches, which are applied behind the ear, contain 1.5 mg scopolamine.

ACTIVE INGREDIENTS Dry leaves contain 0.2-0.65% tropane alkaloids, of which hyoscyamine (up to 70%) and scopolamine (=hyoscine) (up to 20%) are the main compounds. Hyoscyamine forms a racemic mixture upon isolation (=atropine). Also present are withastramonolide and coumarins (umbelliferon, scopolin).

PHARMACOLOGICAL EFFECTS Scopolamine and hyoscyamine inhibit muscarinic acetylcholine receptors and are therefore parasympatholytics. They increase the heart rate, relax smooth muscles, decrease secretions and dilate the pupils. Scopolamine has central sedative, hypnotic and depressant effects and at high doses leads to hallucinogenic effects that may last for several hours.

WARNING The plant and its alkaloids are very poisonous. Accidental and deliberate human fatalities are not rare.

NOTE *D. innoxia*, *D. metel* and *Brugmansia arborea* have been used in homoeopathy and as narcotics and hallucinogens.

STATUS Traditional medicine; modern medicine: atropine, scopolamine; Pharm.

Datura stramonium L.

family: Solanaceae

stramoine (French); *Stechapfel* (German); *stramonio* (Italian); *estramonio* (Spanish)

Daucus carota

wild carrot

Daucus carota subsp. *carota* flowers

Carrots

Daucus carota subsp. *carota* plant

DESCRIPTION Wild carrot is a biennial herb with a single, erect stem, feathery leaves, small white flowers and small dry fruits in characteristic clusters (umbels) surrounded by finely branched bracts. Wild carrot – *D. carota* subsp. *carota* – has a thin, white inedible root, while the common cultivated carrot – *D. carota* subsp. *sativa* has a thick, fleshy taproot.

ORIGIN Europe to central Asia, where it is wild-harvested.

PARTS USED Aerial parts (*Dauci carotae herba*) or the dried root (*Dauci carotae radix; synon. Radix Dauci*); sometimes also the fruits (*Dauci carotae fructus; synon. Fructus Dauci*) or the fruit oil.

THERAPEUTIC CATEGORY Diuretic, carminative.

USES AND PROPERTIES Wild carrot herb is traditionally used to treat kidney and bladder conditions, notably urinary calculus or gravel, lithuria, cystitis and also as an anthelmintic. The herb and the fruits are used in case of indigestion, spasms, flatulence and gout. Carrot juice is an important health drink because it contains high levels of carotene which is converted to vitamin A in the liver.

PREPARATION AND DOSAGE An infusion of 2-4 g of the herb is taken three times per day.

ACTIVE INGREDIENTS The chemical composition of the fruits and the essential oil obtained from them are better known than the leaf. Leaves contain flavonoids and furanocoumarins (5-methoxypsoralen, and 8-methoxypsoralen). Fruits have high levels of flavones (apigenin, luteolin and chrysin) and flavonols (quercitin, kaempferol), together with a complex essential oil comprising monoterpenoids (α-pinene, β-pinene, geraniol, limonene, α-terpinen, terpinen-4-ol and others) and sesquiterpenoids (β-bisabolene, caryophyllene, β-elemene, carotol and daucol) and a phenylpropanoid (asarone).

PHARMACOLOGICAL EFFECTS The diuretic effect of wild carrot has not yet been documented in animals or humans. One of the main constituents of the oil, terpinen-4-ol, however, has documented diuretic activity (it is the diuretic renal irritant present in juniper oil).

WARNING Wild carrot may cause slight skin allergic reactions in some people and there may be a slight photosensitising effect due to the furanocoumarins.

STATUS Traditional medicine; Pharm.

Daucus carota L.   family: Apiaceae

carotte (French); *Wilde Möhre* (German); *carota* (Italian)

Digitalis lanata

Grecian foxglove • woolly foxglove

Digitalis lanata

Digitalis purpurea

Digitalis lutea

DESCRIPTION A perennial with smooth, pointed leaves and long flowering stalks bearing numerous pale yellow or cream-coloured flowers. The bracts and calyces are characteristically hairy. *D. purpurea* (common or purple foxglove) forms a dense rosette of leaves in the first year and slender flowering stalks of up to 2 m in height in the second year. Two other species with yellow flowers are rarely used: the small-flowered *D. lutea* (straw foxglove) and the large-flowered *D. grandiflora* (yellow foxglove).

ORIGIN Central and southeastern Europe (naturalised in North America); purple foxglove occurs naturally in the Mediterranean region and Europe. *D. lanata* and *D. purpurea* are both cultivated for medicinal purposes (the latter also as ornamental in gardens).

PARTS USED Leaves (*Digitalis lanatae folium* or *Digitalis purpureae folium*).

THERAPEUTIC CATEGORY Cardiac stimulant.

USES AND PROPERTIES The plants are a source of digitalis, used since 1785 to treat the symptoms of heart insufficiency, hypertonia and rhythm abnormalities. The typical symptoms of a weak heart are oedema, also known by the outdated term "dropsy" – the legs become swollen due to an accumulation of fluids.

PREPARATION AND DOSAGE The raw herb is no longer used, but carefully prepared formulations of pure heart glycosides as prescription drugs for oral use (tablets or drops) or for injection. The doses vary from 0.1-2 mg per day (sometimes in several smaller doses). The treatment is specialised and adjusted to each individual patient.

ACTIVE INGREDIENTS *Digitalis* species are well known sources of complex mixtures of (up to 80) cardenolides – *D. lanata* contains digoxin, lanatosides, gitoxin and related constituents (about 1.5%), while *D. purpurea* has mainly digitoxin and purpurea-glycosides (up to 0.4%). These drugs are also rich in saponins.

PHARMACOLOGICAL EFFECTS Cardenolides selectively inhibit Na^+, K^+-ATPase and indirectly increase the Ca^{++} concentration in heart muscle cells. Consequently the force and efficiency of contraction of the heart muscle are enhanced.

WARNING Digitalis is quite toxic and not suitable for self-medication.

STATUS Traditional medicine; Pharm.; modern medicine: heart glycosides.

Digitalis lanata Ehrh.   family Scrophulariaceae

digitale laineuse (French); *Wolliger Fingerhut* (German); *digitale lanata* (Italian)

Dioscorea villosa

wild yam

Dioscorea villosa

Dioscorea batatas

DESCRIPTION *Dioscorea* plants (there are more than 800 species) are twining climbers with simple, heart-shaped leaves, small white flowers and tuberous rhizomes as storage organs. *D. villosa* is said to be one of the first commercial sources of steroidal saponins. *D. batatas* (=*D. opposita*) is the *shan yao* of traditional Chinese medicine.

ORIGIN Central America (*D. villosa*) or Asia (*D. opposita*). *D. floribunda*, *D. composita*, *D. mexicana*, *D. deltoidea* and *D. macrostachya* have been cultivated commercially.

PARTS USED Tuber or rhizome; source of diosgenin.

THERAPEUTIC CATEGORY Contraceptive, steroidal therapy.

USES AND PROPERTIES It is important to note that wild yam as a herb has no contraceptive or steroidal uses. It merely provides the starting material from which steroidal hormones are manufactured through semi-synthesis and microbial transformations. Wild yams, including *D. villosa* and *D. batatas*, are nevertheless widely used in traditional medicine. *D. villosa* is stated to have expectorant, anti-inflammatory, anti-spasmodic and cholagogue activities and is used to treat rheumatism and bilious colic. *D. batatas* is included in mixtures but on its own acts as a general tonic.

PREPARATION AND DOSAGE Steroidal hormones and oral contraceptives are used only as standardised, mostly prescription medicines and must be monitored by a health care professional.

ACTIVE INGREDIENTS *Dioscorea* species contain saponins such as dioscin (aglycone diosgenin) (the main compound in *D. villosa*), a useful starting material in the semi-synthesis of steroidal hormones and oral contraceptives. Also of pharmacological interest is the presence of alkaloids in *D. dregeana* and other traditional sedatives and tranquillisers.

PHARMACOLOGICAL EFFECTS Steroidal hormones have contraceptive (oestrogens, gestagens) and anti-inflammatory activities (cortisol) or regulate ion homoeostasis (mineralocorticoids).

WARNING Wild yam is not a source of progesterone and there is no evidence that it can be beneficial in the treatment of menopausal and menstrual symptoms.

NOTES Steroidal products were once mainly derived from yams, but are now also synthesised from natural sterols occurring in soy oil (see *Glycine max*).

STATUS Traditional medicine; Pharm.; modern medicine: steroid hormones.

Dioscorea villosa L.   family: Dioscoreaceae

igname sauvage, racines de colique (French); *Zottige Yamswurzel* (German); *dioscorea* (Italian)

Dorema ammoniacum

ammoniacum • dorema

Dorema ammoniacum leaf

Dorema ammoniacum plant

Dorema ammoniacum fruits

DESCRIPTION Ammoniacum is a robust perennial herb of up to 3 m in height, with thick stems, large leaves and massive flowering stalks bearing small white flowers in characteristic umbels. The small, dry fruits (schizocarps) split into two halves (mericarps) at maturity. It is a monocarpic plant (i.e. it dies after flowering and fruiting).

ORIGIN Iran to Turkestan, Afghanistan, southern Siberia, Pakistan and India. Commercial product is collected mainly from wild plants of *D. ammoniacum* and possibly other species as well.

PARTS USED Oleogum resin (*Gummiresina Ammoniacum*). This is the dried resinous exudate that flows from the stems and leaf stalks following insect damage or incisions. The best quality product is collected as small, pale yellow solid crystals or tears (*Ammoniacum in lacrimis* see photo on page 17); blocks or lumps (up to 600 g) (*Ammoniacum in massis*) are inferior.

THERAPEUTIC CATEGORY Expectorant, antispasmodic, counter-irritant.

USES AND PROPERTIES Ammoniacum is an expectorant, antispasmodic and diaphoretic that is used mainly to treat bronchitis, respiratory ailments and menstrual disorders. It is said to be effective in treating persistent dry coughs. It is an ingredient of counter-irritant plasters (often together with tolu balsam) to treat arthritis and swollen joints. Ammoniacum is a traditional medicine that has been used for a wide range of ailments since ancient times, especially in North Africa, Arabia and western Asia. It is mentioned as an ingredient of abortifacients in old Arabic texts. Strong tinctures are used in perfumery.

PREPARATION AND DOSAGE The powdered gum may be taken orally in doses of about 0.3-1 g, three times per day, or as a strong tincture in equivalent concentrations.

ACTIVE INGREDIENTS The gum contains 60-70% resin, about 12% gum, 0.1-0.3% volatile oil (with linaloolacetate, citronellylacetate, sesquiterpenes). Resin is composed of prenylated coumarins (ammoresinol and doremon A). Also found are salicylic acid and methylsalicylate. The gum is formed by polysaccharides.

PHARMACOLOGICAL EFFECTS Despite its historic importance, the uses and presumed efficacy of ammoniacum in the treatment of respiratory ailments appear to be based on experience and tradition only.

STATUS Traditional medicine; Pharm.

Dorema ammoniacum D. Don

family: Apiaceae

ammoniaque, dorema (French); *Ammoniakpflanze* (German); *ammoniaco* (Italian)

Drosera rotundifolia

sundew

Drosera rotundifolia flowering plant

Drosera rotundifolia plants

Drosera rotundifolia leaves

DESCRIPTION This sundew is a very small perennial rosette with rounded leaf blades on long stalks, characteristically covered in sticky, red, glandular hairs. Small, white flowers are borne at the ends of slender flowering stalks. The glands contain proteolytic enzymes that digest the proteins of small insects that are caught by the sticky hairs, thereby supplementing the nitrogen supply of the plant (it grows in leached, nitrogen-poor soils). Other *Drosera* species are similar but differ in the size of the flowers and in the size, shape and disposition of the leaves. Since *D. rotundifolia* has become very rare, the herb is nowadays obtained from *D. ramentacea*, *D. peltata*, *D. intermedia* and various other species.

ORIGIN Europe (*D. rotundifolia*), Madagascar and eastern Africa (*D. ramentacea*) or eastern Asia, from India to Malaysia and China (*D. peltata*). *Drosera* is not yet cultivated on a commercial scale but wild-harvesting is unlikely to be sustainable in the long term.

PARTS USED Dried, whole plant, including the above and below-ground parts (*Droserae herba*).

THERAPEUTIC CATEGORY Antispasmodic, antitussive.

USES AND PROPERTIES The herb is used in phytotherapy to treat whooping cough (especially dry and chesty cough) and is an ingredient of proprietary cough syrups. Traditional use: internally as a spasmolytic and antidyspeptic, externally to treat skin disorders.

PREPARATION AND DOSAGE A daily dose of 3 g of the dried herb is recommended.

ACTIVE INGREDIENTS *Drosera* contains naphthoquinones, of which ramentaceone and plumbagin are usually the main compounds (in *D. rotundifolia* and related species, at a level of up to 1% of the dried product). *D. ramentacea* contains ramentaceone and some plumbagin but in quite low concentrations, while *D. peltata* has plumbagin and droserone as the main compounds.

PHARMACOLOGICAL EFFECTS Sundew is anti-inflammatory, spasmolytic and prevents bronchospasms. The naphthoquinones are known to be broncholytic and secretolytic, thus providing relief from a dry cough. Plumbagin is antibiotic at low concentrations and cytotoxic at high concentrations.

NOTES It appears that there is some confusion about the botanical source of product and that the identification of raw material to species level is not always easy.

STATUS Traditional medicine; Pharm.; Comm.E+.

Drosera rotundifolia L.   family: Droseraceae

rossolis à feuilles rondes (French); *Rundblättriger Sonnentau* (German); *rosolida*, *rorella* (Italian)

Echinacea pallida

pale purple coneflower

Echinacea pallida

Echinacea angustifolia

DESCRIPTION Pale purple coneflower is a small perennial herb with short, mostly unbranched stems and narrow leaves in a basal tuft. The slender flowering stalks are up to 1 m in height, bearing a single head of flowers with pale purple, drooping, long ray florets (40–90 mm long) and white pollen. Narrow-leaved coneflower (*E. angustifolia*) has branched stems, slightly shorter inflorescences (up to 0.6 m), short ray florets (up to 38 mm long) which are more spreading and yellow pollen. Both these species differ from *E. purpurea* in their long, unbranched flowering stalks borne above a very short, sparsely branched plant.

ORIGIN North America (central parts – not in the western or eastern regions). *Echinacea angustifolia* occurs in the USA and Canada; *E. pallida* only in the USA. Commercially grown in North America and Europe.

PARTS USED Fresh or dried roots (*Echinaceae pallidae radix; Echinaceae angustifoliae radix*).

THERAPEUTIC CATEGORY Immune stimulant.

USES AND PROPERTIES Preparations and extracts are taken orally and used in supportive therapy for colds and influenza. In Germany, only *E. pallida* is an approved herb, not *E. angustifolia*.

PREPARATION AND DOSAGE A daily dose of 900 mg of the powdered root (or equivalent doses in the form of tinctures and dried extracts) is recommended.

ACTIVE INGREDIENTS The roots contain polysaccharides, alkylamides (echinacein), polyacetylenes (trideca-1-en-3,5,7,9,11-pentain, ponticaepoxide), and several caffeic acid derivates, such as echinacoside, chicoric acid and cynarin. Cynarin is unique to *E. angustifolia*. Traces of pyrrolizidine alkaloids (tussilagine) are present.

PHARMACOLOGICAL EFFECTS The immune stimulant effects are mainly derived from *in vitro* experiments with immune cells, showing increased mobility and phagocytosis. The drug also exhibits anti-inflammatory, antibacterial and antiviral properties. All the various compounds in the roots seem to contribute to the overall effect. Controlled clinical studies with patients suffering from flu have shown efficacy for the stated indications; the duration of illness was significantly shortened.

WARNING Do not use in cases of systemic diseases such as tuberculosis, multiple sclerosis and HIV-AIDS.

STATUS Pharm.; Comm.E+; ESCOP 6; WHO 1; clinical trials+.

Echinacea pallida (Nutt.) Nutt.

family: Asteraceae

échinacée (French); *Blasser Sonnenhut* (German); *rudbeckia, pigna rossa* (Italian)

Echinacea purpurea
echinacea • purple coneflower

Echinacea purpurea plant

Echinacea purpurea flower head

DESCRIPTION Purple coneflower is a perennial herb of up to 1 m in height, with erect, much-branched stems and broad, bristly-hairy leaves. Attractive, large, purple flower heads are borne on relatively short stalks. In *E. purpurea*, the flowering stalks are much shorter than the leafy part of the plant, while in *E. pallida* and *E. angustifolia* it is the other way round (see *E. pallida*).

ORIGIN Southern and central USA (see *E. pallida*). The plant is commonly cultivated in many parts of the world.

PARTS USED Fresh plant juice (pressed from the fresh, flowering aerial parts), the dried whole herb (*Echinaceae purpureae herba*) or root (*Echinaceae purpureae radix*).

THERAPEUTIC CATEGORY Immunostimulant.

USES AND PROPERTIES The juice or dry herb is used in supportive treatment of colds and infections of the respiratory and urinary tract; externally to treat wounds, ulcers, and skin inflammations.

PREPARATION AND DOSAGE A daily dose of 6-9 ml of fresh plant juice is recommended. Preparations are also injected. Ointments and creams containing at least 15% pressed juice are used for topical applications.

ACTIVE INGREDIENTS Purple coneflower contains polysaccharides, of which two have become reasonably well known: PS I, a 4-O-methylglucurono-arabinoxylan (molecular mass 35 kilodalton), and PS II, an acid rhamnoarabinogalactan (450 kilodalton). Caffeic acid derivatives are present, such as chicoric acid (up to 2%, low or absent in other species). The plant also contains lipophilic polyacetylenes and alkylamides (mainly isobutylamides, such as echinaceine).

PHARMACOLOGICAL EFFECTS Immune stimulant properties are ascribed to the polysaccharides but the amides and caffeic acid derivatives also contribute to antimicrobial and anti-inflammatory effects in alcoholic extracts. Polysaccharides are known to be active *in vivo* after injection only, so that their oral efficacy has yet to be convincingly demonstrated. Wound-healing was shown using a polysaccharide fraction, echinacin B. Most of the controlled clinical studies show at least some statistically significant improvement in infections and cold symptoms.

STATUS Pharm.; Comm.E+; ESCOP 6; WHO 1; clinical studies+.

Echinacea purpurea (L.) Moench ⎯⎯⎯⎯⎯⎯⎯⎯⎯⎯⎯⎯⎯⎯⎯⎯⎯⎯ family: Asteraceae

échinacée, rudbeckie poupre (French); *Purpur-Sonnenhut* (German); *rudbeckia rossa, echinacea* (Italian)

Elettaria cardamomum

cardamom

Elettaria cardamomum flowers

Elettaria cardamomum plant

Cardamom fruits and seeds

DESCRIPTION Cardamom is a leafy perennial herb with hairless leaves neatly arranged along thick fleshy stalks. The attractive flowers are borne at ground level on much-branched flowering stems and they develop into small green, white or brown three-valved capsules, each containing several brown seeds.

ORIGIN India and Sri Lanka. It is commonly cultivated in India, Malaysia, Indonesia and Guatemala.

PARTS USED Fruits and seeds (*Cardamomi fructus*) or the seed oil (*Cardamomi aetheroleum*), rarely the rhizomes. The seed capsules are hand-harvested just before they split open and are dried in the sun. Cardamom seeds are easily adulterated with seeds of other species; the capsules less easily. As a result, whole fruits with seeds are preferred as raw material, even though the capsules on their own do not contribute to the yield of essential oil.

THERAPEUTIC CATEGORY Cholagogue, antimicrobial.

USES AND PROPERTIES The seeds have been widely used as a spice since ancient times but are also an important Ayurvedic aphrodisiac and remedy in case of digestive problems, asthma, bronchitis and urinary complaints. It is used against bad breath, cough and nausea and may be combined with laxatives to treat indigestion,

stomach pain, griping and flatulence.

PREPARATION AND DOSAGE A daily dose of 1.5 g crushed or ground seeds (or equivalent extracts and tinctures) is recommended.

ACTIVE INGREDIENTS The seeds contain essential oil in concentrations of about 4% of dry weight. The main compound is 1,8-cineole (representing 50% or more), with smaller amounts of α-terpineol, borneol, camphor, limonene and α-terpenyl acetate.

PHARMACOLOGICAL EFFECTS The monoterpenes show antibacterial, antimycotic and antiviral activities and spasmolytic properties. These constituents would also plausibly explain the claimed carminative, antispasmodic and expectorant effects. Fruit extracts promoted the secretion of gastric juices and bile in rats and rabbits.

WARNING According to Ayurvedic practice, cardamom should be avoided during pregnancy; not recommended for patients with gallstones.

NOTES Cardamom is an important spice and flavourant, used in cooking (e.g. curry powders), baking and various drinks. The essential oil is an ingredient of perfumes.

STATUS Traditional medicine; Pharm.; Comm.E+.

Elettaria cardamomum (L.) Maton   family: Zingiberaceae
cardamomier (French); *Kardamompflanze* (German); *cardamomo* (Italian)

Eleutherococcus senticosus

Siberian ginseng • eleuthero

Eleutherococcus senticosus

Aralia racemosa

DESCRIPTION Siberian ginseng is a woody shrub with erect, prickly stems, compound leaves and inconspicuous flowers produced in multi-flowered umbels. It is closely related to various North American species of *Aralia* that are also used in traditional medicine and is sometimes confused with them. These are American spikenard (*Aralia racemosa*), the roots and rhizomes of which are a traditional panacea (cure all) of the Native Americans, wild sarsaparilla (*A. nudicaulis*) which is used in much the same way and Hercule's club (*A. spinosa*), the bark of which has been used in the eastern parts of the USA as traditional medicine.

ORIGIN North-eastern Asia (eastern Siberia).

PARTS USED Dried roots and rhizomes (*Eleutherococci radix*).

THERAPEUTIC CATEGORY Tonic.

USES AND PROPERTIES Siberian ginseng is used as an adaptogenic tonic, in the same way as real ginseng (*Panax ginseng*). It is used to counteract fatigue and stress, decreasing physical and mental capacity and as support during convalescence. It was used by Russian athletes in the 1984 Moscow Olympics and has become a popular tonic in the former USSR.

PREPARATION AND DOSAGE A daily dose of 2-3 g of dry root, taken as tea or as alcoholic extracts (or equivalent preparations), is recommended.

ACTIVE INGREDIENTS The roots and rhizomes contain a diversity of phytochemicals – so-called eleutherosides (a confusing name, since various classes of compounds are involved, such as coumarins, lignans, and phenylpropanoids). These include triterpenoids and triterpene saponins (eleutherosides I-M), lignans and their glycosides (such as sesamin and syringa-resinol), coumarins (isofraxidin), β-sitosterol, daucosterol, liriodendrin and polysaccharides.

PHARMACOLOGICAL EFFECTS Several animal and human studies have been carried out in Russia, indicating that the product is comparable to real ginseng. It appears to improve endurance, immune competence and stress resistance.

WARNING The use of Siberian ginseng should be limited to a maximum period of three months and is considered unsafe for persons with high blood pressure.

STATUS Traditional medicine; Pharm.; Comm.E+; WHO 2.

Eleutherococcus senticosus (Rupr. & Maxim.) Maxim. [=*Acanthopanax senticosus* (Rupr. & Maxim.) Harms] family: Araliaceae
éleuthérocoque, ginseng de Sibérie (French); *Stachelpanax, Sibirischer Ginseng* (German); *eleuterococco* (Italian)

Elymus repens

couchgrass • twitch • witch grass

Elymus repens with open flowers

Elymus repens with closed flowers

DESCRIPTION Couchgrass is a weedy perennial with slender culms growing from creeping rhizomes. The inconspicuous flowers are arranged in two rows to form long thin spikes. This grass is better known as *Agropyron repens* and will be found under this name in most plant books.

ORIGIN Asia, Europe, North and South America. The plant is a cosmopolitan weed and is wild-harvested.

PARTS USED Dried rhizomes and roots (*Agropyri repentis rhizoma*; =*Graminis rhizoma*).

THERAPEUTIC CATEGORY Diuretic.

USES AND PROPERTIES Couch grass is traditionally used to treat inflammations of the respiratory tract and the urinary tract, and also to prevent kidney gravel. It is thought to be useful in the treatment of cystitis, urethritis, prostate problems and to a lesser extent, gout and rheumatism.

PREPARATION AND DOSAGE The grass is added to galenicals and is taken in the form of tablets or tinctures. Decoctions of the dry rhizome (4-9 g per day) may be taken.

ACTIVE INGREDIENTS The rhizome contains mucilage and polysaccharides (3-10% fructans). Triticin

is reported to be one of the main polyfructosans. Also present are small amounts of sugar alcohols, and essential oil (containing mainly carvacrol, thymol, and carvone).

PHARMACOLOGICAL EFFECTS Herbal medicine containing polysaccharides such as inulin are traditionally used as diuretics but there is no clear scientific evidence for the efficacy of couchgrass. The mucilage forms a protective layer over inflamed mucous membranes. The essential oil has antimicrobial activity and might contribute to diuretic properties.

NOTES Grass flowers (*Graminis flos*) are a folk remedy for chilblains, lumbago, neurasthenia and especially rheumatic pains (500 g of dried flowers soaked in boiling water are added to a hot bath). It may also be used as an inhalant in case of throat and nasal congestion (5-10 g in 1 litre of boiling water). The active ingredients or pharmacological effects are not known. Another grass of medicinal importance is the common corn or maize (see *Zea mays*). The various uses of grass pollen and pollen extracts (to treat urological problems and weight loss) are described under *Zea mays*.

STATUS Traditional medicine; Pharm.; Comm.E+.

Elymus repens (L.) Gould [=*Agropyron repens* (L.) P.B.]
family: Poaceae

chiendent officinal (French); *Gemeine Quecke* (German); *gramigna canina* (Italian)

Ephedra sinica

ephedra • desert tea

Ephedra sinica plant

Ephedra distachya flowers

Ephedra distachya stems and fleshy cones

DESCRIPTION A lax, wiry perennial shrub (up to 1 m) with a greyish green colour. It has thin, practically leafless, striated stems, inconspicuous male flowers in small clusters and female flowers that form small, fleshy, bright red cones. Other alkaloid-containing species can also be used, including *E. equisetina*, *E. distachya* (=*E. gerardiana*), *E. intermedia* and *E. shennungiana*.

ORIGIN China (*E. sinica*) (used for more than 4 000 years). Most of other species listed are Asian (except *E. distachya* which is Mediterranean).

PARTS USED Dried stems or aerial parts (*Ephedra herba* or *ma huang*), more rarely the roots (*Ephedra radix*; *ma huang gen*).

THERAPEUTIC CATEGORY Bronchodilator, analeptic, central stimulant.

USES AND PROPERTIES Traditionally used to treat asthma and bronchitis, as well as nasal congestion (rhinitis and sinusitis). It is included in weight loss products and in boosters to improve athletic performance.

PREPARATION AND DOSAGE Dried drug, extracts, tinctures or isolated alkaloid. The maximum daily dose is 300 mg total alkaloid (2 mg per kg body weight in children). Single adult dose: 15-30 mg of alkaloid.

ACTIVE INGREDIENTS The main compound is almost always (–)-ephedrine (a phenylethylamine alkaloid), with smaller amounts of (+)-pseudoephedrine and other minor alkaloids (total content about 2%, depending on the species). Also present are flavonoids, catechols, lignans, tannins and polysaccharides. Roots contain tyrosine derivatives, spermine alkaloids and procyanidins.

PHARMACOLOGICAL EFFECTS Ephedrine stimulates α- and β-adrenergic receptors by increasing the release of noradrenaline from catecholic synapses and inhibiting its re-uptake. Ephedrine is responsible for the central stimulatory effects, the bronchodilation and peripheral vasoconstriction (increases blood pressure). The central stimulation is similar to, but weaker than that of amphetamine: enhanced concentration and a decrease in the sensations of fatigue, hunger and pain.

WARNING Ephedrine is regarded as an illegal dope in sports. Continued prolonged use may lead to dependency. In view of a large number of contra-indications and drug interactions, these products should not be used without medical supervision.

STATUS Traditional medicine; Pharm.; Comm.E+; WHO 1; modern medicine: ephedrine.

Ephedra sinica Stapf
family: Ephedraceae

ma huang (Chinese); *ephedra, raisin de mer* (French); *Ephedra, Meerträubel* (German); *efedra, uva marina* (Italian)

Epilobium parviflorum
small-flowered willow-herb

Epilobium angustifolium

Epilobium parviflorum

Epilobium hirsutum

DESCRIPTION A perennial plant bearing soft-textured, opposite, stalkless leaves, pink flowers with four sepals, four petals and a narrow, stalk-like ovary that develops into a slender capsule containing numerous hairy seeds. *E. parviflorum* is very variable and has several varieties. Other species used for phytotherapy include hairy willow-herb (*E. hirsutum*), bog willow-herb (*E. palustre*), pedicelled willow-herb (*E. roseum*) and pale willow-herb (*E. collinum*). They differ in their hairiness and in the presence or absence of leaf stalks. *E. angustifolium* can easily be recognised by the alternate leaves (opposite in all the others).

ORIGIN Europe (partly Asia, North America); widely distributed and wild-collected in central and eastern Europe.

PARTS USED Whole herb (all aboveground parts) of the flowering and fruiting plant (*Epilobii herba*).

THERAPEUTIC CATEGORY Benign prostate hyperplasia.

USES AND PROPERTIES The herb is used in case of urinary problems, more specifically micturition complaints resulting from benign prostate hypertrophy. *E. angustifolium* is used topically in wound-healing and as a traditional tea to treat respiratory complaints, indigestion and constipation. It is included in commercial skin care products and employed in Chinese medicine for menstrual disorders.

PREPARATION AND DOSAGE A tea, prepared from 1.5-2 g of dried herb in a cup of boiling water is taken twice a day.

ACTIVE INGREDIENTS Numerous flavonoids have been found in *E. parviflorum* and related species, including quercetin, myricetin and kaempferol and the corresponding glycosides. Also present are (up to 0.55%) phytosterols (β-sitosterol, sitosterol glucosides and sitosterol esters) and gallic acid derivates (*E. hirsutum; E. angustifolium*)

PHARMACOLOGICAL EFFECTS No scientific support is yet available for the traditional use, but the herb (especially myricetin-3-O-β-D-glucuronide) is known to inhibit prostaglandin formation that would explain its antiphlogistic activity. For *E. angustifolium*, anti-inflammatory and antimicrobial properties have been reported. Phytosterols may be responsible for the benefits in prostatitis as they can inhibit aromatase, 5α-reductase and the binding of dihydrotestosterone within the prostate (see *Cucurbita pepo*).

STATUS Traditional medicine.

Epilobium parviflorum Schreber

family: Onagraceae

épilobe à petites fleurs (French); *Kleinblütiges Weidenröschen* (German); *epilobio* (Italian)

Equisetum arvense

horsetail • field horsetail

Sterile branch of *Equisetum arvense*

Equisetum arvense cone

DESCRIPTION The horsetail family was already present in the Carboniferous age and is a relict of the early evolution of land plants. Horsetail produces un-branched fertile stems in the early spring, with brownish spore-bearing cones at the tips. In summer, several sterile stems of up to 0.5 m emerge, each having numerous nodes with four or five side branches around each node. The leaves are reduced to minute bracts arranged in a circle at each node. Also used are *E. hyemale* and *E. fluviatile*. The drug is sometimes adulterated with marsh horsetail (*E. palustre*). The latter is distinguished from other species by the length of the first internode of the lateral branches, which is shorter than the leaf sheath around the main stem where it is attached.

ORIGIN Northern temperate zone (North America, Europe and Asia). The sterile summer branches are wild-harvested in eastern Europe.

PARTS USED Dried stems (*Equiseti herba*).

THERAPEUTIC CATEGORY Diuretic, traditional haemostyptic.

USES AND PROPERTIES The herb is used mainly as a diuretic to treat inflammation of the lower urinary tract, kidney gravel and post-traumatic and static oedema. Traditionally, it is used externally for slow healing wounds and other skin disorders; internally in case of enhanced menstrual bleeding.

PREPARATION AND DOSAGE For internal use, a tea is made of 2-4 g of the dried herb (daily dose about 6 g) and for external use, 10 g per litre of water.

ACTIVE INGREDIENTS The herb contains 5-8% silicic acid (including water-soluble silicates), and 1.5% potassium and aluminum salts. Several flavonoids (glycosides and esters of quercetin and kaempferol), equisetolic acid (a dicarboxylic acid) and traces of alkaloids (nicotine, palustrine) are present. *E. palustre* contains the enzyme thiaminase that breaks down thiamine (=vitamin B1) and causes (sometimes fatal) poisoning of horses and other livestock. It also contains potentially toxic spermidine alkaloids such as palustrine.

PHARMACOLOGICAL EFFECTS The uses of *Equisetum* are mainly based on tradition. Flavonoids, silica and potassium salts could be responsible for the weak diuretic activity, wound-healing and the repair of bone and skin tissue.

STATUS Traditional medicine; Pharm.; Comm.E+.

Equisetum arvense L.

family: Equisetaceae

prêle de champs (French); *Ackerschachtelhalm* (German); *coda di cavallo, equiseto dei campi* (Italian)

Erythroxylum coca

coca plant

Erythroxylum coca leaves and flower

Erythroxylum coca fruits

DESCRIPTION The coca plant is a perennial shrub of up to 1 m, with dark green, hairless leaves, small white flowers and bright red berries (drupes). Cultivated forms include *E. coca* var. *coca* (the wild form; with warty stems) and var. *ipadu* (a cultigen), together with two varieties of *E. novogranatense* (with smooth stems).

ORIGIN South America: eastern Andes – Peru, Bolivia (*E. coca*) and Peru, Venezuela and Colombia (*E. novogranatense var. novogranatense*). The plant has been cultivated since ancient, pre-Incan times.

PARTS USED Leaves (*Cocae folium*)

THERAPEUTIC CATEGORY Anesthetic, intoxicant.

USES AND PROPERTIES Coca leaves are a traditional masticatory of the Andes region, still chewed every day to relieve hunger and fatigue. It is also the source of cocaine, the world's first commercial anaesthetic that no longer has much medicinal relevance but that has become a popular illicit drug used by millions of people. American cola was originally an imitation of coca-containing "Coca des Incas" and "Vin Mariani" tonic wine (with alcohol, and caffeine) the latter sanctioned by the Pope. First alcohol was omitted from cola, then coca and nowadays even caffeine.

PREPARATION AND DOSAGE The pure alkaloid had been used medicinally as a local anaesthetic until it was widely replaced by derived synthetics (first xylocaine, then many others). Thousands of Andean people still use the leaves, mixed with lime, every day as a masticatory or in the form of tea bags to brew an infusion known as *mate de coca*. Drug users most commonly snort thin lines of cocaine (in the free base form) from a flat surface through a straw.

ACTIVE INGREDIENTS Coca leaves contain more than 18 tropane alkaloids with cocaine as the main compound (total alkaloids 0.1-0.7%) and hygrine, cuskhygrine as minor components. Young leaves are rich in cinnamoylcocaine. Also present in the leaves are other compounds such as *cis*-hexenol, *trans*-hexenal, methylsalicylate and tannins.

PHARMACOLOGICAL EFFECTS Cocaine is a local anaesthetic and euphoric. The activity results from blocking Na^+ channels in neurons and inhibition of the re-uptake of dopamine and noradrenaline. Cocaine induces a strong psychic but no physical dependence.

NOTES The non-medicinal use of cocaine is illegal.

STATUS Traditional and modern medicine: cocaine.

Erythroxylum coca Lam.   family: Erythroxylaceae

cocalier (French); *Kokastrauch* (German); *coca* (Italian); *cocal* (Spanish)

Eschscholzia californica

Californian poppy

Eschscholzia californica

DESCRIPTION Californian poppy is an attractive annual herb with deeply dissected greyish green leaves and large, bright orange, tulip-shaped flowers that close at night. The four petals fall off after the flower is pollinated and the ovary develops into a capsule that opens explosively by two valves to release the seeds.

ORIGIN California in the USA, where it is the state flower. It is widely cultivated as an attractive garden plant and has become a naturalised weed in some parts of the world.

PARTS USED Dried aerial parts (*Eschscholziae herba*).

THERAPEUTIC CATEGORY Sedative.

USES AND PROPERTIES The herb or preparations containing it are used to treat minor sleeplessness in adults and children. It is also employed in case of anxiety, minor nervous disturbances, neuralgic pains and liver/gall complaints. The North American Indians traditionally used the latex against toothache and ectoparasites.

PREPARATION AND DOSAGE A tea can be made using 0.5-1 g of dried herb in a cup of boiling water. Standardised preparations and capsules with powdered drug are available.

ACTIVE INGREDIENTS Californian poppy contains numerous isoquinoline alkaloids to which the activity is usually ascribed. In aerial parts, the alkaloid content is around 0.5-1.2%, while it is much higher in roots (at least 2%). The main alkaloids in leaves are pavines (californidine and escholzine), together with protopine and only trace amounts of benzophenanthridine and aporphine alkaloids. In roots, however, benzophenanthridine alkaloids, such as chelerythrine and sanguinarine, together with allocryptopine and protopine are the main alkaloids.

PHARMACOLOGICAL EFFECTS The spasmolytic, sedative and anxiolytic properties have been confirmed in animal studies. The time it takes to fall asleep is reduced, and sleep quality is improved. It is likely that these effects can be ascribed to the alkaloids, since many of them affect neuroreceptors and modulate enzyme activities. In the case of protopine, experimental evidence shows definite antispasmodic, antiarrhythmic, anticholinergic and antibacterial activities. Of interest is the fact that this alkaloid increases the binding of GABA (α-aminobutyric acid) to receptors.

STATUS Traditional medicine.

Eschscholzia californica Cham.   family: Papaveraceae

pavot de Californie (French); *Goldmohn, Kalifornischer Mohn* (German); *papavero della California* (Italian); *amapolla* (Spanish)

Eucalyptus globulus

eucalyptus • bluegum

Eucalyptus globulus tree

Eucalyptus globulus flowers and fruits

Foliage: mature (left) and juvenile (right).

DESCRIPTION The bluegum is a very large tree (up to 60 m) with a characteristic shedding bark, greyish foliage and large white flowers. The leaves are dimorphic – broad, rounded and opposite in the basal or juvenile leaves; narrow, falcate or scythe-shaped, alternate and pendulous in upper, mature leaves. Also distinctive are the large, solitary flowers and the large woody capsules.

ORIGIN Australia. Several of the more than 600 species of *Eucalyptus* have become important commercial timber trees and ornamentals in other parts of the world. Bluegum is grown in many countries, but Spain and Marocco have traditionally been important suppliers of the medicinal product. Oil from *E. fruticetorum* (=*E. polybractea*) and *E. smithii* is also acceptable.

PARTS USED Mature (upper) leaves (*Eucalypti folium*), essential oil (*Eucalypti aetheroleum*).

THERAPEUTIC CATEGORY Antiseptic, expectorant.

USES AND PROPERTIES Eucalyptus leaves or essential oil are used to treat the common cold, nasal congestion, bronchial disease and other respiratory problems. The oil is applied externally as a counter-irritant for the relief of rheumatism and minor skin ailments.

PREPARATION AND DOSAGE The leaves can be used to prepare a tea (1.5-2 g of cut leaves in 150 ml water) taken three times a day. The essential oil is used orally but at a low dose (0.3-0.6 ml per day). Cream and ointments should contain 5-20%, or a few drops of the oil itself can be rubbed into the skin.

ACTIVE INGREDIENTS Essential oil is present in the leaves (1.5-3.5%), with 1,8-cineole (=cineole or eucalyptol) as the main ingredient (70-90%), together with α-pinene, *p*-cymene, limonene and several other minor monoterpenoids. Leaves also contain sesquiterpenes (aromadendren, globulol), euglobals (acylphloroglucin derivatives) and flavonoids.

PHARMACOLOGICAL EFFECTS The monoterpenes show antimicrobial, anti-inflammatory, expectorant, secretomotoric and surfactant properties. The "decongestant" sensation in case of a blocked nose is thought to result from the stimulation of cold receptors. The oil is readily absorbed when taken orally and is partially excreted through the lungs. Leaf extracts show diuretic, anti-diabetic and anti-tumour activities.

STATUS Traditional medicine; Pharm.; Comm.E+; ESCOP 6; WHO 2.

Eucalyptus globulus Labill.   family: Myrtaceae

eucalyptus (French); *Eukalyptus, Blaugummibaum* (German); *eucalipto* (Italian); *eucalypto* (Spanish)

Eupatorium perfoliatum

boneset • Indian sage

Eupatorium perfoliatum

Eupatorium purpureum

DESCRIPTION Boneset is an erect perennial herb of more than 1 m in height, with lance-shaped leaves and numerous small purple or white flower heads borne in branched clusters. It should not be confused with gravel root or Joe-Pye-herb/weed (*Eupatorium purpureum*) that has oblong leaves and dark pink flower heads.

ORIGIN North America (eastern USA); material is mainly wild-harvested.

PARTS USED Aerial parts (*Eupatorii perfoliati herba*).

THERAPEUTIC CATEGORY Immune stimulant, cold treatment.

USES AND PROPERTIES The herb was traditionally used as a tonic to treat fever (probably influenza) and rheumatism; it is still mainly employed in case of cold and flu, acute bronchitis and congestion of the nose and throat.

PREPARATION AND DOSAGE A tea is made from 1-2 g of dry herb in a cup of boiling water and is taken three times a day. Liquid extracts (1-2 ml of a 1:1 extract in 25% alcohol) or tinctures (1-4 ml of a 1:5 extract in 45% alcohol) are taken three times a day.

ACTIVE INGREDIENTS Boneset is rich in sesquiterpene lactones, including germacranolides (euperfolin), guianolides (eufoliatin) and others. Also present are diterpenes (dendroidinic acid), triterpenes, phytosterols (sitosterol, stigmasterol), polysaccharides, flavonoids, tannins and essential oil.

PHARMACOLOGICAL EFFECTS Animal studies have shown that both the sesquiterpene lactones and the polysaccharides have immune stimulant activity, thus supporting the traditional use of the herb in treating flu.

NOTES *Eupatorium purpureum* (gravel root), also from the eastern parts of the USA, is a traditional diuretic that has been used to treat various ailments of the urinary tract, including cystitis, prostatitis, urethritis, kidney stones and urinary stones (gravel). *Eupatorium cannabinum*, known as hemp agrimony, has leaflets resembling those of cannabis. Leaves of this species show choleretic, liver-protecting, diuretic, wound-healing and immune stimulant activities, as well as cytotoxic effects on tumour cells.

WARNING *E. purpureum* and *E. cannabinum* contain pyrrolizidine alkaloids (PAs), that have liver toxic and carcinogenic properties. PAs alkylate DNA and are therefore mutagenic. Internal use is thus not recommended.

STATUS Traditional medicine.

Eupatorium perfoliatum L.   family: Asteraceae

herbe à la fièvre (French); *Durchwachsener Wasserdost* (German); *eupatorio*, (Italian)

Euphrasia officinalis
eyebright

Euphrasia officinalis

DESCRIPTION Eyebright is an annual herb of up to 0.4 m in height, with small, deeply toothed leaves arranged in opposite pairs. The flowers are white or pink with a yellow spot and have a dark area in the centre formed by purplish veins. *Euphrasia officinalis* is a species complex of several closely related taxa (including *E. minima, E. nemorosa, E. rostkoviana, E. stricta*). The typical form of the herb is sometimes regarded as *E. rostkoviana*.

ORIGIN Europe (eyebright and related species). The commercial herb is harvested in the wild during the flowering period, mainly in eastern Europe.

PARTS USED Aerial parts (*Euphrasiae herba*).

THERAPEUTIC CATEGORY Traditional eye lotion, anti-inflammatory.

USES AND PROPERTIES Eyebright herb has been used for centuries to treat eye complaints (irritation, inflammation, blepharitis, disturbed vision, eye fatigue, conjunctivitis). It is traditionally taken orally as a stomachic, and to treat coughs and hoarseness, hay fever and sinusitis and externally in case of skin conditions.

PREPARATION AND DOSAGE A 2% decoction is used three or four times a day as eye wash. For internal use, a tea is prepared from 2-3 g of the dried herb.

ACTIVE INGREDIENTS The plant contains several iridoid glycosides (up to 0.9%), including aucubin, catalpol and euphroside. Of interest is also the presence of dehydrodiconiferylalcohol 4β-D-glucoside (a lignane) and eukovoside (a phenylpropane glycoside). Other compounds reported include tannins and several phenolcarboxylic acids (caffeic acid, *p*-hydroxyphenylpyruvic acid and vanillic acid) and various flavonoids.

PHARMACOLOGICAL EFFECTS Iridoid glycosides or the metabolites formed in the body appear to inhibit prostaglandin formation and are therefore anti-inflammatory. Phenolics, such as phenyl-carboxylic acids and flavonoids contribute to the antibacterial effects. Some of the traditional uses are thus plausible but have not been demonstrated for extracts of eyebright. The German Commission E found no convincing scientific evidence in support of the traditional uses.

NOTES Eyebright herb is often quoted as an example of the "doctrine of signatures" because the bright flowers are thought to resemble eyes and hence suggest therapeutic value in treating eye ailments.

STATUS Traditional medicine; Pharm.

Euphrasia officinalis L.   family: Scrophulariaceae
Echter Augentrost (German); *euphraise officinale, casse-lunettes* (French); *eufrasia, erba degli occhi* (Italian)

Fagopyrum esculentum
buckwheat

Fagopyrum esculentum flowers

Fagopyrum esculentum fruit

Fagopyrum esculentum plants

DESCRIPTION Buckwheat is an annual herb (up to 0.7 m), with soft-textured, heart-shaped leaves and small white or pinkish flowers arranged in clusters at the tips of the stems. The fruits are small, strongly angular nutlets with a floury endosperm, known as buckwheat. It is a pseudocereal, the flour of which has been used since ancient times.

ORIGIN Central and northern Asia. The plant is cultivated in many parts of the world as a cereal crop, and also for the extraction of flavonoids.

PARTS USED Aerial parts (*Fagopyri herba*).

THERAPEUTIC CATEGORY Venotonic.

USES AND PROPERTIES The herb is used to treat the symptoms of capillary and venous disorders (including bleeding, varicose veins, bruising, retinal haemorrhage, oedema, haemorrhoids, bleeding gums and poor circulation). It has become popular as a food supplement ("functional food") and is available in health food stores. It is an important natural source for the isolation of rutin (see below). Others are (yield figures in brackets) *Eucalyptus macrorhyncha* leaves (10-24%), *Viola tricolor* var. *maxima* flowers (20%) and *Styphnolobium japonicum* flower buds (up to 30%). The

latter is a tree formerly known as *Sophora japonica*.

PREPARATION AND DOSAGE A tea can be made by adding 2 g of the dried herb to 150 ml water. Two to three cups are taken daily for a period of four to eight weeks. Preparations are available that contain the dried herb, enriched extracts or pure flavonoid extracts.

ACTIVE INGREDIENTS The activity of buckwheat leaves is attributed mainly to flavonoids (or so-called bioflavonoids) of which rutin (quercetin-3-rutinoside) occurs in high yields (normally 2-3%, and up to 8% in improved cultivars). The flowers and seed husks contain dianthrones (0.03%), notably fagopyrine.

PHARMACOLOGICAL EFFECTS Rutin and other flavonoids exhibit vascular protective, anti-inflammatory and antioxidant properties. They help to improve the elasticity of veins and to promote circulation but also have a wide range of other biological activities (because their phenolic hydroxyl groups can interact unspecifically with proteins).

NOTES The fruits are sometimes used to stuff pillows. Fagopyrine may cause phototoxicity in animals when large amounts of the plant have been consumed.

STATUS Traditional medicine; source of rutin.

Fagopyrum esculentum Moench — family: Polygonaceae

sarrasin (French); *Echter Buchweizen* (German); *grano saraceno* (Italian)

Ferula assa-foetida

asafoetida • devil's dung

Ferula assa-foetida plant

Ferula assa-foetida fruit

Devil's dung (asafoetida)

DESCRIPTION An erect perennial herb of up to 2 m in height, with a fleshy taproot, deeply dissected leaves and inconspicuous yellow flowers borne in compound umbels. Asafoetida or similar oleogum resins are obtained from *F. assa-foetida*, *F. foetida* and *F. narthex*; gum galbanum from *F. galbaniflua* (=*F. gummosa*) and *F. rubicaulis* (see also *Dorema ammoniacum*).

ORIGIN Iran and Asian deserts. The various Apiaceae gums are produced from wild plants in a large area that stretches from Iran to Afghanistan, Pakistan and India.

PARTS USED Oleogum resin (devil's dung – *Asa foetida*), obtained as secretions of the upper parts of the roots of the plants by incision.

THERAPEUTIC CATEGORY Carminative, antispasmodic, expectorant.

USES AND PROPERTIES Asafoetida is used to treat dyspepsia with flatulent colic, but also to treat bronchitis, coughs and nervous disorders. Externally it is counter-irritant. Despite being considered the most foul smelling of all natural substances, it is widely used as a natural food flavourant. Galbanum is said to be a digestive stimulant with antimicrobial, antispasmodic, carminative and expectorant properties. It has wound-healing properties and is used in perfumes as a fixative and to give a grassy note.

PREPARATION AND DOSAGE Powdered asafoetida can be taken in doses of 0.3-1 g, three times per day (or as 2-4 ml of a strong tincture).

ACTIVE INGREDIENTS These oleoresin gums have a complex composition; they contain sesquiterpene-coumarin ethers (such as asacoumarin B and farnesiferol A-C), and a volatile oil rich in sulphurous compounds, with which the smell and medicinal activity of asafoetida and galbanum are associated: disulphides and polysulphanes in asafoetida; propenyldisulphides with various other compounds in galbanum.

PHARMACOLOGICAL EFFECTS The disulphides can open and form new disulphide bonds with proteins and thus alter the activity of enzymes, receptors etc. This would explain the wide variety of symptoms treated with asafoetida. Relief from respiratory ailments is a common theme, and this may be linked to the sulphur compounds that are partly excreted through the lungs (see *Allium sativum*).

STATUS Traditional medicine; Pharm.

Ferula assa-foetida L.   family: Apiaceae

férule persique, ase fétide (French); *Stinkasant, Teufelsdreck* (German); *assafetida* (Italian)

Filipendula ulmaria

meadowsweet • queen-of-the-meadow

Filipendula ulmaria

Filipendula ulmaria leaves and flowers

Filipendula ulmaria flowers

DESCRIPTION A perennial herb of wet places, with erect angular and grooved stems, alternate compound leaves bearing three to nine pairs of dentate leaves. The flowers are yellowish white and are borne in multi-flowered corymbs on the stem tips. The famous aspirin (Aspirin™) was named after *Spiraea ulmaria* (the old name for *F. ulmaria*).

ORIGIN Europe and Asia (naturalised in North America); wild-harvested during the flowering season.

PARTS USED Dried flowers (*Spiraeae flos*) or dried aboveground parts (*Spiraeae herba*).

THERAPEUTIC CATEGORY Anti-inflammatory, analgesic.

USES AND PROPERTIES Used in supportive treatment of colds accompanied by fever. It is a traditional diuretic and commonly used in folk medicine against arthritis and rheumatism. Other uses relate to antiseptic, astringent, anti-inflammatory and anti-ulcer properties.

PREPARATION AND DOSAGE A tea is made of 4-6 g of the dried herb, and taken three times per day. Other sources recommend a daily dose of 2.5-3.5 g of the flowers and 4-5 g of the herb. The powdered herb or extracts are used in herbal teas, tablets and tinctures.

ACTIVE INGREDIENTS The drug is rich in flavonoids (up to 6% in flowers), with spiraeoside (=kaempferol 4'-glucoside), rutin, hyperoside and other flavonol glycosides. Gallo- and ellagitannins are present in concentrations of up to 20% (esters of gallic acid, di- and trigalloyl moieties with glucose; such as rugosin D). The volatile oil is rich in methylsalicylate and salicyl-aldehyde; both are present as corresponding glycosides (about 0.5%) in the intact plant (spiraein and mono-tropitin, respectively).

PHARMACOLOGICAL EFFECTS Tannins can form non-covalent bonds with various proteins (enzymes, receptors, transporters) and are therefore astringent, antimicrobial, antioxidant and anti-inflammatory. These effects are probably enhanced by the flavonoids. Salicylates inhibit cyclooxygenase and thus the formation of prostaglandins, involved in inflammations. In analogy to salicin, it appears likely that the spiraein and monotropin are hydrolysed in the intestine and liver, thus converting the "prodrug" into an active medicine. The analgesic, anti-inflammatory and anti-rheumatic properties of meadowsweet thus appear plausible.

STATUS Traditional medicine; Pharm.; Comm.E+.

Filipendula ulmaria (L.) Maxim. (= *Spiraea ulmaria* L.)   family: Rosaceae

reine des prés (French); *Echtes Mädesüß* (German); *regina dei prati, olmaria* (Italian)

Foeniculum vulgare

fennel

Foeniculum vulgare plants

Foeniculum vulgare

Fennel fruit

DESCRIPTION An erect, robust perennial herb of up to 1.5 m in height. The leaf stalks form sheaths around the thick stems and the leaves are finely divided, giving them a feathery appearance. Small yellow flowers are borne in distinctive umbels. Two subspecies, *piperitum* and *vulgare* are distinguished. Among the medicinally used subsp. *vulgare*, a bitter (var. *vulgare*) and sweet variety (var. *dulce*) are recognised.

ORIGIN Mediterranean region. Cultivated worldwide.

PARTS USED Dry fruits (*Foeniculi frutus*), and the essential oil (*Foeniculi aetheroleum*) are mostly used.

THERAPEUTIC CATEGORY Carminative, expectorant, aromatic.

USES AND PROPERTIES Used since ancient times to treat menstrual disorders, dyspepsia, flatulence and cough, and to reduce the griping effect of laxatives. Syrups made from the fruit or the juice extracted from the fresh herb are used for chronic coughs and catarrh of the upper respiratory tract in adults and children. Fruits are traditional ingredients of domestic gripe water to treat flatulence in infants. External uses include skin disorders, conjunctivitis and blepharitis of the eye. Fennel oil has an anis seed flavour and is used like the fruit.

PREPARATION AND DOSAGE A daily dose of 5-7 g of fruits, 10-20 g of fennel syrup or 0.1-0.6 ml of fennel oil is recommended. Fennel syrup contains 0.5 g oil per kg syrup.

ACTIVE INGREDIENTS Fennel oil is rich in phenylpropanoids, mainly *trans*-anethole. Two types of oil are distinguished: bitter fennel oil (30-75% anethole, 12-33% fenchone, α-pinene>limonene) and sweet fennel oil (80-90% anethole, 1-10% fenchon, limonene > α-pinene). Fennel fruits also contain various flavonoids and furanocoumarins and are an industrial source of anethole, used as a flavouring agent in the cosmetic and liquor industries (absinth, ouzo, sambucco).

PHARMACOLOGICAL EFFECTS Fennel oil, especially anethole, has spasmolytic, carminative, anti-inflammatory, oestrogenic, and antimicrobial properties and promotes gastrointestinal motility. Anethole and fenchone are proven secretolytics and stimulants. Anethole is toxic in high concentrations.

WARNING Oils containing high amounts of estragol (tumour-inducing activity in mice), should be avoided.

STATUS Traditional medicine; Pharm.; Comm.E+; ESCOP 1.

Foeniculum vulgare Mill.   family: Apiaceae

fenouil (French); *Fenchel* (German); *finocchio* (Italian); *hinojo* (Spanish)

Fragaria vesca

wild strawberry

Fragaria vesca

DESCRIPTION Wild strawberry is a mat-forming perennial herb that spreads along the ground by numerous runners (stolons) that root at the nodes to produce new plants. The leaves are divided into three broad leaflets with toothed margins and silky hairs on the lower surfaces. Small white flowers are borne on slender stalks, followed by small, red edible fruits (technically a fleshy receptable with numerous achenes on the surface). Several other species and hybrids, including *F. viridis* and *F. moschata* are also sometimes used.

ORIGIN Europe and Asia. The herb is cultivated for medicinal use in central and eastern Europe.

PARTS USED Leaves collected in the flowering stage (wild strawberry leaf – *Fragariae folium*), rarely the fruit (*Fragariae fructus*) or the rhizomes (*Fragariae radix*).

THERAPEUTIC CATEGORY Astringent, anti-diarrhoeal.

USES AND PROPERTIES Leaves and rhizomes are traditionally used as a mild astringent to treat diarrhoea and mucosal inflammations of the mouth (as a gargle). The leaves and the fruit have a wide range of traditional applications and are considered to be diuretic (urinary tract disorders), antirheumatic, cooling and calming. Young leaves have been used as a substitute for black tea and are sometimes taken as a bulking agent (filler) in medicinal herbal teas. The fruits are used in tea mixtures and in liqueurs.

PREPARATION AND DOSAGE An infusion of 1 g of chopped leaves in a cup of boiling water is drunk several times a day.

ACTIVE INGREDIENTS Strawberry leaves are rich in condensed tannins and ellagitannins such as agrimoniin and pedunculagin, together with proanthocyanins, flavonoids (quercetin, rutin) and phenolic acids (salicylic acid, caffeic acid, chlorogenic acid). The rhizomes have a high tannin content (about 10%). Acids, sugar and pectins are present in the ripe fruit.

PHARMACOLOGICAL EFFECTS Tannins and oligomeric proanthocyanidins can form non-covalent bonds with various proteins (enzymes, receptors, transporters) and thus change their conformation and activity. They are therefore astringent, antimicrobial, antioxidant and anti-inflammatory. The use of the drug to treat diarrhoea and mucosal inflammations therefore appears to be plausible.

STATUS Traditional medicine.

Fragaria vesca L.   family: Rosaceae

fraisier des bois (French); *Wild Walderdbeere* (German); *fragola di bosco* (Italian); *fresera* (Spanish)

Fraxinus excelsior

common ash • European ash

Fraxinus excelsior

Fraxinus ornus

DESCRIPTION Ash is a deciduous tree (up to 40 m), with compound leaves (three to six pairs of leaflets), inconspicuous flowers and winged fruits. The small white warty spots (lenticels) on the twigs and the black leaf buds are characteristic. Manna ash (*F. ornus*) is a small tree with five to nine leaflets per leaf and white flowers.

ORIGIN Europe and southwestern Asia (*F. excelsior*); Europe and western Asia (*F. ornus*). Products are obtained through wild-harvesting (common ash) or commercial cultivation in the Mediterranean region (manna ash).

PARTS USED Bark of young branches (*Fraxini cortex*) and leaves (*Fraxini folium*); *F. ornus* yields manna (*Manna cannelata*) – dried sugary exudate that flows after insect damage or after deliberate incisions of the bark during warm, dry weather.

THERAPEUTIC CATEGORY Anti-inflammatory (*F. excelsior*); osmotic laxative (*F. ornus*).

USES AND PROPERTIES Ash bark is a traditional tonic, especially in cases of fever and rheumatism, while the leaves are used to treat minor pains in the joints, bladder complaints, constipation (nowadays in weight loss programmes). Externally it is used to treat wounds and ulcers. Manna is a useful laxative, especially when a soft stool is required (in cases of painful haemorrhoids, anal fissures or after surgery).

PREPARATION AND DOSAGE Ash bark and ash leaf are rarely used in modern medicine. Manna is given at a daily dose of 20-30 g for adults and 2-16 g for children.

ACTIVE INGREDIENTS Ash bark and ash leaf contain tannins, flavonoids (rutin), coumaroyl glucosides (isofraxin, aesculin), secoiridoid glucosides (syringoxide, 10-hydroxyligstroside) and phenolic acids (ferulic acid, sinapic acid) and triterpenes. Manna is composed mainly of D-mannitol (70-90%), with smaller amounts of D-glucose, D-fructose and oligosaccharides.

PHARMACOLOGICAL EFFECTS Isolated coumarins and iridoids of *Fraxinus* inhibit prostaglandin and leucotriene formation; this would explain anti-inflammatory and analgesic activity. Mannitol is a natural osmotic laxative (salts or sugars retain or increase the water content of the stool simply by their osmotic action).

Note *F. chinensis*, *F. americana*, and *F. rhynchophylla* have been used in a similar way to *F. excelsior*.

STATUS Traditional medicine; Pharm.; Comm.E+ (manna only).

Fraxinus excelsior L.

family: Oleaceae

frêne élevé (French); *Gemeine Esche* (German); *frassino* (Italian); *fresno* (Spanish)

Fumaria officinalis
fumitory

Fumaria officinalis plant

Fumaria officinalis flowers

DESCRIPTION A climbing, weedy annual herb with bluish green, somewhat fleshy, deeply dissected leaves, characteristic pink flowers with a dark-tipped spur and small, spherical dry fruits containing a single seed. It was previously included in a separate family, the Fumariaceae, but is now part of the poppy family (Papaveraceae).

ORIGIN Europe and the Mediterranean region to the Middle East, it has become a weed in many parts of the world. The plant is wild-harvested in eastern Europe.

PARTS USED Dried, aboveground parts, gathered during the flowering season (*Fumariae herba*).

THERAPEUTIC CATEGORY Cholagogue, spasmolytic.

USES AND PROPERTIES The herb is used to treat biliary and dyspeptic disorders, especially spastic discomfort of the gastrointestinal tract, the gall-bladder and bile ducts. It is also traditionally used as diuretic and laxative medicine, and externally for the relief of psoriasis and chronic eczema.

PREPARATION AND DOSAGE A tea is made by adding 2-3 g of the dry herb to a cup of boiling water. For bile disorders, a cupful is drunk before every meal.

ACTIVE INGREDIENTS In common with other members of the poppy family, fumitory herb contains several alkaloids (1%): protoberberine (scoulerine) and protopine (=fumarine, the main alkaloid), also spirobenzylisoquinoline (fumaricine, fumariline) and indenbenzazepine (fumaritine, fumarofine) alkaloids. Also present are chlorogenic acid and flavonol glycosides (rutin, quercetin).

PHARMACOLOGICAL EFFECTS The drug has spasmolytic (e.g. on Oddi's sphincter in the bile duct) and choleretic properties. In addition, anticholinergic, antiarrhythmic, antibacterial and GABA-stimulating effects have been described. Synthetic fumaric acid is included in modern psoriasis and eczema remedies.

NOTES *Corydalis* species (*C. cava*, *C. solida*, and *C. yanhusuo*, also Papaveraceae) are rich in isoquinoline alkaloids, with aporphines (mainly bulbocapnine used medicinally as a pure compound), protoberberines (coptisine, corydaline, canadine, scoulerine), protopines (protopine, corycavine) and benzophenanthridines. The alkaloids have sedative and spasmolytic properties. Isolated bulbocapnine is used in neurology to treat chorea, tremors and spasms.

STATUS Traditional medicine; Pharm.; Comm.E+.

Fumaria officinalis L.   family: Papaveraceae

fumeterre officinale (French); *Echter Erdrauch* (German); *fumaria, cresta di gallo* (Italian)

Galanthus nivalis

common snowdrop • snowdrop

Galanthus nivalis

Galanthus nivalis

DESCRIPTION The snowdrop is a small bulbous plant with narrow, longitudinally ridged leaves and a cluster of attractive white, nodding flowers. Several species have been described but they are all closely related and intermediates are common. *G. nivalis* and *G. woronowii* (Caucasian snowdrop) are used as sources of raw material.

ORIGIN Southern, central and eastern parts of Europe, naturalised in Britain (*G. nivalis*); alkaloid-rich forms are cultivated in Bulgaria; *G. woronowii* is endemic to the western Caucasus region and is cultivated in southern parts of the former USSR.

PARTS USED Dried and powdered bulbs of both species (*Galanthi bulbus*), used for alkaloid extraction.

THERAPEUTIC CATEGORY Cholineesterase inhibitor.

USES AND PROPERTIES The isolated alkaloid, galanthamine, is used to alleviate the symptoms of neuromuscular ailments such as neuritis and neuralgia, as well as *myasthenia gravis* and *poliomyelitis*. The greatest interest, however, is in the treatment of Alzheimer's disease and galanthamine products have regulatory approval for treating this condition in most countries.

PREPARATION AND DOSAGE The bulbs are not used as medicine. About 0.15-0.35 mg of galanthamine per kg body weight is administered by intravenous injection.

ACTIVE INGREDIENTS *Galanthus* species contain numerous Amaryllidaceae alkaloids (up to 1.6%), including galanthamine (the main compound, up to 0.8% dry weight in *G. woronowii*), haemanthamine, galanthine, lycorine and narciclasine. A tetrameric lectin has been isolated from bulbs of *G. nivalis*.

PHARMACOLOGICAL EFFECTS Alzheimer's disease (one of the most common forms of dementia, leading to the loss of memory and other cognitive functions) is partly due to a deficiency of acetylcholine in parts of the brain. Acetylcholineesterase is an enzyme that splits acetylcholine, one of the body's most important neurotransmitters. By inhibiting the enzyme, galanthamine appears to help to increase the local concentration of acetylcholine. Lycorine has antiviral properties.

WARNING The plant and its alkaloids are very toxic and not suitable for self-medication.

STATUS Modern medicine: galanthamine; clinical studies+ (galanthamine).

Galanthus nivalis L.   family: Amaryllidaceae

perce-neige, galanthe des neiges (French); *Gemeines Schneeglöckchen* (German); *bucaneve, foraneve* (Italian)

Galega officinalis
goat's rue

Galega officinalis plant

Galega officinalis flowers

DESCRIPTION Goat's rue is a perennial herb of up to 1 m in height, with pinnately compound leaves and attractive white or pink legume flowers arranged in dense, many-flowered clusters.

ORIGIN Europe (central, southern and eastern parts) and northern Arabia. The herb is cultivated to some extent, but mainly as a fodder plant.

PARTS USED Dried, aboveground parts (*Galegae herba*).

THERAPEUTIC CATEGORY Diuretic, hypoglycaemic.

USES AND PROPERTIES The herb is traditionally used as a diuretic and especially as an antidiabetic. It is still widely used in folk medicine, also to treat skin ulcers. When fed to domestic animal (cows, goats) it is believed that milk flow is increased.

PREPARATION AND DOSAGE A tea can be prepared by adding 2 g of the herb to a cup of boiling water. The herb is included in various antidiabetic preparations. One of the reasons why goat's rue is not recommended for self-medication in diabetes is the difficulty in determining an accurate dose in variable plant material.

ACTIVE INGREDIENTS The main active compound is galegine (up to 0.5%), a guanidine derivative that occurs together with 4-hydroxygalegine and quinoline alkaloids (up to 0.35%) such as peganine (=vasicine) and vasicinone. Also present are flavonoids (luteolin), canavanine (a non-protein amino acid), tannins, steroids, saponins and chromium salts (3.7 ppm), all of which could perhaps contribute to the medicinal activity of the plant.

PHARMACOLOGICAL EFFECTS The drug inhibits platelet aggregation, and exhibits hypoglycaemic and lactagogue activities. Glucose transport into cultured cells is inhibited by *Galega* extracts. Galegine and synthetic derivatives of guanidine lower blood sugar levels. Chromium in the diet is known to be important for normal blood sugar metabolism and it has been speculated that the chromium in goat's rue may partly account for the historical use as anti-diabetic. Thus, some evidence exists for hypoglycaemic properties.

WARNING Diabetes is a serious condition and it is therefore no longer considered advisable to use a herbal remedy when safe and effective modern treatments are available. Diabetes should only be treated under the supervision of a health care professional.

STATUS Traditional medicine; Pharm.

Galega officinalis L.   family: Fabaceae

rue de chèvre (French); *Echte Geißraute* (German); *capraggine, ruta di capra* (Italian)

Galeopsis segetum

downy hemp-nettle

Galeopsis segetum flower

Galeopsis segetum plant

Galeopsis tetrahit

DESCRIPTION Hemp-nettle is a weedy herbaceous annual of up to 0.5 m in height with angular stems bearing dentate leaves in opposite pairs. The pale yellow, two-lipped flowers are arranged in clusters at each node and each have two hollow, tooth-like lobes on the lower lip. The plant was previously known as *Galeopsis ochroleuca*.

ORIGIN Central and southern Europe. The herb is wild-harvested during the flowering season in eastern Europe.

PARTS USED Dried, aboveground parts (hemp-nettle herb – *Galeopsidis herba*; synon. *Herba Galeopsidis*).

THERAPEUTIC CATEGORY Expectorant, astringent.

USES AND PROPERTIES Hemp-nettle is traditionally used in central Europe as an expectorant and astringent to treat coughs, bronchitis and catarrh of the respiratory tract. It has also been employed as a diuretic.

PREPARATION AND DOSAGE The herb is used as a tea (2 g added to a cup of boiling water, or 2 g added to cold water and then brought to the boil). A cup of the tea (sweetened with honey if necessary) is taken several times a day. It is included in some herbal teas and extracts are added to commercial preparations.

ACTIVE INGREDIENTS Tannins are present in concentrations of up to 5-10% and silicic acid (including soluble silicates) at up to 1% (the level of soluble silicates is stated to be about 0.1-0.2%). Several flavonoids have been identified, including 8-hydroxyflavone derivatives as main compounds. Both neutral and acidic saponins occur in the herb. Of interest is also the presence of iridoids, notably harpagide, 8-O-acetylharpagide, antirrhinoside and 5-O-glucosylantirrhinoside.

PHARMACOLOGICAL EFFECTS Tannins can form non-covalent bonds with various proteins (enzymes, receptors, transporters) and therefore have astringent, antimicrobial, antioxidant and anti-inflammatory properties. Iridoid glycosides appear to inhibit the formation of prostaglandins and can contribute to anti-inflammatory and analgesic activities. These properties explain some of the traditional medicinal indications but the drug needs a thorough pharmacological investigation.

NOTES The commercial herb is sometimes adulterated with the common hemp-nettle (*G. tetrahit*) and other similar species.

STATUS Traditional medicine; Pharm.; Comm.E+.

Galeopsis segetum Necker (=*G. ochroleuca* Lam., *G. dubia* Leers)   family: Lamiaceae
galéopsis douteux, chanvre bâtard (French); *Gelber Hohlzahn* (German); *canapa selvatica* (Italian)

Galium verum

lady's bedstraw

Galium aparine

Galium verum

Galium odoratum

DESCRIPTION Lady's bedstraw is a wiry perennial herb of up to 0.5 m in height, with slender, angled stems and narrowly linear leaves arranged in whorls along the branches. The inconspicuous flowers are golden yellow in colour. Several other *Galium* species (and the closely related *Rubia*) are used as medicinal plants in various parts of the world, including North Africa, southern Africa and Asia. The best-known ones in Europe are G. *aparine*, known as clivers, or sticky willy and G. *odoratum*, known as sweet woodruff. Both these species differ from G. *verum* in their white flowers. Sticky willy is a creeping and climbing weedy herb with hooked prickles on the leaves and fruits that make them stick to clothing (the model for Velcro fastener).

ORIGIN Europe, North Africa and Asia (G. *verum*, G. *aparine* and G. *odoratum*). The plants are wild-harvested.

PARTS USED Dried aboveground parts (*Galii lutei herba*; *Galii aparinis herba*; *Galii odorati herba*), collected while flowering.

THERAPEUTIC CATEGORY Diuretic (G. *verum*) or diuretic and astringent (G. *aparine*).

USES AND PROPERTIES *Galium* species are mainly used as diuretics to treat minor complaints of the uri-

nary tract, and in the case of G. *aparine*, enlarged lymph nodes. Externally, both G. *verum* and G. *aparine* are used to treat slow healing wounds, psoriasis and other skin ailments. Numerous traditional uses have been recorded for G. *odorata*, ranging from diseases of the respiratory tract, minor disorders of the gastrointestinal tract to sleep disorders and wound treatment.

PREPARATION AND DOSAGE A tea made of 2-4 g of the dry herb in a cup of boiling water is taken two or three times a day. This applies to all three species.

ACTIVE INGREDIENTS *Galium* species contain tannins, phenolic acids, flavonoids and iridoid glycosides. The main iridoid glycosides are asperuloside and monotropeine; coumarins occur in G. *odoratum*. Roots of *Galium* contain anthraquinones (alizarin, lucidin, rubiadin) and naphthoquinones.

PHARMACOLOGICAL EFFECTS The astringent effects are linked to the tannins; iridoid glycosides are anti-inflammatory, while the anthraquinones are laxative and diuretic. Sedative effects of G. *odoratum* are associated with its coumarin content. Detailed pharmacological studies do not exist for *Galium* extracts.

STATUS Traditional medicine; Pharm.

Galium verum L.   family: Rubiaceae

caille-lait jaune, gaillet vrai (French); *Echtes Labkraut* (German); *caglio giallo* (Italian)

Gaultheria procumbens
wintergreen • checkerberry

Gaultheria procumbens

DESCRIPTION A mat-forming woody shrub that can spread to a width of several metres. It has smooth red-brown bark, bright green leathery leaves and small, white or pinkish bell-shaped flowers. The small red berries are edible.

ORIGIN North America (eastern USA and Canada); cultivated to a limited extent but commercial sources are wild-harvested.

PARTS USED Leaves (*Gaultheriae folium*), essential oil (*Gaultheriae aetheroleum*).

THERAPEUTIC CATEGORY Anti-inflammatory, analgesic, counter-irritant.

USES AND PROPERTIES Used externally as a counter-irritant to treat painful muscles and joints, including rheumatism. Infusions, decoctions or small amounts of the oil are rarely taken internally, as tonic, to treat rheumatism and to relieve minor stomach upsets. Canadian Indians traditionally made a refreshing tea from the leaves. Natural wintergreen is rarely used nowadays except in North America.

PREPARATION AND DOSAGE The oil is included in ointments, creams and liniments, at a concentration of about 20%. For oral use in treating rheumatism, 10-20 drops of the oil are included in capsules. It also forms part of cosmetics and oral hygiene products. The leaves are used to make a refreshing tea ("mountain tea").

ACTIVE INGREDIENTS Methyl salicylate is the main ingredient of the oil (99% of the total). It occurs in the plant as monotropitoside (=gautherin; a glycoside with glucose and xylose). In analogy to salicin, it appears likely that the monotropitoside is hydrolysed in the intestine and liver, thus converting the "prodrug" into an active medicine. Also present in the herb are arbutin and tannins. Methyl salicylate is obtained from the bark of *Betula lenta*, leaves of *Filipendula ulmaria* and other plants. It has a very characteristic smell and a sweetish taste. Nowadays, synthetic methyl salicylate has largely replaced the natural product.

PHARMACOLOGICAL EFFECTS Salicylates inhibit cyclooxygenase and thus the formation of prostaglandins, involved in inflammation and pain. The analgesic, anti-inflammatory and anti-rheumatic properties of wintergreen thus appear plausible. It can be toxic when taken internally and should be avoided by people who are allergic to aspirin.

STATUS Traditional medicine.

Gaultheria procumbens L.   family: Ericaceae

gaulthérie du Canada (French); *Niederliegende Scheinbeere, Wintergrün* (German); *uva di monte* (Italian)

Gelsemium sempervirens

yellow jasmine • false jasmine • evening trumpet flower

Gelsemium sempervirens plant

Gelsemium sempervirens flowers

DESCRIPTION Yellow jasmine is an attractive climber (vine) with glossy green, hairless leaves arranged in opposite pairs and bright yellow, tubular flowers. It is closely related to G. *elegans*, a poisonous plant that is traditionally used for murder and suicide in Indomalaysia.

ORIGIN North America (southeastern parts of the USA. It is the state flower of South Carolina). The plant is commonly cultivated as an ornamental climber.

PARTS USED Rhizomes and roots (*Gelsemii rhizoma*).

THERAPEUTIC CATEGORY Antispasmodic, analgesic, sedative.

USES AND PROPERTIES Yellow jasmine or its extracted alkaloids are mainly used to treat neuralgia (intense pain caused by damaged or irritated nerves), especially of the face and mouth (facial and dental neuralgia). It has been used in cough syrups (to treat whooping cough and asthma) and externally to treat various pains resulting from pressure on a nerve, especially in the spinal cord. It is claimed to be of use against migraine and neurological disorders and bleeding (haemorrhoids and the uterus). Fresh rhizomes are popular in homoeopathy to treat migraine, irregular heartbeat, dysmenorrhoea and anxiety.

PREPARATION AND DOSAGE Tinctures (13 drops or 0.3 g per treatment) or more often extracts (3 drops per treatment) are used.

ACTIVE INGREDIENTS Monoterpene indole alkaloids at a concentration of about 0.5% – mainly gelsemine, gelseverine, gelsemicine, gelsedine, sempervirine and various hydroxylated derivates. Coumarins, iridoid glycosides (gelsemide, semperoside) and steroids of the pregnane-type are also present.

PHARMACOLOGICAL EFFECTS The alkaloids (especially gelsemine) inhibit acetylcholine receptors (especially muscarinic AChR), acetylcholine esterase and the synaptic re-uptake of dopamine, noradrenaline and serotonine. These properties explain the observed antispasmodic, analgesic, hypotonic and sedative activities. The plant and its alkaloids (especially gelsemine and gelsemicine) are very poisonous – a single flower or 1.2-3 g of the tincture are said to be potentially lethal to a child. The alkaloids cause respiratory arrest.

WARNING Yellow jasmine can only be used by an experienced health care professional – self-medication can be dangerous or even fatal.

STATUS Traditional medicine.

Gelsemium sempervirens (L.) J. St-Hil.   family: Gelsemiaceae

jasmin sauvage (French); *Falscher Jasmin, Giftjasmin* (German); *gelsemino* (Italian)

Gentiana lutea

yellow gentian

Gentiana lutea flowers

Gentiana lutea plant

Veratrum album

DESCRIPTION Yellow gentian is a robust leafy perennial herb (up to 1.5 m) with large, parallel-veined leaves emerging every year from a persistent rootstock. The yellow flowers are borne in dense clusters along a sturdy flowering stalk. Other commercial sources include G. *purpurea* , G. *punctata*, G. *pannonica*, G. *asclepiadea*, G. *cruciata* and G. *scabrae*.

ORIGIN Europe (typically at high elevations).

PARTS USED Rhizome and root (*Gentianae radix*).

THERAPEUTIC CATEGORY Digestive bitter (*amarum*), cholagogue, stomachic.

USES AND PROPERTIES Gentian root is a traditional bitter tonic that stimulates appetite. It is a roborant and cholagogue, and is used in case of poor appetite, flatulence and bloating, as well as for dyspepsia with anorexia. It is also popular in homoeopathy.

PREPARATION AND DOSAGE A tea can be made by adding 1-2 g of dried root to a cup of boiling water. A daily dose of 2-4 g of root is recommended (for tinctures, 1-3 g per day). Gentian root is included in a wide range of herbal teas and stomachic medicines (tincture, drops, tablets, extracts). It is commercially used mainly to flavour liqueurs.

ACTIVE INGREDIENTS The compounds of special interest are the strongly bitter secoiridoids, of which gentiopicroside (also known as gentiopicrin) is the main constituent (2-3%), together with smaller quantities of swertiamarin and sweroside. The bitter taste is mainly due to amarogentin, a minor compound (only up to 0.084% dry weight!) but with a bitterness value of 50 000 000. This is one of the most intensely bitter substances known. Xanthones such as gentisin, isogentisin and gentioside are also present, and give the roots their characteristic yellow colour. In addition, the rhizomes and roots contain phytosterols, phenolic acids, trisaccharides (gentianose) and polysaccharides (pectin).

PHARMACOLOGICAL EFFECTS The bitter substances stimulate the taste buds and promote (as reflex via the *nervus vagus*) the flow of saliva, gastric juices and bile. In addition, gentian extracts show antimicrobial and immuno-modulatory properties.

WARNING The toxic *Veratrum album* has similar leaves and might be confused with yellow gentian.

STATUS Traditional medicine; Pharm.; Comm.E+; ESCOP 4.

Gentiana lutea L.

family: Gentianaceae

gentiane jaune (French); *Gelber Enzian* (German); *genziana maggiore* (Italian)

Geranium robertianum

herb Robert

Geranium robertianum plant

Geranium robertianum flowers and fruits

DESCRIPTION A short-lived plant (up to 0.5 m), with highly aromatic, deeply dissected, red-green leaves, small pink flowers and oblong, pointed fruits resembling a stork's bill. Other species used in traditional medicine (and as garden plants) include *G. maculatum* (American cranesbill), *G. dissectum* (English cranesbill) and *G. sanguineum* (bloody cranesbill). *Geranium nepalense* and *G. wallichianum* are used for tanning and dyeing.

ORIGIN Europe and Asia, and naturalised in North and South America (*G. robertianum*); eastern and central parts of North America (*G. maculatum*).

PARTS USED Whole dried herb (*Geranii robertiani herba*).

THERAPEUTIC CATEGORY Anti-inflammatory, anti-diarrhoeal.

USES AND PROPERTIES Herb Robert is traditionally used to treat mild diarrhoea and infections of the urinary tract. Externally used as a styptic and to cure slowly healing wounds, eczema and mucosal inflammations. It is said to be useful in treating heavy menstrual bleeding, stomach ulcers and irritable bowel syndrome. American cranesbill is used in the same way. Fresh rhizomes of *G. robertianum* are used in homoeopathy.

PREPARATION AND DOSAGE An infusion of two teaspoons (dried herb) or one teaspoon (dry root). It is also used in homeopathy, mostly at a potency of D1. Extracts of both herb Robert and American cranesbill are included in tablets and tinctures.

ACTIVE INGREDIENTS Essential oil with an unpleasant smell (it contains geraniol, germacren D, limonene, linalool and terpineol) can be isolated from the leaves. Ferulic acid, caffeic acid, rutin, kaempferol and quercetin are the main phenolics of leaves. Geranium species are rich in gallo- and ellagitannins (up to 30%). The main compound in *G. robertianum* is geraniin.

PHARMACOLOGICAL EFFECTS Tannins are astringent and have antiseptic and anti-inflammatory effects because of their ability to non-selectively denature proteins. They have anti-diarrhoeal effects, form protective layers over the skin and mucosa and have a vasoconstricting effect on small vessels, thereby reducing fluid losses from the skin.

WARNING Severe diarrhoea (especially in children) is dangerous due to the risk of dehydration and should be treated by a health care professional.

STATUS Traditional medicine.

Geranium robertianum L.   family: Geraniaceae

géranium robertin, herbe à Robert (French); *Ruprechtskraut* (German); *erba roberta, cicuta rossa* (Italian); *hierba de San Roberto* (Spanish)

Geum urbanum

wood avens • herb

Geum urbanum plant

Geum urbanum flower and fruit

DESCRIPTION Wood avens is an erect perennial herb with slender stems bearing widely spaced, compound leaves with broad, dentate leaflets. The small flowers are yellow. Particularly characteristic are the compound fruits, made up of numerous reddish styles and separate carpels, ending in a hooked, bristly tip. Other species used medicinally include *G. rivale* (water avens) and *G. japonicum* (Japanese avens).

ORIGIN Europe, Asia and North America. The herb is wild-harvested, mainly in eastern and southeastern Europe.

PARTS USED Rhizomes and roots (*Caryophyllatae rhizoma*).

THERAPEUTIC CATEGORY Astringent, tonic, antidiarrhoeal.

USES AND PROPERTIES The rhizome is a traditional remedy to treat mild diarrhoea, dyspepsia and appetite loss. It is used as an astringent (as a gargle) in case of inflamed mucosa of the mouth and throat, chilblains, haemorrhoids and other skin disorders. It is also considered to be a bitter tonic and stomachic. An additive to liqueurs, brandies, toothpastes and mouthwashes.

PREPARATION AND DOSAGE To treat mild diarrhoea, a tea is prepared by adding half a teaspoon to one teaspoon of chopped root to a cup of boiling water. One cup of the lukewarm infusion is taken several times a day. Another source recommends a dose of 1-4 g, taken as an infusion three times per day. To prepare a mouthwash, one teaspoon of root is added to cold water and boiled for a few minutes.

ACTIVE INGREDIENTS The active compounds are tannins (up to 30%). Various complex gallo- and ellagitannins (gemin A,D; pedunculagin, sanguiin H-6) and condensed catechol tannins are present, together with phenolic acids (caffeic, chlorogenic, ellagic, gallic and protocatechuic acids). Small amounts (0.15%) of volatile oil is present, containing eugenol as the main and myrtenal as minor component. Eugenol occurs as a glycoside (gein) and is hydrolysed by the enzyme gease when the plant is wounded or during the drying process.

PHARMACOLOGICAL EFFECTS Tannins are well known for their astringent and antiseptic effects. They are non-specific protein inactivators because their phenolic hydroxyl groups form hydrogen and ionic bonds. Eugenol shows pronounced antimicrobial properties. Traditional uses are therefore plausible.

STATUS Traditional medicine; Pharm.

Geum urbanum L.   family: Rosaceae

benoîte commune (French); *Echte Nelkenwurz* (German); *erba benedetta, cariofillata* (Italian)

Ginkgo biloba

ginkgo • maidenhair tree

Ginkgo biloba leaves

Ginkgo biloba tree

Ginkgo biloba female cones

DESCRIPTION A large tree (up to 35 m in height), with male and female cones borne on separate trees. The leaves are fan-shaped, often notched at the tip (bilobed) and with an unusual system of parallel veins. The female cones have a fleshy outer layer with an unpleasant smell of rancid butter, but the inner part is edible and much sought after in China ("white nuts").

ORIGIN China. A popular ornamental tree and cultivated on a commercial scale in China, France and the USA. As "living fossil" it has maintained its morphology for nearly 200 million years.

PARTS USED Leaves (also seeds).

THERAPEUTIC CATEGORY Central and peripheral circulatory disturbances.

USES AND PROPERTIES Special leaf extracts are used to treat the symptoms of various forms of cerebrovascular insufficiency and dementia (including memory loss, disturbed concentration, dizziness, sleep disturbances, mood swings, decreased stamina and debilitation, morbus Alzheimer). It is also specifically used to treat patients with peripheral arterial occlusive disease (improvement of the pain-free walking distance). Leaves have been part of Chinese medicine

for at least 2 800 years and are still used to strengthen the heart and lungs, and to treat chilblains. The seeds are employed as antitussive and expectorant medicine in China and Japan.

PREPARATION AND DOSAGE Special acetone-water extracts (such as EGb 761) are produced to eliminate both inactive and potentially harmful substances and are widely used in phytotherapy. The recommended daily dose is in the range of 120-240 mg of extract, and the duration of treatment is usually no less than 6-8 weeks.

ACTIVE INGREDIENTS Flavonoids (mainly flavonol glycosides and non-glycosidic biflavonoids), unique diterpene lactones (known as ginkgolides A, B, C, J and M) and a sesquiterpenoid (bilobalide). Extracts contain only negligible amounts of ginkgolic acids.

PHARMACOLOGICAL EFFECTS Special extracts show a wide range of biological activities, including the inhibition of the platelet activating factor (PAF) and of acetylcholine esterase. Clinical trials have shown the efficacy of ginkgo extracts to treat patients with dementia, tinnitus and peripheral circulatory disorders.

STATUS Traditional medicine; Comm.E+ (extracts only); clinical trials+.

Ginkgo biloba L.   family: Ginkgoaceae

ginkgo (French); Ginkgo (German); *ginkgo biloba* (Italian); *arbol de los escudos* (Spanish)

Glycine max

soybean

Glycine max flowers and fruit

Soybeans – *Glycine max* seeds

DESCRIPTION An erect, hairy annual herb with trifoliate leaves and small flowers borne close to the stem. The fruit is a pod containing up to four seeds of variable colour and size, depending on the cultivar.

ORIGIN Central and eastern Asia; thought to be a cultigen derived from *G. soya* as the wild ancestor; cultivated in China since ancient times and now a major world crop.

PARTS USED Seeds (*Sojae semen*), lecithin and oil (*Lecithinum ex soja*; *Sojae oleum*).

THERAPEUTIC CATEGORY Blood lipid reduction; phytoestrogenic.

USES AND PROPERTIES Soybeans may have important dietary value in reducing blood lipid (especially cholesterol) levels, enhancing liver physiology, reducing the symptoms of menopause and the incidence of prostatic and breast cancer. These assumptions are mainly based on comparisons of East Asian people (eating soy as a staple diet) with people from other parts of the world. In Germany, soy lecithin is recommended for the treatment of hypercholesterolemia and other disturbances in the lipid metabolism, as well as in cases of appetite loss, chronic liver disease, including chronic

hepatitis. The use of soy isoflavonoids as phytoestrogens in hormone replacement therapy is increasing but somewhat controversial.

PREPARATION AND DOSAGE The recommended single daily dose of soybean lecithin fraction (for hypercholesterolemia and liver support) is in the order of 1.5-2.7 g.

ACTIVE INGREDIENTS Soybean phospholipids (so-called essential phospholipids, mainly phosphatidylcholine; 2%), soy proteins (40%) and protease inhibitors, together with isoflavonoids (such as genistein, daidzein and corresponding glycosides) and triterpene saponins (various soyasaponins) are the main compounds.

PHARMACOLOGICAL EFFECTS Phospholipids and soy proteins appear to reduce triglyceride and cholesterol levels. Isoflavones weakly bind to oestrogen receptors and can thus modulate oestrogen-regulated genes, especially during menopause (when endogenous oestrogen levels are reduced). Genistein specifically inhibits a tyrosine kinase, that plays a role in cell division (often enhanced in tumour cells). Protease inhibitors could also contribute to anti-tumour activities. Soyasaponins appear to be anti-thrombotic and liver-protectant.

STATUS Pharm.; Comm.E+.

Glycine max (L.) Merr.

family: Fabaceae

fève de soja (French); *Sojabohne* (German); *soia* (Italian)

Glycyrrhiza glabra

liquorice • licorice

Glycyrrhiza glabra leaves and flowers

Glycyrrhiza glabra fruits

Liquorice root

DESCRIPTION Liquorice is a perennial herb of up to 1 m high, with branched rhizomes and woody stems bearing compound leaves and pale purple or white flowers. Chinese liquorice or *gan cao* (*G. uralensis*), is used in much the same way as ordinary liquorice.

ORIGIN Mediterranean region to Central Asia; cultivated in many parts of the world.

PARTS USED Dried rhizomes (*Liquiritiae radix*).

THERAPEUTIC CATEGORY Expectorant, anti-inflammatory, antispasmodic.

USES AND PROPERTIES Since ancient times, the herb has been used to treat chronic gastric and duodenal ulcers, gastritis, epigastric bloating, flatulence, coughs and externally for skin disorders. Rhizomes are important for the extraction of glycyrrhizic acid, which is used externally for its anti-inflammatory properties, especially in pruritis, piles, sunburn and insect bites. Liquorice is also employed as a sweetening agent, in order to hide the unpleasant taste of medicinal formulations.

PREPARATION AND DOSAGE An infusion with 1-1.5 g of chopped rhizome in 150 ml of boiling water. Decoctions and extracts are included in preparations, both as active ingredient and as taste enhancer.

ACTIVE INGREDIENTS Several flavonoids, isoflavonoids and chalcones are present. The main flavonoids and chalcones in the fresh root (liquiritin and isoliquiritin, respectively) are partially hydrolysed upon drying. The main triterpene saponin is glycyrrhizic acid (2-15%) and its aglycone, glycyrrhetinic acid, that occur with 24-hydroxyglycyrrhetinic acid (the latter is 50 to 100 times sweeter than sugar) and several other saponins.

PHARMACOLOGICAL EFFECTS Anti-inflammatory activity (glycyrrhizic and glycyrrhetic acids weakly bind to receptors of corticoids, i.e. glucocorticoids, aldosterone); expectorant, secretolytic and secretomotoric properties (presence of saponins). Liquorice also shows some antiviral, antibacterial, cytotoxic (towards tumour cells), antihepatotoxic, antioxidant, anti-histaminic and immune stimulating properties. So far clinical studies have failed to demonstrate anti-ulcerogenic qualities.

WARNING The mineralocorticoid activities of liquorice, when taken in large doses over prolonged periods (four weeks), can promote hypertonia.

STATUS Traditional medicine; Pharm.; Comm.E+; WHO 1.

Glycyrrhiza glabra L.   family: Fabaceae

réglisse officinale (French); *Spanisches Süßholz, Lakritze* (German); *liquirizia* (Italian); *regalicia* (Spanish)

Grindelia squarrosa

curly-cup gumweed • scaly grindelia

Grindelia squarrosa

Grindelia robusta

DESCRIPTION Gumweed is a perennial plant with toothed, simple leaves and attractive dark yellow flower heads borne on leafy stalks. Surrounding each flowering head are prominent, sharp-tipped, green involucral bracts that give a bristly, thistle-like appearance to the unopened heads. *G. camporum* is an acceptable alternative source of material and can be used interchangeably with *G. squarrosa*. Two other useful species are *G. robusta* and *G. humilis*.

ORIGIN North America – northwestern parts of the USA (*G. squarrosa*) or the southwestern parts of the USA and Mexico (*G. camporum*). *G. squarrosa* has become a weed in Britain and Australia and is nowadays often a source of raw material.

PARTS USED Dried flowering tops and leaves (gumweed herb – *Grindeliae herba*).

THERAPEUTIC CATEGORY Antitussive, spasmolytic.

USES AND PROPERTIES Gumweeds are traditionally used to treat coughs and catarrh of the respiratory tract, including asthma and bronchitis. Externally it is considered to be effective against skin problems, wounds and eczema. Traditionally to treat inflammations of the urinary tract, gastrointestinal spasms and arteriosclerosis.

PREPARATION AND DOSAGE A daily dose of 4-6 g is recommended, taken as a tea. Alternatively, a daily dose of 1.5-3 ml of a tincture can be taken (a 1:10 or 1:5 ratio of herb to ethanol ratio, using 60-80% ethanol). Extracts are sometimes combined with other products.

ACTIVE INGREDIENTS *Grindelia* species contain a resin consisting of numerous diterpenes of the labdane type (grindelic acid is a main compound). Also present are phenolic acids, a volatile oil (mainly borneol, camphor, limonene and methyleugenol), flavonoids (kaempferol, luteolin), gallo- and ellagitannins, polyacetylenes (matricarianol) and triterpene saponins.

PHARMACOLOGICAL EFFECTS Gumweeds are known to have *in vitro* antibacterial and antifungal activity, which is plausible considering its content of various terpenoids that interfere with the stability of biomembranes and phenolic compounds, that inactivate proteins via non-covalent bond formation with phenolic OH-groups. Spasmolytic and anti-inflammatory effects were also shown experimentally.

NOTES The gum of *G. camporum* is said to be chewed liked chewing gum.

STATUS Traditional medicine; Pharm.; Comm.E+.

Grindelia squarrosa (Pursh) Dunal · family: Asteraceae

grindélia (French); *Sperrige Grindelie, Gummikraut* (German); *grindelia* (Italian)

Guaiacum officinale

guaiac • lignum vitae

Guaiacum officinale leaves

Guaiacum officinale young leaves

Guaiac resin

DESCRIPTION Guaiac is an evergreen tree (up to 10 m in height), with compound leaves ending in a pair of leaflets, deep blue flowers and small fruit capsules. Both G. officinale and G. sanctum are used as a source of the product.

ORIGIN Central and South America (West Indies and the north coast of South America). The trees are felled for their timber, which is used not only medicinally but also for construction work.

PARTS USED The heartwood and sapwood, usually in the form of wood shavings (Lignum vitae, Guaiaci lignum), or the resin obtained by heating the wood (Guaiaci resina). Lignum vitae is one of the hardest of all commercial timbers, and has a specific gravity of 1.333. It was formerly used to make bowls for lawn bowling.

THERAPEUTIC CATEGORY Anti-inflammatory, antioxidant.

USES AND PROPERTIES The wood shavings are used for decoctions taken internally to treat rheumatic complaints (chronic rheumatism and rheumatoid arthritis). The resin is said to be a circulatory stimulant and is also used externally to rub into painful joints and to treat skin disorders. In former times, decoctions were mixed with mercury as a cure of syphilis.

PREPARATION AND DOSAGE Decoctions of 1-2 g of wood or wood shavings are taken three times a day. A liquid extract (1 part herb to 1 part 80% alcohol) can be taken three times daily in doses of 1-2 ml.

ACTIVE INGREDIENTS The resin contains numerous lignans (including α-guaiaconic acid, guaiaretic acid, dehydroguaiaretic acid, guaiacin and isoguaiacin), together with various furanolignans and an enedione lignan. Essential oil obtained by steam distillation contains mainly guajol, which can be converted by semisynthesis to guaiazulene, a valuable aromatherapy compound. Phytosterols and triterpene saponins are also present.

PHARMACOLOGICAL EFFECTS The resin is stated to have anti-rheumatic, anti-inflammatory, diuretic, mild laxative and diaphoretic properties. Guaiazulene is similar to chamazulene in its antiphlogistic activity. One of the lignans (known as meso-nordihydro-guaiaretic acid) is thought to induce renal lithiasis. The resin is used in food products as a powerful antioxidant (the activity is ascribed to α-guaiaconic acid).

STATUS Traditional medicine; Pharm.; Comm.E+.

Guaiacum officinale L.   family: Zygophyllaceae

bois de gaïac, bois de vie (French); Guajakholzbaum, Schlangenholz (German); guaiaco, legno santo (Italian); guajacum, palosanto (Spanish)

Gypsophila paniculata
baby's breath • gypsophila

Gypsophila paniculata plants

Gypsophila paniculata flowers

DESCRIPTION Baby's breath is a perennial herb with a long, fleshy taproot, greyish green, narrow leaves and large, intricately branched, sparse clusters of small white flowers. *Gypsophila paniculata* and *G. elegans* are best known for their use as cut flowers (called baby's breath) in wedding bouquets. Other *Gypsophila* species used in phytotherapy include *G. arrostii* (Mediterranean), *G. fastigiata* (central and east Europe), *G. perfoliata* (east Europe) and *G. struthium* (Mediterranean, Near East) Another saponin-rich species is common soapwort (*Saponaria officinalis*) which is an erect plant with much larger, distinctly tubular flowers arranged in compact, more or less rounded clusters.

ORIGIN Central Europe to Central Asia. The plants are widely cultivated as commercial cut flowers, less commonly for medicinal purposes.

PARTS USED Dried, underground parts (*Saponariae albae radix*; *Gypsophilae radix*, white soapwort root).

THERAPEUTIC CATEGORY Expectorant.

USES AND PROPERTIES White soapwort root is used to treat catarrh of the upper respiratory tract. It is still used as an ingredient of various expectorant preparations. Externally, to treat skin disorders.

PREPARATION AND DOSAGE A daily dose of 30-150 mg of the dried herb is recommended (or 3-15 mg of *Gypsophila* saponin).

ACTIVE INGREDIENTS Triterpene saponins (up to 20%) with saponaside A and saponaside D as main glycosides. These two compounds are bidesmosides that yield, upon hydrolysis, gypsogenin as the only aglycone. *G. struthium* is rich is phytosterols (spinasterol).

PHARMACOLOGICAL EFFECTS Saponins affect the *nervus vagus* in the mucous membrane of the stomach, promoting water secretion in the bronchia. A secretolytic and antitussive effect is the consequence (typical for most saponin containing drugs). Saponins can interfere with biomembranes in humans, animals and microbes, making them leaky (known as haemolytic effect). Therefore saponins (especially their monodesmosides) have anti-microbial, spermicidal and cytotoxic properties. Saponins are weakly toxic when administered orally and at low concentrations, but are quite toxic if given intravenously (causing haemolysis).

NOTE Plant saponins have been used as mild washing powders for wool and furs.

STATUS Traditional medicine; Pharm.; Comm.E+.

Gypsophila paniculata L.   family: Caryophyllaceae

gypsophile, brouillard (French); *Schleierkraut, Rispiges Gipskraut* (German); *gypsophila* (Italian)

163

Hamamelis virginiana

witch hazel

Hamamelis virginiana leaves and flowers

Hamamelis virginiana fruits

DESCRIPTION Witch hazel is a shrub or small tree of about 2-3 m in height (rarely up to 10 m) with thin, forked branches having a zigzag pattern between the nodes. The characteristic leaves are broad, with a dentate margin and an unsymmetrical base. Characteristic yellow flowers with long, narrow petals are produced just before spring and develop slowly into paired, woody and hairy capsules that mature in the next summer. Witch hazel should not be confused with the common hazel nut (*Corylus avellana*), a European species that has been used for similar indications.

ORIGIN North America (Canada and eastern USA). The plant is grown in gardens and parks in Europe. Witch hazel is wild-harvested in the USA and represents a substantial industry.

PARTS USED Leaves, bark and twigs (witch hazel leaf and bark – *Hamamelidis folium et cortex*).

THERAPEUTIC CATEGORY Astringent, anti-haemorrhagic, anti-inflammatory.

USES AND PROPERTIES Witch hazel is mainly used to treat diarrhoea and as a mouth rinse and gargle for inflammation of the gums and throat. It is also used for various skin ailments, venous disorders and haemorrhage, including wounds, bruises, abrasions, varicose veins, excessive menstruation, haemorrhoids and localised swellings.

PREPARATION AND DOSAGE About 0.1-1 g of the herb (or equivalent), several times a day. It is often an ingredient of lotions and ointments to treat wounds, skin ailments and varicose veins, and suppositories to treat haemorrhoids. Especially popular is "hamamelis water" (e.g. in cosmetics), a product made by steam distillation of dormant branches, to which ethanol is added. It is used undiluted or diluted 1:3 with water.

ACTIVE INGREDIENTS Both leaves and bark contain up to 10% tannins. Bark mainly contains a mixture of hamamelitannins (=digalloylhamamelose) and catechols, while the leaves have mainly proanthocyanidins, ellagitannins and 0.5% essential oil (safrol, ionon).

PHARMACOLOGICAL EFFECTS The tannins strongly interact with proteins and have proven astringent, antiseptic, haemostatic and anti-haemorrhoidal activities. Clinical studies appear to support some of the indications.

STATUS Pharm.; Comm.E+; ESCOP 5; WHO 2; clinical studies+.

Hamamelis virginiana L.

family: Hamamelidaceae

hamamélis de Virginie (French); *Hamamelis, Zaubernuss* (German); *amamelide, nocciolo delle streche* (Italian)

Harpagophytum procumbens

devil's claw

Harpagophytum procumbens flowers

Harpagophytum procumbens leaves and flowers

Harpagophytum procumbens fruit

DESCRIPTION Devil's claw is a weedy, perennial herb with creeping stems spreading from a thick, carrot-like, primary root surrounded by several tuberous secondary roots. It bears greyish-green, irregularly lobed leaves, tubular yellow and violet flowers and characteristic thorny fruits (to which the common name refers). Two species are known. In *H. procumbens*, the thorny arms on the fruit are longer than the width of the fruit, while they are as long as or shorter than the width of the fruit in the other species, *H. zeyheri*. The latter is chemically variable and not always suitable for medicinal use.

ORIGIN Southern Africa (Kalahari region, from Angola to Namibia, Botswana and South Africa). Experimental cultivation has been initiated, but practically all commercial product is still wild-harvested.

PARTS USED Sliced and dried secondary roots (devil's claw root – *Harpagophyti radix*).

THERAPEUTIC CATEGORY Bitter tonic, anti-inflammatory, anti-rheumatic, weak analgesic.

USES AND PROPERTIES In recent years, devil's claw has become very popular as a general tonic and stomachic, and for the treatment of rheumatism and ar-thritis. An ointment is made from the root material that is applied to sores, ulcers and boils. It is traditionally used as a tonic and general medicine for a wide range of ailments, including digestive complaints, lack of appetite and to treat pain, during and after labour.

PREPARATION AND DOSAGE A daily dose of up to 9 g of the dried root, taken as infusion (1-3 g at a time), is recommended. Standardised extracts and capsules are available.

ACTIVE INGREDIENTS The main compounds of interest are iridoid glycosides (about 3% of dry weight) – mainly harpagoside (0.5-2%), together with harpagide, procumbide and their cinnamic or coumaric acid esters. Also present are phenolic glycosides such as acteoside and isoacteoside.

PHARMACOLOGICAL EFFECTS Clinical studies showed definite benefits in the treatment of rheumatic conditions and low back pain. Iridoid glycosides (or their metabolites) inhibit cyclooxygenase, which explains the slight analgesic and anti-inflammatory activity. The bitter taste (and possibly the value in treating digestive disturbances) is due to the iridoid glycosides.

STATUS Pharm.; Comm.E+; ESCOP 2; clinical studies+.

Harpagophytum procumbens DC. ex Meissn.

family: Pedaliaceae

griffe du diable (French); *Afrikanische Teufelskralle* (German); *artiglio del diavolo, arpagofito* (Italian)

Harungana madagascariensis

haronga

Harungana madagascariensis flowers

Harungana madagascariensis leaves and fruits

Harungana madagascariensis bark

DESCRIPTION Haronga is a shrub or small evergreen tree with reddish bark and bright orange-coloured sap. The large, opposite leaves are prominently veined and densely covered with rusty hairs. Numerous small, white, fragrant flowers are borne in clusters at the branch ends, followed by rounded, fleshy fruits of 2-4 mm in diameter. The plant has also been known as *Haronga madagascariensis* and is still found under this name in some books.

ORIGIN Madagascar, eastern and southern Africa. The tree is a pioneer of disturbed and open places such as forest margins and has become invasive in parts of Australia.

PARTS USED Bark and leaves (haronga bark and leaf – *Harunganae madagascariensis cortex et folium; synon. Folium et cortex Harongae*).

THERAPEUTIC CATEGORY Secretolytic, choleretic, cholekinetic.

USES AND PROPERTIES Haronga bark and leaf is mainly used to treat dyspepsia and mild exocrine pancreatic insufficiency. It is considered effective in stimulating the production of gastric juices and increasing bile flow. In African countries the reddish sap obtained from the bark or stems is used as a styptic and is applied topically to treat various skin diseases, wounds, leprosy and itch. Bark extracts are also traditionally used to treat unspecified stomach ailments.

PREPARATION AND DOSAGE Dried alcoholic extracts can be taken three times per day, with a recommended daily dose of 7.5–15 mg. This corresponds to a daily dose of 25–50 mg of the crude herb. Commercial preparations made from haronga bark extract are available.

ACTIVE INGREDIENTS Haronga bark and leaf contain 1,8-dihydroxyanthracene derivatives. The bark yields harunganin and madagascin, while the leaves have hypericin and pseudohypericin as some of the main compounds. Also present are flavonol glycosides, tannins (especially condensed epicatechins and proanthocyanidins) and phytosterols.

PHARMACOLOGICAL EFFECTS Studies have shown that bark and leaf extracts are choleretic and cholekinetic. Furthermore, the drug stimulates secretion of digestive juices from both the pancreas and the stomach. Hypericin is also found in *Hypericum perforatum*, and has known antiviral and mild antidepressant effects.

STATUS Traditional medicine.

Harungana madagascariensis Lam. ex Poiret (=*Haronga madagascariensis*)   family: Clusiaceae or Hypericaceae
harongana (French); *Haronga, Drachenblutbaum* (German); *aronga* (Italian)

Hedera helix

ivy

Hedera helix flowers (variegated form)

Hedera helix berries

Hedera helix vegetative leaves

DESCRIPTION A woody climber with creeping stems that cling to objects by means of aerial climbing roots. Vegetative leaves are three- to five-lobed and much smaller than those of flowering stems (larger and ovate, without distinct lobes). Inconspicuous flowers are borne in spherical groups and are followed by black berries.

ORIGIN Western Asia and Europe (central, western and southern parts, including the Mediterranean region).

PARTS USED Leaves (*Hederae folium*), sometimes the woody stems (homoeopathy).

THERAPEUTIC CATEGORY Expectorant, spasmolytic, secretolytic.

USES AND PROPERTIES Extracts of dried leaves are used to treat coughs (including pertussis), spastic bronchitis and chronic catarrhs of the respiratory tract. It also shows promise as an antifungal agent against *Candida albicans* and is active against parasites and molluscs. Wood extracts are mostly used as an ingredient of creams, lotions, shampoos (as emollients and for itch relief in skin disorders) and topical anticellulitis products.

PREPARATION AND DOSAGE The recommended daily dose of ivy leaf is 0.3 g per day, or 1.5 g twice per day (depending on the source).

ACTIVE INGREDIENTS The leaves contain 5-8% bidesmosidic saponins of oleanolic acid, hederagenin and bayogenin, known as hederasaponins or hederacosides B to I. Of these, hederasaponin C (also known as hederacoside C) is the main compound, with levels of up to 7%. In dried leaves the more potent monodesmosidic saponines can be formed upon hydrolysis. Also present are various phenolics, as well as polyacetylenes, typically falcarinol, falcarinone and 11-dehydrofalcarinol. Seeds contain large amounts of saponins and are considered to be toxic to humans.

PHARMACOLOGICAL EFFECTS The expectorant properties of the saponins can be explained by an indirect stimulation of the *nervus vagus* in the stomach. Several double-blind placebo-controlled studies have shown efficacy in chronic obstructive bronchitis, with few or no side effects at doses equivalent to 200 mg of crude drug per day (children) or 400 mg (adults). The saponins (or their monodesmoside derivatives) are cytotoxic and haemolytic in higher concentrations. Falcarinol is a skin allergen and is known from other Araliaceae, including *Schefflera* species.

STATUS Pharm.; Comm.E+; clinical studies+.

Hedera helix L.   family: Araliaceae

lierre grimpant, lierre commun (French); *Efeu* (German); *edera* (Italian); *hiedra* (Spanish)

Helichrysum arenarium

sandy everlasting

Antennaria dioica

Helichrysum arenarium

Helichrysum italicum

DESCRIPTION A small perennial herb with narrow, silver-hairy leaves and small, yellow flower heads arranged in cymes. It should not be confused with cat's ear flower, *Antennaria dioica*. The latter is a small, mat-forming perennial herb with silvery leaves and attractive pink or white flower heads borne in rounded clusters. Also well known is the curry plant, *H. italicum*– a shrubby species with narrow leaves and small, yellow flower heads used mainly as a culinary herb.

ORIGIN Central, eastern and southern Europe. The herb is wild-harvested in eastern Europe.

PARTS USED Flower heads, collected and dried before they open (*Helichrysi flos; synon. Flores Stoechados citrinae or Flores Gnaphalii arenarii*).

THERAPEUTIC CATEGORY Choleretic, diuretic.

USES AND PROPERTIES The herb is used for peptic discomfort and is also an additive to tea mixtures, mainly to improve their appearance. It is nevertheless a traditional diuretic tea that has value in the supportive treatment of cholecystitis and spastic disorders of the gall bladder and urinary tract. Extracts are included in commercial cholagogues. Cat's ear flower (*Antennaria dioica*) is also used in tea mixtures, mainly to treat liver complaints and diarrhoea, and as expectorants. The curry plant (*Helichrysum italicum*) has anti-inflammatory, antiviral and antiallergic activity and has been used to treat chronic chest ailments.

PREPARATION AND DOSAGE Tea is prepared with 3-4 g of the finely chopped flowers, and is taken three times a day.

ACTIVE INGREDIENTS *Helichrysum* flowers contain several flavonoids. Isosalipurposide, a chalcone, is responsible for the yellow colour of the bracts. It occurs with the bitter tasting naringenin, naringenin-5-O-diglucoside, helichrysin A, helichrysin B (=salipurposide) and various glycosides of apigenin, luteolin, kaempferol and quercetin. Also noteworthy is the presence of an unidentified antibacterial mixture known as arenarin, and bitter substances presumed to be sesquiterpenoid lactones.

PHARMACOLOGICAL EFFECTS The activity of the herb is poorly known and its use is based mainly on tradition but antibacterial, mild choleretic and spasmolytic effects have been recorded. It is also said to promote gastric and pancreatic secretions.

STATUS Pharm.; Comm.E+.

Helichrysum arenarium (L.) Moench.   family: Asteraceae

immortelle des sables (French); *Sand-Strohblume, Gelbes Katzenpfötchen* (German); *semprevivo, elicriso arenario* (Italian)

Herniaria glabra

smooth rupturewort • glabrous rupturewort • herniary

Herniaria glabra leaves and flowers

Herniaria glabra plant

Herniaria hirsuta

DESCRIPTION Rupturewort is a mat-forming, short-lived perennial herb with very small, inconspicuous leaves, flower and fruits. Two species are used, namely glabrous or smooth rupturewort (*H. glabra*) and hairy rupturewort (*H. hirsuta*). In *H. glabra* all parts are practically hairless and bright green, while the stems and leaves of *H. hirsuta* are greyish green and conspicuously hairy.

ORIGIN Europe and Asia (*H. glabra*) and central Europe, the Mediterranean region and North Africa (*H. hirsuta*). The herb is occasionally grown in gardens but commercial material is mostly wild-harvested.

PARTS USED Dried, aboveground parts (rupturewort herb – *Herniariae herba*) of both species.

THERAPEUTIC CATEGORY Traditional diuretic (urological).

USES AND PROPERTIES A traditional diuretic that is taken for kidney and bladder disorders. In folk medicine, it is used to treat chronic cystitis, urethritis, bladder tenesmus (straining in attempting to urinate) and ailments of the respiratory tract, arthritis, rheumatism and for "blood purification". The name *Herniaria* reflects the belief that the plant can heal hernias.

PREPARATION AND DOSAGE For use as diuretic, 1.5 g of the herb is added to cold water and boiled for a short time. A cupful is taken two or three times a day. Some commercial urological preparations and teas (kidney and bladder tea) contain rupturewort or extracts thereof.

ACTIVE INGREDIENTS Saponins are present in yields of up to 9%, with derivatives of medicagenic acid, 16α-hydroxymedicagenic acid and gypsogenic acid as main compounds. Flavonoids represent up to 1.2% of dry weight (mainly quercetin and isorhamnetin derivatives). Tannins and coumarins such as umbelliferone and herniarin are present in small amounts. The two species are closely similar but some quantitative differences in the major compounds can be expected.

PHARMACOLOGICAL EFFECTS The saponins and flavonoids are considered to be the main active ingredients but their pharmacological effects have not been studied. The herb is known to be weakly spasmolytic but its efficacy and therapeutic value in the treatment of disorders of the urinary tract have not yet been demonstrated by modern studies.

STATUS Traditional medicine; Pharm.; Comm.E+.

Herniaria glabra L.   family: Caryophyllaceae

herniaire (French); *Kahles Bruchkraut* (German); *erniaria* (Italian)

Hibiscus sabdariffa

hibiscus • red-sorrel • roselle • Jamaica sorrel

Hibiscus sabdariffa flower

Hibiscus sabdariffa leaves and flower

Hibiscus flowers (=dried calyces and epicalyces)

DESCRIPTION This hibiscus is an erect annual that can reach 4 m in height. It has lobed leaves and yellow flowers, each with a bright red, fleshy calyx and epicalyx (the epicalyx is a whorl of bracts that resemble a second row of sepals). The calyx and epicalyx are persistent and are collected in the fruiting stage. These edible and sweet-sour structures are known as "hibiscus flowers".

ORIGIN Africa (Angola): now cultivated in all tropical regions. The main producers are in North Africa, Mexico, India, Thailand and China.

PARTS USED Dried calyces and epicalyces (hibiscus flowers – *Hibisci flos*).

THERAPEUTIC CATEGORY Health tea.

USES AND PROPERTIES Hibiscus flower is mainly used in herbal tea – on its own as a sweet-sour, caffeine-free health drink, or more commonly in tea mixtures as a tasty and colourful additive. The health properties are therefore not the primary reason for the popularity of the tea, although it is traditionally used to treat appetite loss, colds, catarrh of the respiratory tract, circulatory ailments and as gentle expectorant, laxative and diuretic. Hibiscus flower is included in ointments (and decoctions intended for topical application) to treat allergic eczema and various other skin conditions.

PREPARATION AND DOSAGE A tea made of 1.5 g of herb in a cup of boiling water can be taken five to ten times per day.

ACTIVE INGREDIENTS In watery extracts, up to 15% mucilage polysaccharides and 2% pectins are present. Typical are organic acids (15–30%), such as the unique hibiscus acid, together with ascorbic, citric, malic, and tartaric acids. The polysaccharides are mainly of the arabinan and arabinogalactan type, and occur with galacturonic acid, rhamnose, galactose and arabinose. The deep red colour is due to 1.5% anthocyanins, including the 3-sambubiosides of delphinidin and cyanidin.

PHARMACOLOGICAL EFFECTS Sugars and acids contribute to the refreshing taste. The polysaccharides might have mild immune-modulating activity; they form a protective film on inflamed mucosal tissues. Anthocyanins provide colour and some antioxidant effects. The laxative effect can be explained by the presence of organic acids that cannot be resorbed in the intestines and therefore lead to water retention.

STATUS Traditional medicine; Pharm.; Comm.E+.

Hibiscus sabdariffa L.

family: Malvaceae

karkadé (French); *Hibiscus, Sabdariffa-Eibisch* (German); *carcade* (Italian)

Hoodia pilifera

hoodia • ghaap • South African "desert cactus"

Hoodia pilifera subsp. *pilifera*

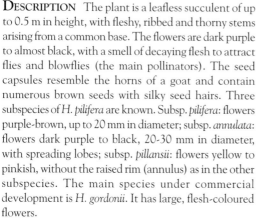

Hoodia pilifera subsp. *annulata*

Hoodia gordonii

DESCRIPTION The plant is a leafless succulent of up to 0.5 m in height, with fleshy, ribbed and thorny stems arising from a common base. The flowers are dark purple to almost black, with a smell of decaying flesh to attract flies and blowflies (the main pollinators). The seed capsules resemble the horns of a goat and contain numerous brown seeds with silky seed hairs. Three subspecies of *H. pilifera* are known. Subsp. *pilifera*: flowers purple-brown, up to 20 mm in diameter; subsp. *annulata*: flowers dark purple to black, 20-30 mm in diameter, with spreading lobes; subsp. *pillansii*: flowers yellow to pinkish, without the raised rim (annulus) as in the other subspecies. The main species under commercial development is *H. gordonii*. It has large, flesh-coloured flowers.

ORIGIN Southern Africa (arid parts). Hoodia is grown on an experimental scale and is not yet fully commercialised.

PARTS USED The fleshy stems.

THERAPEUTIC CATEGORY Appetite suppressant.

USES AND PROPERTIES The stems of *Hoodia* species and several other succulents known as carrion flowers or stapeliads (locally referred to as "ghaap") are tradi-tionally used by the Khoi-San herders of South Africa and Namibia as appetite and thirst suppressants. The appetite suppressant principle has been isolated, iden-tified and patented and is currently being studied with the aim of developing an anti-obesity drug.

PREPARATION AND DOSAGE A small piece of the stem is peeled to remove the thorns and is eaten fresh. The optimal dose of the active compound is not yet known.

ACTIVE INGREDIENTS Like many members of the family, these plants contain cardiac glycosides or bio-chemically related compounds, such as pregnane de-rivatives. The main active compound in *Hoodia* is a pregnane glycoside known as P57.

PHARMACOLOGICAL EFFECTS P57 has powerful appetite-suppressant effects that were demonstrated in animal experiments. Clinical trials are underway to determine the safety and efficacy of the isolated com-pound.

NOTES Another potential natural slimming agent is the fruit rind of the Malabar tamarind, *Garcinia cam-bogia* (family Clusiaceae).

STATUS Traditional medicine (functional food); clinical studies+.

Hoodia pilifera (L.f.) Plowes (=*Trichocaulon piliferum* L.f.)   family: Apocynaceae
hoodia (French); *Hoodia* (German); *hoodia* (Italian)

Humulus lupulus

hop plant

Humulus lupulus plants

Humulus lupulus leaves and female flower clusters

DESCRIPTION A perennial creeper (vine) of up to 10 m in height with branches emerging each year from a woody rhizome or crown. The leaves are deeply lobed, with toothed margins. Male and female flowers occur on separate plants (to prevent pollination, the males are usually eradicated; females are propagated vegetatively). Hops is the cone-like female flower cluster, with several small flowers hidden by overlapping, leafy structures (bracts and bracteoles; they bear numerous orange-yellow glands, producing a resinous exudate).

ORIGIN Northern temperate areas (Asia, Europe and North America). Hop plants have been cultivated for centuries to provide hops for beer brewing.

PARTS USED Hops – the dried, cone-like female flower clusters (*Lupuli strobulus*) or hops grains (the small glands obtained by sieving; *Lupuli glandula*).

THERAPEUTIC CATEGORY Sedative, bitter tonic (*amarum*).

USES AND PROPERTIES Hops has a long history of use as a traditional bitter tonic and diuretic. In modern times, however, the main emphasis is on the sedative and calming effects. It is used to treat mood and sleep disturbances, anxiety and restlessness.

PREPARATION AND DOSAGE A dose of 0.5 g, taken as an infusion, is recommended. Hops or extracts thereof have become popular as an ingredient of sleep-promoting teas and especially of numerous sedative remedies.

ACTIVE INGREDIENTS The bitter substances in hops (up to 5%) are prenylated derivatives of 1-acyl-phloroglucinol and include lupulone and humulone as main compounds. Upon storage, they are slowly split through oxidation to produce a C_5-alcohol, 2-methyl-3-buten-2-ol. Hops also contains several phenolics (2-4%), such as rutin, quercetrin, and proanthocyanidins, as well as up to 1% essential oil, with caryophyllene, humulene and β-myrcene as main terpenoids.

PHARMACOLOGICAL EFFECTS The sedative activity appears to be due to 2-methyl-3-buten-2-ol that is already present in the drug or which is formed internally after oral intake of hops. Humulone and lupulone are known to be antibacterial (they act as preservatives in beer, but have little effect on yeasts and fungi) and are probably oestrogenic. The bitter compounds stimulate appetite and gastric secretions.

STATUS Traditional medicine; Pharm.; Comm.E+; ESCOP 4.

Humulus lupulus L.

family: Cannabaceae

houblon (French); *Hopfen* (German); *luppolo* (Italian); *lupulo* (Spanish)

Hydrastis canadensis

goldenseal

Hydrastis canadensis leaves and flower

Hydrastis canadensis plant with fruit

DESCRIPTION Goldenseal is a perennial herb with a few stems bearing only one to three leaves that emerge every year from a creeping rhizome below the ground. The large, soft leaves are deeply divided into five segments and have toothed margins. Inconspicuous, solitary green and white flowers are produced above the leaves. They soon develop into a small, red, inedible, raspberry-like fruit.

ORIGIN North America (southern Canada and the USA). The plants are mainly wild-harvested in nature and there is some concern about the conservation status of the plant.

PARTS USED Dried rhizome and root (*Hydrastis rhizoma*).

THERAPEUTIC CATEGORY Haemostatic, stomachic, laxative.

USES AND PROPERTIES Goldenseal is mainly used as a haemostatic to stop bleeding (e.g. after birth) and is employed as a substitute for ergot alkaloids. It is also taken as an antibacterial remedy to stop diarrhoea, and as a bitter tonic, digestive stimulant, mild laxative, antihaemorrhagic and general medicine for numerous other complaints. It is externally used to treat stomatitis.

PREPARATION AND DOSAGE An infusion of 0.5-1 g of dried herb is taken three times a day. Liquid extracts and tinctures are also popular, as are numerous preparations with the pure herb or combinations.

ACTIVE INGREDIENTS The main active ingredients are isoquinoline alkaloids: hydrastine (1.5-4% of dry weight of the root) and berberine (up to 6%), canadine (1%) and some other minor compounds.

PHARMACOLOGICAL EFFECTS Most of the activity of the drug is ascribed to the alkaloids – hydrastine and berberine. They possess a large number of pharmacological activities, including the inhibition of several receptors and enzymes. The antimicrobial effects of berberine and hydrastine (which are mainly caused by DNA intercalation) explain the main use of goldenseal as antidiarrhoeal medicine and its use in eye drops.

NOTES It has been suggested that, in the interest of conservation, barberry (*Berberis vulgaris*) and Oregon grape (*Mahonia aquifolium*) should be investigated as sustainable natural sources of berberine rather than *Hydrastis*. Since the alkaloids modulate receptors in the uterus, this drug should not be taken during pregnancy.

STATUS Traditional medicine.

Hydrastis canadensis L.   family: Ranunculaceae

hydrastis (French); *Kanadische Gelbwurzel* (German); *sigillo d'oro* (Italian)

Hyoscyamus niger

henbane

Hyoscyamus niger

Hyoscyamus albus

DESCRIPTION Henbane is an annual or biennial herb of up to 0.5 m in height, with soft hairy stems bearing pale green, lobed and hairy leaves. The calyx is bell-like and toothed, and the petals are greyish yellow with dark purple veins towards their bases. Less commonly used are European henbane or white henbane (*H. albus*) and Egyptian henbane (*H. muticus*). The latter occurs from Egypt to Iran, has a relatively high alkaloid content of up to 1% or more and is therefore used as a commercial source of tropane alkaloids.

ORIGIN Europe and Asia (*H. niger*). The plant is a common weed of disturbed places and is naturalised in North America.

PARTS USED Leaves (*Hyoscyami folium*). Seeds (*Hyoscyami semen*) or roots (*Hyoscyami radix*) are also used to some extent.

THERAPEUTIC CATEGORY Antispasmodic, narcotic.

USES AND PROPERTIES Henbane leaf and the isolated hyoscyamine (and atropine, its racemate) are used in modern phytotherapy mainly to treat spasms of the gastrointestinal tract. It is sometimes included as a sedative in herbal mixtures and combination products. The leaves were formerly smoked to treat asthma (hyoscyamine has bronchodilatory effects), in the same way as *Atropa* leaf or *Datura* leaf. Henbane has a long and interesting history (as a narcotic, e.g. during surgery, and as hallucinogen in witchcraft). It has been used since ancient times to treat pain, toothache and nervous disorders such as mania and hysteria.

PREPARATION AND DOSAGE Standardised henbane powder (containing 0.5-0.7 mg total alkaloid) and pure hyoscyamine are used. Recommended daily dose: 3 g of powder (1.5-2.1 mg total alkaloid); maximum single dose: 1 g of powder (0.5-0.7 mg total alkaloid).

ACTIVE INGREDIENTS The active compounds are the tropane alkaloids hyoscyamine (the major compound) and scopolamine (also in high yield). Alkaloids occur in concentrations of 0.04-0.15% of dry weight in the leaves and up to 0.3% in the seeds. Cases of accidental or deliberate poisoning are rare.

PHARMACOLOGICAL EFFECTS Tropane alkaloids are parasympatholytics and have a spasmolytic and sedative effect on the central nervous system (see details under *Atropa* and *Datura*).

STATUS Trad. medicine; modern medicine: atropine, scopolamine; Pharm.; Comm.E+; clinical studies+.

Hyoscyamus niger L.   family: Solanaceae

jusquiame noire (French); *Bilsenkraut* (German); *giusquiamo nero* (Italian): *veleño negro* (Spanish)

Hypericum perforatum

St. John's wort • perforate St. John's wort

Hypericum perforatum plant

Hypericum perforatum flowers

DESCRIPTION A perennial herb or shrublet (up to 0.6 m), with small, gland-dotted leaves. Oil glands are visible as translucent dots, hence the botanical name "*perforatum*". The bright yellow flowers have numerous stamens and are dotted with small dark-coloured glands.

ORIGIN Europe and Asia; naturalised (e.g. North America, Australia). Selected strains are cultivated.

PARTS USED Dried flowering tops (St. John's wort – *Hyperici herba*).

THERAPEUTIC CATEGORY Antidepressant, wound-healing.

USES AND PROPERTIES Used for healing since ancient times but today mainly for treating mild depression, mood disturbances, anxiety and nervous conditions. It is popular to treat wounds and burns; inflammations of stomach and intestines; against internal worms.

PREPARATION AND DOSAGE Dry herb is sometimes used (daily dose 2-4 g; by infusion three times per day), but more often extracts. To be effective, they should contain 0.1-0.3% hypericin and 1-6% hyperforin (see below). Hypericum oil, which is made by macerating fresh flowers in wheatgerm oil or olive oil, is traditionally used on wounds and burns.

ACTIVE INGREDIENTS *Hypericum* is rich in phenolic compounds and various terpenoids but the chemical constituents of special interest are hyperforin (a phloroglucinol derivative) and hypericin (a dianthrone). The latter occurs with smaller quantities of pseudohypericin, protohypericin and others, and gives the red colour to the isolated oil.

PHARMACOLOGICAL EFFECTS Both hypericin and hyperforin are apparently responsible for a calming and mild antidepressant effect (supported by clinical studies). Whereas a MAO inhibiting activity was considered formerly, today an inhibition of neurotransmitter re-uptake provides a more plausible hypothesis. Hypericin is a photodynamic sensitiser and may cause phototoxic effects in fair-skinned people (but only at very high doses and in the presence of sunlight). Experiments have also shown anti-viral effects, of which a suppression of the HIV-1 virus created considerable interest. Hyperforin is related to the antimicrobial compounds in hops and likewise shows antibacterial effects (important for wound-healing).

STATUS Pharm.; Comm.E+; ESCOP 1; WHO 2; clinical studies+.

Hypericum perforatum L.   family: Clusiaceae or Hypericaceae

millepertuis perforé (French); *Echtes Johanniskraut, Tüpfel-Johanniskraut* (German); *iperico, erba di San Giovanni* (Italian)

Hypoxis hemerocallidea

hypoxis • star flower • "African potato"

Hypoxis hemerocallidea plant

Hypoxis hemerocallidea leaves and flowers

Hypoxis hemerocallidea corms

DESCRIPTION A tuberous perennial with broad, strap-shaped, slightly hairy leaves that are arranged one above the other to form three distinct groups spreading outwards from the centre of the plant. Bright yellow, star-shaped flowers are borne on slender stalks.

ORIGIN Southern Africa. All material is wild-harvested.

PARTS USED The tuberous rootstock (corm), which is blackish outside and yellow within when freshly cut.

THERAPEUTIC CATEGORY Tonic; prostate hyperplasia.

USES AND PROPERTIES Hypoxis was once used in preparations to treat prostate hypertrophy. These products no longer contain any Hypoxis, however, but only isolated phytosterols from other sources. Hypoxis corms or extracts are used to a limited extent as general tonics in African traditional medicine (e.g. decoctions have been given to weak children) and the juice is applied to burns. Stems and leaves are mixed with other ingredients to treat prostate problems and urinary infections.

PREPARATION AND DOSAGE Commercial preparations and traditional decoctions contain the equivalent of about 2-4 g of dry root in a daily dose. Phytomedicines marketed as general tonics and uro-logical tonics nowadays contain pure phytosterols and no longer Hypoxis extracts. The daily dose is about 30-60 mg per day.

ACTIVE INGREDIENTS The activity of Hypoxis against prostatic hyperplasia is ascribed to phytosterols (β-sitosterol and phytosterol glycosides such as sitosterolin). The medicinal value is also associated with hypoxoside and its aglycone, rooperol.

PHARMACOLOGICAL EFFECTS The activity of sitosterols is ascribed to the inhibition of 5α-reductase and aromatase or to decreased binding of dihydro-testosterone within the prostate. An inhibition of prostaglandins has also been postulated which could explain the effects seen in the treatment of chronic polyarthritis. Sceptics point out that 150-300 mg of sitosterol is ingested daily in a normal diet, which is several times more than the amount recommended for dietary supplements. Anti-cancer, anti-HIV and anti-inflammatory activities are ascribed to rooperol. It is markedly anti-mutagenic and cytotoxic to cancer cells but the results of clinical studies in cancer treatment were disappointing.

STATUS Traditional medicine; clinical studies+.

Hypoxis hemerocallidea Fisch. & C.A.Mey. (=H. rooperi S.Moore)　　　family: Hypoxidaceae
hypoxis (French); Hypoxis (German); hypoxis (Italian); inkomfe (Zulu)

Hyssopus officinalis

hyssop

Hyssopus officinalis plant

Hyssopus officinalis flowers

DESCRIPTION Hyssop is an erect perennial herb of up to 0.6 m in height, with square stems, small oblong leaves and attractive, deep blue flowers arranged in oblong, terminal clusters. Cultivars with pale blue, violet, pink or white flowers are sometimes encountered.

ORIGIN Southern and southeastern Europe. The plant is commonly cultivated in herb gardens. The biblical hyssop (referred to at the Crucifixion, for example) is *Origanum syriacum*, a species from the Middle East. See also *O. vulgare* and *O. dictamnus*.

PARTS USED Fresh or dried aboveground parts, collected during flowering (hyssop herb – *Hyssopi herba*), or the essential oil obtained by steam distillation (hyssop oil – *Hyssopi aetheroleum*).

THERAPEUTIC CATEGORY Expectorant, antiseptic, stimulant.

USES AND PROPERTIES Hyssop herb and oil are traditionally used to treat respiratory ailments (coughs, bronchial inflammation and nasal congestion). The oil is a gentle stimulant of circulation and is also used in eyewashes and as a gargle.

PREPARATION AND DOSAGE Weak infusions of the herb can be taken or the oil is applied as chest rubs to treat congestion and coughs. Hyssop extracts and hyssop oil are included in various commercial cough and catarrh mixtures.

ACTIVE INGREDIENTS Hyssop is rich in flavonoids (e.g. 6–9% diosmin) and phenolic acids (including rosmarinic acid), diterpenoid lactones (marrubiin) and triterpenoids (oleanolic acid). The essential oil (up to 1% of dry weight) contains two ketones (pinocamphone and isopinocamphone) as main constituents.

PHARMACOLOGICAL EFFECTS Expectorant properties are linked to the presence of marrubiin, while the antiseptic, spasmolytic and stimulant effects are ascribed to the essential oil. Pinocamphone and isopinocamphone are neurotoxic and thus similar to thujone. They are thought to inhibit cell respiration, resulting in spasms and epileptic fits at toxic doses. The essential oil should not be taken internally except in dilute form.

NOTES Hyssop is popular as a culinary herb that is added in small quantities to salads, soups, sauces and meat dishes. It is thought to aid digestion, especially when eaten with oily foods.

STATUS Traditional medicine.

Hyssopus officinalis L.

family: Lamiaceae

hysope (French); Ysop (German); issopo (Italian)

177

Iberis amara

bitter candytuft • white candytuft • clown's mustard plant

Iberis amara plant

Iberis amara flowers

DESCRIPTION Bitter candytuft is an annual (or rarely biennial) herb with oblong, toothed leaves, attractive white or purplish flowers arranged in many-flowered clusters and characteristic flat, rounded dry fruits.

ORIGIN Europe (mainly the Mediterranean region, including Algeria); commonly cultivated as an ornamental plant and commercially on a relatively small scale for medicinal purposes.

PARTS USED Fresh flowering plant (*Iberidis herba*), rarely also the seeds.

THERAPEUTIC CATEGORY Bitter tonic (*amarum*); choleretic.

USES AND PROPERTIES The herb or the seeds are used in folk medicine as bitter tonics to stimulate the secretion of gastric juices and also for their choleretic effects. Numerous other traditional uses, covering a wide range of indications, have been recorded. It is included (with eight other herbs) in a liquid product known as Iberogast™ that is used for the treatment of dyspeptic complaints and various other ailments of the gastrointestinal tract.

PREPARATION AND DOSAGE Dosage information for the herb or seeds is not available. Up to 20 drops of a liquid preparation in a glass of warm water are used three times a day, taken before or during a meal.

ACTIVE INGREDIENTS Iberis herb contains bitter triterpenoids (mainly cucurbitacins E and I), flavonoids (various glycosides of kaempferol and quercetin), glucosinolates (glucoiberin and other minor glycosides), the corresponding isothiocyanates, formed upon enzymatic hydrolysis, and amines (mainly 3-methylthio-N-propylamine).

PHARMACOLOGICAL EFFECTS Experiments have shown antispasmodic, anti-ulcerogenic, anti-exudative, anti-inflammatory and antimicrobial activities. A clinical study indicated some benefit in patients with irritable colon but the results were not statistically significant. In addition to the obvious bitter tonic effects, the bitter cucurbitacins may possibly have corticomimetic activity. The antiviral, antibacterial and antifungal properties of isothiocyanates (mustard oil) are associated with their ability to form covalent bonds with proteins (see *Tropaeolum*).

STATUS Traditional medicine.

Iberis amara L.   family: Brassicaceae

ibéris amer, thlaspi blanc (French); *Bittere Schleifenblume, Bitterer Bauernsenf* (German); *iberide bianca* (Italian)

Ilex paraguariensis

maté

Ilex paraguariensis leaves

Ilex paraguariensis shrub

Ilex vomitoria

DESCRIPTION Maté is an evergreen shrub or tree with bright green, oblong, leathery leaves, small white flowers and spherical red berries.

ORIGIN South America (Brazil). The tree is grown commercially mainly in Brazil but also in Argentina and Paraguay.

PARTS USED Dried leaves (*Mate folium; synon. Herba Ilicis paraguariensis*).

THERAPEUTIC CATEGORY Stimulant, diuretic.

USES AND PROPERTIES Maté is used as a diuretic and to overcome mental and physical fatigue. It is considered to be a tonic, and stimulant, and is commonly used as a natural slimming remedy. Some people simply enjoy maté as a refreshing alternative to tea or coffee. In South America, the traditional way to drink the infusion is to suck it up from a small gourd, through a silver tube (fitted with a strainer at the bottom).

PREPARATION AND DOSAGE Hot water is poured over about 3 g of dried leaves and allowed to steep briefly before it is strained. As with ordinary tea, even brief boiling will result in an astringent taste because the tannins will also be dissolved. The herb is available in crude form or in a wide range of herbal tea mixtures (kidney and bladder tea, laxative tea, headache tea, and so on).

ACTIVE INGREDIENTS The main active component is caffeine, the well-known alkaloidal stimulant in tea and coffee. It occurs in maté at a level of up to 2% of dry weight. Minor alkaloids are theobromine (up to 0.4%) and traces of theophylline. Also present are phenolic substances (12% chlorogenic acid, 4-16% condensed catechols) together with flavonoids, triterpene saponins and 0.3% essential oils.

PHARMACOLOGICAL EFFECTS The pharmacological activity of caffeine is well known: it binds to adenosine receptors and inhibits phosphodiesterase. These molecular interactions lead to a stimulation of the central nervous system, diuresis, respiration and smooth muscle relaxation. High doses can lead to undesirable side effects such as anxiety, palpitations and sleeplessness.

NOTES Indians in the southeastern USA brew a ceremonial tea (*casseena*) from leaves of *Ilex vomitoria*.

STATUS Traditional medicine; Pharm.; Comm.E+.

Ilex paraguariensis A.St.-Hil.

family: Aquifoliaceae

maté (French); Mate (German); *matè* (Italian); *yerba mate* (Spanish)

Illicium verum

star anise • Chinese anise

Illicium verum leaves

Illicium verum fruits

DESCRIPTION An evergreen small tree of up to 10 m in height, with dark green simple leaves and attractive yellowish green to reddish, solitary flowers. The distinctive star-shaped fruits are made up of eight separate carpels that each form a small capsule with a single, pale brown, shiny seed inside. Oil cells are in the pericarp. Star anise can be confused with Japanese anise, also known as bastard anise or *shikimi* (*Illicium anisatum*) – a toxic adulterant of star anise. It differs in the more irregular shape, smaller size, more yellowish colour and the broader follicles that have distinctly curved tips.

ORIGIN Northeastern Vietnam and southeastern China (*I. verum*) or Japan and Korea (*I. anisatum*). The plant is no longer found in nature but it is widely cultivated in China, Japan and India to the Philippines.

PARTS USED Ripe fruit or syncarp (star anise fruit – *Anisi stellati fructus*).

THERAPEUTIC CATEGORY Expectorant, antispasmodic (stomachic).

USES AND PROPERTIES Star anise is used to treat respiratory ailments (notably inflammation of the respiratory tract), and also dyspepsia (stomach discomfort, indigestion, bloating).

PREPARATION AND DOSAGE The average daily dose is about 3 g of the fruit, or 0.3 g of the essential oil.

ACTIVE INGREDIENTS Star anise is rich in an essential oil that can be present in concentrations of up to 8% of dry weight. It is dominated by one main component, *trans*-anethole (80-90%), occurring with anisaldehyde, methylchavicol (= estragole) and some monoterpenoids (α-pinene, limonene and linalool). Real anis oil (see *Pimpinella anisum*) does not have these monoterpenoids. Japanese anise has myristicin (absent in star anise) and sesquiterpene lactones such as anisatin, neoanisatin and pseudoanisatin, as well as shikimic acid (18%).

PHARMACOLOGICAL EFFECTS The fruits have proven antispasmodic and carminative properties. Anise-flavoured oils increase the tone and contraction of the smooth intestine muscles. Anisatin has convulsive properties and is responsible for toxic effects in *I. anisatum*.

NOTES Star anise is a spice and the oil is sometimes used in beverages and perfumes instead of the more expensive anise oil.

STATUS Traditional medicine; Pharm.; Comm.E+.

Illicium verum Hook.f.

family: Illiciaceae

ba jiao hui xian (Chinese); *badiane de Chine, anis étoilé* (French); *Echter Sternanis* (German); *anice stellato* (Italian); *anis estallado* (Spanish)

Inula helenium

elecampane • elfdock

Inula helenium plant

Inula helenium flower head

DESCRIPTION A large, leafy perennial herb of up to 2.5 m in height, with erect stems bearing broad, irregularly toothed leaves and large, yellow flower heads. The large heads (up to 80 mm in diameter) and slender ligulate florets are quite distinct.

ORIGIN Asia Minor and southeastern Europe; naturalised in Europe, North America and eastern Asia; cultivated in China and eastern Europe.

PARTS USED Dried rhizomes and roots of two to three-year-old cultivated plants (elecampane – *Helenii rhizoma; synon. Radix inulae*).

THERAPEUTIC CATEGORY Expectorant.

USES AND PROPERTIES Elecampane is mostly used as an expectorant for the treatment of coughs (including pertussis) and bronchial catarrh. It is a traditional bitter tonic, stomachic, carminative, cholagogue, diaphoretic and diuretic. The root (or isolated alantolactone, see below) is used as an anthelmintic against several intestinal parasites and for infections of the urinary tract. Externally, extracts are applied as antiseptic to treat skin conditions.

PREPARATION AND DOSAGE As an expectorant, 1-4 g of chopped material is taken as tea three or four times per day. Alantolactone is taken in doses of 300 mg for adults and 50-200 mg for children, daily for two five-day courses (with an interval of 10 days between courses). Also in use is the essential oil.

ACTIVE INGREDIENTS The rhizomes and roots contain a mixture of sesquiterpene lactones often referred to as "helenin" or "elecampane camphor". These compounds also occur in the volatile oil (1-3%) (with alantolactone and some degradation products; mainly alantol and alantic acid). Also present are inulin (up to 44%), polyacetylenes, phytosterols and triterpenoids.

PHARMACOLOGICAL EFFECTS Experiments have shown antibiotic, diuretic, choleretic and secretolytic activities (probably due to the lactones – mainly alantolactone and isoalantolactone).

WARNING The free methylene group of alantolactone is highly reactive and can form covalent bonds with proteins and nucleic acids. The lactones in the herb may cause allergic reactions when applied to the skin.

NOTES *Helianthus tuberosus* (also Asteraceae) is an important source of inulin.

STATUS Traditional medicine; Pharm.

Inula helenium L.   family: Asteraceae

aunée (French); *Echter Alant* (German); *enula campana* (Italian); *enula campana* (Spanish)

Iris germanica

garden iris • common German flag

Iris florentina flower

Iris germanica plant

Orris root

DESCRIPTION Orris is derived from various forms of the common garden iris and related species. These are all perennial herbs with fans of strap-shaped leaves growing from a creeping, fleshy, branched rhizome. A robust flowering stalk of up to 0.8 m in height emerges in the spring, bearing several large and attractive mauve and violet flowers. The flowers are easily recognised by their three erect petals (standards), the three pendant petals (falls) and three broad style-branches that resemble petals. In addition to I. *germanica*, orris is also obtained from I. *florentina* – Florentine iris, sometimes referred to as I. *germanica* var. *florentina* (it has white or cream-coloured flowers) – and I. *pallida* – Dalmatian iris.

ORIGIN Europe to the Ural Mountains.

PARTS USED The peeled and cut rhizome, known as orris root (*Iridis rhizoma*). It is interesting to note that the distinct fragrance (like violets) only develops when the dried product is stored.

THERAPEUTIC CATEGORY Traditional expectorant and emulcent.

USES AND PROPERTIES Orris root is not used on its own, but is included in numerous cough remedies and antitussive medicines (cough teas, bronchial teas). It is added to potpourris as a fixative and was once used to powder wigs and hair. Some liqueurs, toothpastes, and tooth powders are flavoured with orris root. Small children were given iris roots to chew in times when they developed new teeth.

PREPARATION AND DOSAGE The dry herb is not used on its own.

ACTIVE INGREDIENTS Several classes of compounds are present: triterpenes (including α- and β-irigermanal), isoflavones (including irilone and irisolone), aromatic aldehydes and sesquiterpenoids. Of special interest is the essential oil, which contains irone (10-20%) as the main fragrant compound (it smells like violets, and is present in numerous isomers and stereoisomers). The irones develop only after long-term (2-3 year) storage of the dried root, and are released as byproducts of the oxidative degradation of bicyclic triterpenoids known as iridals (mainly iripallidal and iriflorentinal). Polysaccharides (starch, mucilages) are present (up to 50%).

PHARMACOLOGICAL EFFECTS The traditional uses have not yet been substantiated by scientific studies.

STATUS Traditional medicine; Pharm.

Iris germanica L.   family: Iridaceae

iris commun, iris d'Allemagne (French); *Deutsche Schwertlilie* (German); *iris* (Italian)

Juglans regia

walnut • English walnut • Black Sea walnut

Juglans regia

Juglans regia fruit

Juglans nigra

DESCRIPTION Walnut is a tree of up to 25 m in height, with large compound leaves bearing five to nine leaflets. The fruit is a drupe with a fleshy outer pericarp and a bony endocarp that encloses the two edible cotyledons (known as walnuts). Other sources of nuts are the black walnut or American walnut (*J. nigra*) and the butternut (*J. cinerea*).

ORIGIN Asia Minor; exact origin uncertain, it has been cultivated for centuries. Black walnut and butternut both occur in the eastern parts of the USA.

PARTS USED Leaves (walnut leaf – *Juglandis folium* or the fruit husks – *Juglandis fructus cortex*).

THERAPEUTIC CATEGORY Astringent, anti-diarrhoeal.

USES AND PROPERTIES Walnut (and butternut) is mostly applied topically (baths, washes) for skin ailments, including acne, eczema, fungal infections, inflammation, sunburn, perspiration, itchy scalp and ulcers. It has been used to treat infections of the mouth and throat, gastrointestinal ailments and diarrhoea. Infusions are taken orally as supportive treatment for skin problems. Decoctions are traditionally used against bedbugs and lice. The edible seeds contain high amounts of linoleic acid, an important dietary component.

PREPARATION AND DOSAGE An infusion is made by heating 1.5 g of the herb in a cup of water to boiling point. For dressings or lotions, a decoction of 5 g in 200 ml water is recommended.

ACTIVE INGREDIENTS The leaves contain tannins (mainly ellagitannins and catechols) at concentrations of about 10%, together with various flavonoids (3-4%) and organic acids. The naphthoquinone juglone (5-hydroxy-1,4-naphthoquinone) and hydrojuglone are present in the form of glycosides. The brown and black pigments that form when walnuts are damaged are unstable polymers of juglone (therefore they do not occur in high levels in the dried leaves). Small amounts of essential oil are present, containing germacrene D as the main constituent.

PHARMACOLOGICAL EFFECTS The value of walnut leaf to treat skin disorders is mainly ascribed to the tannins (astringent, anti-inflammatory, antimicrobial) but also to juglone and germacrene D, all of which have antimicrobial activity.

STATUS Traditional medicine; Pharm.; Comm.E+.

Juglans regia L.   family: Juglandaceae
noyer royal (French); *Walnuss* (German); *noce* (Italian)

Juniperus communis

Juniper

Juniperus communis leaves and fleshy cones

Juniperus communis trees

Juniperus communis foliage

DESCRIPTION A shrub or small tree, usually up to 5 m in height, with densely crowded needle-like leaves, inconspicuous male and female flowers on separate plants, and small, spherical, blue to black, fleshy, berry-like cones.

ORIGIN North temperate region (Europe, Asia and North America); protected in parts of central Europe but berries are wild-harvested in several countries.

PARTS USED Ripe, fresh or dried female cones, commonly referred to as berries (*Juniperi fructus*) and rarely also dried wood chips.

THERAPEUTIC CATEGORY Diuretic, antiseptic, antirheumatic.

USES AND PROPERTIES Fruits are traditionally used as diuretic and as urinary antiseptic (in case of pyeletis and cystitis), but also as stomachic, carminative and for dyspepsia. Juniper berries are best known for their use in flavouring gin (from *genever*, the Dutch word for juniper). External applications of the essential oils lead to skin irritation and in consequence to an enhanced blood circulation.

PREPARATION AND DOSAGE An infusion is made with 0.5 g freshly crushed berries in 150 ml water. Dry extracts of the wood are included in various diuretic and urological teas and preparations. The essential oil from the fruit is sometimes used, or juniper spirit, which is a mixture of 0.5 g juniper oil in 100 g ethanol-water (2:1), containing 0.1% camphor.

ACTIVE INGREDIENTS The essential oil (up to 2%) contains mainly α- and β-pinene (80%), sabinene, limonene, terpinen-4-ol, borneol and geraniol, together with sesquiterpenes (including α- and β-cadinene). Furthermore, phenolics (3-4%) with flavonoids, catechol tannins and proanthocyanins are present in the fruits. The wood contains unusual diterpenes, such as communis acid, sugiol and xanthoperol, as well as sesquiterpenes, and lignans (such as the cytotoxic podophyllotoxin).

PHARMACOLOGICAL EFFECTS Terpinen-4-ol is considered to be the main diuretic compound and is known to be non-irritant. Because of other compounds, however, the essential oil is not considered to be a safe diuretic, because it works through irritation of the kidney and may cause hematuria. The phenolic compounds are potentially active as antioxidants and may contribute to some extent to the medicinal value of juniper berry.

STATUS Traditional medicine; Pharm.; Comm.E+; ESCOP 3.

Juniperus communis L.   family: Cupressaceae

geniévrier (French); *Gewöhnlicher Wacholder* (German); *ginepro* (Italian); *enebro común* (Spanish)

Kigelia africana

sausage tree

Kigelia africana flowers

Kigelia africana fruits

DESCRIPTION A large, rounded tree of about 12 m in height, with a thick trunk, smooth grey bark, compound leaves with seven to 11 leaflets, very large, attractive, maroon-coloured flowers borne on pendulous stalks (adapted for pollination by bats). The enormous, greyish brown, sausage-shaped fruits are up to 1 m in length and contain a fibrous pulp and numerous seeds.

ORIGIN Tropical Africa; trees are sometimes planted in garden and parks but the medicinal material is wild-collected.

PARTS USED The fruits, rarely the bark.

THERAPEUTIC CATEGORY Wound-healing, skin care.

USES AND PROPERTIES Extracts of the fruit have become popular as an ingredient of commercial skin care products, considered to be of value in the prevention and treatment of sunburn, solar keratoses, eczema, psoriasis, skin pigmentation and even certain types of cancers. There are countless vernacular names and medicinal uses in African traditional medicine. The dried fruit is powdered and used as a dressing for ulcers, sores, syphilis and is also applied locally for rheumatism. Bark or fruit decoctions are commonly used orally or as enema for treating stomach ailments in children.

PREPARATION AND DOSAGE Decoctions are used, but exact dosages are not recorded.

ACTIVE INGREDIENTS The roots and bark have the naphthoquinone lapachol and the dihydroisocoumarin kigelin as major compounds, together with several catalpol-type iridoids (specioside, verminoside, minecoside) and a breakdown product, norviburtinal. Several other compounds, including kigelinone, pinnatal, isopinnatal, stigmasterol, β-sitosterol and γ-sitosterol have been isolated from the bark, roots or fruits.

PHARMACOLOGICAL EFFECTS Naphthoquinones (especially kigelinone and isopinnatal) and the various dihydroisocoumarins (such as kigelin) and their glycosides are antimicrobial and have antifungal activity (including activity against *Candida*). In addition, norviburtinal showed cytotoxic effects against cultured melanoma cells. The reported anti-inflammatory effects could be due to iridoid glycosides or their metabolites, since they are known to interfere with the formation of prostaglandins (that enhances inflammation and pain).

STATUS Traditional medicine.

Kigelia africana (Lam.) Benth.   family: Bignoniaceae

kigelia (French); *Leberwurstbaum* (German); *kigelia* (Italian)

Krameria lappacea

rhatany • Peruvian rhatany

Krameria lappacea leaves and flowers

DESCRIPTION A branched low shrub of up to 1 m in height, with small, silky hairy leaves. The small, solitary, purplish red flowers are borne in the leaf axils. They have four hairy sepals that are purple inside and four reddish purple to pink petals. The plant was previously known as *Krameria triandra* and will be found under this name in most literature sources.

ORIGIN South America (Andes of Bolivia, Ecuador and Peru). The roots are wild-harvested.

PARTS USED Dried roots (rhatany root – *Ratanhiae radix*).

THERAPEUTIC CATEGORY Astringent, anti-diarrhoeal.

USES AND PROPERTIES Rhatany root is used mainly to treat diarrhoea, mucosal infections of the mouth and throat, and also various problems associated with vascular insufficiency (including haemorrhage, wounds, burns, capillary fragility, haemorrhoids). Preparations of the dried roots are used in homoeopathy, for example to treat haemorrhoidal ailments associated with constipation.

PREPARATION AND DOSAGE A decoction is made by boiling 1.5-2 g of the root for 10-15 minutes. The tincture, however, is more popular. Five to ten drops in a glass of water can be taken orally or gargled two or three times per day. The undiluted tincture (often mixed with tincture of myrrh) can be used as an oral paint to treat inflammation of the gums, tongue and throat.

ACTIVE INGREDIENTS Condensed tannins are present in yields of up to 15%, mainly localised in the root bark. They occur as oligomeric proanthocyanidins and prodelphinidins in a ratio of 2:1 (mostly as tetramers). Also of interest are neolignans or so-called ratanhia phenols, which are composed of two phenylpropanoid units. Polymeric phenols form "ratanhia-red", a phlobaphen.

PHARMACOLOGICAL EFFECTS Rhatany root has proven antibacterial and antifungal activity (ascribed mainly to the high tannin content that interferes with proteins in an unspecific way). Also the treatment of mucosal infections and of diarrhoea appears plausible.

NOTES *Krameria* species are important sources of traditional dyes. Raw material for medicinal use is no longer freely available and it has been suggested that the tannin-rich roots of *Potentilla erecta* are a suitable alternative.

STATUS Traditional medicine; Pharm.; Comm.E+.

Krameria lappacea (Domb.) Burd. & Simp. (=*K. triandra* Ruíz & Pavón)　　　　　family: Krameriaceae

ratanhia (French); *Ratanhia* (German); *ratania* (Italian); *ratania* (Spanish)

Lamium album

white dead nettle

Lamium album

DESCRIPTION White dead nettle is a perennial herb (up to 0.5 m), with branched rhizomes and erect branches bearing heart-shaped, toothed leaves in opposite pairs. The white, tubular and two-lipped flowers form small clusters in the axils of the upper leaves. When not in flower, it resembles nettle (*Urtica dioica*), hence the common name.

ORIGIN Europe and Asia; naturalised in parts of North America. Commercial harvesting is done in eastern Europe.

PARTS USED Dried flowering tops (white dead nettle herb – *Lamii albi herba*) or the dried petals (white dead nettle flower – *Lamii albi flos; synon. Flores Lamii albi*).

THERAPEUTIC CATEGORY Traditional expectorant.

USES AND PROPERTIES The herb is used to treat respiratory complaints (to remove phlegm and catarrh) and stomach disorders (flatulence, gastritis, dyspepsia). It has been used specifically in case of leucorrhoea (*fluor albus*), but also against menopausal and urogenital problems. It is considered to be a diuretic and "blood cleanser". Poultices are applied to swellings, bruises, varicose veins and other skin inflammations. The herb is said to be effective against dandruff and an itching scalp and is included in tea mixtures and sedative teas. Extracts are used in lotions, shampoos, rinses and baths.

PREPARATION AND DOSAGE As an expectorant, tea is made from 1 g of the dry material, often sweetened with honey, and sipped several times a day. The recommended daily dose is 3 g. The dose for one sitzbath is 5 g of the dry flowers.

ACTIVE INGREDIENTS The main active ingredients are considered to be iridoid glycosides (lamalbide is a major compound, together with 6-desoxylamalbide, caryoptin and albosides A and B). It is also said to contain mucilage, triterpene saponins, tannins (5-14%), phenolic acids (chlorogenic acid, lamalboside, acteoside) and flavonoids (rutin, quercetin, kaempferol). However, some of these compounds have not been thoroughly studied in *L. album*.

PHARMACOLOGICAL EFFECTS Experiments have shown anti-inflammatory, weak diuretic and antimicrobial activity which could be attributed to the iridoids, tannins and triterpene saponins.

STATUS Traditional medicine; Pharm.; Comm.E+ (flowers only).

Lamium album L.   family: Lamiaceae

ortie blanche (French); *Weiße Taubnessel* (German); *ortica bianca* (Italian); *ortiga blanca* (Spanish)

Laurus nobilis

bay • bay laurel • sweet bay • true laurel

Laurus nobilis leaves and male flowers

Laurus nobilis fruits

DESCRIPTION A large shrub or small tree (rarely up to 20 m) bearing simple, leathery leaves with somewhat wavy margins. Male and female flowers are usually borne on separate trees. Inconspicuous, yellowish white flowers occur in small clusters and develop, in the case of female trees, into black fruits resembling small olives. *L. azorica* is also used medicinally.

ORIGIN Mediterranean region. The true laurel tree was important in Greek mythology and history, and is still a part of the modern vocabulary in such expressions as "a crown of laurel", "baccalaureus Scientiae" – bachelor of science, "poet laureate" or "resting on your laurels".

PARTS USED Leaves (*Lauri folia*) and the essential oil from the leaves (*Lauri aetheroleum*), rarely the fruit (*Lauri fructus*).

THERAPEUTIC CATEGORY Digestive tonic (*amarum*).

USES AND PROPERTIES Bay leaf is used in traditional medicine mainly for gastrointestinal complaints (indigestion, dyspepsia and flatulence). It has been used as a general medicine since ancient times but the efficacy for historical indications (especially kidney and bladder ailments) is not well documented.

The essential oil has become popular in aromatherapy. It should be well diluted in suitable carrier oil and can be rubbed as a counter-irritant onto rheumatic or sprained limbs and bruised skin. The main use of laurel (both the leaves and the leaf oil) is in the food industry, as spice and as flavouring agent. The essential oil shows insecticidal effects.

PREPARATION AND DOSAGE A weak infusion is made of the fresh or dried leaves and can be taken with meals to improve digestion.

ACTIVE INGREDIENTS Essential oil in the leaves (up to 1% of dry weight) has 1,8-cineole, eugenol, linalool, costunolide and deacetyllaurenobiolide as main ingredienjts. In addition, leaves contain isoquinoline alkaloids (reticuline), aporphine alkaloids (boldine and others; similar to those in *Peumus boldus*), flavonoids, lignan glycosides and sesquiterpene lactones (costunolide).

PHARMACOLOGICAL EFFECTS Monoterpenes and sesquiterpene lactones are diuretic, spasmolytic, antimicrobial; they are considered to be responsible for the digestive effects. Also the alkaloids and lignans are biologically active.

STATUS Traditional medicine; Pharm.

Laurus nobilis L.   family: Lauraceae

laurier d'Apollon (French); *Lorbeer* (German); *alloro* (Italian); *laurel* (Spanish)

Lavandula angustifolia

lavender

Lavandula angustifolia plant

Lavandula angustifolia flowers

DESCRIPTION A brittle perennial shrublet of up to 1 m in height, with narrowly oblong, silvery leaves and small purple-blue flowers borne in attractive slender spikes. Commercial cultivation is mainly with so-called lavandin (forms of *L. x intermedia*), spontaneous hybrids between *L. angustifolia* and broad-leaved lavender, *L. latifolia*. Also used are French lavender (*L. dentata*) and Spanish lavender (*L. stoechas*).

ORIGIN Western Mediterranean region. The commercial production of oil has expanded to other regions, including eastern Europe.

PARTS USED Dried flower spikes (*Lavandulae flos*) or oil, distilled from the fresh flowering tops just before the flowers open (*Lavandulae aetheroleum*).

THERAPEUTIC CATEGORY Sedative, spasmolytic, anti-microbial.

USES AND PROPERTIES Lavender flowers are traditionally used as a calming herb in case of dyspepsia and minor nervous disorders, such as restlessness, insomnia and nervous intestinal complaints. The oil is applied topically as a mild antiseptic and stimulant to treat wounds, burns, sunburn and muscular pains. In aromatherapy it is popular to treat headache, migraine, tension and emotional upsets. The oil is used on a massive scale in cosmetic products.

PREPARATION AND DOSAGE The herb is taken as a tea (1.5 g) or 1-4 drops of oil (20-80 ml) can be taken internally in dilute form. A lavender bath can be prepared with 20-100 g of the dried herb in 20 litres of water. The herb or oil is included in calming teas and prepared sedatives, cholagogues and tonics.

ACTIVE INGREDIENTS An essential oil (1-3%) that contains monoterpenoids (up to 75% linaloyl acetate and linalool; furthermore *cis*-β-ocimene, *trans*-β-ocimene, 1-terpenen-4-ol, together with smaller amounts of limonene, 1,8-cineole, camphor, α-terpineol), a sesquiterpenoid (caryophyllene epoxide) and 3-octanone. Leaves contain rosmarinic acid and other tannins (around 12%), coumarins (umbelliferone), triterpenes, and phenolic acids.

PHARMACOLOGICAL EFFECTS Lipophilic monoterpenes interact with biomembranes and modify the activity of ion channels, transporters and receptors. This can explain the sedative, spasmolytic and antibacterial properties of the oil.

STATUS Traditional medicine; Pharm.; Comm.E+.

Lavandula angustifolia Mill. (= *L. officinalis* Chaix, *L. vera* DC.) family: Lamiaceae
lavande (French); *Echter Lavendel* (German); *lavanda* (Italian); *lavanda* (Spanish)

Lawsonia inermis

henna

Lawsonia inermis flowers (white form)

Lawsonia inermis leaves

Lawsonia inermis flowers (pink form)

DESCRIPTION An evergreen shrub of up to 5 m in height, with narrowly oblong, pointed leaves, small, fragrant, white or reddish flowers and black berries. *L. alba* is also used.

ORIGIN India, Middle East and the Mediterranean region. The plant is cultivated on a large scale, especially in Egypt and India.

PARTS USED Powdered leaves (*Hennae folium*).

THERAPEUTIC CATEGORY Astringent, antimicrobial.

USES AND PROPERTIES Henna leaf is a traditional medicine in India, Arabia and North Africa and is used medicinally mainly to treat wounds, sores and skin infections. It is gargled for sore throat and taken internally in case of diarrhoea, dysentery, stomach ulcers and tapeworms. It is also considered to be anti-epileptic and abortifacient. The main use in modern times is as a colouring agent for hair and nails (and traditionally also for hands and feet, especially of brides). Powdered leaves of various grades are added to shampoos and hair dyes to give attractive reddish or bronze tints, depending on the natural colour of the hair. Indigo leaves (*Indigofera tinctoria*) are some-

times mixed with henna to obtain natural brown or black colours. Moisture and some heat are required to obtain an optimum colour reaction. Lawsone produces a long-lasting dyeing effect on the skin and hair by chemically bonding with proteins.

PREPARATION AND DOSAGE Decoctions and infusions may be used, or a paste made of the leaf powder, applied to the skin or the hair.

ACTIVE INGREDIENTS The main compound of interest is lawsone, a 2-hydroxy-1,4-naphthoquinone that is released from glycosides in the fresh leaf through hydrolysis (1% lawsone in dry leaf powder). Also of importance are tannins (up to 10%), other naphthoquinone derivatives, coumarins, flavonoids, phenolic acids, sterols and xanthones, all of which may possibly contribute to some extent to the medicinal properties.

PHARMACOLOGICAL EFFECTS The astringent properties are ascribed to the tannins. Like other naphthoquinones, lawsone is a strong oxidant and can interact with various cellular components, especially with proteins. This would explain its antibacterial, antifungal, anti-amoebic and anthelmintic properties.

STATUS Traditional medicine.

Lawsonia inermis L.   family: Lythraceae

henné (French); *Hennastrauch* (German); *hennè* (Italian)

Leonurus cardiaca

motherwort

Leonurus cardiaca plant

Leonurus cardiaca flowers

DESCRIPTION Motherwort is an erect perennial herb of up to 1.5 m in height, with distinctive toothed, usually drooping leaves and small pink flowers arranged in axillary clusters on the elongated flowering branches. Chinese motherwort or *yi mu cao* (*L. heterophyllus*, = *L. japonicus*), Siberian motherwort or *marahuanilla* (*L. sibiricus*), and *L. quinquelobatus* have been used in the same way as *L. cardiaca*.

ORIGIN Central Europe, northern Europe and Asia; naturalised in North America. The herb is wild-harvested during the flowering season in summer, and is commonly cultivated in gardens.

PARTS USED Aboveground parts (*Leonuri herba*).

THERAPEUTIC CATEGORY Cardiotonic.

USES AND PROPERTIES The main use of the herb is to treat nervous heart conditions (as the name "*cardiaca*" implies); also employed in the supportive treatment of thyroid hyperactivity. Traditionally used as a spasmolytic, hypotensive and in case of climacteric ailments. The English common name refers to the traditional use of calming anxiety during childbirth and it is considered to be a uterine contractant.

PREPARATION AND DOSAGE A tea can be made from 2-4 g of the dried herb and taken three times a day. An average daily dose of 4.5 g or equivalent preparations has been recommended. The herb is mainly taken as an ingredient of various cardiovascular teas and combination products. In folk medicine, mixtures of volatile oils including motherwort extract are applied topically to specified areas around the heart.

ACTIVE INGREDIENTS The main compounds of interest are alkaloids (stachydrine, leonurine), iridoid glycosides (such as ajugol, ajugoside, galiridoside), labdane diterpenes and diterpene lactones (leocardin, marrubiaside), flavonoids, phenolic acids and tannins.

PHARMACOLOGICAL EFFECTS The iridoid glycosides (or the metabolites formed in the body) are likely to interfere with prostaglandin formation, the alkaloids with neuroreceptors and the various phenolics with proteins. It is likely that the diterpenes and diterpene lactones exhibit biological activities (they show some weak structural resemblance to cardenolides). Cardioactivity, uterotonic and oxytocic effects have been documented. Experimental studies, that would explain these properties, are not available.

STATUS Traditional medicine; Pharm.; Comm.E+.

Leonurus cardiaca L.

family: Lamiaceae

agripaume (French); *Herzgespann* (German); *cardiaco* (Italian); *agripalma* (Spanish)

191

Levisticum officinale

lovage

Levisticum officinale plant

Levisticum officinale leaves and flowers

DESCRIPTION A robust perennial herb of up to 2 m in height, with broad, lobed, compound leaves and small yellow flowers arranged in double umbels.

ORIGIN Eastern Mediterranean region. The plant has been cultivated since ancient times and has become naturalised in Europe and North America. Commercial supplies of raw material come from cultivated plants.

PARTS USED Dried rhizome and roots (*Levistici radix*), sometimes also fruits and leaves.

THERAPEUTIC CATEGORY Carminative, diuretic.

USES AND PROPERTIES The main use of the root is as diuretic to treat oedema, inflammation of the lower urinary tract and to prevent kidney gravel. Traditionally it has been taken to improve digestion (as a stomachic and carminative) and as expectorant and emmenagogue. Lovage is also used as a spice and in liqueurs (bitters).

PREPARATION AND DOSAGE A tea is made by pouring boiling water over 1.5-3 g of the dry herb. When used as a diuretic, the tea is taken two or three times a day (or as stomachic, half an hour before a meal). Lovage root is used as an ingredient of various combination products, especially urological and cardiotonic medicines.

ACTIVE INGREDIENTS The roots contain an essential oil (around 1% of dry weight) with up to 70% alkylphthalides. These compounds, with their characteristic smell, include 3-butylphthalide and *cis-* and *trans-*ligustilide as main constituents, with various other phthalides (ligusticum lactone, sedanenolide and angeolide – these are actually *cis* and *trans* isomers, as well as dimers). Other oil components include mono- and sesquiterpenoids (α- and β-pinene, pentacyclohexadiene, α- and β-phellandrene, myrcene and others), as well as coumarins and furanocoumarins (bergapten, coumarin, psoralen and umbelliferone) and polyacetylenes (falcarindiol). Various organic acids have also been reported, including ferulic, caffeic, angelic and isovaleric acids.

PHARMACOLOGICAL EFFECTS Ligustilide and butylidenephthalides are antispasmodic, while the phthalides in general are known to stimulate the secretion of saliva and gastric juices. Butylphthalide and sedanenolide have sedative effects. The furanocoumarins are unlikely to cause phototoxicity because they are poorly soluble in water and therefore practically absent from the tea.

STATUS Traditional medicine; Pharm.; Comm.E+.

Levisticum officinale Koch (=*Ligusticum levisticum* L.)
family: Apiaceae

livèche (French); *Liebstöckel, Maggikraut* (German); *levistico* (Italian); *ligustico* (Spanish)

Linum usitatissimum

flax • linseed

Linum usitatissimum flowers and fruit

Linum usitatissimum plant

Linseeds

DESCRIPTION An erect annual herb of up to 1 m in height with slender stems bearing small, hairless leaves and attractive blue flowers. The fruit capsules contain reddish-brown, smooth seeds. Some cultivars are grown for stem fibres (flax); others for the seeds or seed oil.

ORIGIN Mediterranean region and western Europe. Flax is an ancient cultigen (probably derived from *L. angustifolium*) with large, indehiscent capsules and large seeds.

PARTS USED The ripe, dried seeds (linseed; *Lini semen*).

THERAPEUTIC CATEGORY Bulk laxative.

USES AND PROPERTIES Whole or crushed linseeds are taken orally as a bulk-forming laxative to treat chronic constipation and symptoms of irritable colon, spasmodic colitis and diverticulitis. The mucilage is beneficial in cases of gastritis and enteritis. Seeds or seed flour can be applied externally to treat local inflammations.

PREPARATION AND DOSAGE One tablespoon of whole or cracked (not ground) seeds with 150 ml of water is taken three times per day. A compress or cataplasm can be made with 30-50 g of linseed flour.

ACTIVE INGREDIENTS Large amounts (6-10%) of mucilage are present in the external wall of the outer cell layer of the seed coat. The seed itself contains 35-45% oil (including linoleic acid and α-linolenic acid, ALA), 20-25% proteins and 25% fibres. Also present are sterols and triterpenes (cholesterol, campesterol, stigmasterol, sitosterol and others) together with up to 1% cyanogenic di- and monoglycosides (linustatin, neolinustatin, and linamarin, lotaustralin, respectively).

PHARMACOLOGICAL EFFECTS The mucilage causes an increase in the volume of the colon contents (leading to the stimulation of peristalsis) and lubricates the stools. If cracked seeds are ingested, the oil adds to the lubricating and emulcent effects. Overweight people should use only whole seeds to avoid unnecessary calories. The cyanogenic glycosides release cyanide (HCN) which is rapidly inactivated in the human body; there is no danger of intoxication (especially if whole seeds are ingested). Linseed lowers triglyceride and cholesterol levels. Antibiotic, hypoglycaemic and anticarcinogenic effects have been observed.

NOTES *L. catharticum* contains lignans (such as podophyllotoxins) and has been used as a purgative.

STATUS Pharm.; Comm. E+; ESCOP 1; clinical studies+.

Linum usitatissimum L.   family: Linaceae

lin (French); *Lein, Flachs* (German); *lino* (Italian); *lino* (Spanish)

Lobelia inflata

Indian tobacco • asthma weed

Lobelia inflata flowers and fruit

Lobelia siphilitica flowers

Lobelia tupa

DESCRIPTION Indian tobacco is a small, much-branched annual herb of up to 0.5 m in height, with soft, stalkless leaves and small, pale blue flowers borne amongst leafy bracts along the branch tips. The calyx of the flower is characteristically swollen, hence the botanical name *inflata*. Several other *Lobelia* species have been used in folk medicine. Chinese lobelia (*L. chinensis*) is a traditional diuretic; blue cardinal flower (*L. siphilitica*) has a reputation of being a syphilis cure, while the Chilean cardinal flower (*L. tupa*) is a traditional narcotic and toothache remedy.

ORIGIN North America. The other species mentioned are from China (*L. chinensis*), eastern North America (*L. siphilitica*) and Chile (*L. tupa*). Indian tobacco is cultivated in North America, Russia and India. Many *Lobelia* species are popular garden plants.

PARTS USED Stems and leaves (*Lobeliae herba*).

THERAPEUTIC CATEGORY Respiratory stimulant; cough treatment.

USES AND PROPERTIES Extracts are still included in preparations for the symptomatic treatment of asthma, bronchitis and pertussis. An isolated ingredient, lobeline, is used in oral anti-smoking preparations to lessen the symptoms of nicotine withdrawal. Extracts were once injected as resuscitation treatment for asphyxia and apnoea in babies but is no longer used because of undesirable side effects. North American Indians used the plant as a tobacco substitute (hence the common name) and as an emetic.

PREPARATION AND DOSAGE A dose of 0.2-0.6 g of the herb is taken as an infusion or decoction three times per day. Liquid extracts or tinctures (1:1 in 50% ethanol) are taken in 0.2-0.6 ml quantities, three times daily.

ACTIVE INGREDIENTS The herb contains several piperidine alkaloids (up to 0.5% of dry weight), of which lobeline is the major compound. The alkaloids are also found in the latex and are complexed with chelidonic acid.

PHARMACOLOGICAL EFFECTS Lobeline activates nicotinic acetylcholine receptors (similar to nicotine). It is a respiratory stimulant which accelerates respiratory movements by a direct action on the central nervous system. It also acts as a bronchodilator and ganglionic stimulant. The herb is stated to have antispasmodic, expectorant and emetic properties.

STATUS Traditional medicine; Pharm.

Lobelia inflata L.   family: Campanulaceae

lobélie enflée (French); *Aufgeblasene Lobelie, Indianertabak* (German); *lobelia* (Italian)

Lycium chinense

Chinese wolfberry • Chinese boxthorn

Lycium chinense flower and fruit

Lycium chinense leaves

Lycium chinense dried fruit

DESCRIPTION Chinese wolfberry is a woody shrub of 1 m in height, with thorny stems bearing bright green, hairless, lance-shaped leaves (broadest in the lower half), purple flowers with a tube of 1.5 mm long and bright orange-red berries, about 10 mm long. A close relative is the so-called Duke of Argyll's tea-tree (*L. barbarum*, = *L. halimifolium*). It is a larger shrub of up to 3 m in height with larger berries (up to 20 mm long), ovate-lanceolate leaves (broadest in the middle) and a longer corolla tube (2.5-3 mm).

ORIGIN Eastern Asia (*L. chinense*); China, mainly Ningxia Province (*L. barbarum*). Both species are naturalised in North America (*L. barbarum* in Europe) and are cultivated in China and Malaysia.

PARTS USED Fresh or dried berries of both species (*gou qi zi – Lycii fructus*), nowadays also the dried roots (*Lycii radicis cortex*). The leaves of *L. chinense* are a popular green vegetable in Chinese cooking and are produced commercially on a large scale.

THERAPEUTIC CATEGORY Traditional tonic.

USES AND PROPERTIES The berries are one of the most important traditional medicines in China. They are used as a general tonic to improve the blood, strengthen the body, treat wasting diseases, protect the liver and specifically to improve eyesight.

PREPARATION AND DOSAGE A daily dose of 50 g of dry berries is recommended. The berries are often used in stews or soups as a functional food. Root infusions are sometimes used to lower blood pressure or to treat fevers.

ACTIVE INGREDIENTS The berries contain large quantities of amino acids (up to 5%), polysaccharides and carotenoids (including zeaxanthin, physalien and cryptoxanthin). The berries also contain essential oil with sesquiterpenoids (dehydro-α-cyperone and solavetivone). Numerous triterpenes and steroidal triterpenoids have been isolated from the seeds. The bark is rich in polyamines (kukoamine A) and small peptides (lyciumamide, lyciumine A); leaves contain several steroids, including withanolide A.

PHARMACOLOGICAL EFFECTS Lyciumine A and B inhibit renin and ACE (angiotensin-converting enzyme); kukoamine A reduces blood pressure. Chinese studies have shown antioxidant, hypoglycaemic, lipid-lowering, hypotensive and immune stimulating effects.

STATUS Traditional medicine.

Lycium chinense Mill. family: Solanaceae

lyciet (French); *Chinesischer Bocksdorn* (German); *licio* (Italian)

Lycopus europaeus

bugleweed • gipsywort • water horehound

Lycopus europaeus

Lycopus virginicus

DESCRIPTION Bugleweed is an erect perennial herb of about 0.5 m in height. It has square stems and opposite pairs of lance-shaped leaves with markedly toothed margins. The small, white or pink, two-lipped flowers are borne in multi-flowered, rounded clusters. *L. virginicus* is closely similar and is used in the same way.

ORIGIN Europe and Asia (*L. europaeus*); naturalised in North America. *L. virginicus* is indigenous to North America. Both species are often found in or near water.

PARTS USED Dried aboveground parts (*Lycopi herba*) of flowering plants.

THERAPEUTIC CATEGORY Antithyrotropic; mastodynia.

USES AND PROPERTIES The herb is used to treat an overactive thyroid gland (e.g. *Morbus Basedow*) and associated symptoms, especially nervousness and heart palpitations. It is also used to treat mastodynia (tension and pain in the breast).

PREPARATION AND DOSAGE A daily dose of 1-2 g of the dried herb is taken three times a day as an infusion. Alternatively, tinctures may be taken in doses of 5-10 drops three times daily. Extracts are included in commercial preparations. Each person has a unique

optimum level of thyroid hormones, so that the dosage should be adapted to individual needs.

ACTIVE INGREDIENTS Various phenolic acids (derivatives of hydroxycinnamic acid; caffeic, lithospermic acid and rosmarinic acid) are present. The herb also contains flavonoids (luteolin-7-glucoside and others), tannins, various di- and triterpenes and small amounts of essential oil (bornylacetate, camphene, *p*-cymol).

PHARMACOLOGICAL EFFECTS Depsides of hydroxycinnamic acids appear to be responsible for the observed activities. Experiments have shown antigonadotropic and antithyrotropic activities. It lowers the level of prolactin in blood serum. If treatment is abruptly discontinued, prolactin secretion may increase.

WARNING High doses and continued use of the herb over long periods may lead to an enlargement of the thyroid. The herb should not be administered to people who are already under treatment with other thyroid preparations or people with thyroid insufficiency. Diagnostic procedures that make use of radioactive isotopes are disrupted by bugleweed therapy.

STATUS Traditional medicine; Comm. E+; clinical studies+.

Lycopus europaeus L.   family: Lamiaceae

pied-de-loup (French); *Gemeiner Wolfstrapp* (German); *marrubio d'acqua* (Italian); *manta de lobo* (Spanish)

Malva sylvestris

mallow • common mallow

Malva sylvestris flower

Malva sylvestris leaves and flowers

Malva sylvestris plant

DESCRIPTION Mallow is a biennial herb or shrublet (up to 1 m) with rounded, lobed and dentate leaves. The attractive pink flowers each have five petals with characteristic dark veins at their bases. A second species, known as dwarf mallow (*M. neglecta*), is sometimes also used as a source of leaf material. Both M. *sylvestris* subsp. *sylvestris* and M. *sylvestris* subsp. *mauritiana* are considered suitable as sources of mallow flowers. These flowers should not be confused with *Malvae arboreae flos*, which is harvested from *Alcea rosea* (the garden hollyhock).

ORIGIN Europe and Asia; they have become weeds in other parts of the world.

PARTS USED Dried leaves (*Malvae folium*) or flowers (*Malvae flos*).

THERAPEUTIC CATEGORY Demulcent; cough medicine.

USES AND PROPERTIES The main use of the herb is to treat mucosal irritations of the mouth and throat, that result in dry, irritating cough. It is also considered useful as a mild astringent to treat gastroenteritis. Traditionally it was used internally in case of bladder complaints and externally as a poultice for wounds.

PREPARATION AND DOSAGE About 5 g of dried leaves or flowers (or the equivalent thereof, in extracted form) are used.

ACTIVE INGREDIENTS Like other members of the family (see *Althaea officinalis*), mallow contains mucilage (slime). Mucilage is present in concentrations of 10% and 8% of dry weight in flowers and leaves, respectively. On hydrolysis, the mucilage yields various sugars, including arabinose, galactose, glucose and rhamnose, together with galacturonic acid. Of importance are quite high yields of anthocyanins in the flowers (about 7% of dry weight), including malvin (malvidin 3,5-diglucoside), malvidin 3-glucoside and cyanidin 3-glucoside. Also present are small amounts of tannins (rosmarinic acid) and proanthocyanins.

PHARMACOLOGICAL EFFECTS The mucilage in mallow is emulcent and therefore forms a protective film over inflamed mucous membranes. Anthocyanins and the other phenolics have antioxidant activities; they are responsible for the mild astringent and anti-inflammatory properties.

NOTES The flowers are sometimes included in other products as a natural colourant.

STATUS Traditional medicine; Pharm.; Comm.E+.

Malva sylvestris L.   family: Malvaceae

mauve sauvage (French); *Wilde Malve, Große Käsepappel* (German); *malva riondela* (Italian); *malva* (Spanish)

Marrubium vulgare
white horehound

Marrubium vulgare flowers

Marrubium vulgare plant with fruit

DESCRIPTION A perennial herb of less than 0.5 m high, with angular stems, densely hairy, conspicuously veined leaves (often greyish green) and rounded clusters of small, white, two-lipped flowers at each node.

ORIGIN Southern Europe and Asia. The herb is thought to have originated in the Mediterranean region but is now widely dispersed in most continents of the world, where it has become a common roadside weed.

PARTS USED The fresh or dried aboveground parts (*Marrubii herba*) are used.

THERAPEUTIC CATEGORY Choleretic and expectorant.

USES AND PROPERTIES White horehound is used mainly for two conditions: digestive complaints (lack of appetite, indigestion, dyspepsia, biliary complaints and flatulence) and dry coughs (acute or chronic bronchitis). Traditionally, it is a treatment in cases of menstrual disorders and inflammations of mucous membranes and skin.

PREPARATION AND DOSAGE A daily dose of 4.5 g of dried herb (or equivalent dose) is recommended. It is usually taken as a tea, but the product is also included in ready-made expectorants and digestive medicines.

ACTIVE INGREDIENTS The main compound of interest is marrubiin (up to 1%), a diterpene lactone of the labdane type. It is thought that a precursor, premarrubiin, is actually present in the plant and that it is converted to marrubiin and further to marrubiinic acid. Other diterpenoids include marrubenol, peregrinol and vulgarol. Flavonoids (glycosides of apigenin, luteolin and quercetin), tannins and phenolic acids, betonicine, choline and small amounts of essential oil (with camphene, limonene, sabinene and other mono- and sesquiterpenoids) are present.

PHARMACOLOGICAL EFFECTS Choleretic effects are ascribed to marrubiin or marrubiinic acid (it stimulates bile secretion). Marrubiin is considered to be the main expectorant principle as it is thought to stimulate secretion of the bronchial mucosa, but the volatile oil in the plant will also contribute to the spasmolytic, expectorant and vasodilatory activities.

WARNING At high doses, white horehound may possibly be cardioactive and have uterine stimulant effects, so care should be taken not to ingest large amounts.

STATUS Traditional medicine; Pharm.; Comm.E+.

Marrubium vulgare L.   family: Lamiaceae

marrube blanc (French); *Gemeiner Andorn* (German); *marrobio* (Italian); *marrubio* (Spanish)

Marsdenia cundurango

condurango • condor plant

Marsdenia astephanoides

Marsdenia coulteri

Marsdenia cundurango bark

DESCRIPTION Condurango is a woody creeper (vine) with hairy shoots, large heart-shaped leaves and small greenish white flowers. The fruits are follicles. Over 250 species have been described for the genus *Marsdenia*, which occur in the tropics of the Old and New World.

ORIGIN South America. The plant is indigenous to the Andes region of Ecuador and Peru, and grows on the western slopes of the Cordillera mountains. It is cultivated in East Africa.

PARTS USED Dried bark, collected from the trunk and branches (*Condurango cortex*).

THERAPEUTIC CATEGORY Digestive (bitter tonic).

USES AND PROPERTIES Condurango is used as a bitter tonic to stimulate appetite and to reduce nausea. The reputation of the plant seems mainly based on early reports that it can cure stomach cancer, but there is no convincing scientific evidence to support this claim. It is also traditionally used in case of liver and menstrual disorders. As a commercial product, condurango is mainly of historical interest and it is rarely used nowadays.

PREPARATION AND DOSAGE Daily doses of 2-5 g (tincture) or 0.2-0.5 g (extract) are recommended. Tea can be used in a single dose per day: 1.5 g well cut or pulverised bark is briefly boiled in water, cooled and strained.

ACTIVE INGREDIENTS The main active ingredients are considered to be a complex mixture of steroidal saponins, bitter pregnane derivatives (condurango glycosides) known collectively as condurangin. They seem to replace cardiac glycosides that are common in other members of the Asclepiadaceae. In addition, several other metabolites are known from the bark, including condurangamines A and B, chlorogenic acid, caffeic acid, cyclitols, flavonoids and phytosterols.

PHARMACOLOGICAL EFFECTS It is known that the product stimulates the secretion of saliva and gastric juices by stimulating the *nervus vagus* in the stomach and therefore has value as a digestive medicine. However, no clinical trials seem to have been done, and the pharmacological properties of condurango are as yet poorly explored. Extracts exhibit anti-tumour activities against Ehrlich carcinoma in mice. Condurangin is quite toxic (LD_{50} values for cats and dogs are 40-50 mg/kg body weight).

STATUS Traditional medicine; Pharm.; Comm.E+.

Marsdenia cundurango Reichb.f.   family: Asclepiadaceae

condurango (French); *Kondurangostrauch, Kondorliane* (German); *vite aquilina* (Italian); *condurango blanco* (Spanish)

Matricaria recutita

chamomile • German chamomile

Matricaria recutita

DESCRIPTION An annual herb with feathery leaves and attractive flower heads. The base of the flower head is characteristically hollow, while it is solid in Roman chamomile, *Chamaemelum nobile*.

ORIGIN Eastern Europe and the Near East; widely cultivated (especially in Argentina) for medicinal use – the consumption is 5 000 tons per year.

PARTS USED Dried flower heads (*Matricariae flos*), essential oil distilled from the flowers (*Matricariae aetheroleum*) or liquid extracts.

THERAPEUTIC CATEGORY Anti-inflammatory, antispasmodic, carminative, antiseptic.

USES AND PROPERTIES Used topically to treat inflammations of the skin and mucosa, and other skin disorders (including surgical wounds); internally against flatulent nervous dyspepsia (adults and children), gastritis, diarrhoea, travel sickness and mild anxiety. The volatile oil is inhaled to treat nasal catarrh, inflammation and irritation of the respiratory tract.

PREPARATION AND DOSAGE One or two teaspoons is taken by infusion (or 1-4 ml of a 1:1 tincture in ethanol), three times per day. A product known as Kamillosan has over many years shown positive results in various skin disorders. Recommended dosage for douches is 3-10% infusion and for bathing, 50 g of dry herb per 10 litres of water. Creams and semisolid products should contain 3-10% of the crude herb.

ACTIVE INGREDIENTS Activity is ascribed to essential oil constituents (45% *trans*-β-farnesene), the flavonoids (apigenin-, luteolin- and patuletin-7-glycosides) and coumarins (umbelliferone, herniarin). The oil has cyclic sesquiterpenoids, predominantly α-bisabolol (up to 50%) and chamazulene (up to 15%). Chamazulene is an artefact formed from matricin during steam distillation and gives the oil a deep blue colour. Also present are polyacetylenes (*cis*-en-in-dicycloether) and polysaccharides.

PHARMACOLOGICAL EFFECTS In human studies, anti-inflammatory (e.g. gastritis), antiseptic, antispasmodic and sedative effects are evident, which are related to the sesquiterpenes and flavonoids. Antibiotic and anti-inflammatory activities were noted in topical use.

WARNING Allergic reactions are mostly due to contamination with *Anthemis cotula*, which contains anthecotulide, a contact allergen.

STATUS Traditional medicine; Pharm.; Comm.E+; ESCOP 6; WHO 1.

Matricaria recutita L. [=*Chamomilla recutita* (L.) Rauschert; =*Matricaria chamomilla* L.] family: Asteraceae
camomille (French); *Echte Kamille* (German); *camomilla* (Italian); *camomilla, manzanilla* (Spanish)

Medicago sativa
alfalfa • lucerne

Medicago sativa flowers

Medicago sativa plant

Medicago sativa seeds (bottom) and sprouts (top)

DESCRIPTION Lucerne is a perennial herb with trifoliate leaves, clusters of small flowers that range from yellow to blue or purple and characteristically coiled pods.

ORIGIN Indigenous to southwestern Asia (Turkey) but naturalised in Europe for many centuries, and in all temperate and tropical parts of North America and Africa. It has become one of the most important of all cultivated pasture and fodder plants.

PARTS USED Stems and leaves (*Medicago sativae herba*), seeds and sprouts.

THERAPEUTIC CATEGORY General tonic (possibly cholesterol-lowering).

USES AND PROPERTIES Lucerne is better known as a fodder and food than as a medicinal plant. The sprouts (germinated seeds) are popular as a health food and ground dried herb may be given to convalescents as a dietary supplement and general tonic because it is rich in minerals and vitamins. It is considered useful in lowering cholesterol levels.

PREPARATION AND DOSAGE About 5-10 g of the dried herb is taken three times a day.

ACTIVE INGREDIENTS Leaves and seeds contain a large number of chemical compounds, including organic acids, free amino acids, non-protein amino acids (especially canavanine), stachydrine, coumarins (medicagol), isoflavonoids (coumestrol, genistein and others), saponins (glycosides of hederagenin, medicagenic acid and soyasapogenols), steroids (mainly β-sitosterol, some campesterol, stigmasterol, and others).

PHARMACOLOGICAL EFFECTS Animal studies have indicated that the saponins decrease intestinal absorption of cholesterol (and lower its concentration in blood) and prevent arteriosclerosis. In a human study, it was found that 40 g of seeds three times a day helped to normalise cholesterol levels in the blood serum of hyperlipoproteinaemic patients. Also high levels of manganese (45.5 mg/kg) are thought to lower cholesterol in some people. Coumestrol and genistein have documented oestrogenic effects.

WARNING Massive amounts of alfalfa in the diet could result in symptoms of systemic lupus erythematosus (SLE) or in reversible pancytopenia. Excessive ingestion of the seeds should therefore be avoided, particularly in persons with a history of SLE. In the USA, alfalfa is listed as GRAS ("Generally Regarded as Safe").

STATUS Traditional medicine (dietary supplement).

Medicago sativa L.   family: Fabaceae

luzerne (French); *Luzerne* (German); *alfa-alfa* (Italian)

Melaleuca alternifolia

tea tree

Melaleuca alternifolia tree

Melaleuca alternifolia leaves and flowers

DESCRIPTION A medium-sized tree with papery bark, linear leaves and white flowers resembling bottle-brushes. The long, conspicuous stamens are arranged in five bundles in each flower. Tea tree should not be confused with ordinary black tea (*Camellia sinensis*).

ORIGIN Australia (mainly New South Wales); cultivated mostly in Australia. It is said to have been a traditional medicine of the Aborigines.

PARTS USED Essential oil (*Melaleucae aetheroleum*), obtained from the leaves by steam distillation.

THERAPEUTIC CATEGORY Antimicrobial, expectorant.

USES AND PROPERTIES The oil is widely used in ointments and creams to treat insect bites, wounds, abrasions, acne, skin infections, fungal infections (including athlete's foot and thrush). It is popular in aromatherapy because it can be used directly on the skin and does not irritate mucous membranes. Dilute oil is sometimes used internally as a mouthwash in case of mucosal inflammations, such as tonsillitis, pharyngitis and sinusitis and to treat catarrh of upper respiratory tract. The oil is used as an antiseptic and preservative in cosmetic products.

PREPARATION AND DOSAGE Pure or dilute oil is used externally, often in combination with other ingredients. Internal use should be supervised by a health care professional.

ACTIVE INGREDIENTS More than 60 terpenoids have been identified in the volatile oil; 1-terpinen-4-ol should constitute at least 30% of total terpenoids in high quality oil. Other compounds present are α- and γ-terpinene (about 40%) and 1,8-cineole (=eucalyptol; maximum of 15% in high quality oil).

PHARMACOLOGICAL EFFECTS The monoterpenes interact with biomembranes and membrane proteins, thus explaining the observed antibacterial, antifungal and antiviral activities. A few clinical studies have shown positive results in the treatment of acne and fungal infections.

NOTES Cajuput or cajeput oil is obtained from M. *leucadendra* (=M. *leucadendron*) or M. *cajuputi* that occur in Australia, Malaysia and New Caledonia. It is used in aromatherapy and as an antiseptic in nose drops. Niaouli oil (obtained from M. *viridiflora*) contains 1,8-cineole as main ingredient (35-60%) and is used in aromatherapy and in proprietary medicines.

STATUS Pharm.; WHO 2; clinical studies +.

Melaleuca alternifolia Cheel.   family: Myrtaceae

melaleuca (French); *Teebaum* (German); *melaleuca* (Italian)

Melilotus officinalis

sweet clover • ribbed or common melilot

Melilotus officinalis flowers and fruits

Melilotus officinalis plant

Melilotus alba

DESCRIPTION An erect herb with trifoliolate dentate leaves, small yellow flowers in dense oblong clusters and small, almost spherical, indehiscent pods. *M. alba, M. altissima* and *M. indica* have also been used.

ORIGIN Widely distributed in Europe, Asia and North Africa; now a roadside weed in many parts of the world.

PARTS USED Fresh or dried leaves and flowering branches of *M. officinalis* or *M. altissima* (*Meliloti herba*).

THERAPEUTIC CATEGORY Anti-oedemic, venotonic.

USES AND PROPERTIES Extracts are used to treat the symptoms of venous and lymphatic insufficiency and capillary fragility, such as varicose veins, pruritus, cramp in the calf and in acute attacks of haemorrhoids. Preparations are available for topical and oral treatment of minor sleep disturbances and minor gastrointestinal disorders.

PREPARATION AND DOSAGE For internal use, the dosage corresponds to 3-30 mg of coumarin (1-7.5 mg for parenteral use). For external application, an effective dose of the herb should be guaranteed.

ACTIVE INGREDIENTS The main (up to1%) active ingredient is coumarin, formed enzymatically from melilo-

toside (2'-hydroxycinnamic acid glucoside) upon drying or tissue breakdown. Also present are melilotin (3,4-dihydrocoumarin), various phenolic acids (caffeic acid, ferulic acid), monoterpenes, triterpene saponins (soyasapogenol) and flavonoids. Fungal infection of the plant may lead to the formation of phytoalexins. The well-known anticoagulant (anti-clotting factor) dicoumarol derives from hydroxycinnamic acid upon inadequate drying (not present in fresh or carefully dried herb).

PHARMACOLOGICAL EFFECTS Coumarin shows anti-oedemic and anti-exudative activities and accelerates wound-healing. It increases the flow rate in veins (and the lymph system) and decreases capillary permeability but has no anticoagulant properties. Coumarin can induce tumours in rats when given at high doses over prolonged periods.

WARNING It is risky to take the herb while using anticoagulants.

NOTES Synthetic coumarin-type anticoagulants (e.g. warfarin, phenprocoumon in Marcoumar™) were developed with dicoumaroyl as a model.

STATUS Traditional medicine; Pharm; Comm.E+; ESCOP 4.

Melilotus officinalis (L.) Medikus

family: Fabaceae

mélilot officinal (French); *Echter Steinklee* (German); *meliloto, trifoglio cavallino* (Italian)

Melissa officinalis

lemon balm • balm • sweet balm

Melissa officinalis plant

Melissa officinalis leaves and flowers

DESCRIPTION A herbaceous perennial of up to 0.9 m in height with angular stems, rugosely veined leaves in opposite pairs and cream-coloured to white flowers.

ORIGIN Eastern Mediterranean and Asia Minor; commercial cultivation is centred in southwestern, central and eastern Europe.

PARTS USED Dried leaves of *Melissa officinalis* subsp. *officinalis* (*Melissae folium*) and essential oil (*Melissae aetheroleum*)

THERAPEUTIC CATEGORY Sedative, carminative, spasmolytic, antiviral.

USES AND PROPERTIES In modern times, lemon balm has become popular as a calming and soothing herb, mainly for the treatment of minor sleeplessness and nervous stomach disorders in adults and children. It is said to stimulate appetite. Extracts of the herb have demonstrated activity against bacteria, fungi and viruses (including herpes) and are an ingredient of ointments and creams for topical use.

PREPARATION AND DOSAGE A cup of lemon balm tea (1.5-4.5 g of dried leaf) may be taken several times a day. Various products are available, mainly for oral use. Lemon balm is often used as a minor ingredient and then it is unlikely to have any therapeutic effect.

ACTIVE INGREDIENTS The drug should contain at least 0.05% of essential oil (a complex mixture of monoterpenoids and sesquiterpenoids). The main ingredient is citronellal (about 30-40%), together with 10-30% citral. Citral actually comprises two compounds, citral a (geranial) and citral b (neral) in a ratio of 4:3. Major sesquiterpenoids include germacrene D and β-caryophyllene. The drug contains about 4% rosmarinic acid (also known as labiate tannin), phenolic acids, triterpenes, monoterpene glycosides and flavonoids.

PHARMACOLOGICAL EFFECTS The essential oil has spasmolytic and sedative properties and is known for its antibacterial and antifungal activities. This is plausible with regard to the biochemical properties of lipophilic monoterpenes with aldehyde groups. Watery extracts containing rosmarinic acid have virustatic effects (especially against *herpes simplex*). They also exhibit antihormonal and antithyreotropic effects.

NOTES The herb has a long history of medicinal use in Europe, associated with bees and honey, hence the name *Melissa* (*mel* is the Latin for honey).

STATUS Pharm.; Comm.E+; ESCOP 2; WHO 2.

Melissa officinalis L.   family: Lamiaceae

mélisse (French); *Zitronenmelisse* (German); *melissa, cedronella* (Italian); *melissa* (Spanish)

Mentha arvensis

field mint • corn mint • Japanese mint

Mentha arvensis leaves

Mentha arvensis flowers

DESCRIPTION Field mint is a rhizomatous herb with hairy stems (up to 0.6 m), distinctly hairy, broad and rounded leaves. The flowers are usually lilac, rarely white, and are borne in widely spaced clusters. It differs from peppermint (M. x piperita) in the fresh green colour, the hairy leaves and stems and the sparse flower clusters (see M. x piperita and M. spicata).

ORIGIN Eurasia. It is the only mint that thrives in the subtropics – others require a more temperate climate. Production occurs in China, Brazil, India and Paraguay.

PARTS USED Essential oil (Menthae arvensis aetheroleum). It is distilled from the stems and leaves, mainly to produce pure menthol. The common method for obtaining crystalline menthol is to gradually cool the oil at 2°C per day from 35°C to 5°C – part of the menthol crystallises, so that the menthol content of the remaining oil drops to about 30-45%. This dementholated oil is used medicinally, in toothpaste and chewing gum.

THERAPEUTIC CATEGORY Antibacterial, cooling, carminative, cholagogue.

USES AND PROPERTIES Field mint oil is widely used, internally and topically, for a variety of ailments. It is traditionally used in Europe for treating flatulence, gastrointestinal and gall bladder disorders and catarrhs of the upper respiratory tract. Oil is topically applied in case of myalgic and neuralgic pain. It is emollient, itch-relieving and widely used in oral hygiene.

PREPARATION AND DOSAGE For internal use, a daily dose of 3-6 drops is recommended. For inhalation, 3-4 drops are added to hot water, while several drops may be rubbed into the skin. Preparations intended for nasal application should contain 1-5% of the oil. Ointment and creams for external application typically contain 5-20% essential oil.

ACTIVE INGREDIENTS Dementholated oil contains menthol (30-45%), menthone (17-35%), isomenthone (5-13%), menthyl acetate (2-7%) and limonene (1.5-7%). Other ingredients should be in low concentration: carvone (the major component of spearmint oil) – 2% and pulegone (the main component of pennyroyal oil) – 1.5%.

PHARMACOLOGICAL EFFECTS Experimental evidence exists for most of the activities listed under therapeutic category above.

WARNING See under M. x piperita.

STATUS Pharm.; Comm.E+.

Mentha arvensis L. (=M. arvensis L. var. piperascens Malinv.)   family: Lamiaceae
bo he (Chinese); menthe, baume de champs (French); Ackerminze (German); menta selvatica (Italian)

Mentha x *piperita*

peppermint

Mentha x *piperita*   *Mentha* x *piperita* var. *citrata*

DESCRIPTION Peppermint has reddish purple, usually hairless stems (up to 0.9 m) and leaves, and the flowers (invariably lilac-pink) are arranged in dense, elongated terminal clusters. Eau-de-cologne mint (*M. x piperita var. citrata*) has some use in perfumery.

ORIGIN Peppermint does not occur in nature but is a sterile triple hybrid between *M. aquatica* and *M. spicata* (the latter itself is a hybrid between *M. suaveolens* and *M. longifolia*). Most of the annual production of more than 3 000 tons of oil comes from the USA.

PARTS USED Fresh or dried leaves (*Menthae piperitae folium*) and the essential oil obtained by steam distillation (*Menthae piperitae aetheroleum*).

THERAPEUTIC CATEGORY Leaves: choleretic, carminative; oil: antibacterial, cooling, carminative, cholagogue, spasmolytic.

USES AND PROPERTIES The drug is used to treat digestive disorders and to mask the unpleasant taste of other herbs. It is specifically employed in case of spastic complaints (including irritable bowel syndrome), ailments of the gall bladder and bile duct, and catarrhs of the respiratory tract. The oil is antimicrobial, antiviral and mildly anaesthetic, and can be used topically to relieve pain, including headache (but not migraine) and mucosal inflammations of the mouth.

PREPARATION AND DOSAGE Leaves are used as tea and the oil taken orally (daily dose 6-12 drops) or as part of proprietary medicines and in slow-release formulations to treat spastic colon. A few drops of oil may be rubbed into affected parts (forehead and temples in the case of tension headaches).

ACTIVE INGREDIENTS The activity is ascribed mainly to the essential oil components, which include menthol (30-40% or more), (–)-menthone (15-25%), (–)-menthyl acetate (up to 10%), (–)-menthofuran (preferably less than 5%, because it has an unpleasant smell). Carvone and pulegone should preferably be absent.

PHARMACOLOGICAL EFFECTS Animal studies and clinical trials support most of the claimed therapeutic benefits listed above. The cooling effect is due to the presence of menthol which affects cold receptors.

WARNING Peppermint oil should not be applied to the facial region or near the nose of small children (risk of spasms and respiratory arrest).

STATUS Pharm.; Comm.E+; ESCOP 3; WHO 2; clinical studies+.

Mentha x *piperita* L.   family: Lamiaceae

menthe poivrée (French); *Pfefferminze* (German); *menta piperina* (Italian); *la menta* (Spanish)

Mentha spicata

Spearmint • garden mint

Mentha spicata

Mentha suaveolens 'Variegata'

Mentha longifolia

Mentha pulegium

DESCRIPTION Spearmint is a rhizomatous herb with oblong, bright green, usually hairless leaves with strongly dentate and wavy margins, and elongated clusters of white flowers. It is superficially similar to field mint (M. *arvensis*) but differs in the white flowers and the distinctive, non-cooling, spearmint smell (menthol is absent). The form that is commonly cultivated in gardens is known as M. *spicata* var. *crispa* (previously considered to be a distinct species, M. *crispa*). Another European mint is pennyroyal (M. *pulegium*), a creeping herb with tiny leaves and a distinctive smell.

ORIGIN The common garden mint or spearmint is thought to have originated in Europe as a garden hybrid between M. *suaveolens* (apple mint or woolly mint; the cultivar Variegata is generally known as pineapple mint) and M. *longifolia* (horse mint or longleaf mint). Commercial cultivation for spearmint oil is centred in the USA (Washington state, Oregon and Idaho) but dried leaf is also produced in Egypt and eastern European countries.

PARTS USED Leaves (*Menthae crispae folium*) or the essential oil (*Menthae crispae aetheroleum*).

THERAPEUTIC CATEGORY Leaves: stomachic, carminative; oil: antibiotic, decongestant.

USES AND PROPERTIES Spearmint leaf is used in much the same way as peppermint leaf to treat digestive complaints, but not for most of the other indications. The oil is used mainly for inhalation, to treat catarrh. It is incorporated in mouthwashes and toothpastes, as well as chewing gum.

PREPARATION AND DOSAGE About 1-1.5 g of dried leaf in a cup of boiling water is taken several times a day.

ACTIVE INGREDIENTS Spearmint oil contains at least 50% carvone as the main ingredient, together with smaller amounts of limonene. Other constituents should be less than 2% each, and pulegone should be less than 0.5%. The leaf also contains flavonoids and tannins. Pulegone, the main component of pennyroyal oil, is an arbortifacient and is known to be hepatotoxic (ingestion of 30 ml can be fatal). It is useful against ectoparasites.

PHARMACOLOGICAL EFFECTS Spearmint leaf has limited use in medicine but the oil is important in oral hygiene.

STATUS Traditional medicine; Pharm.

Mentha spicata L. Danert

family: Lamiaceae

menthe douce (French); *Krauseminze* (German); *menta ricciuta* (Italian)

Menyanthes trifoliata

bogbean

Menyanthes trifoliata plants

Menyanthes trifoliata flowers and fruit

Menyanthes trifoliata in its natural habitat

DESCRIPTION Bogbean is a leafy, water-loving plant that grows in marshes and on lake margins. It has large, trifoliate, basally sheathing leaves resembling the leaves of beans (hence the common name bogbean) and attractive white and pink flowers with distinctive fringed petals. *Menyanthes* is chemically similar to members of the Gentianaceae.

ORIGIN Northern temperate zone (North America, Europe and Asia). The plant is not cultivated but is wild-harvested in midsummer.

PARTS USED Dried leaves (*Menyanthidis folium*; synon. *Trifolii fibrini folium*).

THERAPEUTIC CATEGORY Bitter tonic (*amarum*).

USES AND PROPERTIES Bogbean leaves are used for loss of appetite and dyspeptic complaints. It is also employed as an ingredient in cholagogues, geriatric medicines and especially in anti-inflammatory and antirheumatic formulations. Traditionally, it is used to treat skin disorders, cold and fever. Industrially it is a hop substitute and an ingredient of bitter liqueurs.

PREPARATION AND DOSAGE Unsweetened tea, made from 0.5-1 g of finely chopped leaves is taken half an hour before meals. The daily dose is 1.5-3 g.

ACTIVE INGREDIENTS The leaves contain bitter-tasting secoiridoid glycosides, including dehydro-menthiafolin (main component), menthiafolin and loganin, as well as coumarins (scopoletin, scoparone, braylin). Also present are phenolic acids, tannins, flavonoids (kaempherol, quercetin, O-methylquercetin and their glycosides), a volatile oil (benzaldehyde, citronellol), triterpenes and traces of alkaloids (gentianine, gentianidine).

PHARMACOLOGICAL EFFECTS Bogbean is closely related to gentian and other members of the Gentianaceae (see *Gentiana lutea* and *Centaurium erythraea*) and is similarly used as bitter tonic. The varied herbal uses have not yet been thoroughly investigated from a pharmacological point of view. Scopoletin and scoparone are known to act as cholagogues and choleretics and have antihepatotoxic activity. Scopoletin is stated to have a spasmolytic effect. Extracts show antimicrobial properties (probably due to the activity of iridoids, tannins and terpenoids).

WARNING Very large doses may cause diarrhoea, nausea and vomiting.

STATUS Traditional medicine; Pharm.; Comm.E+.

Menyanthes trifoliata L.   family: Menyanthaceae

trèfle d'eau (French); *Bitterklee, Fieberklee* (German); *trifoglio d'acqua* (Italian); *trébol acuático* (Spanish)

Myrica cerifera

bayberry • wax myrtle • waxberry

Myrica cordifolia

Myrica cerifera

Myrica gale

DESCRIPTION Bayberry is an evergreen shrub or small tree of up to 10 m in height, with oblong leaves, inconspicuous yellow flowers in elongated clusters and grey waxy berries. Related species are bog myrtle (*M. gale*) and dune waxberry (*M. cordifolia*). See notes below.

ORIGIN North America; eastern and southern parts, mostly in the coastal Atlantic regions.

PARTS USED Root bark (candleberry bark, wax myrtle bark).

THERAPEUTIC CATEGORY Emetic, astringent, anticatarrhal.

USES AND PROPERTIES The product is mainly used to treat mucous colitis but numerous other uses have been recorded, including the treatment of diarrhoea, colds and flu, sore throat, heavy menstruation, leucorrhoea (as a douche) and ulcers.

PREPARATION AND DOSAGE Infusion, decoctions or tinctures of 0.6-2.0 g of powdered bark may be taken three times a day. Powdered bark may be applied to ulcers. Bark extracts are included in numerous commercial preparations.

ACTIVE INGREDIENTS The root bark contains the flavonoid myricitrin, together with tannins and triterpenoids (including myricadiol, taraxerol and taraxerone). The wax (actually a lipid obtained from the skin of the fruits) contains esters of palmitic, myristic and lauric acids.

PHARMACOLOGICAL EFFECTS It is speculated that myricitrin may account for the reported antibacterial and choleretic effects. Tannins are astringent and provide a plausible explanation for some of the traditional uses.

WARNING Myricadiol has documented mineralocorticoid activity. It has also been suggested that large doses may interfere with steroid treatment or with medication for hypotension or hypertension.

NOTES The specific epithet *cerifera* means wax-bearing. In former times, the wax was a substitute for bees wax and used to make candles and scented bayberry soap. In South Africa, the wax of *Myrica cordifolia* (dune waxberry) is used to make candles and floor polish. Leaves of the European and North America *M. gale*, *Myrti brabantici folia*, contain 0.4% essential oil (rich in 1,8-cineole) and flavonoids (myricetin). It is a traditional medicine that was used against parasites and to treat skin disorders.

STATUS Traditional medicine; Pharm.

Myrica cerifera L. (= *M. pensylvanica* Loisel.)
arbre à suif (French); *Wachsmyrte* (German); *corteccia* (Italian)

family: Myricaceae

Myristica fragrans

nutmeg tree

Myristica fragrans female flower

Myristica fragrans leaves and fruit

Nutmeg and mace

DESCRIPTION Nutmeg is an evergreen tree of up to 20 m in height. Female trees produce a pale brownish yellow, fleshy fruit that splits into two at maturity. Inside is a large, hard seed, surrounded by a peculiar bright red aril that forms a thin, net-like fleshy layer.

ORIGIN Southeast Asia; indigenous to Amboine Island, one of the Molucca Islands. It was introduced to Mauritius, Malaysia, Sri Lanka, Sumatra and the Caribbean Islands. Most of the commercial product comes from Malaysia, Indonesia and the West Indies (Grenada).

PARTS USED The dried, dehusked seeds (*Myristicae semen*), the dried seed arils (mace – *Myristicae arillus*) and essential oil (*Myristicae aetheroleum*).

THERAPEUTIC CATEGORY Antispasmodic, digestive (central stimulant).

USES AND PROPERTIES Nutmeg and/or mace is used to treat complaints of the digestive tract, such as bloating, stomach cramps and diarrhoea, as well as catarrh of respiratory tract. Nutmeg oil is traditionally applied as a counter-irritant for relief of aches and pains.

PREPARATION AND DOSAGE Small amounts of the powdered product (0.3-1.0 g) is taken three times a day with a little water. Larger doses may cause headache and dizziness. Doses of 5 g or more are dangerous and may cause psychic disturbances, hallucinations, heart palpitations and abortion.

ACTIVE INGREDIENTS Nutmeg and mace contain an essential oil (up to 15% of dry weight). The main compounds are sabinen, α-pinene and β-pinene (80%) and myristicine (10%), together with other phenylpropanoids, elemicin, eugenol, isoeugenol, methyleugenol, safrol and others. Seeds contain up to 75% of fatty oil (known as nutmeg butter) and various lignans and neolignans.

PHARMACOLOGICAL EFFECTS The drug has pronounced antimicrobial and anti-inflammatory activities (inhibition of prostaglandin formation was demonstrated). The essential oil is known to have a spasmolytic activity and relieves stomach cramps and flatulence. The addictive and hallucinogenic effects are ascribed to myristicin and elemicin that are converted to amphetamine-like compounds.

WARNING Large quantities of nutmeg and mace can be dangerous (use medicinally only under proper supervision).

STATUS Traditional medicine; Pharm.

Myristica fragrans L.   family: Myristicaceae

noix muscade (French); *Muskatnussbaum* (German); *noce moscata* (Italian); *nuez moscada* (Spanish)

Myroxylon balsamum
Tolu balsam tree

Myroxylon balsamum leaves

Peruvian balsam

DESCRIPTION This is a tall, evergreen tree (up to 19 m) with compound, hairy, gland-dotted leaves, white flowers and pale brown seed pods. M. balsamum var. balsamum (= M. toluiferum) is the source of Tolu balsam and M. balsamum var. pereirae, the source of Peruvian balsam.

ORIGIN South and Central America. Tolu balsam comes from the town of Tolu in Columbia; Peruvian balsam comes mainly from San Salvador but also Costa Rica, Guatemala and Mexico (not from Peru!).

PARTS USED The oleoresin (Tolu balsam – *Balsamum tolutanum*), which oozes out of damaged bark; Peruvian balsam is an aromatic, dark brown oily liquid obtained from smoked trees.

THERAPEUTIC CATEGORY Antiseptic, expectorant, wound-healing.

USES AND PROPERTIES Tolu balsam is mainly included in cough and throat syrups. It is antiseptic, expectorant, and stimulating, and has a pleasant taste. It is an ingredient of friar's balsam, a traditional inhalant to treat catarrh and colds. Peruvian balsam is rarely taken orally but is used mainly in ointments and preparations to treat slow healing wounds, burns, ulcers, frost-bite, haemorrhoids and bruises caused by protheses.

PREPARATION AND DOSAGE An average daily dose of 0.6 g of Tolu balsam is recommended, while topical skin preparations of Peruvian balsam may contain up to 20% of the product.

ACTIVE INGREDIENTS Balsams are defined as oleoresins that contain benzoic acid, cinnamic acid and their esters. Tolu balsam contains benzoic acid (up to 20%), cinnamic acid (10-15%) and benzyl benzoate, together with resin, volatile oil, phenylpropanoids (including eugenol and traces of vanillin). Peruvian balsam contains about 45-70% benzyl benzoate and benzyl cinnamate, known collectively as cinnamein, together with several other esters and alcohols of benzoic and cinnamic acid. Other ingredients include α-nerolidol, β-nerolidol and small amounts of vanillin.

PHARMACOLOGICAL EFFECTS Benzoic acid and derivatives are strongly antibacterial. The utilisation of Tolu balsam as an antiseptic and mild expectorant can therefore be plausibly explained. Peruvian balsam promotes wound-healing by stimulating the granulation process. Benzyl benzoate works against ectoparasites, especially scabies.

STATUS Traditional medicine; Pharm.; Comm.E+.

Myroxylon balsamum (L.) Harms   family: Fabaceae
baumier de Tolu (French); *Tolubalsambaum* (German); *balsamo del Tolù* (Italian)

Myrtus communis

myrtle

Myrtus communis flowers and fruits

DESCRIPTION An evergreen shrub (up to 3 m, depending on cultivar) with small, dark green, glossy leaves, attractive white flower resembling those of *Eucalyptus* species and purple to black berries.

ORIGIN Unknown; The plant has been cultivated since ancient times and is now found from the Mediterranean to southern Asia. Myrtle is a symbol of purity and was commonly used in rituals in ancient Greece. Essential oil is produced mainly in Morocco, Tunisia, Lebanon, the former Yugoslavia and Corsica.

PARTS USED Leaves (*Myrti folium*), the essential oil (*Myrti aetheroleum*) or the ripe fruits.

THERAPEUTIC CATEGORY Expectorant, astringent, urinary tract antiseptic.

USES AND PROPERTIES Myrtle leaf or myrtle oil are relatively uncommon in modern phytotherapy but have been used since ancient times as an ingredient of cough syrups to treat chest infections, congestion, sinusitis and disorders of the urinary tract (considered to be a urinary tract disinfectant). The oil and leaves are applied externally to treat wounds, acne, piles and gum diseases. It has become popular in aromatherapy. A fraction of the oil, known as myrtol, is widely used as expectorant. A cough remedy based purely on myrtol is one of the top-selling phytomedicines in Germany.

PREPARATION AND DOSAGE Oil: 0.2 g; leaves: tea with 15-30 g per litre.

ACTIVE INGREDIENTS Essential oil (0.3-0.5%) with 1,8-cineole (12-45%), α-pinene (15-38%), myrtenol, myrtenyl acetate (4-20%), camphene, nerol, geraniol and dipentene. Leaves also contain a bitter substance and tannins. Myrtol is a fraction of the essential oil that contains mainly 1,8-cineole, limonene and α-pinene. The best quality is said to come from Corsica. Leaves are rich in gallotannins (8%), condensed tannins (14%) and phloroglucins (myrtucommulone A, B).

PHARMACOLOGICAL EFFECTS The oil exhibits spasmolytic, antibacterial and antifungal properties and is active against ectoparasites (lice, fleas). Considering the biological properties of the monoterpenes present (membrane disturbance; modulation of membrane proteins) the medicinal uses appear plausible (see *Eucalyptus globulus*).

NOTES The oil is important in the perfume industry and is an ingredient of "eau 'd Ange".

STATUS Traditional medicine; Pharm.

Myrtus communis L.

family: Myrtaceae

myrte (French); *Echte Myrte* (German); *mirto* (Italian)

Nelumbo nucifera

lotus • sacred lotus

Lotus leaves

Lotus rhizomes

Nelumbo nucifera (white form)

DESCRIPTION Lotus is a water plant with thick, fleshy rhizomes growing in the mud and large, umbrella-shaped leaves borne on long stalks. The large, solitary, waxy flowers are attractive, fragrant and usually red or pink but sometimes white. Also characteristic are the cup-shaped fruits, each bearing several hard but edible seeds.

ORIGIN Southern Asia (mainly India, Tibet and China), to tropical Australia. It was introduced to the Nile in Egypt in early times but is no longer found there. Commercial cultivation for food and traditional medicine has been practised in China since ancient times. It is grown as ornamental plant in ponds and lakes in many parts of the world. The plant is sacred in the Hindu and Buddhist religions and is a symbol of vitality and purity.

PARTS USED Most parts of the plant are used in traditional Chinese medicine and in Ayurvedic medicine, including the leaves (*he ye* or *Folium Nelumbinis*), rhizomes (*ou jie*), seeds (*lian zi*), seed embryos (*lian zi xin*) and even the stamens of the flower (*lian xu*).

THERAPEUTIC CATEGORY Leaves and flowers: astringent, haemostatic; rhizomes, seeds and seed embryos: demulcent and tonic.

USES AND PROPERTIES Leaves and flowers are used to treat a wide range of bleeding disorders, including menorrhagia and haemorrhoids, as well as fever, diarrhoea and nervous conditions. Pastes are applied to inflamed skin. The seeds are eaten as a functional food or tonic and are said to be beneficial in case of nausea, indigestion, nervous disorders and insomnia. Lotus is traditionally used in China as an antidote for mushroom poisoning.

PREPARATION AND DOSAGE A daily dose of 5-8 g of rhizome or seeds is taken by mouth. Leaves, flowers and stamens are rarely used alone but are usually mixed with various other herbs.

ACTIVE INGREDIENTS The plant is exceptionally rich in alkaloids (such as nuciferine, neferine, lotusine, roemerine and anonaine). Leaves and flowers contain flavonoids (quercetin and isoquercitrin).

PHARMACOLOGICAL EFFECTS Animal studies have shown CNS-depressant, anti-inflammatory, hypoglycemic and antipyretic effects.

NOTES The rhizomes (Chinese arrowroot) and seeds are popular food items in China.

STATUS Traditional medicine.

Nelumbo nucifera Gaertner   family: Nymphaeaceae

lian (Chinese); *kamala* (Sanskrit); *kanwal* (Hindi); *nelumbo* (French); *Lotosblume* (German); *nelumbo* (Italian)

213

Nepeta cataria

catnip • catnep

Nepeta cataria (wild form)

Nepeta cataria (garden cultivar)

DESCRIPTION A perennial herb of up to 1 m in height, with opposite pairs of hairy leaves and numerous small, white, pink or blue flowers arranged in rounded clusters. Various cultivars, differing in growth form, flower colour and essential oil composition, have been developed.

ORIGIN Eastern Mediterranean region, southern Asia and central Asia.

PARTS USED Leaves or flowering tops (*Nepetae catariae herba*); essential oil.

THERAPEUTIC CATEGORY Mild sedative, mild soporific, digestive.

USES AND PROPERTIES Catnip tea is mainly used as a calming and sleep-inducing herbal remedy, usually taken at bedtime. It also eases indigestion, promotes sweating and controls the symptoms of diarrhoea. Folk uses include the treatment of infections, toothache, headache, stress, colic, scalp irritations, arthritis, rheumatism, eye inflammation, allergies and haemorrhoids. Catnip tea was once commonly used in Europe as a relaxing and multi-purpose hot beverage before real tea was introduced. It was one of the main healing plants grown in the herb gardens of medieval monasteries.

PREPARATION AND DOSAGE A tea prepared from about 10 g of dried herb in a cup of boiling water can be taken twice a day. It is also used as tinctures, extracts or capsules.

ACTIVE INGREDIENTS An essential oil, rich in nepetalactone (the main compound); nepetalic acid, epinepetalactone, caryophyllene, citral, citronellol, linonen and camphor are present. Nepetalactone and related compounds are iridoids similar to those found in valerian (see *Valeriana officinalis*).

PHARMACOLOGICAL EFFECTS The calming effect of catnip is ascribed to nepetalactone and related compounds. Nepetalactone and nepetalic acid were shown to significantly increase sleeping time in mice. Catnip oil is known to cause CNS depression in humans when taken in large amounts.

NOTES The common name is derived from the effect it has on cats – the plant acts like cannabis in these animals. Nepetalactone is thought to have aphrodisiac and pheromone activity associated with feline courtship behaviour and catnip is therefore used by manufacturers of cat toys with the aim of causing playful behaviour. It is also an effective insect and rodent repellent.

STATUS Traditional medicine.

Nepeta cataria L.

family: Lamiaceae

herbe aux chats (French); *Katzenminze* (German); *cataire, nepeta* (Italian)

Nerium oleander

oleander • rose laurel • rose bay

Nerium oleander flowers and fruit

DESCRIPTION A shrub or small tree (up to 5 m), with oblong, bright green leathery leaves, each with a prominent white midrib. The flowers are attractive, fragrant and usually pink in colour, but a multitude of colour forms and double varieties have been developed for use as garden ornamentals.

ORIGIN Mediterranean region; widely cultivated.

PARTS USED Leaves (*Oleandri folium*).

THERAPEUTIC CATEGORY Heart stimulant; skin treatment.

USES AND PROPERTIES Oleander leaves or tea made thereof are traditionally used to treat functional disorders of the heart, especially as a substitute for digitalis or ouabain. It is extremely poisonous however. The herb has also been used topically to treat skin rashes and scabies.

PREPARATION AND DOSAGE Due to the difficulty of standardising herbal preparations, the use of oleander in self-medication is no longer considered safe. Extreme plant to plant variation and geographical variation are known. In former times, oleander leaf powder (*Oleandri pulvis normatus*) was standardised (using guinea-pigs) to have an activity equal to 0.5% oleandrin.

ACTIVE INGREDIENTS Oleander leaf contains a very large number of cardiac glycosides (cardenolides) (1-2%); aglycones are digitoxigenin, gitoxigenin, oleandrigenin, adynerigenin, neriagenin, oleagennin and uzarigenin. Also present are flavonoid glycosides (neriin, rutin), pregnane glycosides, pentacyclic triterpenes, saponins, tannins and essential oil.

PHARMACOLOGICAL EFFECTS Cardenolides inhibit Na^+, K^+-ATPase, thereby increasing the Ca^{++} level in heart muscle cells. As a result, oleandrin (and possibly other cardenolides) strengthens the contraction of the heart muscle while lowering the heartbeat. It is said to be weaker in action than digitoxin and ouabain. In addition, cardenolides exhibit diuretic effects.

WARNING All parts of the plant are very poisonous and accidental deaths (especially amongst children) are known.

NOTES Yellow oleander (*Thevetia peruviana*) is a related South American plant containing numerous cardiac glycosides (mainly thevetin A and B, once commercially available as a heart stimulant, thevetin). Seeds (*Thevetiae semen*) contain about 10% cardenolides.

STATUS Traditional medicine; Pharm.

Nerium oleander L.   family: Apocynaceae

laurier rose (French); *Oleander* (German); *oleandro* (Italian); *adelfa* (Spanish)

Nigella sativa

black cumin • black seed • kalonji

Nigella sativa plant

Nigella sativa flowers

Nigella sativa seeds

DESCRIPTION An erect annual herb (up to 0.4 m) with finely dissected leaves, attractive white flowers and pointed, segmented, many-seeded fruit capsules.

ORIGIN Southern Europe, North Africa and western Asia. Early domestication probably took place in Mesopotamia or ancient Egypt (seeds were found in Tutankhamen's tomb). In southern and central Europe, seeds were formerly a condiment; still widely used in Pakistan, India, Arabia and Egypt.

PARTS USED Seeds or seed oil.

THERAPEUTIC CATEGORY Immune stimulation (tonic), antispasmodic, diuretic, digestive, antiseptic.

USES AND PROPERTIES Black cumin is important in Arabian and Islamic folk medicine for a wide range of ailments. It is mainly used to treat stomach upsets and colic, but is also considered effective against spasms, asthma, headache and intestinal worms. In large quantities it is diuretic and promotes lactation. The seeds are best known for their culinary uses in Indian and Middle Eastern cuisine (as pepper substitute, spice and especially to flavour bread – e.g. *naan* bread).

PREPARATION AND DOSAGE A tea made from a teaspoon of crushed seeds in a cup of boiling water can be taken twice daily as a tonic. Extracts and tinctures are used in various commercial preparations.

ACTIVE INGREDIENTS The seeds contain a fixed oil (up to 40% of dry weight) with several phytosterols and an essential oil rich in thymoquinone (the main ingredient), *p*-cymene and thymol. Seeds also contain α-hederin (a triterpene saponin) and nigellone (polythymoquinone), together with triglycosides of quercetin and kaempferol, and nigelline (an alkaloid with a characteristic smell). The seed cake is rich in proteins and amino acids (especially high in valine).

PHARMACOLOGICAL EFFECTS Thymoquinone and nigellone have shown a wide range of pharmacological activities in animal studies. They suppress 5-lipoxygenase and inducible nitric oxide synthase and may therefore be of value in inflammatory and autoimmune conditions. Evidence of hypoglycaemic, antioxidant, liver-protecting, analgesic, antithrombotic, spasmolytic, bronchodilatory, antitumour (ascribed to α-hederin) and antibacterial effects was published in recent years.

NOTES The essential oil of *N. damascena* (containing damascenin) is used as a perfume.

STATUS Traditional medicine.

Nigella sativa L.   family: Ranunculaceae

nigelle, poivrette (French); *Schwarzkümmel* (German); *nigella* (Italian)

Ocimum basilicum

basil • sweet basil

Ocimum basilicum

Ocimum tenuiflorum

DESCRIPTION Sweet basil is a robust, aromatic annual (up to 0.7 m), with soft, hairless leaves and broad spikes of white flowers. Sacred basil, holy basil or *tulsi* in Hindi (*O. tenuiflorum*, often called *O. sanctum*) is a short-lived perennial with hairy stems, hairy leaves and slender clusters of purple, lilac or white flowers. A third species is hairy basil or hoary basil (*O. canum*), an annual with tapering, glandular, practically hairless leaves but with hairy calyces around the small white flowers.

ORIGIN Tropical regions throughout Africa, the Middle East, India and Southeast Asia. Since all three species mentioned above have been used as culinary and medicinal herbs for centuries (first in India and North Africa; later in southern and central Europe), the exact origins of the cultivated forms are not known.

PARTS USED Dried aboveground parts (*Basilici herba; Ocimi sancti herba*) or the essential oil; rarely the seeds or roots.

THERAPEUTIC CATEGORY Tonic (aromatic), carminative, diuretic, anthelmintic.

USES AND PROPERTIES Basil species are widely used in traditional medicine as tonics and general medicines against indigestion, flatulence, loss of ap-

petite and internal parasites. Sweet basil has been considered a useful diuretic since ancient times and is sometimes included in wound-healing ointments. Leaf infusions or fresh leaf juice of holy basil is used in India mainly against cough, upper respiratory infections, stress-related skin disorders and indigestion. The seeds are considered to be a nutritional tonic.

PREPARATION AND DOSAGE Tea made from 2-4 g of the dried herb is taken two or three times per day.

ACTIVE INGREDIENTS The essential oil (up to 1%) of *O. basilicum* has methylchavicol (=estragole) and linalool as main component (both may reach 70% or more), together with eugenol, ocimene and cineole. Also present are tannins and flavonoids.

PHARMACOLOGICAL EFFECTS Antibacterial, anti-ulcerogenic and anthelmintic activities have been reported which can be plausibly explained by the secondary metabolites present.

WARNING Estragole is carcinogenic at higher doses, so that basil should not be taken over long periods of time, or be given to pregnant women and young children.

STATUS Traditional medicine; WHO 2 (*Ocimi sancti herba*).

Ocimum basilicum L.   family: Lamiaceae

basilic (French); *Basilikum* (German); *basilico* (Italian)

Oenothera biennis

evening primrose

Oenothera biennis plant

Oenothera biennis flowers and young fruit

DESCRIPTION Evening primrose is a biennial or short-lived perennial forming a basal rosette of leaves in the first year, and a sturdy flowering stalk (up to 1.5 m) in the second year. The large, yellow, tubular flowers open in the evening and are pollinated by moths. Numerous minute seeds are produced in oblong seed capsules (up to 150 000 seeds per plant).

ORIGIN North America (from Canada to Florida and Mexico). The plant has become a roadside weed in many parts of the world and an important cash crop for the production of evening primrose oil. The total world production of the seed is estimated at 4 000 tons.

PARTS USED Seeds (seed oil; *Oenotherae biennis oleum*).

THERAPEUTIC CATEGORY Nutritional supplement (treatment of atopic eczema).

USES AND PROPERTIES The seed oil contains high levels of a polyunsaturated fatty acid known as γ-linolenic acid (gamma-linolenic acid; GLA). GLA is taken for the symptomatic relief of skin disorders, especially atopic eczema (but also in cases of pruritus and skin inflammations). It is said to have benefits in irritable bowel syndrome, menopausal problems, circulatory and rheumatic disorders.

PREPARATION AND DOSAGE A daily dose of 2-3 g is recommended (sometimes as much as 3-5 g of oil per day). Capsules are available that contain 0.5 g of oil corresponding to 40 mg of GLA.

ACTIVE INGREDIENTS Seeds contain up to 25% oil, of which about 8-14% is GLA (the rest, 60-80%, is linoleic acid).

PHARMACOLOGICAL EFFECTS GLA is one of the essential fatty acids required by humans to maintain normal body function, because it is a precursor of dihomo-γ-linolenic acid and arachidonic acid, from which prostaglandins and leucotrienes derive. The latter are hormone-like substances that affect cholesterol levels, dilation of blood vessels and inflammation. Some people (about 10-20% of the population), especially those with neurodermatitis, are apparently deficient in the enzyme that converts linoleic acid to γ-linolenic acid. Several clinical trials have shown the efficacy of GLA in treating eczema.

NOTES High levels of GLA have also been found in borage and blackcurrant seeds.

STATUS Pharm.; WHO 2; clinical studies+.

Oenothera biennis L.   family: Onagraceae

onagre bisannuelle (French); *Gemeine Nachtkerze* (German); *enothera* (Italian)

Olea europaea

olive tree

Olea europaea flowers

Olea europaea fruit

Olea europaea trees

DESCRIPTION Trees of up to 10 m in height, easily recognised by their irregular, often gnarled trunks, opposite pairs of oblong, dark green leaves that are silvery below, small, white flowers that have only two stamens and distinctive fruits (olives).

ORIGIN The cultivated olive is a cultigen of the Mediterranean region (Europe, North Africa and western Asia). Commercially grown in the Mediterranean (90%), but also Africa, Australia and South America.

PARTS USED Dried leaf (*Oleae folium*) and fruit oil (*Olivae oleum*; cold-pressed from the oily mesocarp).

THERAPEUTIC CATEGORY Traditional anti-hypertensive and diuretic (leaf); cholagogue, mild laxative (oil, internal use); demulcent and emollient (oil, external use).

USES AND PROPERTIES Olive leaf is used in Mediterranean countries as a traditional remedy for a wide variety of ailments, mainly as antihypertensive and diuretic. It is also used for its hypoglycaemic, antipyretic and antispasmodic activities, to name only a few. In addition to its use as cholagogue and laxative, the oil is useful as a solvent for some drugs and in refined form for parenteral preparations.

PREPARATION AND DOSAGE A daily dose of about 1-2 g of olive leaf has been recommended (taken as infusion, tincture or tablet). For internal use, 15-30 ml of oil is taken with meals; for external use, the pure oil is applied or it is slightly warmed to body temperature for application to the rectal region or ears.

ACTIVE INGREDIENTS Leaves contain secoiridoids, including oleuropein (the main compound), ligustroside and oleacein, triterpenoids (oleanolic acid, uvaol), sterols, flavonoids (chrysoeriol and apigenin and luteolin glycosides) and various phenolic acids. Olive oil represents about 30% of the ripe fruit and is rich in triglycerides consisting mainly of oleic acid and linoleic acid.

PHARMACOLOGICAL EFFECTS It is known that oleuropein lowers blood pressure by increasing coronary flow; furthermore, a recent study has shown that oleacein inhibits the angiotensin converting enzyme (ACE). The German Commission E does not recommend olive leaves or olive oil to treat hypertension. Oleuropein has significant antispasmodic, antioxidant and lipid-lowering activities.

STATUS Traditional medicine; Pharm.

Olea europaea L.

family: Oleaceae

olivier (French); *Ölbaum* (German); *olivo, ulivo* (Italian); *olivo* (Spanish)

Ononis spinosa

spiny restharrow

Ononis spinosa plant

Ononis spinosa flowers

DESCRIPTION The plant is a spiny subshrub of less than 1 m in height bearing trifoliate leaves on the lower branches and simple leaves higher up. Attractive pink and white flowers are produced in summer, followed by small seed pods.

ORIGIN Europe, western Asia and North Africa. Commercial product is wild-harvested in southeastern Europe.

PARTS USED Dried roots, harvested in autumn (*Ononidis radix*). The roots have a characteristic radiate structure in transverse section, due to broad medullary rays.

THERAPEUTIC CATEGORY Diuretic.

USES AND PROPERTIES Spiny restharrow is a mild diuretic that has been used since ancient times. In traditional medicine it is employed to treat rheumatism and gout. In modern times it is used in irrigation therapy as a diuretic medicine for inflammatory conditions of the lower urinary tract and for preventing and treating kidney gravel.

PREPARATION AND DOSAGE A tea is prepared by pouring boiling water over 2-2.5 g of the coarsely powdered root. It is taken several times a day. The recommended daily dose is 6-12 g of the herb. It is included in herbal mixtures and diuretic preparations.

ACTIVE INGREDIENTS The active ingredient responsible for the diuretic effect is not yet known but it has been speculated that it could be α-onocerin, also known as onocol, a triterpene. It co-occurs with sterols, mainly sitosterol, and various phenolic acids. Also of interest is the presence of isoflavones (compounds characteristic of the roots of members of the Fabaceae). Ononin (formononetin7-glucoside), formononetin, genistein, and biochanin A 7-glucoside, together with their 6"-malonates are the main isoflavonoids. Small amounts of essential oil (up to 0.2%) are found, with trans-anethole, carvone and menthol as major constituents.

PHARMACOLOGICAL EFFECTS The diuretic effects of restharrow root has been well established by experiments in animals. The isoflavones could exhibit oestrogenic effects.

WARNING Treatment should be combined with ample intake of fluids. Irrigation therapy can be harmful in cases of oedema due to cardiac or renal insufficiency.

STATUS Traditional medicine; Pharm.; Comm.E+; ESCOP 5.

Ononis spinosa L.   family: Fabaceae

bugrane épineuse, arrête-boeuf (French); *Dornige Hauhechel* (German); *bonaga, ononide* (Italian); *gatuña* (Spanish)

Origanum vulgare

oregano

Origanum majorana

Origanum vulgare

Origanum dictamnus

DESCRIPTION Oregano is an aromatic perennial herb (up to 0.9 m) with hairy, opposite leaves and white or pink flowers congested towards the branch ends. It is very similar to marjoram or sweet marjoram (*O. majorana*) and the two species (both popular culinary herbs) are often confused. Several species have been used in folk medicine, including *O. compactum*, *O. dictamnus*, *O. heracleoticum*, *O. onites* and *O. syriacum*. *O. syriacum* is the hyssop of the Bible (mentioned at the Crucifixion). *O. dictamnus*, the dittany of Crete (or *dictamon* in Greek), has woolly leaves and large floral bracts. In Greek mythology, it is the herb that was used by Aphrodite to heal the wounds of the trojan hero Aenèas.

ORIGIN Europe to central Asia (*O. vulgare*), Mediterranean region (*O. majorana*), Middle East (*O. syriacum*) and Crete (*O. dictamnus*). Oregano, and to a lesser extent marjoram, are commercially grown as spices (oregano gives the characteristic flavour to pizza). Dittany and related species have been developed as ornamental garden plants. The herb is still a popular medicine in Greece and especially in Crete, where it is said to be endemic.

PARTS USED Dried aboveground parts (oregano –

Origani vulgaris herba; marjoram herb – *Majoranae herba*); essential oil (oregano oil – *Origani vulgaris aetheroleum* and marjoram oil – *Majoranae aetheroleum*).

THERAPEUTIC CATEGORY Stomachic, expectorant.

USES AND PROPERTIES Oregano, sweet marjoram and dittany are mainly used to treat bronchitis, catarrh, cold and flu, colic and dyspepsia. These herbs or their dilute oils are sometimes used topically for mouth hygiene, to treat nasal congestion, wounds and itching skin. The essential oils of oregano and marjoram are used in aromatherapy.

PREPARATION AND DOSAGE Tea made from 1-2 g of dried herb can be taken three times a day. The oil should never be taken internally.

ACTIVE INGREDIENTS Oregano and dittany oil contains carvacrol (40-70%), p-cymene and γ-terpinen, while marjoram oil mainly has terpinen-4-ol, α-terpineol, sabinen, linalool and carvacrol.

PHARMACOLOGICAL EFFECTS The essential oils of *Origanum* species interfere with biomembranes and are known to be antibacterial, anti-fungal, antiviral, spasmolytic and anti-inflammatory.

STATUS Traditional medicine; Pharm.; Comm.E+.

Origanum vulgare L.   family: Lamiaceae

origan (French); *Echter Dost* (German); *origano* (Italian); *orégano* (Spanish)

Orthosiphon aristatus

long-stamened orthosiphon

Orthosiphon aristatus

Orthosiphon grandiflorus flowers

DESCRIPTION A perennial herb (up to 0.8 m) with opposite, hairy, distinctly toothed leaves borne on short petioles. Small, tubular, white or lilac flowers with long, protruding stamens are borne in oblong clusters. The very long stamens are a distinctive feature, as reflected in Dutch-Indonesian, German and French names. *O. grandiflorus* is a closely related species.

ORIGIN Southeast Asia, Malaysia and Australia. It is cultivated in Indonesia (Java) and Australia, Georgia (Caucasus) and Vietnam.

PARTS USED Dried leaves (*Orthosiphonis folium*).

THERAPEUTIC CATEGORY Urological (diuretic, weak antispasmodic).

USES AND PROPERTIES Java tea is mainly used as a diuretic in cases of chronic inflammation of the kidney and bladder and in bladder catarrh, kidney catarrh, bacteriuria and irritable bladder. The product is used on its own or in combination with tea mixtures and urological preparations.

PREPARATION AND DOSAGE Tea is made with 2-3 g of the finely chopped leaves in 150 ml boiling water. The recommended maximum daily dose is 6-12 g of the herb. Tinctures and tablets are also available, usually standardised according to the flavonoid content.

ACTIVE INGREDIENTS Large amounts of potassium salts (about 3%) and only small amounts (up to 0.3%) of a complex essential oil, yielding mostly borneol, limonene, thymol and sesquiterpenoids. Of interest are several methoxylated flavonoids such as eupatorin, rhamnazin, scutellarein tetramethyl ether, salvigenin and sinensetin, as well as flavonol glycosides. Caffeic acid esters are present in the form of rosmarinic acid, together with mono- and dicaffeoyl-tartaric acids and smaller amounts of lithospermic acid. There are also diterpenes derived from pimarane, known as orthosiphol A-E, some triterpenes and saponins.

PHARMACOLOGICAL EFFECTS *Orthosiphon* extracts show antimicrobial, anti-inflammatory and distinct diuretic properties. Triterpenes, saponins, flavonoids and monoterpenes could be responsible for these properties. Sinensetin and scutellarein inhibit 5-lipoxygenase, which would partly explain the anti-inflammatory effects. It has been proposed that the herb may cause a widening of the ureters, so that small renal calculi may be eliminated with the urine.

STATUS Traditional medicine; Pharm.; Comm.E+; ESCOP 1.

Orthosiphon aristatus (Blume) Miq. [(= *O. spicatus* (Thunb.) Bak., = *O. stamineus* Benth.]   family: Lamiaceae
kumis kutjing (Indonesian); *koemis koetjing* (Indonesian); *moustache de chat* (French); *Katzenbart* (German); *tè de Giava* (Italian)

Paeonia lactiflora

white peony

Paeonia lactiflora leaves and flowers

Paeonia officinalis

DESCRIPTION A leafy perennial herb with a strongly branched root. The leaves are compound, with oblong, red-veined segments. Attractive, large flowers are characteristic – they are usually white but may also be red or purple. Large seeds are borne in a segmented fruit comprising 3-5 few-seeded follicles. In European folk medicine, the seeds of *P. officinalis* were an epilepsy remedy and the petals are included in herbal teas, mainly to enhance their appearance. In China and Japan, species such as *P. veitchii* (*chi shao*, red peony) and *P. moutan* (=*P. suffruticosa*), the source of *mudan pi* (moudan root bark), are listed in pharmacopoeias.

ORIGIN China, Japan and India (*P. lactiflora*); southern Europe (*P. officinalis*).

PARTS USED Dried root (*Paeoniae radix rubra*); in Europe, also the petals of *P. officinalis* (*Paeoniae flos*).

THERAPEUTIC CATEGORY Antispasmodic, anti-inflammatory, analgesic.

USES AND PROPERTIES The main use of the root in Chinese medicine is to treat menstrual disorders, such as amenorrhoea, dysmenorrhoea, and dyspepsia (stomach spasms, liver problems). Other uses in the traditional system of medicine include dementia, head-

ache, vertigo, allergies and as an anticoagulant. In Chinese folk medicine it is considered to be useful in case of fevers and externally to treat atopic eczema, wounds, boils, sores and burns. In European medicine, roots and seeds of *P. officinalis* have been considered useful against epilepsy, arthritis, stomach complaints, cough and various skin disorders but they are no longer used.

PREPARATION AND DOSAGE The maximum daily oral dose is 6-15 g of the crude plant material.

ACTIVE INGREDIENTS The main active principle in white peony root is a monoterpenoid glycoside known as paeoniflorin (up to 5%) and various derivatives. Gallotannins are present in the roots and flowers. The petals typically contain anthocyanins such as paeonin (=paeonidin 3,5-diglucoside) and flavonoids (kaempferol derivatives).

PHARMACOLOGICAL EFFECTS Paeoniflorin showed analgesic, antipyretic, anti-inflammatory, uterus-contractant, sedative and vasodilatory effects in test animals.

STATUS Traditional medicine; Pharm. (*P. officinalis*); WHO 1 (*P. lactiflora*).

Paeonia lactiflora Pallas (= *P. albiflora*)   family: Paeoniaceae

bai shao yao (Chinese); *pivoine* (French); *Chinesische Pfingstrose, Päonie* (German); *peonia* (Italian)

Panax ginseng

ginseng • Asian ginseng • Korean ginseng

Panax ginseng plants

Panax ginseng fruits

Ginseng roots

DESCRIPTION A small perennial geophyte with a single stem emerging every year from a short rhizome attached to a fleshy root. One to four palmately compound leaves are formed at a single node which also bears a single cluster of small white flowers that each develop into a fleshy, two-celled, bright red fruit. American ginseng (*Panax quinquefolius*) is said to differ by the rounded rather than tapered leaflet bases, but it is difficult to distinguish between the two species.

ORIGIN Mountain forests of eastern Asia. Grown as a crop in China, Russia, Korea and Japan. American ginseng occurs naturally over a large part of the USA and Canada and is also cultivated there on a large scale for export to China.

PARTS USED Fresh or mostly dried root (*Ginseng radix*).

THERAPEUTIC CATEGORY Adaptogenic tonic.

USES AND PROPERTIES This is the most famous of all Chinese medicinal plants and has a great reputation as an adaptogen – a remedy that enhances nonspecifically the body's own defense against stress and disease. The root has been used in China for thousands of years and should not be judged as a medicine because it is not aimed at any particular disease. It is rather aimed at counteracting weakness, fatigue, declining stamina and concentration, and at enhancing convalescence.

PREPARATION AND DOSAGE A daily dose is 1-2 g (up to 3 g) of dried root (or 200-600 mg extract). It may be directly chewed, or taken as an infusion (instant tea, 3 g teabags or ginseng preparations are available). Treatment should last for at least three to four weeks (up to three months).

ACTIVE INGREDIENTS A complex mixture of triterpenoid saponins with 20(S)-protopanaxadiol and 20(S)-protopanaxatriol as aglycones, collectively known as ginsenosides (up to 6%). The most important ones are the ginsenosides Rg_1, Rc, Rd, Rb_1, Rb_2 and Rb_0. Also present is a series of polyacetylenes (the ginsenoynes A-K) and small amounts of essential oil.

PHARMACOLOGICAL EFFECTS Controlled clinical studies have shown that ginseng improves mood, physical and intellectual performance, convalescence and various other metabolic parameters (including immune response).

STATUS Pharm.; Comm.E+; WHO 1; clinical studies +.

Panax ginseng C. A. Mey.

family Araliaceae

ginseng (French); Ginseng (German); ginseng (Italian)

Papaver somniferum

opium poppy

Papaver somniferum fruit capsules

Papaver somniferum flowers

Papaver rhoeas

DESCRIPTION An erect annual (up to 1.5 m), bearing hairless, grey-green leaves, attractive white, red or purple flowers and characteristic spherical fruit capsules containing numerous greyish to black seeds.

ORIGIN Southwestern Asia; an ancient cultigen of uncertain origin, grown in Europe, North Africa and Asia for centuries. Two types can be distinguished – those grown for opium (legal production mainly in India, Turkey) and those grown for poppy seed and seed oil.

PARTS USED The dried latex (raw opium – *Opium*). Opium is produced by making shallow cuts in the unripe fruit – the white latex that oozes out soon turns brown and is collected and dried. The world demand for opiates is nearly 200 tons of alkaloid per year.

THERAPEUTIC CATEGORY Analgesic, euphoric (morphine, codeine); antitussive (codeine, noscapine).

USES AND PROPERTIES Pure alkaloids are nowadays used in standardised modern medicines intended for oral and parenteral use – mainly to treat intense pain (e.g. in cancer patients) and as antitussive medicines (to treat difficult, non-productive coughs). Opium powder and opium extract have become less important. Morphine can be converted into heroine, an important intoxicant. Opium and morphine cause constipation (used as anti-diarrhoeal).

PREPARATION AND DOSAGE Pure morphine is administered in doses of 10-40 mg per day. Codeine is used in doses of 30 mg every four hours.

ACTIVE INGREDIENTS Opium poppy and opium contain numerous isoquinoline alkaloids. Morphine is the most important opium alkaloid (10-12%), followed by (–)-noscapine (=narcotine, 2-10%) and codeine (2.5-10%). Most of the pure morphine obtained through extraction is converted chemically to codeine.

PHARMACOLOGICAL EFFECTS Morphine modulates endorphine receptors and acts as a powerful analgesic but is unfortunately highly addictive. Codeine is an effective painkiller (though less active than morphine, but also less addictive). It sedates the cough centre and has antitussive activity. Noscapine is a specific antitussive.

NOTES The dried petals of the corn poppy (*P. rhoeas*) are a traditional sedative but is nowadays used mainly in tea mixtures, to enhance their appearance.

STATUS Traditional and modern medicine: morphine and other isolated alkaloids; Pharm.; source of pure alkaloids.

Papaver somniferum L.   family: Papaveraceae

pavot somnifère (French); *Schlafmohn* (German); *pavot officinal, papavero domestico* (Italian)

Parietaria officinalis

pellitory of the wall

Parietaria officinalis

Parietaria officinalis leaves and flowers

Parietaria judaica

DESCRIPTION This inhabitant of walls and dry stony places is a perennial with dark green leaves, small greenish flowers and small capsules containing dark brown to blackish seeds. The female flowers are borne on the tips of the stems, while the male flowers are clustered in the leaf axils. A closely related species, *P. judaica* (=*P. diffusa*) is used in the same way as *P. officinalis*. It is similar to the latter but is a much smaller herb with smaller leaves. The name *Parietaria* is derived from *paries*, the Latin word for wall, in reference to the main habitat (cracks in walls) of the two species. *Parietaria* species are related to stinging nettle (*Urtica* species) but their glossy upper leaf surfaces are distinct.

ORIGIN Central and southern Europe (*P. officinalis*) or western and southern Europe (*P. judaica*). These plants have become weeds in many parts of the world. They are wild-harvested to a limited extent for medicinal use and are not cultivated.

PARTS USED Whole herb (aerial parts).

THERAPEUTIC CATEGORY Traditional diuretic and anti-inflammatory.

USES AND PROPERTIES The herb is traditionally used to treat kidney and bladder disorders, urinary tract infections, cystitis, urinary stones and related ailments. It is also a traditional cough medicine and may be used to alleviate the pain of wounds and burns and to promote their healing.

PREPARATION AND DOSAGE Infusions or decoctions are used internally or externally but effective or safe doses are not specified.

ACTIVE INGREDIENTS The plants contain organic acids, especially caffeoylmalic acid, together with tannins and flavonoids.

PHARMACOLOGICAL EFFECTS Almost nothing is known about the pharmacological effects or the compounds responsible for the diuretic and anti-inflammatory effects observed in traditional use. The phenolic acids and tannins are likely candidates responsible for part of the activities.

WARNING The pollen of *P. officinalis* is known to cause severe allergic reactions in some people. Present in the pollen is a dodecapeptide containing Par o 1, the major allergen.

STATUS Traditional medicine.

Parietaria officinalis L.   family: Urticaceae

pariétaire officinale (French); *Aufrechtes Glaskraut* (German); parietaria (Italian)

Passiflora incarnata

passion flower • apricot vine

Passiflora incarnata leaves and fruit

Passiflora incarnata flower

DESCRIPTION A woody perennial creeper (vine) that climbs with the aid of coiled tendrils. It has hairless, lobed leaves, large stipules and solitary, very characteristic, open, white and violet flowers, with conspicuous flower parts that have given rise to the vernacular name "passion flower". The origin is said to be a "Calvary Lesson" by Catholic missionaries in South America. The numerous petaloid corona threads are seen as a symbol for the Crown of Thorns, the five stamens for the Wounds, the three stigmas for the Nails on the Cross and the five sepals and five petals as the ten apostles (excluding Judas and Peter). The fruit is a characteristic many-seeded berry with delicious, juicy fruit pulp.

ORIGIN Eastern and southern parts of North America. It is cultivated to a limited extent.

PARTS USED Dried whole herb, mainly leaves and thin stems (*Passiflorae herba*).

THERAPEUTIC CATEGORY Sedative.

USES AND PROPERTIES The main use of passion flower herb is as a mild sedative to treat nervousness, restlessness, sleeplessness and nervous gastrointestinal disorders, especially in children.

PREPARATION AND DOSAGE A tea can be made with 2 g of finely chopped herb. Two or three cups are taken throughout the day, or one or two cups at bedtime (maximum daily dose is 4-8 g of herb). Extracts are used in a large number of sedative preparations and combinations; also in some cardiotonics.

ACTIVE INGREDIENTS The herb contains flavonoids (C-glycosides of vitexin, isovitexin, apigenin and luteolin), γ-pyrone derivatives (maltol and ethylmaltol), a polyacetylene (passicol) and a cyanogenic glycoside (gynocardin). Previous reports mention indole alkaloids of the harmine type. A re-evaluation, using a sensitive HPLC method, failed to find evidence of alkaloids.

PHARMACOLOGICAL EFFECTS Passion flower has sedative, hypnotic and anti-spasmodic activity, as shown in animal studies. It is not yet clear which compounds are responsible; β-carboline alkaloids inhibit MAO and bind to serotonin receptors; they would be good candidates for a sedative but their presence has been disputed. Maltol and ethylmaltol have CNS sedating and anticonvulsant effects.

STATUS Traditional medicine; Pharm.; Comm.E+; ESCOP 4.

Passiflora incarnata L.

family: Passifloraceae

passiflore, fleur de la passion (French); *Fleischfarbene Passionsblume* (German); *passiflora* (Italian); *pasiflora* (Spanish)

Paullinia cupana

guaraná • Brasilian cocoa

Paullinia cupana leaves and climbing tendril

Paullinia cupana seeds

Theobroma cacao fruit

DESCRIPTION A woody creeper (vine) with compound leaves, coiled tendrils, inconspicuous yellowish flowers and small, bright red fruits that contain spherical, brown seeds. The seeds have shiny dark spots on their tips, resembling eyes (hence a common association between guaraná seeds and human eyes in folklore and traditions of the Maués Indians of Brazil).

ORIGIN South America (lower Amazon region); cultivated in Brazil.

PARTS USED Seeds (or a dried paste prepared from roasted, powdered seeds and water, known as *guaraná*).

THERAPEUTIC CATEGORY Stimulant tonic, anti-diarrhoeal, diuretic.

USES AND PROPERTIES Guaraná preparations and drinks are tonics that counteract fatigue. The product is used to some extent to treat mild diarrhoea, functional asthenia (a technical term for diminishing strength and energy) and as supportive treatment in weight loss programmes. Traditionally it is a tonic and potential aphrodisiac. The main use nowadays is as an ingredient of non-alcoholic, fizzy soft drinks (known as *guaraná* or *cupana*) that are extremely popular in South America. In recent years, these "energy drinks" (with taurine) have become fashionable especially amongst young people in western Europe.

PREPARATION AND DOSAGE The traditional product is a dried paste made from powdered seeds. Soft drinks contain up to 1.3 g extract per 100 g.

ACTIVE INGREDIENTS Guaraná paste contains a minimum of 3% caffeine (the seeds at least 3.5%, but up to 6%). It generally has three to fives times more caffeine than coffee, making it the most caffeine-rich of all products. Also of pharmaceutical interest is the high yield of phenolics (12%), which include catechin, epicatechin and proanthocyanidins.

PHARMACOLOGICAL EFFECTS Caffeine is a well-known central stimulant and diuretic (see *Coffea arabica*), so that its benefit in tonics and weight loss preparations is obvious. The anti-diarrhoeal effects are ascribed to tannins. Caffeine is considered safe to use but may cause palpitations, lack of concentration and sleeplessness when taken in higher doses.

NOTES Seeds of *Theobroma cacao* (family Sterculiaceae) contain caffeine (but mainly theobromine) and are used in chocolate production.

STATUS Traditional medicine; functional food.

Paullinia cupana Kunth   family: Sapindaceae

guarana (French); *Guarana-Strauch* (German); *cupana* (Spanish)

Pausinystalia johimbe

yohimbe tree

Pausinystalia johimbe leaves

Pausinystalia johimbe bark

DESCRIPTION Yohimbe is a large forest tree of up to 30 m in height bearing narrowly oblong, bright green simple leaves and small, tubular, white or yellowish flowers. The fruits are small capsules containing winged seeds.

ORIGIN West and Central Africa (Cameroon to Congo). The tree is not yet cultivated commercially to any extent, and concern has been expressed about the conservation status of the species.

PARTS USED Bark, harvested from the stem or smaller branches of the tree (*Yohimbe cortex*).

THERAPEUTIC CATEGORY Aphrodisiac, urological.

USES AND PROPERTIES Extracts of the bark are traditional stimulants and male tonics in tropical Africa. In modern phytomedicine it has been used to regulate micturition and has become extremely popular for treating impotence and frigidity. Beneficial effects against hypertension and fatigue have been reported.

PREPARATION AND DOSAGE The average and maximum daily doses of bark is 3 g and 10 g respectively. The safe and effective dose of yohimbine in stimulant preparations and sexual tonics is said to be less than 10 mg. Higher doses of 50-100 mg are hallu-cinogenic; more than 100 mg are considered unpleasant and dangerous.

ACTIVE INGREDIENTS The bark contains several monoterpene indole alkaloids of the yohimbine type (3-6%), of which (+)-yohimbine is the main compound.

PHARMACOLOGICAL EFFECTS The alkaloid yohimbine inhibit α-adrenergic receptors; they thus affect the sympatic nervous system, leading to vasodilatation and a decreased blood pressure. Yohimbine is a central stimulant and can enhance general anxiety and excitability of the lower abdomen. As a result, the use in urinary incontinence (weak bladder) and impotence is plausibly explained. Yohimbine was shown to increase copulation frequency in rats and a double blinded study with humans gave positive results in treating male erectile dysfuntion.

WARNING Self-medication can be dangerous, especially in patients with low blood pressure, diabetes, heart and kidney diseases or when taking anti-depressive drugs, benzodiazepins, sympathomimetics and tyramine-rich foods. Side effects include overstimulation, irritability and anxiety attacks.

STATUS Traditional medicine; modern medicine: yohimbine: Pharm.; clinical studies+.

Pausinystalia johimbe (K. Schum.) Beille (= *Corynanthe yohimbe* K. Schum.)   family: Rubiaceae
yohimbe (French); *Yohimbebaum* (German); *yohimbe* (Italian)

Peganum harmala

harmala • African rue

Peganum harmala shrub

Peganum harmala flowers

DESCRIPTION A small, erect shrub of about 0.5 m in height, with linear leaves and attractive cream-coloured flowers. The seeds are borne in trilocular capsules.

ORIGIN Mediterranean region (Europe and North Africa), Arabia and western Asia; typical of dry places.

PARTS USED Mainly the seeds (*Harmalae semen*); rarely roots.

THERAPEUTIC CATEGORY Hallucinogen, intoxicant.

USES AND PROPERTIES Seeds have been used to a limited extent against stomach pain and externally to treat wounds and rashes. The plant is toxic but has interesting traditional uses, especially for ailments requiring antispasmodic and painkilling effects. These include Parkinson's disease, eye diseases, rheumatism, nervous disorders and impotence. Smoke from burning seeds is a traditional intoxicant and sexual stimulant in central Asia. It is claimed that the intricate patterns on oriental carpets, as well as the concept of flying carpets, were inspired by the hallucinogenic effects of the seed alkaloids.

PREPARATION AND DOSAGE Harmala seeds are no longer used. Pure alkaloids were once extracted for medicinal use.

ACTIVE INGREDIENTS The toxicity and hallucinogenic effects are due to β-carboline (indole) alkaloids, also known as harman alkaloids (mainly harmine, with harmane, harmol, and harmatol). Pure alkaloid was formerly used to treat Parkinson's disease.

PHARMACOLOGICAL EFFECTS The alkaloids interact with the central nervous system. They can activate serotonine receptors because of the structural similarity of serotonine and β-carboline alkaloids. They also inhibit monoamine oxidase, an enzyme that breaks down catechole amines. As a consequence, serotoninergic and dopaminergic synapses are stimulated, leading to euphoric and hallucinogenic effects.

WARNING *Peganum* is toxic and should not be used under any circumstances.

NOTES Harmine and related alkaloids are also found in *Banisteriopsis caapi* (family Malpighiaceae), a woody climber(vine) from tropical South America (Amazonia, Ecuador, Colombia, Peru). Bark infusions, known as *caapi* in Brazil, *ayahuasca* in Peru and *yagé* or *yajé* in Colombia, are of traditional importance as an intoxicant in religious rites.

STATUS Traditional medicine.

Peganum harmala L.   family: Zygophyllaceae

harmel (French); *Steppenraute* (German); *peganum* (Italian)

Pelargonium sidoides

umckaloabo

Pelargonium sidoides

Pelargonium sidoides flowers

Pelargonium sidoides roots

DESCRIPTION A small perennial herb with tuberous roots, rounded to heart-shaped and slightly silky leaves, and small tubular flowers that are dark maroon red to almost black. They are pink in the closely related and formerly used *P. reniforme*. Shrubby pelargoniums grown for their essential oil are also of some medicinal interest, particularly the famous rose geraniums (cultivars derived from *P. graveolens*, *P.capitatum* and *P. radens*).

ORIGIN South Africa. *P. sidoides* is cultivated on a small scale in South Africa. Rose geranium oil (especially Bourbon oil) has been produced on the small Indian Ocean island of Réunion for many years but the plants are nowadays also grown in other parts.

PARTS USED The fleshy roots are used, fresh or dried.

THERAPEUTIC CATEGORY Antibiotic, immune-stimulant.

USES AND PROPERTIES Root extracts are used in preparations to treat acute and chronic infections of the nose, ears and chest. It is said to be particularly effective for bronchitis in children and as supportive treatment in tuberculosis and chronic bronchitis. Rose geranium oil is used in perfumery and aromatherapy (as a substitute for rose oil, from *Rosa damascena*).

PREPARATION AND DOSAGE An ethanolic extract is used in a proprietary herbal tincture known as Umkaloabo™. Infusions or decoctions are traditionally used but dosage information on the crude herb is not available.

ACTIVE INGREDIENTS The main ingredients are coumarins (mainly 7-hydroxy-5,6-dimethoxycoumarin, also known as umckalin, that co-occurs with at least seven other coumarins), gallic acid derivates (including gallic acid and gallic acid methyl ester), oligomeric proanthocyanidins, flavan-3-ols (e.g. catechin) and flavonoids (e.g. quercetin). *Pelargonium* oils contain various monoterpenoids such as geraniol, (+)-iso-menthone, citronellol and phenylethyl alcohol (responsible for the rose smell).

PHARMACOLOGICAL EFFECTS The gallic acid derivatives and other phenolic compounds in the roots have powerful antibacterial and antiviral activity and these compounds, together with the coumarins, provide a rationale for the proven immunomodulatory activity. *Pelargonium* oil is antibacterial; citronellol is a known insect repellent.

STATUS Traditional medicine; clinical studies+.

Pelargonium sidoides DC.

family: Geraniaceae

Pelargonium sidoides (French); *Umckaloabo* (German); *Pelargonium sidoides* (Italian)

Persea americana
avocado

Persea americana leaves and flowers

Persea americana fruit

Argania spinosa flower and fruit

DESCRIPTION An evergreen tree (up to 40 m) with large, simple, bright green leaves that are characteristically paler green below. Small, yellowish flowers are borne near the branch tips and they are followed by large, usually pear-shaped, green or purple fruits. The fruit has a thin leathery skin with a thick layer of greenish yellow, butter-textured flesh around a very large seed.

ORIGIN Central America; probably cultivated since ancient times for its delicious and nutritious fruits. Commercial production is centred mainly in California, Mexico, Chile, Israel, Australia and South Africa.

PARTS USED Oil, extracted from the fruit flesh (*Avocado oleum*); also the leaves (*Perseae folium*).

THERAPEUTIC CATEGORY Emollient, cosmetic.

USES AND PROPERTIES Avocado oil has become popular as a natural oil used as a carrier and base for aromatherapy oils and cosmetic products. It is a popular ingredient of "natural" or "organic" skin care products such as ointments, skin creams, soaps and shampoos. Leaves have been used in Mexico to treat menstrual disorders and for contraception.

PREPARATION AND DOSAGE The oil is used as carrier in aromatherapy or in various combinations with other cosmetic ingredients.

ACTIVE INGREDIENTS Unsaponifiable matter (non-glyceride constituents) occur in avocado oil up to 1%. Branched hydrocarbons, phytosterols and triterpene alcohols, such as cycloartenol, methylcycloartenol, make up the bulk of the 1%. The oil itself is variable in composition but contains oleic acid as main constituent, together with substantial quantities of palmitic acid, palmitoleic acid, linoleic acid and small amounts of γ-linolenic acid. Leaves produce an essential oil (with estragol, caryophyllen, eugenol and monoterpenes).

PHARMACOLOGICAL EFFECTS The unsaponifiable fraction of avocado pear oil, in combination with that of soybean oil, has been tested for use against ailments of the mouth (in stomatology) and as treatment for gum diseases (periodontitis). It is considered to be of potential value in the supportive treatment of arthritis pain.

NOTES Another example of a natural cosmetic oil is argan oil, obtained from the fruits of a thorny Moroccan tree, *Argania spinosa* (Sapotaceae).

STATUS Traditional medicine; Pharm.

Persea americana L. (= *P. gratissima* Gaertn.)   family: Lauraceae

avocatier (French); *Avocado* (German); *avocado* (Italian); *ahuacate* (Spanish)

Persicaria bistorta

bistort

Persicaria bistorta

Persicaria odorata

DESCRIPTION A small, weedy perennial herb of damp places with creeping rhizomes, long, narrow basal leaves and attractive clusters of pink flowers in dense oblong spikes. *Persicaria* species were until recently included in the genus *Polygonum*, so that bistort will be found under the name *Polygonum bistorta* in most text books. Some species have remained in *Polygonum* (see *Polygonum aviculare*). Several *Persicaria* species are used in traditional medicine (and as food plants) in various parts of the world. Well-known examples are *P. chinense*, *P. hydropiper* and *P. odorata*. Leaves of the last-mentioned, known as *rau ram*, Vietnamese mint or Vietnamese coriander, are important in Vietnamese and Chinese cooking. They yield an essential oil known as kesom oil that is being developed for the food and fragrance industries.

ORIGIN Europe, Asia and North America. The herb is wild-harvested.

PARTS USED Mostly the dried rhizomes (*Bistortae rhizoma*).

THERAPEUTIC CATEGORY Astringent, anti-diarrhoeal, anti-catarrhal, anti-inflammatory.

USES AND PROPERTIES Bistort is used mainly to treat diarrhoea and dysentery and catarrh of the up-per respiratory tract. It is said to be helpful in case of cystitis and is used externally in mouthwashes, gargles, douches, baths and ointments to treat inflamed and infected mucosa and skin.

PREPARATION AND DOSAGE The herb may be used as a tea (1-2 g as infusion, taken up to three times a day). Infusions and decoctions may also be prepared for topical use.

ACTIVE INGREDIENTS The main active compounds are considered to be tannins (oligomeric proantho-cyanidins, galloyl and catechol tannins), that are present in very high yields in the rhizomes (15-36%). In addition, rhizomes and aerial parts accumulate silicic acid. Anthraquinones that are typical for Polygonaceae (see *Rheum palmatum*) are almost absent in *Persicaria*.

PHARMACOLOGICAL EFFECTS Tannins are known for their astringent properties (they cause tissues and veins to contract, thus reducing bleeding) and also for their antibacterial effects. Tannins act non-specifically on microbial proteins, disrupt their proliferation and in this way help to "detoxify" the digestive system in cases of infection and diarrhoea or dysentery.

STATUS Traditional medicine.

Persicaria bistorta (L.) Samp. (=*Polygonum bistorta* L.) family: Polygonaceae
bistorte (French); *Wiesen-Knöterich, Schlangen-Knöterich* (German); *bistorta* (Italian)

Petasites hybridus

butterbur

Petasites hybridus

DESCRIPTION A robust perennial herb with an underground rhizome and very large leaves that have a greyish hairy layer on the lower surfaces. The pale purple or rarely yellow tubular florets are borne in small discoid heads aggregated into large clusters along the stem. Flowering occurs in spring, before the leaves emerge.

ORIGIN Europe and northwestern Asia; introduced to North America. Material is mostly wild-harvested.

PARTS USED Dried leaves (*Petasitidis folium*) or the rhizomes (*Petasitidis rhizoma*).

THERAPEUTIC CATEGORY Antispasmodic, analgesic, against migraine.

USES AND PROPERTIES The rhizomes are used to treat spastic pain of the head and in the gastrointestinal and urinary tract (especially in the case of kidney and bladder stones) and bronchial spasms. Leaves are no longer much used but are a traditional remedy for nervous cramps (tranquilliser), dysmenorrhoea, pain (including headache) and colic. They have also been taken to treat wounds and skin disorders.

PREPARATION AND DOSAGE The main interest is in standardised extracts without pyrrolizidine alkaloids (PAs). PA can be removed by ion-exchange chromatography; alternatively, rhizomes are extracted with CO_2 (these extracts contain sesquiterpenes but no PAs). Extracts and proprietary preparations are used as sedatives, spasmolytics and against headache.

ACTIVE INGREDIENTS The activity of rhizomes and leaves is ascribed mainly to petasin and isopetasin (0.36% of dry weight of the leaf) and several similar sesquiterpenoids (esters of eremophilane-type sesquiterpene alcohols). Of toxicological interest is the presence, in low amounts (up to 0.05%), of macrocyclic pyrrolizidine alkaloids with a 1,2-unsaturated necine structure such as senecionine, senkirkine and integerrimine.

PHARMACOLOGICAL EFFECTS The sesquiterpenes inhibit the formation of leucotrienes and exhibit spasmolytic and analgesic properties. Controlled clinical studies show a positive effect in the treatment of patients with chronic headache and migraine.

WARNING The maximum daily intake of PAs and their N-oxides (cumulative liver toxins and potential carcinogens) should not exceed 1 μg (most drug preparations exceed this level, but PA-free preparations are available).

STATUS Traditional medicine; Comm.E+ (rhizome only); clinical studies+.

Petasites hybridus (L.) Gaertner, Meyer & Scherb.   family: Asteraceae

pétasite vulgaire (French); *Gemeine Pestwurz* (German); *farfaraccio* (Italian)

Petroselinum crispum

parsley

Petroselinum crispum (cultivated form)

Petroselinum crispum var. neapolitanum

DESCRIPTION Parsley is a biennial herb (up to 1 m) with a fleshy root and finely divided, compound and curly leaves in a basal rosette. Greenish yellow flowers and small dry fruits are formed on erect double umbels in the second growing season. The wild form of common parsley, as well as the cultivated Italian parsley (var. *neapolitanum*) have flat, non-curly leaves. Turnip-rooted parsley is a cultivar with edible roots.

ORIGIN Europe and western Asia. It is cultivated as a garnish, salad ingredient, spice and to a limited extent as a medicinal plant in many parts of the world.

PARTS USED Mainly the leaves (*Petroselini herba*) and roots (*Petroselini radix*), less commonly the fruits (*Petroselini fructus*).

THERAPEUTIC CATEGORY Diuretic.

USES AND PROPERTIES Parsley leaf and root are employed to treat gastrointestinal and urinary tract disorders (treatment and prophylaxis of kidney gravel). The fruits have a more powerful effect and were traditionally used for painful periods but are no longer very popular because of potential negative side effects (abortifacient). Leaves have been applied topically as emulcent and itch-relieving treatment for skin problems.

PREPARATION AND DOSAGE A daily dose of up to 6 g of the dry leaf or root is recommended. Tea made from 2 g herb in a cup of boiling water can be taken three times per day. Parsley leaf, root or fruits (or more often extracts) are commonly included in diuretic, laxative and "slimming" teas and in other diuretic preparations.

ACTIVE INGREDIENTS Parsley contains an essential oil (fruits: 2-6%; herb: 0.5%) which has very high levels of the phenylpropanoids apiol, myristicin or allyl-tetramethoxybenzol. Furthermore, biologically active flavonoids (including apiin) and traces of furano-coumarins (e.g. bergapten, oxypeucedanin, psoralen).

PHARMACOLOGICAL EFFECTS Myristin and apiol have a terminal methylene group that is chemically highly reactive. They can bond to proteins or DNA. The diuretic activity is ascribed to the irritant and stimulant effects of the phenylpropanoids and flavonoids on the kidneys. Pure apiol is abortifacient in high doses. Myristicin is the stimulant and hallucinogenic principle present in nutmeg oil (*Myristica fragrans*).

STATUS Traditional medicine; Pharm.; Comm.E+ (root, herb).

Petroselinum crispum (Mill.) A.W. Hill   family: Apiaceae

persil (French); *Petersilie* (German); *prezzemolo* (Italian); *perejil* (Spanish)

Peumus boldus

boldo

Peumus boldus leaves

Peumus boldus tree

Peumus boldus fruit

DESCRIPTION Boldo is a shrub or small tree of up to 7 m in height with broad, leathery leaves, easily recognised by the numerous small, warty protuberances on the upper surface and the slightly rolled-in margins. The flowers are small, bell-shaped and yellowish in colour, and the fruits are small, yellow, edible berries.

ORIGIN South America (Chile). The plant is cultivated to a limited extent.

PARTS USED Dried leaves (boldo leaf – *Boldo folium*).

THERAPEUTIC CATEGORY Choleretic, mild diuretic, stomachic, mild sedative.

USES AND PROPERTIES The main use of boldo leaf is as a choleretic medicine to treat dyspepsia and mild spastic complaints. It is also considered to be a good general medicine and tonic. Leaf extracts are commonly included in cholagogues and biliary preparations, including teas, instant teas, teabags, powders and drops. Preparations that are standardised for their alkaloid content are preferred. Boldo is also a traditional anthelmintic in Chile.

PREPARATION AND DOSAGE A choleretic tea can be made with 1-2 g of chopped leaf and drunk two or three times a day (an average daily dose of 3 g).

Standardised preparations and teas can also be used.

ACTIVE INGREDIENTS Boldo leaves contain 0.2% aporphine alkaloids of which boldine is the main compound. An essential oil is present at a yield of 2-3% of leaf dry weight, with *p*-cymene (30%), ascaridole (40-50%), 1,8-cineole, linalool, and other minor mono-terpenoids. The leaves also contain small amounts of flavonols and their glycosides (e.g. boldoglucin, isorhamnetin).

PHARMACOLOGICAL EFFECTS Boldine stimulates the production of bile, its secretion from the gall bladder and the secretion of gastric juices. It also has mild diuretic and weak hypnotic activities, and stimulates the excretion of uric acid. The liver protective activity observed in animal studies is thought to be due to boldine, but not the anti-inflammatory effects that were recorded. Ascaridole is a major component of the oil and has known anthelmintic and emetic effects (see *Chenopodium ambrosioides*). It is toxic to humans (symptoms: ringing in the ears, spasms and coma) so that the pure oil is not suitable for internal use.

STATUS Traditional medicine; Pharm.; Comm.E+; ESCOP 1.

Peumus boldus Mol.   family: Monimiaceae

boldo (French); *Boldo* (German); *boldo* (Italian); *boldo* (Spanish)

Phaseolus vulgaris

common bean • kidney bean • French bean

Phaseolus vulgaris (climbing cultivar)

Phaseolus vulgaris (bushy cultivar)

DESCRIPTION The common bean is a twining or bushy annual with trifoliolate leaves, small white or pink flowers and narrowly oblong, multi-seeded pods. The seeds are more or less kidney-shaped and variable in size, shape and colour, depending on the cultivar. Beans are grown as a vegetable (young pods) or as a pulse (ripe seeds).

ORIGIN Tropical America. Beans are now cultivated in all parts of the world and a multitude of cultivars and bean types have been developed.

PARTS USED The dried bean pods, without the seeds – *Phaseoli pericarpium* (*Phaseoli fructus sine semine*).

THERAPEUTIC CATEGORY Diuretic.

USES AND PROPERTIES The herb is included in many herbal teas, tea bags and other preparations intended for the promotion of kidney and bladder health. It is a weak diuretic and is traditionally used to treat ailments of the urinary tract, gout and itchy skin. It has a long history of use as weak anti-diabetic.

PREPARATION AND DOSAGE To prepare a tea, 2.5-5 g of the drug is added to 150 ml of boiling water and steeped for 10-15 minutes. One cup is taken two or three times per day. The daily dose is around 5-15 g. Many herbal teas and proprietary products have bean pods as an ingredient.

ACTIVE INGREDIENTS Bean pods are rich in amino acids (mainly asparagine, arginine, leucine, tyrosine, tryptophan and lysine) and trigonelline (= 1-methylnicotinic acid), an alkaloid also found in the seeds of *Trigonella foenum-graecum*, *Coffea arabica* and *Cannabis sativa*. Only silicic acid and arginine have so far been considered as possible active compounds that may explain the observed diuretic and claimed anti-diabetic activity. Recently, chromium salts – bean pods contain about 1 ppm – have been discussed in this context.

PHARMACOLOGICAL EFFECTS More research is needed to explain the diuretic and anti-diabetic effects.

NOTES Another member of the legume family that has medicinal properties is lupin (genus *Lupinus*). Several species from Europe (*L. albus*, *L. luteus*, *L. angustifolius*) and South America (*L. mutabilis*) are known as medicinal plants. Lupins contain lupanine and other quinolizidine alkaloids, saponins and isoflavonoids. They have been used traditionally to treat skin disorders, ectoparasites and diabetes.

STATUS Traditional medicine; Pharm.; Comm.E+.

Phaseolus vulgaris L.

family: Fabaceae

haricot (French); *Gartenbohne* (German); *fagiolo* (Italian)

Phytolacca americana

pokeweed • pigeonberry • inkberry

Phytolacca americana flowers

Phytolacca americana berries

DESCRIPTION A perennial herb of up to 3 m in height, bearing soft fleshy leaves, small greenish-white flowers and elongated clusters of dark purple berries. The plant was previously known as *P. decandra*. Also used in traditional medicine are *shang-lu*, *P. acinosa*, from East Asia and soapberry or *endod*, *P. dodecandra*, from Africa.

ORIGIN North America; sometimes a weed of disturbed places, especially in the Mediterranean region.

PARTS USED Berries (*Phytolaccae americanae fructus*) and roots (*Phytolaccae americanae radix*).

THERAPEUTIC CATEGORY Traditional medicine (anti-inflammatory).

USES AND PROPERTIES Roots or berries are considered to be anti-rheumatic, emetic, analgesic, anti-inflammatory, anti-catarrhal, purgative, immune stimulant and lymphatic system stimulant. Externally the drug is applied to treat inflammatory conditions and skin ailments. In homoeopathy, pokeweed is popular for treating rheumatism, mastitis, sore throat and tonsillitis. In parts of Africa, the berries of *P. dodecandra*, whose saponins are molluscicidal, are used as a cheap and effective measure to control bilharzias (caused by *Schistosoma* species).

PREPARATION AND DOSAGE A dose of 60-100 mg of powdered root has been recommended, but treatment should be supervised by a health care professional.

ACTIVE INGREDIENTS Fruits contain coloured alkaloids (betacyanins) of the betalain type, such as betanidine, betanine, phytolaccine and others (formerly used to colour weak red wines). The presence of saponins in all plant parts is well known, represented by various phytolaccosides and several different triterpenoid aglycones (e.g. phytolaccagenin, or oleanolic acid and phytolaccagenic acid in the case of *P. dodecandra*. Furthermore, a lectin (pokeweed mitogen, PWM), an antiviral protein (pokeweed antiviral protein, PAP) and neolignans (isoamericanin A and others) are present in the roots.

PHARMACOLOGICAL EFFECTS Saponins, lignans and lectins are probably responsible for the observed anti-inflammatory, hypotensive, diuretic, molluscicidal, spermicidal and abortive effects. The lectins and saponins are quite toxic, especially when applied by injection. The medicinal properties need to be evaluated by clinical studies.

STATUS Traditional medicine; formerly Pharm.

Phytolacca americana L. (=*P. decandra* L.)   family: Phytolaccaceae

phytolaque (French); *Kermesbeere* (German); *fitolacca, uva turca* (Italian)

Pilocarpus jaborandi
jaborandi

Pilocarpus pennatifolius leaves and flowers

DESCRIPTION Jaborandi is a shrub or small tree of up to 3 m in height, with large, hairless compound leaves and small pinkish flowers borne in slender clusters. In addition to *P. jaborandi*, several other species are also known as "jaborandi" and are listed as acceptable alternative sources of the herb, including *P. microphyllus*, *P. pennatifolius* and *P. racemosus*.

ORIGIN South and Central America (*P. jaborandi* mainly in Brazil). Material is wild-harvested and there is some concern about the sustainability of the resource.

PARTS USED Dried leaves (*Jaborandi folium*).

THERAPEUTIC CATEGORY Glaucoma treatment; anti-inflammatory.

USES AND PROPERTIES Leaves are traditionally used for a wide range of ailments (fever, dry mouth, bronchitis, influenza and tonsillitis). It is an ingredient of topical products used against psoriasis and baldness. In modern phytotherapy, the isolated alkaloids are used in ophthalmology to lower intraocular pressure in cases of glaucoma.

PREPARATION AND DOSAGE A daily dose of 6 g of the dried leaves can be taken as tea or in tinctures (the maximum single dose is 2 g). Pure pilocarpine (see below) or a mixture of pilocarpine and another alkaloid, physostigmine, is included in tablets (5 mg) and in eye ointments (usually 0.2%).

ACTIVE INGREDIENTS Leaves contain numerous imidazole alkaloids (up to 1% of dry weight), including pilocarpine (the main compound), isopilocarpine, pilocarpidine, and isopilocarpidine. Also present in *P. jaborandi* leaves is an essential oil with limonene as main compound and smaller amounts of 2-undecanone.

PHARMACOLOGICAL EFFECTS Pilocarpine acts as a miotic (it constricts the pupil of the eye) and reduces intraocular pressure. It is highly active as a diaphoretic (increases perspiration) and salivation. The value of the alkaloid in anti-baldness products is attributed to its ability to open skin pores, increase capillary blood circulation and to promote transdermal penetration of other pharmaceutical compounds. Pilocarpine is an agonist at muscarinergic acetylcholine receptors.

NOTES Physostigmine, obtained from the calabar bean (*Physostigma venenosum*) is a powerful acetylcholine-esterase inhibitor.

STATUS Traditional medicine; Pharm.; modern medicine: pilocarpine; clinical studies+ (pilocarpine).

Pilocarpus jaborandi Holmes   family: Rutaceae

jaborandi (French); *Gewöhnlicher Jaborandistrauch* (German); *iaborandi* (Italian); *jaborandi* (Spanish)

Pimpinella anisum

anise

Pimpinella anisum seedlings

Pimpinella anisum flowering plants

Anise fruits

DESCRIPTION A sparse, erect annual (up to 0.5 m) bearing variable leaves on slender stalks. The basal leaves are more or less round and undivided, while the upper ones become increasingly more divided. Numerous small white flowers are borne in a typical umbel, and are followed by small greyish green fruits (about 2 mm long).

ORIGIN Eastern Mediterranean (probably mainly Greece and Egypt) and western Asia; cultivated in many parts of the world.

PARTS USED Ripe, dried fruits (*Anisi fructus*) and the essential oil, distilled from the ripe fruits (*Anisi aetheroleum*).

THERAPEUTIC CATEGORY Expectorant, carminative.

USES AND PROPERTIES The fruit and the oil are a traditional remedy for catarrh of the respiratory tract (colds and flu, cough, bronchitis) and also for dyspeptic complaints (indigestion, flatulence, colic). At high doses, the oil is antiseptic and antispasmodic, and has been used as a stimulating liniment and against ectoparasites. Many cough remedies and other medicinal products contain aniseed extract or aniseed oil, not only for its medicinal properties (antitussive, expectorant) but also to improve the flavour and taste.

PREPARATION AND DOSAGE A tea is prepared from 3 g of ripe fruits, crushed immediately before use. The daily dose should not exceed 5 g of fruit, or 0.3 g of oil.

ACTIVE INGREDIENTS The fruit yields up to 5% essential oil, in which *trans*-anethole is the dominant compound (up to 90%), and also responsible for the taste and smell. Minor constituents of the oil include estragole (=methylchavicol; up to 4%), anise ketone, anisaldehyde and anisic acid. Oil stored at room temperature and exposed to light may produce small amounts of 4,4′-dimethoxystilbene, an oestrogen.

PHARMACOLOGICAL EFFECTS Anethole has documented expectorant, antispasmodic and antimicrobial activities. The carminative effect is less pronounced than with other oils (caraway, fennel). Distinct expectorant activity is linked to the ability of anethole to stimulate ciliary movement of the bronchial epithelium.

NOTES Anise is a popular spice and is easily recognised by its distinctive flavour in food and alcoholic drinks (e.g. absinthe, anis, anisette, pernod, pastis and sambuca).

STATUS Traditional medicine; Pharm.; Comm.E+; ESCOP 3.

Pimpinella anisum L.   family: Apiaceae

anis vert (French); *Anis* (German); *anice verde* (Italian); *anis* (Spanish)

Pimpinella major

greater burnet saxifrage

Pimpinella major

Pimpinella major leaves and flowers

DESCRIPTION A perennial herb or shrublet of up to 1 m in height, with erect stems bearing compound, feathery leaves, slender, leafless flowering stalks, white, hairless flowers in double umbels and small, hairless fruit. It is closely related to *P. saxifraga* (burnet saxifrage). *P. peregrina* from the eastern Mediterranean is regarded as an adulterant of *Pimpinella radix*.

ORIGIN The whole of Europe and western Asia; naturalised in North America. The plants are wild-harvested.

PARTS USED Mostly the dried rhizomes and roots of *P. major* and *P. saxifraga* (*Pimpinellae radix*); traditionally also the aboveground parts of the herb.

THERAPEUTIC CATEGORY Antitussive and mild expectorant, antiseptic.

USES AND PROPERTIES The rhizomes and roots are used mainly for catarrh and infections of the upper respiratory tract. Infusions or tinctures are gargled to treat inflammations of the mouth and throat. The powdered product or extracts are frequently an ingredient of bronchial remedies. Pimpinella herb (aboveground parts) is traditionally used: internally to treat lung ailments, disorders of the urinary tract, and as a digestive; externally for varicose veins and slow-healing wounds. Efficacy has not yet been scientifically proven for any of these indications.

PREPARATION AND DOSAGE A suitable daily dose is 6-12 g of the dry rhizome and root, taken as a tea or as pimpinel tincture (with a herb to solvent ratio of 1:5). As cough medicine, the infusion or tincture, sweetened with honey, can be taken several times a day.

ACTIVE INGREDIENTS The underground parts contain an essential oil (up to 0.7%) with the tiglic acid ester or 2-methylbutyric acid ester of epoxypseudo-isoeugenol as main compounds. Also present in the oil are several tri-nor-sesquiterpenes (C12) such as geijerene, pregeijerene, and sesquiterpenes (β-bisabolene and 1,4-dimethylazulene). Several furanocoumarins have been found (up to 2%), together with sitosterol, phenolic acids and traces of polyacetylenes.

PHARMACOLOGICAL EFFECTS It is likely that the essential oil and perhaps the saponins are responsible for both secretomotoric and secretolytic activities that account for the antitussive and expectorant uses of the drugs.

STATUS Traditional medicine; Comm.E+ (roots only).

Pimpinella major (L.) Hudson

family: Apiaceae

grand boucage (French); *Große Bibernelle* (German); *pimpinella* (Italian)

Pinus sylvestris

Scots pine

Pinus sylvestris trees

Pinus sylvestris needles and cones

Picea abies needles and cone

DESCRIPTION A large tree (up to 30 m) with characteristic reddish brown bark, needle-shaped leaves and small, almost spherical cones. Several species are used to produce turpentine (oleoresin) and essential oil (by steam distillation), including pumilio pine (*Pinus mugo* subsp. *pumilio*), maritime pine (*P. pinaster*), pitch pine (*P. palustris*), common spruce (*Picea abies*), common fir (*Abies alba*) and common larch (*Larix decidua*). *Cedrus deodora* (Himalyan cedar or *deodar*) is popular in Ayurvedic medicine.

ORIGIN Europe, western and northern Asia. Pines, spruces and firs occur almost exclusively in the northern hemisphere.

PARTS USED Fresh/dried young branches (pine sprouts – *Pini turiones*), essential oil from the leaves and young branches (pine needle oil – *Pini aetheroleum*) or essential oil from turpentine (purified turpentine oil – *Terebinthinae aetheroleum rectificatum*). Also used are fresh fir sprouts (*Piceae turiones recentes*) and fir needle oil (*Piceae aetheroleum*). In the case of larch, a balsam is tapped from the trunks (larch turpentine – *Terebinthina laricina*).

THERAPEUTIC CATEGORY Expectorant, counter-irritant.

USES AND PROPERTIES Needle oils and turpentine oils are traditional expectorants used to treat catarrh of the upper and lower respiratory tract. Turpentine oil is specifically used against chronic bronchial disease with heavy secretion. The oil or formulated products (tinctures, ointments, gels, emulsions) are rubbed into the skin as a counter-irritant to treat mild muscular pain, neuralgia and rheumatism. Larix balsam is used as inhalant but also for rheumatic and neuralgic conditions.

PREPARATION AND DOSAGE The products are included in cough medicines or are used as inhalants. The sprouts may be taken as teas, tinctures or syrups.

ACTIVE INGREDIENTS Turpentine oil contains mainly α-pinene, β-pinene, camphene, β-phyllandrene, Δ³-carene and limonene. Pine needle oil has similar monoterpenoids, but the distinctive odour is due to esters, mainly (–)-bornyl acetate.

PHARMACOLOGICAL EFFECTS Turpentine oil and needle oils are antiseptic and secretolytic. Topical use of turpentine or pine needle oil stimulates peripheral circulation (hyperaemic properties).

STATUS Pharm.; Comm.E+ (pine sprouts, oil, turpentine; fir shoots, oil; larix balsam).

Pinus sylvestris L.   family: Pinaceae

pin sauvage (French); *Waldkiefer* (German); *pino silvestre* (Italian); *pino silvestre* (Spanish)

Piper methysticum
kava kava • kava

Piper methysticum

DESCRIPTION An evergreen woody, scrambling shrub of up to 3 m in height bearing large heart-shaped leaves and oblong clusters of inconspicuous flowers (male and female ones on different plants). The branched, fleshy rhizomes can weight up to 10 kg. Several other *Piper* species are of medicinal value.

ORIGIN Polynesia; apparently an ancient cultigen derived from *P. wichmannii*; it is grown in the western Pacific (mainly the islands of Fiji, Samoa, Tonga and Vanuata). Traditional kava drink was prepared by women and children chewing the roots and then mixing it with water to ferment.

PARTS USED Rhizomes and roots (*Piperis methystici rhizoma*).

THERAPEUTIC CATEGORY Sedative (anxiolytic).

USES AND PROPERTIES In modern phytotherapy, kava roots and extracts thereof are used mainly to treat sleep disturbances, anxiety and stress.

PREPARATION AND DOSAGE Crude herb or preparations equivalent to a daily dose of 60-210 mg of kava pyrones is recommended. The treatment should last no longer than three months.

ACTIVE INGREDIENTS Kava root contains styrylpyrones, also known as kavapyrones or kavalactones (at a level of at least 3.5% of dry weight in high quality product). The main compounds are kawain, methysticin, dihydrokawain, dihydromethysticin, yangonin and desmethoxy-yangonin.

PHARMACOLOGICAL EFFECTS Kavalactones bind to various neuroreceptors, especially GABA and dopamine receptors, and inhibit Na^+-channels. These interactions explain the observed sedative, muscle relaxing, anti-convulsive, tranquillising and analgesic effects. Kava can be seen as the herbal alternative to synthetic anxiolytics such as benzodiazepines, with no evidence of physical or psychological dependency. Several controlled clinical trials have shown efficacy for kava to treat patients with anxiety, tension and agitation or psychosomatic menopausal complaints.

WARNING Chronic abuse of kava may lead to serious toxic effects. Although the herb is considered safe at therapeutic doses (provided there is no history of liver disorders or alcoholism) drugs have been taken from the herbal markets in Germany and other countries.

STATUS Traditional medicine; Pharm.; Comm.E+; WHO 2; clinical trials+.

Piper methysticum Forster f.   family: Piperaceae

kava, kava kava (French); *Kawapfeffer, Rauschpfeffer* (German); *kava-kava* (Italian)

Piper nigrum

pepper • Madagascar pepper

Piper nigrum leaves and fruits

Piper betle

Black pepper

DESCRIPTION An evergreen perennial climber (up to 5 m) with bright green, heart-shaped leaves. It bears clusters of small flowers and small spherical fruits that turn red when they ripen. Several other *Piper* species are medicinally interesting. The leaves of betel vine (*P. betle*) of Indo-Malaysia are wrapped around betel palm nuts (*Areca catechu*) to make a traditional stimulant masticatory. Cubebs or Java pepper represents the fruits of *P. cubeba* of Indonesia, a digestive medicine and expectorant. It contains antiseptic volatile oil that is used in aromatherapy. Leaves of *matico* (*P. angustifolium* = *P. elongatum*) of South America are used as diuretic, urinary tract disinfectant, anti-diarrhoeal, and externally for skin complaints and haemorrhoids. See also kava (*P. methysticum*).

ORIGIN Southern India (Malabar coast – used as a spice since antiquity). Pepper is now cultivated in most tropical parts of the world.

PARTS USED Fruits ("peppercorns"). Green pepper is the whole fresh berry, frozen or preserved. White pepper is the fully mature fruits from which the outer fleshy layers had been removed before drying (*Piper albi fructus*). Black pepper is the almost mature, complete berries, dried and separated from their stalks (*Piper nigri fructus*).

THERAPEUTIC CATEGORY Digestive.

USES AND PROPERTIES Black pepper is an important item in Ayurvedic medicine. It stimulates the digestive system and may be used against nausea, dyspeptic complaints and lack of appetite. The essential oil is used topically to treat toothache, rheumatic pains and ectoparasites.

PREPARATION AND DOSAGE Internally: 0.3-0.6 g; maximally 1.5 g per day.

ACTIVE INGREDIENTS Pepper contains an essential oil (up to 3.5%) and 5-10% pungent acid-amides (pseudoalkaloids), with piperine as main compound and several others (e.g. piperyline, piperoleines and piperamine). The sharp smell is due to essential oil, which contains mainly sabinene, pinene, phellandrene, linalool and limonene. Long pepper (*P. longum*) has similar constituents.

PHARMACOLOGICAL EFFECTS Piperine has known CNS depressant and anticonvulsive effects. Pepper is antimicrobial and can stimulate both the digestive system (cholagogue) and the circulatory system. Piperine shows insecticidal properties.

STATUS Traditional medicine.

Piper nigrum L.   family: Piperaceae

poivre (French); *Pfeffer* (German); *pepe* (Italian); *pimienta* (Spanish)

Plantago afra

psyllium • fleawort

Plantago arenaria

Plantago afra

Fleaseed and blond psyllium (*ispaghula*)

DESCRIPTION Psyllium is a small, erect, annual herb with glandular, hairy, narrowly oblong leaves borne in whorls at each node. The inconspicuous flowers are grouped together in dense, oblong clusters that mature into membranous, two-celled capsules, each bearing two small oblong, dark brown seeds (resembling fleas, hence the name flea seed). Real psyllium is derived mainly from *P. afra* (previously *P. psyllium*) or from *P. arenaria* (=*P. indica*) (an acceptable substitute). Blond psyllium or pale psyllium, also known as Indian psyllium or more often by the Hindi name *ispaghula* comes from *P. ovata*, previously *P. ispaghula*. Japanese psyllium, *shazen-shi* or *che-qian-zi* is derived from *P. asiatica*.

ORIGIN Mediterranean and Central Europe (*P. afra* and *P. indica*), India and Iran (*P. ovata*), Japan (*P. asiatica*); commercially grown mainly in India, Pakistan, Iran and southern Europe.

PARTS USED Ripe seeds (*Psyllii semen*) – pinkish brown in *P. ovata*, blackish brown in *P. psyllium*. The seed husks of blond psyllium are readily separated from the seed and is a separate product, psyllium seed husk (*Plantaginis ovatae testa*).

THERAPEUTIC CATEGORY Bulking laxative.

USES AND PROPERTIES The seeds and seed husks are gentle laxatives to treat chronic constipation and to produce a soft stool because they lubricate, soften and increase faecal volume and viscosity. The product is also used against diarrhoea and to treat cases of irritable colon and other inflammations of the gastrointestinal tract.

PREPARATION AND DOSAGE About 5-15 g of seeds are soaked in 150 ml water for several hours and then taken orally. The daily dose is 12-40 g (seeds) or 4-20 g (husk alone). Drink 150 ml of water per 5 g of drug.

ACTIVE INGREDIENTS The epidermis of the seed husk contains mucilages (10-12%); by swelling they can absorb large volumes of water. Up to 0.2% aucubin (an iridoid glycoside) is present in the seeds.

PHARMACOLOGICAL EFFECTS Increasing the faecal mass (due to more fibres, water and faecal bacteria) promotes peristalsis and at the same time retains moisture and lubricates the intestines. The drug lowers blood lipids and blood pressure and shows weak anti-inflammatory activities.

STATUS Pharm.; Comm.E+; ESCOP 2 (isphaghula); ESCOP 5 (psyllium); WHO 1.

Plantago afra L. family: Plantaginaceae

herbe aux puces (French); *Flohkraut* (German); *psillio* (Italian); *psilio* (Spanish) (=*P. psyllium* L.)

Plantago lanceolata

ribwort plantain

Plantago lanceolata

Plantago major

Plantago media

DESCRIPTION A rosette-forming perennial herb bearing narrowly oblong, sparsely hairy and distinctly parallel-veined leaves, distinctly ridged flowering stalks and numerous inconspicuous white or pale pink flowers in a dense solitary cluster. Also used are greater plantain (*P. major*) and hoary plantain (*P. media*); easily recognised by a rosette of broad or hairy leaves, respectively.

ORIGIN Europe, central and northern Asia (all three species), naturalised in America and Australia.

PARTS USED Leaves (*Plantaginis lanceolatae folium*) or aboveground parts – *Plantaginis lanceolatae herba*.

THERAPEUTIC CATEGORY Anti-inflammatory, expectorant (*P. lanceolata*); diuretic and haemostyptic (*P. major*).

USES AND PROPERTIES Plantain ribwort is used mainly against catarrhs of the respiratory tract and inflammation of the mouth and throat. It is externally used to treat wounds and inflammation of the skin. Greater plantain herb is traditionally used against cystitis, haematuria and for relief from irritating and bleeding haemorrhoids. It is used against colds and flu in modern Chinese herbalism.

PREPARATION AND DOSAGE A tea is prepared from 2-4 g of the dry herb, with an average daily dose of 3-6 g. Fresh plant juice or powdered herb is included in ointments for topical application. Extracts form ingredients of antitussive, expectorant and broncho-spasmolytic preparations. Greater plantain herb is used in much the same way (2-4 g of herb by infusion, three times per day).

ACTIVE INGREDIENTS Iridoid glycosides (up to 2.5% of dry weight). The main compound is aucubin, accompanied by catalpol and asperuloside. Furthermore, 2% mucilage, together with tannins (6.5%), phenolic acids (chlorogenic and caffeic acid), unidentified saponins and flavonoids. *P. major* and *P. media* have similar constituents.

PHARMACOLOGICAL EFFECTS Astringent, anti-inflammatory and antibacterial. Antimicrobial activities have been ascribed to aucubin or more specifically its aglycone, aucubigenin. Aucubin, the other iridoid glycosides or their metabolites inhibit prostaglandin formation, which would explain their anti-inflammatory properties. The drugs have shown bronchodilatory, hypotensive, mild laxative and hepatoprotective effects (mechanisms as yet unknown).

STATUS Traditional medicine; Pharm.; Comm.E+.

Plantago lanceolata L.   family: Plantaginaceae

plantain lancéole (French); *Spitzwegerich* (German); *plantaggine* (Italian); *llantén menor* (Spanish)

Platycodon grandiflorus

Chinese bellflower • balloon flower

Platycodon grandiflorus plant

Platycodon grandiflorus flower

DESCRIPTION Chinese bellflower is an erect perennial herb of about 0.5 m in height, with fleshy, white, finger-shaped roots and straight stems bearing hairless, stalkless, coarsely toothed leaves that are slightly paler on their lower sides. The upper stems bear leaves that are much reduced in size and very attractive, solitary or paired, bell-shaped, usually violet-blue but sometimes white, flowers. The fruits are egg-shaped capsules that split open at the top. There is only this one species in the genus *Platycodon*, which is closely related to the well-known bellflowers (genera *Codonopsis* and *Campanula*) – they differ mainly in details of the fruit.

ORIGIN North-eastern Asia (east Siberia, China, Japan, Korea). The plant is commonly cultivated in gardens and various colour forms, including double-flowered cultivars, have been developed.

PARTS USED Dried roots (*Platycodi radix*).

THERAPEUTIC CATEGORY Expectorant, anti-inflammatory.

USES AND PROPERTIES The herb has become very popular in modern Chinese herbalism to treat coughs, colds, bronchitis, congestion, throat infections and tonsillitis. Several other uses have been recorded in tra-

ditional Chinese medicine, including asthma, peptic ulcers, chronic inflammations, viral infections and high blood pressure.

PREPARATION AND DOSAGE The roots are taken as infusions, decoctions or as extracts at a dosage corresponding to 2-9 g of dry root per day.

ACTIVE INGREDIENTS The major compounds of interest are triterpene saponins (2% or more in the dry root). Most of the saponins are derivatives of two sapogenins, platycodigenin and polygala acid. These include platycodins A-I and platycoside C.

PHARMACOLOGICAL EFFECTS Animal experiments have clearly shown antibacterial, anti-inflammatory, antitussive, expectorant and anti-ulcer activities. All of these effects are attributed to the platycodins which appear to induce the secretion of endogenous antiphlogistic corticosterone. The herb stimulates the flow of saliva and bronchial secretion but inhibits gastric secretion and thus prevents peptic ulcers. Blood cholesterol- and triglyceride-lowering effects were reported in rats.

NOTES *Platycodon* root is eaten as a functional food in China and Korea and is often an ingredient of herbal teas.

STATUS Traditional medicine; WHO 1.

Platycodon grandiflorus (Jacq.) A.DC.   family: Campanulaceae

chieh keng (Chinese); *platycodon à grandes fleurs* (French); *Ballonblume* (German); *platycodon* (Italian)

Podophyllum peltatum

may apple • American mandrake

Podophyllum peltatum plants

Podophyllum hexandrum leaf and fruit

DESCRIPTION A peculiar perennial plant with branched rhizomes spreading below the ground, a single pair of large, soft and deeply lobed umbrella-like leaves and a single white flower. The oblong, fleshy fruit is toxic when green but edible when ripe. The most important of the four Asian species is the Himalayan may apple (*P. hexandrum*) that tends to form dense clumps.

ORIGIN Eastern North America (*P. peltatum*) or Himalayas (*P. hexandrum* – one of four species in East Asia).

PARTS USED Dried rhizome (*Podophylli peltati rhizoma*), used for podophyllin extraction or traditionally a powdered mixture of resins (*Podophylli resina*).

THERAPEUTIC CATEGORY Purgative; treatment of cancer and warts.

USES AND PROPERTIES Traditionally used as a strong purgative and to remove condylomata. Lignans from may apple are chemically converted into etoposide, mitoposide and teniposide, that are useful chemotherapeutics for the treatment of tumours (including testicular carcinomas and lymphomas).

PREPARATION AND DOSAGE The removal of warts is normally done under medical supervision – 1.5-3 g of root or 1.5-3 g fluid extract is applied to the affected area, taking care to avoid the adjacent skin.

ACTIVE INGREDIENTS The rhizome and roots contain up to 6% of a resinous substance known as podophyllum resin or podophyllin. This is a rich source (up to 50%) of podophyllotoxin, a lignane (1-aryltetrahydronaphthalene) with antimitotic activity. Related compounds are α- and β-peltatins, deosoxypodophyllotoxin and their glycosides. Podophyllotoxin is converted into stable derivatives.

PHARMACOLOGICAL EFFECTS Podophyllotoxin and peltatins (both highly toxic when ingested) inhibit the growth of tumours by acting as mitotic spindle poisons – they stop cell division at the beginning of metaphase. Semisynthetic derivatives with similar anticancer activity (they inhibit DNA topoisomerase) but with fewer side effects have been developed. These products cause necrosis when applied to external carcinomas and warts of less than four cubic centimeters.

WARNING Internal and parenteral use only under strict medical supervision; do not use during pregnancy.

STATUS Traditional medicine; Pharm.; Comm.E+; source of podophyllotoxin.

Podophyllum peltatum L.

family: Berberidaceae

podophylle pelté, pomme de mai (French); *Gewöhnlicher Maiapfel* (German); *podofillo* (Italian)

Pogostemon cablin

patchouli • patchouly

Pogostemon cablin

DESCRIPTION An aromatic perennial herb of up to 1 m in height, with hairy, square stems and opposite pairs of soft, broad leaves. Pale pink tubular flowers are borne in whorls along an elongated floral axis, but the plant usually remains vegetative and rarely flowers. Indian patchouli or Java patchouli (*P. heyneanus*) is also a commercial source of essential oil. It differs from *P. cablin* in the smooth stems and the fact that it flowers regularly.

ORIGIN Indo-Malaysia (from India to the Philippines and Malaysia; also on Réunion and Mauritius). The plant is now widely cultivated in warm climates.

PARTS USED Leaves (fresh or dried) (*Patchouli folium*), essential oil (*Patchoulia aetheroleum*).

THERAPEUTIC CATEGORY Traditional aphrodisiac (herb); cosmetic, insect repellent (oil).

USES AND PROPERTIES Patchouli is important in traditional medicine in China, Malaysia and India, not only of its alleged aphrodisiac properties, but also to treat a wide range of ailments, including colds and flu, fever and headache. Externally it is applied to repel insects and to alleviate an itching and inflamed skin. The essential oil extracted from the leaves and stems by steam distillation has become very popular in aromatherapy, to treat menstrual pains, mild depression, anxiety and skin complaints. It is used to give fragrance to cosmetics and shampoos, and specifically in insect repellents and leech repellents.

PREPARATION AND DOSAGE Fresh or dried leaves are used as tea but the use of the oil (on its own or in formulated preparations) has become more important in recent years.

ACTIVE INGREDIENTS The essential oil contains numerous monoterpenes and sesquiterpenoids. The main ingredient is known as patchouli alcohol or patchoulol, a unique sesquiterpene. Furthermore, dhelwangin (an antibacterial sesquiterpene), and several phenylpropanoids, such as eugenol, benzaldehyde, have been recorded.

PHARMACOLOGICAL EFFECTS The pharmacological properties of the herb and its oil are relatively poorly studied. The observed antimicrobial properties are plausibly explained by the presence of sesquiterpenes and eugenol. An anti-emetic effect has been described. The insect-repellent activity of the oil has been the main focus of research.

STATUS Traditional medicine.

Pogostemon cablin (Blanco) Benth. (= *P. patchouli* Pellet.) family: Lamiaceae
patchouli (French); *Patschulipflanze* (German); *patchouly* (Italian)

Polygala senega

senega snakeroot • senega

Polygala senega

Polygala senega flowers

DESCRIPTION A small perennial herb of up to 0.5 m in height, with erect, mostly unbranched stems arising from a branched root. The leaves are alternate, small, lance-shaped and practically without stalks. Small, white flowers are arranged in oblong clusters at the tips of the stems. Each flower has five petal-like sepals of unequal size and a small tuft (corona) at the tip of the short petals. *Polygala* species are widely used as traditional medicine. *P. fruticosa* and *P. virgata* for example, are popular in Zulu medicine, while *P. amara* (bitter milkwort) and related species have been used in folk medicine as expectorant, stomachic and galactogogue (mirrored in scientific name) in central Europe.

ORIGIN North America (eastern and midwestern USA and over most of Canada). Roots are still wild-harvested but the plant has been cultivated on a limited scale. The roots were used by the Canadian Seneca Indians to treat rattlesnake bites (hence the scientific and common names).

PARTS USED Dried, mostly sliced roots (senega root – *Polygalae radix*).

THERAPEUTIC CATEGORY Expectorant, secretolytic, antitussive.

USES AND PROPERTIES Senega snakeroot is mainly used in cough medicines to treat bronchitis (especially chronic bronchitis), chronic asthma, dry coughs, catarrh of the respiratory tract and emphysema. It is also gargled to treat throat infections.

PREPARATION AND DOSAGE Dry root (0.5-1 g) is taken by infusion three times per day. Liquid extracts (0.3-1 ml per day) and tinctures (2.5-5 ml per day) may also be used. The herb is most often used as part of proprietary preparations against coughs and bronchitis.

ACTIVE INGREDIENTS The roots contain triterpenoid saponins of the so-called bidesmoside type with presenegin as aglycone, in concentrations of up to 12%. The compounds are known as senegasaponins A-D (presenegenin is the main sapogenin). Also present are methyl salicylate and organic acids.

PHARMACOLOGICAL EFFECTS The mechanisms of action have not been studied in detail; but it is likely that the anti-inflammatory, antitussive, expectorant and secretolytic effects are due to the saponins and methyl salicylate (see *Gypsophila paniculata*).

STATUS Traditional and homoeopathic medicine; Pharm.; Comm.E+; ESCOP 3; WHO 2.

Polygala senega L.   family: Polygalaceae

Senega Klapperschlangenwurzel (German); *polygala sénéga* (French); *poligala, serpentella* (Italian)

Polygonum aviculare

knotweed • knotgrass

Polygonum aviculare

Polygonum aviculare flowers

DESCRIPTION A spreading, wiry annual weed with sparse, slender stems, distinct nodes covered by translucent stipular sheaths (these have lacerated edges and are dark-coloured at their bases, giving the stems a distinctive "knotty" appearance) and small, narrow, almost stalkless leaves. Minute reddish flowers are borne in the leaf axils. Several *Polygonum* species have been moved to the genus *Persicaria* (see *Persicaria bistorta*). Roots of flowery knotweed or *he shou wu* (*Polygonum multiflorum* or *Fallopia multiflora*) is important in Chinese medicine.

ORIGIN Europe and Asia; it has become a weed of cultivation in all temperate parts of the world and is collected mainly in eastern Europe.

PARTS USED Whole herb, including the roots (knotweed herb – *Polygoni avicularis herba*).

THERAPEUTIC CATEGORY Traditional expectorant.

USES AND PROPERTIES Knotweed herb is mainly used, to this day, to treat coughs, bronchial catarrh and inflammation of the mouth and upper respiratory tract. In China and the eastern Mediterranean region it has been used since ancient times as a diuretic and in folk medicine also for throat and bronchial ailments, as haemostyptic and to treat skin problems. *He shou wu* is

a tonic herb used in China for numerous and diverse indications (including liver ailments, kidney problems, nervous conditions, premature ageing and infertility).

PREPARATION AND DOSAGE A cup of tea can be made from 1.5 g of the chopped dry herb, and taken three to five times a day for coughs and catarrh. The herb or extracts thereof form ingredients of cough teas and various proprietary products used as antitussive and diuretic medicines.

ACTIVE INGREDIENTS It has been speculated that the tannins (3.6% gallo- and catechol tannins) are the main active compounds. Other potentially active constituents present are flavonoids (such as avicularin, quercetin 3-arabinoside, hyperoside, vitexin), mucilage, silicic acid (1%), phenolcarboxylic acids and some coumarins.

PHARMACOLOGICAL EFFECTS Tannins unspecifically inhibit enzymes and receptors; it is plausible to attribute antimicrobial, anti-inflammatory and haemostyptic properties to tannins and other phenolic compounds. Silicic acid and flavonoids might enhance diuresis.

STATUS Traditional medicine; Comm.E+.

Polygonum aviculare L.

family: Polygonaceae

renouée des oiseaux (French); *Vogelknöterich* (German); *centinodia* (Italian)

Populus tremuloides

American aspen • Canadian aspen

Populus tremuloides trees

Populus tremuloides leaves

Populus tremula leaves

DESCRIPTION American/Canadian aspen is a deciduous tree of about 20 m in height, with small, oval, dentate leaves on long stalks that quiver markedly in the wind. Aspen (*P. tremula*) and black poplar (*P. nigra*) are also used. Poplar buds, however, are most often obtained from the balsam poplar (*P. balsamifera*) or balm of Gilead (*Populus candicans*), sometimes called *P. gileadensis* or *P.* x *jackii* 'Gileadensis' (known only as a cultigen). Balm of Gilead is a confusing term because it represents several products from unrelated plants (*Abies balsamea, Commiphora gileadensis, Liquidambar orientalis* and *Populus* species).

ORIGIN North America (*P. tremuloides, P. candicans*); Europe and Asia (*P. tremula, P. nigra*).

PARTS USED Bark (*Populi cortex*) and buds (dried, unopened leaf buds – *Populi gemmae*), rarely the leaves (*Populi folium*).

THERAPEUTIC CATEGORY Anti-inflammatory, antirheumatic (bark); expectorant, counter-irritant (buds).

USES AND PROPERTIES Poplar bark is a traditional medicine against rheumatoid arthritis and other rheumatic conditions, but also cystitis, diarrhoea and the common cold. The leaves and bark are used for urinary problems resulting from an enlarged prostate. Buds are used against chronic bronchitis and rheumatism and externally for treating superficial wounds, external haemorrhoids, frostbite and sunburn (and as an ointment for myalgia).

PREPARATION AND DOSAGE Dosage depends on the treatment, but a typical dose would be a decoction of 1-4 g of bark, taken three times per day. Buds are included in semi-solid preparations (ointments and creams; *Populi unguentum*) (concentration 20-30%).

ACTIVE INGREDIENTS Poplar bark is similar to willow bark and also contains salicin (about 2.4%), salicortin and various benzoyl esters of salicin – mainly populin (salicin-5-benzoate), tremulacin and tremuloidin. Also present are tannins and triterpenes. The buds contain essential oil and flavonoids in addition to salicin and related phenolic glycosides.

PHARMACOLOGICAL EFFECTS Salicin and salicin derivates are converted to salicylalcohol in the intestine. In the liver it is further oxidised to salicylic acid, the active compound, known for its anti-inflammatory and analgesic properties (see *Salix*).

STATUS Traditional medicine; Comm.E+ (buds only).

Populus tremuloides Michaux family: Salicaceae

peuplier faux-tremble (French); *Amerikanische Espe* (German); *pioppo* (Italian)

Potentilla anserina

silverweed

Potentilla anserina

DESCRIPTION A low perennial herb that spreads through long runners. It has pinnately compound leaves, with markedly dentate and densely silky leaflets, giving them a silvery appearance. The yellow flowers are typical of the family (five petals, numerous stamens) and are borne on long stalks. It is one of two *Potentilla* species that are used in traditional medicine (see *P. erecta*).

ORIGIN Asia, Europe and North America. The plants grow in grasslands and are wild-harvested shortly before or during flowering, mainly in eastern Europe.

PARTS USED Fresh or dried leaves (silverweed herb – Anserinae herba).

THERAPEUTIC CATEGORY Astringent.

USES AND PROPERTIES The herb is used mainly to treat nonspecific diarrhoea and mucosal inflammations of the mouth and throat. It is also used in case of minor menstrual disorders. Traditionally it is recommended against cramps and spasms, and to treat colic. As an astringent it is said to be an effective treatment for bleeding haemorrhoids, sores and eczema.

PREPARATION AND DOSAGE An infusion made from 2 g of the dried herb can be taken three times a day. The infusion can also be applied to the skin, or gargled, in the case of mouth and throat infections.

ACTIVE INGREDIENTS The leaves contain at least 5-10% tannins, to which the astringent qualities are ascribed. The tannins are of the ellagic acid type, and both monomeric and dimeric ellagitannins are present. Flavonoids (kaempferol, myricetin, quercetin), proanthocyanidins and phenolic acids (ferulic, caffeic acid) may also contribute to some extent to the medicinal properties of the plant.

PHARMACOLOGICAL EFFECTS Silverweed is mainly used for its astringent properties, which are clearly related to the high tannin content. Tannins can interact with its multitude of hydroxy groups with proteins; they alter the conformation of enzymes, receptors and transporters and often inactivate them. This would explain the antimicrobial, anti-inflammatory and haemostyptic activities observed. Animal studies have shown that the drug has an effect on the tone and contraction frequency of uterine muscles, so that the traditional use against mild dysmenorrhoea seems plausible. The reported spasmolytic activity needs re-evaluation.

STATUS Traditional medicine; Pharm.; Comm.E+.

Potentilla anserina L.   family: Rosaceae

herbe d'ansérine, argentine (French); *Gänsefingerkraut* (German); *argentina anserina, potentilla* (Italian)

Potentilla erecta

tormentil

Potentilla erecta

DESCRIPTION Tormentil is a small, much-branched herb. The sparsely hairy leaves are digitately dissected into four or five dentate leaflets which are borne directly on the stems (leaf stalks are absent). The flowers are solitary, relatively small, yellow and differ markedly from those of all other *Potentilla* species (and most other Rosaceae) in the presence of four rather than the more usual five petals.

ORIGIN Central and eastern Europe. The product is wild-harvested mainly in eastern Europe.

PARTS USED The sliced and dried rhizomes, with the roots removed (*Tormentillae rhizoma*).

THERAPEUTIC CATEGORY Astringent.

USES AND PROPERTIES Tormentil is taken orally in case of diarrhoea, dysentery, gastroenteritis, and enterocolitis. It is also used as a gargle or rinse to treat inflammation of the mucous membranes of the mouth and throat. It can be applied externally to sores, wounds and other skin disorders.

PREPARATION AND DOSAGE An infusion of 2-3 g of the dried rhizome is made in a cup of boiling water. One cup is taken two to three times per day between meals to treat diarrhoea and related disorders. The infusion may also be used externally. Tinctures can be diluted (10-20 drops in a glass of water) to rinse the mouth and throat. Tormentil is included in many commercial stomachic, anti-diarrhoeal preparations and mouth sprays.

ACTIVE INGREDIENTS The rhizomes contain large amounts of tannins (up to 22%), mainly of the catechol type. Non-hydrolysable tannin is present in the form of oligomeric proanthocyanidins (up to 20%); the main hydrolysable tannin is agrimoniin and other ellagitannins and catechol gallates. Also present is tormentoside, a triterpene saponin known as a glucoside of tormentillic acid.

PHARMACOLOGICAL EFFECTS The tannins and triterpenes are apparently responsible for at least some of the medicinal activities of the drug. Tannins are astringent and interact widely with proteins, resulting in antimicrobial, antiviral and anti-diarrhoeal properties. Triterpenes can act as cortisone mimics, and might contribute to the anti-inflammatory, hypoglycaemic, antihypertensive, immune stimulant, anti-allergic, and interferon-inducing effects, that have been reported.

STATUS Traditional medicine; Pharm.; Comm.E+.

Potentilla erecta (L.) Räusch (=*Potentilla tormentilla* Stokes)　　　　　　family: Rosaceae
tormentille (French); *Blutwurz* (German); *tormentilla* (Italian)

Primula veris

cowslip

Primula veris

Primula elatior

DESCRIPTION An attractive perennial herb with a basal rosette of wrinkled leaves arising each spring from a fleshy rhizome. Golden yellow, strongly scented flowers are borne in multi-flowered clusters on slender stalks. *Primula veris* (Latin: "firstling of spring") was previously known as *P. officinalis*. A closely related species and alternative source of raw material is the oxlip, *P. elatior*. It is slightly larger and has pale yellow, weakly scented flowers that are borne in few-flowered clusters. Also used are *P. auricula* and *P. farinosa*.

ORIGIN Europe and Asia (*P. veris* and *P. elatior*).

PARTS USED The dried flowers, with calyces (*Primulae flos cum calycibus*) or the dried rhizomes and roots (*Primulae radix*).

THERAPEUTIC CATEGORY Expectorant, secretolytic.

USES AND PROPERTIES Primrose flower and root are traditionally used as expectorants to treat bronchitis, coughs with sticky mucus, colds and catarrh of the nose and throat. The flowers have a much milder action than the roots. In traditional medicine, the flowers are also used for nervous conditions, headaches and as cardiac tonic but none of these indications is supported by scientific evidence.

PREPARATION AND DOSAGE A tea can be made from 2-4 g of the flower or 0.2-0.5 g of the root. As an expectorant, the infusion is sweetened with honey and taken every two or three hours.

ACTIVE INGREDIENTS The roots contain large amounts (5-10%) saponins, present as glycosides of several structurally similar aglycones such as protoprimulagenin A and priverogenin A, B. Also present are phenolic glycosides such as primulaverin (=primulaveroside) and primverin which give the characteristic "wintergreen" smell to the roots when broken down by enzymatic hydrolysis to methoxysalicylate methyl ester. The flowers have small amounts of saponins and flavonoids.

PHARMACOLOGICAL EFFECTS Saponins in the roots (and to a lesser extent the flowers) are responsible for the mucous-expelling and secretolytic actions. Saponins affect the *nervus vagus* in the mucous membrane of the stomach, promoting in a reflectory way water secretion in the bronchia (resulting in secretolytic and antitussive effects, typical of most saponin-containing drugs). Salicylates show anti-inflammatory activity.

STATUS Traditional medicine; Pharm.; Comm.E+; ESCOP 3.

Primula veris L. [=*P. officinalis* (L.) Hill.]   family: Primulaceae

primevère officinale, coucou (French); *Wiesen-Schlüsselblume* (German); *primavera* (Italian)

Prunus africana

red stinkwood • pygeum

Prunus africana fruits

Prunus africana flowers

Prunus africana bark

DESCRIPTION This tall forest tree may reach a height of more than 30 m. Buttress roots are often present. The dark green, glossy leaves have minute serrations along the edges and smell of almonds when crushed. Small white flowers in elongated clusters are followed by reddish brown berries of about 10 mm in diameter. The tree was previously known as *Pygeum africanum*. Several other species of *Prunus* have medicinal value (see *P. spinosa*).

ORIGIN The tree occurs in tropical and subtropical parts of Africa. Wild-harvesting of bark is very destructive and some attempts have been made to establish plantations for sustainable bark production.

PARTS USED Stem bark (*Pygei africani cortex*)

THERAPEUTIC CATEGORY Urological; benign prostrate hyperplasia.

USES AND PROPERTIES Bark extracts have become popular in Europe (France, Italy and Switzerland) as the main therapy for benign prostate hypertrophy.

PREPARATION AND DOSAGE Lipophilic and phytosterol extracts (100 mg per day in six to eight week cycles) are most commonly used in Europe. Proprietary extracts, often in combination with nettle root

(*Urtica dioica*) and saw palmetto (*Serenoa repens*) are available and widely used. Bark decoctions are traditionally used in African traditional medicine.

ACTIVE INGREDIENTS Phytosterols (free and glycosylated β-sitosterol, campesterol) and tannins are present in the bark, together with pentacyclic triterpenoid esters and various linear aliphatic alcohols and their ferulic acid esters. The presence of amygdalin, a cyanogenic glycoside, has been reported.

PHARMACOLOGICAL EFFECTS The activity of extracts against prostatic adenoma is possibly due to β-sitosterol, which is also found in other plants that are traditionally used for the same purpose (see *Serenoa repens* and *Cucurbita pepo*). Experimental studies suggest that the phytosterols may inhibit the binding of dihydrotestosterone within the prostate, or perhaps work through inhibition of 5α-reductase and aromatase. It is possible that the terpenoids and ferulic acids esters contribute to the beneficial effects. Controlled clinical trials have shown statistically significant improvements in a number of symptoms associated with prostatitis.

STATUS Traditional medicine; Pharm.; WHO 2; clinical trials+.

Prunus africana (Hook. f.) Kalkman (= *Pygeum africanum* Hook.f.)   family: Rosaceae
pygeum (French); *Pygeum africanum* (German); *pygeum* (Italian)

Prunus spinosa

blackthorn • sloe

Prunus spinosa

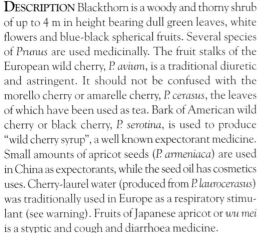

Prunus serotina

Prunus laurocerasus

DESCRIPTION Blackthorn is a woody and thorny shrub of up to 4 m in height bearing dull green leaves, white flowers and blue-black spherical fruits. Several species of *Prunus* are used medicinally. The fruit stalks of the European wild cherry, *P. avium*, is a traditional diuretic and astringent. It should not be confused with the morello cherry or amarelle cherry, *P. cerasus*, the leaves of which have been used as tea. Bark of American wild cherry or black cherry, *P. serotina*, is used to produce "wild cherry syrup", a well known expectorant medicine. Small amounts of apricot seeds (*P. armeniaca*) are used in China as expectorants, while the seed oil has cosmetics uses. Cherry-laurel water (produced from *P. laurocerasus*) was traditionally used in Europe as a respiratory stimulant (see warning). Fruits of Japanese apricot or *wu mei* is a styptic and cough and diarrhoea medicine.

ORIGIN Europe, western Asia and North Africa (*P. spinosa*). The products are wild-harvested in eastern Europe. Other species listed above are European and Asian in origin, except the North American *P. serotina*.

PARTS USED Dried flowers (*Pruni spinosae flos*) and fresh or dried ripe fruits (*Pruni spinosae fructus*).

THERAPEUTIC CATEGORY Astringent, diuretic.

USES AND PROPERTIES The dried fruits (or fruit juice) are used to treat inflammation of the mouth, gums and throat. Numerous medicinal properties have been ascribed to the flowers (expectorant, mild laxative, diuretic and diaphoretic).

PREPARATION AND DOSAGE A tea is made from 1-2 g of dried flowers, and one or two cups are taken during the day or at night. To treat inflammation of the mouth and throat, an infusion of 2-4 g of the dried fruit or fresh fruit juice is made as an oral gargle.

ACTIVE INGREDIENTS Mainly present are tannins, flavonoids and cyanogenic glycosides; prunasin produces prussic acid (hydrogen cyanide, HCN) and benzaldehyde (with a "marzipan" smell) upon enzymatic hydrolysis.

PHARMACOLOGICAL EFFECTS Tannins are known for their antiseptic, anti-diarrhoeal and anti-inflammatory effects.

WARNING HCN is a strong toxin; 5-12 seeds of bitter almonds (*P. dulcis* var. *amara*) can be lethal for children. Cherry-laurel water may contain HCN.

STATUS Traditional medicine; Pharm.; Comm.E+ (fruit only).

Prunus spinosa L. family: Rosaceae

prunellier (French); *Schlehdorn, Schlehe* (German); *prugnolo* (Italian)

Psidium guajava

guava tree

Psidium guajava flowers

Psidium guajava fruits

DESCRIPTION The guava is a shrub or small tree, usually up to 4 m in height. The bark peels off in flakes, revealing the characteristically smooth, pale-coloured trunk and branches. The large leaves have prominent veins and are borne opposite each other in pairs. Small white flowers, with numerous stamens develop into rounded or pear-shaped, yellow, many-seeded fruits. Guavas have pink or yellow fruit flesh, are delicious to eat and have a high vitamin C content.

ORIGIN Central America. The guava has become naturalised in many parts of the world and is widely cultivated as a commercial fruit crop.

PARTS USED Fresh or dried leaves (*Djamboe folium*; synon. *Psidii pyriferi folium*).

THERAPEUTIC CATEGORY Anti-diarrhoeal, traditional anti-diabetic.

USES AND PROPERTIES Leaves are commonly used in traditional medicine, mainly to treat gastrointestinal disorders (such as diarrhoea) and diabetes, but also fever (including malaria), cough, ulcers, boils and wounds.

PREPARATION AND DOSAGE Infusions of leaves are taken as tea. For severe diarrhoea, the recommended dose is one crushed leaf in a litre of water.

ACTIVE INGREDIENTS Guava leaf is rich in tannins (9-12%) and other phenolic compounds, of which amritoside (a glycoside – gentiobioside – of ellagic acid) is of particular interest. Another biologically interesting compound is guiajaverin, a glycoside (arabinopyroside) of quercetin. The leaves also contain 0.3% essential oils (with eugenol) and triterpenoids that may contribute to the overall medicinal activity.

PHARMACOLOGICAL EFFECTS Tannins are known intestinal astringents and haemostatics, so that their presence can plausibly explain the therapeutic value of the plant against diarrhoea and dysentery. The tannins have vasoconstricting activity, form a protective layer on the skin and mucosas and are antibacterial and antifungal, so that they are effective against both internal and external infections. Quercetin (and its glycosides) are known for antioxidant, anti-carcinogenic, anti-HIV and antibiotic activities. In addition, hypoglycemic effects have been documented. Eugenol has definite antibacterial properties.

STATUS Traditional medicine.

Psidium guajava L.

family: Myrtaceae

goyave, goyavier (French); *Guayavebaum* (German); *guava* (Italian)

Psychotria ipecacuanha

ipecac • Brazilian ipecac • ipecacuanha

Psychotria ipecacuanha

DESCRIPTION Ipecac is a small shrublet (up to 0.4 m) with bright green opposite leaves and distinctive interpetiolar stipules. Small white flowers are borne in compact clusters (cymes). The plant was previously known as *Cephaelis ipecacuanha*. An acceptable alternative source of the drug is the so-called Cartagena, Panama, Costa Rica or Nicaragua ipecacuanha, hitherto known as *Cephaelis acuminata*. Several tropical American species have been used as inferior substitutes or adulterants of ipecac, including *C. tomentosa*, *C. humboldtiana*, *C. barcella* and *C. elata*. The term ipecac or ipecacuanha has been used not only for "real" ipecac but also (incorrectly) for various other emetic roots.

ORIGIN Brazil. Roots are wild-collected, mainly in Matto Grosso, Brazil. Attempts at cultivating the plants in Malaysia were not very successful.

PARTS USED Dried roots (*Ipecacuanhae radix*) or standardised root powder (*Ipecacuanhae pulvis normatus*); isolated alkaloids (emetine).

THERAPEUTIC CATEGORY Expectorant, emetic.

USES AND PROPERTIES Ipecac is mainly used against chronic bronchitis accompanied by a dry cough. At about 10 times the therapeutic dose, it is strongly emetic and therefore the active ingredient in emetic syrups. They are used to induce vomiting in cases of accidental poisoning.

PREPARATION AND DOSAGE The crude drug is not suitable for self-medication as the dose has to be very carefully measured. The expectorant dose is about 10 ml of a 0.5% infusion, while the emetic dose is 0.5-2 g of dried root or root powder.

ACTIVE INGREDIENTS The root contains numerous isoquinoline alkaloids (up to 4%), of which emetine and cephaeline are the most important compounds.

PHARMACOLOGICAL EFFECTS Emetine and cephaeline are almost equal to each other in their activity. The alkaloids irritate the *nervus vagus* in the stomach; this stimulates water secretion in bronchial tissues in a reflectory way, resulting in the known expectorant and secretolytic activities (note that saponins apparently work in the same way!). The alkaloids are also strongly emetic at high doses, and overdoses can be dangerous. Emetine strongly intercalates DNA and blocks protein biosynthesis; this is the base for its use as a cytotoxic and anti-amoebic drug.

STATUS Traditional medicine; Pharm.

Psychotria ipecacuanha (Brot.) Stokes [=*Cephalis ipecacuanha* (Brot.)A. Rich.]   family: Rubiaceae
ipécacuanha (French); *Brechwurzel, Ruhrwurzel* (German); *ipecacuana* (Italian); *ipecacuana* (Spanish)

Pueraria lobata

kudzu vine • Japanese arrowroot

Pueraria lobata plant

Pueraria lobata leaves

DESCRIPTION A robust climber that can reach up to 30 m or more in height. It has woody stems arising from a very large tuberous root below the ground. The stems bear deciduous, compound (pinnately trifoliate) leaves, twining tendrils and clusters of purple flowers.

ORIGIN India, China and Japan. The plant is naturalised in the USA and has become a troublesome invader. It is cultivated in parts of China.

PARTS USED Dried roots (*Puerariae radix*) or more rarely the flowers (*Puerariae flos*).

THERAPEUTIC CATEGORY Claimed to be spasmolytic, against alcohol abuse.

USES AND PROPERTIES In China, kudzu vine is an ancient remedy, mainly against colds and flu, feverish conditions, muscle aches, gastritis, dysentery, hypertension, migraines and *angina pectoris* (a condition characterised by intense pain in the chest). It is said to be an old Chinese antidote for alcohol abuse. Most of the interest in modern times has focused on this application.

PREPARATION AND DOSAGE In Chinese tradition, the root is often used in combination with other herbs.

A daily dose of 9-15 g of dried root is recommended. For *angina pectoris*, tablets containing 10 mg of standardised extract (equivalent to 1.5 g of root) are taken two or three times per day.

ACTIVE INGREDIENTS The activity of the medicine is mainly ascribed to isoflavonoids, of which puerarin, daidzein and daidzin are some of the main compounds. The effect of the herb against alcohol abuse has been ascribed to daidzin and daidzein.

PHARMACOLOGICAL EFFECTS Studies have shown that flavonoid extracts of the root increase blood flow to the brain and heart, and that they also have a spasmolytic effect. This may partly account for some of the traditional uses. Animal studies indicated antidipsotropic effects, but it was later shown that various fruit juices and a chocolate drink also significantly reduced alcohol intake under free choice conditions. A clinical trial on alcoholic adults, given 1.2 g of kudzu root twice a day, failed to show any benefits.

NOTES Kudzu vine has been used in China for centuries as a source of textile fibre and cordage.

STATUS Traditional medicine.

Pueraria lobata (Willd.) Ohwi [=*P. montana* (Lour.) Merr. var. *lobata* (Willd.) Maesen & S. Almeida]   family: Fabaceae
kudzu (French); *ge gen* (Chinese); *Kudzubohne* (German); *kudzu* (Italian)

Pulmonaria officinalis

lungwort

Pulmonaria officinalis leaves

Pulmonaria officinalis flowers

DESCRIPTION Lungwort is a hairy, bristly perennial herb of up to 0.3 m in height, with large, oval leaves dotted with white spots. The tubular flowers are borne in small clusters and turn from red to blue as they mature. It is interesting to note that the herb was used against lung diseases in former times, because the spotted leaves resemble diseased lungs ("doctrine of signatures").

ORIGIN Europe. The plant is commonly cultivated.

PARTS USED Leaves (*Pulmonariae herba*).

THERAPEUTIC CATEGORY Expectorant.

USES AND PROPERTIES Lungwort is mainly used in folk medicine and as a medicinal herb it is nowadays considered to be mostly of historical interest. It is, however, still used as an expectorant and is sometimes utilised in case of ailments of the gastrointestinal and urinary tract. Externally, the herb is applied in case of haemorrhoids and wounds.

PREPARATION AND DOSAGE A tea is prepared from 1.5 g of the finely chopped herb. It is sweetened with honey and taken as a bronchial tea in small sips several times a day.

ACTIVE INGREDIENTS The herb contains mucilage, flavonoids (O-glycosides of kaempferol and quercetin), 4% catecholtannins, 2% gallotannins, up to 5% silicic acid and up to 1.2% allantoin (this compound is also present in *Symphytum officinale* and other members of the family Boraginaceae). It has been suggested that *Pulmonaria*, like other Boraginaceae (see *Borago*, *Symphytum*), may contain potentially toxic pyrrolizidine alkaloids. In a careful screening of plant material from different localities, no pyrrolizidine alkaloids could be detected.

PHARMACOLOGICAL EFFECTS The demulcent effects may be due to mucilage and the diuretic effect to flavonoids and silicic acid. Allantoin helps to destroy necrotic tissue and enhances tissue proliferation and the formation of new epithelia. It is therefore used to treat wounds and burns, ulcers and eczema. The presence of allantoin may provide a rationale for the healing effects when the herb is applied topically but there is not yet any scientific support for the numerous other folk uses.

STATUS Traditional medicine; Pharm.

Pulmonaria officinalis L.

family: Boraginaceae

pulmonaire (French); *Echtes Lungenkraut* (German); *polmonaria* (Italian); *pulmonaria* (Spanish)

Pulsatilla vulgaris

pasque flower • pulsatilla

Pulsatilla vulgaris fruiting plant

Pulsatilla vulgaris flower

DESCRIPTION Pasque flower is a small perennial herb with hairy stems, finely dissected compound leaves, and large, bell-shaped purplish flowers. Each carpel in the flower develops into a seed with a hairlike tip, so that the seed heads have an attractive feathery appearance. The meadow pasque flower (*P. pratensis*) and several other species are alternate sources of raw material. Roots of *P. chinensis* is the *bai tou weng* of Chinese medicine.

ORIGIN Europe. The traditional use of *Pulsatilla vulgaris* is more or less restricted to central and eastern Europe.

PARTS USED Dried (rarely fresh) aboveground parts (*Pulsatillae herba*).

THERAPEUTIC CATEGORY Antispasmodic, antimicrobial.

USES AND PROPERTIES Preparations are traditionally used to treat cough, menstrual pains, neurotonic disorders and sleeplessness. Also listed as traditional uses are gastrointestinal and urinary tract disorders, genital disorders, inflammation of the skin and mucosa, neuralgia and migraine. Pasque flower herb is one of the most popular of all homoeopathic remedies and is used against a wide range of conditions, including depression, headache, stomach pain, irregular menstruation and ailments of the lungs, kidneys, liver, bladder and skin. In China, the roots of *P. chinensis* (*bai tou weng*) are considered to be effective against dysentery.

PREPARATION AND DOSAGE Small amounts of the dry herb are traditionally taken as a tea, or more often extracts are incorporated into preparations and supplements.

ACTIVE INGREDIENTS The fresh herb contains the glucoside ranunculin, a terpenoid lactone, that is broken down to protoanemonin when the plant is dried (and then dimerises to non-toxic anemonin).

PHARMACOLOGICAL EFFECTS Protoanemonin is highly reactive due to the exocyclic methylene group; it can bond with proteins and DNA. Protoanemonin may cause severe allergic dermatitis (itching, rashes, blisters) when exposed to the skin. It is strongly anti-bacterial and causes paralysis of the central nervous system.

WARNING Fresh pulsatilla may cause severe irritation of the skin, or of the kidneys and urinary tract if ingested. The extent to which ranunculin and protoanemonin have been degraded during drying is not always known; therefore, the dry drug should be taken with caution.

STATUS Traditional medicine.

Pulsatilla vulgaris Mill. (=*Anemone pratensis* L.)   family: Ranunculaceae

anémone pulsatille (French); *Gemeine Küchenschelle* (German); *pulsatilla* (Italian)

Punica granatum

pomegranate

Punica granatum fruit

Punica granatum flowers

Punica granatum fruit rind and roots

DESCRIPTION Pomegranate is a spiny, deciduous shrub or small tree of about 5 m in height. It has small leaves clustered at the branch tips, attractive orange-red flowers, a characteristic large fleshy fruit crowned with a persistent calyx and numerous seeds, each with a bright red, fleshy, edible layer.

ORIGIN Southeastern Europe. The plant appears to be an ancient cultigen (suggested to be Eve's apple in the Bible) and is still a minor fruit crop and medicinal plant in the Mediterranean region.

PARTS USED Fruit pericarp (pomegranate fruit rind – *Granati pericarpium*) or the stem and root bark (*Granati cortex*).

THERAPEUTIC CATEGORY Antidiarrhoeal; anthelminthic.

USES AND PROPERTIES Root bark is traditionally used as a vermifuge to treat intestinal parasites, mainly tapeworm. The dried fruit rind or the fruit pulp is a common remedy for upset stomachs and especially to treat diarrhoea. Fruits are used to produce grenadine, a cordial, and the rind to tan leather.

PREPARATION AND DOSAGE In traditional medicine, infusions or tinctures of the fresh or dried fruit rind are taken, usually with honey added to counter the bitter taste. Decoctions of the root bark (sometimes with stem bark, leaves or young fruit added) were widely used as a tapeworm remedy up to the first half of the twentieth century.

ACTIVE INGREDIENTS The fruit rind contains gallo/ellagitannins – mainly punicalin and punicalagin, at very high concentrations (up to 28%). Several piperidine alkaloids are present in the roots, bark, leaves and young fruit but not in the rind. The major active alkaloids are pelletierine (=isopelletierine) and N-methylisopelletierine. Also present is a homotropane alkaloid, pseudopelletierine.

PHARMACOLOGICAL EFFECTS The very high tannin content easily explains the antidiarrhoeal effect. The alkaloids interact strongly with nicotinic acetylcholine receptors. They will narcotise tapeworms so that they lose their grip, and are expelled. Unfortunately, the alkaloids are absorbed through the intestine and cause undesirable CNS effects.

WARNING The alkaloids are highly toxic and self-medication can be dangerous.

STATUS Traditional medicine; Pharm.

Punica granatum L.   family: Punicaceae

grenadier (French); *Granatapfelbaum* (German); *melograno* (Italian)

Quassia amara
quassia • Surinam quassia

Quassia amara flowers

Quassia amara leaves

Quassia amara tree

DESCRIPTION A shrub or small tree of about 4 m in height bearing compound leaves with a winged leaf rachis and attractive bright red flowers. Another source of quassia or bitterwood is Jamaica quassia, *Picrasma excelsa* (Simaroubaceae), a large forest tree with compound, stipulate leaves, yellow flowers and small black fruit.

ORIGIN South America (*Q. amara*); central America (*P. excelsa*); *Q. amara* is commonly cultivated in Indo-Malaysia and worldwide as an ornamental tree.

PARTS USED Wood or wood chips (*Quassiae lignum*).

THERAPEUTIC CATEGORY Bitter tonic (*amarum*), antimicrobial.

USES AND PROPERTIES The extremely bitter wood or extracts thereof were formerly much used as a bitter tonic to stimulate appetite and as a digestive. Traditionally used as anthelmintic and insecticide (on fly paper against flies or against ectoparasites).

PREPARATION AND DOSAGE A tea made from 0.5 g of powdered wood is drunk half an hour before meals. The product is more commonly used as a component of several stomachics and cholagogues.

ACTIVE INGREDIENTS The extremely bitter taste is due to the presence of several seco-triterpenes known as quassinoids. Quassin (bitter value 17 000 000), neoquassin and 18-hydroxyquassin are the main compounds. Also present are indole alkaloids including various β-carboline (such as *N*-methoxy-2-vinyl-β-carboline) and several canthinone-type alkaloids (such canthin-6-one, 4-methoxy-5-hydroxy-canthin-6-one).

PHARMACOLOGICAL EFFECTS Quassinoids and canthinone alkaloids show antibacterial, antifungal, antiviral, antiparasitic (amoeba, trypanosomes, worms, insects), antitumour and positive inotropic activities. β-Carboline and canthinone alkaloids inhibit cAMP-phosphodiesterase. Bitter compounds stimulate appetite, partly by increasing the secretion of gastric juices. A clinical study showed the insecticidal efficacy in treating patients with lice.

NOTES The bitter bark of the tropical American angostura tree (*Galipea officinalis*, family Rutaceae) is a traditional tonic; extracts were once included in digestive bitters and cocktails. In this case the bitter substances are alkaloids.

STATUS Traditional medicine; Pharm.

Quassia amara L.   family: Simaroubaceae

bois amer (French); *Quassiaholzbaum* (German); *quassia* (Italian); *quassia surinam* (Spanish)

Quercus robur

oak • common oak

Quercus robur

Quercus robur leaves and fruit (acorns)

DESCRIPTION A large deciduous tree (up to 50 m), easily recognised by the shortly stalked (almost sessile) leaves, lobed wavy leaf margins, long flowering stalks and the characteristic fruits (acorns). It is similar to sessile oak (*Q. petraea*), which has stalked leaves but stalkless flower clusters. In Europe, oak bark was much used in former times for tanning in the leather industry, while oak wood remains an important industrial source of tannins, especially for taste improvement in the wine and spirits industries. Other tannin sources include blackwattle bark from *Acacia mearnsii* (South Africa, Kenya, Brazil), bark from *Schinopsis* species (South America), bark from *Myrica esculenta* (China) and black myrobalan fruits from *Terminalia chebula* (India).

ORIGIN Europe. Commercially from eastern Europe.

PARTS USED The bark from young branches and trunks of young trees (*Q. petraea, Q. robur*) is harvested in spring (*Quercus cortex*).

THERAPEUTIC CATEGORY Antidiarrhoeal, astringent, antimicrobial.

USES AND PROPERTIES Oak bark and extracts thereof are used against acute diarrhoea and stomach cramps. It is applied externally against inflammations of the skin or mucosa, particularly of the mouth and throat, but also the genital and anal region; furthermore to treat wounds, eczema, and foot perspiration.

PREPARATION AND DOSAGE For internal use, about 3 g of the drug are taken as a decoction. Oral rinses, gargles and compresses are prepared from 20 g of the bark in 1 litre of water. For bathing, 5 g per litre of water is used.

ACTIVE INGREDIENTS The main constituents in the bark are condensed tannins (up to 20%), mainly ellagitannins (such as castalagin, roburin), catechins and oligomeric proanthocyanidins.

PHARMACOLOGICAL EFFECTS Tannins non-specifically inhibit or denature proteins, such as enzymes and receptors; it is plausible to attribute antimicrobial, antiviral, anthelmintic, anti-inflammatory and haemostyptic properties to tannins.

WARNING If diarrhoea persists after three to four days, a doctor should be consulted.

NOTES Oak galls (*gallae*) are especially rich in gallotannins and very astringent and are sometimes used as the main source of medicinal tannins.

STATUS Traditional medicine; Pharm.; Comm.E+.

Quercus robur L.

family: Fagaceae

chêne blanc (French); *Stieleiche* (German); *quercia commune* (Italian)

Rauvolfia serpentina
Indian snakeroot

Rauvolfia vomitoria

Rauvolfia serpentina

Rauvolfia tetraphylla

DESCRIPTION An erect woody shrublet (about 0.5 m), with pointed leaves arranged in whorls of three to five. Clusters of small white or pinkish flowers are followed by red berries that turn black when they ripen. Also of medicinal interest are *R. vomitoria* from West Africa and *R. tetraphylla* from Central and South America.

ORIGIN Pakistan and India to Indonesia. The plant has been overharvested in the wild in India, so that a ban was placed on exports in 1997. African *R. vomitoria* has become an important alternative source of reserpine.

PARTS USED Dried roots, known as Indian snakeroot (*Rauvolfiae radix*); isolated alkaloids.

THERAPEUTIC CATEGORY Antihypertensive, tranquilliser.

USES AND PROPERTIES The powdered root or extracts thereof are given for mild hypertension and as a tranquilliser against anxiety and mental disorders. Numerous traditional uses have been recorded, including the treatment of snake and insect bites, constipation, insomnia, liver diseases and rheumatism.

PREPARATION AND DOSAGE A daily dose of 600 mg of powdered root (6 mg total alkaloids), is recommended; several isolated alkaloids are used medicinally.

ACTIVE INGREDIENTS The product contains up to 60 different monoterpene indole alkaloids (1-2%) of the yohimbane-, heteroyohimbane-, sarpagane- and ajmalane- types. The main hypertensive alkaloids are reserpine and rescinnamine (=reserpinine). Other important alkaloids are serpentine, ajmalicine, and ajmaline.

PHARMACOLOGICAL EFFECTS Reserpine inhibits the re-uptake of noradrenaline in synaptic vesicles of adrenergic neurones. The neurotransmitter is therefore degraded by MAO and COMT and no longer available. This explains the activity against high blood pressure: reserpine depletes the tissue stores of catecholamines from peripheral areas of the body, while the sedative effects are ascribed to depletion of noradrenaline and serotonin from the brain. Vasodilation and hypotension or central sedation are a consequence. The use against mild essential hypertension is supported by clinical data.

WARNING The alkaloids may cause mental depression that could persist long after the treatment has been stopped. Persons with a history of depression and suicidal tendencies should not be treated.

STATUS Traditional and modern medicine: reserpine and other isolated alkaloids; Pharm.; Comm.E+; WHO 1.

Rauvolfia serpentina (L.) Benth. ex Kurz   family: Apocynaceae

sarpagandha (Hindi); *rauwolfia, arbre aux serpents* (French); *Rauwolfia, Schlangenholz* (German); *rauvolfia, serpentina indiana* (Italian)

Rhamnus catharticus

buckthorn

Rhamnus catharticus

Rhamnus catharticus leaves and fruit

DESCRIPTION Buckthorn is a woody shrub of 3 m in height, with opposite, finely toothed leaves borne on spiny branches. Inconspicuous yellowish green flowers are borne in clusters in the leaf axils. These are followed by spherical, shiny fruits (drupes) of about 5-8 mm in diameter that are initially red but black when they ripen.

ORIGIN Europe, Asia and North Africa. Berries are wild-harvested, mainly in the former USSR.

PARTS USED Dried berries (*Rhamni cathartici fructus*).

THERAPEUTIC CATEGORY Stimulant laxative.

USES AND PROPERTIES The product is used as a laxative in cases where a soft stool is desirable (e.g. haemorrhoids, rectal-anal surgery). In folk medicine, the berries have been used as diuretic medicine and as a so-called "blood purifier".

PREPARATION AND DOSAGE A tea made from 2-5 g of the dry berries in 150 ml water is taken in the morning and/or evening. The minimum dose required for a soft stool should be taken – this differs from person to person and some experimentation is required. The daily dose should not exceed 5 g.

ACTIVE INGREDIENTS The fruits contain anthraquinone glycosides (2-5%; up to 1.4 mg/fruit). Free emodin and emodinanthrone, as well as glucofrangulins and frangulins, have been detected, mainly in the seeds. Also present are organic acids (including ascorbic acid), pectins, flavonoids (1%), tannins (3-4%), and anthocyanins.

PHARMACOLOGICAL EFFECTS Anthranoids of the emodin type (1,8-dihydroxyanthracene derivatives) are present as β-glycosides. These are merely the prodrugs, that are neither absorbed nor hydrolysed in the upper gastrointestinal tract, but are broken down into anthrones only when they reach the colon. The resulting anthrones are the active laxatives that act on the colon motility, resulting in faster bowel movements. Molecular targets include a chloride channel and less importantly the Na^+, K^+-ATPase. Anthrones enhance the secretion of water and inhibit its resorption in the colon, so that a liquefied stool and a gentle laxative effect is obtained.

WARNING The herb is contraindicated in cases of obstruction or inflammation of the intestines (appendicitis, colitis and Crohn's disease) and during pregnancy; not to be administered to children under the age of 12.

STATUS Traditional medicine; Pharm.; Comm.E+.

Rhamnus catharticus L.   family: Rhamnaceae

nerprun purgatif (French); *Echter Kreuzdorn* (German); *spina cervina* (Italian); *espino cerval* (Spanish)

Rhamnus frangula
alder buckthorn

Rhamnus frangula

DESCRIPTION A woody shrub of 3-5 m in height, with non-thorny, brittle branches (*frangere* is the Latin for break) that have an unpleasant odour (hence *Faulbaum* in German) and broad leaves with prominent, arching secondary veins. Small greenish flowers are followed by small, two- or three-seeded fruit (drupes) that change from red to black as they ripen. The tree is sometimes called buckthorn and may therefore be confused with real buckthorn (*Rhamnus catharticus*).

ORIGIN Europe, Mediterranean region (including North Africa) and northwestern Asia. The product is wild-collected mainly in eastern Europe and Russia.

PARTS USED Dried bark of the trunk and branches (*Frangulae cortex*). Fresh bark has to be aged – stored for one year or heat treated before use (see below).

THERAPEUTIC CATEGORY Stimulant laxative.

USES AND PROPERTIES The dry bark may be used as a laxative, but more often the powdered bark or bark extracts are included as ingredients in proprietary products. It is sometimes part of combination products (with antispasmodic herbs and bulk laxatives).

PREPARATION AND DOSAGE Cut or powdered bark or bark extracts are used for making teas or decoctions.

About 2 g of chopped bark is typically steeped in 150 ml of boiling water. The daily dose should not exceed 20-30 mg of total hydroxyanthracenes.

ACTIVE INGREDIENTS In the fresh bark, the active compounds are present as anthrone- or dianthrone-glycosides (frangularoside and glucofrangularoside) (6%). With storage or heat treatment, these are oxidised to anthraquinone glycosides, mainly glucofrangulin A (bis-glycoside with glucose and rhamnose), glucofrangulin B (bis-glycoside with glucose and apiose), frangulins A and B (monoglycosides with only apiose) and frangulaemodin 8-*O*-glucoside. Also present are free emodin, physcion and chrysophanol.

PHARMACOLOGICAL EFFECTS The anthracene glycosides act as prodrugs and are partly converted to the active anthrones and anthranols in the large intestine (see *Rhamnus catharticus* above).

WARNING Stimulant laxatives should never be used for more than a week or two without seeking medical advice. They should also not be used during pregnancy (risk of abortion) or while breastfeeding.

STATUS Traditional medicine; Pharm.; Comm.E+; ESCOP 5; WHO 2.

Rhamnus frangula L. (=*Frangula alnus* Mill.)   family: Rhamnaceae

bourdaine (French); *Faulbaum* (German); *frangola* (Italian); *frangola* (Spanish)

Rhamnus purshianus
cascara buckthorn • cascara sagrada tree

Rhamnus purshianus

DESCRIPTION The plant is a large, deciduous shrub or small tree of up to 12 m in height. It has oblong leaves with prominent parallel veins, small greenish flowers and red fruits (drupes) of about 10 mm in diameter that turn black when they ripen. Cascara sagrada is the Spanish for "holy bark".

ORIGIN Western coastal region of North America (from Canada to southern California). Commercial supplies come from plantations in the USA and Canada.

PARTS USED Dried trunk and stem bark (*Rhamni purshiani cortex*). Fresh bark tends to cause nausea and griping, so it is stored for one year (or artificially aged) before use.

THERAPEUTIC CATEGORY Stimulant laxative.

USES AND PROPERTIES The bark has mild purgative properties and is used as a laxative to treat constipation. Cascara sagrada is still very popular and is an ingredient in several hundred different medicinal products. The annual harvest of bark has been estimated to reach 2 000 tons in some years.

PREPARATION AND DOSAGE Teas or decoctions are made at the same dose than is used for *Rhamnus frangula* (2 g in 150 ml water, or a total of 20-30 mg total hydroxyanthracene derivatives per day).

ACTIVE INGREDIENTS The dry bark contains 6-9% hydroxyanthraquinone glycosides, the bulk of which is made up of O-glycosides of aloeemodin, chrysophanol and emodin or C-glycosides (so-called cascarosides A, B, C and D; also aloin A, B).

PHARMACOLOGICAL EFFECTS Stimulant laxatives influence the motility of the colon and speed up the movement of the bowels, resulting in a reduction in liquid absorption. Part of the glycosides are degraded by bacterial enzymes in the colon to form anthrones, the active laxative compounds.

WARNING The product should not be used during pregnancy or lactation. Stimulant laxatives should not be used for periods longer than one or two weeks, and then only after a change in diet or the use of bulk laxatives were found to be ineffective. Anthraquinones appear to have mutagenic properties.

STATUS Traditional medicine; Pharm.; Comm.E+; ESCOP 5; WHO 2.

Rhamnus purshianus DC.   family: Rhamnaceae

sacrée (French); Amerikanischer Faulbaum (German); cascara sagrada (Italian); cáscara sagrada (Spanish)

Rheum palmatum

rhubarb • Chinese rhubarb

Rheum palmatum leaves

Rheum palmatum flowers

Rheum officinale

DESCRIPTION A leafy perennial herb with large leaves arising directly by thick and fleshy stalks from an underground rhizome. The leaves are palmately lobed in *R. palmatum*, or rounded and often toothed in the closely related *R. officinale*. Both species form enormous panicles of inconspicuous flowers, followed by winged fruit. Rhapontic rhubarb (*Rheum rhaponticum*) is no longer recommended. Also used are *R. emodi*, *R. webbianum* and *R. rhabarbarum*; petioles of the latter (rich in oxalates), are widely used as vegetable.

ORIGIN Northwestern China and Tibet; cultivated mainly in China, but also Korea, India and Pakistan. Any of the two species (or their hybrids, or mixtures) are acceptable.

PARTS USED Sliced and dried rhizomes (*Rhei radix*).

THERAPEUTIC CATEGORY Stimulant laxative.

USES AND PROPERTIES Rhubarb root is used as a stimulant laxative to treat constipation. At low doses, it is a useful astringent and antimicrobial haemostyptic, and stomachic against diarrhoea and liver complaints.

PREPARATION AND DOSAGE The laxative dose is about 1-2 g of powdered rhizome, taken as a tea. As stomachic, 0.1-0.2 g of powdered drug may be used (often mixed with other herbs to improve the taste). Powdered rhizomes or extracts are included in laxative medicines, stomachic bitters, cholagogues, slimming preparations or "blood-cleansing" teas.

ACTIVE INGREDIENTS Rhubarb root contains a large and variable numbers of hydroxyanthracene derivatives (3-12%), together with tannins (5-10%), stilbene glucosides (1%) and flavonoids (2-3%). Most of the anthracenes are present as anthraquinone glycosides of the main aglycones – chrysophanol, emodin, aloe-emodin, rhein and physcion (e.g. pulmatin, chrysophanein and physcionin). The tannins are a mixture of gallotannins and esters with gallic-, hydroxycinnamic- and coumaric acids. Rhapontic rhubarb has rhaponticoside, a stilbene derivative; it is present in certain varieties of *R. palmatum*.

PHARMACOLOGICAL EFFECTS The anthrones and dianthrones have laxative properties (see *Rhamnus catharticus*). Tannins have an astringent action (see *Quercus robur*). Rhaponticin has weak oestrogenic properties and poses a slight health risk.

STATUS Traditional medicine; Pharm.; Comm.E+; ESCOP 6; WHO 1.

Rheum palmatum L.

family: Polygonaceae

dai hoàng, da huang (Chinese); *rhubarbe* (French); *Medizinal-Rhabarber* (German); *rabarbaro* (Italian)

Rhodiola rosea

roseroot • arctic root

Rhodiola rosea

Rhodiola rosea leaves

Rhodiola rosea flowers

Sedum acre

DESCRIPTION A perennial succulent of up to 0.6 m in height with fleshy rhizomes, stems and oblong leaves bearing small yellow flowers. The genus *Rhodiola* is nowadays considered to be a subgenus of *Sedum*.

ORIGIN Arctic region (mainly Scandinavia and Siberia). The plant has a long history of medicinal use and was mentioned by Dioscorides.

PARTS USED Rhizomes; nowadays as standardised extracts. The freshly cut rhizome has a fragrance reminiscent of attar-of-roses (hence the scientific name).

THERAPEUTIC CATEGORY Adaptogen.

USES AND PROPERTIES Rhodiola has been extensively used in folk medicine (e.g. the Vikings and Siberians) to increase physical strength and endurance, resistance to cold and disease, and to promote fertility and longevity. The herb was distributed along ancient trade routes and became popular also in Mongolia and China. In Sweden, it is considered to be a stimulant and antifatigue agent. The modern use is as an adaptogenic tonic, to increase physical and mental endurance, reduce the symptoms of asthenia (fatigue, decreased capacity for work, irritability), alleviate sexual disorders, promote fertility, and to moderate the symptoms

associated with old age and some neurological disorders.

PREPARATION AND DOSAGE In recent years, exclusively as extracts (in 40% ethanol), standardised to contain 3% rosavins and 0.8-1% salidroside (see below). The usual daily dose is 200-600 mg of extract (equal to about 20-60 drops of tincture), taken two or three times per day (for up to four months).

ACTIVE INGREDIENTS Phenylpropanoids (rosavin, rosin and rosarin; the so-called rosavins), together with phenylethanol derivatives (mainly salidroside, =rhodioloside). Also present are flavonoids (e.g. rodiolin), monoterpenoids (rosiridol, rosaridin), phytosterols and phenolic acids.

PHARMACOLOGICAL EFFECTS In several controlled clinical studies, extracts were shown to significantly improve physical strength and endurance and to alleviate symptoms associated with asthenia and a wide range of neurological disorders.

NOTES The related *Sedum acre* (stonecrop or wall pepper) is a traditional medicine in Europe. It contains piperidine alkaloids and was once popular as an emetic, purgative and abortifacient.

STATUS Pharm.; clinical studies+.

Rhodiola rosea L. [=*Sedum rosea* (L.) Scop.]   family: Crassulaceae

rosenrot (Swedish); *rhodiole rose* (French); *Rosenwurz* (German); *rodiola rosea* (Italian)

Rhododendron tomentosum

marsh tea

Rhododendron tomentosum

DESCRIPTION Marsh tea is a woody shrub of up to 1.5 m in height, with narrowly oblong, leathery leaves and attractive white or pink flowers. The plant is better known by the original name, *Ledum palustre* (the genus *Ledum* has been included in *Rhododendron*). *Rhododendron* species used in traditional medicine include R. *aureum* from Asia, R. *campylocarpum* from Asia, R. *ferrugineum* (European mountains) and R. *ponticum* (Europe, Asia Minor).

ORIGIN Northern Europe, northern Asia and America. Plant material is wild-harvested.

PARTS USED Leaves and twigs (*Ledi palustris herba*).

THERAPEUTIC CATEGORY Traditional expectorant, anti-inflammatory.

USES AND PROPERTIES Marsh tea extracts are mainly used as ingredients of cough mixtures and anti-rheumatic preparations. They have been used specifically against whooping cough and also as emetic, diuretic and diaphoretic medicines. Extracts are nowadays used in low concentrations in homoeopathic preparations, mainly to treat bronchitis, rheumatism, gout and skin ailments.

PREPARATION AND DOSAGE In view of the known toxicity, the herb is no longer considered suitable for self-medication. Its use is limited to homoeopathic preparations. The Vikings used the plant to enforce their beer. It was traditionally used as insecticide against moths and bedbugs.

ACTIVE INGREDIENTS An essential oil is present (up to 2.5% of dry weight) with two sesquiterpenes (palustrol and ledol) as main components. Also present are carvacrol, thymol and coumarins such as fraxin and esculin. Typical ingredients of *Rhododendron* are tetracyclic diterpenes (such as grayanotoxin I, andromedol, or similar compounds).

PHARMACOLOGICAL EFFECTS The herb irritates the skin and mucous membranes and is known to be antitussive and anti-inflammatory. Ledol exhibits intoxicant and narcotic properties; it is also insecticidal. Human poisoning has been frequently reported, leading to abortion and sometimes narcotic intoxication, followed by paralysis. The tetracyclic diterpenes in other *Rhododendron* species produce symptoms of central nervous system stimulation and show anti-hypertensive effects.

STATUS Traditional medicine; Pharm. (now obsolete).

Rhododendron tomentosum Harmaja (=*Ledum palustre* L.) family: Ericaceae
lède, lédier, bois de savane (French); *Sumpfporst* (German); *ledum palustre* (Italian)

Ribes nigrum

blackcurrant

Ribes nigrum leaves and fruit

Ribes nigrum

Ribes rubrum

DESCRIPTION Blackcurrant is a shrub of about 2 m in height, with deeply lobed, reticulately veined and doubly dentate leaves. The white flowers are borne in short clusters, and develop into brownish black, shiny fruits, each tipped by the persistent calyx. It is closely related to redcurrant, *R. rubrum*, a species grown for its glistening, bright red fruit. The fruit of both species are used to make jam and jelly.

ORIGIN Central and eastern Europe. It is cultivated in cold temperate regions.

PARTS USED Mainly the leaves (blackcurrant leaf – *Ribis nigri folium*) but also the fruit and seed oil.

THERAPEUTIC CATEGORY Traditional diuretic.

USES AND PROPERTIES Leaves are a folk medicine and are taken against arthritis, spasmodic cough and diarrhoea. Leaves and buds are taken in cases of rheumatism and urinary problems. As a tasty source of vitamin C, the fruits are useful as a dietary supplement during the cold and flu season. Fresh ripe fruits and fruit juice are useful in cases of mild diarrhoea. Seed oil has become popular as an alternative to evening primrose oil. It contains about 15% γ-linolenic acid.

PREPARATION AND DOSAGE A tea is made from 2-4 g of finely chopped leaves and is taken several times a day. The leaves are sometimes included in diuretic tea mixtures and other herbal teas.

ACTIVE INGREDIENTS Flavonoids (about 0.5%) are present, including derivatives of quercetin, kaempferol, myricetin, isorhamnetin and sakuranetin. Essential oil, 0.4% proanthocyanidins, diterpenes and ascorbic acid (0.3%) are reported to be present.

PHARMACOLOGICAL EFFECTS Experiments with rats and cats show diuretic and hypotensive effects; the flavonoids decrease the permeability of capillaries and the formation of prostaglandins. Oligomeric proanthocyanidins and perhaps anthocyanidins in the fruit are likely to have antimicrobial and antioxidant effects. These properties may explain some of the medicinal uses of the drug.

NOTES Blackcurrent fruits are used for jam or soft drinks. They are especially famous for making a liqueur known as *Crème de cassis*, which is traditionally mixed with dry white wine or champagne (this tasty mixture is known as "kir"). A valuable essential oil is distilled from the buds.

STATUS Traditional medicine; ESCOP 4.

Ribes nigrum L. family: Grossulariaceae

cassis (French); *Schwarze Johannisbeere* (German); *ribes nero* (Italian)

Ricinus communis

castor oil plant

Ricinus communis flowers

Ricinus communis fruit capsules

Ricinus communis seeds

DESCRIPTION This is a shrub or small tree (up to 4 m), with very large, hand-shaped leaves. Female and male flowers appear separately near the tips of the branches and the fruit is a three-seeded capsule with spine-like projections. Each seed is about 10 mm long, conspicuously shiny and irregularly mottled with silver, brown and black.

ORIGIN Probably north-east Africa and India (an ornamental plant and naturalised weed in the tropics and subtropics); product comes from India, China and Brazil.

PARTS USED Seed oil (*Ricini oleum*), extracted by cold pressing, to avoid toxic lectins from dissolving in the oil.

THERAPEUTIC CATEGORY Laxative.

USES AND PROPERTIES Castor oil is a well-known and effective purgative medicine. During the 17th and 18th centuries, a fortnightly purging was considered necessary for good health, but the ritualised purgation of children and the excessive use of laxatives have virtually disappeared in modern times. Root and leaf poultices are used in folk medicine to treat wounds, sores and boils. Castor oil is nowadays mainly an industrial product (lubricant and starting material in the manufacture of polymers).

PREPARATION AND DOSAGE One to two teaspoons (5-10 g) of the oil are usually taken as a laxative (maximally 30 g per day).

ACTIVE INGREDIENTS Castor oil contains a fatty acid known as ricinoleic acid, which accounts for about 90% of the triglyceride fatty acids in the oil. The seeds contain two highly toxic substances not present in the oil – ricinine (a pyridine alkaloid) and ricin (a lectin). The latter is among the most toxic compounds; two seeds may be fatal.

PHARMACOLOGICAL EFFECTS Ricinoleic acid, which is formed from triglycerides under the influence of lipase in the small intestine, enhances the formation of prostaglandin E2, endogenous NO and the release of serotonin and histamine. These properties reduce the net resorption of fluids and electrolytes, and stimulate peristalsis.

WARNING Do not use in case of intestinal inflammation.

NOTES Another member of the Euphorbiaceae, *Croton tiglium*, yields croton oil rich in co-carcinogenic phorbol esters, the most powerful but obsolete purgatives known to man.

STATUS Traditional medicine; Pharm.

Ricinus communis L.   family: Euphorbiaceae

ricin (French); *Rizinus, Christuspalme* (German); *ricino* (Italian); *ricino* (Spanish)

Rosa canina

rose • dog rose

Rosa canina flowers

Rosa x centifolia

Rosa canina fruit (rose hips)

DESCRIPTION The dog rose is a woody creeper (up to 5 m), with curved thorns on the stem, leaves with about three pairs of toothed leaflets, attractive pink flowers and fleshy red fruits known as rose hips. Various species are acceptable sources of rose hips and seeds. Extracts of the distinctive thorny hips of R. roxburghii are a nutritional supplement in China.

ORIGIN R. canina is indigenous to Europe and Asia (naturalised in North America). R. gallica (common rose), considered to be of Iranian origin, has given rise to a bewildering diversity of cultivars through crossing and backcrossing with other species.

PARTS USED Dried, ripe fruit with the seeds removed (Rosae pseudofructus), dried seeds, dried flowers and essential oil distilled from flowers.

THERAPEUTIC CATEGORY Diuretic.

USES AND PROPERTIES Rose hips (with or without seeds) are traditionally used to treat a diversity of ailments of the gastrointestinal tract and nowadays mainly to enhance the flavour of tea mixtures. Seeds are a traditional diuretic and used against various disorders of the urinary tract. Dried petals of Rosa gallica and

R. x centifolia are used in mouth rinses to treat mild inflammation. The essential oil of R. x centifolia and R. x damascena ("attar of rose") is very popular in aromatherapy (said to have mild sedative, antidepressant and anti-inflammatory activity). Rosewater is a traditional eye lotion.

PREPARATION AND DOSAGE Infusions are made of 2-2.5 g crushed rose hips (with or without seeds), 1-2 g of powdered seeds and 1-2 g of rose flower.

ACTIVE INGREDIENTS Rose hips contain ascorbic acid (up to 2.4% vitamin C), pectins, carotenoids (mainly rubixanthin, lycopene and β-carotene), flavonoids, tannins, organic acids (malic and citric acid) and sugars. Seeds are rich in γ-linolenic acid and linoleic acid. Petals contain tannins.

PHARMACOLOGICAL EFFECTS Diuretic, hypoglycaemic and antioxidant and astringent (petals) effects have been shown experimentally. The seed oil of R. moschata helps to reduce scars (from acne, surgery) and wrinkles.

STATUS Traditional medicine; Pharm.; Comm.E+ (petals only).

Rosa canina L.   family: Rosaceae

églantier (French); *Hundsrose, Gemeine Heckenrose* (German); *rosa canina* (Italian)

Rosmarinus officinalis

rosemary

Rosmarinus officinalis

Rosmarinus officinalis leaves and flowers

DESCRIPTION Rosemary is an aromatic evergreen shrub (about 1 m) bearing narrow leaves that are bright green above, with rolled-in margins and densely hairy below, and small, pale purple or bluish flowers.

ORIGIN Mediterranean region; widely cultivated as a culinary herb; commercially in the Mediterranean.

PARTS USED Dried leaves (*Rosmarini folium*), essential oil (*Rosmarini aetheroleum*).

THERAPEUTIC CATEGORY General tonic, antimicrobial, spasmolytic.

USES AND PROPERTIES Rosemary is a carminative and stomachic to treat stomach cramps and flatulence, and to stimulate appetite and the secretion of gastric juices. It is considered to be useful against headache and nervous complaints. When used externally (in ointments and bath oils), the oil stimulates blood circulation and has antibacterial, antifungal, antiparasitic and mild analgesic activity (it provides some relief from muscle aches and joint pains).

PREPARATION AND DOSAGE A tea made of 2 g of dry herb is taken three times per day. For internal use, a maximum of 20 drops of oil (1 ml) should be taken per day, in doses of no more that 2 drops. For preparing a bath, 50 g of the herb is boiled in a litre of water.

ACTIVE INGREDIENTS Essential oil is present (2.5%), with 1,8-cineole, α-pinene, and camphor as main components, and smaller amounts of β-pinene, borneol, isobornyl acetate, limonene, linalool, 3-octanone, terpineol and verbinol. Also reported in leaves are phenolic acids (rosmarinic acid), bitter diterpenes (carnosol, rosmanol), triterpenes (oleanic and ursolic acid), triterpene alcohols (α-amyrin, β-amyrin, betulin), as well as several flavonoids and their glycosides (diosmetin, luteolin, genkwanin).

PHARMACOLOGICAL EFFECTS Animal and laboratory studies have confirmed the reported antibacterial, antifungal, antiviral, spasmolytic, antioxidant, smooth-muscle modulating, analgesic, anti-inflammatory and venotonic effects. The herb acts as mild cholagogue and choleretic.

NOTES Rosemary is an ingredient in cosmetics and in liqueurs such as bénédictine.

STATUS Traditional Medicine; Pharm.; Comm.E+; ESCOP 3.

Rosmarinus officinalis L.   family: Lamiaceae

romarin (French); *Rosmarin* (German); *rosmarino* (Italian); *roméro* (Spanish)

Rubus fruticosus

bramble • blackberry

Rubus fruticosus (wild type)

Rubus fruticosus cultivar

Rubus idaeus

DESCRIPTION R. fruticosus comprises a species complex with more than 100 separate species; it is a sprawling and prickly shrub (up to 3 m) bearing compound leaves with prickles along the midrib, and sparse hairs on the lower surface. The flowers are white to pale pink and are followed by clusters of black berries. Raspberry (*R. idaeus*) is less prickly but has a dense layer of white hairs on the lower surface of the leaves and the fruit is pinkish red when ripe (unlike bramble, the berry separates from the common receptable when ripe).

ORIGIN Europe and the Mediterranean region, but naturalised on all continents. Raspberry occurs naturally in Europe, Asia and North America. Both species have given rise to commercial cultivars, grown for their delicious fruit.

PARTS USED Enzymatically fermented and dried leaves. Bramble leaf (*Rubi fruticosi folium*) and raspberry leaf (*Rubi idaei folium*) are both used.

THERAPEUTIC CATEGORY Astringent.

USES AND PROPERTIES Bramble leaf is recommended as an astringent and for treating non-specific acute diarrhoea and inflammation of the mouth and throat. Dried or fermented leaves are included in tea mixtures. Raspberry leaves are mainly used for their astringent properties (to treat diarrhoea and as gargle for mouth or throat infections) and as ingredients in commercial herbal tea mixtures. Raspberry leaf is traditionally used to ease labour in childbirth.

PREPARATION AND DOSAGE A tea made from 1.5 g of leaves (both bramble and raspberry) is taken up to three times per day.

ACTIVE INGREDIENTS Bramble leaf contains about 10% hydrolysable tannins (gallotannins, dimeric ellagitannins), and flavonoids. Gallotannins, ellagitannins and flavonoids have also been found in raspberry leaf.

PHARMACOLOGICAL EFFECTS The tannin content of the leaves is clearly in agreement with the observed astringent and antidiarrhoeic effects. Limited information on other indications is available. Animal and human studies have indicated that raspberry leaf has uteronic activity, causing contraction of uterine muscles.

STATUS Traditional medicine; Pharm.; Comm.E+ (blackberry leaf).

Rumex crispus

yellow dock

Rumex crispus

Rumex crispus fruit

DESCRIPTION Yellow dock is a robust, leafy herb of up to 1.5 m in height, bearing large leaves with distinctive sheathing leaf bases. Numerous small greenish flowers are produced on an extensive panicle, followed by small, reddish brown, winged fruit. The various *Rumex* species are difficult to tell apart. *Rumex* species are closely related to the well-known medicinal plants known as rhubarbs (*Rheum* species).

ORIGIN Europe and Asia. It has become a weed in many parts of the world.

PARTS USED Sliced and dried roots.

THERAPEUTIC CATEGORY Stimulant laxative.

USES AND PROPERTIES Infusions and decoctions are traditionally used as laxatives to treat constipation, liver problems and arthritis. It is regarded as a cleansing herb, useful to clear chronic skin problems. In traditional medicine, the root is a remedy against internal parasites (tapeworm and roundworm). The whole plant is also said to be widely employed in case of vascular disorders and internal bleeding. Externally, it is applied to ulcers, boils and tumours.

PREPARATION AND DOSAGE Decoctions or infusions can be prepared from 1-2 g of the crushed root in 150 ml water. For topical use, a hot poultice is made from the pounded roots and leaves.

ACTIVE INGREDIENTS Members of the Polygonaceae are well known for the presence of anthraquinones. *Rumex* roots contain glycosides of emodin and chrysophanol (such as chrysophanein) and also tannins. Oxalic acid is typical for *Rumex*.

PHARMACOLOGICAL EFFECTS The laxative effect of *Rumex* root is due to chrysophanol and related anthracene glycosides, that are also found in *Rheum* and *Aloe*. Oxalic acid is toxic in high concentrations, but is medicinally used (5% solution, together with 5% malonic acid) as a haemostatic agent.

WARNING As with all stimulant laxatives, yellow dock should not be used continuously for more than a week or two. Do not use during pregnancy, while breastfeeding, in young children or in persons suffering from inflammatory diseases of the gastrointestinal tract.

NOTES *Rumex acetosa*, *R. acetosella* and *Oxalis acetosella* (Oxalidaceae) contain high amounts of oxalic acid and its salts. They are used as vegetables and medicinally as diuretics and against skin disorders.

STATUS Traditional medicine; Pharm.

Rumex crispus L.

family: Polygonaceae

rumex crépu, patience crépue (French); *Krauser Ampfer* (German); *romice crespo* (Italian)

Ruscus aculeatus
butcher's broom

Ruscus aculeatus

Ruscus aculeatus berries

DESCRIPTION The plant is an evergreen perennial (up to 1 m), with peculiar leaflike, leathery branches or false leaves called phylloclades. Small, greenish flowers are borne on the phylloclades and the attractive fruits are bright red, fleshy berries.

ORIGIN Western Europe and Mediterranean region to western Asia; commonly grown in gardens. Butchers in Europe formerly used the branches as brooms, hence the common name.

PARTS USED Sliced and dried rhizome and root (*Rusci aculeati rhizoma*).

THERAPEUTIC CATEGORY Venotonic, anti-inflammatory, diuretic.

USES AND PROPERTIES Extracts are used to treat the symptoms of chronic venous insufficiency (varicose veins), such as swelling, itching, pain and heaviness. It is also considered to be effective in relieving the discomfort of haemorrhoids (itching, burning) and is included in proprietary preparations for both oral and topical use. Butcher's broom is a traditional diuretic and is said to be mildly laxative.

PREPARATION AND DOSAGE Extracts, equivalent to a daily dose of 7-11 mg ruscogenin, are taken orally.

ACTIVE INGREDIENTS The activity of the product is ascribed to steroidal saponins (up to 6% of dry weight). The main saponins are ruscin (monodesmosidic spirostane type) and ruscoside (bidesmosidic furostane type), that co-occur with the corresponding aglycones ruscogenin (1β-hydroxydiosgenin) and neoruscogenin.

PHARMACOLOGICAL EFFECTS Experiments have shown that extracts of butcher's broom are associated with the stimulation of the α-adrenergic receptors of the smooth muscle cells in the vascular wall. In this way, dilated venous vessels are supported and strengthened. Ruscogenin and related compounds are used in ointments and suppositories for the symptomatic relief of pain and discomfort associated with varicose veins and acute attacks of piles. The *Ruscus* saponins are known to be absorbed when taken orally and are included in combination products intended for oral use against the symptoms of venous and lymphatic vessel insufficiency.

NOTES Figwort or pilewort, *Ranunculus ficaria* (family Ranunculaceae) is a traditional and effective anti-haemorrhoidal treatment. The activity is ascribed to saponins (glycosides of hederagenin and oleanolic acid).

STATUS Traditional medicine; Comm.E.+.

Ruscus aculeatus L.   family: Ruscaceae or Asparagaceae

petit houx (French); *Stechender Mäusedorn* (German); *pungitopo* (Italian)

Ruta graveolens

rue • herb of grace

Ruta graveolens flowers

Ruta graveolens fruit

DESCRIPTION Rue is a woody, strongly aromatic, perennial shrub (about 1 m), bearing irregularly divided, compound leaves covered with minute, translucent glands, clusters of small yellow flowers and four-lobed fruit capsules. The Mediterranean Aleppo rue (*R. chalepensis*) is traditionally used in a similar way.

ORIGIN Southern Europe; commonly cultivated in many parts of the world.

PARTS USED Dried leaves (*Rutae folium*) or dried, aboveground parts (*Rutae herba*).

THERAPEUTIC CATEGORY Traditional tonic.

USES AND PROPERTIES Rue is traditionally used for a very wide range of ailments, including menstrual disorders, spasms, loss of appetite, dyspeptic complaints, circulatory disorders, fever, high blood pressure, heart palpitations, inflamed mucosa, toothache, hysteria, arthritis, sprains, injuries and skin diseases. It has been used as a uterine stimulant and for inducing abortion – a dangerous practice that has led to fatalities. Rue was formerly used to improve and stabilise wine of bad quality.

PREPARATION AND DOSAGE Extreme care should be taken because rue can cause severe photodermatitis.

It is toxic and abortive if taken in high doses. Bruised leaves may be placed on a tooth and in the ears to alleviate pain.

ACTIVE INGREDIENTS A large number of chemical compounds are known from *R. graveolens*. Examples of interest are the coumarins (coumarin, herniarin, gravelliferon, rutaretin), furanocoumarins (bergapten, psoralen, rutamarin), furanoquinoline alkaloids (dictamnine, skimmianine, rutacridone and various derivatives) and the flavonoid rutin (5%). Methyl nonyl ketone (2-undecanone) is a major component of the volatile oil and is used in perfumery and flavourings.

PHARMACOLOGICAL EFFECTS Reported antimicrobial, antispasmodic, anti-exudative, analgesic and ion channel inhibiting activities are probably due to furanocoumarin and furanoquinoline alkaloids. Rutin is a well-known capillary protectant, and is used together with coumarins as a supplementary treatment for chronic venous diseases.

WARNING Furanocoumarins and related alkaloids are mutagenic and should be avoided during pregnancy.

STATUS Traditional medicine; Pharm. (now obsolete).

Ruta graveolens L.

family: Rutaceae

rue (French); *Weinraute* (German); *ruta* (Italian); *ruda común* (Spanish)

Salix alba

white willow

Salix alba tree

Salix alba leaves and fruit

DESCRIPTION White willow is a deciduous tree (up to 20 m), with erect branches bearing oblong, somewhat silvery leaves and attractive catkins (spikes of naked flowers) – those on male trees with protruding yellow stamens, those on female trees with green styles. Several salicin-rich species such as the basket willow (*S. purpurea*) and crack or brittle willow (*S. fragilis*) are recommended today for commercial bark harvesting. A cultivar of *S. alba* is famous as the traditional source of timber for making cricket bats.

ORIGIN Europe and Asia (*S. alba*, *S. fragilis*); Europe and North Africa to Asia (*S. purpurea*). Willow bark is produced mainly in eastern and southeastern Europe.

PARTS USED Dried bark, from two to three year old branches (*Salicis cortex*) (today mainly from *S. purpurea*).

THERAPEUTIC CATEGORY Anti-inflammatory, analgesic, antipyretic.

USES AND PROPERTIES Willow bark is traditionally used against fever, flu, rheumatism, headaches and other minor pain.

PREPARATION AND DOSAGE A tea can be made by adding 2-3 g of chopped or powdered bark to a cup of cold water and heating it to boiling point. A cupful is drunk three or four times per day. Extracts of willow bark are ingredients of various commercial phytomedicines (analgesics, antirheumatics, sedatives and stomachics).

ACTIVE INGREDIENTS The main active ingredients are phenolic glycosides, such as salicylates (salicortin, salicin, tremulacin), syringin, and triandrin; furthermore phenolic acids (chlorogenic acid) and oligomeric proanthocyanidins (1%). Salicortin is hydrolysed to salicin (either in the plant or after ingestion) and the salicin in turn is converted (by intestinal hydrolysis) to saligenin (=salicyl alcohol). Saligenin is absorbed into the bloodstream and oxidised in the liver to salicylic acid (the main active substance). The acetylated form of salicylic acid is the well known analgesic, aspirin.

PHARMACOLOGICAL EFFECTS Salicylic acid inhibits cyclooxygenase, the key enzyme of prostaglandin biosynthesis. As prostaglandins mediate pain and inflammation, the observed anti-inflammatory, antirheumatic and analgesic effects appear plausible. Controlled clinical studies support these claims. Salicin, unlike aspirin, does not irritate the stomach.

STATUS Pharm.; Comm.E+; ESCOP 4; clinical studies+

Salix alba L.   family: Salicaceae

saule blanc (French); *Silberweide* (German); *salice bianco* (Italian)

Salvadora persica

mustard tree • toothbrush tree

Salvadora persica leaves and berries

Salvadora persica tree

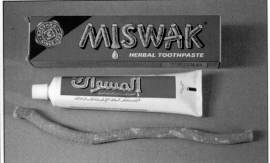

Root, known as *miswak*

DESCRIPTION The mustard tree is a shrub or small tree of up to 5 m in height, with opposite, pale green, somewhat fleshy leaves and minute yellowish green flowers in short clusters. The fruits are edible, rounded berries that are up to 10 mm in diameter and turn pink to red when they ripen. In Arabia, the tree, widely known as *arak*, is found in large numbers in depressions and saline habitats. The fruits have a sweet but peppery taste and are said to be the "mustard seed" mentioned in the Bible.

ORIGIN Southern Africa to North Africa, Arabia and India.

PARTS USED Roots (in pieces of about 100-200 mm long by 10 mm in diameter). These are known as *siwak* or more commonly *miswak*, and are sold as toothbrush sticks or chewing sticks on local markets. Commercial root extracts are also used.

THERAPEUTIC CATEGORY Dental care.

USES AND PROPERTIES Miswak is commonly used in the Arabic world as toothbrushes or chewing sticks to clean the teeth. Extracts of the roots, known as "peelu extract" (*peelu* is the Urdu name for the tree)

are included in commercial toothpastes. Public dental care is totally acceptable and encouraged, and is found only amongst men, mainly from the older generation.

PREPARATION AND DOSAGE To use the root, bark is removed from the tip (for about 10 mm) and the end is chewed until the fibres separate. Brushing is done by rubbing the teeth up and down in vertical strokes, from the gums to the cutting edges.

ACTIVE INGREDIENTS The roots produce lignan glycosides (liriodendrin and salvadoraside), together with a benzyl glycoside (salvadoside), a phenolic glycoside (syringin) and a phytosterol glycoside. Also present are salvadoricine (an indole alkaloid), salvadourea and thiodiamin (urea derivates), resin, silica, triethylamine and vitamin C, all of which are thought to contribute to the promotion of healthy teeth and gums.

PHARMACOLOGICAL EFFECTS Root extracts are known to have powerful antibacterial and antiplaque activity. Human studies have shown definite beneficial effects in oral hygiene.

STATUS Traditional medicine.

Salvadora persica L.   family: Salvadoraceae

arak (Arabic); *salvadora persica* (French); *Senfbaum, Zahnbürstenbaum* (German); *salvadora persica* (Italian)

Salvia officinalis

sage • garden sage • common sage

Salvia officinalis

Salva officinalis 'Purpurascens'

DESCRIPTION Sage is a perennial shrublet (up to 0.6 m) with square stems bearing opposite pairs of grey, rough-textured leaves and attractive purplish blue flowers. Closely related, with similar uses are *S. fruticosa* (= *S. triloba*), known as trilobed or Greek sage (the leaves are lobed at their base) and *S. lavandulifolia* (a source of medicinal oil). See also *Salvia sclarea*.

ORIGIN Eastern Mediterranean region and southern Europe (*S. officinalis*, *S. lavandulifolia*); Italy to the Middle East (*S. fruticosa*). Commercial cultivation mainly in eastern Europe, Asia, USA and South Africa.

PARTS USED Dried leaves (*Salviae folium*, *Salviae trilobae folium*).

THERAPEUTIC CATEGORY Antiseptic, antispasmodic, carminative.

USES AND PROPERTIES Sage is a popular remedy against gingivitis and mucosal inflammation of the mouth and throat. It is a digestive medicine to treat upset stomachs, flatulence and diarrhoea and is considered effective as antisudorific to treat night sweats and excessive perspiration. The drug has been used as an antidiabetic. Sage is best known as a culinary herb.

PREPARATION AND DOSAGE Daily doses equivalent to 4-6 g of the dried herb or up to 0.3 g of essential oil are recommended for internal use. For gargles and rinses, use 2.5 g of herb or 3 drops of oil in 100 ml water.

ACTIVE INGREDIENTS Essential oil (up to 3.6%) rich in α-thujone (usually the major compound) and β-thujone (together up to 60%), with smaller amounts of camphor, 1,8-cineole and other monoterpenes. Also present are phenolic acids (6%) such as rosmarinic acid (Labiate "tannin"), various flavonoids, diterpenoids such as carnosol (=picrosalvin; bitter value 14 000) and rosmanol, together with triterpenes (oleanic acid and derivatives). The oil of *S. fruticosa* is low in thujone (up to 7%); that of *S. lavandulifolia* practically thujone free.

PHARMACOLOGICAL EFFECTS Experimental evidence supports the claimed antispasmodic, antisudorific, antimicrobial, and antiviral effects. The neurotoxicity of the oil is ascribed to thujone (see *Chrysanthemum vulgare*) so that the internal use of *S. officinalis* and its products is restricted.

WARNING Do not use internally in large amounts or for prolonged periods.

STATUS Traditional medicine; Pharm.; Comm.E+; ESCOP 2.

Salvia officinalis L.   family: Lamiaceae

sauge officinale, sauge commune (French); *Echter Salbei, Gartensalbei* (German); *salvia* (Italian); *salvia officinal* (Spanish)

Salvia sclarea

clary sage

Salvia sclarea

Salvia sclarea flowers

DESCRIPTION Clary sage is a robust perennial herb of up to 1 m in height, with square stems, large green leaves and attractive blue and white flowers borne amongst leafy, violet-coloured bracts. The name *Salvia* is derived from the Latin *salvere* (to feel well) or *salvus* (healthy) and several species are used medicinally. Best known are *S. officinalis*, *S. fruticosa* and *S. lavandulifolia* (see *S. officinalis*). In China, the roots of red sage or *danshen* (*S. miltiorrhiza*) are used for circulatory problems. In southern Africa, *S. africana-caerulea* and others are traditional cold and flu remedies. In Mexico, a cultigen known botanically as *S. divinorum* is used as a hallucinogen.

ORIGIN Southern Europe to central Asia (*S. sclarea*). Commercial cultivation occurs mainly in eastern Europe, Russia and Asia.

PARTS USED Dried leaves (*Salviae sclareae herba*) or the essential oil.

THERAPEUTIC CATEGORY Antiseptic, carminative, astringent.

USES AND PROPERTIES Clary sage is particularly popular for the treatment of wounds, dyspeptic, urinary and menstrual disorders; the essential oil is becoming popular in aromatherapy. It is used in much the same way as common sage (see *S. officinalis*) but is considered to be less effective. The oil is used in soaps and perfumes (e.g. *eau-de-cologne*) and in alcoholic beverages (e.g. vermouth and liqueurs).

PREPARATION AND DOSAGE Clary sage is used in much the same way as common sage (see *S. officinalis*).

ACTIVE INGREDIENTS Like other *Salvia* species, the herb is rich in flavonoids (flavones), rosmarinic acid (up to 4.6%) and essential oil. The oil differs markedly from that of *S. officinalis* in that it is rich in linalool (up to 30%), linalyl acetate (up to 75%), β-caryophyllene and myrcene (up to 4.5%). Extracts contain a diterpene, sclareol, that is used as a starting material in chemical synthesis of other diterpenes (such as amber oxide) and in the perfume industry.

PHARMACOLOGICAL EFFECTS Clary sage is considered to be pharmacologically similar to common sage but the oil constituents suggest that the two are not the same. Clary sage oil is thought to be less toxic.

STATUS Traditional medicine.

Salvia sclarea L. family: Lamiaceae

sauge sclarée (French); *Muskateller-Salbei* (German); *moscatella* (Italian); *salvia esclarea* (Spanish)

Sambucus nigra

elder • elderberry tree

Sambucus nigra fruit

Sambucus nigra flowers

Sambucus ebulus

DESCRIPTION Elder is a shrub or small tree (up to 6 m), with sparse, pithy stems bearing compound leaves and flat-topped cymes with a multitude of tiny white flowers. The fruits are fleshy black drupes, each with three oblong seeds. It is similar to American elder (*S. canadensis*, an ornamental with edible fruit); also used are dwarf elder (*S. ebulus*) leaves, fruits and roots.

ORIGIN Europe, Asia and North Africa (*S. nigra*); eastern parts of North America (*S. canadensis*). Mostly wild-harvested in eastern Europe and western Asia but plantations are known, e.g. in Hungary.

PARTS USED Dried, sieved flowers, without stalks (*Sambuci flos*); fresh or dried fruits (*Sambuci fructus*), leaves and roots.

THERAPEUTIC CATEGORY Traditional diaphoretic (flowers, fruit); diuretic, laxative (fruit).

USES AND PROPERTIES Elder flowers are traditionally used to treat colds and catarrh of the upper respiratory tract, as well as hay fever. The dried fruits or fresh juice are used to some extent as an analgesic, diuretic, laxative and diaphoretic in cases of feverish catarrhal conditions. Elder flowers are commonly included in tea mixtures or other herbal remedies and are used for light alcoholic beverages. The berries are widely used as a natural colouring agent in food products.

PREPARATION AND DOSAGE Tea (3 g of flowers, or 10 g of fruits in 150 ml boiling water) are taken several times a day (average daily dose is 10-15 g). Extracts and tinctures are also used.

ACTIVE INGREDIENTS Rutin (about 2%), isoquercitrin and hyperoside are the main flavonols in the flowers and fruits. Flowers also contain chlorogenic acid (about 3%), other organic acids and triterpenoids – mainly α-amyrin and β-amyrin (about 1%), while the fruits have 3% tannins and several anthocyanins (sambucin, sambucyanin and chrysanthemin, all glycosides of cyanidin). Cyanogenic glycosides (including sambunigrin, prunasin and holocalin) occur in the seeds; lectins in the fruit.

PHARMACOLOGICAL EFFECTS There is some evidence that the flower ingredients possess diuretic, laxative, mild anti-inflammatory and antiviral activity. Antioxidant effects have been ascribed to the fruits due to their anthocyanin content.

STATUS Traditional medicine; Pharm.; Comm.E+ (flowers); WHO 2 (flowers).

Sambucus nigra L.   family: Caprifoliaceae

grand sureau (French); *Schwarzer Holunder* (German); *sambuco* (Italian); *sauco* (Spanish)

Sanguinaria canadensis

bloodroot

Sanguinaria canadensis

Macleaya cordata

DESCRIPTION Bloodroot is a small perennial herb (up to 0.4 m), producing a red sap or latex. It has solitary leaves and flowers emerging from a creeping, fleshy, red rhizome. The leaf has a rounded, markedly lobed blade. The attractive flower has four to 16 white petals and develops into a narrow, two-valved capsule containing numerous small seeds.

ORIGIN North America; mainly wild-harvested in the eastern parts of the USA.

PARTS USED Dried rhizome, with the roots removed (*Sanguinariae canadensis rhizoma*).

THERAPEUTIC CATEGORY Antibiotic, anti-inflammatory, dental hygiene.

USES AND PROPERTIES Traditionally used as an emetic, expectorant and spasmolytic to treat bronchitis and asthma, as well as other ailments of the respiratory tract (cough, croup, laryngitis and pharyngitis). In former times, it was applied topically against skin ulcers, warts and cancer. Despite its toxicity, bloodroot is still included in several commercial expectorants, cough syrups and stomachics. The most common modern use is as an ingredient of mouth rinses and toothpaste to counteract dental plaque and gingivitis.

PREPARATION AND DOSAGE Up to 0.5 g of dried rhizome is taken as an infusion (or equivalent extracts or tinctures) three times per day. The emetic dose is 1-2 g.

ACTIVE INGREDIENTS Isoquinoline alkaloids (up to 9%), with sanguinarine (a benzophenanthridine) as the main compound (about 50%) and several others, including chelerythrine, sanguilutine, allocryptopine, protopine, berberine, coptisine.

PHARMACOLOGICAL EFFECTS The activity is ascribed mainly to sanguinarine. It intercalates DNA, binds to proteins (including various receptors) and shows anti-inflammatory, antifungal, antimicrobial activity. It effectively inhibits dental plaque (as demonstrated in controlled clinical studies). The expectorant and emetic effect is probably due to the alkaloids (irritation of the *nervus vagus*, see *Psychotria ipecacuanha*).

WARNING Since sanguinarine and some of the other alkaloids can intercalate DNA, they are potential mutagens. There is new evidence that prolonged use in oral hygiene products may be harmful.

NOTES Sanguinarine may also be obtained from the Asian plume poppy, *Macleaya cordata*.

STATUS Traditional medicine; Pharm.; clinical studies+.

Sanguinaria canadensis L.   family: Papaveraceae

sanguinaire du Canada (French); *Kanadische Blutwurzel* (German); *sanguinaria* (Italian)

Sanguisorba officinalis
burnet • greater burnet • garden burnet

Sanguisorba officinalis

Sanguisorba minor

DESCRIPTION Burnet is an erect perennial herb of up to 1 m in height, with feathery compound leaves and slender, branched flowering stalks bearing dense, oblong heads of inconspicuous purple flowers. The plant was previously known as *Poterium officinalis*. Salad burnet (*Sanguisorba minor*) is a much smaller plant that is sometimes added to salads, cheeses and herb butter. It has been used medicinally in much the same way as greater burnet. *S. anistroides* has been used against diabetes.

ORIGIN Europe and Asia (*S. officinalis*) or southern and central Europe (*S. minor*). *Sanguisorba officinalis* is naturalised in North America. Both species are commonly cultivated in herb gardens.

PARTS USED Mostly the dried roots (*Sanguisorbae rhizoma et radix*), sometimes the dried aboveground parts (*Sanguisorbae herba*).

THERAPEUTIC CATEGORY Astringent, haemostyptic, antihaemorrhoidal.

USES AND PROPERTIES The roots of burnet are known to be effective against acute diarrhoea. The herb also has antihaemorrhagic properties and has been used to treat ulcerative colitis, metrorrhagia (uterine bleeding) and topically against haemorrhoids, various skin conditions (wounds, ulcers, burns and eczema) and mucosal inflammations (included in gargles and tooth pastes). The main traditional use (in Europe and China) is to stop bleeding, as is reflected in the generic name *sanguis* (blood) and *sorbeo* (I absorb).

PREPARATION AND DOSAGE An infusion of 2-6 g may be taken three times a day (or liquid extracts or tinctures). Extracts are included in ointments and lotions for topical application.

ACTIVE INGREDIENTS Roots contain hydrolysable and condensed tannins, mostly derivatives of gallic acid and ellagic acid (e.g. 3,3,4-tri-*O*-methylellagic acid, gambiirin A, gambiirin B, sanguiin, eugeniin). Furthermore, flavonoids (rutoside, quercetin, kaempferol), oligomeric proanthocyanidins, and various monodesmosidic triterpene saponins have been reported, including pomolic acid glycosides (also known as sanguisorbin).

PHARMACOLOGICAL EFFECTS The tannin and saponin contents are clearly in agreement with the observed astringent, antimicrobial, anti-inflammatory, haemostyptic and antidiarrhoeic effects (see *Quercus robur*).

STATUS Traditional medicine.

Sanguisorba officinalis L.

family: Rosaceae

sanguisorbe; grande pimprenelle (French); Großer Wiesenknopf (German); sorbastrella (Italian)

Sanicula europaea

sanicle • wood sanicle

Sanicula europaea flowers

Sanicula europaea plant with fruit

Sanicula europaea leaves

DESCRIPTION Sanicle is a small, shade-loving, perennial herb with deeply lobed, hand-shaped leaves emerging every year from an underground rootstock. Small white flowers are borne on slender flowering stalks of up to 0.4 m in height, followed by bristly fruits that are dispersed by animals. Old traditional herb, as indicated by the name (*sanare*: to heal). *S. marilandica* from North America is also used in folk medicine.

ORIGIN Europe, Asia and Africa; material is wild-collected.

PARTS USED The dried herb (*Saniculae herba*), more rarely the dried roots (*Saniculae radix*).

THERAPEUTIC CATEGORY Astringent, expectorant.

USES AND PROPERTIES Sanicle herb has been used mainly to treat catarrh of the upper respiratory tract and was a popular remedy for diarrhoea, stomach upsets, flatulence, excessive bleeding. As a gargle is was used in cases of sore throat, mouth infections and gingivitis. Leaves were once popular as a compress to treat wounds, bruises, burns, skin infections and haemorrhoids. In central Europe, sanicle is still popular in folk medicine, especially as an ingredient of tea mixtures taken for flatulence and diarrhoea. The roots are used in much the same way as the leaves, except that they are also considered to be a useful astringent.

PREPARATION AND DOSAGE An infusion of 1-2 g of the herb is taken two or three times a day (daily dose of 4-6 g) to treat respiratory infections. Stronger infusions or decoctions are used as gargles and for topical use.

ACTIVE INGREDIENTS Large amounts (more than 10%) of monodesmosidic triterpene saponins (esters of saniculoside A-D), together with flavonoids (rutin, astragalin) various organic acids (chlorogenic acid, 0.6%; rosmarinic acid, 1.7%; ascorbic acid, 0.1%) and mucilage. The herb is said to contain tannins, allantoin and traces of essential oil (this needs confirmation).

PHARMACOLOGICAL EFFECTS Antimicrobial and anti-inflammatory effects of the drug have been shown experimentally. Expectorant properties are likely to be due to the saponins, while the astringent and styptic properties are ascribed to the tannins.

STATUS Traditional medicine; Comm.E+ (*Saniculae herba* only).

Sanicula europaea L.   family: Apiaceae

sanicle (French); *Sanikel* (German); *sanicola, erba fragolina* (Italian); *saniculu* (Spanish)

Santalum album

sandalwood • white sandalwood

Santalum album

White sandalwood

Red sandalwood

DESCRIPTION An evergreen, semi-parasitic tree of up to 10 m in height, with pointed green leaves, small yellowish flowers and dark purple berries. It should not be confused with red sandalwood (*Pterocarpus santalinus*; Fabaceae), a traditional source of red dye.

ORIGIN India (both *S. album* and *P. santalinus*). Trees of both species are cultivated to some extent in India and in Southeast Asia.

PARTS USED Wood from the trunk or branches, known as white sandalwood (*Santali lignum albi*), or the essential oil distilled from the wood. The bark, known as *chandanam* in Sanskrit, is also used in Ayurvedic medicine. In the case of red sandalwood (*Santali lignum rubri*), only the dark-coloured heartwood is used.

THERAPEUTIC CATEGORY Urological.

USES AND PROPERTIES White sandalwood is used to treat infections of the lower urinary tract, especially cystitis and gonorrhoea. Extracts of the wood (or the bark) is used topically to treat skin conditions and internally as a cooling medicine to cure dizziness, chest complaints and indigestion. The essential oil is used in aromatherapy against nervous disorders and as antispasmodic. Red sandalwood is a traditional diuretic, anti-diarrhoeal and stomachic but in modern times, it is used only as a natural dye to colour herbal mixtures and toothpaste.

PREPARATION AND DOSAGE Infusions or decoctions of wood chips are taken. A total daily dose of 10-20 g is recommended. The oil should not be taken internally in its natural state. When used for the treatment of urological problems, it should be enclosed in a resistant coating that can withstand gastric juices. Taken in this way, the daily dose is 1-1.5 g.

ACTIVE INGREDIENTS White sandalwood is rich in essential oil (about 5%) that contains the sesquiterpene alcohols α-santalol and β-santalol as main compounds. Red sandalwood contains two red pigments (benzoxanthenone derivatives; santalin A,B).

PHARMACOLOGICAL EFFECTS Known antibacterial and spasmolytic properties of the drug can be attributed to the lipophilic sesquiterpenes. Today, antibiotics have widely replaced the drug.

STATUS Traditional medicine; Comm.E+.

Santalum album L.   family: Santalaceae

santal blanc (French); *Weißer Sandelbaum* (German); *sandalo* (Italian); *leño de santalo citrino* (Spanish)

Saponaria officinalis

soapwort • red soapwort

Saponaria officinalis flowers

Saponaria officinalis

Quillaja saponaria

DESCRIPTION Soapwort is a perennial herb (up to 0.5 m), with leafy stems arising from thin, underground rhizomes. The bright green leaves are borne in opposite pairs and the attractive, tubular pink flowers occur in clusters at the tips of the stems.

ORIGIN Europe and Asia (naturalised in North America); a popular garden ornamental, commercially grown mainly in China, Iran and Turkey.

PARTS USED Dried roots and rhizomes (*Saponariae rubrae radix*), less often the herb.

THERAPEUTIC CATEGORY Expectorant.

USES AND PROPERTIES Soapwort is traditionally used to treat cough, bronchitis and other diseases of the respiratory tract. In folk medicine, the herb or root is used as diuretic, antirheumatic and topically for skin conditions such as eczema. The dried rhizomes or herb (or extracts thereof) are ingredients of a few commercial cough medicines but are no longer very popular. In former times, soapwort was used as a household detergent and soap substitute. *Saponaria* is derived from the Latin for soap (*sapo*).

PREPARATION AND DOSAGE A tea can be made from 0.4 g of the dried rhizomes (slightly higher doses of the aboveground parts). The recommended daily dose of rhizomes is 1.5 g.

ACTIVE INGREDIENTS All parts are rich in saponins (triterpene glycosides); up to 8% of dry weight. The main compound is quillaic acid but saponarosides, saponasides A,D and gypsogenin has also been reported.

PHARMACOLOGICAL EFFECTS Soapwort is thought to exert an expectorant action through irritation of *nervus vagus* in the gastric mucosa and in a reflectory way by stimulating water excretion in bronchial tissues. Saponins might exert their anti-inflammatory activity via a corticomimetic effect.

NOTES Another rich source of saponins is soap bark, obtained from *Quillaja saponaria* (family Rosaceae). It contains so-called quillaja saponin, a mixture of complex acylated triterpenoid saponins. Extracts are included in shampoos and skin care products because of itch-relieving and emollient activity. It lowers blood cholesterol levels but is suspected of being poisonous.

STATUS Traditional medicine; Comm.E+ (root only).

Saponaria officinalis L. ___ family: Caryophyllaceae

saponaire (French); *Gewöhnliches Seifenkraut* (German); *saponaria* (Italian); *hierba japonera* (Spanish)

Satureja montana

winter savoury

Satureja montana

Satureja montana flowers

DESCRIPTION Winter savoury is a small, perennial shrublet of up to 0.3 m in height, with small, dark green leaves borne in opposite pairs and small white or pinkish flowers in oblong clusters along the branch ends. Summer savoury (*Satureja hortensis*, an annual plant), is a popular culinary herb also used to some extent in traditional medicine. It is rich in volatile oil with carvacrol (spasmolytic, carminative properties) as the main ingredient.

ORIGIN Southern Europe and North Africa (*S. montana*); southeastern Europe (*S. hortensis*).

PARTS USED Dried flowering tops (*Saturejae montanae herba*) or the essential oil (*Saturejae montanae aetheroleum*).

THERAPEUTIC CATEGORY Stomachic, carminative.

USES AND PROPERTIES Winter savoury is mainly used to treat stomach disorders, including indigestion, flatulence and colic. It is also used as an antiseptic to treat infections of the respiratory and urinary tracts, as well as fungal infections. The herb or the essential oil is used in much the same way as lavender, to treat wounds, burns and skin infections. In central Europe, summer savoury is used in much the same way as winter savoury or thyme. Mixed with honey, it is taken as a tea to treat cough and asthma. It is used as a cosmetic in soap and washing powder.

PREPARATION AND DOSAGE A tea may be prepared from 2-4 g of the dried herb in a cup of boiling water (taken two or three times per day). The essential oil or extracts of the plant are applied topically or added to bath water.

ACTIVE INGREDIENTS The essential oil is rich in carvacrol (40-60%), accompanied by *p*-cymol (10-20%) and γ-terpinene (15-20%), with smaller amounts of linalool and thymol. The level of essential oil in the commercial product should not be less than 0.7%. The herb contains rosmarinic acid and derivatives of hydroxycinnamic acid.

PHARMACOLOGICAL EFFECTS Carvacrol and the other monoterpenes are lipophilic and easily interact with biomembranes and membrane proteins. These properties plausibly explain the observed antispasmodic, diuretic, antimicrobial and secretomotoric effects.

STATUS Traditional medicine.

Satureja montana L.   family: Lamiaceae

sarriette des montagnes (French); *Bergbohnenkraut* (German); *santoreggia, erba peverella* (Italian)

Sceletium tortuosum

sceletium

Sceletium tortuosum plant

Sceletium tortuosum flowers

Traditional product

DESCRIPTION Sceletium is a short-lived perennial succulent plant with creeping stems and overlapping pairs of leaves that have glistening, crystal-like water cells on their surfaces. The leaves become "skeletonised" when they dry out – the persistent leaf veins remain on the plant – hence the generic name *Sceletium*. Pale to bright yellow or orange-yellow flowers are borne along the branch tips, followed by pale brown, papery capsules containing numerous small, reddish brown, kidney-shaped seeds. There are eight species of *Sceletium*, but only *S. tortuosum* is well known and used in commercial products.

ORIGIN South Africa (southwestern parts of the Cape and Namaqualand). Selected strains with a high alkaloid content are grown commercially on a small scale in South Africa.

PARTS USED Dried whole plant.

THERAPEUTIC CATEGORY Hypnotic, sedative.

USES AND PROPERTIES The plant is used to elevate mood and to counteract anxiety, stress and tension. Numerous traditional uses have been recorded, including relief of hunger and thirst, treatment of colic in infants and as replacement therapy for alcoholics.

PREPARATION AND DOSAGE The fermented and dried herb is traditionally chewed (hence the Afrikaans name *kougoed*, literally meaning "chewing stuff"). It can also be used as a tea, decoction and tincture. A dose of 100-200 mg of the dried, powdered herb is included in tablets and capsules (about 1-4 mg of alkaloid) and taken two or three times a day.

ACTIVE INGREDIENTS Sceletium contains mesembrine-type alkaloids (mesembrine, mesembrenone, mesembrenol, tortuosamine and others) at concentrations ranging from 0.05-2.3% of the dry product. Mesembrine is usually the main ingredient in leaves.

PHARMACOLOGICAL EFFECTS Mesembrine is a potent serotonin-uptake inhibitor and the other alkaloids appear to be active at other neuroreceptors. An interesting feature of this unique plant is the apparent absence of physical and psychological dependency, even after many years of habitual use. No adverse side effects have been recorded. High doses may cause euphoria but the plant is not hallucinogenic.

STATUS Traditional medicine.

Sceletium tortuosum (L.) N.E. Br.   family: Mesembryanthemaceae

kanna (Khoi); *kougoed* (Afrikaans); *sceletium* (French); *Sceletium* (German); *sceletium* (Italian)

Scopolia carniolica

scopolia

Scopolia carniolica plant

Scopolia carniolica flowers

Scopolia carniolica dried rhizomes

DESCRIPTION A perennial herb (up to 0.5 m) with erect stems emerging every year from persistent rhizomes. The oblong, soft leaves have long stalks and wavy margins. Small, purplish brown, bell-shaped flowers are borne in the leaf axils.

ORIGIN Southeast Europe (east Alps, Carpathian mountains). The plant is sometimes grown in gardens and has been cultivated commercially for tropane alkaloid production.

PARTS USED Mostly the dried rhizomes (*Scopolia rhizoma*), ("roots"). The leaves can be used as a source of raw material for alkaloid extraction.

THERAPEUTIC CATEGORY Antispasmodic.

USES AND PROPERTIES Scopolia is used specifically to treat spasms of the gastrointestinal tract, bile ducts and urinary tract. It is sometimes used externally for relief of rheumatic pain. Indications are similar to those of *Atropa belladonna*.

PREPARATION AND DOSAGE Carefully controlled doses are used, so that the daily dose does not exceed 3 mg of total alkaloids (average single dose 0.25 mg; the maximum single dose 1 mg).

ACTIVE INGREDIENTS The dry rhizomes contain 0.3-0.8% tropane alkaloids. L-hyoscyamine is the main compound, together with small amounts of L-scopolamine and atropine (racemic mixture of hyoscyamine) and atroscine (racemic mixture of scopolamine). Leaves contain hyoscyamine, scopolamine, cuscohygrine and 3α-tigloyloxytropane (up to 0.5% (total alkaloids).

PHARMACOLOGICAL EFFECTS Tropane alkaloids from scopolia rhizomes have parasympatholytic properties and cause relaxation of smooth muscles (see *Atropa belladonna* and *Datura stramonium*). As a result, it is effective in treating intestinal spasms.

WARNING High doses are toxic and side effects (including hyperthermia, tachycardia, hallucinogenic sensations) are not trivial, so that scopolia should only be used under medical supervision.

NOTES Another European plant rich in tropane alkaloids and much used in ancient and medieval times (famous in mythology) is mandrake, *Mandragora officinarum*. The main commercial source for tropane alkaloids nowadays is the leaves of the Australian trees *Duboisia myoporoides* and *D. leichardtii* (Solanaceae).

STATUS Traditional and modern medicine: alkaloids; Comm.E+.

Scopolia carniolica Jacq.   family: Solanaceae

scopolia (French); *Glockenbilsenkraut* (German); *scopolia* (Italian)

Scrophularia nodosa

figwort • common figwort

Scrophularia nodosa

Scrophularia nodosa flowers and fruit

DESCRIPTION Figwort is a perennial herb of up to 0.7 m in height, with erect leafy branches sprouting from an underground rhizome. Numerous small, brownish red flowers are borne in a large sparse cluster along the branch end. The scientific name is derived from the traditional use of the plant against scrofula, a form of tuberculosis affecting the lymph nodes. According to the "doctrine of signatures", the nodular rhizomes resemble swollen lymph glands, thereby indicating that the plant may be effective in treating swellings and swollen glands.

ORIGIN Europe, Asia and North America; commonly found in damp places and wild-harvested while in flower.

PARTS USED Dried aboveground parts (*Scrophulariae herba*).

THERAPEUTIC CATEGORY Dermatological, anti-inflammatory, mild diuretic.

USES AND PROPERTIES Figwort is mainly used externally to treat chronic skin conditions such as eczema and psoriasis, and to a lesser extent for wounds, burns, sunburns, diaper rashes, ulcers and swellings. It is also taken internally as a bitter tonic, mild diuretic and antirheumatic. It is said to increase myocardial contraction.

PREPARATION AND DOSAGE A dose of 2-8 g of dried herb may be taken as an infusion, or equivalent quantities in the form of tinctures and extracts.

ACTIVE INGREDIENTS Several iridoid glycosides are present, such as harpagoside, harpagide, procumbide, aucubin and catalpol; also flavonoids and saponins. The iridoid composition resembles that of devil's claw (see *Harpagophytum*) but the harpagoside content is lower.

PHARMACOLOGICAL EFFECTS The iridoid glycosides (more likely the metabolites formed in the body) are considered to be anti-inflammatory (especially when applied topically), since they appear to inhibit the formation of prostaglandins (mediators of inflammation). They are also bitter substances, indicating general tonic and digestive uses.

NOTES Balmony (*Chelone glabra*) is a related North American species that also contains catalpol derivatives. It is used against gall stones, digestive disorders and as an anthelmintic.

WARNING Persons with heart conditions, diabetes and pregnant or lactating women should not use the drug internally.

STATUS Traditional medicine; Pharm.

Scrophularia nodosa L.

family: Scrophulariaceae

scrofulaire noueuse (French); *Knotige Braunwurz* (German); *castagnola* (Italian)

Scutellaria lateriflora

skullcap • Virginia-skullcap • helmet flower

Scutellaria lateriflora

Scutellaria lateriflora flowers

Scutellaria baicalensis

DESCRIPTION Skullcap is a leafy perennial herb of about 0.5 m in height, with erect branches bearing opposite pairs of oblong leaves and numerous bluish or violet flowers borne in a cluster. It is similar to Baical skullcap or *huang quin* (*S. baicalensis*) and European skullcap (*S. galericulata*). The common names refer to the helmet-shaped flowers.

ORIGIN North America (*S. lateriflora*), Russia to China and Japan (*S. baicalensis*) and Europe (*S. galericulata*).

PARTS USED Dried aerial parts (*S. lateriflora*); dried roots (*S. baicalensis*).

THERAPEUTIC CATEGORY Anticonvulsant, sedative (*S. lateriflora*, *S. galericulata*); anti-inflammatory, anti-allergic, circulatory (*S. baicalensis*).

USES AND PROPERTIES The American and European skullcaps are traditional nerve tonics and sedatives. The American species became well known as a treatment for epilepsy, *grand mal*, hysteria and nervous conditions. It is today widely used in commercial preparations, mainly for nervous conditions – tension, anxiety and insomnia. Baical skullcap is one of the most important Chinese remedies and is very popular for a wide variety of ailments, including the treatment of allergies, inflammation, arteriosclerosis, dermatitis and high blood lipids.

PREPARATION AND DOSAGE An infusion of 1-2 g of the dried herb is taken three times per day (or equivalent doses in the form of tinctures and extracts).

ACTIVE INGREDIENTS *Scutellaria* species are known for their rich diversity and abundance of flavonoids, to which most of the medicinal properties are ascribed. *S. lateriflora* is said to contain apigenin, hispidulin, luteolin, scutellarein and scutellarin as main flavonoids, together with catalpol (an iridoid glycoside). The roots of *S. baicalensis* have numerous flavonoids (up to 20%), with flavone-*O*-glycosides (mainly baicalin and and wogonoside) as main compounds.

PHARMACOLOGICAL EFFECTS Several studies have been carried out with *S. baicalensis* (mostly on lipid metabolism and histamine) but very few on *S. lateriflora*. Baical skullcap does not appear to have any antispasmodic activity but has shown efficacy in the treatment of the symptoms of cerebral thrombosis and paralysis caused by stroke.

STATUS Traditional medicine; Pharm.

Scutellaria lateriflora L.

family: Lamiaceae

scutellaire, scutellaire latériflore (French); *Virginia-Helmkraut* (German); *scutellaria* (Italian)

Securidaca longepedunculata

violet tree

Securidaca longepedunculata

Securidaca longepedunculata flowers

Securidaca longepedunculata root bark

DESCRIPTION The violet tree is up to 6 m in height and has a characteristic pale grey, smooth bark. The oblong leaves are crowded towards the stem tips, where clusters of attractive pink to purple flowers are borne in early summer. The fruit is a round nut with a single large, curved wing. The plant has a very distinctive appearance and is not likely to be confused with any others.

ORIGIN Tropical Africa. The tree is not cultivated.

PARTS USED Mainly the roots, sometimes also the stem bark or leaves.

THERAPEUTIC CATEGORY Traditional panacea and general tonic, antirheumatic, antitussive.

USES AND PROPERTIES The violet tree is one of the most popular of all traditional medicines in Africa and is used for almost any conceivable ailment. Amongst the numerous uses, it is particularly popular for coughs, chest complaints, rheumatism, toothache, headache, constipation and as contraceptive. It is applied externally for the treatment of wounds, sores and rheumatic pain. The bark has been used as an ingredient of arrow poison and as ordeal poison.

PREPARATION AND DOSAGE The safe dosage has not been recorded. Decoctions are taken for chest com-plaints, while the roots are chewed to relieve tooth-ache. A hot water poultice of the roots is said to give symptomatic relief of rheumatism, while powdered root or wood scrapings are rubbed into scarifications on the forehead to treat headaches.

ACTIVE INGREDIENTS The volatile oil of the roots contains large amounts of methyl salicylate. Various triterpene saponins, with presenegenin as aglycone, the toxic indole alkaloid securinine and some other alkaloids (including ergot alkaloids) have been re-ported.

PHARMACOLOGICAL EFFECTS The presence of salicylates may partly explain the wide diversity of uses. Methyl salicylate is known as a counter-irritant that penetrates the skin and underlying tissue to act as a potent anti-inflammatory agent. It is also known to be useful in oral hygiene. Saponins have secretolytic properties and thus would explain the antitussive ef-fects of the drug. The toxicity is ascribed mainly to securinine.

WARNING The plant is known to be very poison-ous and is not suitable for self-medication.

STATUS Traditional medicine.

Securidaca longepedunculata Fres. (often given as "*S. longipedunculata*" in the literature)   family: Polygalaceae
securidaca (French); *Securidaca* (German); *securidaca* (Italian)

Senecio ovatus

alpine ragwort

Senecio ovatus

Senecio jacobaea

DESCRIPTION An erect perennial herb of up to 1 m in height, with narrow, finely toothed leaves and large numbers of flower heads borne in loose clusters. Each flower head is somewhat tubular in shape and has relatively few ligulate florets. The plant is well known by the older names (*S. fuchsii* and *S. nemorensis*). Several *Senecio* species have been traditionally used as medicinal plants, including groundsel (*S. vulgaris*), common ragwort (*S. jacobaea*) and liferoot (*S. aureus*).

ORIGIN Central Europe (*S. ovatus*); Europe, weed worldwide (*S. vulgaris*); Europe, Asia, and naturalised in North America (*S. jacobaea*); eastern North America (*S. aureus*). Commercial product of *S. ovatus* is mainly collected from the wild.

PARTS USED Dried aboveground parts (*Senecionis herba*).

THERAPEUTIC CATEGORY Haemostyptic.

USES AND PROPERTIES Extracts of various *Senecio* species are used to treat capillary and arterial bleeding, especially in various gynaecological conditions and in hypertrophic gingivitis. The North American liferoot (*S. aureus*) has also been widely used to treat gynaecological problems – mainly to induce menstrua-

tion and to reduce excessive bleeding (as douche). Other uses include the improvement of circulation (*S. vulgaris*); pain and inflammation (*S. jacobaea*, used externally as poultice).

PREPARATION AND DOSAGE In former times, a tea was prepared using 1 g of dried herb in a cup of water. Internal use is restricted (see warning below). External application is also problematic, especially when applied to broken skin.

ACTIVE INGREDIENTS *Senecio* species contain pyrrolizidine alkaloids (PAs) with an unsaturated base, such as senecionine, integerrimine, nemorensine and retrorsine. In *S. ovatus*, the main compounds are reported to be fuchsisenecionine and senecionine (about 100-1 000 μg total alkaloid per g fresh weight).

PHARMACOLOGICAL EFFECTS Animal studies have confirmed the haemostyptic properties of PAs. They are converted in the liver into chemically reactive pyrrol derivatives that alkylate DNA. PAs are cumulative liver toxins and also mutagenic and carcinogenic.

WARNING *Senecio* species are no longer considered safe for internal use (upper limit for PAs is 1 μg per day).

STATUS Traditional medicine.

Senecio ovatus (Gaertn., Mey. & Scherb.) Willd. (= *S. fuchsii* C.C.Gmel.)   family: Asteraceae
séneçon (French); *Fuchskreuzkraut* (German); *senecione alpino* (Italian)

Senna alexandrina

senna

Senna alexandrina

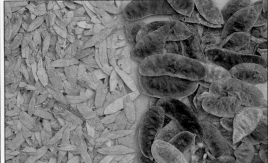

Senna alexandrina flowers

Senna leaves and pods

DESCRIPTION Senna is a shrub (up to 2 m) with compound, feathery leaves and small yellow flowers. Two cultivars or forms, previously considered to be two different species of the genus *Cassia*, are Alexandrian senna or Khartoum senna (previously *C. senna* or *C. acutifolia*) and Tinnevelly senna (previously *C. angustifolia*). The former is a somewhat smaller shrub with a higher anthranoid content. *Cassia* species with straight stamens (as opposed to curved stamens) were moved to the genus *Senna*, and the correct name for the combined species is *Senna alexandrina*.

ORIGIN Northeastern Africa and the Middle East. Raw material comes from Egypt and Sudan (still known in the trade as Alexandrian or Khartoum senna) or from cultivated plants in India and Malaysia (Tinnevelly senna).

PARTS USED Dried leaves (*Sennae folium*) or pods (*Sennae fructus*).

THERAPEUTIC CATEGORY Laxative.

USES AND PROPERTIES Senna leaves and pods are widely used as a laxative to treat acute constipation. After anal-rectal surgery, or when painful haemorrhoids are present, senna is used to ensure a soft stool. The popularity of senna leaves and senna pods can be judged by the fact that millions of tons are produced each year. It is an ingredient of many laxative teas and other commercial preparations.

PREPARATION AND DOSAGE A tea is prepared with 1 g Alexandrian or 2 g Tinnevelly senna leaves or pods in a cup of hot (but not boiling) water. Depending on body mass and age, the effective daily dose of sennosides ranges from about 10-30 mg.

ACTIVE INGREDIENTS Both leaves and pods contain several dianthrone glycosides (about 3%), including sennosides A and B. Also present are anthraquinone glycosides such as the 8-glycosides of aloe-emodin and rhein, mucilage (10%) and flavonoids (mainly kaempferol derivatives).

PHARMACOLOGICAL EFFECTS The sennosides are broken down by bacterial enzymes in the colon to rhein anthrone. Rhein acts as stimulant and irritant laxative by promoting the active secretion of water into the colon and by preventing its reabsorption.

WARNING Senna should not be used for chronic constipation; danger of severe K^+ loss (see *Rhamnus*).

STATUS Traditional medicine; Pharm.; Comm.E+; ESCOP 5; WHO 1.

Senna alexandrina Mill. (= *Cassia senna* L., *C. angustifolia* Vahl., *C. acutifolia* Del.)   family: Fabaceae
senna (French); *Senna* (German); *senna* (Italian); *sen* (Spanish)

Serenoa repens

saw palmetto • sabal

Serenoa repens

Dried fruits

DESCRIPTION A more or less stemless palm (about 2 m), with greyish green, fan-shaped leaves having thorny teeth along the margins of the leaf stalk. It has dense clusters of small flowers and oblong, single-seeded fruits ("berries") of about 30 mm long that turn black when they mature.

ORIGIN Southeastern USA. The plants form dense thickets and the fruits are mainly wild-harvested.

PARTS USED Dried fruits (*Sabal fructus*).

THERAPEUTIC CATEGORY Benign prostate hyperplasia (BPH).

USES AND PROPERTIES Fruits are used to treat urination problems associated with an enlarged prostate gland. The medication does not reduce the enlargement but only alleviates the symptoms: an increase in the frequency of urination (pollakiuria), urination at night (nycturia), as well as a weak urinary stream and a delayed onset of urination. A more advanced stage of BPH (stage II) (a condition ascribed to the accumulation of dihydrotestosterone in the prostate) is characterised by residual urine and a frequent urge to urinate.

PREPARATION AND DOSAGE A daily dose of 1-2 g of dried fruit or 320 mg of lipophilic extract is recom-

mended. Solvent extracts, using hexane or ethanol (or liquid carbon dioxide) are most often used. These are included in various commercial preparations.

ACTIVE INGREDIENTS The seed oil is rich in short chain fatty acids (especially lauric acid) and their glycerides. Extracts also contain various phytosterols – sitosterol (both free and esterified forms), campesterol and cycloartenol.

PHARMACOLOGICAL EFFECTS Saw palmetto apparently inhibits the binding of dihydrotestosterone at androgen receptors, and the enzymes 5α-reductase and aromatase (thereby preventing the male hormone testosterone from being converted into dehydrotestosterone and oestrogen). These activities are usually ascribed to phytosterols and provide a base for the use of saw palmetto, pumpkin seeds, hypoxis corms and pygeum bark in BPH therapy. Palmetto extracts also have anti-inflammatory activity. Several controlled clinical studies have shown significant improvements in the symptoms of prostate adenoma as compared with placebo controls.

WARNING If you suffer from this disorder, consult your doctor at regular intervals.

STATUS Pharm.; Comm.E+; WHO 2; clinical studies+.

Serenoa repens (Bartram) Small (=*Sabal serrulata* Rohm. & Schult.)   family Palmae/Arecaceae
palmier de l'Amérique du Nord (French); *Sägepalme, Zwergpalme* (German); *palmetta di Florida* (Italian)

Silybum marianum
milk-thistle • St. Mary's thistle

Silybum marianum flower head

Silybum marianum

Silybum marianum fruits

DESCRIPTION Milk-thistle is a biennial herb (up to 2 m) bearing dark green leaves mottled with white along the veins and with toothed, spiny margins. Numerous purple florets are borne in large, spiny heads. The fruits are brown to blackish achenes of about 6 mm long.

ORIGIN Southern Europe, North Africa and western Asia. It has become naturalised in North America, South America, Australia and central Europe. The product is harvested from cultivated plants.

PARTS USED Ripe fruit (*Cardui mariae fructus*); less commonly the aerial parts.

THERAPEUTIC CATEGORY Digestive tonic; hepatoprotective.

USES AND PROPERTIES Fruits are taken as a bitter digestive tonic in case of dyspepsia and disorders of the biliary system, while extracts are used for their hepatoprotective properties (toxic liver damage, especially after poisoning by *Amanita* toxins – phalloidin and α-amanitin – , chronic liver inflammation and cirrhosis). Leaves and aboveground parts are thought to have cholagogue properties and have been used in supportive treatment of biliary conditions and liver disorders.

PREPARATION AND DOSAGE A daily dose of about 12-15 g of dry fruits is recommended, while an extract containing 200-400 mg of silymarin is considered an effective dose.

ACTIVE INGREDIENTS Up to 30% lipids and 30% proteins are the main ingredients of fruits, but the hepatoprotective activity is ascribed to a mixture of flavonolignans (2-3%) known as silymarin. It contains about 50% silybinin (a benzodioxane) and smaller amounts of isosilybinin, silychristin and silydianin.

PHARMACOLOGICAL EFFECTS Silymarin shows antihepatotoxic effects (it prevents liver toxins from entering the liver cells and also stimulates regeneration and the formation of new liver cells). Silymarin significantly improves survival of patients with chronic liver disease (usually caused by alcohol abuse). Silybinin infusion therapy has resulted in a decline in fatal mushroom poisoning caused by the death cap, *Amanita phalloides*. Silybinin reactivates protein synthesis in the liver that is normally blocked by amanitin and other mushroom toxins. The efficacy of the drug to treat patients with toxic liver defects and liver cirrhosis was demonstrated in controlled clinical studies.

STATUS Pharm.; Comm.E+; WHO 2; clinical studies+.

Silybum marianum (L.) Gaertn.   family: Asteraceae

chardon Marie (French); *Mariendistel* (German); *carduo mariano* (Italian); *cardo mariano* (Spanish)

Simmondsia chinensis

jojoba

Simmondsia chinensis male flowers

Simmondsia chinensis

Simmondsia chinensis fruit

DESCRIPTION Jojoba is a dioecious, evergreen shrub or small tree of about 4 m in height, with small, bluish green, leathery leaves and inconspicuous, wind-pollinated flowers. Flowers on male plants are borne in clusters in the leaf axils; those on female plants are usually solitary on the branch tips and have persistent petals that expand as the fruit matures. The fruit capsule has three locules, only one of which contains a single seed. In commercial plantations, female plants obviously predominate, but male plants are planted every 20 rows or so to ensure effective pollination and seed set.

ORIGIN Sonora desert (northern Mexico and southwestern USA). The plant is cultivated as an oil crop in South America, Africa and Israel.

PARTS USED The seed oil, which is actually a liquid wax.

THERAPEUTIC CATEGORY Hair and skin care.

USES AND PROPERTIES Native Indians used the drug to treat skin disorders. Jojoba oil is mainly included in hair and skin care products (lotions, creams, soaps and lipstick). The oil is also an excellent non-greasy lubricant that is used to some extent as a sub-stitute for sperm whale oil in the lubrication of fine machinery. Despite the possibility of producing a valuable oil in arid regions, and the numerous commercial and industrial applications that have been proposed for jojoba oil, the industry has developed very slowly.

PREPARATION AND DOSAGE Jojoba oil is usually hydrogenated before use in cosmetics. It is a liquid wax, even at low temperatures; after hydrogenation it remains solid (at temperatures of up to 65 °C).

ACTIVE INGREDIENTS Jojoba seeds contain up to 60% of a mixture of wax esters, including fatty acids and alcohols of chain lengths C20 to C26 (eicosenoic acid, docosenoic acid, eicosenol, docosenol and hexacosenol). It is chemically different from other seed oils in that it lacks triglycerides. Also present in seeds are nitrile glycosides (simmondsin; cyanomethylene derivatives).

PHARMACOLOGICAL EFFECTS The oil is said to easily penetrate the upper layers of human skin, hence its popularity in cosmetics. Jojoba oil is considered unsuitable for internal use as there are indications of undesirable side effects.

STATUS Traditional medicine; source of cosmetic oil.

Simmondsia chinensis (Link) C. Schneider   family: Simmondsiaceae

jojoba (French); *Jojobastrauch* (German); *jojoba* (Italian); *jojoba* (Spanish)

Siphonochilus aethiopicus

wild ginger • African ginger

Siphonochilus aethiopicus flower

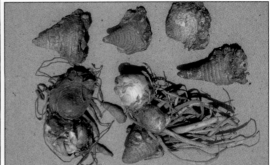

Siphonochilus aethiopicus

Siphonochilus aethiopicus rhizomes and roots

DESCRIPTION Wild ginger is a leafy perennial herb of up to 0.5 m in height. The leaves resemble those of ginger (*Zingiber officinale*) and emerge every year (in the rainy season) from a conical, fleshy rhizome below the ground. Large, attractive pink flowers are borne at ground level, followed by a small fruit (berry) that forms below the ground or at ground level. Wild ginger is a southern African plant and should not be confused with several other plants also known as wild ginger.

ORIGIN Southern tropical Africa (south of Malawi to the eastern part of South Africa). The plant has become rare in some parts but is now cultivated on a small commercial scale. There is some evidence that the form of wild ginger traditionally used by the Zulu people of South Africa is an ancient cultigen and crop plant.

PARTS USED The rhizomes and thick, fleshy roots. These are traditionally used fresh but are nowadays freeze-dried and powdered for commercial use.

THERAPEUTIC CATEGORY Anti-inflammatory, bronchodilator.

USES AND PROPERTIES Wild ginger is used against a wide range of ailments. It is an important traditional medicine against malaria, oral and vaginal thrush, fever, headache, colds, chest ailments, asthma and coughs. Tablets are available and other commercial products are being developed.

PREPARATION AND DOSAGE About 200 mg of dried, powdered herb is taken three or more times per day. In traditional medicine, the fresh rhizome and roots are chewed. For topical use, chewed rhizome or rhizome decoctions are applied.

ACTIVE INGREDIENTS Wild ginger contains a ses-quiterpene of the furanoid type as the main volatile component but a large number of other terpenoids are present in the essential oil. Also present are compounds structurally related to curcumin, the main anti-inflammatory in turmeric (see *Curcuma*).

PHARMACOLOGICAL EFFECTS The pharmacological activity of wild ginger is poorly known. The anti-malarial and antifungal effects are thought to be at least partly due to the sesquiterpenoids, while the anti-inflammatory properties probably result from the curcumin-like compounds.

STATUS Traditional medicine.

Siphonochilus aethiopicus (Schweinf.) B.L.Burtt [= *S. natalensis* (Schltr. & K. Schum.) J.M. Wood & Franks] family: Zingiberaceae
gingembre Africaine (French); *Afrikanischer Ingwer* (German); *zenzero Africano* (Italian)

302

Smilax aristolochiaefolia

sarsaparilla • Mexican sarsaparilla

Smilax regelii

Smilax china

DESCRIPTION Sarsaparilla is a woody climber of about 4 m in height with broad leaves that have prominent veins arising from the base. It has conspicuous tendrils, small greenish flowers and red berries. Several species of *Smilax* are used in traditional medicine in various parts of the world, but the main commercial ones are Mexican sarsaparilla (*S. aristolochiaefolia*, previously known as *S. medica*), Honduras sarsaparilla (*S. regelii*, previously known as *S. officinalis* or *S. utilis*), Ecuadorian sarsaparilla (*S. febrifuga*) and Chinese sarsaparilla (*S. china*).

ORIGIN Central America and the northern parts of South America (*S. aristolochiaefolia*). Commercially cultivated in central America.

PARTS USED Roots of *S. aristolochiaefolia* and several other species, including *S. cordifolia*, *S. regelii*, and *S. tonduzii* (*Sarsaparilla radix*).

THERAPEUTIC CATEGORY Skin treatment (psoriasis, antipruritic, antirheumatic).

USES AND PROPERTIES Sarsaparilla is traditionally used to treat psoriasis and various other skin conditions. It has also been used as a diuretic against rheumatism, rheumatoid arthritis, leprosy and venereal disease. Preparations were once popular amongst gym enthusiasts as sarsaparilla was believed to increase lean body mass. In Mexico, it is used as a tonic and aphrodisiac. Root extracts are a traditional ingredient of root beer and are included in herbal teas.

PREPARATION AND DOSAGE Decoctions of 1-4 g of dried root are taken three times per day. Extracts and tinctures are also used.

ACTIVE INGREDIENTS Sarsaparilla root contains 1-3% steroidal saponins (various species have sarsasapogenin, smilagenin and diosgenin as main compounds). These are used as starting materials for the synthesis of cortisone and other steroids (see *Dioscorea villosa*). Also present are organic acids, flavonoids and phytosterols (sitosterol, stigmasterol).

PHARMACOLOGICAL EFFECTS There is some evidence that sarsaparilla has anti-inflammatory activity and that it is effective in treating psoriasis. It is said to improve appetite and digestion; it is believed to have testosterogenic and progesterogenic effects. In general, the herbal use of sarsaparilla is regarded with scepticism as no convincing scientific evidence of its reputed pharmacological actions seems to have been published.

STATUS Traditional medicine; Pharm.

Smilax aristolochiaefolia Mill.   family: Smilacaceae

salsepareille (French); *Mexiko-Sarsaparille* (German); *salsapariglia smilace* (Italian)

Solanum dulcamara

bittersweet • woody nightshade

Solanum dulcamara

DESCRIPTION A deciduous woody climber (up to 5 m), bearing simple or lobed leaves, dark purple flowers and attractive berries that are bright red when mature.

ORIGIN Europe and Asia (naturalised in North America). The plant is cultivated to some extent but commercial product is wild-harvested in early spring or late autumn, when the stems are leafless.

PARTS USED Dried two- or three-year-old stems (*Dulcamarae stipites / Dulcamarae stipes*).

THERAPEUTIC CATEGORY Anti-eczema, antipruritic.

USES AND PROPERTIES Bittersweet is taken orally in supportive treatment of chronic eczema and pruritic skin conditions. Traditional uses include the treatment of catarrh of the upper respiratory tract, bronchitis, asthma and rheumatic conditions. It is applied externally for various skin ailments (mainly eczema and pruritis), as well as rheumatism.

PREPARATION AND DOSAGE For internal use, a tea is prepared from up to 1 g of dry herb in a cup of water, taken three times per day (daily dose of up to 3 g). For external application, an infusion or decoction of 1-2 g in a cup of water is recommended.

ACTIVE INGREDIENTS The main active compounds are steroidal alkaloids and steroidal saponins. Depending on the source, the main alkaloids are glycosides of soladulcidine, tomatidenol or solasodine. The saponins are yamoginosides A and B (these are bidesmosides of a furostanol, protoyamogenin) or soladulcosides (monodesmosides of spirostan-26-one). Tannins are also present, and probably contribute to the medicinal activity.

PHARMACOLOGICAL EFFECTS The herb is known to possess anticholinergic and antiphlogistic effects. It is also astringent, antibacterial and antifungal. The saponins can produce the observed secretolytic and antimicrobial effects. A clinical trial has shown definite symptomatic relief in cases of eczema and pruritis.

NOTES Other *Solanum* species used in traditional medicine include the ordinary potato, *S. tuberosum* (fresh juice is taken for gastric ulcers), eggplant or aubergine, *S. melongena* (externally used for skin conditions), *kantakari*, *S. xanthocarpum* (seeds are used as expectorant) and *intuma*, *S. aculeastrum* and other species (green fruits are used as local anaesthetic to treat toothache).

STATUS Traditional medicine; Comm.E+; clinical trials +.

Solanum dulcamara L.   family: Solanaceae

douce-amère (French); *Bittersüßer Nachtschatten* (German); *dulcamara* (Italian)

Solidago virgaurea

goldenrod • European goldenrod

Solidago virgaurea

Solidago virgaurea flower heads

Solidago canadensis

DESCRIPTION Goldenrod is an erect herb (up to 1 m), bearing oblong leaves and numerous flower heads in oblong clusters at the branch ends. The bright yellow flower heads are relatively large, with the ray florets about 6-10 mm long. Other species used for similar indications are the early goldenrod, *S. gigantea* var. *serotina* (hairless stems and ray florets) and Canadian goldenrod, *S. canadensis* (hairy stems and very small ray florets).

ORIGIN Temperate parts of Europe, Asia, North Africa and North America (*S. virgaurea*); North America but widely naturalised in Europe (*S. gigantea* and *S. canadensis*). Commercial product (of all three species, often in mixtures) is harvested in the wild, mainly in eastern Europe. *S. virgaurea* is cultivated on a small scale.

PARTS USED Dried aboveground parts, collected during flowering (*Solidaginis virgaureae herba*). The name *Herba Solidaginis* is used when the exact source is not specified, or *Herba Serotinae* for early goldenrod.

THERAPEUTIC CATEGORY Diuretic.

USES AND PROPERTIES Goldenrod is mainly used as diuretic and urinary antiseptic to treat kidney and bladder infections, as well as urinary calculi and kidney gravel. It is included in cough medicines and antirheumatic preparations. The herb is used externally as a mouth and throat rinse against mucosal inflammation and applied to the skin to treat sores and slow healing wounds.

PREPARATION AND DOSAGE Tea is made from 2-3 g of the herb, steeped or briefly boiled in a cup of water. As diuretic, it is taken three to five times a day – the recommended daily dose is 6-12 g.

ACTIVE INGREDIENTS Goldenrod contains complex mixtures of flavonoids (including glycosides of quercetin, isoquercetin and kaempferol), mono- and bidesmosidic triterpene saponins (e.g. polygalic acid derivatives – virgaureasaponins 1-3), phenolic glycosides (e.g. the bisdesmosides leiocarposide and virgaureoside A), a volatile oil (0.5%) with monoterpenes, organic acids and polysaccharides.

PHARMACOLOGICAL EFFECTS The herb has diuretic activity (usually ascribed to leiocarposide), as well as antiphlogistic, analgesic, antifungal and mild antispasmodic effects. These activities can be attributed to the saponins and phenolics, present in the drug.

STATUS Pharm.; Comm.E+; ESCOP 2.

Solidago virgaurea L.

family: Asteraceae

solidago, verge d'or (French); *Echte Goldrute* (German); *verga d'oro* (Italian)

Sorbus aucuparia

mountain ash

Sorbus acuparia tree

Sorbus acuparia leaves and fruit

DESCRIPTION Mountain ash is a small tree of about 10 m in height, with compound leaves, small, unpleasant-smelling white flowers and clusters of orange-red berries resembling minute apples.

ORIGIN Europe and southwestern Asia. Trees are commonly cultivated as ornamentals; the drug comes from eastern Europe.

PARTS USED Mature, ripe berries (sometimes cooked and dried). The pharmaceutical name is *Sorbi aucupariae fructus*.

THERAPEUTIC CATEGORY Osmotic laxative; sweetener for diabetics.

USES AND PROPERTIES Mountain ash berries are traditionally used for a wide range of ailments, including diabetes, scurvy, kidney disorders, arthritis, diarrhoea, haemorrhoids and "blood purification". Nowadays, the main compound (sorbitol) is produced synthetically (by reduction of glucose) and can be used as a sugar substitute for diabetics – sorbitol is about half as sweet as sucrose. It was also used as cholagogue to treat dyspepsia and as a mild laxative for constipation. Sorbitol is widely used in pharmaceutical technology (as moisture regulator, stabiliser and plasticiser) and in the food industry.

PREPARATION AND DOSAGE An oral dose of 20-30 g of sorbitol is laxative and smaller amounts are used as sweeteners.

ACTIVE INGREDIENTS The main active compound in the berries is the common sugar alcohol known as sorbitol (D-glucitol). Sorbitol occurs in many different Rosaceae fruits (apples, pears, plums, cherries) but *Sorbus* berries have a relatively high concentration (about 10%). The seeds are cyanogenic (containing amygdalin) and should be avoided. The berries also contain ascorbic acid (0.13%) and an irritant, parasorbic acid, that is largely broken down during the drying process and completely degraded during cooking.

PHARMACOLOGICAL EFFECTS Sorbitol is absorbed in the gastrointestinal tract and is converted to fructose in the liver. The advantage to diabetics is that no glucose is released into the bloodstream. Sorbitol is well known as an osmotic laxative.

STATUS Traditional medicine; source of sorbitol (now obsolete).

Sorbus aucuparia L.   family: Rosaceae

sorbier des oiseleurs (French); *Eberesche* (German); *sorbo degli uccellatori* (Italian); *serbal de cazadores* (Spanish)

Spilanthes acmella

spilanthes • toothache plant • pará cress

Spilanthes acmella

DESCRIPTION Spilanthes is a weedy annual of up to 0.4 m in height, with soft, somewhat purple-flushed leaves and solitary flower heads borne in the leaf axils. Each flower head is maroon and yellow, with no ligulate florets. A variety or cultivar known as Brazilian cress or pará cress, *S. acmella* var. *oleracea* or simply *S. acmella* 'Oleracea' (formerly *S. oleracea*) is a popular salad plant in South America. In a new classification system it is listed as *Acmella oleracea*.

ORIGIN South America. The plant is thought to be an ancient cultigen of Peruvian origin. Cultivation has spread to most tropical parts of the world.

PARTS USED Dried, aboveground parts, harvested during the flowering period (*Spilanthis oleraceae herba*). Flower heads are harvested for commercial extraction of spilanthol (see below).

THERAPEUTIC CATEGORY Local anaesthetic (dental care), antibiotic, antiphlogistic, sialagogue (stimulates the flow of saliva).

USES AND PROPERTIES Spilanthes is used as a stimulating tonic and antibiotic in traditional medicine, mainly to treat inflammation of the mouth and gums, toothache, digestive complaints, intestinal worms, colds, flu, respiratory tract infections, ear infections, headache, cold sores and herpes. The leaves are eaten fresh as salad or used in soups and stews. Extracts may soon be included in soft drinks with the aim of adding a tingling effect.

PREPARATION AND DOSAGE The fresh or dried herb is taken orally, in doses of 0.5-2 g, depending on the quality of the material. Strong infusions or tinctures may be used, especially for topical application. For treating toothache, a strong tincture is applied to the affected area with cotton wool.

ACTIVE INGREDIENTS The main compound of interest is the pungent spilanthol, an isobutylamide. It reaches levels of 1.2% or more in flower heads. The presence of several minor isobutylamides, choline, tannins and resin have been recorded.

PHARMACOLOGICAL EFFECTS When chewed, the flower heads produce a remarkable tingling sensation in the mouth, a local anaesthetic effect and a pronounced increase in saliva flow. These effects are due to spilanthol, which also has strong insecticidal and antimicrobial activities.

STATUS Traditional medicine; source of spilanthol.

Spilanthes acmella (L.) Murr. [(=*Spilanthes oleracea* L., =*Acmella oleracea* (L.) R.K. Jansen)]   family: Asteraceae
cresson de Para, spilanthe des potagers (French); *Parakresse* (German); *spilante* (Italian)

Stachys officinalis

wood betony

Stachys officinalis

Stachys officinalis flowers

DESCRIPTION Betony is a perennial herb of up to 0.6 m in height, with square stems bearing hairy, heart-shaped to oblong leaves and clusters of attractive, small, tubular, purple flowers at the tips. Three other well known species are *S. palustris* (marsh palustris), *S. recta* that are sometimes used in traditional medicine and *S. byzantina*, the familiar garden plant known as lamb's ears. A species with edible tubers is the Japanese artichoke, *S. affinis* (=*S. tuberifera*).

ORIGIN Europe and Asia. The plant is commonly cultivated as an ornamental plant and is often seen in herb gardens.

PARTS USED Dried, aboveground parts, harvested during the flowering period (*Betonicae herba*).

THERAPEUTIC CATEGORY Sedative, bitter tonic.

USES AND PROPERTIES Wood betony has been used as a panacea since ancient times and is traditionally accepted to be effective against almost any disease. In central Europe it is taken mainly to treat diarrhoea, indigestion and catarrh of the upper respiratory tract, or it is gargled against mouth ulcers and gingivitis. In modern times, it is mainly used against headache and neuralgia. The herb is also considered to be a useful bitter tonic to aid in digestion and to relieve stress and tension. In homoeopathy, the fresh flowering herb is used.

PREPARATION AND DOSAGE About 1-2 g of the dry herb is steeped in a cup of boiling water and taken one to three times per day.

ACTIVE INGREDIENTS The chemical variation in wood betony is not well studied. However, the plant contains alkaloids such as stachydrine and betonicine, as well as tannins (15%) and unspecified bitter substances. Aerial parts of the plant contain several phenylethanoid glycosides, including acetoside, two epimers of campneoside II, forsythoside B, leucosceptoside B and betonyosides A-F.

PHARMACOLOGICAL EFFECTS Tannins are likely to be responsible for the antidiarrhoeal, antimicrobial and anti-inflammatory effects, while the sedative properties have been ascribed to the alkaloids. The contribution of the phenylethanoids to the medicinal activity of the herb is not clear.

STATUS Traditional medicine.

Stachys officinalis (L.) Trev. (=*Stachys betonica*, = *Betonica officinalis* L.) family: Lamiaceae
bétoine (French); *Betonie, Heilziest* (German); *betonica* (Italian)

308

Stellaria media

chickweed • starweed

Stellaria media

DESCRIPTION Chickweed is a small, creeping, annual herb of up to 0.1 m in height but which can spread up to 0.4 m wide under favourable conditions. It has soft, fleshy stems bearing small, oblong leaves in opposite pairs, inconspicuous, white, star-shaped flowers and small, nodding fruits that are enclosed in persistent green calyx lobes.

ORIGIN Europe, North Africa, north Asia. Chickweed thrives in moist places and has become a cosmopolitan weed. It is exceptionally common and can be found in almost any garden.

PARTS USED Fresh or dried aboveground parts (*Stellariae media herba; = Herba alsines*).

THERAPEUTIC CATEGORY Treatment of skin disorders.

USES AND PROPERTIES Fresh or dried herb is used mainly to treat the itchiness caused by rashes, eczema, haemorrhoids, varicose veins, psoriasis, inflammation, nettle burns and other skin disorders. Internally it is traditionally used against rheumatism. Fresh flowering plants are used in homoeopathy against inflammation of the joints and rheumatism.

PREPARATION AND DOSAGE The fresh juice, poultices, ointments or creams are used to treat itchy skin. Decoctions of the fresh or dry herb can be taken orally to treat rheumatism. The fresh herb is edible and may be cooked as a vegetable or added fresh to a salad.

ACTIVE INGREDIENTS Triterpene saponins, to which the itch-relieving properties are ascribed. Also present are coumarins, phytosterols, flavonoids (mainly apigenin C-glycosides, rutin), organic acids and vitamin C. The Asian species *S. yunnanensis, S. dichotoma* and others have yielded several cyclopeptides but these or similar compounds have not yet been reported from *S. media*.

PHARMACOLOGICAL EFFECTS The efficacy of the herb in treating itching skin is attributed to the saponins (said to be emollient and healing) but the actual mechanism of action appears to be unknown (possibly a corticomimetic activity).

NOTES Members of the family Caryophyllaceae typically produce saponins and several of them are used medicinally as secretolytics (see *Gypsophila* and *Saponaria*). Furthermore, whereas anthocyanins are normally responsible for blue and red colours of flowers, betalains take this role in the order Caryophyllales.

STATUS Traditional medicine.

Stellaria media (L.) Vill.   family: Caryophyllaceae

mouron blanc (French); *Vogelmiere* (German); *stellaria* (Italian)

Strophanthus gratus

strophanthus

Strophanthus kombe

Strophanthus gratus

Acokanthera oppositifolia

DESCRIPTION *Strophanthus gratus* is a woody climber that can grow up to 10 m in height. It has robust stems, simple glossy leaves and large, attractive, bright pink or purple flowers. The seeds are borne in long narrow pods. Also commercially important is *S. kombe*. It has large hairy leaves and beautiful yellow and white flowers with the tips of the petals drawn out into extremely long, wiry lobes.

ORIGIN Tropical West Africa (*S. gratus*) and tropical South and East Africa (*S. kombe*). The seeds are mostly wild-harvested but *S. gratus* (and to some extent *S. kombe*) are cultivated on a small scale.

PARTS USED Ripe seeds (*Strophanthi grati semen*).

THERAPEUTIC CATEGORY Cardiac insufficiency.

USES AND PROPERTIES Cardiac glycosides extracted from the seeds are used as heart tonics to slow down the heart rate but to increase the force and efficiency of the contractions. *Strophanthus* in its crude form is not suitable for medicinal use, but carefully purified extracts are injected (often as emergency treatment) in cases of heart failure. Some commercial preparations containing pure heart glycosides of both *S. gratus* and *S. kombe* and also from *Acokanthera*

oppositifolia are still available. Species from both genera are very poisonous and are traditional arrow and spear poisons in Africa.

PREPARATION AND DOSAGE The main heart glycoside, ouabain, is administered intravenously only because it is very poorly absorbed in the digestive tract. Cardenolides are extremely toxic and doses are carefully adapted to individual needs by health care professionals.

ACTIVE INGREDIENTS Over 30 cardiac glycosides; with ouabain (g-strophanthin) as the main component (3-8%). It is crystallised from the crude extract, where it forms 90-95% of total glycosides. Seeds of *S. kombe* contain a complex mixture of cardiac glycosides (up to 10%), with k-strophanthin as main compound.

PHARMACOLOGICAL EFFECTS Heart glycosides such as ouabain act in different ways. They inhibit Na^+, K^+-ATPase and indirectly increase the concentrations of cellular Ca^{++} ions that trigger muscle contraction. Cardenolides are known to increase the strength of contraction of the heart muscle. They lower the pulse and slow down the pacemaker function.

STATUS Traditional medicine; source of ouabain.

Strophanthus gratus (Wallich & Hook.) Baillon — family: Apocynaceae

strophanthus (French); *Strophanthus* (German); *strofanto* (Italian)

Strychnos nux-vomica

nux vomica

Strychnos nux-vomica

Strychnos nux-vomica seeds

DESCRIPTION Nux vomica is an evergreen tree of about 25 m in height, with spiny branches bearing broad, three-veined leaves and small, white, tubular flowers. It has large yellow fruits containing up to eight disc-shaped seeds.

ORIGIN Southern Asia. It is wild-harvested and also cultivated in tropical areas of Asia and West Africa.

PARTS USED Ripe seeds (*Strychni semen*).

THERAPEUTIC CATEGORY Stimulant, bitter tonic.

USES AND PROPERTIES Nux vomica is no longer used to any extent in modern phytomedicine, except in homoeopathy. It has been used as stimulant and bitter tonic, and as analgesic in ointments. In former times, the seeds were mainly used to kill rodents and other pests.

PREPARATION AND DOSAGE The maximum daily dose of strychnine is 20 mg, and the maximum single dose is 10 mg. More than 60 mg are lethal. Because of the extreme toxicity, the use of nux vomica, even as bitter tonic in low doses, is no longer considered safe.

ACTIVE INGREDIENTS The seeds contain mono-terpene indole alkaloids at levels of 1-3%. The two main compounds are strychnine and a methoxylated derivative known as brucine.

PHARMACOLOGICAL EFFECTS Strychnine inhibits a glycine receptor (an inhibiting neuroreceptor) and thus stimulates all parts of the central nervous system. Poisoning symptoms include anxiety, extreme sensitivity to light and noise, convulsions and death by asphyxia, due to contraction of the diaphragm.

NOTES Various other *Strychnos* species are used in Africa and Southeast Asia as arrow poisons and in traditional medicine. The fruit flesh is often edible and very tasty, while the seeds can be extremely poisonous. A species related to *S. nux-vomica*, known as the St. Ignatius poison nut (*S. ignatii*) is still used as an ingredient of homoeopathic medicine. Several South American species (*S. castelnaei, S. toxifera*) are a source for curare, quaternary bisindole alkaloids, such as C-toxiferine I and others. They block nicotinic acetyl-choline receptors which leads to a paralysis of muscles. This feature is useful in surgery, to prevent contraction of muscles. These alkaloids have been used as arrow poison by South American Indians.

WARNING Nux vomica nuts or extracts thereof are extremely poisonous and are not suitable for self-medication.

STATUS Traditional medicine; Pharm.

Strychnos nux-vomica L.   family: Loganiaceae or Strychnaceae

noix vomique (French); *Brechnussbaum* (German); *noce vomica* (Italian)

Styphnolobium japonicum

pagoda tree • Japanese pagoda tree

Styphnolobium japonicum

DESCRIPTION The pagoda tree is a graceful deciduous tree (up to 20 m) and has characteristic bright green twigs with prominent white dots (lenticels). Compound leaves are borne along the branch ends, and clusters of white, pea-like flowers appear in summer. The fruits are greenish yellow, fleshy pods that are usually markedly constricted between the seeds.

ORIGIN China and Korea. Popular as an ornamental tree and now found as a garden and street tree in many parts of the world.

PARTS USED Dried, unopened flower buds (*Sophoreae flos, Sophorae gemmae*) are used for extraction of flavonoids.

THERAPEUTIC CATEGORY Venotonic.

USES AND PROPERTIES The main flavonoid in the flower buds is used to treat symptoms of capillary and venous insufficiency, including swollen legs, varicose veins, cramps, haemorrhage, piles and circulatory disorders affecting skin and mucosa. Extracts are used topically in creams and ointments. The flower buds are also the source of a yellow dye, traditionally used to colour silk.

PREPARATION AND DOSAGE In order to be effective, very high doses are usually prescribed – typically 1 g of pure rutin per day over a period of eight weeks to improve the symptoms of venous insufficiency. Even higher doses (up to 2 g) are considered appropriate for relief of haemorrhoids.

ACTIVE INGREDIENTS The main active compound in the flower buds is rutin (quercetin 3-rutinoside), which occurs in concentrations of 15-20%. The flavonoid (flavonol glycoside) is extracted with boiling water and then crystallised in pure form. An alternative source is the leaves of buckwheat (see *Fagopyrum esculentum*) but the extraction is more complicated because of interfering substances.

PHARMACOLOGICAL EFFECTS The venotonic properties of flavonoids were mostly demonstrated in laboratory experiments and there are very few studies showing efficacy in humans. Nevertheless, flavonoids, anthocyanins and proanthocyanidins are widely considered to strengthen capillaries and to reduce capillary permeability, apart from their free radical scavenging and antioxidant properties. A partial synthetic derivative of rutin, Venoruton™, shows better bioavailability and is used to treat venous disorders.

STATUS Pharm. (rutin).

Styphnolobium japonicum (L.) Schott (= *Sophora japonica* L.)   family: Fabaceae

sophora japonica (French); *Japanischer Schnurbaum* (German); *sofora* (Italian)

Sutherlandia frutescens

cancer bush • sutherlandia

Sutherlandia frutescens flowers and fruit

Sutherlandia frutescens flowers

Sutherlandia microphylla

DESCRIPTION Cancer bush is a perennial shrub (up to 2 m), with compound leaves, bright red flowers and inflated, bladdery pods. The various inland species of Sutherlandia (including a form with narrow pods known as *S. microphylla*) are regarded by some botanists as a single, variable species, *S. frutescens*. Sutherlandia is very closely related to the genus *Lessertia* and is sometimes considered to be part of the latter.

ORIGIN Southern Africa. The plants are commonly cultivated as garden ornamentals. Raw material is wild-harvested to some extent but a selected chemotype is nowadays cultivated on a commercial scale.

PARTS USED Dried twigs and leaves.

THERAPEUTIC CATEGORY Adaptogenic tonic.

USES AND PROPERTIES Cancer bush has a long history of traditional use. It is a bitter tonic and adaptogen that has been used against numerous ailments, including colds and influenza, cough, asthma, bronchitis, fever, indigestion, poor appetite, gastritis, peptic ulcers, dysentery, diabetes, liver conditions, rheumatism, urinary tract infections, tuberculosis, stress and anxiety. It has been used in the treatment and prevention of cancer, hence the common name. Recent anecdotes and observations indicate immune stimulatory properties (similar to those of *Astragalus*) and significant benefits in the treatment of wasting in cancer and AIDS. Extracts are used topically in the treatment of burns, wounds and inflammatory skin conditions.

PREPARATION AND DOSAGE A daily dose of about 1-2 g of the dry herb is taken as tea, decoction or tablets (one or two tablets containing 300 mg of the dry herb, three times per day).

ACTIVE INGREDIENTS Leaves contain complex mixtures of bitter triterpenoid glycosides, several flavonoids, high levels of free amino acids (including *L*-canavanine, a non-protein amino acid) and pinitol (a cyclitol).

PHARMACOLOGICAL EFFECTS The triterpenoids might have corticomimetic activity besides their obvious bitter tonic effects. Canavanine is an arginine mimic that reduces the uptake of essential amino acids from the intestines and disturbs protein biosynthesis; it has documented anticancer and antiviral activity and is known to inhibit nitric oxide synthase. Pinitol is a known antidiabetic agent with potential for treating wasting in cancer and AIDS.

STATUS Traditional medicine.

Sutherlandia frutescens (L.) R. Br. [= *Lessertia frutescens* (L.) P. Goldblatt & J.C. Manning]   family: Fabaceae
sutherlandia (French); Sutherlandia (German); sutherlandia (Italian)

Symphytum officinale

comfrey

Symphytum officinale plants

Symphytum officinale

Symphytum officinale flowers

DESCRIPTION A leafy perennial herb with erect flowering stems (up to 1 m) arising each year from a fleshy rhizome. Large hairy leaves are borne along the stems and tubular blue or yellowish white flowers in one-sided clusters at the tips.

ORIGIN Europe and western Asia; naturalised in North America and widely grown as a garden subject. Commercial products are obtained from cultivated plants.

PARTS USED Mainly the dried rhizome and roots (*Symphyti radix, Consolidae radix*), sometimes also the aboveground parts (*Symphyti herba*).

THERAPEUTIC CATEGORY Wound-healing.

USES AND PROPERTIES Mainly used externally for the treatment of inflammation, bruises, sprains, dislocations, pulled ligaments and muscles, arthritis, glandular swellings, slow healing wounds and boils. Traditionally, roots or leaves were taken internally against lung disorders, gastritis, stomach ulcers, and bleeding.

PREPARATION AND DOSAGE Poultices and pastes are prepared from the fresh root for external use. A decoction of 1 part dry roots to 10 parts of water is a suitable alternative. A daily dose of 5-10 g of dry roots was traditionally taken in the form of tea but internal use is now obsolete because of liver damage.

ACTIVE INGREDIENTS The roots contain about 0.8% allantoin and large amounts of mucilage (fructans). Also present are pyrrolizidine alkaloids (PAs) and their N-oxides (up to 0.4%, including intermedine, symphytine and echimidine), as well as 4-6% tannins, triterpenes, and organic acids (including rosmarinic acid).

PHARMACOLOGICAL EFFECTS The wound-healing activity is attributed especially to allantoin (the compound is known to promote granulation and tissue regeneration) and to the mucilage (demulcent effects). Rosmarinic acid has proven anti-inflammatory activity. PAs are haemostyptic but also hepatotoxic, carcinogenic and mutagenic.

WARNING The internal use of comfrey should be discouraged, as the PAs alkylate DNA and can therefore become carcinogenic. Albeit limited, absorption of externally applied alkaloids does takes place; the level of PAs should not exceed 10 µg per day. Application on broken skin should be avoided. Do not eat comfrey (such as *S. uplandicum*) as a vegetable.

STATUS Traditional medicine; Pharm.; Comm.E+ (external use only).

Symphytum officinale L. (= *S. consolida* Gueldenst. ex Ledeb.)   family: Boraginaceae

grande consoude (French); *Gemeiner Beinwell* (German); *consolida maggiore* (Italian)

Syzygium aromaticum
clove tree

Syzygium aromaticum tree

Syzygium aromaticum leaves and flowers

Cloves

DESCRIPTION The clove tree is an evergreen tropical plant that may reach 12 m, bearing simple, glossy green leaves and small white flowers with numerous prominent stamens. Another species of *Syzygium* that is well known for its medicinal properties is the jambolan, *S. cumini*.

ORIGIN Southeast Asia (Moluccas Islands); traditionally cultivated in Tanzania (Zanzibar), Madagascar and other East African islands, but is nowadays found as a crop in almost all tropical parts of the world. The jambolan originates from southern Asia; grown as a crop in many tropical regions.

PARTS USED Hand-picked and dried flower buds, known as cloves (*Caryophylli flos*) or the essential oil distilled from them (clove oil; *Caryophylli aetheroleum*). In the case of jambolan, the bark or seeds are used.

THERAPEUTIC CATEGORY Local anaesthetic, carminative.

USES AND PROPERTIES Cloves or clove oil are used as a first aid remedy for toothache and to treat mucosal inflammations of mouth and throat; in traditional medicine internally as carminative and anti-emetic, externally against rheumatism and myalgia. It is often included in stomachic medicines and tonics. The oil can be used as an insect repellent. Cloves are famous as a spice. In Indonesia, they form an important component of the local cigarettes. Jambolan bark is used against diarrhoea and topically against inflammation of the mouth, throat and skin.

PREPARATION AND DOSAGE Clove oil is used in its pure form for topical application against toothache. For mouthwashes, extracts or dilutions corresponding to 5% essential oil may be used. The daily dose of jambolan bark is 3-6 g.

ACTIVE INGREDIENTS The essential oil occurs in large quantities in the buds (15-20% of dry weight), with eugenol as the main component (up to 85%) and smaller amounts of eugenyl acetate (up to 15%) and β-caryophyllene (up to 7%). Cloves also contain flavonoids, galloyltannins, phenolic acids and triterpenes.

PHARMACOLOGICAL EFFECTS Clove oil has known local anaesthetic, antiseptic, antispasmodic and carminative activity. Eugenol inhibits prostaglandin formation, explaining its analgesic and anti-inflammatory properties.

WARNING The oil can cause allergies.

STATUS Traditional medicine; Pharm.; Comm.E+. (cloves, jambolan bark); WHO 2.

Syzygium aromaticum (L.) Merr.& Perry (= *Eugenia caryophyllus* (C.Spreng.) Bull. & Harr.)   family Myrtaceae
giroflier (French); *Gewürznelkenbaum* (German); *chiodi di garofano* (Italian); *clavero* (Spanish)

Tabebuia impetiginosa

pau d'arco • lapacho

Tabebuia impetiginosa flowers

DESCRIPTION An evergreen tree of up to 25 m in height, with palmately compound leaves and rounded clusters of attractive tubular flowers. They are predominantly pink but have a yellow throat. The narrowly oblong fruits produce numerous flat, winged seeds. *T. avellanedae* was previously considered to be a distinct species but is now included in *T. impetiginosa*. *Tabebuia* species are best known as sources of valuable timber and as ornamental trees (e.g. *T. rosea* and *T. chrysantha*).

ORIGIN Northern Mexico to Argentina; bark is harvested in the wild.

PARTS USED Dried inner bark (*Tabebuiae cortex*).

THERAPEUTIC CATEGORY Antimicrobial; anti-inflammatory.

USES AND PROPERTIES In modern herbal medicine, the bark is used mainly to treat candida infections, bacterial infections, chronic venereal diseases and as supportive treatment in cancer. South Americans traditionally used lapacho as a cure-all to treat various conditions, including cancer, rheumatism, gastritis, bronchitis, fever, eczema and fungal infections.

PREPARATION AND DOSAGE The bark is infused and used as a tea, or is powdered and used to manufac-ture capsules and tablets.

ACTIVE INGREDIENTS Bark contains anthraquinones, naphthoquinones and furanonaphthoquinones as main active constituents. Of particular interest is the naphthoquinone lapachol, that co-occurs with dehydroiso-α-lapachone and dehydro-α-lapachone. Commercial products often contain little or no naphthoquinones, despite the fact that the bark produces 2-7% lapachol. Various other compounds are present, including various benzoic acid derivatives and iridoid glycosides (6-epimonomelittoside).

PHARMACOLOGICAL EFFECTS The quinones are chemically reactive as oxidants; furanonaphthoquinones can form covalent bonds with proteins and DNA. In various *in vitro* and *in vivo* studies, the naphthoquinones (or bark extracts) showed definite antibacterial, antiviral, antifungal, analgesic, anti-inflammatory, and cancer preventative activities. Even at very low concentrations, the naphthoquinones act as non-specific immune stimulants. Anticancer activity has been ascribed to lapachol but the results of clinical trials have thus far been ambiguous.

STATUS Traditional medicine.

Tabebuia impetiginosa (DC.) Standley   family: Bignoniaceae

pau d'arco (Portuguese); *lapacho* (Spanish); *pau d'arco* (French); *Ipêbaum, Lapacho* (German); *ipê roxo, pau d'arco* (Italian)

Tamarindus indica

tamarind • Indian date

Tamarindus indica tree

Tamarindus indica leaves and flowers

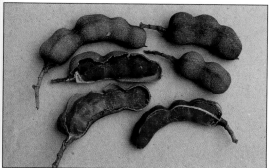

Tamarindus indica pods and fruit pulp

DESCRIPTION Tamarind is an evergreen tree of up to 25 m in height, with sparse branches bearing pinnately compound leaves and attractive yellow and orange flowers. The fruit is an oblong, greyish brown, indehiscent pod with up to 12 seeds surrounded by a fleshy, edible fruit pulp.

ORIGIN The tree is an ancient cultigen of unknown origin (probably from tropical Africa), from where it spread to other warm parts of the world. It is commonly cultivated for the fruit pulp and has become a popular ornamental tree.

PARTS USED Fruit pulp – the fleshy, reddish brown, edible mesocarp of the pod (*Tamarindorum pulpa*). The pulp is either used in its crude form (*Tamarindorum pulpa cruda*), or as purified pulp (*Tamarindorum pulpa depurata*). It is purified by dissolving the crude product in hot water, filtering to remove insoluble fractions and then concentrating and drying the thickened extract, often after one part of powdered sugar has been added.

THERAPEUTIC CATEGORY Mild laxative.

USES AND PROPERTIES Fruit pulp (or extracts thereof) is eaten for its mild laxative effects and is sometimes combined with senna leaf powder. It has a delicious sweet-sour taste and is widely used as a tonic to improve appetite and digestion. Numerous other traditional uses, such as treatment of liver and bile disorders, have been recorded. In India, for example, a beverage made from the fruit is taken for feverish conditions. In the food industry, the pulp is used in drinks, chutneys and as an ingredient of Worcester sauce.

PREPARATION AND DOSAGE Dried fruit pulp is added to commercial constipation remedies or the fresh pulp is eaten.

ACTIVE INGREDIENTS The pulp is rich in pectin, monosaccharides and organic acids (mainly as potassium hydrogen tartrate, but also as free acids – including tartaric acid, malic acid and citric acid). The total acid content is about 12-15%. The distinctive odour is ascribed to pyrazinen and thiazols and to essential oil (in low concentration) which contains monoterpenoids and aromatic cinnamates.

PHARMACOLOGICAL EFFECTS Tamarind fruit pulp is astringent, mildly antiseptic and helps to moisten and lubricate the intestines. It has a mild laxative effect.

STATUS Traditional medicine; Pharm.

Tamarindus indica L.

family: Fabaceae

tamarinier (French); *Tamarinde* (German); *tamarindo* (Italian)

Taraxacum officinale

dandelion

Taraxacum officinale

DESCRIPTION Dandelion is a leafy perennial herb with a fleshy taproot and a rosette of markedly toothed leaves. Solitary yellow flower heads are borne on hollow, unbranched stalks. The small brown fruits (achenes) each has a hairy "parachute" for wind dispersal. All parts of the plant exude a bitter, milky juice when cut or broken. The common dandelion is actually a complicated mixture of microspecies and races that are difficult to identify (the name *T. officinale* is loosely applied to the species complex as a whole). *Dandelion* is a corruption of *dent de lion* (lion's tooth) in reference to the sharp teeth on the leaves.

ORIGIN All parts of the northern hemisphere (now a cosmopolitan weeds); widely cultivated for salad, but medicinal product comes mainly from eastern Europe.

PARTS USED The fresh or dried leaves, roots, or both (*Taraxaci radix cum herba*). The young leaves are eaten as a salad (traditionally a "spring salad" in Europe), while roots collected in autumn (when rich in inulin) are dried and roasted as a coffee substitute.

THERAPEUTIC CATEGORY Diuretic, bitter tonic.

USES AND PROPERTIES Dandelion is mainly used as a diuretic but it is also an appetite-stimulating bitter tonic, thought to be useful to treat stomach, liver, gall bladder and rheumatic complaints. It is applied externally for eczema and other skin conditions. Because of the high inulin content dandelion tea can be useful for patients with diabetes.

PREPARATION AND DOSAGE A dose of 4-10 g of the herb is taken as infusion or tincture three times per day.

ACTIVE INGREDIENTS The main constituents are sesquiterpene lactones (tetrahydroridentin B, taraxacolide β-D-glucoside, and others), a phenolic acid derivative (taraxacoside) and triterpenoids (taraxasterol and derivatives). Also present are high levels of potassium (up to 4.5%) and inulin (up to 40% in autumn).

PHARMACOLOGICAL EFFECTS There is some experimental evidence for the diuretic (reflected in French common name!) and cholagogic activities (linked to the bitter sesqui- and triterpenoids). Extracts showed moderate anti-inflammatory activity.

WARNING Repeated exposure to the milky latex may cause contact dermatitis.

STATUS Traditional medicine; Pharm.; Comm.E+; ESCOP 2.

Taraxacum officinale Weber ex Wigg.   family: Asteraceae

pissenlit, dent de lion (French); *Gemeiner Löwenzahn* (German); *taraxaco* (Italian); *diente de leon* (Spanish)

Taxus baccata

yew • English yew

Taxus baccata leaves and fleshy cones

DESCRIPTION A slow-growing, long-lived, evergreen tree (up to 20 m), with reddish brown bark and dark green leaves arranged in two ranks. The inconspicuous male cones have about 10 shield-shaped anthers, while the female cone is a hard, egg-shaped structure surrounded by a bright red, fleshy aril. There are about seven closely related species of yew (some consider them mere varieties). The discovery of anticancer properties was first made with taxol, a diterpene extracted from the bark of Pacific yew (*T. brevifolia*).

ORIGIN Europe and the Mediterranean region (*T. baccata*) or the western coastal regions of North America (*T. brevifolia*).

PARTS USED Bark (originally); nowadays the leaves (a renewable and sustainable resource, obtained from *T. baccata*, *T. x media* and *T. wallichiana*).

THERAPEUTIC CATEGORY Cancer treatment.

USES AND PROPERTIES Yew bark or leaves are not suitable for self-medication but they are the source of taxol and similar compounds that are highly effective in the treatment of advanced ovarian cancer, breast cancer and possibly other tumours.

PREPARATION AND DOSAGE Pure chemical compounds are given in doses of about 110-250 mg/m^2 per day, at intervals of three to four weeks.

ACTIVE INGREDIENTS Numerous diterpenes with a taxane nucleus occur in yew trees. Taxol, also known as paclitaxel (a diterpene pseudoalkaloid) was the first compound to be extracted and used (the word Taxol™ – with a capital T – is a registered trademark). Nowadays, diterpenes such as 10-deacetylbaccatin III are extracted from the leaves of *T. baccata* and other species and converted by partial synthesis into structural analogues of taxol, such as docetaxel (marketed as Taxotere™).

PHARMACOLOGICAL EFFECTS Taxol and docetaxel are spindle poisons that inhibit cell division, thus preventing tumour growth. While colchicine and *Catharanthus* alkaloids inhibit the polymerisation of tubulin (a protein) to form the microtubules of the spindle, taxol and docetaxel prevent the depolymerisation of the microtubules. The efficacy was demonstrated in clinical trials.

WARNING It is important to stress that all parts of the yew tree (except the aril) are extremely poisonous.

STATUS Pharm; modern medicine: taxol; clinical studies+ (pure alkaloids).

Taxus baccata L.
family: Taxaceae
if (French); *Eibe* (German); *tasso* (Italian)

Terminalia chebula

black myrobalan • chebulic myrobalan

Terminalia chebula

Terminalia bellirica

Phyllanthus emblica

DESCRIPTION A large deciduous tree of up to 25 m in height, with large oblong leaves that are hairy below. Small yellow flowers are borne in clusters in the leaf axils and have an unpleasant odour. The fruits are large oblong drupes that turn yellowish brown when they ripen. Several species of *Terminalia* are used in traditional medicine in various parts of the world. Of special importance in Ayurvedic medicine are the bark of the arjun tree (*T. arjuna*) from India (a traditional heart tonic) and the fruit of beleric (belliric) myrobalan (*T. bellirica*) from India and Indonesia. The ripe or unripe fruit of the latter (known as bedda nuts or *bahira* in Hindi) have numerous uses in Asian folk medicine (mainly a bitter tonic and antiseptic against various ailments of the gastrointestinal and respiratory tracts).

ORIGIN India to China and Malaysia (*T. chebula*).

PARTS USED Dried, ripe fruits (black chebulic or black myrobalan; *Myrobalani fructus*; *abhaya* in Sanskrit), rarely the bark.

THERAPEUTIC CATEGORY Astringent, laxative, digestive, antiseptic.

USES AND PROPERTIES Black chebulic is a general medicine traditionally used mainly against digestive disorders and inflammation of mucus membranes. The fruits are used as part of a standard mixture in Ayurvedic medicine known as *triphala* (meaning "three fruit"). This mixture of the fruits of *T. chebula*, *T. bellirica* and *Phyllanthus emblica* is a famous panacea or general tonic. Dried fruits are used on a large scale as an industrial source of tannins for the leather industry.

PREPARATION AND DOSAGE The daily dose is 3-9 g, often used in decoctions with other herbs.

ACTIVE INGREDIENTS The drug contains high concentrations of gallotannins (including terchebulin, terflavin A, corilagin, punicalagin and chebulinic acid), together with triterpene saponins.

PHARMACOLOGICAL EFFECTS Beneficial effects in treating gastrointestinal ailments are clearly linked to the astringent and antimicrobial properties of the tannins. Experiments have shown cardiotonic and cholesterol lowering activities.

STATUS Traditional medicine.

Terminalia chebula Retz.

family: Combretaceae

myrobalan noire (French); *Chebula-Myrobalane* (German)

Teucrium chamaedrys

germander • wall germander

Teucrium scordium

Teucrium chamaedrys

Teucrium trifidum

DESCRIPTION Germander is a small perennial herb of about 0.2 m in height, with small opposite leaves and clusters of pink or purple flowers borne on the branch tips. Several other species have been used in folk medicine. In Europe, the wood germander or wood sage (*T. scorodonia*) is well known, but other traditional medicinal species include cat thyme (*T. marum*), mountain germander (*T. montanum*), poley (*T. polium*), and water germander (*T. scordium*). In Africa, *T. africanum* and *T. trifidum* are popular remedies for dysentery and haemorrhoids.

ORIGIN Mediterranean, southern central Europe to western Asia (*T. chamaedrys*); mostly wild-harvested for medicinal use.

PARTS USED Dried, aboveground parts, collected while flowering (*Teucrii chamaedryos herba*).

THERAPEUTIC CATEGORY Bitter tonic, astringent.

USES AND PROPERTIES Germander is a traditional tonic, diuretic, anti-diarrhoeal medicine and mouthwash that was mainly used in France and Italy. It has also become popular as a supportive treatment in weight loss programmes. The herb is no longer used to any extent, as several cases of liver damage have been re-ported. Wood sage (*T. scorodonia*) was once popular in the treatment of bronchitis.

PREPARATION AND DOSAGE Infusions and decoctions of the herb were formerly used, but studies are needed to evaluate safety and to determine an appropriate and safe dosage.

ACTIVE INGREDIENTS Diterpene lactones of the *ent*-clerodan-type are present, including dihydroteugin, teucrins A to G, teufline, teuflidin and isoteuflidin. Germander contains triterpenes, essential oil, flavonoids and complex phenolic acid glycosides (teucrioside). The other *Teucrium* species are also rich in diterpene lactones and iridoid glycosides (harpagide, 8-O-acetylharpagide).

PHARMACOLOGICAL EFFECTS The pharmacological activity of the various compounds has not been studied. The terpenoid lactones are bitter substances that are perhaps also responsible for the stimulant and anticatarrh effects. It is not known which compound(s) are responsible for the reported cases of acute hepatitis.

WARNING Germander may cause liver damage and preparations have been formally banned in France.

STATUS Traditional medicine.

Teucrium chamaedrys L.   family: Lamiaceae

germandrée chamaedrys (French); *Echter Gamander* (German); *camedrio querciola* (Italian)

Thuja occidentalis

American arbor-vitae • white cedar

Thuja occidentalis – branches with female cones

DESCRIPTION Arbor-vitae is an evergreen tree of up to 20 m in height, with flattened branches bearing scale-like leaves, inconspicuous male cones and small oblong female cones with overlapping cone scales.

ORIGIN Eastern parts of North America. The tree produces a useful, soft, fragrant timber and is commonly cultivated in gardens (variegated forms, known as "golden cypress", and dwarf forms are popular).

PARTS USED Leaves (actually the young, flattened branches –*Thujae summitates*) or the essential oil (*Thujae aetheroleum*).

THERAPEUTIC CATEGORY Traditional diuretic, expectorant; immune stimulant.

USES AND PROPERTIES Extracts are used to treat fever, colds, headache, rheumatism, bronchitis and cystitis. It is considered to be an effective decongestant and expectorant. The fresh young twigs are popular in homoeopathy to formulate products against warts, skin rashes, rheumatism and the common cold. Thuja or thuja oil is traditionally used to induce abortion – sometimes with fatal results.

PREPARATION AND DOSAGE Infusions are rarely used because the dosage should be determined accu-rately. Alcoholic extracts are usually preferred (used in commercial preparations). The oil or extracts may be rubbed into the skin as a counter-irritant to treat rheumatic pain, warts, stiff muscles and skin infections, rashes and neuralgia.

ACTIVE INGREDIENTS Volatile oil (0.4-1%);the main compound is thujone (both α-thujone and β-thujone, up to 65% of the total oil), together with α-pinene, camphor, borneol and fenchone. Also present are sesquiterpenes, flavonoids and polysaccharides.

PHARMACOLOGICAL EFFECTS Thujone is known to be neurotoxic (see *Artemisia absinthium*) so that internal use is not recommended. Ingestion over a long period may be particularly harmful due to cumulative effects. A tincture was successful in treating warts and epitheliomes. The water-soluble polysaccharide fraction shows immune stimulant properties. A combination of *Echinacea*, *Thuja*, and *Baptisia tinctoria* is used in phytotherapy as an immune stimulant (Esberitox™).

NOTES The essential oil is used commercially in disinfectants, hair cosmetics, liquid soaps, insecticides and deodorants. Powdered leaves are said to kill flies and ticks.

STATUS Traditional medicine; Pharm.

Thuja occidentalis L.   family: Cupressaceae

thuya d'occident, thuya américain (French); *Abendländischer Lebensbaum* (German); *thuja* (Italian)

Thymus vulgaris

thyme • garden thyme

Thymus vulgaris

Thymus serpyllum

DESCRIPTION A small perennial herb or shrublet with thin stems bearing small, greyish green leaves in opposite pairs and minute violet flowers. Spanish thyme (*T. zygis*) is an accepted alternative source of the herb. Often used but less effective are wild thyme (*T. serpyllum*), larger wild thyme (*T. pulegioides*), African wild thyme (*T. schimperi*) and lemon thyme (*T. x citriodora* – a garden hybrid between *T. vulgaris* and *T. pulegioides*).

ORIGIN Southern and southeastern Europe (*T. vulgaris*), Spain and Portugal (*T. zygis*), western and northern Europe to the Ukraine (*T. serpyllum*) and most parts of Europe (*T. pulegioides*). Grown in herb gardens; cultivated commercially in many parts of the world.

PARTS USED Dried leaves and flowers (*Thymi herba*); volatile oil (*Thymi aetheroleum*).

THERAPEUTIC CATEGORY Expectorant, spasmolytic, antibiotic.

USES AND PROPERTIES The herb is mostly taken against gastrointestinal disturbances and for the treatment of coughs, colds, bronchitis and inflammation of the upper respiratory tract. It is locally applied against mucosal inflammation of mouth and throat, and for treating minor wounds. The oil is added to baths in case of bronchial catarrh and itching skin.

PREPARATION AND DOSAGE A tea made from 1-4 g of the herb can be taken several times a day (expectorant use) or before or during meals (stomachic use). The herb, extracts of the herb, the essential oil or isolated thymol are used in commercial preparations, including cough teas, cough drops, gargles and antiseptic ointments.

ACTIVE INGREDIENTS The essential oil is very variable but good quality oil is rich in thymol (30-50%) and carvacrol (1-5%), with smaller amounts of linalool, p-cymene, cineole, thujan-4-ol and α-pinene. The herb is rich in labiate tannins (up to 7%), several polymethoxyflavones, triterpenes and polysaccharides..

PHARMACOLOGICAL EFFECTS Thyme oil and thymol are strongly antibiotic (thymol is 25 times more effective than phenol). Antispasmodic, anti-inflammatory and antitussive activities are ascribed to the polymethoxyflavones and monoterpenes.

NOTES Thyme and thyme oil are commonly used in cosmetics and to flavour food and liqueurs.

STATUS Traditional medicine; Pharm.; Comm.E+; ESCOP 1; WHO 1.

Thymus vulgaris L.   family: Lamiaceae

thym (French); *Echter Thymian* (German); *timo* (Italian); *tomillo* (Spanish)

Tilia cordata

lime • linden • small-leaved lime

Tilia platyphyllos

Tilia cordata

Tilia cordata tree

DESCRIPTION Lime or linden is a deciduous tree of up to 30 m in height bearing large, heart-shaped leaves with serrate margins and brown hairs along the veins on the lower sides. Groups of five to ten greenish yellow flowers with numerous stamens are characteristically borne on a slender stalk hanging down from a large, oblong, leaf-like bract. *T. cordata* and *T. platyphyllos* (large-leaved lime) are both used. The latter has fewer flowers (two to five per bract) and the leaves have white hairs along the veins.

ORIGIN Europe (*T. cordata*) and Europe to southwestern Asia (*T. platyphyllos*). Both species are commonly cultivated. The product comes mainly from eastern Europe, southwestern Asia and China. Traditionally court was held under a linden tree in Central Europe.

PARTS USED Dried flowers and bracts of both species (*Tiliae flos*). Sometimes also the wood (actually the inner bark together with the adjoining newly-formed wood – usually referred to as sapwood), or more rarely charcoal made from lime wood.

THERAPEUTIC CATEGORY Traditional diaphoretic and mild sedative.

USES AND PROPERTIES Lime flowers are used mainly to treat feverish colds, cough and sore throat, but also traditionally as sedative, antispasmodic, stomachic and diuretic (as demulcent for relief of itching skin ailments). The sapwood is used as spasmolytic, hypotensive, diuretic, and to increase bile flow. Charcoal is used in case of intestinal disorders and abscesses of the leg.

PREPARATION AND DOSAGE As a tea, about 2-4 g of dried flowers are used daily. Extracts and tinctures of both the flowers and sapwood are used as such or are included in several commercial preparations.

ACTIVE INGREDIENTS Flowers are rich in mucilage and phenolics (about 1% flavonoids, together with proanthocyanidins, gallocatechol tannins and phenolic acids). Small amounts of essential oil occur in the bracts (mainly aldehydes) or flowers (mainly mono- and sesquiterpenoids, such as linalool, germacrene, farnesen). Sapwood contains phenolic acids and polyphenols.

PHARMACOLOGICAL EFFECTS The claimed diaphoretic, sedative, spasmolytic and diuretic activities of the flowers are based on anecdotal rather than clinical evidence but there is better support for the stated uses of the sapwood.

STATUS Traditional medicine; Pharm.; Comm.E+.

Tilia cordata Mill.   family: Tiliaceae

tilleul à petites feuilles (French); *Winterlinde* (German); *tiglio* (Italian)

Trigonella foenum-graecum

fenugreek

Trigonella foenum-graecum

Trigonella foenum-graecum seeds

DESCRIPTION Fenugreek is a small annual herb (up to 0.5 m), bearing trifoliate leaves and inconspicuous pale yellow flowers in the leaf axils. The fruits are long, thin, often curved and sharply pointed pods with 10 to 20 angular seeds (3-5 mm long).

ORIGIN Mediterranean region, northeastern Africa and western Asia; cultivated since ancient times; nowadays mainly in France, Turkey, India, and China.

PARTS USED Ripe, dried seeds (*Foenugraeci semen*).

THERAPEUTIC CATEGORY Digestive tonic, demulcent, expectorant.

USES AND PROPERTIES Seeds are mainly used to treat loss of appetite, anorexia and weight loss, and externally as a poultice against skin inflammation, boils, ulcers and eczema. Traditional uses are many and varied, and include the treatment of sore throat (seed powder used as roborant), stomach ulcers, stomach pain, late-onset diabetes, high cholesterol, impotence and loss of libido. The seeds or sprouts are nutritional supplements (in Ethiopia, for example, the seeds are used to prepare a milk substitute for infants). The distinctive flavour is used in Middle Eastern and Indian cooking.

PREPARATION AND DOSAGE For internal use, a daily dose of 3-18 g of seeds (powdered or crushed) is recommended. For external use, 50 g of powdered seeds are mixed with 250 ml of water (also as gels, liniments, ointments and oils).

ACTIVE INGREDIENTS The seeds are rich in mucilage (mainly galactomannans), lipids, proteins (up to 30%) and protease inhibitors. Numerous steroid saponins are present; the most common aglycone is diosgenin and its epimer yamogenin. Also present are furostanol glycosides (trigofoenoside A-G). Small amounts of an alkaloid (trigonelline) and a steroidal peptide (foenugraecin) may contribute to the medicinal properties. The characteristic fenugreek smell is ascribed to 3-hydroxy-4,5-dimethyl-2[5H]-furanone; the bitter taste to the furostanol glycosides.

PHARMACOLOGICAL EFFECTS The saponins could be responsible for the observed anti-diabetic, lipid and cholesterol lowering activities. Also recorded are secretolytic, hyperglycaemic, anti-inflammatory, uterotonic, cardiotonic and mild antiseptic effects.

NOTES Fenugreek might be an industrial source of diosgenin for the production of steroidal hormones.

STATUS Traditional medicine; Pharm.; Comm.E+.

Trigonella foenum-graecum L.   family: Fabaceae

fénugrec (French); *Griechischer Bockshornklee* (German); *fieno-greco* (Italian): *fenugreco* (Spanish)

Tropaeolum majus

nasturtium

Tropaeolum majus (nasturtium)

Rorippa nasturtium-aquaticum (watercress)

DESCRIPTION The nasturtium is a perennial (in frost-free areas) with fleshy stems and distinctive peltate leaves borne on long stalks. The attractive, trumpet-shaped flowers are usually orange or yellow, and have prominent nectar spurs at their bases. The seeds are round and fleshy. A plant with similar secondary metabolites is watercress (now correctly known as *Rorippa nasturtium-aquaticum* but until recently *Nasturtium officinale*). Nasturtium and watercress are both popular salad plants that are also used for medicinal purposes.

ORIGIN Peru (*Tropaeolum*). Nasturtium cultivars are popular garden plants. Watercress is a cosmopolitan weed of wet places.

PARTS USED Fresh or dried leaves (*Tropaeoli herba*). In the case of watercress, the fresh or dried above-ground parts (*Nasturtii herba*).

THERAPEUTIC CATEGORY Antibiotic; diuretic, cholagogue.

USES AND PROPERTIES *Tropaeolum* is used as a natural antibiotic to treat infections of the urinary tract and respiratory tract. It is applied topically against various fungal infections, including candida and as a counter-irritant in case of muscle pain. Fresh water-cress (*Rorippa*) is used in folk medicine as a diuretic and traditional "spring tonic", while the dried herb is extracted for use in commercial cholagogue formulations. It is also used against catarrh of the respiratory tract.

PREPARATION AND DOSAGE In the case of water-cress, about 4-6 g of the dried herb, 20-30 g of the fresh herb and 60-150 g of fresh leaf juice are recommended. Similar quantities are suitable in the case of *Tropaeolum*.

ACTIVE INGREDIENTS *Tropaeolum*: benzyl glucosinolate (=glucotropaeolin) which is hydrolysed by myrosinase to benzyl isothiocyanate (=benzyl mustard oil). *Rorippa*: phenylethyl glucosinolate (=gluconasturtiin) that is converted into phenylethyl isothiocyanate.

PHARMACOLOGICAL EFFECTS Mustard oils are easily resorbed and form covalent bonds with proteins. This plausibly explains their antiviral, antifungal and antibacterial activity. In addition, benzyl mustard oil is an antineoplastic agent but is also a severe irritant.

NOTES Chinese watercress, *Rorippa montana* is used in the same way as *T. majus* and *R. nasturtium-aquaticum* to effectively treat respiratory ailments.

STATUS Traditional medicine; Comm.E+.

Tropaeolum majus L.   family: Tropaeolaceae

capucine grande, cresson d'Inde (French); *Große Kapuzinerkresse* (German); *nasturzio* (Italian)

Turnera diffusa

damiana

Turnera diffusa

DESCRIPTION Damiana is an aromatic shrub of up to 2 m in height, with erect stems bearing simple, toothed leaves. Yellow, solitary flowers are borne at the branch tips.

ORIGIN Tropical America (Caribbean Islands, Mexico and southern California). The shrub is cultivated to a limited extent, but most of the raw material is obtained from wild-harvesting.

PARTS USED Dried leaves (*Damianae folium*).

THERAPEUTIC CATEGORY General tonic, traditional aphrodisiac.

USES AND PROPERTIES Damiana is claimed to be a stimulant and aphrodisiac that is used for the prevention and treatment of sexual disturbances, loss of libido, menstrual problems, impotence and prostate problems. It is considered useful for countering fatigue, overwork, depression and stress. In aromatherapy, the essential oil is considered to be uplifting. In Mexico, an infusion is drunk like ordinary black tea.

PREPARATION AND DOSAGE An infusion of 2-4 g of dried herb is taken three times per day. Extracts and tinctures are also used, and are included as an ingredi-

ent of various urinary formulations, tablets and tonics.

ACTIVE INGREDIENTS The herb is chemically poorly known. It contains a cyanogenic glycoside (tetraphyllin B) and low levels (up to 0.7%) arbutin (a phenolic glycoside – see *Arctostaphylos*). The plant yields an essential oil containing various monoterpenoids and sesquiterpenoids (including α-pinene, β-pinene, calamene, α-copaene, δ-cadinene, thymol and possibly also 1,8-cineole and p-cymene). The presence of unspecified gum, tannins, bitter principles, phytosterols and resins has been reported.

PHARMACOLOGICAL EFFECTS There is no scientific evidence to justify the traditional use of damiana herb as aphrodisiac. Hypoglycaemic and uterotonic effects have been noted. Arbutin is known as a diuretic and urinary tract disinfectant but the levels in damiana are considered too low to be therapeutically significant.

WARNING Excessive use of the herb should be avoided (especially during pregnancy and lactation) as there is no reliable toxicity data.

STATUS Traditional medicine; Pharm.

Turnera diffusa Willd. [=*Damiana diffusa* var. *aphrodisiaca* (L.F. Ward.) Urb.]   family: Turneraceae

damiana (French); *Damiana* (German); *damiana* (Italian)

Tussilago farfara

coltsfoot

Tussilago farfara leaves

Tussilago farfara flower heads

DESCRIPTION Coltsfoot is a small perennial herb with distinctive heart-shaped leaves that are bright green above and silvery below due to a felt-like layer of white hairs. Bright yellow flower heads are produced on scaly stalks in early spring, before the leaves emerge.

ORIGIN Asia, Europe and North Africa. The raw material is wild-harvested in eastern and southeastern Europe.

PARTS USED Mainly the dried leaves (*Farfarae folium*; synon. *Tussilaginis folium*). In former times the dried flower heads, whole herb or roots were also used.

THERAPEUTIC CATEGORY Expectorant, antitussive.

USES AND PROPERTIES The herb has a long history of use as an effective cough medicine and it is still used to treat mouth and throat inflammation, asthma, bronchitis and other respiratory ailments. Coltsfoot is no longer very popular because it contains pyrrolizidine alkaloids (see below). Flower heads and roots are no longer used.

PREPARATION AND DOSAGE A tea may be prepared from 0.6-2.5 g of dried leaves, taken three times per day. Liquid extracts, tinctures and syrups are also used. Leaves and leaf extracts are included in cough teas and commercial cough preparations. Some experts argue that pyrrolizidine alkaloids (PAs) should be completely avoided, while others consider the very low levels not to be harmful, provided the daily intake does not exceed 1 μg alkaloid and that the period of use not exceeds six weeks per year (see *Senecio ovatus*).

ACTIVE INGREDIENTS The cough-relieving effects are usually ascribed to mucilage, that occurs in levels of up to 10% of the dry herb. Also of interest is the presence of a sesquiterpene ester, known as tussilagone. The flower heads and leaves contain 100 μg per g (0.01% dry weight) of pyrrolizidine alkaloids and their N-oxides – mainly senkirkine and tussilagine but also senecionine in some sources of raw material.

PHARMACOLOGICAL EFFECTS Mucilage forms a protective layer over the inflamed mucous membranes of the throat and mouth and thereby counteracts the urge to cough. Animal studies have shown that tussilagone is a respiratory stimulant.

WARNING PAs can be carcinogenic; do not use PA-rich coltsfoot (especially during pregnancy).

STATUS Traditional medicine; Pharm.; Comm.E+ (leaf only).

Tussilago farfara L.   family Asteraceae

pas d'âne, tussilage (French); *Huflattich* (German); *farfaro* (Italian); *farfara* (Spanish)

Ulmus rubra

slippery elm • red elm

Ulmus rubra

DESCRIPTION Slippery elm is a large deciduous tree of up to 20 m in height, with a rounded crown, hairy young twigs, large oblong, pointed leaves and rounded, somewhat hairy fruits of about 20 mm long. The tree was previously known as *U. fulva*.

ORIGIN Central and southern parts of the USA.

PARTS USED The inner bark, which is harvested in spring (*Ulmi fulvae cortex*).

THERAPEUTIC CATEGORY Demulcent, emollient.

USES AND PROPERTIES Slippery elm is highly mucilaginous and is used mainly to treat inflammation and ulceration of the mucous membranes of the mouth, throat, stomach or duodenum. It is considered useful for convalescence (as nutrient supplement) and against colitis, heartburn, gastritis and diarrhoea. Externally it is applied as a poultice to wounds, burns, abscesses, boils and ulcers. Indian women used the drug to ease birth.

PREPARATION AND DOSAGE As a nutritional supplement, 4 g of powdered bark steeped in 500 ml of water is taken three times a day. Powdered bark is boiled in water (ratio 1:8) and 4-16 ml of the decoction can be taken three times daily, or 5 ml of a tincture (1 part bark in 1 part 60% ethanol) three times a day. For topical application, the coarsely ground bark is soaked in boiling water.

ACTIVE INGREDIENTS The mucilage (slime) is the main constituent in the product. It consists of pentose, methylpentose and hexose sugars, together with two polyuronides. When hydrolysed, glucose, galactose, galacturonic acid and rhamnose are released. The product also contains substantial quantities of tannins and phytosterols.

PHARMACOLOGICAL EFFECTS The presence of mucilage justifies the use of slippery elm for its demulcent and antitussive effects. Mucilage forms a soothing and protective layer over inflamed mucous membranes. Tannins are known to be astringent and antimicrobial, so they can help to detoxify the gastrointestinal tract and act as an antiseptic in wound treatment by killing harmful bacteria.

NOTES A number of European species, such as White elm, *Ulmus laevis*, common elm, *U. carpinifolius* and Scots elm, *U.glabra* have been used for similar indications in traditional medicine.

STATUS Traditional medicine; Pharm.

Ulmus rubra Muhl. (=*U. fulva* Michx.)   family: Ulmaceae

Rotulme (German)

Uncaria tomentosa

cat's claw

Uncaria tomentosa flower heads

Uncaria tomentosa leaves and thorns

Uncaria tomentosa young plant

DESCRIPTION A woody and thorny creeper (vine) up to 60 m long with modified flowering stalks acting as tendrils, simple leaves in opposite pairs and cream-coloured flowers in rounded clusters. The vernacular name is derived from the claw-like thorns; but there are numerous unrelated plants that are also known in Latin America as *uña de gato* or cat's claw.

ORIGIN Tropical South and Central America. The plant is predominantly wild-harvested.

PARTS USED Root (*Uncariae tomentosae radix*) or stem bark (*Uncariae tomentosae cortex*).

THERAPEUTIC CATEGORY Immune regulant.

USES AND PROPERTIES Used for diverse indications, including AIDS, cancer, herpes, chronic fatigue syndrome, asthma, diabetes, circulatory problems and arthritis. It appears to be an adaptogenic tonic, as it is claimed to be immune modulating, anti-inflammatory, antimutagenic, anti-carcinogenic, antiviral and antioxidant.

PREPARATION AND DOSAGE The recommended daily dose is 2-6 g (for tea) or preparations of 20–60 mg standardized extracts (1:10).

ACTIVE INGREDIENTS Several monoterpene indole alkaloids and triterpene saponins derived from quinovic acid are present. The plant occurs in two chemotypes, one containing mainly pentacyclic oxindoles (e.g. pteropodine, isopteropodine, isomitraphylline), while the other has predominantly tetracyclic oxindoles, such as rhynchophylline and isorhynchophylline.

PHARMACOLOGICAL EFFECTS *In vitro* studies have indicated immune modulating, anti-inflammatory, antimutagenic, antitumour, antiviral and antioxidant effects, but clinical trials are needed to substantiate the claims that *U. tomentosa* is effective against serious health conditions. One double-blinded trial with a standardized extract (absence of tetracyclics) of the root of the pentacyclic chemotype has demonstrated clinical relief in patients with rheumatoid arthritis.

NOTES *U. guianensis* is the second South American *Uncaria*, not closely related to *U. tomentosa* – it has reddish flowers, more prominently curved thorns and contains a considerably lower content of oxindole alkaloids. In China, the stems and thorns of *U. rhynchophylla* (*gou teng*) are a traditional sedative and antispasmodic. Also used are *U. acida, U. bernaysii, U. elliptica, U. gambir, U. hirsuta, U. lanosa* and *U. sinensis*.

STATUS Traditional medicine.

Uncaria tomentosa DC.   family: Rubiaceae

Katzenkralle (German); *uña de gato* (Spanish)

Urginea maritima

sea squill • sea onion

Urginea maritima

Urginea maritima flowers

Urginea maritima plants

DESCRIPTION A bulbous perennial with a basal rosette of leaves and a tall flowering stalk of up to 1 m or more in height, with numerous small white flowers along the top. The onion-like bulbs can weigh several kilograms and are white in colour. The plant is also known as *Scilla maritima* or *Drimia maritima* and is considered to represent a complex of several closely related species that occur in the Mediterranean region. For commercial extraction, *U. indica* can be used as a substitute. Species with red bulbs are traditionally used as rat poisons.

ORIGIN True *U. maritima* occurs only on the Iberian peninsula, while other species of the complex are found in other parts of the Mediterranean region. *U. indica* is an Indian and African plant.

PARTS USED The sliced and dried fleshy inner bulb scales (*Scillae bulbus*).

THERAPEUTIC CATEGORY Heart tonic, diuretic, expectorant.

USES AND PROPERTIES Squill is considered to be a safe heart tonic (NYHA I and II) and diuretic. It has been traditionally used as an expectorant in cough mixtures, also for chronic bronchitis (especially of a type with unproductive cough), asthmatic bronchitis and whooping cough. Externally it is employed to disinfect wounds.

PREPARATION AND DOSAGE Standardised powder containing 0.15-2% cardiac glycosides is used in average daily doses of 0.1-0.5 g. The main glycoside is administered orally at an initial dose of 1.5-2.5 mg per day and thereafter 1-2 mg per day.

ACTIVE INGREDIENTS *Urginea* species contain cardiac glycosides of the bufadienolide type (1.8%), as well as unusual flavonoids. The main glycosides in true squill are glucoscillaren A and scillaren A, together with the 11β-hydroxylated derivatives scillaphaeoside and glucoscillaphaeoside. Scillaren A may lose, through enzymatic hydrolysis, one glucose molecule to yield proscillaridin A. *U. indica* has similar compounds but lacks glucoscillaren A.

PHARMACOLOGICAL EFFECTS Bufadienolides exhibit positive inotropic and weakly negative chronotropic heart activity. They also have expectorant, diuretic and emetic activities. Vomiting is stimulated mainly by gastric irritation.

WARNING Squill powder or extracts are poisonous and should only be used under professional supervision.

STATUS Traditional medicine; Pharm.; Comm.E+.

Urginea maritima (L.) Baker [=*Drimia maritima* (L.) Stearn]   family: Hyacinthaceae
scille maritime (French); *Meerzwiebel* (German); *cipolla marina, squilla* (Italian)

Urtica dioica

stinging nettle

Urtica dioica

Urtica urens

DESCRIPTION Perennial stinging nettle (*U. dioica*) is an erect herb (up to 1.5 m) with drooping, somewhat greyish leaves. The slender flower clusters are longer than the leaf stalks in both male and female plants. Annual stinging nettle (*U. urens*) is smaller, with bright green leaves and flower clusters that are shorter than the leaf stalks.

ORIGIN Europe and Asia (*U. dioica*), entire northern hemisphere (*U. urens*). Both have become weeds in many countries.

PARTS USED Of both species, the aboveground parts or leaves (*Urticae herba, -folium*) or roots (*Urticae radix*).

THERAPEUTIC CATEGORY Antirheumatic (herb and leaf); urological (roots).

USES AND PROPERTIES Leaves and roots are used in supportive treatment of rheumatic complaints, and to a lesser extent inflammation of the urinary tract and the prevention and treatment of kidney gravel. Dried roots or root extracts are used to treat the symptoms of an enlarged prostate. The leaves are rich in minerals and vitamins and have been used as a nutritional supplement.

PREPARATION AND DOSAGE Daily doses of 8-12 g (leaf) and 4-6 g (roots) are recommended.

ACTIVE INGREDIENTS Nettle leaf contains minerals, (especially silicic acid; up to 5%), amines (histamine, acetylcholine, serotonin), flavonol glycosides, phenolic acids, scopoletin, β-sitosterol and tannins. Roots contain polysaccharides, a lectin (UDA), several phenolics (including lignans, coumarins) and sterols, including β-sitosterol, 7α- and 7β-hydroxysitosterol and their glycosides. The stinging hairs act like miniature syringes and inject histamine and acetylcholine, causing extreme irritation.

PHARMACOLOGICAL EFFECTS Leaves show a mild diuretic, analgesic, and anti-inflammatory action (the dose of non-steroidal anti-inflammatory drugs in the treatment of arthritis can be reduced, if *Urtica* is taken concomitantly – phenolic compounds are responsible for this activity). Nettle roots interact with testosterone-binding proteins, 5α-reductase and aromatase. Nettle lectins appear to be an immune stimulant. Controlled clinical studies support efficacy for the treatment of benign prostate hypertrophy and the traditional diuretic and anti-inflammatory uses in treating arthritis.

STATUS Traditional medicine; Pharm.; Comm.E+; ESCOP 2 (radix), 4 (*folium/herba*); WHO 2 (radix); clinical studies+.

Urtica dioica L.   family: Urticaceae

ortie brulante (French); *Große Brennessel* (German); *ortica maschio* (Italian); *ortiga mayor* (Spanish)

Vaccinium myrtillus
bilberry • blueberry

Vaccinium myrtillus plant

Vaccinium myrtillus fruit

Vaccinium vitis-idaea

DESCRIPTION Bilberry is a common shrublet (up to 0.8 m) with small toothed leaves, white, bell-shaped flowers and purplish blue berries (8 mm diameter).

ORIGIN Cold temperate parts of the northern hemisphere (common in Europe, but also in Asia and North America). Berries and leaves are wild-harvested.

PARTS USED Dried, ripe berries (*Myrtilli fructus*) and to a lesser extent the leaves (*Myrtilli folium*).

THERAPEUTIC CATEGORY Anti-diarrhoeal.

USES AND PROPERTIES Fruits and fruit extracts are recommended for treating diarrhoea, especially in children. They are used locally to treat inflammation of the mucous membranes of the mouth and throat. Traditional uses include improvement of the cardiovascular system and vision. Leaves are traditionally used against diabetes, arthritis, gout, poor circulation, and complaints of the digestive system, kidneys and urinary tract and externally against mucosal inflammations, dermatitis, haemorrhoids and other skin conditions.

PREPARATION AND DOSAGE A daily dose of 20-60 g of dried berries is recommended. The leaves are no longer recommended because prolonged use seemed to have toxic side effects.

ACTIVE INGREDIENTS The main active ingredients are mostly catechol tannins (up to 12%) and proanthocyanidins. Also present are anthocyanins, flavonoids, iridoids glycosides (asperuloside, monotropein) and phenolic acids. Similar compounds are present in the leaves. Aerial parts contain a simple bicyclic quinolizidine alkaloid, epimyrtine. Arbutin and other hydroquinones (see *Arctostaphylos*) are more or less absent.

PHARMACOLOGICAL EFFECTS The drug reduces the levels of blood lipids and glucose; it has antimicrobial, antiviral, anti-exudative and anti-ulcer activity, improves the permeability of capillaries and wound-healing and inhibits platelet aggregation. These properties can be partly explained by the secondary metabolites present; clinical studies are needed to substantiate the claims.

NOTES Bog bilberry (*V. uliginosum*) has similar phytochemicals and is used like bilberry. Cowberry (*V. vitis-idaea*) is rich in tannins, proanthocyanins and arbutin. Leaves are a traditional antiseptic diuretic (see *Arctostaphylos*) used to treat infections of the urinary tract.

STATUS Traditional medicine; Pharm.; Comm.E+ (fruit only).

Vaccinium myrtillus L.
family: Ericaceae

airelle myrtille (French); *Heidelbeere, Blaubeere* (Germany); *mirtillo* (Italian); *arandano commun* (Spanish)

Vaccinium oxycoccos
European cranberry • small cranberry

Vaccinium oxycoccos leaves

Vaccinium oxycoccos flowers and fruit

DESCRIPTION Small cranberry is a creeping and mat-forming evergreen perennial of boggy habitats with slender and sparse branches bearing attractive pink flowers and bright red, edible berries of up to 13 mm in diameter. Large cranberry (*V. macrocarpon*) differs in the broader, green (not red) bracts below the flower, the rounded (not pointed) leaf tips and the larger (10-25 mm) berries.

ORIGIN *V. oxycoccos* is widely distributed in all parts of the northern hemisphere, while *V. macrocarpon* is indigenous to North America, where it co-occurs with small cranberry. Cranberry has become the basis of an important industry in North America.

PARTS USED Ripe fruit, fruit extract or fruit juice.

THERAPEUTIC CATEGORY Urinary tract infections.

USES AND PROPERTIES Cranberry juice is recommended for the prevention and treatment of urinary tract infections (including cystitis) and kidney disorders. It is rich in vitamin C and has been used against scurvy.

PREPARATION AND DOSAGE One litre of juice per day is suggested as an appropriate dose, or the equivalent thereof in the form of an extract in capsules.

ACTIVE INGREDIENTS The fruits are rich in organic acids (30%), including quinic, malic, citric, and hippuric acid, anthocyanins and vitamin C.

PHARMACOLOGICAL EFFECTS It had been formerly assumed that cranberry juice makes the urine acidic and that bacteria are unable to flourish in a low pH environment. This assumption has subsequently been disproved. Presently it is assumed that cranberry contains substances which prevent the adhesion of *E. coli* to bladder wall linings. If *E. coli* cannot adhere, there is no infection. Controlled clinical studies have demonstrated the efficacy of cranberry to treat bladder infections.

NOTES In the USA, several members of the Ericaceae family with edible berries are known as cranberry, not only *V. oxycoccus* (small cranberry) but also *V. macrocarpon* (large or common cranberry) and *Arctostaphylos uva-ursi* (upland cranberry). The latter is another herb that is used to treat urinary infections (see *Arctostaphylos*). Leaves and fruit of the strawberry tree (*Arbutus unedo*, Ericaceae) have been similarly used in Europe.

STATUS Traditional medicine; clinical studies+.

Vaccinium oxycoccos L.   family: Ericaceae
canneberge (French); *Gewöhnliche Moosbeere* (German); *mirtillo palustre* (Italian)

Valeriana officinalis

valerian • common valerian

Valeriana officinalis flowers

Valeriana officinalis

Dried roots

DESCRIPTION Valerian represents a species complex; it is an erect perennial herb with creeping, aromatically smelly rhizomes, somewhat fleshy roots, hollow stems, compound leaves and small white or pinkish flowers arranged in flat-topped terminal clusters.

ORIGIN Europe and Asia (naturalised in North America); cultivated in several European countries, in Japan and the USA.

PARTS USED Rhizomes and roots (*Valerianae radix*).

THERAPEUTIC CATEGORY Sedative (tranquilliser).

USES AND PROPERTIES One of the most important herbal sedatives and incorporated into numerous products. It is a non-addictive tranquilliser that is specifically recommended against restlessness, sleeplessness, minor nervous conditions, the symptoms of menopause and the anxiety associated with premenstrual syndrome. Traditional uses include the supportive treatment of gastrointestinal pain and spastic colitis.

PREPARATION AND DOSAGE A daily dose of 10 g of dried root can be used, in doses of 2-3 g, taken one to five times per day. For external use, 100 g in a full bath is recommended.

ACTIVE INGREDIENTS The drug contains volatile oil (usually less than 1%), with bornyl acetate as the main constituent, together with β-caryophyllene, valeranone, valerenal, bornyl isovalerate and valerenic acid. Valepotriates (unusual iridoid derivatives) are present in carefully dried root at levels of 0.5-2% (mainly valtrate and acevaltrate, with smaller amounts of other valepotriates). Three cyclopentane sesquiterpenoids (valerenic acid, acetoxyvalerenic acid and valerenal) are characteristic of *V. officinalis* and do not occur in other species.

PHARMACOLOGICAL EFFECTS Experiments show that aqueous and alcoholic extracts interact mainly with the $GABA_A$- and benzodiazepine receptors. Valepotriates (mainly valtrate or dihydrovaltrate) are spasmolytic. Clinical studies imply that valerian is effective in easing sleep disturbances and minor nervous conditions if taken over a period of several weeks.

NOTES Other valerians with sedative activities include *V. edulis* (=*V. mexicana*), *V. fauriei* and *V. jatamansi* (=*V. wallichii*).

WARNING Valepotriates are potential mutagens (tea is therefore more safe than alcoholic extracts).

STATUS Traditional medicine; Pharm.; Comm.E+; ESCOP 4; WHO 1; clinical studies+.

Valeriana officinalis L.

family: Valerianaceae or Caprifoliaceae

valériane officinale (French); *Gemeiner Baldrian, Arzneibaldrian* (German); *valeriana* (Italian)

Verbascum phlomoides

mullein • orange mullein

Verbascum phlomoides

Verbascum phlomoides flowers

DESCRIPTION Mullein is a leafy biennial herb with a robust rosette of woolly leaves. A *branched* panicle with erect spikes (up to 2 m), densely packed with yellow flowers, develops in the second year of growth. Mostly used are orange mullein, *V. phlomoides* and large-flowered mullein, *V. densiflorum* (= *V. thapsiforme*). They are distinguished mainly by the size of the flowers and the hairiness of the stamens. A third species, great mullein (*V. thapsus*), is sometimes not distinguished from *V. phlomoides* and is also an acceptable source of raw material.

ORIGIN Central, eastern and southern Europe, Asia Minor and North Africa (*V. phlomoides* and *V. densiflorum*); commercially grown in Egypt and eastern Europe.

PARTS USED Dried flower petals, including the corolla and stamens (*Verbasci flos*), rarely the leaves (*Verbasci folium*).

THERAPEUTIC CATEGORY Respiratory catarrh, diuretic.

USES AND PROPERTIES *Verbasci flos* are mainly used to treat catarrh of the respiratory tract. The drug shows demulcent and secretolytic properties. It is therefore widely used to treat coughs, influenza and bronchitis and is included in herbal tea mixtures. The herb is also considered to be diaphoretic and diuretic, and is used externally to treat wounds and other skin disorders. Dried leaves are used in a similar way.

PREPARATION AND DOSAGE A daily dose of 3-4 g is recommended, taken as a tea (1 g in 150 ml boiling water). Extracts are included in soothing syrups and also in ointments and oils to treat earache, haemorrhoids, sores and boils.

ACTIVE INGREDIENTS Triterpene saponins, including verbascosaponin are present, together with about 3% mucilage (after hydrolysis it yields mainly galactose, arabinose and uronic acids). Other main components are iridoid glycosides (aucubin, catalpol and related compounds), flavonoids (up to 4%, mainly rutin and hesperidin) and various phenolic acids.

PHARMACOLOGICAL EFFECTS The saponins are secretolytic and expectorant, the mucilage demulcent, the flavonoids thought to be weakly diuretic and the iridoid glycosides anti-inflammatory. Antiviral effects have also been demonstrated, but clinical studies are needed to confirm the traditional indications.

STATUS Traditional medicine; Pharm.; Comm.E+ (flowers only).

Verbascum phlomoides L.   family: Scrophulariaceae

molène faux-phlomis (French); *Filz-Königskerze* (German); *barbarasco* (Italian)

Verbena officinalis

vervain

Verbena officinalis

Verbena officinalis flowers

DESCRIPTION Vervain is a weedy perennial herb of up to 1 m in height, with angular stems, widely spaced, unevenly dissected leaves in opposite pairs, and slender, sparsely flowered spikes of small lilac flowers.

ORIGIN Probably Mediterranean; today widely distributed in Europe, Asia, North Africa and North America. It is wild-harvested in southeastern Europe.

PARTS USED Whole herb (aboveground parts, collected while flowering), known as verbena herb (*Verbenae herba*).

THERAPEUTIC CATEGORY Diuretic, expectorant, bitter tonic.

USES AND PROPERTIES A bitter tonic, diuretic and demulcent to treat various skin disorders and slow healing wounds. It is still used to some extent against kidney and bladder complaints and rheumatism, and for stimulating milk flow during breastfeeding. Numerous traditional uses have been recorded, including the treatment of fever, cough, sore throat, asthma, pain, liver problems and other metabolic disorders. The fresh, flowering herb is used in homoeopathy to treat mental exhaustion and epilepsy.

PREPARATION AND DOSAGE An infusion of 1.5 g of the herb in 150 ml water is taken three times per day, or 5-10 g in 1 litre water for topical use.

ACTIVE INGREDIENTS The main active principles appear to be iridoid glycosides such as verbenalin, verbenin and hastatoside, that occur at levels of up to 0.5% of dry weight. Caffeic acid derivatives, such as verbascoside (0.8%), are present.

PHARMACOLOGICAL EFFECTS Extracts show antimicrobial, antiviral, immune stimulant, cytotoxic, diuretic, antitussive, secretolytic and anti-inflammatory effects. Iridoid glycosides and the verbascoside or more likely the metabolites formed in the body could be, at least partly, responsible for the observed effects. The emetic iridoids could exert their secretolytic properties in a reflectory way (in the same way as saponins). The bitter taste and tonic (*amarum*) use in stimulating digestion, are ascribed to the iridoids. Clinical studies are needed to demonstrate the efficacy of the traditional indications.

NOTES American vervain, *V. hastata* is also rich in iridoid glycosides and has been used in traditional medicine to treat colds and catarrhs of the respiratory tract.

STATUS Traditional medicine; Pharm.; Comm.E+.

Verbena officinalis L.   family: Verbenaceae

ma bian cao (Chinese); *verveine officinelle* (French); *Eisenkraut* (German); *verbena commune* (Italian); *verbena medicinal* (Spanish)

Veronica officinalis

speedwell • veronica

Veronica officinalis

Veronica officinalis plants

Veronicastrum virginicum

DESCRIPTION Speedwell is a spreading perennial herb of up to 0.2 m in height with small, hairy leaves borne in opposite pairs on rounded (non-angular) stems, and erect clusters of pale blue flowers.

ORIGIN Europe, western Asia and North America; it is wild-harvested mainly in eastern Europe.

PARTS USED Dried aboveground parts, known as speedwell herb or veronica herb (*Veronicae herba*).

THERAPEUTIC CATEGORY Traditional expectorant, general tonic.

USES AND PROPERTIES Speedwell is a traditional medicinal plant that is not much used in modern phytotherapy except occasionally as an expectorant in cases of catarrhs of the respiratory tract, in cases of dyspepsia, biliary complaints, as gargle to treat inflammation of the mucous membranes of the mouth and throat, as topical application to promote wound-healing, to relieve skin itching and to counter perspiration of the feet. It has been used in folk medicine as an expectorant, antiarthritic, appetite stimulant, tonic, diaphoretic, and many more. The fresh and dried herb is popular in homoeopathy.

PREPARATION AND DOSAGE A dose of 1.5 g in 150 ml water may be taken two or three times per day. For topical use, an infusion or decoction of 10-20 g of the herb in a litre of water can be prepared.

ACTIVE INGREDIENTS Small amounts (up to 1%) of iridoid glycosides (aucubin, catalpol, esters of catalpol, such as veronicoside and verproside, ladroside), flavonoids (luteolin glycosides), organic acids (chlorogenic acid, caffeic acid), tannins, triterpenoids and β-sitosterol have been found in the plant.

PHARMACOLOGICAL EFFECTS Experimental data suggest ulcus-protective activities. Iridoid glycosides of other drugs have shown antimicrobial, anti-inflammatory and secretolytic effects, that would explain part of the traditional indications. Detailed clinical studies are required to substantiate the indications of speedwell herb.

NOTES The related *Veronicastrum virginicum* (black root or Culver's root) is a traditional North American Indian medicine. The rhizome is a strong purgative and emetic, and has been used to treat chronic constipation, liver complaints and gall bladder inflammation. The pharmacology and chemistry are poorly known.

STATUS Traditional medicine.

Veronica officinalis L.   family: Scrophulariaceae

véronique officinale (French); *Echter Ehrenpreis, Wald-Ehrenpreis* (German); *veronica* (Italian)

Viburnum prunifolium

black haw • American sloe

Viburnum prunifolium

Viburnum opulus (wild form)

DESCRIPTION Black haw is a woody, deciduous shrub of up to 4 m in height, with lobed leaves, clusters of small, white flowers and black berries. It is closely related to the guelder rose or crampbark (*V. opulus*). The latter is a deciduous shrub with lobed leaves, attractive rounded (globose) clusters of white flowers and bright red berries.

ORIGIN Central and eastern parts of the USA (*V. prunifolium*); Europe, Asia and the Mediterranean region (*V. opulus*). Both species are commonly cultivated as ornamental garden shrubs.

PARTS USED Stem bark (black haw bark – *Viburni prunifolii cortex*). The bark of *V. opulus* (*Viburni opuli cortex*) is also used to some extent.

THERAPEUTIC CATEGORY Spasmolytic.

USES AND PROPERTIES Black haw bark is specifically used to treat menstrual cramps, uterine pain and menstrual disorders. In folk medicine it is also used against morning sickness and the symptoms of menopause. The closely related crampbark (*V. opulus*) appears to be less specific in its actions but it has been considered in former times as a remedy for menstrual disorders and to prevent a miscarriage. It is traditionally used (both inter- nally and topically) to relieve stomach cramps, colic, muscle spasms and high blood pressure.

PREPARATION AND DOSAGE About 1 g of finely chopped bark of black haw is taken two or three times a day as an infusion.

ACTIVE INGREDIENTS Numerous chemical com- pounds are known from black haw bark, including amentoflavone and other flavonoids, triterpenoids (α- and β-amyrin, oleanolic acid, ursolic acid and deriva- tives), coumarins (aesculin, scopoletin, scopolin), or- ganic acids (chlorogenic acid, isochlorogenic acid and salicylic acid), a phenol glucoside (arbutin) and sito- sterols. Arbutin and four iridoid glycoside esters have been isolated from *V. opulus* leaves; the bark com- pounds are similar to those of *V. prunifolium*.

PHARMACOLOGICAL EFFECTS Aesculetin and scopoletin are known to be active as musculotropic spasmolytics, but the active ingredient responsible for the spasmolytic effects on the uterus is not yet known.

NOTES Black haw bark and crampbark are rarely employed in modern phytomedicine. They should preferably be used only under professional supervision.

STATUS Traditional medicine; Pharm.

Viburnum prunifolium L.   family: Caprifoliaceae

viorne à feuilles de prunier (French); *Amerikanischer Schneeball* (German); *viburno prunifolio* (Italian)

Vinca minor

periwinkle • common periwinkle • lesser periwinkle

Vinca minor flowers

Vinca minor leaves

Vinca major

DESCRIPTION The common periwinkle is a small herbaceous perennial that spreads with trailing branches. It has shiny, opposite leaves and attractive blue flowers. Greater periwinkle (*V. major*) is very similar but has larger flowers.

ORIGIN Europe (often in the vicinity of castles and old human settlements); commonly cultivated as an ornamental plant.

PARTS USED Leaves or aboveground parts (*Vincae minoris folium*); today mainly the isolated vincamine.

THERAPEUTIC CATEGORY Cerebral circulatory stimulant.

USES AND PROPERTIES Periwinkle is no longer used to any extent as a traditional remedy, but is of more interest as a source material to extract pure alkaloids. The main alkaloid, vincamine, can be used to treat cerebral senility (dizziness, memory loss and other symptoms of old age) and several other cerebrovascular disorders.

PREPARATION AND DOSAGE Due to potential side effects (leukocytopaenia, lymphocytopenia), the herb itself is rarely used. Vincamine is given orally (as a prescription medicine) at a level of 40-60 mg per day.

ACTIVE INGREDIENTS The plant contains about thirty monoterpene indole alkaloids at a level of up to 1% of dry weight (wild plants), or up to 4% (in cultivation). Vincamine is the major constituent and represents about 10% of the total alkaloids. A bitter principle, vincine, is also present, together with phenolic compounds.

PHARMACOLOGICAL EFFECTS Extracts showed hypotensive, spasmolytic, hypoglycaemic, immune-stimulant, cytotoxic, and analgesic properties. Animal and human studies have shown that vincamine reduces the blood pressure, and increases blood flow to the brain and thus the oxygen and glucose supply.

NOTES Vincamine has a low bioavailability, so that slow-release formulations have been developed. The alkaloid is nowadays largely produced through semisynthesis from tabersonine, an alkaloid extracted from the seeds of the tropical African *Voacanga africana* and *V. thouarsii*. The term "vinca alkaloids" usually refers to the alkaloids obtained from Madagascar periwinkle (*Catharanthus roseus*, previously known as *Vinca rosea*).

WARNING Periwinkle or its extracts are not recommended for medicinal use in most countries.

STATUS Traditional and modern medicine: vincamine.

Vinca minor L.   family: Apocynaceae

petite pervenche (French); Kleines Immergrün (German); *pervinca minore* (Italian); *vincapervinca menor* (Spanish)

Viola tricolor

wild pansy • heartsease

Viola tricolor (cultivated form)

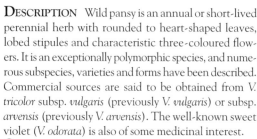

Viola tricolor (wild form)

Viola odorata

DESCRIPTION Wild pansy is an annual or short-lived perennial herb with rounded to heart-shaped leaves, lobed stipules and characteristic three-coloured flowers. It is an exceptionally polymorphic species, and numerous subspecies, varieties and forms have been described. Commercial sources are said to be obtained from *V. tricolor* subsp. *vulgaris* (previously *V. vulgaris*) or subsp. *arvensis* (previously *V. arvensis*). The well-known sweet violet (*V. odorata*) is also of some medicinal interest.

ORIGIN Europe and Asia. The plant is wild-harvested in the flowering period and is also cultivated.

PARTS USED Dried aboveground parts (*Violae tricoloris herba*).

THERAPEUTIC CATEGORY Supportive treatment of various skin conditions.

USES AND PROPERTIES Nowadays, the main use of the herb is to treat eczema, impetigo, pruritis and acne. Traditionally, it is an expectorant, diuretic and anti-inflammatory. It is gargled against throat infections and is sometimes used as antitussive, cholagogue, antirheumatic and tonic.

PREPARATION AND DOSAGE A tea can be made with 1.5 g of the dried product in 150 ml of water, taken up to three times per day. Poultices of fresh herb or a decoction of 4 g dry herb in 150 ml water can be prepared for external use.

ACTIVE INGREDIENTS The drug contains methylsalicylic acid and violutoside (the glucosidoarabinoside of salicylic acid methyl ester), numerous flavonoids (including rutin, violanthin, scoparin, vicenin 2, and C-glycosides of vitexin, saponaretin, orientin and iso-orientin), anthocyanins, violaxanthin and derivatives, and coumarins (umbelliferone). Also of interest are mucilage (about 10%), tannins and 5% triterpene saponins with ursolic acid as an aglycone. *Viola odorata* (sweet violet) contains mucilage, flavonoids and saponins, and has been used as expectorant and as ingredient of skin creams.

PHARMACOLOGICAL EFFECTS The triterpenes, flavonoids and methylsalicylates exhibit anti-inflammatory and secretolytic effects. These substances would plausibly explain the use of *Viola tricolor* as an expectorant and antiphlogistic remedy to treat catarrhs and skin inflammations. Clinical studies are needed to confirm the efficacy of the treatments.

STATUS Traditional medicine; Comm.E+ (external use).

Viola tricolor L.   family: Violaceae

pensée sauvage (French); *Feldstiefmütterchen* (German); *viola del pensiero* (Italian)

Viscum album

mistletoe • European mistletoe

Viscum album

Viscum album leaves and berries

DESCRIPTION Mistletoe is a semi-parasitic, woody shrub that grows on trees. It has leathery, yellowish green leaves, inconspicuous flowers and spherical, white, sticky berries. Three subspecies are recognised: one grows only on broadleaf trees, one mainly on pines and larches (*Pinus* and *Larix*) and one only on fir (*Abies*).

ORIGIN Europe and Asia. The product is wild-harvested.

PARTS USED The fresh or dried herb (*Visci herba*) or leaves only (*Visci folium*), mainly to make proprietary products for injection.

THERAPEUTIC CATEGORY Cytostatic, non-specific immune stimulation (by injection only).

USES AND PROPERTIES Supportive treatment of cancer, degenerative inflammation, high blood pressure, poor circulation (as heart tonic), and as sedative. *Viscum* tea is traditionally used to treat high blood pressure.

PREPARATION AND DOSAGE Proprietary products and isolated constituents are injected. For supportive treatment of high blood pressure, 2.5 g of the dried herb is soaked in 150 ml cold water for 10-12 hours. It can be slightly heated before drinking (one or two cups per day).

ACTIVE INGREDIENTS A clear distinction should be made between compounds that are active when injected, or active when taken by mouth (they may not be absorbed). The plant is rich in lectins (0.1%) (glycoproteins that can bind to specific sugar motives; mistle lectin I-III; =Ml I-III), each of which comprises numerous isolectins. Of special interest are up to 0.1% viscotoxins, polypeptides (viscotoxins A, B, P) composed of 46 amino acids. Also present are mucilage, polysaccharides, phenylpropanes, caffeic acid derivatives and flavonoids. Secondary metabolites of the host plant can influence the pharmacological activity of the drug.

PHARMACOLOGICAL EFFECTS When injected at low concentrations, mistletoe preparations (especially the lectins and viscotoxins) show immune-stimulating effects; at higher concentrations the cytoxic and anti-tumour activities predominate. Some clinical studies showed significant benefits in the treatment of malignant metastasic tumours. The value of oral use (hypotensive effects) have yet to be convincingly demonstrated.

NOTES *Viscum capense* is a traditional tonic tea.

WARNING Mistletoe is not suitable for self-medication.

STATUS Pharm.; Comm.E+; source of extracts for injection; clinical studies +.

Viscum album L.   family: Viscaceae

gui blanc (French); *Mistel* (German); *vischio* (Italian); *muérdago* (Spanish)

Vitex agnus-castus

chaste tree

Vitex agnus-castus leaves

Vitex agnus-castus

Vitex agnus-castus flowers and fruit

DESCRIPTION A shrub or small tree of up to 5 m in height. Characteristic are the hairy, compound leaves, with up to nine oblong leaflets radiating from the leaf stalk, the oblong clusters of lilac to blue (rarely white) flowers and the small, hard, four-seeded berries.

ORIGIN Southern Europe and Asia (mainly Mediterranean region). It is grown as a garden ornamental and has become naturalised in tropical regions.

PARTS USED Ripe, dried fruits (chaste tree fruit – *Agni casti fructus*).

THERAPEUTIC CATEGORY Gynaecological.

USES AND PROPERTIES Fruits or fruit extracts are used for a variety of menstrual disorders, including premenstrual syndrome, dysmenorrhoea, *corpus luteum* deficiency, as well as menopausal problems and mastodynia. Since ancient times, the chaste tree has been considered a symbol of chastity. The fruits are traditionally used as anaphrodisiacs and were called "monk's pepper" because they were considered to be helpful to medieval monks in keeping their vow of celibacy. The fruits are used in homoeopathy in preparations to treat impotence, depression and hypogalactia (inadequate milk secretion).

PREPARATION AND DOSAGE Treatment is given in the form of dry extracts or liquids (infusions or tinctures). The recommended dose varies from extracts corresponding to 30-40 mg of dry fruit, as recommended by the German Commission E, to up to 3 g of crushed fruits (or equivalent preparations) per day.

ACTIVE INGREDIENTS The fruits contain essential oil, iridoid glycosides (agnuside and aucubin), flavones and flavonoids (casticin, penduletin, chrysospenol-D), diterpenoids (vitexilactone, rotundifurane) and low yields (about 1.2%) of essential oil containing 1,8-cineole, limonene and pinene.

PHARMACOLOGICAL EFFECTS The beneficial effects are ascribed to diterpenes in the fruit which has a dopaminergic action in the pituitary gland, resulting in the inhibition of prolactin secretion. Animal and controlled clinical studies provide scientific support for activity of the drug in treating gynaecological disorders (including premenstrual syndrome, dysmenorrhoea, and *corpus luteum* deficiency).

STATUS Traditional medicine; Comm.E+; clinical studies+.

Vitex agnus-castus L.   family: Verbenaceae

gattilier agneau-chaste (French); *Keuschlamm, Mönchspfeffer* (German); *agnocasto* (Italian)

Vitis vinifera

grape vine

Vitis vinifera flowers

Vitis vinifera fruit (berries)

Grape vines

DESCRIPTION The grape vine is a woody climber with large, lobed leaves, coiled climbing tendrils, inconspicuous flowers and bunches of red or green berries.

ORIGIN The cultivated form is thought to be Mediterranean in origin, from where it was introduced to practically all temperate regions of the world.

PARTS USED Seeds (for extracts), very rarely the leaves.

THERAPEUTIC CATEGORY Antioxidant.

USES AND PROPERTIES Grape seed is an important commercial source of so-called botanical antioxidants (free-radical scavengers), that are taken to help the body resist diseases. Red grape leaves have been used to some extent in traditional medicine to treat diarrhoea, improve circulation and to help control bleeding. Wine, especially red wine, is considered to be healthy if taken in moderation.

PREPARATION AND DOSAGE Grape seed oil is used in relatively large doses. The extract is concentrated and standardised to contain 80-85% procyanidins. About 50-100 mg of such extracts (or equivalent quantities) are recommended as an effective daily dose.

ACTIVE INGREDIENTS The active ingredients in grape seed oil are nonhydrolysable or condensed tannins, better known by numerous other names (procyanidins, proanthocyanidins, leucoanthocyanidins, polyphenols or pycnogenols). Also of importance are the anthocyanins (mainly 3-glycosides of cyanidin and peonidin), organic acids, tannins and other phenolic compounds in red grapes and red wine.

PHARMACOLOGICAL EFFECTS Oligomeric proanthocyanidins (OPC) are antioxidants, free-radical scavengers and antimutagenics . Because of a large number of phenolic hydroxyl groups OPC can form multiple hydrogen bonds with proteins. OPC inhibit lipid peroxidase, the angiotensin converting enzyme and specifically collagenase and other enzymes associated with capillary fragility. OPC are therefore useful as venotonics. Resveratrol and other phenolics are considered to be the beneficial (anti-arteriosclerotic) ingredients of red wine. Few clinical studies on OPC have focused on specific diseases (but see *Crataegus*).

NOTES Other commercial sources of OPC include green tea (see *Camellia*), maritime pine bark (*Pinus pinaster*) and *Crataegus*.

STATUS Traditional medicine.

Vitis vinifera L.   family: Vitaceae
vigne (French); *Weinrebe* (German); *vite* (Italian)

Warburgia salutaris

pepperbark tree

Warburgia salutaris tree

Warburgia salutaris leaves and flowers

Warburgia salutaris bark

DESCRIPTION Pepperbark is a medium-sized tree of about 10 m in height, with a rough, mottled bark which is reddish on the inner side. The leaves are oblong, glossy green above and paler below. Small, greenish yellow flowers are produced between the leaves on the stem, followed by round, green fruits with several flat seeds inside.

ORIGIN Eastern and southern Africa. In nature, trees have been heavily exploited for their bark. Pepperbark is now cultivated on a small scale for the production of leaves.

PARTS USED Traditionally, the bark or root bark, but in modern times also the dried leaves. All parts have a strong peppery taste.

THERAPEUTIC CATEGORY Antibiotic, general tonic.

USES AND PROPERTIES In southern Africa, pepperbark is a popular and widely used remedy for coughs, colds, chest complaints, bronchial infections and oral thrush. The numerous traditional uses include treatments for headache, malaria, influenza, rheumatism, venereal diseases, toothache and gastric ulcers.

PREPARATION AND DOSAGE Traditionally, cold water infusions of the powdered bark are taken orally as expectorants, or the bark is smoked as a cough and cold remedy. Powdered leaf may be taken in tablet form (or traditionally licked from the hand, and swallowed with some water). The recommended dose for supportive treatment of infections is three (200 mg) tablets per day.

ACTIVE INGREDIENTS The bark contains numerous drimane sesquiterpenoids such as warburganal and polygodial. It is also said to contain mannitol.

PHARMACOLOGICAL EFFECTS The activity of *Warburgia* seems to be due to the drimanes, which are biologically active; as aldehydes they easily form covalent bonds with amino groups of proteins and thus alter their activities. They are potent insect antifeedant with antibacterial and anti-ulcer activity. Mannitol is used for dyspepsia and as a diuretic, and as a sweetener for diabetics.

NOTES Other members of the family are also used in traditional medicine, such as the east African *W. ugandensis* (bark is used as an aromatic bitter and emetic) and *Canella alba* (a mixture of the powdered bark with aloes has been used as an emmenagogue).

STATUS Traditional medicine.

Warburgia salutaris (Bertol.f.) Chiov.   family: Canellaceae

isibhaha (Zulu); *warburgia* (French); *Warburgia, Pfefferrindebaum* (German); *warburgia* (Italian)

Withania somnifera

winter cherry • ashwagandha

Withania somnifera flower

Withania somnifera fruit

DESCRIPTION Winter cherry is a perennial shrublet of up to 1 m in height, with densely velvety stems and leaves, small white or yellowish flowers in short clusters and spherical orange-red berries of about 8 mm in diameter. These are completely enclosed in brown papery and bladdery structures formed by the remains of the sepals, that enlarge markedly as the fruit develops.

ORIGIN *W. somnifera* has a wide natural distribution in Africa, southeastern Europe and Asia and often grows as a weed. It is cultivated in India and elsewhere as a medicinal crop plant.

PARTS USED Mainly the roots, rarely the leaves.

THERAPEUTIC CATEGORY Sedative, adaptogenic tonic (roots), wound-healing (leaves).

USES AND PROPERTIES As perhaps the best known of all the plants used in Ayurvedic medicine, ashwagandha is a sedative, hypnotic and adaptogenic tonic to counter stress. It is widely referred to as "Indian ginseng" because it is, like real ginseng (*Panax ginseng*), used as general tonic and considered to be effective against a large number of ailments. The fleshy roots are indeed superficially similar to ginseng roots. For topical use, leaf poultices are applied to treat open cuts, wounds, abscesses, inflammation, haemorrhoids, rheumatism and syphilis.

PREPARATION AND DOSAGE For internal use, a dose of 3-6 g of dried root, taken in the form of a decoction, infusion or tincture, is normally used. The leaves or the whole plant may be applied to wounds, or ointments are made with fat or oil.

ACTIVE INGREDIENTS The plant contains complex mixtures of chemical compounds – more than 80 constituents have been described. Of special interest are several steroids with an ergostane skeleton, the so-called withanolides, of which withaferin A is a well-known example. Many alkaloids are present, including withasomnine.

PHARMACOLOGICAL EFFECTS The withanolides and other *Withania* compounds have been the subject of numerous studies in which antibiotic, anti-inflammatory, cytotoxic, antitumour and cholesterol lowering activities have been demonstrated. Sedative and hypnotic effects have been ascribed to the alkaloids. Clinical studies are needed to confirm the efficacy of traditional indications.

STATUS Traditional medicine.

Withania somnifera (L.) Dunal   family: Solanaceae

withania (French); *Schlafbeere, Withania* (German); *ashwagandha* (Hindi); *witania, ginseng indiano* (Italian)

Xysmalobium undulatum

uzara • milk bush

Xysmalobium undulatum plants

Xysmalobium undulatum flowers

Uzara root

DESCRIPTION Uzara is a perennial herb of up to 1 m in height, with robust, erect, flowering stems developing from a fleshy root system. The plant has large leaves arranged in opposite pairs (they exude a milky latex when broken), rounded clusters of yellowish brown flowers and large, hairy capsules which contain numerous fluffy seeds.

ORIGIN Southern Africa; limited cultivated.

PARTS USED Dried roots (*Uzarae radix*). They are harvested from two to three year old plants.

THERAPEUTIC CATEGORY Antidiarrhoeal, spasmolytic.

USES AND PROPERTIES Uzara is used in modern phytotherapy to treat non-specific, acute diarrhoea, and to a much lesser extent for the treatment of afterbirth cramps. It is an important traditional medicine in southern Africa and has been used since early times as a remedy for diarrhoea and colic. Numerous other folk uses have been recorded, including the treatment of stomach cramps, headache, oedema (as a diuretic), and dysmenorrhoea. Powdered root is applied to sores and wounds. Other members of the family such as *Asclepias crispa* and various *Pachycarpus* species also

have bitter roots and are used in traditional medicine in much the same way as uzara.

PREPARATION AND DOSAGE A daily dose of 45-90 mg of total glycosides is recommended, after an initial dose of 1 g of the herb (75 mg of total glycosides). For children, 15-30 mg total glycosides is adequate. Tinctures or dried extracts, with a known glycoside content, are available. In traditional medicine, infusions are taken, or the powdered root is snuffed for headache or directly applied to wounds and abscesses.

ACTIVE INGREDIENTS The root contains several cardiac glycosides, of which uzarin (aglycone: uzarigenin) is the major and best known compound.

PHARMACOLOGICAL EFFECTS Uzarin has proven antidiarrhoeal activity, by inhibiting intestinal motility through affecting the visceral smooth muscles. Uzarin inhibits $Na^+,K^+ATPase$, like other cardenolides. Because of its low bioavailability after oral application, digitalis-like symptoms are only found at very high doses. Therefore, the Asclepiadaceae glycosides show a relatively low toxicity and appear to be rather safe.

STATUS Traditional medicine; Comm.E+.

Xysmalobium undulatum R. Br.

family: Asclepiadaceae

ishongwe (Zulu); *uzara* (French); *Uzara* (German); *uzara* (Italian)

Zea mays

corn • maize

Zea mays

Secale cereale

DESCRIPTION Maize is a robust annual grass of up to 3 m in height with thick stems and broad, sheathing leaves. Male flowers are born in clusters at the tips of the branches, while female flowers are arranged in thick spikes in the leaf axils, tipped by long, slender styles visible as a beard-like mass.

ORIGIN Central America (now cultivated in practically all parts of the world).

PARTS USED The styles and stigmas, harvested before fertilisation (corn silk or maize silk – *Maidis stigma*). Maize pollen is a minor component (3%) of a pollen mixture that is used for producing extracts – the rest is 92% rye pollen (*Secale cereale*) and 5% timothy pollen (*Phleum pratense*). Hay flower (*Graminis flos*) is the aboveground parts of various grasses.

THERAPEUTIC CATEGORY Diuretic (styles and stigmas); urological (pollen extract); appetite stimulant (raw pollen); topical hyperaemic (hay flower).

USES AND PROPERTIES Corn stigmas are traditionally used as a weak diuretic to treat disorders of the urinary tract. It is thought to be valuable for slimming, and to treat cystitis, rheumatism and arthritis. Corn silk is known as *yu mi shu* in China – an oedema treatment.

Pollen extract is used against the symptoms of prostate hyperplasia while the pollen itself (or powdered pollen) is taken for weakness and associated appetite loss. Hay flowers are applied externally as hot compresses to treat arthritis.

PREPARATION AND DOSAGE An infusion of stigmas (0.5 g in 150 ml water) is taken several times a day. Pollen extract is used in daily doses of 80-120 mg (for at least three months). A daily dose of 30-40 g of raw pollen is recommended for weakness.

ACTIVE INGREDIENTS Maize stigmas contain some essential oil (with carvacrol and other terpenes) and unidentified saponins, flavonoids, bitter substances, polyphenols, sugars, mucilage and potassium salts. The activity of pollen is ascribed to the presence of sterols.

PHARMACOLOGICAL EFFECTS Experiments have confirmed the diuretic action of corn silk, tentatively attributed to the high potassium level. The efficacy of pollen extracts against prostate hypertrophy was confirmed in clinical studies (for phytosterol activity, see *Cucurbita pepo*).

STATUS Traditional medicine; Pharm.; Comm.E+ (hay flower and pollen only).

Zea mays L.

family: Poaceae

maïs (French); Mais (German); mais (Italian); maíz (Spanish)

Zingiber officinale

ginger

Zingiber officinale

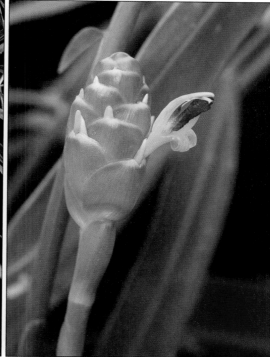

Zingiber officinale flowers

DESCRIPTION A herbaceous perennial of about 1 m in height, with large leaves developing from a branched rhizome. The flowers occur in a dense, scaly spike on an elongated stalk. Each flower has three yellowish orange petals with an additional purplish, lip-like structure.

ORIGIN Probably northeastern India. Ginger is an ancient sterile cultigen and has never been found in nature. It is grown vegetatively as a spice in practically all tropical and subtropical parts of the world.

PARTS USED Fresh or dried rhizomes (*Zingiberis rhizoma*).

THERAPEUTIC CATEGORY Anti-emetic, carminative, cholagogue, and antispasmodic.

USES AND PROPERTIES The fresh or dried rhizomes or extracts thereof are important ingredients of stomachics and tonics to treat dyspepsia and nausea (especially travel sickness). In China, the main use of fresh ginger is for treating fever, coughs and nausea, while dried ginger is used against stomach pain and diarrhoea. Ginger is widely used in folk medicine all over the world. Its pungent taste is sometimes used to mask the unpleasant taste of other medicines.

PREPARATION AND DOSAGE A daily dose of 2-4 g

dried rhizome is recommended. For dyspepsia, 0.5-1.0 g of dried herb can be used to make a tea (or 2 g if used as anti-emetic).

ACTIVE INGREDIENTS The rhizomes are chemically complex. The volatile oil contains monoterpenoids (e.g. camphene, β-phellandrene, neral and geranial), diterpene lactones (e.g. galanolactone) and sesquiterpenoids (e.g. α-zingiberene and *ar*-curcumene). The pungent taste is due to numerous gingerols, of which [6]-gingerol is an example.

PHARMACOLOGICAL EFFECTS Extracts are antibacterial, antifungal, molluscicidal, antiparasitic and anthelmintic. Hypoglycaemic, cholesterol lowering, immune-stimulant, and especially anti-inflammatory properties have been recorded. Ginger has anti-ulcer and cholagogue effects. It stimulates peristalsis and the secretion of saliva and gastric juices. The activity against functional dyspepsia and ulcers is due mostly to [6]-gingerol and [8]-gingerol, as well as α-zingiberene. Clinical studies have shown ginger to be effective in controlling post-operative nausea and travel sickness.

STATUS Traditional medicine; Pharm.; Comm.E+; ESCOP 1; WHO 1; clinical studies+.

Zingiber officinale Roscoe   family: Zingiberaceae

gingembre (French); *Ingwer* (German); *zenzero* (Italian); *jengibre* (Spanish)

Ziziphus jujuba

Chinese date • jujube tree • French jujube

Ziziphus mucronata fruits

Ziziphus jujuba flowers

Ziziphus jujuba fruits

DESCRIPTION A spiny shrub or small tree of up to 6 m in height. It has glossy, three-nerved leaves, inconspicuous yellowish green flowers and oval, reddish brown, edible fruit. Each fruit has a narrowly oblong stone (pip) surrounded by a layer of tasty fruit flesh.

ORIGIN Southeastern Europe to China; widely cultivated in the warmer parts of Europe and Asia.

PARTS USED Ripe fruit (*Jujubae fructus*), seeds.

THERAPEUTIC CATEGORY Antiallergic, anticatarrh, tonic (fruit); sedative (seeds).

USES AND PROPERTIES The delicious and highly nutritious fruits (Chinese dates or *da zao*) are used as a functional food and tonic, to improve general health, to gain weight and to treat disorders of the upper respiratory tract. The seeds are used for nervous conditions and insomnia.

PREPARATION AND DOSAGE No data could be found.

ACTIVE INGREDIENTS *Ziziphus* species are known for accumulating an unusual type of alkaloid usually referred to as peptide alkaloids. Frangufoline (also known as sanjoinine A) occurs in seeds of *Z. jujuba*. The fruit (without the seed) of Chinese date also con-

tain tetracyclic triterpenoid saponins, flavonoids and mucilage.

PHARMACOLOGICAL EFFECTS The sedative and hypnotic effects of the seeds of *Z. jujuba* can be ascribed to the peptide alkaloids. The main compound, frangufoline, is known to have a strong sedative effect. The mucilage can help to reduce cough-inducing irritations of the throat (leading to cough) by forming a protective layer over mucosal tissues. The saponins are secretolytic. Some studies suggested that the fruit helps to strengthen the immune system and to increase endurance. In a human study it was found that Chinese date improved liver function in people with liver ailments.

NOTES Other species of *Ziziphus* that are used in traditional medicine include *Z. spinosa* and *Z. mucronata*. Seeds of *Z. spinosa* (known as *suan zau ren*) are used in China for insomnia and other nervous conditions. In Africa, the leaves and bark of *Z. mucronata* (buffalo thorn) is commonly used in traditional medicine. It is applied to boils and infected wounds, not only to promote healing but also for its sedative effects.

STATUS Traditional medicine.

Ziziphus jujuba Mill. (= *Z. vulgaris* Lam.)   family Rhamnaceae
jujubier (French); *Jujube, Brustbeerbaum* (German); *giuggiolo comune* (Italian)

HEALTH DISORDERS AND MEDICINAL PLANTS

Health disorders and how to treat them with medicinal plants

The human body is extremely complex. Its organisation into differentiated organs, tissues and cells that all have differing functions must be well organised and coordinated to function smoothly. With over 30 000 genes and even more gene products (e.g. proteins with various functions) in 10^{13} cells, the human body represents an extremely complex network that even today, in the age of molecular biology, is only partly understood.

If elements in this regulatory network are missing or are not performing optimally, because of genetic (inherited gene defects; mutations) or environmental influences (such as infections by parasites, bacteria, fungi or viruses; accidents causing wounds, burns, etc.; toxins from diet that modulate the activity and function of proteins in the body), then health disorders or disturbances result.

Health disorders can be treated in various ways. If the cause is known, then a causal treatment becomes possible (e.g. elimination of infecting bacteria with antibiotics). In many cases, disorders are so complex that only a symptomatic treatment is available, relieving pain or discomfort, thus improving quality of life.

For most disorders and disturbances, potent and specific medicines are available, mostly of synthetic origin. These therapeutics are usually powerful, but very often exhibit a number of undesired side effects. Therapeutics derived from plants are usually less specific; they can affect more than one molecular target. This property can be helpful in complex disorders in which the exact causes are not known. Phytomedicine is not the first choice to treat severe and life-threatening diseases, but can be useful in many other instances.

The following list of indications should provide an overview of those conditions for which phytomedicine plays a relevant role. This compilation is not intended as a recipe for self-treatment. In case of a health disorder, the reader is advised to see a health care professional first for a proper diagnosis. Once the diagnosis is established, then phytotherapy can be considered as an alternative or supportive treatment, if appropriate.

Heart and circulation

Heart insufficiency

Heart insufficiency results from an inability of the heart muscle to supply the body with adequate amounts of blood. If the heart is no longer well supplied with oxygen-rich blood, because coronary blood vessels are blocked or become narrow because of arteriosclerosis or are weakend by infections, its pumping ability is reduced. Symptoms are dyspnea (difficulty in breathing), fatigue, tachycardia, nycturia, oedema and cyanosis. The New York Heart Association (NYHA) has published a scale with four stages describing the severity of this disorder: NYHA I and II – complaints under physical activity; NYHA III and IV – complaints under modest activity or when at rest.

TREATMENT A causal therapy cannot be achieved with phytomedicines. Symptomatic treatment depends on the degree of heart insufficiency. According to the NYHA scale stages III and IV are treated with isolated cardiac glycosides, which inhibit Na^+, K^+-ATPase. In response the internal Ca^{++}-level is increased, which stimulates the activity of the heart muscle. Resorption and elimination of cardiac glycosides differ with their structure (e.g. lipophilicity).

Early stages of heart insufficiency (NYHA I and II) can be treated with phytomedicines, such as *Crataegus* extracts, rich in flavonoids and oligomeric proanthocyanidins, that inhibit Na^+,K^+-ATPase, phosphodiesterase and angiotensin converting enzyme (ACE). Blood flow is enhanced by a positive inotropic and dromotropic effect. In addition, vascular resistance is reduced upon medication with standardised *Crataegus* extracts (e.g. WS 1442). Therapy should be accompanied by avoiding risks, inherent in smoking, alcohol, and being overweight.

Several placebo-controlled double-blind clinical studies provide evidence that extracts from *Crataegus* show efficacy for the treatment of patients with heart insufficiency NYHA I, II and even III. It has the same efficacy as the ACE inhibitor captopril. The therapeutic index of *Crataegus* is large and side effects are minimal.

MAIN PLANTS **Plants with cardiac glycosides:** *Adonis vernalis, Apocynum cannabinum, Convallaria majalis, Digitalis purpurea, D. lanata, Helleborus niger, Nerium oleander, Strophanthus gratus, Thevetia peruviana, Urginea maritima.* **Other plants:** *Ammi visnaga, Cinnamomum camphora, Crataegus monogyna* and relatives; *Leonurus cardiaca.* **Plants used in traditional medicine:** *Achillea millefolium, Arnica montana, Cytisus scoparius, Glycyrrhiza glabra, Hypericum perforatum, Ilex paraguariensis, Lavandula angustifolia, Rosmarinus officinalis, Theobroma cacao, Valeriana officinalis, Viscum album.*

Cardiac rhythm disturbance

Disturbances of the pacemaker and conduction systems of the heart can result in irregular heartbeat (arrhythmia), in an enhanced heartbeat (tachycardia; >100 beats/min) or reduced heartbeat (bradycardia; <60 beats/min). Causes are complex and cardiac rhythm disturbances are symptoms of cardiac or other disorders, which can be influenced by psychosomatic factors.

TREATMENT Isolated alkaloids, such as quinidine, ajmaline and sparteine inhibit Na^+ channels and exhibit anti-arrhythmic effects in that they influence the conduction system. Atropine reduces the influence of the vegetative nerve system, by blocking mAChR. Other phytochemicals influence the factors that have brought about cardiac rhythm disturbances, such as hypoxia, blood flow or metabolic imbalances; extracts of *Crataegus* fall into this category.

MAIN PLANTS *Atropa belladonna, Cinchona* species, *Crataegus monogyna* and related species; *Cytisus scoparius, Rauvolfia serpentina.*

Angina pectoris

This is a coronary disorder caused by ischemia; it occurs in irregular attacks, accompanied by intense pains and feeling of constriction and anxiety.

TREATMENT The condition is usually treated with nitrates, beta blockers, and calcium antagonists. A prophylactic treatment can be done with khellin and visnadin, isolated from *Ammi visnaga*. Both compounds are spasmolytic in coronary blood vessels and improve blood flow and oxygen supply in the heart. Clinical studies provide evidence for the efficacy of *Crataegus* (see "heart insufficiency") for this indication. The alkaloids theophylline and papaverine inhibit cAMP-phosphodiesterase and have therefore coronary dilatating properties.

MAIN PLANTS *Ammi visnaga, Camellia sinensis, Crataegus monogyna* and related species, *Papaver somniferum.* **Plants used in traditional medicine:** *Alpinia officinarum, Capsicum annuum, C. frutescens, Zingiber officinale.*

Circulatory disorders (peripheral veno-occlusive arterial disease)

If **peripheral** veins and arteries become obstructed or narrower because of arteriosclerotic deposits or inflammation of arterial walls, circulation of peripheral organs, such as legs, is reduced. As a consequence muscles and other tissues are no longer optimally supplied with oxygen, so that physical efforts become difficult and painful. Four stages are characterised (according to Fontaine): I, no complaints; II, *Claudicatio intermittens* (IIa: leg pains after more than 200 m of walking; IIb: leg pains after less than 200 m of walking); III, pains even when lying horizontally; IV, acral lesions and pains while resting. **Cerebral circulatory** disorder caused by arteriosclerotic or embolic processes lead to a reduced oxygen and glucose supply in the brain that result in metabolic and physiological imbalances of neurones.

TREATMENT Only patients with stages I and II can be treated with phytotherapy. The aim is to improve blood flow by dilatation of blood vessels and increase of cardiac output; control of prostacyclin and thromboxan formation in arteries and thrombocytes. In addition, risk factors, such as enhanced levels of triglycerides, cholesterol, adipositas, lack of physical exercise and smoking, should be observed and eliminated.

Cerebral circulation problems can be improved by increasing oxygen and glucose supply; vasodilatation, e.g. by ajmalicine, reduced ergot alkaloids (dihydroergocristin), theophylline and papaverine can enhance blood flow through cerebral capillaries. The prevention of oedemas, e.g. by aescin or flavonoids (rutin) is also of interest.

Controlled double-blind clinical studies provide evidence (improvement by over 30% as compared to placebo) that Ginkgo extracts (EGb 761) improve symptoms of peripheral and cerebral circulatory disorders.

MAIN PLANTS *Aesculus hippocastanum, Camellia sinensis, Fagopyrum esculentum, Ginkgo biloba, Papaver somniferum, Rauvolfia serpentina, Vinca minor*; ergot alkaloids from *Claviceps purpurea*.

Hypertension and hypotension

Hypertension is characterised by a blood pressure above 140/90 mm Hg; causes are often difficult to define. Hypotension is defined by a blood pressure below 105/60 mm Hg and can be caused by physiological or hormonal imbalances and blood loss.

TREATMENT Treatment of hypertension includes accompanying measures, such as reducing salt (NaCl) and alcohol intake, nicotine abstinence and increasing physical activity. Medicinal treatment involves the application of diuretic, sympathetic, vasodilatative drugs, of ACE inhibitors, Ca-antagonists and aldosteron antagonists. Phytomedicine can provide diurectic, sympathetic, vasodilatative drugs that can be useful in mild forms of hypertension. The alkaloids reserpine, rescinnamine and serpentine (which inhibit the re-uptake of noradrenaline into presynaptic vesicles) have been used to treat severe forms of hypertension. Hypotension can be improved by physical exercise and plant extracts with stimulating properties, such as purine alkaloids (caffeine) or vasoconstricting activities (e.g. ergot alkaloids, ephedrine).

MAIN AND TRADITIONAL PLANTS **Hypertension**: *Adonis vernalis, Allium sativum, Convallaria majalis, Crataegus monogyna* and related species; *Digitalis purpurea, D. lanata, Helleborus niger, Nerium oleander, Rauvolfia serpentina, Urginea maritima*. **Hypotension**: *Camellia sinensis, Claviceps purpurea* (e.g. ergotamine, 9,10-dihydroergotamine), *Coffea arabica, Cola nitida, Cytisus scoparius, Ephedra distachya, Rosmarinus officinalis*; isolated alkaloids from *Claviceps purpurea* (e.g. ergotamine and 9,10-dihydroergotamine).

Other plants: *Betula* species, *Equisetum arvense, Humulus lupulus, Olea europaea, Rhododendron* species, *Solidago virgaurea, Valeriana officinalis, Veratrum album, Viscum album*.

Chronic venous insufficiency (CVI); varicosis

Venous circulatory disorder, especially in lower extremities (legs) can lead to varicosis, thrombophlebitis, and phlebothrombosis and in consequence to chronic venous insufficiency. Endothelia of veins become leaky and by loss of fibrous tissues the valves of veins lose their function. This disorder is thus mainly caused by a reduced venous drainage (obstruction of deep veins or insufficiency of the valves of veins). Symptoms are complex and include a feeling of heaviness in legs, oedema, nightly cramps in the leg, pain and itching.

TREATMENT Besides physical treatment (compression bandages to improve haemodynamics), exercise, and surgery, CVI can be treated medicinally using diuretics and oedema protectant. The latter therapeutic is aimed at reducing the permeability of capillaries and thereby preventing oedema formation. A randomised placebo-controlled clinical study has shown that aescin (100 mg per day of a triterpene fraction from *Aesculus hippocastanum*) improves the symptoms of CVI, especially when accompanied by physical treatment. The flavonoid rutin and partial synthetic derivatives (e.g. troxerutin) also reduce oedema formation.

MAIN AND TRADITIONAL PLANTS *Aesculus hippocastanum, Centella asiatica, Fagopyrum esculentum, Hamamelis virginiana, Melilotus officinalis, Ruscus aculeatus, Styphnolobium japonicum*.

Cerebral disorders

Dementia

Dementia is a loss of individually acquired intellectual capabilities (i.e. memory, concentration, learning, vigilance, power of judgement, spatial orientation, articulation). It also manifests as an inability to cope with ordinary daily problems or to interact properly in a professional and social context (e.g. affective disorders, such as loss of motivation, emotional control or social behaviour). Severe forms of vascular (also called multiinfarct or arteriosclerotic) dementia (frequency: 10–20%) and/or degenerative dementia of the Alzheimer type (50% of all demential illnesses) lead to complete loss of personality and imbecility. In 25% of dementia cases, patients suffer from both vascular dementia and Alzheimer's disease. Degenerative and multiinfarct dementia increases with age: Whereas ca. 5% of the population of 65 years of age suffer from dementia, the frequency is up to 30% in persons over 80–90 years of age. The pathology of dementia is complex and includes increased vasoconstriction, deficiency of certain neurotransmitters, increased platelet aggregation and ischemia (multiinfarct), free radicals, membrane defects, disorder of cerebral metabolism or progressive degeneration of neurones.

TREATMENT Most treatments are symptomatic and can temporarily improve quality of life or delay the progression of Alzheimer's disease by up to 1–2 years. Improvement of central cholinergic systems can be achieved through inhibition of acetylcholine esterase (e.g. by galanthamine, Ginkgo extracts or synthetic drugs, such donepezil, memantine, rivastigmine and tacrine). Furthermore, Ginkgo extracts may protect membranes and neurones from death and apoptosis, improve cerebral metabolism, protect against hypoxia and ischemia, cure cerebral oedemas, improve radical scavenging and haemodynamic and haemorheological properties of the blood (e.g. PAF antagonism). A large number of controlled clinical studies (placebo-controlled, double-blind, randomised trials) have proven the efficacy of Ginkgo extracts, (especially *Ginkgo-biloba*-special extract EGb 761; 240 mg per day). Medicinal therapy should be accompanied by orientation, reminiscence and validation therapy.

MAIN PLANTS *Ginkgo biloba, Galanthus nivalis.*

Dizziness (vertigo)

Dizziness is the result of a disturbance of equilibrium due to the vestibular and optical senses no longer being congruent. Vertigo can be accompanied by anxiety, emesis, nausea, profuse perspiration, tachycardia, labyrinthine ataxia, collapse and nystagmus. The causes of this disorder can be manifold, ranging from disturbances in the vestibule, disorder in the central nervous system, to side effects from medicines (e.g. streptomycin) or alcohol to ophthalmologic, psychiatric or orthopaedic problems.

TREATMENT Vertigo therapy involves a treatment of any basic disorder, physical training and symptomatically by medicines. A few controlled clinical studies over 60 to 90 days have shown that symptoms of dizziness improve after treatment with Ginkgo extracts (240 mg Ginkgo special extract EGb 761).

MAIN PLANTS *Ginkgo biloba.*

Ringing in ear (tinnitus)

This ailment manifests as variable noise in the ears (in absence of external sources), such as whistling, buzzing, ringing or hissing sounds, often accompanied by defective or impaired hearing. Tinnitus can occur sporadically, continuously or synchronously with heartbeat or breathing. It can be caused by infection or nearly any disorder of the ear, by certain medicines (e.g. quinidine; salicylates, aminoglycoside antibiotics), by disorders of heart and circulation (e.g. hypertony; arteriosclerosis), neurodegeneration, tumours, or by *Morbus Ménière*. Tinnitus can lead to insomnia, lack of concentration, anxiety, frustration, depression, headache and psychological disturbances.

TREATMENT Treatment of the basic disorder that has secondarily caused tinnitus is the method of choice. Five placebo-controlled double-blind clinical studies, three reference-controlled studies with 535 patients and 11 open clinical studies with 1 802 patients showed the efficacy of Ginkgo (120–240 mg per day of EGb 761) to reduce the intensity of tinnitus noise.

MAIN PLANTS *Ginkgo biloba.*

Psychological and psychosomatic disturbances

Depression

Psychic diseases and disorders can be caused by disturbance of the equilibrium between neurotransmitters, receptors and transporters of neurotransmitters. A low concentration of noradrenaline and serotonine is often connected with depression whereas their increased concentration can lead to schizophrenic-type disorders. The main symptoms are low spirit, cheerless mood, loss of interest and motivation and fatigue. Side effects are complex and include insomnia, feelings of guilt, low self-confidence and even suicidal thoughts.

TREATMENT The aim of antidepressive drugs is to raise the level of noradrenaline and serotonine. This can be achieved either by application of a neurotransmitter agonist that stimulates the corresponding receptor, by MAO inhibitors, or most commonly by so-called re-uptake inhibitors which block amine transporters at the presynapse. As a result, noradrenaline, serotonine and dopamine stay in the synaptic cleft, are not degraded by MAO or COMT and their local concentration is raised. Phytomedicine has been successfully used to treat mild depressions: extracts from *Hypericum perforatum* block the presynaptic transporters and raise the concentration not only of noradrenaline but also of serotonine, dopamine, GABA and other neurotransmitters. Several controlled double-blind studies have proven the efficacy of *H. perforatum* (compared to placebo and synthetic antidepressants) to improve the mood of patients with mild (not severe) depression. The doses were 900 mg WS 5570 per day.

MAIN PLANTS *Hypericum perforatum.*

Anxiety

Patients with anxiety and fear have the subjective feeling of dangerous threat (even mortal terror), and suffer from psychological and vegetative symptoms, such as nervousness, concentration problems, headaches, paleness, perspiration, trembles, heartbeat, raised blood pressure and diarrhoea. Anxiety, accompanied by tension and restlessness can continue for weeks.

TREATMENT Anxiety is treated with anxiolytics or tranquillisers. The aim is to separate the influence of psychic conditions on the vegetative system. Activation of the GABA receptor with benzodiazepins (at the "benzodiazepin"-receptor), leads to attenuation of the limbic system, to muscle relaxation, sedation and spasmolytic effects. Controlled clinical studies have shown the efficacy of kava kava when compared with synthetic benzodiazepins.

MAIN PLANTS *Humulus lupulus, Hypericum perforatum, Piper methysticum, Rauvolfia serpentina.*

Insomnia, tension and restlessness

Patients with insomnia suffer from a bad sleep quality, difficulties falling asleep and sleeping without interruptions. Patients worry much about their insomnia, fear negative consequences and go through mood swings. They show an increased irritability, general tiredness, often also tension and restlessness.

TREATMENT Insomnia, tension and restlessness can be treated with GABA receptor agonists and other sedatives. A number of plant extracts affect the GABA receptor (including *Valeriana officinalis, Humulus lupulus, Passiflora incarnata*). Plants with essential oils (such as *Lavandula angustifolia, Melissa officinalis*) can be regarded as mild spasmolytic drugs that also alleviate nervousness and tension. A number of controlled clinical studies have shown the efficacy of *Valeriana officinalis* to treat insomnia, often in combination with *Melissa officinalis*.

MAIN PLANTS Symptoms of insomnia, tension and restlessness have been successfully treated with *Humulus lupulus, Hypericum perforatum, Lavandula angustifolia, Melissa officinalis, Mentha x piperita, Passiflora incarnata, Piper methysticum, Rauvolfia serpentina, Valeriana officinalis*. **Plants used in traditional medicine:** *Angelica archangelica, Atropa belladonna, Avena sativa, Citrus aurantium, Corydalis cava, Crocus sativus, Eschscholtzia californica, Lycopus europaeus, Lycopus virginicus, Nardostachys grandiflora, Piscidia piscipula, Tilia cordata*.

Travel sickness

Dizziness followed by vomiting (emesis) is caused by hyperexcitation in the motoric centre of the CNS (vestibular disturbances).

TREATMENT Important plant substances include the tropane alkaloid scopolamine, which blocks muscarinic AChR and therefore sedates motoric and vegetative centres of the brain stem. In addition, *Zingiber officinalis* appears to help to overcome travel sickness, vertigo and nausea (also nausea caused by anaesthetics).

MAIN PLANTS *Datura stramonium* and other plants with scopolamine, *Zingiber officinale*. **Plants used in traditional medicine:** *Anamirta cocculus*.

Exhaustion, weakness, stress

This symptom complex comprises vitality problems, a decrease of psychological and physical vigilance, an increased susceptibility for infections, insomnia and burnout symptoms. It is especially common in elderly people.

TREATMENT Tonics can be regarded as adaptogens that work against exhaustion, weakness and stress. The pharmacology of the mostly complex extracts is not well understood. It has been speculated that adaptogens might have corticomimetic and neuromodulatory effects and that they stimulate cellular metabolism. Therapeutic studies with ginseng have shown a positive effect in this context.

MAIN PLANTS **Tonics and adaptogens:** *Eleutherococcus senticosus, Panax ginseng, Sutherlandia frutescens, Withania somnifera*. **Cognition enhancer:** *Ginkgo biloba*. **Bitter tonics:** *Artemisia abrotanum, Centaurium erythraea, Cinchona* species, *Citrus aurantium, Gentiana lutea, Harungana madagascariensis, Marsdenia cundurango, Menyanthes trifoliata, Taraxacum officinale*. **Pungent tonics:** *Acorus calamus, Alpinia officinarum, Myristica fragrans, Zingiber officinale*. **Stimulants:** Plants with purine alkaloids – *Coffea arabica, Cola acuminata, Theobroma cacao, Paullinia cupana, Ilex paraguariensis*. **Aphrodisiacs:** *Pausinystalia johimbe, Ptychopetalum olacoides, P. uncinatum, Strychnos nux-vomica, Turnera diffusa*, cantharidine from certain insects.

Disorders of the digestive tract

Irritation of the stomach and intestinal tract (including dyspepsia; lack of appetite, spasms)

Disorders of the digestive tract include functional and chronic disturbances, and psychosomatic complaints, such as irritable stomach and colon, and various forms of dyspepsia. Psychosomatic dysfunctions do not result in pathological or morphological changes but are characterised by a disturbance of gut motility and tonicity, or an imbalance of secretion of gastric juice and digestive enzymes and the resorption of nutrients. Symptoms include heartburn, lack of appetite, belching, vomiting, nausea, flatulence and regurgitation.

TREATMENT Besides dietetic measures and the exclusion of certain foods, phytomedicines can be useful. These include plants that modulate the secretion of digestive enzymes and bile, that buffer gastric acid, enhance gut motility, but reduce spasms and are anti-inflammatory.

- Drugs with essential oils or pungent principles (*aromatica, acria*) the former usually termed "carminatives". They enhance the secretion of gastric and digestive fluids in patients with lack of appetite and dyspepsia; they are slightly spasmolytic, and show anti-inflammatory, antibacterial and antifungal effects.
- Drugs with bitter compounds (*amara, amara-aromatica*), such as iridoids and sesquiterpenes, alkaloids, triterpenes, and flavonoids; they enhance the production of saliva, gastric juice and bile.
- Drugs with mucilage (*mucilaginosa*) protect mucous membranes.
- Hydrolytic enzymes (such as papain, bromelain, ficin) can be used to substitute a lack of endogenous enzyme production.
- Drugs with tropanes and other alkaloids are antispasmodic since they inhibit muscarinic AChR of smooth intestinal muscles.

Controlled clinical studies provide evidence that carminatives are efficacious.

Main and traditional plants Carminatives with essential oils: *Achillea millefolium, Angelica archangelica, Artemisia vulgaris, Carum carvi, Coriandrum sativum, Elettaria cardamomum, Foeniculum vulgare, Matricaria recutita, Mentha x piperita, Pimpinella anisum, Rosmarinus officinalis.* **With pungent principles:** *Acorus calamus, Allium cepa, Allium sativum, Allium ursinum, Alpinia officinarum, Brassica nigra, Iberis amara, Sinapis alba, Tropaeolum majus, Zingiber officinale.* **Drugs with bitter principles:** *Artemisia absinthium, Centaurea benedicta (=Cnicus benedictus), Centaurium erythraea, Cichorium intybus, Cinchona pubescens, Citrus aurantium subsp. aurantium, Gentiana lutea, Harungana madagascariensis, Marrubium vulgare, Marsdenia cundurango, Menyanthes trifoliata, Quassia amara.* **Plant enzymes:** *Ananas comosus, Carica papaya, Ficus carica.* **Antispasmodic drugs:** *Atropa belladonna,* and other taxa with tropane alkaloids

Gastritis and ulcers

Acute gastritis can be caused by alcohol, drugs or cold drinks and affect the mucous membranes of the stomach. Chronic gastritis is characterised by a reduced hydrochloric acid (HCl) production or a reflux of gut content into the stomach. In the latter case, ulcers can develop. Ulcers of the stomach and duodenum are the result of a microbial infection by a bacterium, *Helicobacter pylori*, which finds optimal growth conditions when the mucosal membranes are disturbed. The condition can be accompanied by stomach cramps.

Treatment Basically, *H. pylori* is treated with antibiotics, but gastritis and ulcers also benefit from phytomedicines. Gastric acid secretion can be inhibited by tropane alkaloids, such as atropine. Mucous membranes are protected with *mucilaginosa* and anti-inflammatory drugs. Cramps and colics can be treated with phytomedicines containing tropane alkaloids or essential oils that show membrane activity.

Any phytotherapeutic treatment should be supported by dietetic measures (avoiding acidic, very sweet or spicy foods and drinks, alcohol, coffee and ulcerogenic medicines) and a reduction of stress.

Main plants *Achillea millefolium, Althaea officinalis, Alpinia officinarum, Angelica archangelica, Atropa belladonna, Calendula officinalis, Carum carvi, Coriandrum sativum, Glycyrrhiza glabra, Linum usitatissimum, Malva sylvestris, Matricaria recutita, Melissa officinalis, Mentha x piperita, Mentzelia cordifolia.* **Plants used in traditional medicine:** *Citrus aurantium subsp. aurantium, Crocus sativus, Juglans regia, Lavandula angustifolia, Levisticum officinale, Linum usitatissimum, Lythrum salicaria, Thymus serpyllum.*

Diarrhoea, colitis, and diverticulitis

Acute diarrhoea can derive from psychosomatic disturbances, or be caused by infections (viral, bacterial, fungal and parasitic) or intoxication (alcohol, heavy metals, laxatives, antibiotics, and several other xenobiotics). Chronic diarrhoea can result from an acute diarrhoea (and its causes), but also from organic disorders of the gut, from pancreatic insufficiency, food allergies, and hormonal disturbances.

Colitis ulcerosa and *Morbus Crohn* are chronic inflammations of the gut. *Morbus Crohn* affects lower small intestine and colon and is characterised by diarrhoea, abdominal pain, fistula or fever. *Colitis* affects the mucosa of the large intestine and rectum and is accompanied by ulcers. It can be caused by psychosomatic and autoimmune disturbances. Diverticulitis can be a cause of senile atrophy of the rectum and is accompanied by the formation of gut invaginations (diverticles) that are chronically inflamed.

TREATMENT Patients with *Morbus Crohn* and *Colitis ulcerosa* should avoid sugar and cereals (e.g. bread) and keep a strict dietary regime. In addition, plants with calming, spasmolytic, anti-inflammatory, anti-allergic, swelling and carminative properties can be useful. Diarrhoea is treated by calming down gut motility (e.g. opium or *Uzara*), by astringent tannins (that bind receptors and microorganisms), by anti-inflammatory drugs (with mucilage, and essential oils), by adsorption of toxins (e.g. activated charcoal, medicinal coal, clay, kaolin), by filling the gut with swelling substances, by enzyme substitution, by adding special yeasts (e.g. *Saccharomyces boulardii*) and by substituting water and ion losses (electrolytes, glucose).

MAIN PLANTS Astringent plants: *Camellia sinensis, Hamamelis virginiana, Krameria lappacea, Lythrum salicaria, Potentilla erecta, Rubus fruticosus, Quercus robur, Vaccinium myrtillus.* **Plants with anti-inflammatory and carminative properties:** *Carum carvi, Ferula assa-foetida, Foeniculum vulgare, Matricaria recutita, Mentha x piperita, Pimpinella anisum.* **Spasmolytic and calming drugs:** *Pachycarpus* species, *Papaver somniferum, Xysmalobium undulatum.* **Adsorbents and swelling drugs:** agar from red algae; pectins from *Ceratonia siliqua, Citrus, Pyrus, Malus; Linum usitatissimum, Plantago afra, Plantago ovata.* **Plants used in traditional medicine:** *Aesculus hippocastanum, Agrimonia eupatoria, Castanea sativa, Fragaria vesca, Galeopsis segetum, Geum urbanum, Hypericum perforatum, Okoubaka aubrevillei, Potentilla anserina, Rubus idaeus, Veratrum album.*

Constipation

Constipation can be caused by food low in fibres, lack of motility, psychosomatic disturbances, extreme adipositas, medicines (e.g. opium, morphine, anticholinergics, antipyretics, sympathomimetics, antidepressants, laxatives) and organic disorders (haemorrhoids, colon irritability, inflammation and tumours).

TREATMENT The aim is to activate gut motility by bodily exercise and food rich in fibres. If necessary, plant material with swelling or osmotic properties can be used. Stimulant laxatives (with anthranoids) are favoured by patients but should be used with care, since they can lead to chronic constipation. The reduced and deglucosylated anthrone (glycosides are hydrolysed in the gut) and anthranol are the active form of anthranoids. They stimulate the release of histamine and prostaglandins, thus increasing gut motility. The resorption of sodium and chloride ions is reduced thus increasing osmotically the water content in the faeces. In the large intestine, an increased secretion of mucilage takes place. In combination, all these activities lead to a strong laxative effect.

MAIN PLANTS Laxatives: *Aloe vera* (=*A. barbadensis*), *Aloe ferox, Rhamnus catharticus, Rhamnus frangula, Rhamnus purshianus, Rheum officinale, Rheum palmatum, Ricinus communis, Senna alexandrina.* **Fibres and swelling drugs:** Agar from *Gelidium, Ahnfaltia* species, *Astracantha gummifera, Ficus carica, Linum usitatissimum, Plantago afra, Plantago arenaria, Plantago ovata, Tamarindus indica, Triticum aestivum.* **Osmotics:** mannitol, sorbitol from various fruits. **Plants used in traditional medicine:** *Bryonia dioica, Citrullus colocynthis, Convolvulus scammonia, Hibiscus sabdariffa, Ipomoea orizabensis, Ipomoea purga, Prunus spinosa, Rosa canina, Strychnos nux-vomica.*

Haemorrhoids and proctitis

Proctitis is an inflammation of the rectum, often found in patients with *Morbus Crohn* and colitis. They suffer from spasms of the anal sphincter, constipation and pruritus. Haemorrhoids (inner and outer) are dilations of anal arteries that may be inflamed and bleeding.

TREATMENT Proctitis and haemorrhoids are treated locally with anti-inflammatory, astringent, haemostyptic, analgesic, antimicrobial and spasmolytic phytomedicines.

MAIN AND TRADITIONAL PLANTS *Aesculus hippocastanum, Arnica montana, Atropa belladonna, Fagopyrum esculentum, Hamamelis virginiana, Hypericum perforatum, Matricaria recutita, Myroxylon balsamum, Potentilla erecta, Quercus robur, Ruscus aculeatus, Symphytum officinale.*

Disorders of the liver and bile system

Infections of the liver and intoxications

The liver is the main organ of metabolism (e.g. lipid metabolism, protein biosynthesis; glycogen storage) and detoxification in our body. Viral, bacterial and parasitic infections or toxins (toxins from mushrooms, lower fungi, plants or chemical industry) that destroy liver cells, can be life threatening. Liver cirrhosis as a result of long-term alcohol abuse can be considered in this context. Some compounds damage the endothelia of blood vessels in the liver, such as pyrrolizidine alkaloids, arsenic and other toxins. On the other hand, the liver has a high regeneration capability, so that new cells can easily replace the destroyed tissue (once the causative agent has disappeared).

TREATMENT   Only a few medicinal plants exist that can alleviate severe liver damage. Basically, secondary metabolites, such as lignans ("silymarin") in *Silybum marianum*, help to stabilise and seal membranes of liver cells, so that toxins cannot enter. Silymarin is a radical scavenger, stimulates RNA transcription and protein biosynthesis and supports the regeneration of damaged liver tissue. Controlled clinical studies have shown that the lignan fraction of *S. marianum* is useful to treat mushroom poisoning (e.g. by *Amanita phalloides*) and damaged liver (after viral infections, alcohol abuse or chemical intoxications) in doses of 200–400 mg silymarin per day. A placebo-controlled double-blind study with 170 patients suffering from liver cirrhosis provided clear evidence that survival was significantly enhanced in the silymarin treated group.

MAIN PLANTS   *Cynara scolymus*, phospholipids from *Glycine max*, *Silybum marianum*. **Plants used in traditional medicine:** *Agrimonia eupatoria*, *Beta vulgaris*, *Eclipta alba*, *Helichrysum arenarium*, *Phyllanthus amarus*, *Picrorhiza kurrooa*, *Rehmannia glutinosa*, *Schisandra chinensis*, *Wedelia calendulacea*.

Disorders of gall production, gall bladder and bile ducts

Bile is produced in the liver and transported to the intestine via the bile ducts. Bile acids have emulgating properties that help the digestion of lipid material by lipase in the gut. A decreased bile production is therefore bad for intestinal digestion. Bacterial infection of the bile duct and gall bladder and gallstones (resulting from cholesterol, calcium carbonate, bilirubin; *cholelithiasis*) cause inflammation. Disorders include disturbance of motility of bile ducts, painful biliary colics, cramps of the *sphincter oddii*, and abdominal pains in the epigastrium.

TREATMENT   Cholagogues that enhance bile production and flow are divided into choleretics, that stimulate bile production in the liver and cholekinetics, which promote contraction of the gall bladder and of the bile duct and thus bile flow. Several secondary metabolites are transported via the bile duct into the duodenum and can therefore reach target tissues in the bile duct. Drugs with tropane and other alkaloids (*Atropa belladonna*, *Scopolia carniolica*, *Peumus boldo*, *Fumaria officinalis*, *Chelidonium majus*) inhibit muscarinergic acetylcholine receptors and are therefore spasmolytic. Plant drugs with essential oils or lipophilic terpenoids (such as *Artemisia absinthium*, *Mentha* species, *Angelica archangelica*, *Curcuma longa*, *C. xanthorrhiza*, *Elettaria cardamomum* and others) also exhibit a weak spasmolytic effect. Spasmolytic drugs release spasms and reduce pain.

Some of the cholagogues have antibacterial and anti-inflammatory properties, such as *Chelidonium majus* or *Harpagophytum procumbens*. Plants with essential oil and mustard oil may be used as supportive treatment of bacterial infections and inflammation of the biliary tract (*Achillea millefolium*, *Angelica archangelica*, *Curcuma longa*, *C. xanthorrhiza*, *Elettaria cardamomum*, *Raphanus sativus*). Several drugs taste bitter and are considered to have choleretic effects (such as *Marrubium vulgare*, *Cynara scolymus*, *Taraxacum officinale*, *Peumus boldo*, *Helichrysum arenarium*). Controlled clinical studies are not available and the pharmacological properties of the drugs mentioned are sometimes disputed by pharmacologists.

MAIN PLANTS   *Achillea millefolium*, *Artemisia absinthium*, *Curcuma longa*, *C. xanthorrhiza*, *Cynara scolymus*, *Fumaria officinalis*, *Mentha x piperita*, *Peumus boldus*, *Taraxacum officinale*. **Plants used in traditional medicine:** Many plants have been used as cholagogues, including *Allium sativum*, *Angelica archangelica*, *Artemisia abrotanum*, *Atropa belladonna*, *Berberis vulgaris*, *Calendula officinalis*, *Centaurea benedicta* (=*Cnicus* *benedictus*), *Chelidonium majus*, *Cichorium intybus*, *Elettaria cardamomum*, *Gentiana lutea*, *Harpagophytum procumbens*, *Harungana madagascariensis*, *Helichrysum arenarium*, *Inula helenium*, *Marrubium vulgare*, *Raphanus sativus*, *Scopolia carniolica*, *Veronicastrum virginicum*, *Zingiber officinale*.

Disorders of the lipid metabolism

Hyperlipidemia and arteriosclerosis

Arteriosclerosis can result from hyperlipidemia, nicotine abuse, arterial hypertension, Diabetes mellitus, overweight, hereditary disposition and lack of physical exercise.

Hyperlipidemia is characterised by enhanced blood levels of triglycerides (>160 mg per 100 ml) and cholesterol (>260 mg per 100 ml). Raised levels of blood lipids can be a risk factor for the development of arteriosclerosis. The lipid metabolism (which includes lipoproteins, such as HDL, LDL, VLDL and their receptors) and the corresponding arteriosclerotic changes of arterial walls are interrelated in a complex network and often linked with hypertension and other coronary disorders. Arteriosclerosis is a risk factor for cardiac infarction and stroke.

TREATMENT These conditions are mainly treated with synthetic preparations (e.g. fibrates), but phytotherapy (allicin, sitosterols, phospholipids, unsaturated fatty acids) and a fibre rich diet can have a positive effect and can lower blood lipids to some degree (up to 20%). Garlic and onions are rich in the sulfur-containing alliin. Upon tissue damage, alliin is cleaved by alliinase to allicin. Allicin is highly reactive and can bind to any sulfhydryl group of enzymes, receptors or other proteins. It is therefore not surprising that quite a number of molecular targets appear to be affected in the human body and that pharmacological responses are manifold. A number of clinical trials have been performed with garlic, indicating that cholesterol and triglyceride levels can be reduced by 10 to 20%. However, the validity of these studies has been questioned.

MAIN PLANTS *Allium sativum*, *A. cepa*, *Cynara scolymus*. **Plants used in traditional medicine:** *Allium ursinum*, *Camellia sinensis*, *Eleutherococcus senticosus*.

Disorders of the kidneys and urinary tract

Infection of the urinary tract

Bacterial infections may occur internally, either from blood or lymphatic tissues, or from outside, via the urethra. These infections are favoured by urinary obstructions and can lead to inflammation.

TREATMENT Arbutin, present in *Vaccinium uva-ursi* and other Ericaceae, mustard oils (as in *Armoracia rusticana*) and sesquiterpenes in *Santalum album* are eliminated via the urinary tract and show antibacterial activity. Diuretic drugs that are often applied in combination with antibacterial drugs, also help to reduce symptoms because of increased urine production and rinsing effects. In severe cases, treatment with antibiotics becomes necessary.

MAIN AND TRADITIONAL PLANTS *Agathosma betulina*, *Armoracia rusticana*, *Fabiana imbricata*, *Pterocarpus santalinus*, *Santalum album*, *Tropaeolum majus*, *Vaccinium uva-ursi* (see also plants listed as diuretics below).

Inflammation of the urinary tract (including urolithiasis and nephrolithiasis)

Inflammation of the kidneys and urinary tract can be caused by bacterial infections, urinary gravel and stones (formed from urate, oxalate, cystin, xanthine or creatine). Inflammations can be accompanied by spasms.

TREATMENT Diuretic drugs containing terpenoids, coumarins, furanocoumarins, flavonoids, saponins, cardiac glycosides, or their metabolic products, lead to increased urine formation and have a rinsing and anti-inflammatory effect in the urinary tract. More diluted urine prevents stone formation (prophylactic effect). When spastic pains occur, they can be treated with spasmolytic drugs, such as *Scopolia carniolica* or *Petasites hybridus*. In the case of stones and gravel, diuretic, spasmolytic and litholytic drugs can be applied.

MAIN AND TRADITIONAL PLANTS **Diuretic drugs:** *Adonis vernalis, Agathosma betulina, Angelica archangelica, Apium graveolens, Asparagus officinalis, Betula pendula* and related species, *Convallaria majalis, Equisetum arvense, Fagopyrum esculentum, Genista tinctoria, Helichrysum arenarium, Helleborus niger, Herniaria glabra, Hibiscus sabdariffa, Juniperus communis, Lespedeza capitata, Levisticum officinale, Melilotus officinalis* and related species, *Ononis spinosa, Orthosiphon aristatus, Petroselinum crispum, Phaseolus vulgaris, Pimpinella major, Polygonum hydropiper, Rhamnus frangula, Ribes nigrum, Rosa canina, Smilax* species, *Solidago canadensis, S. virgaurea, Taraxacum officinale, Urginea maritima, Urtica dioica, Viola tricolor.* **Antispasmodic and analgesic drugs:** *Ammi visnaga, Atropa belladonna, Berberis vulgaris, Chelidonium majus, Melissa officinalis, Petasites hybridus, Scopolia carniolica.* **Plants with urolithiasis effects:** *Rubia tinctorum.*

Benign prostatic hypertrophy (BPH)

This condition is characterised by an increased size of the prostate caused by growth of fibromuscular and epithelial tissues around urethra. The frequency of BPH increases with age and about 70% of men above 75 have BPH, but only 30–40% of men suffer from it. Symptoms include dysuria, increased urination, urgency to urinate, especially at night (nycturia), and difficulty to urinate. Consequences of urethra constriction through BPH are decreased urine flow and pressure and urine retention in the bladder. It is likely that BPH is caused by a decrease in testosterone production and in its increased conversion to estradiol (by aromatase), dihydrotestosterone (known to induce growth of prostatic epithelia) and androstandiol (5α- and 3α reductase, respectively).

TREATMENT Besides surgery and other invasive treatments, BHP can be treated with chemically defined medicines (e.g. finasteride) and phytotherapy (especially plants with phytosterols). The aim is to inhibit the proliferation of periurethral tissues and to relax urethral and prostatic muscles in order to enhance urethral flow. More than 20 controlled clinical studies (double-blind, randomised) proved the efficacy of *Serenoa* and *Urtica*, alone and in combination (e.g. 320 mg *Serenoa-* and 240 mg *Urtica* extract per day), to reduce BPH symptoms. The benefits were comparable to those of finasteride, but with much less side effects.

MAIN AND TRADITIONAL PLANTS *Cucurbita pepo, Epilobium parviflorum, E. angustifolium, Hypoxis hemerocallidea* (=*H. rooperi*), pollen from *Secale cereale, Phleum pratense, Zea mays* (extractum pollinis siccum), *Populus tremuloides, P. tremula, Prunus africana, Rhus aromatica, Scopolia carniolica, Serenoa repens* (=*Sabal serrulata*), *Urtica dioica.* **Sedative drugs:** *Humulus lupulus, Hypericum perforatum, Piper methysticum, Valeriana officinalis.*

Disorders of the musculoskeletal system

Rheumatism and arthritis

Rheumatic disorders that can be treated with phytomedicines include soft tissue rheumatism, polyarthritis, spondylitis, athrosis and gout. These disorders are complex and involve inflammation and degeneration of skeletal muscles, bones and joints, often accompanied by severe pain.

TREATMENT Because of pain and inflammation, a symptomatic treatment is carried out by inhibiting enzymes of prostaglandin and leucotriene formation, such as cyclooxygenase, and 5-lipoxygenase (e.g. by salicylic acid, iridoid glycosides and derivatives). Another approach uses cortico-mimetic substances (triterpenes, steroids, and other secondary metabolites) that induce endogenous cortisone formation, and thus block the first step of arachidonic acid release, i.e. by inhibiting phospholipase A2 and C. Immune modulating and immune-suppressive therapy can also be useful. Traditional medicine employs counter irritants, drugs against *dyscrasia* as well as hydrolytic enzymes, such as papain, bromelain, ficin, pepsin, trypsin, amylases, and lipases. Controlled clinical studies have shown the efficacy of *Harpagophytum, Salix* and *Urtica* to treat rheumatic disorder.

MAIN AND TRADITIONAL PLANTS **Plants with inhibitors of prostaglandin formation:** *Arnica montana, Boswellia sacra, Chrysanthemum parthenium, Filipendula ulmaria, Gaultheria procumbens, Harpagophytum procumbens, Matricaria recutita, Populus tremula, Primula elatior, P. veris, Salix alba, S. purpurea, Solidago* *virgaurea, Urtica dioica, Viola tricolor.* **Plants with hyperaemic and anti-inflammatory essential oils:** *Arnica montana, Brassica nigra, Bryonia dioica, Capsicum annuum, C. frutescens, Cinnamomum camphora, C. verum, Croton tiglium, Eucalyptus globulus, Juniperus communis, Pinus mugo, P. sylvestris, Rhododendron tomentosum (=Ledum palustre), Rosmarinus officinalis, Spilanthes acmella, Syzygium aromaticum, Taraxacum officinale, Thymus vulgaris, Verbena officinalis, Viscum album.* **Plants with cortico-mimetic properties:** *Boswellia serrata, Bryonia dioica, Calendula officinalis, Glycyrrhiza glabra, Phytolacca americana, Smilax regelii, Solanum dulcamara, Withania somnifera.* **Immune stimulants:** *Echinacea angustifolia* and related species, *Viscum album.* **Enzyme sources:** *Ananas comosus, Carica papaya, Ficus carica.* **Other plants:** *Aconitum napellus, Cardiospermum halicacabum, Commiphora mukul, Gelsemium sempervirens, Gnaphalium polycephalum, Lachnanthes tinctoria, Ruta graveolens, Symphytum officinale.*

Gout

An imbalance of uric acid, known as hyperuricemia (>6.5 mg uric acid/ 100 ml serum) is caused by a disorder of the purine metabolism and leads to a precipitation of sodium urate crystals in the synovial fluids of the big toe (hallux), and less common, of the knee, tarsus, wrist and finger joints. These crystals cause an inflammation and attract leukocytes and macrophages. Macrophages are lysed when digesting the urate crystals and release lysosomal enzymes that aggravate the inflammation. In addition, leukocytes release lactic acid that lowers the local hydrogen ion concentration and decreases the solubility of urate, thus intensifying its crystallisation.

TREATMENT Colchicine is used to stop the vicious cycle: colchicine binds to tubulin and thus inhibits microtubule formation and therefore the motility of macrophages (chemotaxis) which no longer aggregate in the inflamed joints. In addition, colchicine has indirect analgesic properties, as it inhibits the release of prostaglandin. Because colchicine is very toxic (lethal dose 20 mg), not more than 8 mg should be used to treat an acute attack of gout.

MAIN PLANTS *Colchicum autumnale.*

Disorders of the endocrine system

Menstrual disorders

Menstruation (occurring every 28 days) can be too frequent (polymenorrhoea), irregular (oligomenorrhoea), absent (amenorrhoea), painful (dysmenorrhoea), too strong (hypermenorrhoea, menorrhagia) or too weak (hypomenorrhoea). Uterine bleeding that is not connected with menstruation can occur during pregnancy, after birth or may be caused by inflammation, polyps or myomas.

TREATMENT This disorder is often caused by hormonal or endocrine disturbances. Therefore, hormones or hormone mimetics are used for therapy, such as oestrogens or gestagens. However, plant medicines may also play a role in this context.

Antidysmenorrhoics are medicines that reduce menstrual pains and are often spasmolytic, analgesic, astringent or aim to arrest menstrual bleeding. Other medicines (emmenagoga) induce or enhance menstrual bleeding involving a direct or indirect stimulation of the womb. The latter compounds can induce an abortion at higher concentration and should be avoided during pregnancy.

MAIN AND TRADITIONAL PLANTS *Achillea millefolium, Alchemilla vulgaris, Aloe* species, *Aristolochia clematitis* (beware of carcinogenic aristolochic acid!), *Atropa belladonna, Brassica nigra, Capsella bursa-pastoris, Chamaemelum nobile, Chelidonium majus, Chrysanthemum vulgare, Cimicifuga racemosa, Cinchona* species, *Cinnamomum zeylanicum, Claviceps purpurea, Cyclamen europaeum, Cytisus scoparius, Equisetum arvense, Erigeron canadensis, Hyoscyamus niger, Inula helenium, Juniperus sabina, Lamium album, Matricaria recutita, Melissa officinalis, Myristica fragrans, Petroselinum crispum, Polygonum aviculare, P. hydropiper, Potentilla anserina, Pulsatilla vulgaris, Rhamnus frangula, Ricinus communis, Rosmarinus officinalis, Ruta graveolens, Senecio ovatus* (= *S. nemorensis*; beware of carcinogenic PAs!), *Senna alexandrina, Veratrum album, Viburnum prunifolium, Viscum album, Vitex agnus-castus.*

Premenstrual tension and climacteric syndrome

Premenstrual tension (PMS) occurs a few days before menstrual bleeding and is characterised by anxiety, irritability, change of mood, insomnia, headache, pain in swollen breasts (mastodynia), abdominal pains or oedema in the legs. PMS is caused by an imbalance between progesteron and oestrogen and is strongly influenced by psychosomatic factors. Climacteric syndrome describes a disturbance of women over 45 when ovarian functions diminish. It is characterised by a reduced production of oestrogen and gestagens whereas gonadotropic hormone secretion (FSH, LH) is enhanced. Symptoms of the climacteric syndrome are complex and manifold and include menstrual irregularities, dysfunctional bleeding, hot flushes, profuse perspiration, insomnia and depression.

TREATMENT Climacteric syndrome is usually treated with oestrogen or oestrogen/gestagen. For PMS and climacteric problems plant extracts with hormone mimetics and "phytoestrogens" are also useful. Psychosomatic side effects can be treated with antidepressant, spasmolytic and anxiolytic phytomedicines or with plant tonics. Controlled clinical studies with *Cimicifuga racemosa*, *Vitex agnus-castus*, *Piper methysticum* and *Panax ginseng* have provided evidence for efficacy in the treatment of PMS and the climacteric syndrome.

MAIN PLANTS Hormone mimetics: *Cimicifuga racemosa*, *Glycine max*, *Lycopus virginicus*, *Rheum rhaponticum*, *Vitex agnus-castus*. **Treatment of psychosomatic problems:** *Eleutherococcus senticosus*, *Hypericum perforatum*, *Panax ginseng*, *Piper methysticum*. **Plants used in traditional medicine:** *Pulsatilla vulgaris*, *Sanguinaria canadensis*, *Strychnos nux-vomica*, *Viburnum prunifolium*.

Inflammation of the genital tract

Inflammations of female genitalia can be caused by fungal, bacterial or viral infections.

TREATMENT Infections are treated locally or systemically with antimycotics and antibiotics. Treatment with phytomedicine is also useful and includes drugs with anti-inflammatory or antimicrobial secondary metabolites (e.g. tannins, essential oils). An immune-stimulant effect of some plants can enhance the healing process.

MAIN AND TRADITIONAL PLANTS *Achillea millefolium*, *Alchemilla vulgaris*, *Bryonia dioica*, *Echinacea* species, *Lamium album*, *Malva sylvestris*, *Matricaria recutita*, *Polygonum aviculare*, *Quercus robur*, *Rosmarinus officinalis*, *Salvia officinalis*, *Thuja occidentalis*, *Urtica dioica*, *Vaccinium uva-ursi*.

Mastitis

Inflammation of the breast (mastitis) is usually caused by infection within the breast-feeding period. Mastodynia refers to a tension of the breast shortly before onset of menstrual bleeding (see PMS).

TREATMENT In severe cases of mastitis, antibiotics are required and further lactation is blocked by prolactin inhibitors. In traditional medicine, teas with antimicrobial properties have been used.

MAIN AND TRADITIONAL PLANTS *Bellis perennis*, *Conium maculatum*, *Humulus lupulus*, *Juglans regia*, *Phytolacca americana*, *Salvia officinalis*.

Immune system

Immunodeficiency or immunosuppression

Causes of immunodeficiency and immune suppression can be manifold: wrong nutrition and lifestyle (too little or too much food; lack of movement; extensive sport activity; heavy alcohol and nicotine intake), environmental influences (climatic changes, UV-exposure; toxins), severe burns, certain disorders (diabetes, uremia, tumors, severe allergies), medical treatment (chemotherapy, antibiotic treatment) and psychosomatic factors. A suppression of the cellular and humoral immune response can result in increased infection and inflammation rates.

TREATMENT Known immune deficiencies can be treated by stimulation of cellular and humoral immune responses. As this is a complex field and patients show great individual variation, it is difficult to obtain unequivocal pharmacological evidence for efficacy of phytomedicinal treatments. Immune stimulating secondary metabolites include polysaccharides, alkylamide, phenolics, triterpenes and non-protein amino acids. Controlled clinical studies with *Echinacea* and *Eleutherococcus* extracts indicate some positive therapeutic effects in the treatment of infections and common cold. Counter-irritant therapy or iritative therapy uses plants with pungent, hyperaemic, inflammatory or cytotoxic ingredients to stimulate the immune system.

MAIN PLANTS *Baptisia tinctoria, Echinacea purpurea, E. pallida, E. angustifolia, Eleutherococcus senticosus,* medicinal yeast (*Saccharomyces cerevisiae*), *Sutherlandia frutescens, Tabebuia impetiginosa, Thuja occidentalis, Viscum album.* **Plants used in traditional medicine**: *Achyrocline satureoides, Arnica montana, Calendula officinalis, Eupatorium perfoliatum, E. cannabinum* (beware of carcinogenic PAs!), *Matricaria recutita.* **Irritative therapy uses**: *Capsicum annuum, Croton tiglium* (beware of co-carcinogenic phorbol esters!); *Daphne mezereum, Euphorbia* species (beware of co-carcinogenic phorbol esters!); *Rhus toxicodendron, Sinapis nigra,* terpentine from *Pinus* (and toxins from animals, such as *Apis, Lachesis* and *Lytta vesicatoria*).

Disorders of the respiratory tract

Common cold; rhinitis, sinusitis, and otitis

Disorders of the respiratory tract (more than 90%) are caused by various viruses that destroy mucosal cells. The necrotic tissues can secondarily suffer from bacterial infections. Mucosas swell and show an enhanced mucus production. Pollinosis (hayfever) is an allergic disturbance affecting the respiratory tract. This disorder is often a complex with rhinitis, tracheitis, laryngitis, pharyngitis and acute bronchitis. Rhinitis can lead to sinusitis, a painful inflammation of ethmoidal, frontal, maxilliary or sphenoidal sinuses. Otitis is a painful inflammation of the middle ear (otidis media) or outer ear (otitis externa), caused by bacterial infections.

A common cold must be distinguished from viral influenza. The latter disorder is characterised by high fever, intense headache, muscle pains and cough.

TREATMENT Mainly symptomatic – products with anti-inflammatory, antiallergic and mucosa subsiding, mucosa protectant, antibacterial, demulcent, astringent and immunostimulant properties are widely employed. Phytomedicines are usually applied locally (ointments, balsams or inhalations). Immunomodulatory drugs are taken orally (sometimes locally or parenterally). Monoterpenes such as menthol, generate the sensation of cooling, thus relieving the pain and discomfort of cold symptoms. Infants and small children may suffer from severe spasms (glottis, bronchia) when treated with essential oils – be careful!

MAIN AND TRADITIONAL PLANTS **Plants with essential oils**: *Cinnamomum camphora, Commiphora myrrha, Eucalyptus globulus, Foeniculum vulgare, Matricaria recutita, Mentha x piperita* and others, *Picea abies* and others, *Pimpinella anisum, Pinus mugo* and others, *Salvia officinalis, Thymus serpyllum, T. vulgaris.* **Plants with alkaloids and other ingredients**: *Allium cepa, Cinchona* species, *Ephedra distachya, Euphrasia officinalis, Galphimia glauca, Gentiana lutea, Luffa operculata, Phytolacca americana, Primula veris, Verbena officinalis.* **Immunostimulatory drugs**: *Baptisia tinctoria, Echinacea angustifolia* and related species, *Thuja occidentalis.*

Bronchitis

Acute bronchitis is caused by viral, bacterial or fungal infections and is characterised by a disturbance of bronchial mucosa, including hyperemia, oedema, cell death, increase mucus production, cough and dyspnoea. Chronic bronchitis may result from relapsing infections, chronic sinusitis, bronchial allergies and excessive smoking. It is characterised initially by cough and expectoration, then by dyspnoea and respiratory insufficiency and in severe cases by obstructive emphysema. Acute bronchitis can lead to pneumonia, which needs to be treated with antibiotics.

TREATMENT Most phytomedicines used to treat bronchitis are mixtures of several drugs, that are taken orally, by inhalation (essential oils) or topical application (in case of lipophilic essential oils). As an adjuvant therapy to antibiotics and chemotherapy, drugs that stimulate the immune system (immunostimulants) and physical measures (inhalation, topical application, and wet packs) can be useful. Topically applied phytomedicines may have expectorant, anti-inflammatory, spasmolytic and disinfectant properties. Expectorant drugs can be rich in saponins or the alkaloid emetine, which is not resorbed but stimulates the nervus vagus in the stomach. In a reflectory way this stimulation leads to a secretion of water in the bronchia that dilutes the mucus; a secretolytic effect results. Drugs with essential oils stimulate secretion of bronchial endothelia (secretolytic effect) and enhance ciliary activity (secretomotoric effect).

Anti-inflammatory, spasmolytic and disinfectant activities can be further beneficial properties of mono-terpenes, sesquiterpenes and phenylpropanoids present in essential oils. In addition, saponins may exhibit corticomimetic effects. Salicylic acid derivatives present in *Viola* and *Primula* and iridoid glycosides in *Verbena*, *Plantago* and *Veronica* may enhance the anti-inflammatory properties.

Clinical studies provide evidence for the efficacy of essential oils in treating bronchitis.

MAIN AND TRADITIONAL PLANTS **Saponin and iridoid drugs:** *Aesculus hippocastanum*, *Castanea sativa*, *Glycyrrhiza glabra*, *Gypsophila paniculata*, *Hedera helix*, *Plantago lanceolata*, *Polygala senega*, *Primula elatior*, *P. veris*, *Pulmonaria officinalis*, *Rumex crispus*, *Saponaria officinalis*, *Viola tricolor*. **Alkaloid drugs:** *Camellia sinensis*, *Ephedra distachya*, *Hydrastis canadensis*, *Papaver somniferum*, *Psychotria ipecacuanha* (=*Cephaelis ipecacuanha*). **Plants with essential oils:** *Asarum europaeum*, *Cinnamomum camphora*, *Eucalyptus globulus*, *Foeniculum vulgare*, *Glechoma hederacea*, *Hyssopus officinalis*, *Inula helenium*, *Larix decidua*, *Mentha x piperita* and others, *Picea abies* and others, *Pimpinella anisum*, *P. saxifraga*, *Pinus mugo* and others, *Salvia officinalis*, *Thymus vulgaris*, *T. serpyllum*, *T. zygis*, *Verbena officinalis*, *Veronica officinalis*.

Asthma

Asthma (*Asthma bronchiale*) is a complex disorder. It is influenced by infections, toxins and allergens that cause a chronic inflammation but also by stress and other psychosomatic factors. Bronchial hyperreactivity is intermediary to *asthma bronchiale*. An asthma attack starts with the release of cellular mediators from mast cells, granulocytes and macrophages, including leukotrienes, prostaglandins, bradykinine, histamine and others. These compounds induce a contraction of smooth bronchial muscles, and enhance mucus and oedema formation.

TREATMENT Causal treatment may include the avoidance of allergens, a specific hyposensitisation, an anti-infective and psychotherapy. A symptomatic treatment involves the application of bronchodilatory, expectorant, antitussive and anti-inflammatory medicines.

In case of *status asthmaticus* (severe attack) glucocorticoids and isolated alkaloids such as theophylline (broncholytic by inhibition of phosphodiesterase and histamine secretion) and atropine (sympatholytic; spasmolytic on smooth bronchial muscles) (and their derivatives) are used. Ephedrine is an indirect sym-pathomimetic that enhances the release of noradrenaline with bronchodilatory properties. Otherwise, plant extracts with weaker activities can be applied.

MAIN PLANTS *Ammi visnaga*, *Atropa belladonna*, *Camellia sinensis*, *Datura stramonium*, *Ephedra distachya* and other species, *Hyoscyamus niger*. **Plants used in traditional medicine:** *Allium cepa*, *Aralia racemosa*, *Grindelia robusta*, *Lobelia inflata*, *Solanum dulcamara*.

Cough, irritating cough, pertussis

Cough is a symptom of various disorders, including bronchial infections, asthma and chronic bronchitis. Whooping cough (pertussis) is caused by an infection with *Bordetella pertussis*. Cough can be a burden on the heart and circulation.

TREATMENT Cough is a reflex that helps to eliminate (expel) mucus or foreign bodies from the bronchial tract. A complete inhibition of cough is therefore not advisable. Antitussives are indicated in cases of unproductive and distressing cough, especially nightly and dry irritating cough. In the case of productive cough, i.e. when mucus is produced, antitussives are no longer required. Cough can be silenced centrally by affecting the neuronal "cough centre" in the *Medulla oblongata* (e.g. by codeine and noscapine). Most phytomedicines (with mucilage, essential oils) affect peripheral targets, such as nerves in the throat; they are "calmed down" so that cough irritation is suppressed. Plants with quinones, such as plumbagin and droserone have been used to treat pertussis. Phytomedicines that are used to treat bronchitis are also relevant and often useful for relieving cough and irritating cough.

MAIN AND TRADITIONAL PLANTS (see also bronchitis) *Drosera ramentacea, D. rotundifolia, Ephedra distachya, Eryngium planum, Papaver somniferum, Pinguicula vulgaris, Rhododendron tomentosum (=Ledum palustre)*. **Plants with mucilages:** *Althaea officinalis, Cetraria islandica, Malva neglecta, M. sylvestris, Plantago lanceolata, Trigonella foenum-graecum, Tussilago farfara, Verbascum densiflorum* and others.

Mucosal inflammation

Mucosa of the mouth and respiratory tract are subject to viral, bacterial and fungal infections that can lead to painful inflammation. Difficulty in swallowing, hoarseness and swollen tissues are typical symptoms of gingivitis, stomatitis, pharyngitis, laryngitis and tonsillitis.

TREATMENT Treatment with phytomedicines is symptomatic and mainly external, by using extracts for gargling, rinsing, or inhalation. Several plant medicines used for this indication have anti-inflammatory effects. Drugs with tannins, essential oils and mustard oils have antibacterial properties, thus a mild disinfectant effect can also be achieved.

MAIN AND TRADITIONAL PLANTS **Plants with essential oils:** *Achillea millefolium, Chamaemelum nobile, Commiphora erythraea, C. myrrha* and others, *Eucalyptus globulus, Foeniculum vulgare, Matricaria recutita, Mentha x piperita, Salvia officinalis, S. triloba, Santalum album, Syzygium aromaticum, Thymus vulgaris*. **Plants with tannins:** *Geum urbanum, Hamamelis virginiana, Hydrastis canadensis, Krameria lappacea, Potentilla erecta, Quercus robur, Rheum palmatum*. **Plants with glucosinolates:** *Armoracia rusticana, Tropaeolum majus*. **Plants with anti-inflammatory metabolites:** *Plantago lanceolata, Solidago virgaurea, Viola tricolor*.

Disorders of the skin

Wounds and haematoma

A distinction is made between primary wounds – caused by cuts, stabs, abrasions and scratches – and secondary wounds – caused by bites, fissures, burns or contusions (bruises with damaged veins below intact skin). Primary wounds heal within six to eight days without loss of tissue after a scab or scurf has been formed. Secondary wounds are slower to heal since new tissue (granulation tissue) has to be formed and the process is often accompanied by infections and haematomas.

TREATMENT Wounds are treated with medicines or medicinal plants that have haemostyptic, disinfectant, wound cleaning, analgesic, anti-inflammatory and astringent properties. Some of these may also promote the formation of granulation tissue and new epithelia. Responsible compounds include flavonoids, tannins, essential oils, sesquiterpenes, saponins, allantoin, benzoylesters, alkylamides, polysaccharides (e.g. mucilage), fatty oils and enzymes (e.g. papain, bromelain).

MAIN AND TRADITIONAL PLANTS *Achillea millefolium, Allium cepa, Aloe vera, Ananas comosus, Arnica montana, Artemisia abrotanum, Bellis perennis, Calendula officinalis, Carica papaya, Centella asiatica, Cinnamomum camphora, Commiphora myrrha, Echinacea* species, *Eucalyptus globulus, Hamamelis virginiana, Hydnocarpus kurzii, Hypericum perforatum, Juglans regia, Krameria lappacea, Marrubium vulgare, Matricaria recutita, Melaleuca alternifolia, Myroxylon balsamum, Pinus sylvestris, Quercus robur, Rhododendron tomentosum (=Ledum palustre), Rosmarinus officinalis, Ruta graveolens, Symphytum officinale, Syzygium aromaticum, Verbena officinalis*.

Infections (bacteria, fungi, viruses)

The skin can be infected by fungi (e.g. *Candida*), bacteria, and certain viruses (e.g. *Herpes labialis, Herpes zoster*).

TREATMENT Fungi can be treated with specific antimycotics, bacteria with antibiotics and viruses with virustatic or virucidal medicines. Usually, classical antibiotics and chemotherapeutics are used for treatment, since the activity of plant extracts is often too low to overcome severe infections. Nevertheless, plants with phenolics (such as rosmarinic acid), tannins, essential oils, phenylpropanoids (e.g. eugenol), saponins and some alkaloids (e.g. berberine, sanguinarine) exhibit substantial disinfectant, antibacterial, antifungal and antiviral properties.

MAIN AND TRADITIONAL PLANTS *Allium sativum, Cinnamomum camphora, C. verum, Eucalyptus* species, *Matricaria recutita, Melaleuca alternifolia* and related species, *Melissa officinalis, Mentha x piperita, Myroxylon balsamum, Pinus sylvestris* and related species, *Sutherlandia frutescens, Syzygium aromaticum, Thuja occidentalis, Thymus vulgaris*.

Psoriasis

Psoriasis is a complex disorder (influenced by inherited and psychosomatic factors) and characterised by an enhanced proliferation of epidermal cells (keratocytes) that leads to the extensive production of scales. This disorder is often accompanied by inflammation of the skin.

TREATMENT Psoriasis is mainly treated symptomatically. Inflammation can be controlled by anti-inflammatory medicines and the proliferation of epidermal cells by chemotherapy. Synthetic drugs can be used, but phytotherapy also plays a role in the treatment of psoriasis. Plants with cytotoxic alkaloids, such as berberine (e.g. in *Mahonia aquifolium*), with dianthranols (mostly synthetic today; formerly from *Andira araroba*), or with phototoxic furanocoumarins (e.g. abundant in members of the Apiaceae) are employed. Furanocoumarins, such as 8-methoxypsoralen, are lipophilic and easily penetrate the skin. Inside the cells, furanocoumarins intercalate DNA. If the skin is then exposed to UV light (360 nm) these compounds are activated and can form covalent bonds with thymine bases in the DNA. The alkylation stops DNA replication and induces cell death. Longterm utilisation of this treatment (known as phototherapy), which uses mainly isolated compounds, such as 8-methoxypsoralen, can cause skin cancer. Salicylic acid has also been used to treat psoriasis because of its keratolytic properties; vitamin A derivatives, such as retinoids can influence inflammation and cell proliferation. In traditional medicine, tars produced from *Betula, Fagus, Juniperus* and other woody plants, which contain cytotoxic phenols, cresols, anthracenes and naphthalins, have been employed.

MAIN PLANTS *Ammi majus, Angelica archangelica, Levisticum officinale, Mahonia aquifolium.* **Plants used in traditional medicine:** Tars from *Betula, Fagus, Juniperus*; extracts containing steroidal saponins of *Andira araroba, Centella asiatica, Smilax aristolochiaefolia, S. regelii*.

Vitiligo

Vitiligo is characterised by the occurrence of white patches on the skin that can be round or irregular in shape. The origin of vitiligo is uncertain but has been linked to disorders of the nervous system or an inhibition of pigment formation by genetic or immunological factors.

TREATMENT Furanocoumarins, such as psoralen, in combination with UV light (UV-A) induce repigmentation of skin parts with vitiligo. Carotenoids, such as β-carotene or canthaxanthin, are deposited in the epidermis and can slightly compensate for the pigment deficiency.

MAIN PLANTS Plants with furanocoumarins (see psoriasis).

Eczema, neurodermatitis, haemorrhoids, other inflammations

Eczemas are dermal inflammations that affect either the epidermis or cutaneous-vascular tissues. Certain types affect the skin epidermis, e.g. contact dermatitis, allergies and contact eczema, diaper dermatitis and atopic dermatitis (neurodermatitis). The second type of dermatitis includes exanthema caused by chemicals and medicines, plant allergies, urticaria, Quincke's oedema, and photoallergies.

TREATMENT If allergens are responsible for eczema, the obvious treatment is to avoid such allergens in food, cosmetics or the environment. Chronic eczema can be caused by disturbances of the metabolism and a sensible treatment is to improve the basic underlying problems and to induce physiological changes. Treatment with medicinal plants includes the topical application of fatty ointments to protect the skin from unspecific irritations, anti-inflammatory compounds (that block the cascade leading to prostaglandins and leucotrienes; e.g. salicylic acid and corticomimetics) and compounds that suppress itching. Severe allergic skin disorders are usually treated with antihistamines and corticoids. Secondary plant metabolites used to treat eczema include flavonoids, tannins, essential oils, sesquiterpenes, saponins, allantoin, benzoylesters, salicylic acid, alkylamides and polysaccharides (e.g. mucilage).

Oils rich in unsaturated fatty acids (linolic and linoleic acid) that are precursors for the biosynthesis of arachidonic acid (used to make prostaglandins and leucotrienes) have been employed to treat neurodermatitis.

MAIN PLANTS *Echinacea pallida* and related species, *Hamamelis virginiana*, *Linum usitatissimum*, *Matricaria recutita*, *Oenothera biennis*, *Quercus robur*, *Smilax regelii*, *Solanum dulcamara*, *Viola tricolor*. **Plants used in traditional medicine:** *Anacardium occidentale*, *Cardiospermum halicacabum*, *Chelidonium majus*, *Croton tiglium*, *Daphne mezereum*, *Euphrasia officinalis*, *Fagopyrum esculentum*, *Galium* species, *Juglans regia*, *Nerium oleander*, *Urtica dioica*.

Pruritus and insect bites

Pruritus or unpleasant itching is a symptom of most dermal disorders. It can also be symptomatic of a metabolic disorder, such as diabetes, icterus, renal failure and gout. Pruritus can also be caused by allergens or insect bites. Itching occurs when cellular mediators, such as histamine, bradykinin or prostaglandin are released and interact with corresponding receptors. The stings or bites of various insects may induce the release of these mediators.

TREATMENT Medicinal plants or isolated plant products (menthol, thymol, camphor) are used to reduce itching by local cooling, anaesthetic, analgesic, anti-inflammatory or astringent effects.

MAIN PLANTS *Cinnamomum camphora*, *Lavandula angustifolia*, *Matricaria recutita*, *Mentha* species, *Thymus vulgaris*, *Viola tricolor*. **Plants used in traditional medicine:** *Allium cepa*, *Cardiospermum halicacabum*, *Fagopyrum esculentum*, *Mucuna pruriens*, *Plantago lanceolata*. Extracts from honeybees (*Apis mellifera*) are also used.

Acne, seborrhea

Acne is a complex disorder, often prevalent during puberty. It is characterised by an enhanced sebum production (seborrhea) and an increased cornification of the follicles (hyperkeratosis). Acne is often accompanied by inflammation and bacterial infections (by *Corynebacterium acnes*, *Staphylococcus epidermidis*) of the follicle. Sebum production is stimulated by dihydrotestosterone, an androgen derived from testosterone.

TREATMENT Acne is treated topically by reducing sebum production (e.g. by vitamin A-acid, antiandrogens), by eliminating the cornification (e.g. with salicylic acid and retinoids) and by eradicating the bacterial infections (e.g. with antibiotics, such as erythromycin and tetracyclin). Plants containing salicylic acid or antibacterial alkaloids, saponins, and anthranoids can also be used.

MAIN AND TRADITIONAL PLANTS *Aloe ferox*, *Bellis perennis*, *Chelidonium majus*, *Equisetum arvense*, *Filipendula ulmaria*, *Fumaria officinalis*, *Juglans regia*, *Mahonia aquifolium*, *Ononis repens*, *Stellaria media*, *Viola tricolor*.

Hyperhidrosis

Enhanced or excessive perspiration is known as hyperhidrosis. It can be caused by internal, psychic and external factors.

TREATMENT External treatment utilises drugs rich in tannins and salicylic acid. Internally, essential oils (such as extracts from *Salvia officinalis*) and tropane alkaloids have been used. Tropane alkaloids block muscarinic acetylcholine receptors and thus the smooth muscles of sweat glands.

MAIN AND TRADITIONAL PLANTS *Atropa belladonna*, *Pilocarpus jaborandi*, *Quercus robur*, *Salvia officinalis*, *Sanguinaria canadensis*, *Viola tricolor*.

Warts and *Condylomata acuminata*

Warts and *Condylomata acuminata* (warts occurring on genitalia) are caused by viruses of the papilloma group (HPV = Human Papilloma Virus) that induce the growth of their host cells. Warts can also result from hyperkeratosis, an excessive cornification of the palm of the hand and sole of the foot.

TREATMENT Painful plantar warts are removed surgically, whereas other warts are removed by local etching and peeling treatments. A more conservative treatment with plant extracts has been used in traditional medicine. Salicylic acid has a substantial keratolytic effect, whereas the lignan podophyllotoxin (in extracts of *Podophyllum peltatum*) and the alkaloid sanguinarine (in *Chelidonium majus*) exhibit virucidal properties.

Main plants *Podophyllum peltatum*. **Plants used in traditional medicine:** *Chelidonium majus, Lycopodium annotinum, Thuja occidentalis*.

Disorders of the eye

Disorders of the eye comprise a wide range of disturbances. **Glaucoma** is a complex condition characterised by an enhanced inner eye pressure that can lead to reduced vision and blindness. **Inflammation** can affect the iris (iritis), the uvea (uveitis) and cornea (keratitis); symptoms are local pain, enhanced production of tears, avoidance of light, spasms of the eyelids (*blepharospasm*) and disturbance of vision. In addition, the conjunctiva and the eyelid (blepharo-conjunctivitis) and the retina (retinopathy) can become inflamed. A special case is retinopathies, caused by diabetes.

Treatment The treatment of glaucoma is aimed at the reduction of intra-ocular pressure. The plant alkaloids pilocarpine (activates mAChR) and physostigmine (inhibits AChE) are parasympathomimetics and stimulate the contraction of eye muscles (M. *ciliaris*, M. *sphincter pupillae*). Atropine and scopolamine are parasympatholytics and inhibit the ciliary muscle (mydriatic). These alkaloids are used to treat iritis, uveitis and keratitis and are useful for eye diagnostics. Inflammations of conjunctiva and the eyelid (and eye infections) have been treated with plant-derived substances that exhibit antimicrobial and anti-inflammatory activities, such as the alkaloid berberine and extracts containing saponins, essential oils and tannins. Flavonoids, such as rutin (or synthetic derivatives, such as troxerutin) prevent internal bleeding and oedema and exhibit anti-inflammatory effects. It is used for diabetic retinopathies.

Main plants *Atropa belladonna; Berberis vulgaris, Datura stramonium, Physostigma venenosum, Pilocarpus jaborandi*; rutin from *Fagopyrum esculentum, Styphnolobium japonicum* or *Ruta graveolens*. **Plants used in traditional medicine:** *Aesculus hippocastanum, Allium cepa, Arnica montana, Delphinium staphisagria, Digitalis lanata, Euphrasia officinalis, Foeniculum vulgare, Hamamelis virginiana, Matricaria recutita, Prunus spinosa, Rosa canina, Ruta graveolens*.

Parasitic infections

Especially in the tropics, humans suffer from various parasitic infections. Common ones include malaria (caused by *Plasmodium*), amoebiasis (caused by amoebas), schistosomiasis (caused by schistosomes), sleeping sickness (caused by trypanosomes), filariasis (caused by *Filaria*) and various types of intestinal worms.

Treatment Most drugs that affect an intestinal parasite will also affect the host. Amoebas have been treated with emetine from *Psychotria* (it inhibits protein biosynthesis and intercalates DNA) and malaria with quinine from *Cinchona* (inhibits parasitic metabolism and is also a DNA intercalating agent) or artemisinin from *Artemisia annua*. Intestinal worms have traditionally been treated with extracts from ferns (*Dryopteris filix-mas*), and higher plants (*Artemisia cina, Chenopodium ambrosioides, Chrysanthemum vulgare*).

Main and traditional plants *Artemisia maritima* and related species, *Artemisia annua, A. cina, Chenopodium ambrosioides* var. *anthelminticum, Chrysanthemum vulgare, Cinchona succirubra* and related species, *Dryopteris filix-mas, Psychotria ipecacuanha* and related species.

Pain

Intense pain

Some diseases and disorders (such as cancer), fractures, wounds and surgery are accompanied by heavy pain.

Treatment A very potent strategy is the modulation of endorphine receptors with morphine, an opium alkaloid. Opium alkaloids are highly addictive and must therefore be used with special care.

Main plants *Papaver somniferum* (morphine).

Migraine

The pathophysiology of migraine, which affects more women than men, is not fully understood, but involves a disturbance of cerebral blood circulation. Migraine headaches can be accompanied by neurological and somatic disturbances (including nausea and emesis).

TREATMENT Serotonin agonists appear to have a positive influence on migraine and promote vasoconstriction of cerebral arteries. Phytomedicines with these properties include ergot alkaloids from *Claviceps purpurea* (such as ergotamine).

MAIN AND TRADITIONAL PLANTS *Claviceps purpurea* (a fungus from *Secale*); *Chrysanthemum parthenium*, *Gelsemium sempervirens*, *Digitalis purpurea*, *Cyclamen europaeum*, *Iris versicolor*, *Sanguinaria canadensis*, *Cimicifuga racemosa*, *Petasites hybridus*.

Neuralgia

Neuralgia refers to pains along the nerves, which occur in discrete attacks. The pathophysiology is complex.

TREATMENT Neuralgia is mainly treated symptomatically, using analgesic drugs, including phytochemicals.

MAIN AND TRADITIONAL PLANTS *Aconitum napellus* and related species, *Mentha x piperita*, *Salix* species.

Cancer

Cancer comprises a large variety of malignant tumours that can affect nearly all organs of the body. Carcinomas are of epithelial origin. From a primary tumour, metastases can spread to other tissues and organs. Cancer is fatal if a tumour destroys the function of a vital organ.

TREATMENT Treatment includes surgery, radiotherapy and chemotherapy. Cancer cells usually divide much faster than "normal" cells. Therefore, compounds that stop cell division (e.g. alkaloids, such as vinblastine, vincristine, taxol, camptothecine, colchicine, demecolcine, or the lignan podophyllotoxin and partial synthetic derivatives) or compounds that kill cells (cytotoxic substances), are the two most commonly employed means of chemotherapy. Because of high toxicity and small therapeutic indices, extracts from plants are no longer used but rather isolated chemical entities. Another approach uses immune stimulants and cytotoxic peptides, e.g. viscotoxins or mistletoe lectins from *Viscum album*. Results from clinical studies are contradictory; a few show an enhanced survival rate after mistletoe treatment. An unspecific stimulation of the immune system by polysaccharides (from *Echinacea* species, certain mushrooms, e.g. *Lentinus edodes*, *Schizophyllum commune*, *Coriolus versicolor*) and quinones (from *Dionaea*, *Tabebuia*) has been postulated.

MAIN PLANTS *Camptotheca acuminata*, *Catharanthus roseus*, *Colchicum autumnale*, *Podophyllum peltatum*, *P. hexandrum*, *Taxus baccata*, *T. brevifolia*, *Viscum album*. **Plants used in traditional medicine:** *Dionaea muscipula*, *Echinacea purpurea*, *Tabebuia impetiginosa*; also mushrooms (*Lentinus edodes*, *Schizophyllum commune*, *Coriolus versicolor*).

OVERVIEW OF SECONDARY METABOLITES AND THEIR EFFECTS

Secondary metabolites, or "natural products" are low-molecular weight compounds that do not play a role in primary plant metabolism. They constitute the active ingredients of medicinal plants. Although approximately only 20% of higher plants have been investigated in some depth so far, several ten thousands of secondary metabolites (see Table below) have already been isolated and their structures determined by mass spectrometry, nuclear magnetic resonance or X-ray diffraction. Three major groups of secondary metabolites can be recognised: nitrogen-containing substances, terpenes and phenolics. Over 14 000 nitrogen-containing secondary metabolites have been described so far. Alkaloids, amines, non-protein amino acids, cyanogenic glycosides and glucosinolates are the main compounds in this group.

Number of natural products	
With nitrogen	
● Alkaloids (1)	12 000
● Non-protein amino acids (2)	700
● Amines (3)	100
● Cyanogenic glycosides (4)	60
● Glucosinolates (5)	100
● Alkamides	150
Without nitrogen	
● Monoterpenes (6) (incl. iridoids)	2 500
● Sesquiterpenes (7)	5 000
● Diterpenes (8)	2 500
● Triterpenes (9), saponins, steroids	5 000
● Tetraterpenes	500
● Phenylpropanoids, coumarins, lignans	2 000
● Flavonoids (10)	4 000
● Polyacetylenes (11), fatty acids, waxes	1 000
● Polyketides (12)	750
● Carbohydrates	>200

Overview of numbers and representative structures of secondary metabolites

371

Most animals can run or fly away in case of danger when they are threatened by predators or can use an immune system against invading microbes or parasites. Both these means are apparently not available to plants when attacked by herbivores, microbes (bacteria, fungi) and even other plants competing for light, space and nutrients. Plants have evolved numerous defence strategies. The major one is the production of secondary metabolites, which have no direct function in growth or development or primary processes such as photosynthesis, respiration, assimilation of nutrients, transport or differentiation but serve for protection against viruses, bacteria, fungi, competing plants and importantly, against herbivores (e.g. nematodes, slugs and snails, arthropods, vertebrates). In addition, secondary metabolites can serve as signal compounds to attract animals for pollination (fragrant monoterpenes; coloured anthocyanins or carotenoids) and seed dispersal. In addition, some secondary metabolites concomitantly exhibit physiological functions, for example they can serve as mobile and toxic nitrogen transport and storage compounds or for UV-protection. Besides chemical defence a number of plants use mechanical and morphological features for protection, such as thorns, spikes, glandular and stinging hairs (often filled with noxious chemicals), or develop an almost impenetrable bark (especially woody perennials).

We have to know the secondary metabolites present in a medicinal plant and their biological activities in order to understand and evaluate the effects and efficacy of phytomedicines.

ALKALOIDS AND THEIR MODES OF ACTION

Formerly, this class of secondary compounds was restricted to plant bases (if the free base is dissolved in water, an alkaline pH results) with a heterocyclic nitrogen atom. Exocyclic nitrogen bases were termed "pseudo-alkaloids". Other definitions demanded that the skeleton of alkaloids should derive from amino acids or that these bases have pharmacological activities. At present, the definition is much more pragmatic and includes all nitrogen-containing natural products which are not otherwise classified as peptides, antibiotics, non-protein amino acids, amines, cyanogenic glycosides, glucosinolates, cofactors, phytohormones or primary metabolites (such as purine and pyrimidine bases).

Alkaloids have been detected in about 15% of plants, but also occur in bacteria, fungi, and even in animals. Within the Plant Kingdom, they are found in ancient (basal) groups such as *Lycopodium* or *Equisetum*, and in higher plants such as in gymnosperms and angiosperms. In angiosperms some families contain more alkaloidal taxa than others: alkaloid-rich families include the Amaryllidaceae, Papaveraceae, Berberidaceae, Colchicaceae, Fabaceae, Boraginaceae, Apocynaceae (including Asclepiadaceae), Asteraceae, Gnetaceae, Ranunculaceae, Rubiaceae, Solanaceae, Rutaceae and others.

Alkaloids are stored predominantly in tissues that are important for survival and reproduction of the plant producing them, which include actively growing young tissues, root and stem bark, flowers (especially seeds), seedlings and photosynthetically active tissues. In general, alkaloid levels are markedly reduced in senescing tissues, so that fallen leaves are often nearly alkaloid-free. The alkaloid contents in storing organs can be quite high, reaching up to 10% of dry weight in some instances. In several herbaceous plants, alkaloids are stored in epidermal and subepidermal tissues (for example, cocaine, colchicine, aconitine, steroidal alkaloids, nicotine, veratrine, buxine, coniine, lupanine) that have to ward off small enemies (insects, microorganisms) as a first line of defence. To reach these sites of accumulation, short- and long-distance transport via xylem or phloem is required. A number of plants produce latex, which often contains defence chemicals, such as alkaloids (morphine and related benzylisoquinoline alkaloids in Papaveraceae; protoberberine and benzophenanthridine alkaloids in *Chelidonium*; lobeline and other piperidine alkaloids in *Lobelia*) and terpenoids (e.g. phorbol esters). Alkaloid patterns usually vary between the site of synthesis and the sites of accumulation, since a number of secondary substitutions may take place in the latter tissues. Or transport may be selective, resulting in differing alkaloid profiles in sink organs. In addition, alkaloid profiles of seeds and seedlings often differ from those of the mature plant. Both patterns and concentrations usually change during the development of plants and the annual cycle. In general, alkaloids are not end products of metabolism but can be degraded to serve as a nitrogen source when needed. This seems to be plausible because nitrogen is a limited nutrient for plants. Alkaloids stored in seeds are partly degraded during germination and seedling development and their nitrogen is probably used for the synthesis of amino acids. Knowledge of this alkaloidal variation in plants is important in the production of plant medicine because it allows the plants to be collected and harvested at the right time and the right growth stage.

Alkaloids are certainly multipurpose compounds which, depending on the situation, may be active in more than one environmental interaction, e.g. as defence compounds against herbivorous animals, bacteria, fungi, viruses or competing plants. Alkaloids are especially infamous as animal toxins but also represent the active principle of many medicinal plants. The various steps in neuronal signalling and signal transduction, that are unique for animals, provide central targets that are affected by several amines and alkaloids. Targets can be:

- The neuroreceptor itself. Agonists mimic the function of a neurotransmitter (acetylcholine, dopamine, noradrenaline, adrenaline, serotonin, GABA, glutamate, glycine, endorphines, peptides) by binding to its receptor and causing the normal response. Antagonists (often called "blocker") also bind to the receptor but act as an inhibitor of the natural ligand by competing for binding sites on the receptor, thereby blocking the physiological response.
- Voltage-gated Na^+, K^+ and Ca^{2+} channels.
- The enzymes, which deactivate neurotransmitters after they have bound to a receptor, such as acetyl-choline esterase, monoamine oxidase and catechol-O-methyltransferase.
- Transport processes, which are important for the uptake and release of the neurotransmitters in the presynapse or synaptic vesicles. Also Na^+, K^+ and Ca^{2+}-ATPases, which restore the ion gradients, must be considered in this category.
- Modulation of key enzymes of signal pathways:
  - adenylyl cyclase (making cAMP)
  - phosphodiesterase (inactivating cAMP or cGMP)
  - phospholipase C (releasing inositol phosphates such as IP3 and diacylglycerol (DAG)
  - several protein kinases, such as protein kinase C or tyrosine kinase (activating other regulatory proteins or ion channels).

Since alkaloids often derive from the same amino acid precursor as the neurotransmitters serotonin, norad-renaline, dopamine, GABA, glutamic acid or histamine, their structures can often be superimposed on those of neurotransmitters. Other alkaloids are planar and lipophilic; they intercalate DNA (Berberine, Sanguinarine, Emetine). Pyrrolizidine alkaloids and aristolochic acid alkylate DNA alter metabolic activa-tion in the liver. Colchicine, vinblastine, and taxol inhibit the assembly or disassembly of microtubules. Some alkaloids that intercalate and/or affect microtubules, induce apoptosis (programmed cell death). Indolizidine alkaloids inhibit carbohydrate processing enzymes in the endoplasmic reticulum.

It is apparent that alkaloid toxicity and pharmacological activity in animals and humans is clearly corre-lated with their interactions with particular molecular targets.

Pyrrolidine alkaloids

Nicotine

Nicotine (from *Nicotiana* species; Solanaceae; agonist at nicotinic acetylcholine receptor, nAChR; CNS-stimulant).

Pyrrolizidine alkaloids (PA)

Heliotrine   Senecionine

Heliotrine (from *Heliotropium* species; Boraginaceae); **senecionine** (from *Senecio* species, Asteraceae; PAs can affect a number of neuroreceptors; furthermore they are converted into active pyrrols in the liver that can alkylate DNA and proteins; PAs are therefore mutagenic and carcinogenic)

Tropane alkaloids

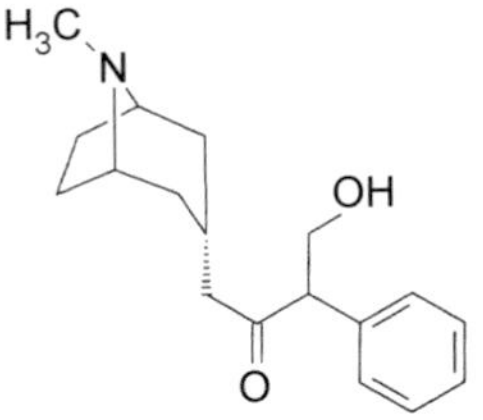

L-Hyoscyamine 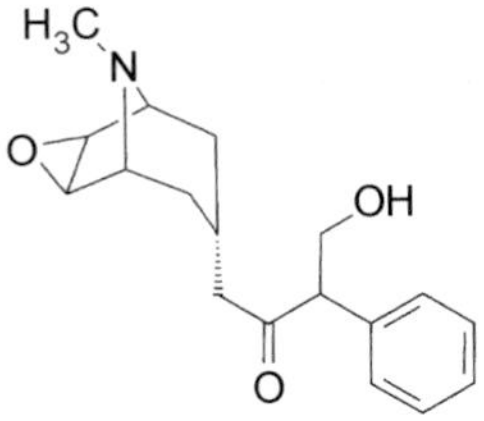   L-Scopolamine 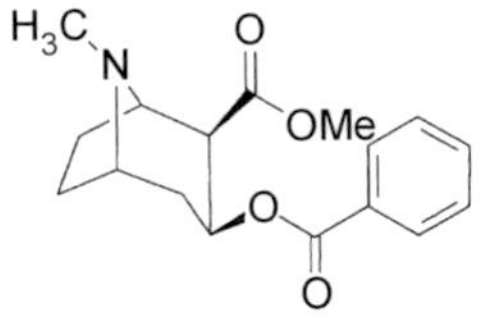   Cocaine

L-Hyoscyamine, L-scopolamine (from *Atropa, Datura, Hyoscyamus, Mandragora, Duboisia*; Solanaceae; strong antagonists at muscarinic acetylcholine receptor, mAChR; inhibition of smooth muscles and thus spasmolytic; hallucinogenic activity in CNS). **Cocaine** (from *Erythroxylon* species; Erythroxylaceae; inhibits the re-uptake of dopamine and noradrenaline, thus CNS stimulant; Na^+ channel blocker with local analgesic properties).

Piperidine alkaloids

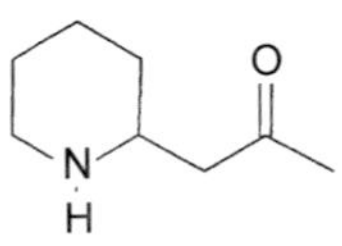

Pelletierine 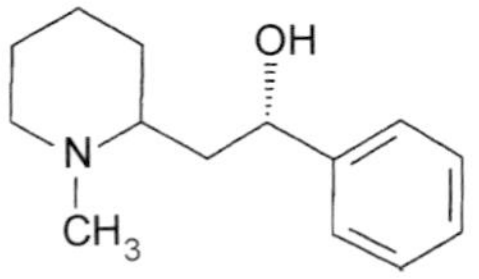   Sedamine 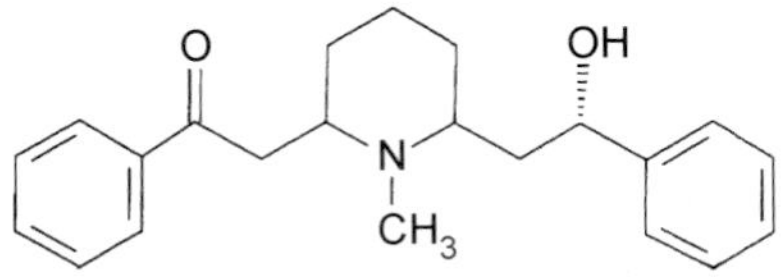   Lobeline

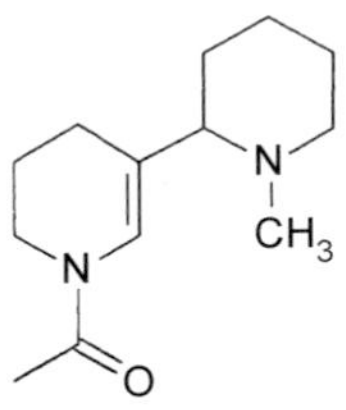

Ammodendrine 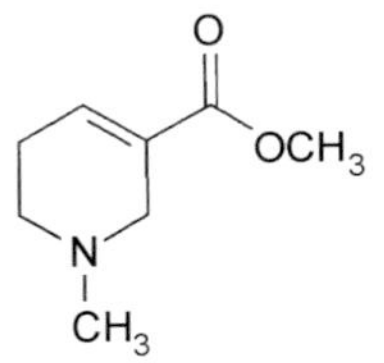   Arecoline 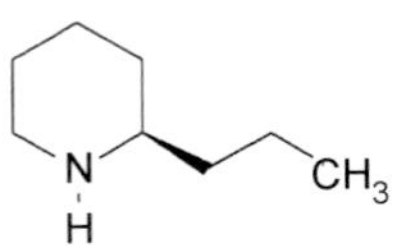   Coniine

Pelletierine (from *Punica granatum*, Punicaceae, and *Sedum* species, Crassulaceae; antagonist at nAChR, paralyses skeletal muscles). **Sedamine** (from *Sedum* species, Crassulaceae; pungent, binds to AChR). **Lobeline** (from *Lobelia* species, Campanulaceae; agonist at nAChR; CNS stimulant). **Ammodendrine** (from *Lupinus* species and other Fabaceae; binds at nAChR; mutagen that causes fetal malformations, so-called crooked calf-disease). **Arecoline** (from *Areca catechu*, Arecaceae; agonist at mAChR, binds nAChR and adrenergic receptors). **Coniine** (from *Conium maculatum*, Apiaceae; antagonist at nAChR; an infamous poison of ancient Greece; used to kill Socrates).

Quinolizidine alkaloids (QA)

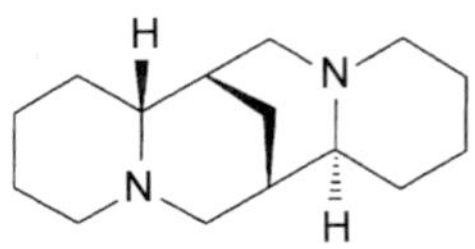

Sparteine 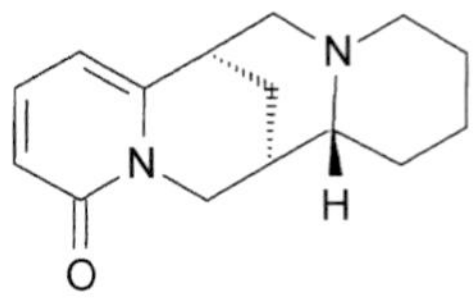   Anagyrine

Sparteine (from *Cytisus, Lupinus* and *Genista* species and other Fabaceae; agonist at mAChR and inhibitor of Na^+ channels; used as antiarrhythmic and uterotonic medicine). **Anagyrine** (from *Baptisia, Sophora* and *Genista* species and other Fabaceae; agonist at nAChR; mutagen that leads to fetal malformations, so called crooked calf-disease).

374

β-Carboline alkaloids

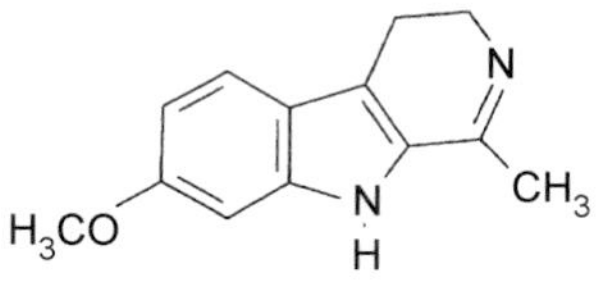

Harmaline

Harmaline (from *Peganum harmala*, Zygophyllaceae, *Banisteriopsis* species, Malpighiaceae; agonist at 5-HT-receptor, MAO-inhibitor; CNS-stimulant and hallucinogen).

Simple indole alkaloids

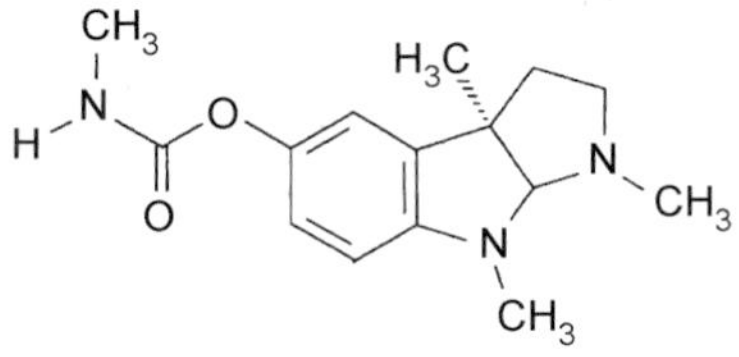

Physostigmine

Physostigmine (from *Physostigma* species, Fabaceae; inhibitor of acetylcholine esterase; indirect parasympathomimetic).

Quinoline alkaloids

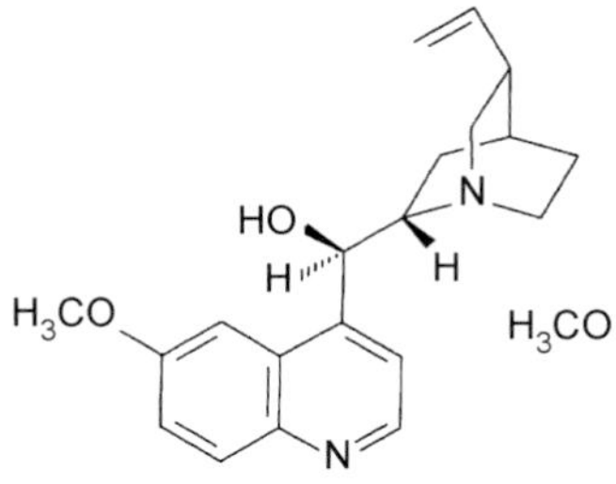

Quinine 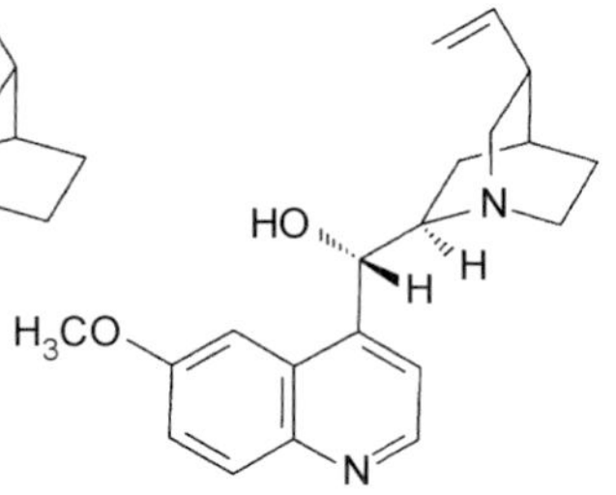   Quinidine 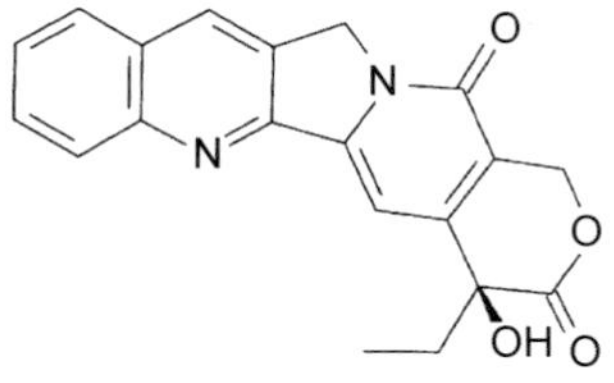   Camptothecine

Quinine (from *Cinchona* species, Rubiaceae; DNA-intercalating; inhibits the metabolism of *Plasmodium* which causes malaria). **Quinidine** (from *Cinchona* species, Rubiaceae; DNA-intercalating; inhibits Na^+ channels, binds to mAChR; used as an antiarrhythmic drug). **Camptothecine** (from *Camptotheca*, Nyssaceae; and *Ophiorrhiza*, Rubiaceae; inhibits DNA topoisomerase and thus replication and cell division. It is used in tumour therapy).

Ergot alkaloids

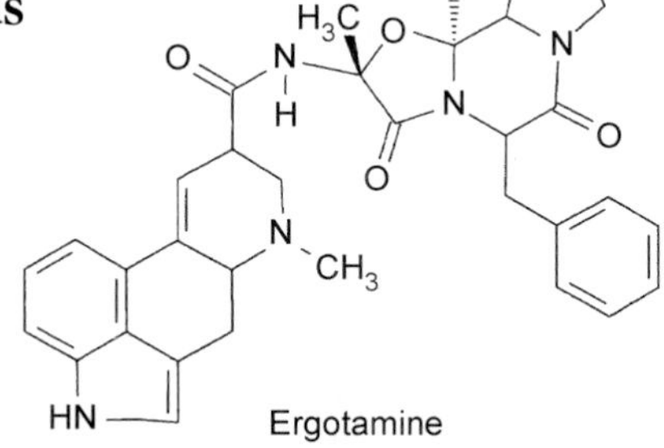

Ergotamine 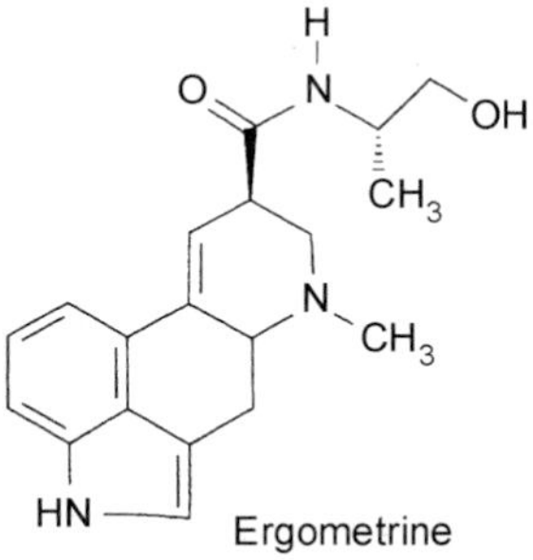   Ergometrine

Ergotamine, Ergometrine (from *Claviceps purpurea*, a symbiotic fungus on *Secale*; with α-sympatholytic activities, bind to receptors of noradrenaline, dopamine and serotonin).

375

Monoterpene indole alkaloids

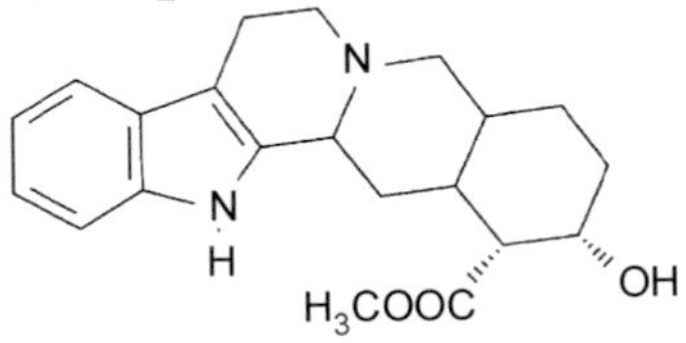

Yohimbine

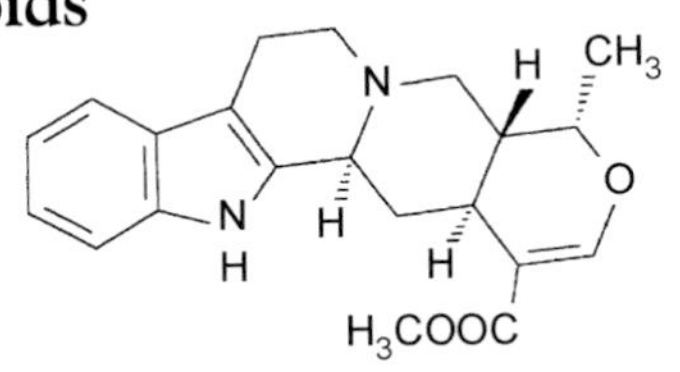

Ajmalicine

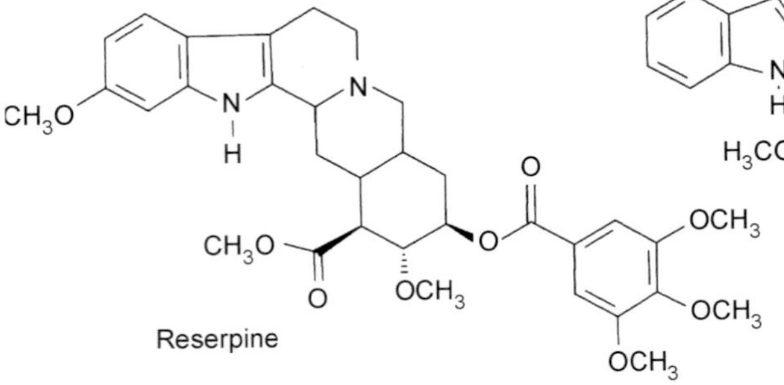

Reserpine

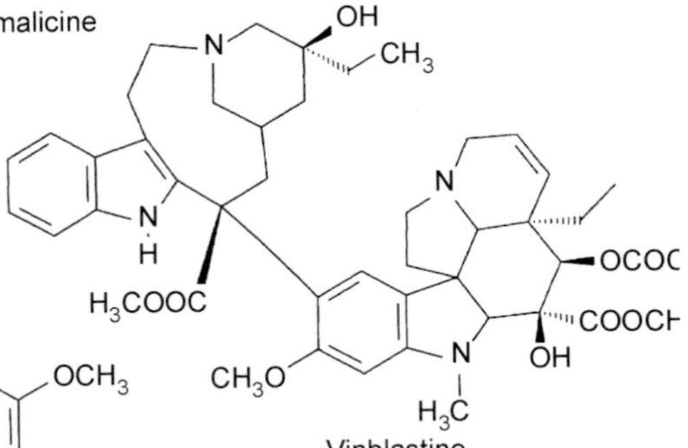

Vinblastine

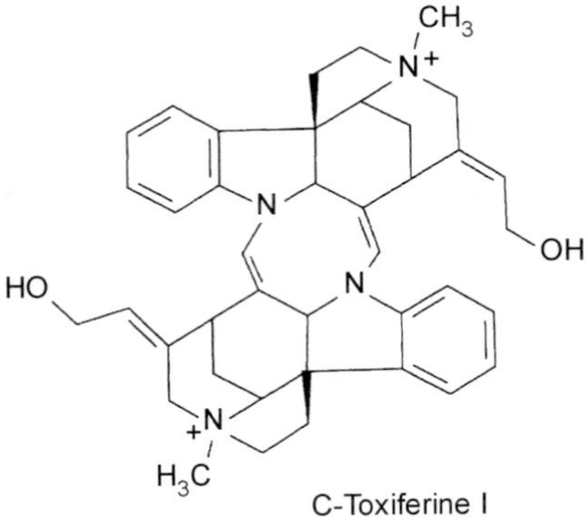

C-Toxiferine I

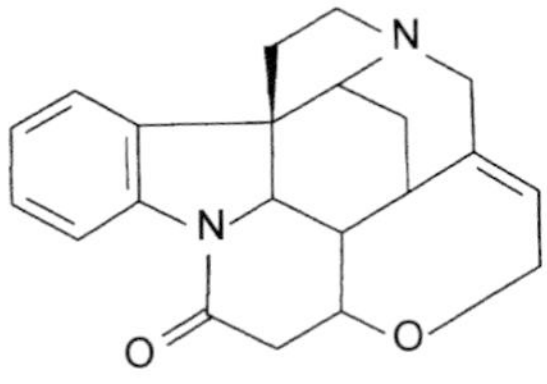

Strychnine

Yohimbine (from *Pausinystalia johimbe*, Rubiaceae; binds to adrenergic receptors, α_2-antagonist). **Ajmalicine** (raubasine) (from *Rauwolfia* species, Apocynaceae; inhibitor of Na^+ channels; used as an antiarrhythmic drug). **Reserpine** (from *Rauwolfia* species, Apocynaceae; inhibits proton pumps at the neurovesicle membrane and thus blocks re-uptake of noradrenaline and dopamine). **Vinblastine** (from *Catharanthus roseus*, Apocynaceae; binds to tubulin and inhibits microtubule formation; DNA-intercalator; important in tumour therapy). **C-Toxiferine I** (a curare alkaloid from *Strychnos* species, Loganiaceae; inhibits nAChR; blocks neuromuscular activity). **Strychnine** (from *Strychnos* species, Loganiaceae; antagonist at glycine gated chloride channel).

Simple phenylethylamines

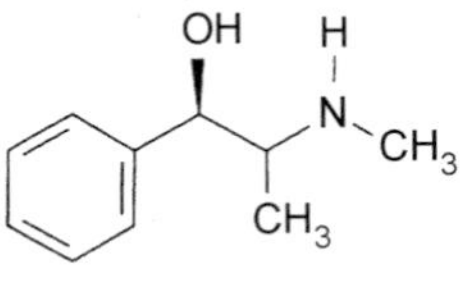

Ephedrine

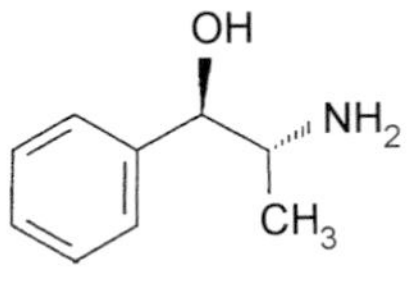

Nor-ψ-ephedrine

Ephedrine (from *Ephedra* species, Ephedraceae; inhibits the re-uptake of catecholamines into the presynapse; indirect sympathomimetic). **Nor-ψ-ephedrine** (Kathine) (from *Catha edulis*, Celastraceae; inhibits the re-uptake of catecholamines into the presynapse; indirect sympathomimetic).

376

Amaryllidaceae alkaloids

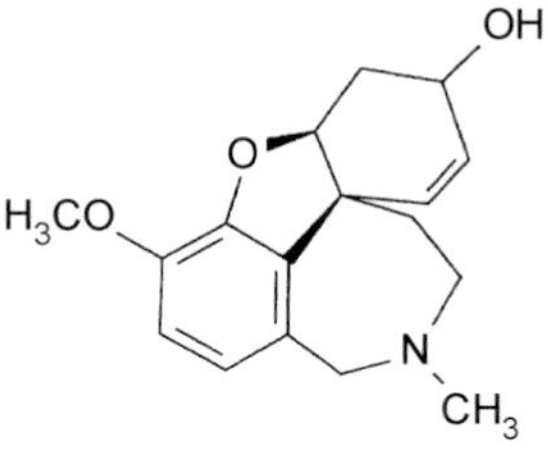

Galanthamine

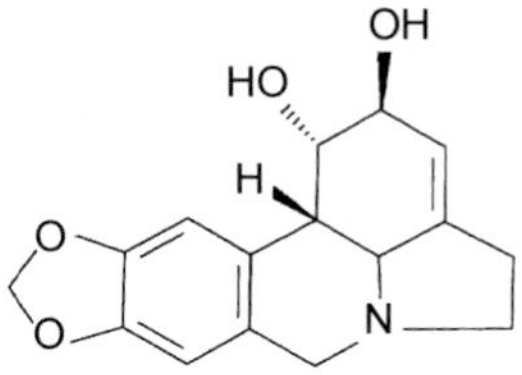

Lycorine

Galanthamine (from *Galanthus* species, Amaryllidaceae; inhibits acetylcholine esterase; used in the therapy of Alzheimer's disease). **Lycorine** (from *Narcissus* species, Amaryllidaceae; inhibitor of protein biosynthesis).

Colchicum alkaloids

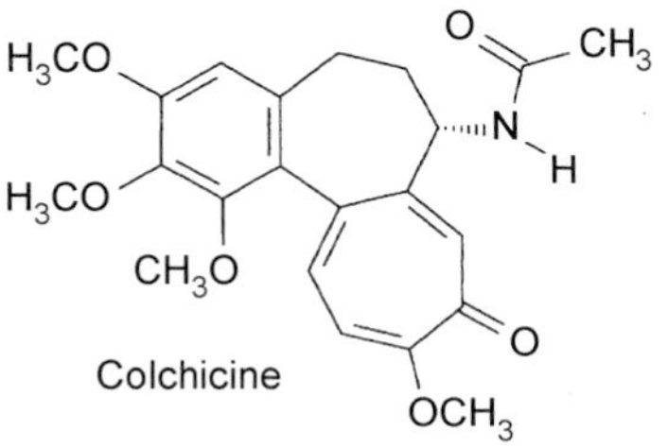

Colchicine

Colchicine (from *Colchicum* species, Cochicaceae; binds to tubulin and inhibits its polymerisation to microtubules; used in the treatment of gout).

Benzylisoquinoline alkaloids

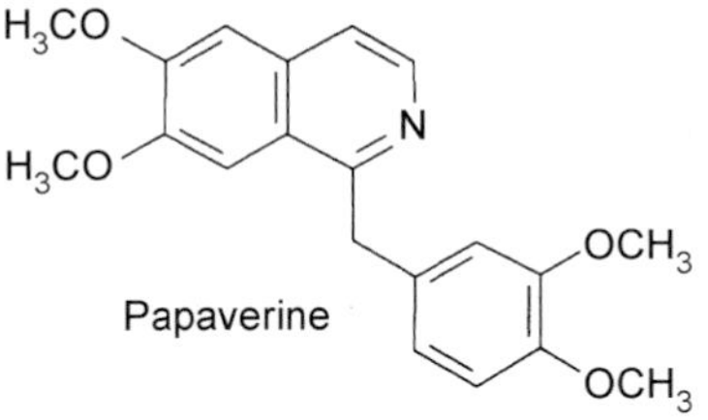

Papaverine

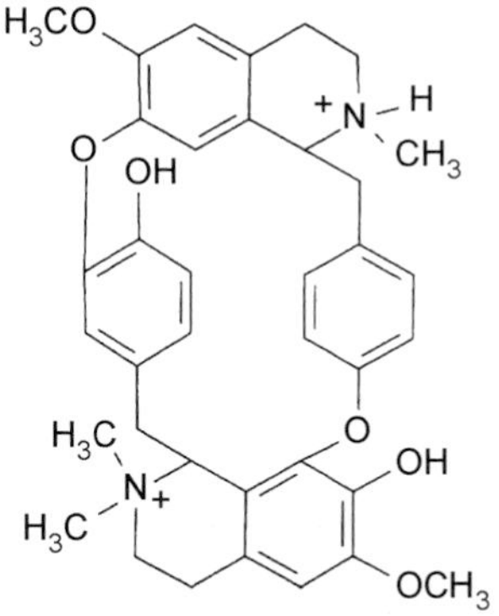

Tubocurarine

Papaverine (from *Papaver* species, Papaveraceae; inhibits cAMP-phosphodiesterase). **Tubocurarine** (from *Chondrodendron* species, Menispermaceae; inhibits nAChR; blocks neuromuscular activity).

Aporphine alkaloids

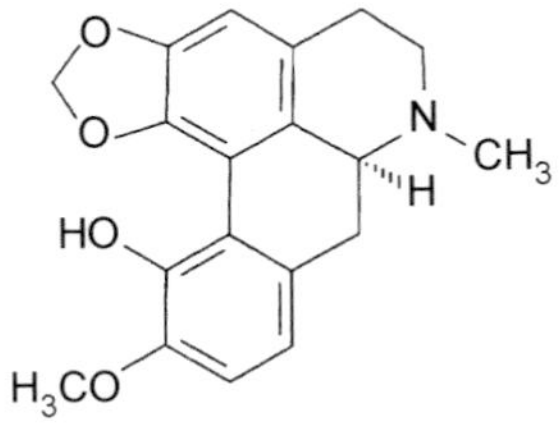

Bulbocapnine

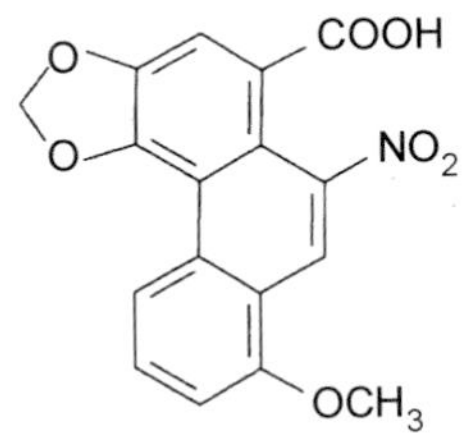

Aristolochic acid I

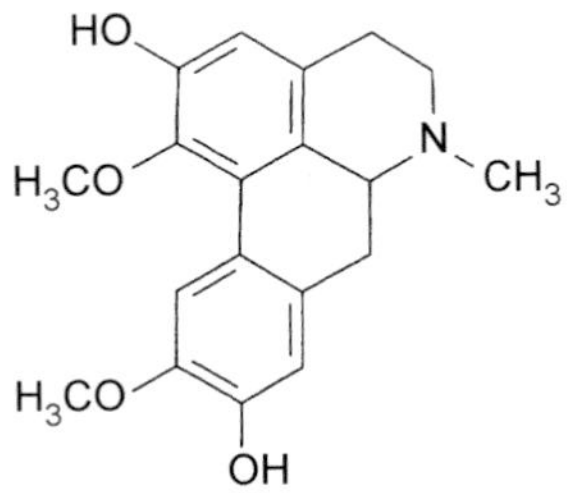

Boldine

Bulbocapnine (from *Corydalis* species, Papaveraceae; antagonist at dopamine receptor). **Aristolochic acid I** (from *Aristolochia* species, Aristolochiaceae; after metabolic activation, DNA-alkylating, mutagenic and carcinogenic activities have been reported). **Boldine** (from *Peumus boldus*, Monimiaceae; antagonist at nAChR and α_1-receptor; binds at mAChR and 5-HT-R.

Morphinane alkaloids

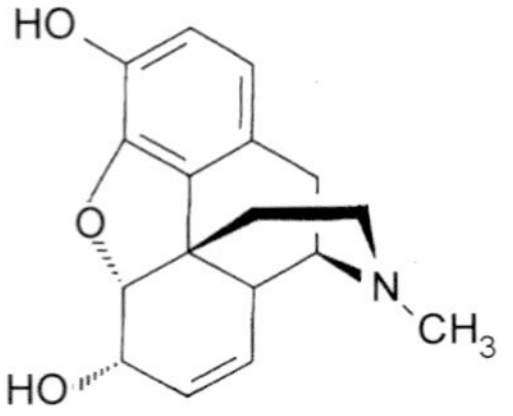

Morphine

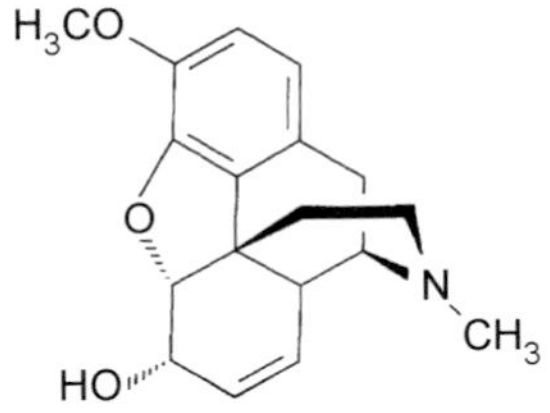

Codeine

Morphine (from *Papaver somniferum*; Papaveraceae; agonist at endorphin receptors; strong analgesic, intoxicant). **Codeine** (from *Papaver* species, Papaveraceae; inhibits the cough centre; analgesic).

Protoberberine alkaloids

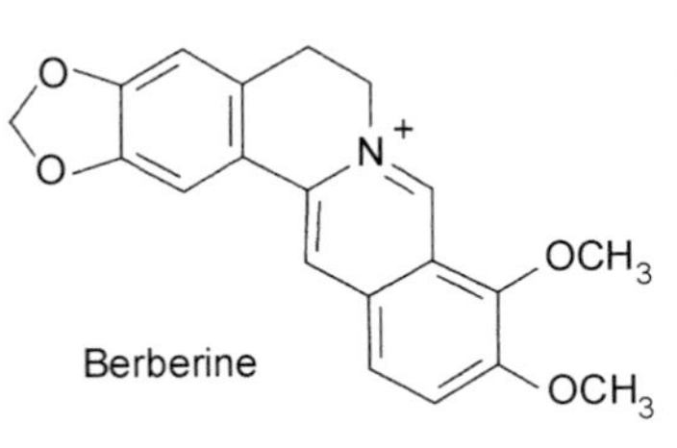

Berberine

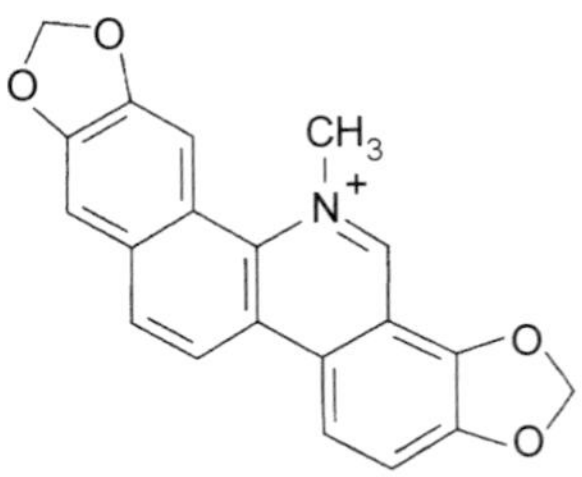

Sanguinarine

Berberine (from *Berberis* and related Berberidaceae; binds to various neuroreceptors; DNA-intercalating). **Sanguinarine** (from *Sanguinaria canadensis*, Papaveraceae; binds to various neuroreceptors; DNA-intercalating).

Purine alkaloids

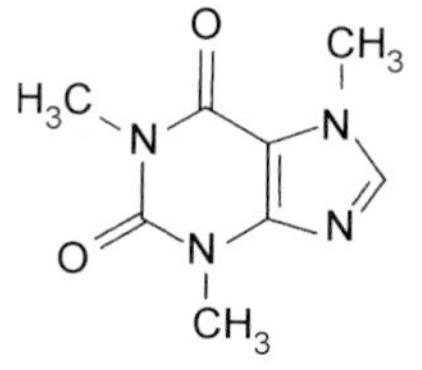

Caffeine

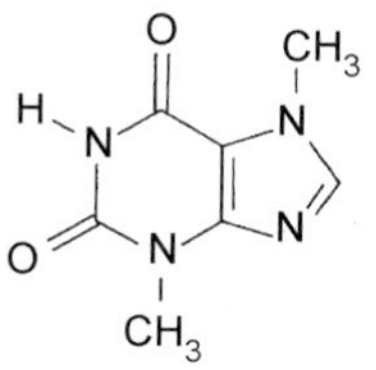

Theobromine

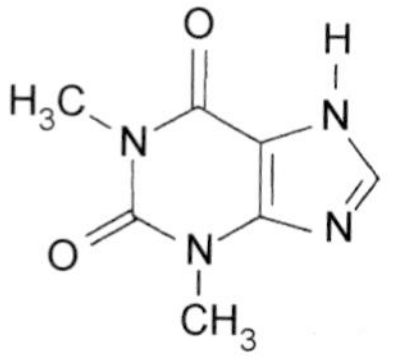

Theophylline

Caffeine, theobromine, theophylline (from *Coffea, Theobroma, Camellia, Cola, Ilex paraguariensis* and *Paullinia*; inhibitors of phosphodiesterase; antagonists at adenosine receptor).

Imidazole alkaloids

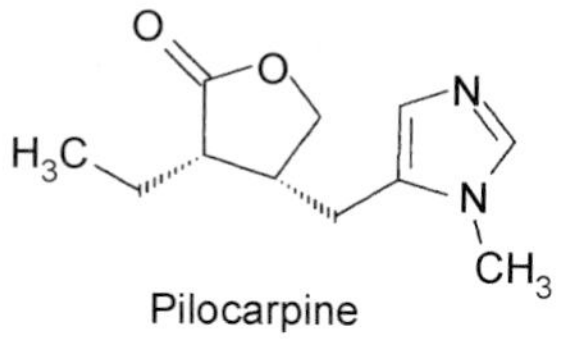

Pilocarpine

Pilocarpine (from *Pilocarpus jaborandi*, Rutaceae; agonist at mAChR; direct parasympathomimetic).

Terpene alkaloids

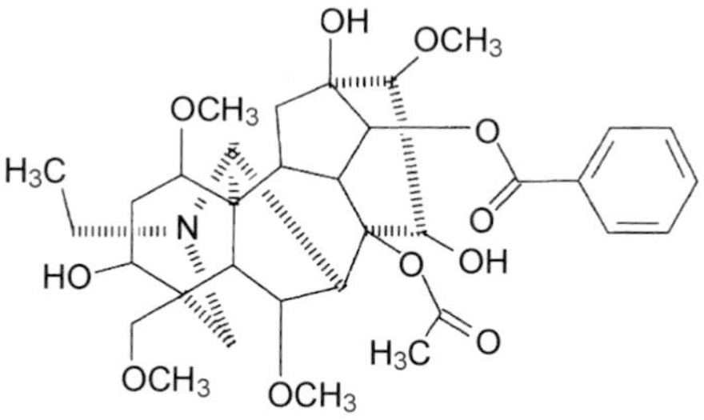

Aconitine

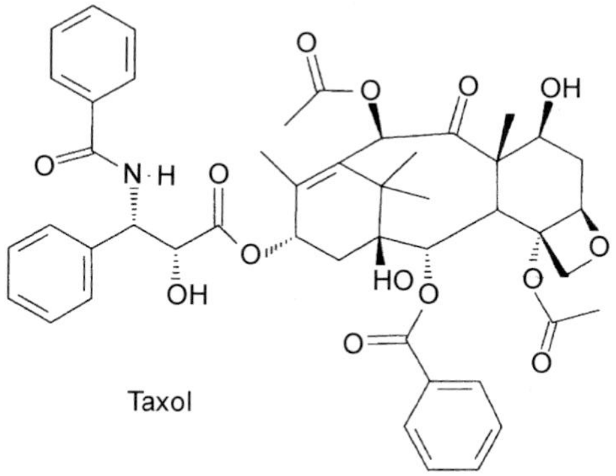

Taxol

Aconitine (from *Aconitum* species, Ranunculaceae; activates Na$^+$ channels, thus analgesic and paralytic).
Taxol (from *Taxus* species, Taxaceae; binds and stabilises microtubules; important anti-tumour drug).

NON-PROTEIN AMINO ACIDS (NPAAS) AND THEIR MODES OF ACTION

Whereas proteins of all organisms are built up by the 20 common L-amino acids, more than 600 other amino acids have been discovered in plants that are not building blocks of proteins (therefore called "non-protein amino acids"). NPAAs are especially abundant in the family Fabaceae and several monocotyledonous families (lily-like groups). Organs rich in these metabolites are seeds (Fabaceae) or rhizomes (monocots). Concentrations in seeds can exceed 8% of dry weight and up to 50% of the nitrogen present can be attributed to them. Since NPAAs are often (at least partly) remobilised during germination they certainly function as nitrogen storage compounds in addition to their role as defence chemicals.

NPAAs often figure as antinutrients or antimetabolites. Many non-protein amino acids resemble protein amino acids and quite often can be considered to be their structural analogues and may interfere with the human metabolism:

- In ribosomal protein biosynthesis NPAAs can be accepted in place of the normal amino acid leading to defective proteins.

- NPAAs may competitively inhibit uptake systems for amino acids.
- NPAAs can inhibit amino acid biosynthesis by substrate competition or by mimicking end product mediated feedback inhibition of earlier key enzymes in the pathway.
- NPAAs may affect other targets, such as DNA-, RNA-related processes (canavanine, mimosine), receptors of neurotransmitters, inhibit collagen biosynthesis (mimosine), or β-oxidation of lipids (L-hypoglycine).

L-Arginine

Canavanine

L-Proline

L-Azetidine-2-carboxylic acid

Canavanine is a structural analogue of **L-arginine** and is widely distributed amongst legumes. **L-Azetidine-2-carboxylic acid** occurs widely in monocots and functions as a structural analogue of **L-proline**.

Alliin

alliinase

Allicin

In garlic and onions a NPAA is present, better known as **alliin**. Upon tissue damage alliin is converted enzymatically into **allicin**, a diallylsulfide. Allylsulfide is quite reactive and can form disulfide bridges with SH-groups of proteins. This would explain the wide range of pharmacological activities that were attributed to garlic.

CYANOGENIC GLYCOSIDES AND THEIR MODES OF ACTION

More than 60 different cyanogenic glycosides (forming glucosides with β-D-glucose) are widely distributed among plants (more than 2 600 cyanogenic taxa have been reported) especially among members of the families Rosaceae, Fabaceae, Gramineae and Araceae.

In case of emergency, i.e. when plants are wounded by herbivores or other organisms, the cellular compartmentation breaks down and vacuolar cyanogenic glycosides come into contact with an active β-glucosidase of broad specificity, which hydrolyses them to yield 2-hydroxynitrile (cyanohydrine). 2-Hydroxynitrile is further cleaved into the corresponding aldehyde or ketone and hydroprussic acid (HCN) by a hydroxynitrile lyase.

Foods that contain cyanogens, such as manihot (*Manihot esculenta*) and sorghum (*Sorghum bicolor*), have repeatedly caused intoxications and even deaths in people and animals. Special care must be taken when such food is prepared; traditionally cyanogens and hydrocyanide are leached out during food processing. In recent years plant breeders have produced varieties in which the pathways leading to cyanogenic glycosides have been down-regulated.

Hydrocyanide (HCN) is highly toxic to animals or microorganisms due to its inhibition of enzymes of the respiratory chain (i.e. cytochrome oxidase) because it blocks the essential ATP production. HCN also binds to other enzymes containing heavy metal ions.

(S)-Prunasin

β-glucosidase

hydroxynitrile lyase

HCN

Benzaldehyde

(R)-Sambunigrin (R=H)
(R)-Dhurrin (R=OH)

Linamarin

S-Prunasin is commonly found in the seeds (sometimes also the leaves) of cherries, plums, apples, apricots and almonds (genus *Prunus*, Rosaceae). **R-Sambunigrin** (R=H) occurs in *Sambucus* species (Caprifoliaceae); **R-Dhurrin** (R= OH) in *Sorghum* species. **Linamarin** occurs in linseeds (*Linum usitatissimum*; Linaceae).

GLUCOSINOLATES AND THEIR MODES OF ACTION

More than 80 different glucosinolates have been found in higher dicotyledonous plants in the order of Capparales, which include the phylogenetically related families Capparidaceae, Brassicaceae, Resedaceae, Moringaceae, Tropaeolaceae and others. Glucosinolates are polar molecules, which are formed in the cytoplasm and stored in vacuoles. All plant parts may accumulate glucosinolates, but seeds and roots are often especially rich in these allelochemicals. Concentrations are in the range of 0.1–0.2 % fresh weight in leaves, up to 0.8% in roots and up to 8% in seeds.

When plants are wounded the resulting tissue decompartmentation brings myrosinase in contact with the glucosinolates. When hydrolysed, glucosinolates liberate D-glucose, sulphate and an unstable aglycone, which may convert at pH 5-8 to isothiocyanate (common name "mustard oil") as the main product.

Isothiocyanates are responsible for the distinctive, pungent flavour and odour of mustards and horseradish. Alkyl-, alkenyl-, methylthioalkyl- and benzylisothiocyanates are lipophilic, volatile allelochemicals that can disturb the fluidity of biomembranes and can covalently bind to free amino groups of enzymes, receptors or other macromolecules. Because isothiocyanates can easily penetrate biomembranes, they can interact with epidermal and mucosal tissues. At higher concentrations painful irritations, bronchitis, pneumonia, gastro-enteritis, diarrhoea, heart and kidney disorders and even abortions can be the result. Isothiocyanates are antibiotic, because besides making bacterial or fungal cells leaky, interactions with proteins and cellular targets are likely.

Sinigrin

Allyl isothiocyanate

Glucotropaeolin

Benzyl isothiocyanate

Sinigrin occurs in *Brassica nigra* (Brassicaceae) and *Armoracia rusticana* (Brassicaceae) and produces **allyl isothiocyanate**. **Glucotropaeolin** is the main GS in *Tropaeolum majus* (Tropaeolaceae) and yields **benzyl isothiocyanate**.

381

TERPENOIDS AND THEIR MODES OF ACTION

Terpenoids represent a large class of plant products. Main groups include monoterpenes (with 10 carbon atoms), sesquiterpenes (15 carbon atoms), diterpenes (20 carbon atoms), triterpenes (30 carbon atoms), steroids (27 carbon atoms or less), tetraterpenes (40 carbon atoms) and polyterpenes. Although their main building blocks are simple, most terpenes represent complex structures because of various chemical groups and secondary ring formations.

Iridoids

A subclass of monoterpenes are the iridoid glycosides (secoiridoids, secologanin derivates) with more than 200 structures distributed in the families Apocynaceae, Gentianaceae, Lamiaceae, Loganiaceae, Menyanthaceae, Plantaginaceae, Rubiaceae, Scrophulariaceae, Valerianaceae and Verbenaceae.

Aucubin

Harpagide

Harpagoside

Gentiopicrin

Valepotriate

Aucubin occurs in *Plantago lanceolata* (Plantaginaceae), *Veronica officinalis* (Scrophulariaceae), in *Euphrasia officinalis* (Scrophulariaceae) and in *Ajuga reptans* (Lamiaceae). These drugs are used against infections and inflammations. **Harpagoside** and **harpagide** have been found in *Harpagophytum procumbens* (Pedaliaceae); harpagide also in *Scrophularia nodosa* (Scrophulariaceae). These iridoids or their metabolites have analgesic and antirheumatic properties.

Iridoid glycosides are cleaved in the animal body to the corresponding aglycons. The lactone ring may open now, generating a reactive aldehyde function that can form covalent bonds with amino groups of proteins. This mechanism could explain anti-inflammatory properties of iridoid drugs; the alkylation could lead to the inhibition of cyclooxygenase and 5-lipoxygenase and can thus interfere with the production of inflammation promotors, such as prostaglandins and leukotrienes.

Some iridoids, such as the gentiopicrosides (e.g. **gentiopicrin**), present in Gentianaceae and Menyanthaceae, have an extremely bitter taste and are used as bitter tonics in phytomedicine to induce the secretion of digestive enzymes ("amara"). **Valepotriates** from *Valeriana officinalis* (Valerianaceae) have sedative properties; they stimulate the GABA receptor. Because of their epoxide group they are reactive and can cause mutations under experimental conditions.

Volatile mono- and sesquiterpenes

Mono- and sesquiterpenes are often volatile and can be isolated through steam distillation as "essential oils". These compounds are usually lipophilic and are stored in specialised oil cells, trichomes, resin channels or other dead cells. They are especially abundant in Asteraceae, Apiaceae, Lamiaceae, Fabaceae, Rutaceae, Lauraceae, Cupressaceae, Pinaceae, Myrtaceae and Zingiberaceae.

Monoterpenes occur as linear molecules or with 1 or 2 ring structures.

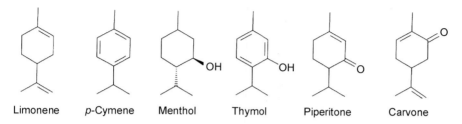

Ocimene   Citral   Nerol   Geraniol

Examples of linear monoterpenes

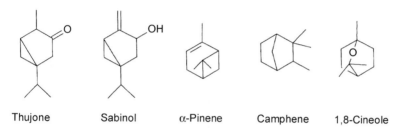

Limonene   *p*-Cymene   Menthol   Thymol   Piperitone   Carvone

Examples of monocyclic monoterpenes

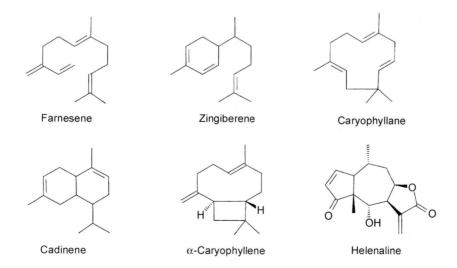

Thujone   Sabinol   α-Pinene   Camphene   1,8-Cineole

Examples of bicyclic monoterpenes

An intriguing number of complex ring structures can be found in sesquiterpenes.

Farnesene   Zingiberene   Caryophyllane

Cadinene   α-Caryophyllene   Helenaline

Artemisinin   Ptaquiloside

Especially reactive sesquiterpenes are sesquiterpene lactones. A well-known representative is **helenaline** of *Arnica* species. Its exocyclic methylene group easily binds to SH-groups of proteins. This explains the broad pharmacological activities of *Arnica*. The sesquiterpene **artemisinin** from *Artemisia annua* with a reactive peroxide function has recently been developed into a potent antimalaria drug, since it is active against *Plasmodium falciparum*. Some sesquiterpenes are highly reactive compounds, such as **ptaquiloside** in the bracken fern (*Pteridium aquilinum*). Bracken is known to cause bladder cancer in humans and livestock.

Diterpenes

Diterpenes occur in several gymnosperms, Asteraceae, Euphorbiaceae, Thymelaeaceae, Lamiaceae and others. Among them we find extremely complex ring structures.

TPA (phorbol ester)   Forskolin

A number of diterpenes are infamous for their toxic properties, such as **phorbol esters** of Euphorbiaceae and Thymelaeaceae; they mimic the endogenous signal molecule diacylglycerol and thus activate protein kinase C and can act as tumour promoters. **Forskolin** from *Coleus forskohlii* (=*Plectranthus barbatus*, Lamiaceae) is an activator of adenynylcyclase and leads to the production of the second messenger cAMP. Another diterpene is taxol A (paclitaxel, Taxol™) that can be isolated from several yew species (including the North American *Taxus brevifolia* and the European *Taxus baccata*). See page 319 for further discussion.

Biological activities of terpenoids

Terpenes (mono-, sesqui-, di- and triterpenes) have a number of common activities that can be discussed together. They are usually highly hydrophobic substances. Most of them readily interact with biomembranes. They can increase the fluidity of the membranes, which can lead to uncontrolled efflux of ions and metabolites, and receptors, or even to cell leakage resulting in cell death. A conformation change of membrane proteins (e.g. ion channels, transporters) can occur when the lipophilic compounds dive into the biomembrane and gather close to membrane proteins. If Na^+, K^+ or Ca^{++} channels are affected, a disturbance of signal transduction could result. The use of essential oils to treat spasms and light pain in case of dyspeptic or gall disorders could thus be plausibly explained. Since the lipophilic terpenes can cross the blood brain barrier, we can also explain the sedative and analeptic effects ascribed to several drugs.

This membrane activity is rather unspecific; therefore, terpenes show antimicrobial and cytotoxic activities against a wide range of organisms, ranging from bacteria, fungi, to insects and vertebrates. The antimicrobial properties explain the wide distribution and utilisation of plants with essential oils as mild antibacterial drugs used to treat bacterial and parasitic infections and disorders of the respiratory tract.

Important functional groups of terpenes are the aldehyde function that forms covalent bonds with free amino groups of proteins (Schiff's bases), and also terminal or exocyclic methylene groups, that couple to SH groups of proteins. Inner oxides or peroxides of terpenes are chemically reactive and can bind to proteins.

The use of essential oils as counter-irritant or as diuretic can be inferred from the membrane disturbances caused on the skin or in the kidneys. This can be both a membrane or a membrane protein interaction.

Essential oils stimulate fluid excretion in the lungs and also activate cilial activity in bronchia. This is the basis on which plants containing these substances are used as secretolytic and secretomotoric drugs.

Considering the known biological properties of terpenoids, also side effects of essential oils (abortifacient, allergenic, narcotic, nephrotoxic and hepatotoxic properties) can be explained plausibly, especially if the drugs were consumed in larger doses.

Triterpenes, steroids and saponins

Triterpenes and steroids (biogenetically derived from C-30 precursors) can occur as free compounds but more often as saponins (with one to several sugar molecules attached to them). Whereas free triterpenes and steroids are lipophilic compounds, the glycosidic saponins are water-soluble and are stored in the vacuole. Saponins are widely distributed in the plant kingdom and approximately 70% of all plants produce them. Steroidal saponins are abundant in monocots of the families Dioscoreaceae, Trilliaceae, Liliaceae, Agavaceae, Asparagaceae, Convallariaceae, Alliaceae and Smilacaceae. Triterpene saponins mainly occur in angiosperm families such as the Caryophyllaceae, Ranunculaceae, Chenopodiaceae, Theaceae, Fabaceae, Apiaceae, Araliaceae, Primulaceae and Sapotaceae. Gymnosperms are apparently without saponins. Saponins are mainly stored as inactive furostanol glycosides or triterpene bidesmosides in the vacuole (the active compounds would destroy the tonoplast of the producing plants!). When attacked by microbes or herbivores these compounds are converted into spirostanol glycosides or triterpene monodesmosides that exhibit membrane activity.

Example of a steroid saponin (**sarsaparilloside**) that is converted to the monodesmosidic spirostanol (**sarsapogenin**).

Example of a bidesmosidic triterpene saponin (hederasaponin C) that is converted into its monodesmosidic counterpart (**α-hederin**).

Quassin

Cucurbitacin B

Quassin, a modified triterpene from *Quassia jamaicensis* (Simaroubaceae) is an especially bitter tasting compound and is used as a bitter, but also as an anthelmintic and insecticide. **Cucurbitacins** from *Bryonia* and other Cucurbitaceae are equally bitter, but exhibit strong laxative properties as well.

Monodesmosidic saponins are amphiphilic compounds (i.e. they have a hydrophilic sugar and a lipophilic terpene moiety), which can complex cholesterol in biomembranes with their lipophilic terpenoid moiety and bind to surface glycoproteins and glycolipids with their sugar side chain. This leads to a severe tension of the biomembrane and leakage. This activity can easily be demonstrated with erythrocytes that lose their haemoglobin through haemolysis when in contact with saponins. This membrane activity is rather unspecific and affects a wide set of organisms from microbes to animals. Also cardiac glycosides and steroidal alkaloids from *Solanum* species react as saponins at higher doses.

The antimicrobial effect partly explains the wide use of saponin drugs in phytotherapy to overcome mainly external infections. Because of general toxicity, an internal use refers to low doses. For example, saponins affect the *Nervus vagus* in the stomach and reflectorily induce a secretion of water in the lungs thus leading to secretolytic effects. Therefore, plants containing saponins are widely used as secretolytic drugs. Higher doses cause an emetic effect or toxicity.

Steroids, triterpenes and saponins of plant drugs sometimes structurally resemble endogenous hormones, e.g. glucocorticoids. The anti-inflammatory effects reported from many drugs could be due to a corticomimetic effect. The triterpenes or steroids could directly interfere with phospholipase (a target of cortical) or they could act at the level of nuclear receptors that modulate gene activity.

COOH

COOH

OH

OH

HOOC

OH

O

OH

OH

OH

Glycyrrhizic acid

A pronounced anti-inflammatory activity has been reported for **glycyrrhizic acid** from *Glycyrrhiza glabra* (Fabaceae), a triterpene saponin with a sweet taste.

Cardiac glycosides

A special case of steroidal saponins are cardiac glycosides that inhibit Na^+,K^+-ATPase and are therefore strong toxins but useful in medicine (doses 1-3 mg/d) to treat heart problems. Cardiac glycosides can be divided in two classes: Cardenolides have been found in Scrophulariaceae (*Digitalis*), Apocynaceae (*Apocynum, Nerium, Strophanthus, Thevetia, Periploca, Xysmalobium*), Brassicaceae (*Erysimum, Cheiranthus*), Celastraceae (*Euonymus*), Convallariaceae (*Convallaria*) and Ranunculaceae (*Adonis*). Bufadienolides occur in Crassulaceae (*Kalanchoe*), Hyacinthaceae (*Urginea*) and Ranunculaceae (*Helleborus*). The varying structures hardly influence the binding of cardiac glycosides at Na^+,K^+-ATPase; however their resorption differs. Polar molecules are resorbed very slowly, but once inside the body their action is rapid. Lipophilic cardiac glycosides easily diffuse into the body but because of their binding to plasma proteins they remain in the system for prolonged periods of time.

OH

OH

OH

HO

OH

rha─O

OH

OH

Ouabain

O

sugars

OH

Digitoxin

O

sugars

OH

Scillaren

Ouabain is a polar cardiac glycoside from *Strophanthus gratus* (Apocynaceae), which is applied intravenously; it has been widely used as an arrow poison in Africa. **Digitoxin** and related substances are isolated from *Digitalis lanata* (Scrophulariaceae) and are administered orally. **Scillaren** is bufadienolide from *Urginea maritima* (Hyacinthaceae).

Tetraterpenes

Carotenoids represent the most important members of tetraterpenes. An example is β-**carotene** (from carrots, *Daucus carota*). They are highly lipophilic compounds and are always associated with biomembranes. In chloroplasts they serve as accessory pigments important for photosynthesis. They also protect against UV light. Some flowers and many fruits are rich in carotenoids: in these instances they help to attract pollinating insects and more importantly to attract seed dispersing animals. Whereas young and immature fruits are usually green (containing toxic secondary metabolites in addition; e.g. steroid alkaloids in tomatoes or in *Solanum dulcamara*), ripe fruit (without noxious secondary metabolites) advertise their physiological state with prominent red colours (that can be detected by birds and mammals). The red and orange colours are due to carotenoids. Carotenoids are the precursors for vitamin A in animals, which is used to produce retinal (a light sensor in the rhodopsin complex) and retinoic acid (retinoids bind to nuclear receptors and are local mediators of vertebrate development). They also exhibit antioxidant activities.

β-Carotene

Polyterpenes

Polyterpenes, consisting of 10 to 1 000 isoprene units, are prominent in latex of Euphorbiaceae, Moraceae, Apocynaceae, Sapotaceae and Asteraceae. Some polyterpenes are used commercially such as rubber (from *Hevea brasiliensis*, Euphorbiaceae) or gutta-percha (from *Palaquium*, Sapotaceae).

PHENOLIC COMPOUNDS: PHENYLPROPANOIDS, COUMARINS, FLAVONOIDS AND TANNINS AND THEIR MODES OF ACTION

Phenylpropanoids derive from phenylalanine and tyrosine via desamination and represent building blocks for a wide variety of phenolic compounds. Phenylpropanoids can occur as simple compounds (as phenylacrylic acids, phenylacrylic aldehydes, or phenylallyl alcohols) that differ by their degree of hydroxylation and methoxylation.

| Cinnamic acid | *p*-Coumaric acid | Caffeic acid | Sinapic acid |

Examples of simple phenylpropanoids

| Syringic acid | Gallic acid | Salicylic acid | Salicin |

Examples of phenolic acids

A shortening of the side chain leads to benzoic acid and corresponding derivates, such as **syringic acid** and **gallic acid**. Especially important in the medicinal context are **salicylic acid**, saligenin and the respective glucoside, **salicin**. Salicylic acid and derivates are useful in medicine because they inhibit a key enzyme of prostaglandin biosynthesis, i.e. cyclooxygenase. These compounds are known from willows (*Salix* species, Salicaceae), poplars (*Populus* species, also Salicaceae), *Filipendula ulmaria* (Rosaceae), *Primula veris* (Primulaceae), and *Viola tricolor* (Violaceae).

Rosmarinic acid

Phenylpropanoids can also be conjugated with a second phenylpropanoid, such as in **rosmarinic acid** (because of the number of phenolic hydroxyl groups this compound has been regarded as a tannin typical of Lamiaceae) or with amines, such as coumaroylputrescine.

| Umbelliferone | Psoralen | Angelicin |

Examples of coumarins and furocoumarins

Phenylpropanoids serve as building blocks for coumarins and furocoumarins. Simple coumarins are stored as coumaroylglucosides in the vacuole. Upon tissue damage these glucosides are hydrolysed by a β-glucosidase. After isomerisation and formation of a lactone ring, simple coumarins are generated, such as **umbelliferone**. Coumarins can reach concentrations of up to 2% in plants and are common in the Apiaceae (most genera), and in certain Fabaceae (e.g. *Dipteryx odorata*, *Melilotus officinalis*), Poaceae (e.g. *Anthoxanthum odoratum*), Rubiaceae (e.g. *Galium odoratum*). Furocoumarins usually have a third furane ring that derives from active isoprene. A linear type (**psoralen**-type) or angular type (**angelicin**-type) are distinguished. The furocoumarins are present in aerial parts such as leaves and fruits but also in roots and rhizomes. They are abundant in Apiaceae (contents up to 4%), but also present in certain genera of the Fabaceae (e.g. *Psoralea bituminosa*) and Rutaceae. Furocoumarins can intercalate DNA and upon illumination with UV light can form cross-links with DNA bases, but also with proteins. They are therefore mutagenic and possibly carcinogenic. In plants they serve as defence compounds against herbivores and pathogens. In medicine, furocoumarins are employed in the treatment of psoriasis and vitiligo.

Phenylpropanoids can form complex dimeric structures, so-called lignans. **Podophyllotoxin**, which occurs in members of the genera *Podophyllum* (Berberidaceae), *Linum* (Linaceae), and *Anthriscus* (Apiaceae) is a potent inhibitor of microtubule formation and thus prevents cell division. Podophyllotoxin and its derivatives have been used in cancer therapy. Condensation of phenylpropanoids forms the complex lignin macromolecules that are important for the mechanical stability of plants, but also show some antimicrobial and antioxidant effects.

Podophyllotoxin

Stilbenes — Resveratrol

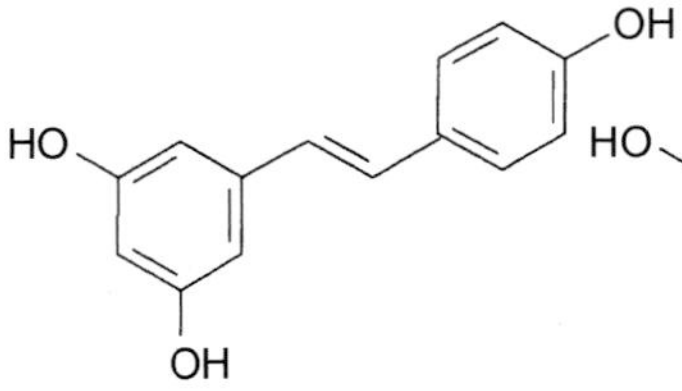

Chalcones — Isoliquiritigenin

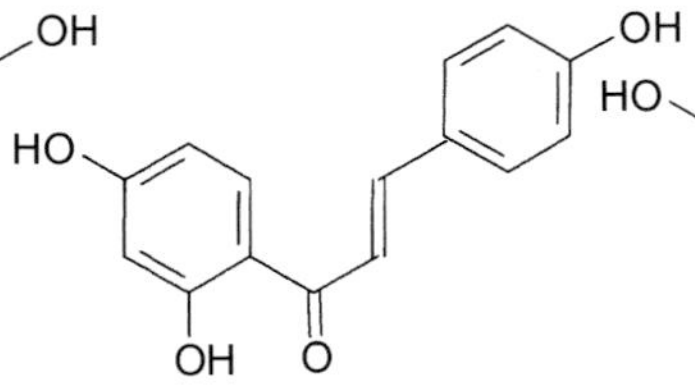

Isoflavones — Genistein

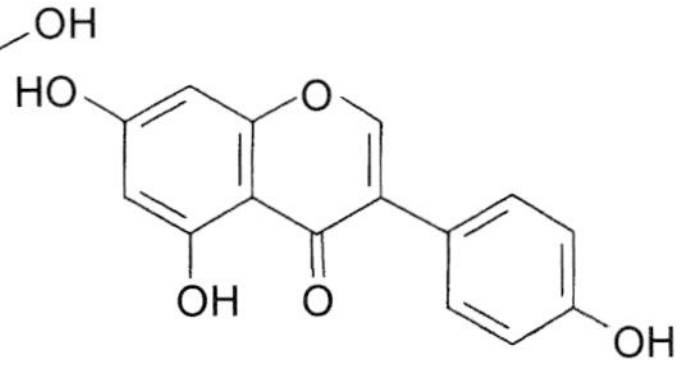

Flavones — Apigenin

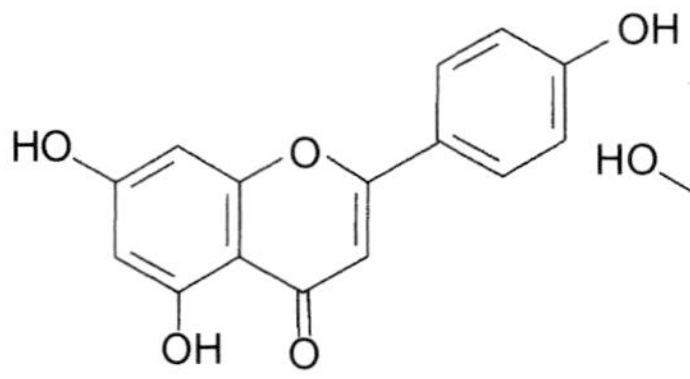

Flavonols — Kaempferol

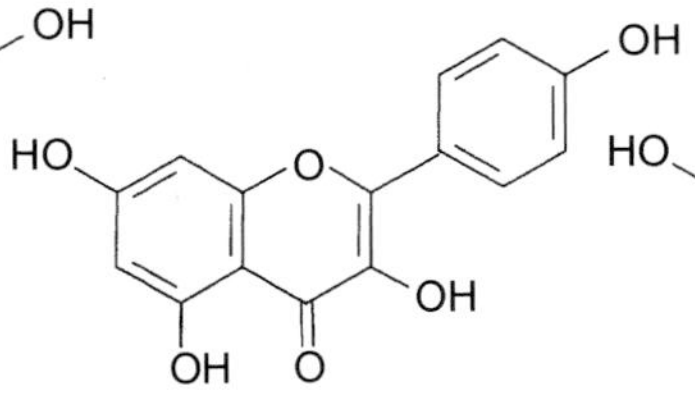

Flavanones — Naringenin

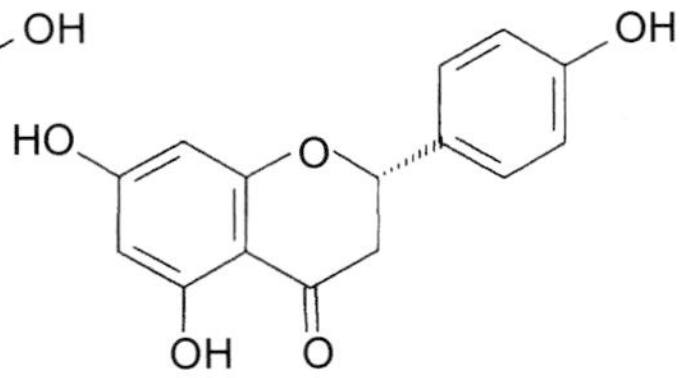

Phenylpropanoids can condense with a polyketide moiety to form flavonoids, chalcones, catechins and anthocyanins. These compounds are characterised by two aromatic rings that carry several phenolic hydroxy or methoxylgroups. In addition, they often occur as glycosides and are stored in vacuoles.

Anthocyanidin — Peonidin

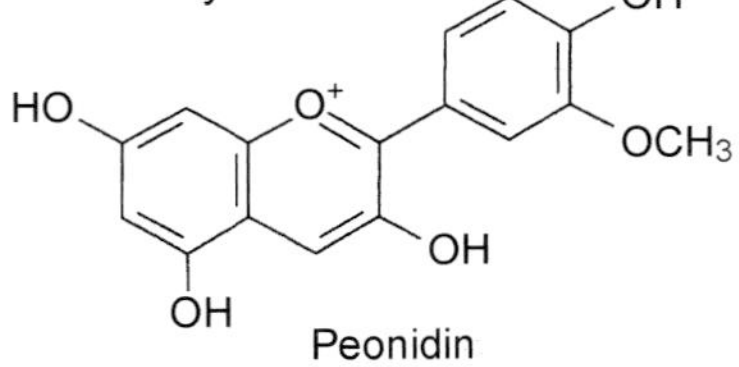

The colour of anthocyanins depends on the degree of glycosylation, hydrogen ion concentration and the presence of certain metals (e.g. aluminum ions) in the vacuole. Parallel to a change in pH of the vacuole in developing flowers, a colour change from pink to dark blue can be observed in several species of the Boraginaceae (e.g. *Symphytum, Echium*). Many of the flavonoids, chalcones and anthocyanins are widely distributed in higher plants and show colours under visual and UV light and are typical secondary metabolites of flowers and fruits. They function to attract pollinating insects or fruit-dispersing animals.

The phenolic hydroxyl groups of flavonoids can interact with proteins to form hydrogen, ionic bonds and thus modulate a multitude of molecular targets. They can be regarded as general protein modifying compounds. Since proteins are involved in most disorders and disturbances, these properties can explain the utility of phenolics in medicine. In consequence, they are apparently the active ingredients in many phytomedicines.

Isoflavones are common secondary metabolites in legumes (subfamily Papilionoideae). They exhibit oestrogenic activities and inhibit tyrosine kinases. Because of these properties they are often regarded as useful compounds that might play a role in the prevention of certain cancers (breast cancer, prostate cancer) and the regulation of hormonal disturbances.

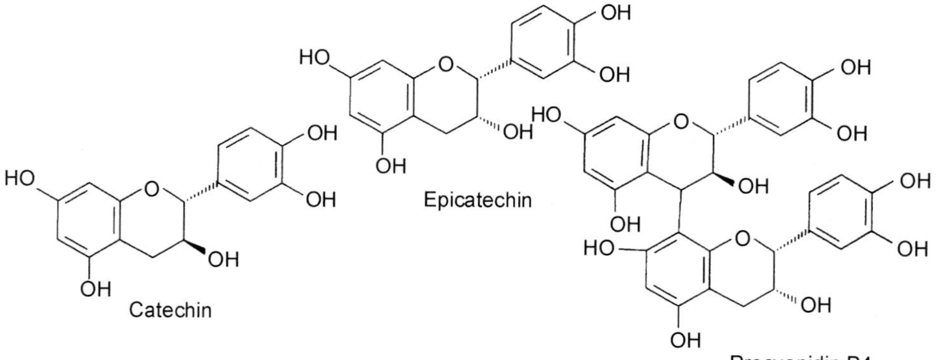

Epicatechin

Catechin

Procyanidin B4

Catechins form a special class of flavonoids, which often dimerise or even polymerise to form **procyanidins** and oligomeric procyanidins. The conjugates (which cannot be hydrolysed; "non-hydrolysable tannins") are characterised by a large number of hydroxyl groups. The phenolic hydroxyl groups can interact with proteins to form hydrogen and ionic bonds and possibly even covalent bonds. If more than 20 hydroxyl groups are present these compounds act as "tannins". These compounds have antimicrobial activities and can inhibit receptors and enzymes – externally, internally and in the digestive tract. The protein interactions are the basis for the utilisation of plants with catechins in phytotherapy (e.g. *Crataegus monogyna* in patients with heart problems).

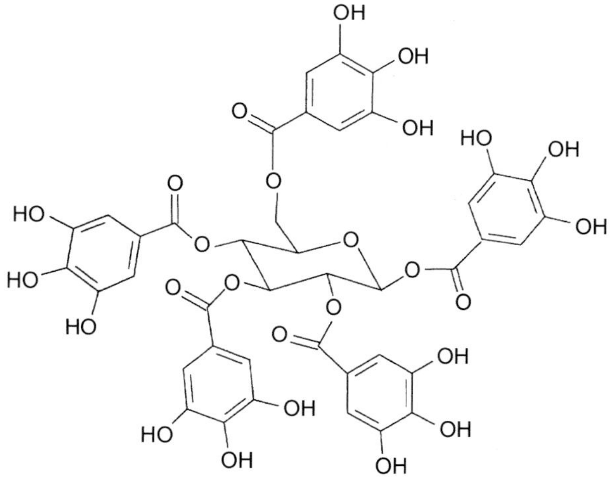

Pentagalloyl glucose

Another important group of tannins is hydrolysable (so-called hydrolysable tannins). They represent esters between gallic acid and sugars; in addition several moieties of gallic acid can be present that are also linked by ester bonds. These gallotannins (an example, **pentagalloyl glucose,** is shown above) are widely distributed in plants, often in bark, leaves and fruits. Especially rich in gallotannins are galls induced by various gall-forming insects. Gallotannins, which can additionally be condensed with catechins, contain a large number of phenolic hydroxyl groups so that they can form stable protein-tannin complexes and thus interact with a wide variety of protein targets in microbes and animals (see also catechins; last paragraph). Tannins are useful in medicine to treat dermal and mucosal infections and disturbances; intestinal problems (such as diarrhoea) have traditionally been treated with tannin-rich phytomedicines.

In summary, flavonoids and phenylpropanoids (including coumarins, furocoumarins, tannins, etc.) exhibit a wide range of biological activities. In several instances, they act as analogues of cellular signal compounds or substrates. Afflicted targets range from prostaglandin and leukotriene formation, enzyme inhibition, oestrogenic properties (coumarins, isoflavones, stilbenes) to DNA alkylation (e.g. by furocoumarins). These molecules usually have several phenolic hydroxyl groups in common, which can form hydrogen bonds or ionic bonds (maybe also covalent bonds) with proteins and peptides. These interactions disturb secondary and tertiary protein structures. The higher the number of phenolic hydroxyl groups, the stronger the astringent and denaturing effect. Tannins form stable protein-tannin complexes and inhibit enzymatic activities very effectively.

POLYKETIDES AND THEIR MODES OF ACTION

Polyketides derive from acetate as a building block and either represent secondary metabolites in their own right (such as anthraquinones), or they form mixed compounds (such as flavonoids). Secondary metabolites with an anthracene skeleton can be present as anthrones, anthraquinones, anthranols, dianthrones, naphthodianthrones and dianthranoles. In plants, anthracene compounds are usually present as mono- or diglycosides. Anthracene derivates are common in certain genera of the Polygonaceae, Rhamnaceae, Fabaceae (Caesalpinioideae), Rubiaceae, Hypericaceae and Asphodelaceae.

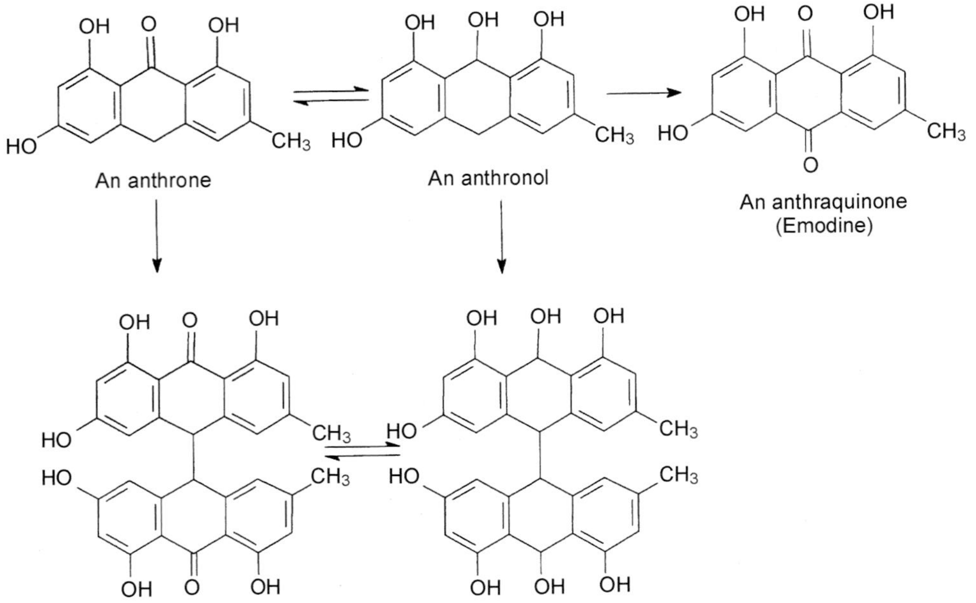

An anthrone

An anthronol

An anthraquinone
(Emodine)

Glycosylated monomeric anthrones exhibit a strong laxative activity by interfering with intestinal Na$^+$,K$^+$-ATPase and adenylyl cyclase. Water content of faeces is increased and gut motility stimulated. They had been used in medicine for several thousand years as laxatives. Anthraquinones also have phenolic OH-groups and can therefore interact with many proteins in the human body. These compounds can also interact with DNA and can probably cause mutations.

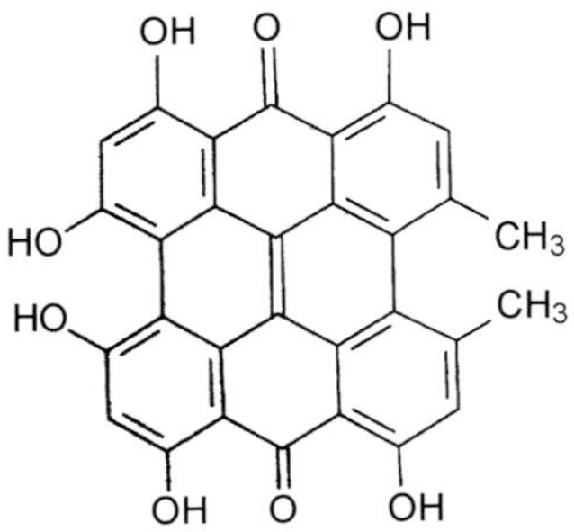

Hypericin

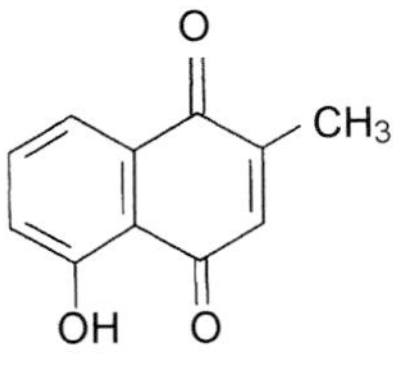

Plumbagin

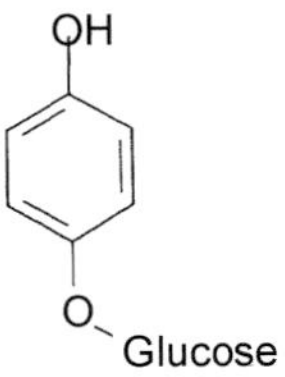

Arbutin

Dimeric anthraquinones (such as **hypericin**) are also present in *Hypericum perforatum* (Hypericaceae) and contribute to its pharmacology. The naphthoquinone **plumbagin** is present in *Drosera* species (Droseraceae) and appears to be responsible for the antitussive effects. **Arbutin**, a simple quinone, is present in many species of the Ericaceae; the free quinone appears to be responsible for the antibacterial effects.

POLYACETYLENES, THIOPHENES, ALKAMIDES, FATTY ACIDS AND WAXES AND THEIR MODES OF ACTION

Polyacetylenes or polyines are aliphatic hydrocarbons with carbon-carbon (C-C) triple and double bonds, such as in **falcarinol**.

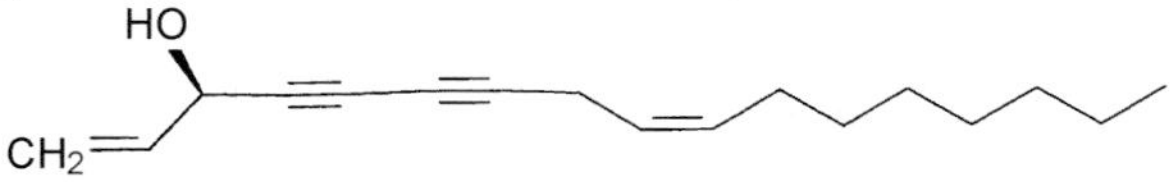

Falcarinol

Polyines are common in Asteraceae, Campanulaceae, Apiaceae, Araliaceae, Oleaceae and Santalaceae. Polyines are reactive molecules that can interfere with membrane proteins (receptors, ion channels, transporters) and other proteins. They are active against bacteria, fungi, insects and nematodes.

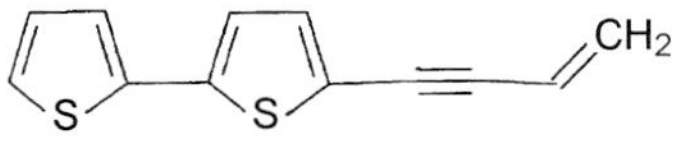

5-(3-Buten-1-ynyl)-2,2'-bithienyl (BBT)

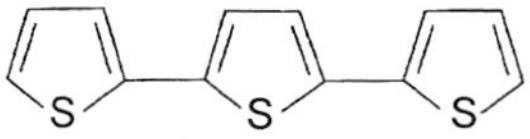

α-Tertienyl

In some plants, we find derivates of polyines in which oxygen or sulphur have been added to the triple bonds and secondary ring formations have occurred. Typical examples are thiophenes from *Tagetes* (Asteraceae) that exhibit a wide range of antimicrobial activities. Two examples are shown above.

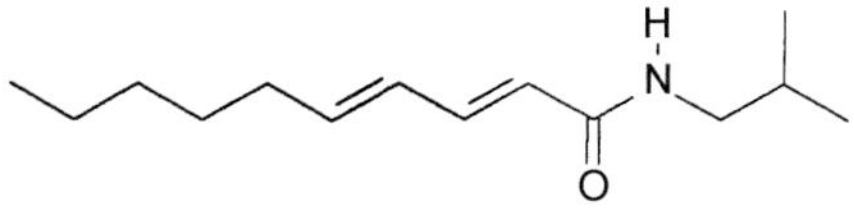

Deca-2E,4E-dienoic acid isobutylamide

Alkamides (150 structures have been reported) can be regarded as polyenes with nitrogen containing substituents. They occur in Piperaceae, Aristolochiaceae, Rutaceae and Asteraceae and appear to be antimicrobial, insecticidal and molluscicidal. Most fatty acids can be regarded as primary metabolites. Some have altered side chains and exhibit strong pharmacological effects, such as the purgative ricinoleic acid from *Ricinus communis*.

CARBOHYDRATES AND THEIR MODES OF ACTION

Plants produce and store several carbohydrates and organic acids, most of which must be regarded as primary metabolites. Several carbohydrates, such as glucose, galactose or mannose are used to form glycosides with secondary metabolites and are thus participants of both primary and secondary metabolism.

Arabinose   Digitalose   Galactose   Mannose

Examples of simple carbohydrates

A special example is phytic acid (a myo-inositol esterified with up to six phosphate groups) that can complex Ca^{++} and Mg^{++} ions and thus functions as antinutritive substance.

Stachyose

Several di-, tri- and oligosaccharides, such as **stachyose**, raffinose (that are typical for seeds and roots) produce substantial flatulence in humans.

Hexoses and pentoses are also the building blocks of important polysaccharides in plants, such as starch, cellulose, hemicellulose and pectin. In addition, a number of plants produce mucilage and specific storage products, such as inulin in Asteraceae and Campanulaceae. Plants rich in mucilage are used in medicine to treat coughs, to improve digestion and topically to soothe inflamed skin. The mucilage can form a protective film over inflamed mucosal tissues.

QUICK GUIDE TO COMMERCIALISED MEDICINAL PLANTS

Origin: A=Africa; SA=Southern Africa, NA=North Africa, WA=West Africa; Eu=Europe, NAm=North America; CAm=Central America; SAm=South America; As=Asia; EAs=East Asia; Aus=Australia.
Plant parts used: S=*semen* (seeds); O=*oleum* (oil); H=*herba* (herb), F=*folium* (leaves), FL= *flores* (flowers), E=*exudatum* (exudate); FR=*fructus* (fruit), R= *radix* (root), RH= *rhizoma* (rhizome or rootstock), B=*bulbus* (bulb); C=*cortex* (bark); L=*lignum* (wood); LE=*lignum extractum* (wood extract); T= *tuber*; G=*gummi* (gum).
Medicinal system (M): TM= traditional medicine; TCM=traditional Chinese medicine; TEM=traditional European medicine; TAM=traditional African medicine; TIM=traditional Indian medicine (including Ayurveda); TNAM=traditional North American medicine; TSAM=traditional Central & South American medicine TAUM=traditional Australian medicine; MM=modern medicine; ExM=experimental medicine.

Bold scientific name: treated and illustrated species

Species; family; common name	Ori-gin	Plant parts used	Active principles	M	Main indications in traditional medicine or homoeopathy; other uses
Abelmoschus moschatus; Malvaceae; musk mallow	EAs	S, O	ambrettolid and other fatty acids	TCM TIM	spasmolytic; digestive disorders; perfume; liqueurs
Abies alba, A. sibirica, A. balsamea; Pinaceae; fir trees	Eu As NAm	O	bornylacetate and other monoterpenes; diterpenes; resveratrol and other phenolics	TEM TNAM	counter-irritant for rheumatism and muscle pains; catarrh; cough, pertussis, bronchitis; urinary tract conditions
Abroma augusta; Sterculiaceae; devil's cotton, *ulat kambal* (Sanskrit)	As	R, C	triterpenes, mucilage	TIM	menstrual disorders, anti-diabetic
Abrus precatorius; Fabaceae; crab's eye ornaments	As	S	abrin (toxic lectin), indole alkaloids	TIM ExM	contraceptive; abortifacient experimental medicine;
Abutilon indicum; Malvaceae; Indian mallow, *atibala*	As	H, S, R	mucilage, tannins	TIM	catarrh; skin disorders, wounds; laxative
Acacia catechu; Fabaceae; catechu acacia	As EAs	LE	catechin, epicatechin (and polymeric flavanoid derivates	TIM	anti-diarrhoeal; haemostyptic; antibiotic
Acacia senegal; Fabaceae; gum acacia; *hashab*	NA	G	gum arabic: a complex mixture of polysaccharides	TAM TEM TIM	softens and soothes skin and mucosa; moisturising, antibiotic, protective; used as pharmaceutical aid (in solid formulations)
Acalypha indica; Euphorbiaceae; Indian acalypha	As	H	acalyphin (cyanogen)	TIM	expectorant; diuretic; topically for skin disorders
Acanthosicyos horridus; Cucurbitaceae; *nara*	SA	A	cucurbitacins; triglycerides	TAM	cosmetics, food (mature seeds)
Acanthus mollis; Acanthaceae; bear's breech	Eu	F, R	mucilage, tannins	TEM	wound healing; inflammation of mucous membranes in respiratory and digestive tract
Achillea millefolium; Asteraceae; yarrow	Eu As	H	pyrroline alkaloids; azulenic compounds; sesquiterpene lactones	TEM	anti-arthritic, antipyretic, anti-inflammatory, diuretic
Achyranthes bidentata; A. aspera; Amaranthaceae; rough chaff, *apamarg, niu xi*	EAs A	R	triterpene saponins; ecdysterone and other phytoecdysteroids;	TCM TIM	expectorant; inflammation of mouth; hypotonic, diuretic, uterus contractant

Achyrocline satureoides and related species; Asteraceae	SAm	H	flavonoids, phloroglucins, caffeic acid	TSAM	antibacterial; immune modulation; anti-exsudative; spasmolytic, analgesic; infections, disorders of intestinal tract
Acokanthera oppositifolia; Apocynaceae; bushman poison	A	S	ouabain and other cardenolides	TEM MM	cardiac disorders; arrow and spear poison
Aconitum carmichaelii; A. kusnezoffii; Ranunculaceae; *chuan wu; chao wu*	EAs	R	diterpenoid alkaloids	TCM	topical application: anti-rheumatic, analgesic, anti-neuralgic; extremely toxic!
Aconitum napellus; Ranunculaceae; monkshood	E	R	diterpenoid alkaloids (mainly aconitine)	TEM MM	topical application: antirheumatic, analgesic, anti-neuralgic; extremely toxic!
Acorus calamus; A. gramineus; Acoraceae; sweet flag, *vacha*	Eu NAm As	RH	monoterpenoids, sesquiterpenoids, phenylpropanoids	TEM TIM TCM	bitter tonic, stimulant; possible harmful effects!
Acronychia pedunculata; Rutaceae	EAs	F, R, C	acridone alkaloids; furoquinoline alkaloids; acrovestone and other phloroglucins	TCM TIM	sedative; cytotoxic; analgesic; skin disorders
Actaea racemosa (see *Cimicifuga racemosa*)					
Adhatoda vasica (see *Justicia adhatoda*)					
Adiantum capillus-veneris; Adiantaceae; maidenhair fern disorders	Eu NAm	H	tannins, mucilage, flavonoids; triterpenes	TEM	disorders of respiratory tract; hypoglycaemic; menstrual
Adlumia fungosa; Papaveraceae; Alleghenny vine, climbing fumitory	NAm	H	isoquinoline alkaloids (adlumine, bicuculline, protopine)	TNAM	sedative; GABA antagonist; stimulation of intestinal and uterine contractions
Adonis vernalis; Ranunculaceae; pheasant's eye	Eu	H	cardiac glycosides	TEM	heart stimulant, diuretic; numerous other uses
Aegle marmelos; Rutaceae; stone apple; *bilwa, bael*	As	H,R,F R	coumarins, tannins, alkaloids	TIM	astringent; laxative, dyspepsia, earache;
Aegopodium podagraria; Apiaceae; ground elder, goutweed	Eu	H, R	falcarindiol and other polyacetylenes; furocoumarins; flavonoids, caffeic acid	TEM	gout and rheumatism; haemorrhoids
Aerva javanica and related species; Amaranthaceae	A As	H,F,R	ecdysterone; sitosterol; triterpenes; saponins; flavonoids	TAM	hypnotic, narcotic, diuretic, antimicrobial, anthelmintic, anti-inflammatory
Aesculus hippocastanum; Hippocastanaceae; horse chestnut	Eu As	S, F, C	triterpene saponins	TEM	anti-inflammatory, venotonic, anti-oedema
Aethusa cynapium; Apiaceae; fool's parsley	Eu As	H	aethusin and other polyacetylenes; flavonoids; vitamin C	TEM	counter-irritant; gastro-intestinal disorders; very toxic!
Aframomum melegueta; Zingiberaceae; grains of paradise, melagueta pepper	WA	S	essential oil, pungent paradol, tannins	TAM	dyspepsia
Agastache rugosa; Lamiaceae; giant hyssop, *huo xiang*	EAs	H	methyl chavicol, anethole, anisaldehyde and other volatiles	TCM	digestive disorders; antifungal
Agathis australis; A. dammara; Araucariaceae; kauri; *bendang*, Manila copal	EAs Aus	resin O	volatile oil with pinene and limonene; diterpenes	TAUM	kauri copal; Manila copal; used for plasters and dentistry; source for lacquers
Agathosma betulina; A. crenulata; Rutaceae; buchu	A	F	essential oil with mono-terpenes, diosphenol; mucilage, flavonoids	TAM	diuretic; inflammation of urinary tract; bitter tonic
Agave americana; A. sisalana; Agavaceae; century plant, sisal	CAm SAm	F	steroidal saponins; isoflavones, coumarins	TSAM	mucosal inflammation; digestive disorders; base for pulque and tequila; fibres

Species; Family; common name	Origin	Part	Constituents	Tradition	Uses
Ageratum conyzoides; Asteraceae; billy-goat weed	CAm	H	volatile oil with precocens and other chromenes; monoterpenes; flavonoids	TAM TSAM	wound treatment; antiseptic; disorders of respiratory tract; juvenile hormone antagonist;
Agrimonia eupatoria; A. procera; Rosaceae; common agrimony; scented agrimony	Eu	H	catechol tannins and gallotannins	TEM	anti-diarrhoeal, astringent, mild diuretic
Agropyron repens (see Elymus repens)					
Agrostemma githago; Caryophyllaceae; corn cockle	Eu As	S	orcylalanine (NPAA); triterpene saponins	TEM	antimycotic; haemolytic; toxic!
Ahnfeltia species; Rhodophyceae	As	algae	acidic polygalactans; agarose, agaropectin (agar)	TEM	laxative, used in galenics and microbiology (agar plates)
Ailanthus altissima; A. malabarica; Simaroubaceae; tree of heaven	EAs	C	quassin, ailanthinone and other quassinoids; tannins; indole alkaloids	TCM	amarum, spasmolytic, dysentery; anthelmintic; amoebicidal; antitumour activities
Ajuga reptans; A decumbens; A. bracteosa; Lamiaceae; bugle	Eu As	H	harpagide and other iridoid glycosides; ajuga-lactones and other ecdysteroids; diterpenes	TEM TCM	astringent; laxative; mild analgesic properties; wound healing
Akebia quinata; Lardiz-abalaceae; chocolate vine	EAs	H	triterpene saponins; flavonoids	TCM	urinary tract infections; digestive disorders
Alchemilla vulgaris (=*A. xanthochlora*) and other species; Rosaceae; lady's mantle	Eu NAm As	H	ellagitannins (agrimoniin and others)	TEM	astringent, antihaemorrhagic
Alchornea cordifolia, A. floribunda; Euphorbiaceae /Alchorniaceae	A	F,R, FR	tannins; alkaloids (alchorneine)	TAM	antimicrobial; antitrypanoso-mal; spasmolytic; antidepres-sant; narcotic hallucinogen
Aletris farinosa; Melanthiaceae/ Liliaceae; ague root, unicorn root	NAm	RH, F	steroid saponins (diosgenin-type), volatile oil	TNAM	estrogenic properties; menstrual disorders; dyspepsia
Alisma plantago-aquatica; Alis-mataceae; water plantain, *ze xie*	Eu As	R	pungent resin; ess. oil; tannins, triterpenes	TCM	diuretic, urinary tract infections
Alkanna tuberculata; Boraginaceae; alkanet	Eu As	R	alkannin, pyrrolizidine alkaloids (carcinogenic!)	TEM	astringent, antimicrobial; skin disorders; red colour
Alliaria petiolata; Brassicaceae; garlic mustard, hedge garlic	Eu As	H	sinigrine and other glucosinolates; sinapine; vitamin C, vitamin A	TEM TIM	colds; wound healing; scurvy
Allium cepa; Alliaceae; onion	Eu	B	sulphur-containing compounds	TEM	antibiotic, antibacterial, lipid-lowering
Allium sativum; A. ursinum; Alliaceae; garlic, wood garlic, *lasuna*	Eu As	B	sulphur-containing compounds	TEM TIM MM	antibacterial, antiviral; against arteriosclerosis, lipid-lowering
Alnus glutinosa, A. incana; A. japonica; Betulaceae; alder	Eu As	C, F	tannins, stilbenes; triterpenes; biarylheptanoids	TEM	astringent; mouthwash to treat inflammations of mucous membranes; wounds; haemostyptic
Aloe ferox; Asphodelaceae; bitter aloe, Cape aloe	SA	E, gel	bitters: aloin (=barbaloin) and chromones; gel: polysaccharides	TAM TEM	bitters: laxative, bitter tonic; gel: health drink, wound-healing, cosmetic
Aloe vera; Asphodelaceae; aloe vera	NA	E, gel	bitters: aloin (=barbaloin) and chromones; gel: polysaccharides	TAM TNAM TEM	bitters: laxative, bitter tonic; gel: health drink, wound-healing, cosmetic
Aloysia triphylla; Verbenaceae; lemon verbena	SAm	F	essential oil; flavonoids	TSAM TEM	digestive, sedative; used in aromatherapy
Alpinia officinarum; Zingiberaceae; lesser galangal, Siamese ginger; *gao liang jiang*	As EAs	RH	monoterpenoids, diarylheptanoids, gingerols	TCM TIM TEM	carminative, digestive tonic, anti-emetic

Alstonia constricta, A. scholaris; Apocynaceae; devil's tree	EAsA US	C	alstonine, reserpine and other monoterpene indole alkaloids	TEM	hypotensive; antispasmodic, febrifuge; laxative, stimulant
Althaea officinalis; Malvaceae; marshmallow	Eu As	R, F, FL	mucilages (polysaccharides)	TEM	demulcent, emollient, expectorant
Amaranthus dubius, A. hypochondriacus; Amaranthaceae; amaranth	CAm EU As	H	tannins, betacyanins, saponins, flavonoids	TEM	astringent, antidiarrhoeal; haemostyptic; inflammations of mucous membranes, diuretic
Ambrosia artemisiifolia; Asteraceae; common ragweed	NAm	F	sesquiterpene lactones	TNAM	allergenic
Ammi visnaga; Apiaceae; visnaga, *khella*, bishop's weed	NA	FR	furanocoumarins (khellin, visnagin, etc.)	TAM TEM	antispasmodic, vasodilator, anti-asthmatic
Amomum aromaticum and related species; Zingiberaceae; Bengal cardamom, *sha ren*	EAs	FR	volatile oil with 1,8-cineol, bornylacetate and other monoterpenes	TCM TIM	disorders of respiratory tract; dyspepsia; carminative
Anacardium occidentale; Anacardiaceae; cashew nut tree	CAm SAm	FR,C, F	anacardic acid (salicylic acid derivative), tannins	TIM TSAM	anti-inflammatory; toothache; skin disorders; hypoglycaemic, hypotensive, counter-irritant, antimicrobial, anthelmintic
Anacyclus pyrethrum; Asteraceae; pyrethrum	Eu	R	anacycline, inulin	TEM	toothache; stimulation of salivation
Anagallis arvensis; Primulaceae; scarlet pimpernel	Eu	H	triterpene saponins, tannins, cucurbitacins	TEM TIM	diuretic, expectorant; diaphoretic; skin disorders; haemorrhoids; fungitoxic
Anamirta cocculus; Menispermaceae; fish-berry plant, Indian berry	EAs	F, FR	picrotoxin and other sesquiterpene lactones; protoberberine alkaloids	TIM	externally against parasites; nerve stimulant; skin disorders; counter-irritant; travel sickness; very toxic!
Ananas comosus; Bromeliaceae; pineapple plant	CAm	pro-teins	bromelain (mixture of proteolytic enzymes)	MM	digestive, anti-inflammatory; treatment of post-traumatic and post-operative oedemas
Anchusa officinalis; Boraginaceae; bugloss	Eu	H	pyrrolizidine alkaloids (carcinogen!); allantoin	TEM	expectorant, sedative, wound healing
Andira araroba; Fabaceae; araroba tree	SAm	F	chrysarobin (anthraquinone), berberine	TEM TSAM	strong irritant; skin disorders; source of Goa powder or araroba
Andira inermis; Fabaceae; angelin, dog almond	CAm SAm	C	N-methyltyrosine; berberine	TEM TSAM	against internal worms; antispasmodic
Andrographis paniculata; Acanthaceae; andrographis, *kalmegh*	EAs	H	diterpene lactones	TIM TEM	tonic; against kidney stones
Anemarrhena asphodeloides; Anthericaceae / Liliaceae; *zhi mu*	EAs	RH	steroid saponins, xanthones, lignans	TCM	inhibits Na^+, K^+-ATPase, and DNA-polymerase; mouth ulcers, infections, fever
Anemone nemorosa, A. ranunculoides, A. sylvestris; A. cylindrica and others; Ranunculaceae; anemone	Eu NAm	H, R	ranunculin, protoanemonin	TEM	counter-irritant (rheumatism), toothache, headache; bronchitis
Anethum graveolens; Apiaceae; dill	Eu NA, As	FR	essential oil with carvone; flavonoids, coumarins	TEM	stomachic, carminative, diuretic
Angelica archangelica; Apiaceae; angelica	Eu As	R, H, FR, oil	essential oil; coumarins; furanocoumarins	TEM	appetite stimulant, stomachic, spasmolytic
Angelica polymorpha var. *sinensis, A. dahurica* and other species; Apiaceae; *dang gui, du huo*; Chinese angelica	As EAs	R	essential oil; coumarins; furanocoumarins	TCM	tonic; anaemia, constipation, irregular menstruation, pain
Antennaria dioica; Asteraceae; cat's ear flower	Eu	H	flavonoids, sesquiterpene lactones	TEM	expectorant; liver complaints, diarrhoea
Anthemis cotula; A. tinctoria; Asteraceae; mayweed; dyer's chamomile	Eu As	FL, H	anthecotulid and other sesquiterpene lactones; volatile oil	TEM TNAM	spasmolytic, fever, skin irritant; menstrual disorders; anthelmintic

Anthriscus cerefolium; Apiaceae; chervil	Eu	H	methylchavicol, coumarins; apiin	TEM	diuretic, skin disorders, spice
Anthyllis vulneraria; Fabaceae; kidney-vetch	Eu As	H, FL	canalin, canavanin (NPAAs); catechol tannins; flavonoids, isoflavones;	TEM	external and internal wounds; expectorant
Aphanes arvensis, Rosaceae; parsley piert	Eu As	H	tannins	TEM	astringent; diuretic, demulcent; inflammations of urinary tract
Apium graveolens; Apiaceae; celery	Eu As	H, FR, R	monoterpenes, butyl-phthalids, coumarins, furocoumarins, flavonoids	TEM TCM	diuretic (urinary tract disorders), carminative, dyspepsia, cough, gout, sedative, spice, aphrodisiac
Apocynum cannabinum; A. androsaemifolium; Apocynaceae; Indian hemp, dogbane	NAm	R	cardenolides, k-stro-phanthoside, cymarin	TEM	cardiac disorders, diuretic
Aquilaria malaccensis, A. sinensis; A. agallocha; Thymelaeaceae; agarwood, aloewood, *akil, agaru*	As	L, resin	sesquiterpenes; couma-royl-lignan, liriodenine (aporphine alkaloid)	TIM TCM	astringent; febrifuge; dyspepsia, diuretic, skin disorders; ectoparasites
Aquilegia vulgaris; Ranunculaceae; columbines	Eu As	H, S	triglochinine (cyanogenic glycoside); triterpene saponins	TEM	scurvy, jaundice; sedative, skin disorders
Arachis hypogaea; Fabaceae; peanut	SAm	S	triglycerides, lectins,	TEM	skin disorders; laxative, base for ointments
Aralia racemosa; A. mandshurica; Araliaceae; American spikenard	NAm EAs	R	volatile oil; tannins, sesqui-, and diterpenes; saponins; falcarinone and other polyacetylenes	TNAM TCM	colds, diaphoretic, cough, skin conditions; sedative tonic
Arbutus unedo; Ericaceae; strawberry tree	Eu	F, FR	up to 2.7% arbutin and related hydroquinones, iridoid glycosides; flavonoids, tannins	TEM	antiseptic for urinary tract infections; astringent, antidiarrhoeal
Arctium lappa; Asteraceae; burdock	Eu	R	polyacetylenes, essential oil	TEM	diuretic, skin disorders eczema, psoriasis, acne, skin infection, etc.)
Arctostaphylos uva-ursi; Ericaceae; bearberry	Eu As NAm	F	Arbutin (a phenolic glycoside) and other hydroquinones; tannins	TEM TNAM	urinary antiseptic; treatment of cystitis, pyelitis, lithuria
Areca catechu; Arecaceae; betel nut palm	As	S	arecoline, catechol tannins	TEM TIM	parasympathomimetic; enhance-ment of glandular secretions; anthelmintic; central nervous stimulant (used in combination with *Piper betle*)
Argania spinosa; Sapotaceae; argan, argan tree	NA	S	triglycerides	TAM	oil similar to olive oil, used in cosmetics; valuable gum
Argemone mexicana; Papaveraceae; Mexican poppy, prickly poppy	Am	H, S	isoquinoline alkaloids	TSAM	analgesic, sedative, purgative
Arisaema consanguineum; Araceae; Jack-in-the-pulpit	EAs	RH	triterpene saponins, benzoic acid	TCM	catarrhs, skin disorders; analgesic, sedative; toxic!
Aristolochia clematitis; Aristolochiaceae; birthworth	Eu	H, R	aristolochic acids (carcinogenic!)	TEM	child birth, abortifacient, wound-healing; very toxic!
Aristolochia fangui and several other species; Aristolochiaceae; Chinese birthworth, *guang fang ji*	As	R	aristolochic acids (carcinogenic!)	TCM	various uses; known to be toxic (kidney damage)
Armoracia rusticana; Brassicaceae; horseradish	Eu	R	glucosinolates: mainly gluconasturtin, sinigrin; peroxidase enzyme	TEM	respiratory and urinary tract disorders; counter-irritant; a popular spice
Arnica chamissonis, A. fulgens and other species; Asteraceae; arnica	NAm	FL (H, R)	sesquiterpene lactones and various other compounds	TNAM TEM	anti-inflammatory, counter-irritant, wound healing; internal use is dangerous!

Arnica montana; Asteraceae; arnica	Eu	FL (H, R)	sesquiterpene lactones and various other compounds	TEM	anti-inflammatory, counter-irritant, wound healing; internal use is dangerous!
Artemisia abrotanum; Asteraceae; southernwood	Eu	H	abrotin; bitters; isofraxidin (a coumarin); ess. oil (1,8-cineol)	TEM	aromatic; anthelmintic, spice
Artemisia absinthium; Asteraceae; wormwood	Eu	H	essential oil with mono- and sesquiterpenoids; sesquiterpene lactones	TEM	bitter tonic, dyspepsia, bile tract disorders; used in alcoholic drinks; neurotoxic (thujone)!
Artemisia afra; Asteraceae; African wormwood; *umhlonyane, lengana, wildeals*	A	H	essential oil with mono- and sesquiterpenoids; sesquiterpene lactones	TAM	bitter tonic, analgesic, anthelmintic; treatment of colds; thujone potentially harmful!
Artemisia annua; Asteraceae; Chinese wormwood, *qing hao*	Eu As	H	artemisinin, a sesquiterpene lactone	TCM MM	effective and cost-effective antimalarial; traditional tonic, febrifuge, antibiotic
Artemisia cina; Asteraceae; santonica	As	FL	santonin, artemisin, ess. oil	TEM	anthelmintic
Artemisia vulgaris and numerous other species; Asteraceae; mugwort	Eu As	H	essential oil with mono- and sesquiterpenoids; sesquiterpene lactones	TEM	stomachic, emmenagogue, cholagogue, anthelmintic
Arum maculatum; Araceae; lords-and-ladies	Eu	RH	polysaccharides, saponins	TEM	tonic, stomachic, topically for ulcers
Arundo donax; Poaceae; giant reed	Eu	RH	indole alkylamines, gramine etc.	TEM	diuretic, uterus stimulant
Asarum europaeum; *A. canadense*; *A. sieboldii*; Aristolochiaceae; asarabacca; wild ginger	Eu NAm EAs	RH	essential oils (pinene and other monoterpenes, asarone, methyleugenol and other phenylpropanoids)	TEM TCM	spasmolytic, disorders of respiratory tract; antibacterial, analgesic; diuretic, abortifacient; menstrual disorders, intestinal disorders; emetic; asarone carcinogenic!
Asclepias fruticosa (*Gomphocarpus fruticosus*); Asclepiadaceae; milkweed	A	R	cardenolides	TEM	heart disorders
Asclepias tuberosa; Asclepiadaceae; pleurisy root	NAm	R	cardiac glycosides, various other compounds	TNAM	expectorant, diaphoretic, antispasmodic
Ascophyllum nodosum; Fucaceae; knotted wrack	NAt-lantic	algae	minerals, trace elements, tannin-like substances (fucosan), iodine	TEM	used in iodine therapy and as ingredient of slimming teas
Aspalathus linearis; Fabaceae; rooibostea plant	SA	H	flavonoid glycosides	TAM	antispasmodic, general health tonic (herbal tea)
Asparagus officinalis; Asparagaceae; asparagus	Eu As, A	RH	phenolics, steroidal saponins, asparagine	TEM	diuretic; anti-inflammatory
Asparagus racemosus; also *A. ascendens*, *A. falcatus*; Asparagaceae; *shatavari*	A As	R	steroidal saponins	TIM	various uses: coolant, aphrodisiac, nerve tonic, antispasmodic
Aspidosperma quebracho-blanco; Apocynaceae; quebracho	SAm	C	aspidospermine, yohimbine and other monoterpene indole alkaloids, tannins	TEM TSAM	expectorant, asthma, bronchitis, wound healing, burns; febrifuge
Asplenium scolopendrium (*Phyllitis scolopendrium*); Polypodiaceae; hartstongue	Eu As Am	H	tannins, mucilage, flavonoids	TEM	digestive disorders; wound healing; expectorant, diuretic
Astracantha gummifera; Fabaceae; traganth	As	G	polysaccharides	TEM	hydrophilic and colloidal agent used in pharmaceutical products
Astragalus membranaceus, *A. mongholicus* and related species; Fabaceae; membranous milk vetch; *huang qi*	As	R	triterpene saponins; polysaccharides, isoflavones	TCM	adaptogenic tonic; immune stimulant
Atractylodes macrocephala; Asteraceae; *pai shu*	EAs	RH	volatile oil with atractylol	TCM	tonic, digestive disorders; antibiotic

Atriplex hortensis, *A. halimus* and related species; Chenopodiaceae; saltbushes	Eu As	H	triterpene saponins, flavonoids, vitamin C, amaranthine (betalain); oxalate	TEM	dyspepsia, expectorant, hypoglycaemic, anti-diabetic, urinary tract disorders
Atropa belladonna; Solanaceae; deadly nightshade	Eu As NA	F, R	tropane alkaloids (mainly atropine)	TEM MM	spasmolytic, hallucinogen; asthma, pain relief, mydriatic
Avena sativa; Poaceae; oats	Eu NA	H, FR	silica, minerals, amino acids, vitamins	TEM	anti-pruritic (oats straw); dietary aid (oats grain); putative sedative (green tops)
Azadirachta indica; Meliaceae; neem tree, *neem*, *nimba*	As	L, C, R, S	triterpenoids (limonoids): azadirachtin	TIM	numerous uses; skin healing
Bacopa monnieri; Scrophulariaceae; *brahmi*, bacopa, *andri*, water hyssop	As	H	bacosides, steroid saponins	TIM TCM	tonic, disorders of the nervous system; dyspepsia, bronchitis
Ballota africana; Lamiaceae; African horehound	A	H	diterpenoids, essential oil	TAM	fever, cough, colds, hysteria, insomnia, pain treatment
Ballota nigra Lamiaceae; black horehound	Eu As	H	diterpenoids (mainly ballotenol); flavonoids	TEM	spasmolytic, sedative; cough, nervous disorders
Bambusa arundiacea; Poaceae; male bamboo, spiny bamboo	As	R, H	silica	TIM	menstrual disorders; diuretic; spasmolytic
Banisteriopsis caapi; Malpighiaceae; *caapi*, *ayahuasca*, *yagé*	SAm	L	harmin and other β-carboline alkaloids	TSAM	central stimulant, hallucinogenic
Baptisia tinctoria; Fabaceae; false indigo	NAm	R	cytisine and other quinolizidine alkaloids	TEM TNAM	laxative, against fever; wound healing; antimicrobial; immune stimulant
Barosma betulina (see *Agathosma betulina*)					
Bellis perennis; Asteraceae; daisies	Eu As	H, FL	triterpene saponins	TEM	expectorant; dyspepsia; inflammation of gall bladder
Benincasa hispida; Cucurbitaceae; wax gourd, white gourd	A As	FR	saponins; guaridine	TCM	bronchitis; diuretic, laxative; anthelmintic
Berberis vulgaris; Berberidaceae; barberry	Eu As	FR, C, R	isoquinoline and protoberberine alkaloids (mainly berberine)	TEM MM	digestive, anti-biotic, liver stimulant; pure berberine is used in eye drops to treat conjunctivitis
Bergenia crassifolia; Saxifragaceae; elephant-ear, Siberian saxifrage	As	R, F	tannins; arbutin	TEM	astringent; antiseptic; haemostyptic
Beta vulgaris var. *conditiva*; Chenopodiaceae; beetroot	Eu	R	betanin and other betacyanins	TEM	liver and kidney disorders; immune stimulant; adjuvant with radiation and chemotherapy
Betula pendula, *B. alba*; Betulaceae; birch	Eu As	F, C, leaf buds	flavonoid glycosides; methylsalicylate	TEM	diuretic (leaf); antipruritic (tar oil)
Bidens tripartita; *B. pilosa*; Asteraceae; blackjack	Eu Am	H	flavonoids, polyacetylenes, tannins	TEM	astringent, diuretic, inflammation of digestive tract; antidiarrhoeal
Bixa orellana; Bixaceae; annato	CAm SAm	S	bixin and other carotenoids	TSAM	astringent; wounds and burns; food colouring; cosmetics
Boerhaavia diffusa; Nyctaginaceae; red spiderling, *punarnava*	As	R, F	alkaloids, sterols, exdysteroids	TIM	anthelmintic; anti-inflammatory, adaptogenic
Borago officinalis; Boraginaceae; borage	Eu	FL, H seed oil	mucilage, pyrrolizidine alkaloids; seed oil rich in gamma-linolenic acid	TEM	emollient; herb not to be taken internally (pyrrolizidine alkaloids)
Boswellia frereana; Burseraceae; olibanum tree	A	E	volatile oil; triterpenoids	TAM	antiseptic, expectorant, sedative

Boswellia papyrifera; Burseraceae; Ethiopian frankincense tree	A	E	volatile oil; triterpenoids	TAM	antiseptic, expectorant, sedative
Boswellia sacra; Burseraceae; frankincense tree	A As	E	volatile oil; triterpenoids; boswellic acid	TAM TEM TCM	antiseptic, expectorant, sedative; anti-inflammatory; anti-rheumatic
Boswellia serrata and other species; Burseraceae; Indian olibanum tree, *salai guggul*	As	E	boswellin and other oleo-resins;	TIM TCM	antiseptic, expectorant, sedative; arthritis treatment
Brassica nigra; Brassicaceae; black mustard	Eu As	S	glucosinolates (mainly sinigrin)	TEM	antibacterial; counter-irritant to treat rheumatic pain)
Brucea javanica; Simaroubaceae; Java brucea	As EAs	FR, S	bitter triterpenoids (bruceosides and related quassinoids)	TIM TCM	anti-dysenteric; anti-malaria; used against infections and intestinal worms
Bryonia dioica; *B. alba*; Cucurbitaceae; red bryony; white bryony	Eu	R	various cucurbitacins (bitter triterpenoids)	TEM	antirheumatic, cathartic, expectorant, emetic
Bupleurum falcatum (=*B. chinense*); Apiaceae; bupleurum, Chinese thorowax	Eu As	R	triterpenoid saponins, polyacetylenic compounds	TCM	tonic, anti-inflammatory, anti-pyretic, liver protective
Butea monosperma; Fabaceae; *dhak*, flame of the forest	As	F,FL, S, C	tannins	TIM	skin disorders; gargle & mouth wash; antidiarrhoeal; vaginitis
Calamintha nepeta; Lamiaceae; common calamint	Eu As	H	pulegone and other monoterpenes	TEM	diaphoretic; carminative; expectorant
Calendula officinalis; Asteraceae; marigold	Eu	FL, ess. oil	flavonoids, saponins, triterpenes, sesquiterpenes	TEM	anti-inflammatory, antispasmodic; wounds and skin ailments; colourant in herbal teas
Calluna vulgaris; Ericaceae; heather, common heather	Eu	H	tannins, arbutin	TEM	antidiarrhoeal; inflammations of urinary tract
Calotropis procera; Asclepiadaceae / Apocynaceae; apple of Sodom	As	R	cardenolides	TIM	multiple uses
Caltha palustris; Ranunculaceae; marsh marigold	Eu	H	ranunculin; protoanemonin	TEM	skin disorders
Camellia sinensis; Theaceae; tea plant	As EAs	F	caffeine; phenolic acids, tannins	TCM TEM	stimulant, antioxidant, possible antimutagen; beverage
Camptotheca acuminata; Cornaceae; camptotheca, cancer tree, happy tree	EAs	F	pentacyclic quinoline alkaloids (camptothecin)	TCM MM	cancer treatment
Cananga odorata; Annonaceae; ylang-ylang tree	EAs	O	monoterpenes, sesqui-terpenes, eugenol, safrole	TCM	sedative, antiseptic; hypotonic; perfume
Canella winterana; Canellaceae; canella bark tree	CAm	C	pinene and other monoterpenes, eugenol	TEM TNAM	tonic, spice, aromatic, anti-septic, cytotoxic, insect repellent
Cannabis sativa; Cannabaceae; marijuana, hemp	As EAs	F, FL, S	phenolic terpenoids (cannabinoids), mainly tetrahydrocannabinol	TCM TIM MM	intoxicant, sedative, analgesic, anti-emetic; an important fibre and oil seed crop
Capparis spinosa; Capparaceae; capers	Eu	FL	glucosinolates, rutin, saponins	TEM	laxative, dyspepsia, spice; haemostyptic, skin conditions
Capsella bursa-pastoris; Brassicaceae; shepherd's purse	Eu	H	flavonoids, amino acids, amines, terpenoids, glucosinolates (sinigrin)	TEM	antihaemorrhagic, urinary antiseptic; eye diseases; against dysentery
Capsicum frutescens; *C. annuum*; Solanaceae; chilli pepper, Tabasco pepper	CAm SAm	FR, S	pungent capsaicinoids, mainly capsaicin; colour due to carotenoids	TSAM TEM	topical analgesic, carminative; counter-irritant; an important spice
Cardiospermum halicacabum; Sapindaceae; balloon vine	CAm SAm	S, H	cyanolipids, saponins	TIM	topical skin disorders; sedative
Carex arenaria; Cyperaceae	Eu	RH	silica; tannins, saponins	TEM	diuretic

402

Carica papaya; Caricaceae; papaya tree, paw paw	CAm SAm	FR, F	proteolytic enzymes (mainly papain) from crude latex of unripe fruit	TSAM TSAM MM	digestive, wound-healing, anthelmintic; cultivated fruit; papain is a meat tenderiser
Carlina acaulis; Asteraceae; stemless carlina	Eu	R	polyacetylenes, inulin	TEM	diuretic, skin disorders
Carthamus tinctorius; Asteraceae; safflower, *hong hua*	NA As	FL, S, seed oil	carthamin and other glucosylated dichalcones, flavonoids, triterpene alcohols	TAM TCM	emmenagogue, anti-inflammatory; gynaecological ailments (China); health food (seed oil, natural dye)
Carum carvi; Apiaceae; caraway	Eu As	FR	volatile oil; mainly carvone	TAM TIM TEM	carminative, stomachic, spasmolytic, expectorant; an important spice
Cassia acutifolia, C. angustifolia (see *Senna alexandrina*)					
Cassia fistula; Fabaceae; purging cassia, Indian laburnum; *aragwadha*	As	R, C, FR pulp	anthraquinone derivatives; fruit pulp contains 60% sugars	TIM	bark and root extracts used against skin conditions; fruit pulp used as purgative
Cassia senna (see *Senna alexandrina*)					
Castanea sativa; Fagaceae; sweet chestnut	Eu As	F, C	tannins (mainly ellagitannins); flavonoids	TEM	astringent, antitussive; gargle to treat mucosal infections; edible nuts
Castanospermum australe; Fabaceae; Australian chestnut	Aus	F	polyhydroxy alkaloids	ExM	glucosidase inhibitor (HIV)
Catalpa bignonioides; Bignoniaceae; Indian bean	NAm	C, FR	catalpine (an iridoid glycoside); tannins	TNAM	sedative, analgesic; cough, bronchitis
Catha edulis; Celastraceae; khat	A	F	phenylethylamines (mainly cathinone)	TAM	stimulant, appetite suppressant; numerous traditional uses
Catharanthus roseus; Apocynaceae; Madagascar periwinkle	A	F, R	monoterpene indole alkaloids	TAM MM	traditionally used to treat diabetes and rheumatism; isolated alkaloids used in modern cancer therapy
Caulophyllum thalictroides; Berberidaceae; blue cohosh, squaw root	NAm As	R	quinolizidine alkaloids; saponins	TNAM	antispasmodic, diuretic, menstrual disorders, ant-inflammatory, diaphoretic
Ceanothus americanus; Rhamnaceae; red root, New Jersey tea	NAm	R, F	macrocyclic peptide alkaloids, triterpenes (e.g. ceanothic acid)	TNAM	haemostyptic, astringent; numerous traditional uses; herbal tea
Cedrus deodara, C. libani; Pinaceae; cedar trees; *devadaru*	As	L, O, C	cedrene and other monoterpenes	TIM TEM	expectorant, antiseptic, bronchitis; diuretic, sedative
Centaurea benedicta (= *Cnicus benedictus*); Asteraceae; holy thistle, blessed thistle	Eu	H	essential oil; cnicin and other bitter sesquiterpene lactones; lignan lactones	TEM	appetite stimulant, dyspepsia; topically used against wounds and ulcers
Centaurea cyanus; Asteraceae; blue cornflower	Eu As	FL	anthocyanins (cyanidin glycosides); sesquiterpene lactones	TEM	general tonic, stomachic, diuretic; lotions, eye washes; colourant in herbal teas
Centaurium erythraea; Gentianaceae; centaury	Eu	H	bitter iridoid glycosides (secoiridoids), mainly swertiamarin	TEM	bitter tonic; numerous traditional uses; bitter food flavouring; some species used in homoeopathy
Centella asiatica; Apiaceae; *gotu cola*, hydrocotyle, *mandukparni*	A As EAs	F	triterpenoids (asiaticoside, asiatic acid, madecassic acid)	TIM TAM MM	venous insufficiency, wound-healing, general tonic; prevention of scar tissue formation; adaptogen
Centhranthus ruber; Valerianaceae; red valerian	Eu	R	valepotriates	TEM	sedatives; source of valepotriates
Cephaelis ipecacuanha (see *Psychotria ipecacuanha*					
Ceratonia siliqua; Fabaceae; carob tree	Eu	FR	sugars, polysaccharides	TEM	antidiarrhoeal; dietetic, celiac disorders

Cetraria islandica; Parmeliaceae; Iceland moss	Arctic	lichen	polysaccharides, mainly lichenin and isolichenin; also bitter lichenolic acids (depsidones)	TEM	antitussive, emollient, bitter tonic; treatment of wounds
Chamaelirium luteum; Melanthiaceae/ Liliaceae; unicorn root	Am	R	steroidal saponins, diosgenin	TNAM	uterine tonic, diuretic; wounds, ulcers
Chamaemelum nobile; Asteraceae; Roman chamomile	Eu	FL	essential oil; azulenic compounds; sesqui-terpenoids, polyacetylenes	TEM	sedative, antispasmodic, anti-inflammatory; topical uses; cosmetics; aromatherapy
Chaenomeles speciosa; Rosaceae; Chinese quince, *mu gua*	As	FR	minerals	TCM	spasmolytic, rheumatic pain
Cheiranthus cheiri (see *Erysimum cheiri*)					
Chelidonium majus; Papaveraceae; greater celandine	Eu As NA	H	protopine, protoberberine and benzophenanthridine alkaloids	TEM	cholagogue, antimicrobial, spasmolytic; topical uses
Chelone glabra; Scrophulariaceae; balmony	NAm	H	resin, bitter substances	TNAM	laxative, cholagogue; anthelmintic
Chenopodium ambrosioides; Chenopodiaceae; wormseed goosefoot	SAm CAm	ess. oil	Essential oil with ascaridol as main ingredient	TSAM TEM	anthelmintic; veterinary uses; toxic!
Chenopodium quinoa; Chenopodiaceae; quinoa	SAm	S	saponins; protein, starch	TSAM	diaphoretic, expectorant; food
Chimaphila umbellata; Ericaceae/Pyrolaceae; prince's pine	Eu NAm	H	arbutin; tannins; methyl salicylates;	TNAM	diuretic, disinfectant, astringent, disorders of urinary tract
Chionanthus virginicus; Oleaceae; fringe tree, old man's beard	NAm	R	saponins, lignan glycosides, secoiridoids	TNAM	cholagogue, liver tonic; bitter tonic, anti-emetic, laxative; wounds
Chondrodendron tomentosum; Menispermaceae; pareira root	SAm	R	tubocurarine and other alkaloids	TSAM MM	diuretic, muscle relaxant; spasmolytic, menstrual disorders; surgery; arrow poisons
Chondrus crispus; Gigartinaceae; Irish moss, caragheen (a seaweed)	NAt-lantic	algae	carrageenans (galactans, polymers of sulphated galactose); iodine	TEM	demulcent; industrial thickening and gelling agents
Chrysanthemum balsamita; Asteraceae; alecost, costmary	Eu	F	essential oil; bitter sesquiterpene lactones	TEM	traditional vermifuge; formerly used as bitter flavour in ale
Chrysanthemum cinerariifolium; Asteraceae; pyrethrum	Eu As	FL	pyrethrins	TEM	traditional and modern insecticide
Chrysanthemum x morifolium; Asteraceae; chrysanthemum, *ju hua*	EAs	FL	triterpene alcohols (e.g. helianol)	TCM	general tonic, anti-inflammatory; ingredient of herbal teas
Chrysanthemum parthenium; Asteraceae; feverfew	Eu As	F, H	parthenolide and other sesquiterpene lactones	TEM	migraine prophylactic; anti-inflammatory
Chrysanthemum vulgare; (= *Tanacetum vulgare*); Asteraceae; tansy	Eu As	FL, H	essential oil (mainly thujone); sesquiterpene lactones; triterpenoids	TEM	traditional vermifuge; various other uses; very toxic!
Cichorium intybus; Asteraceae; chicory	Eu As	R	lactucin and other sesquiterpene lactones	TEM TIM	bitter tonic; "blood purifier"; laxative, diuretic; coffee substitute and additive
Cicuta virosa; Apiaceae; cowbane, water hemlock	Eu	H	polyacetylenes	TEM	antispasmodic; rheumatism; topically as analgesic; antileucemic effects
Cimicifuga racemosa; Asteraceae; black cohosh, snakeroot	NAm	R, RH	tetracyclic triterpenoid glycosides; isoflavonoid (formononetin); organic acids, gallotannins	TNAM TEM	menstrual disorders; sedative; several other species used in Chinese and Ayurvedic medicine

Cinchona pubescens; Rubiaceae; Peruvian bark tree	SAm	C	quinoline alkaloids (quinine, quinidine and others)	TSAM TEM MM	bitter tonic; traditional antimalarial; pure alkaloids are used as anti-malarial and antiarrhythmic drugs
Cinnamomum aromaticum (=*C. cassia*); Lauraceae; cassia bark tree	EAs	C, FL	essential oil (mainly cinnamaldehyde); procyanidins in bark	TCM TIM TEM	appetite stimulant; dyspeptic disorders; an important spice
Cinnamomum camphora; Lauraceae; camphor tree	As EAs	L, F	essential oil with camphor and cineol	TCM TEM	circulatory and respiratory stimulant; counter-irritant; common ingredient of topical preparations
Cinnamomum tamala; Lauraceae; Indian cinnamon; *pathram*	As	L, R	essential oil	TIM	aromatic; mouth ulcers
Cinnamomum verum; Lauraceae; cinnamon bark tree, true cinnamon	As	C	essential oil (mainly cinnamaldehyde, with eugenol); procyanidins	TIM TEM	dyspeptic disorders; astringent; an important spice (sometimes adulterated with *C. aromaticum*)
Cinnamomum zeylanicum (see *C. verum*)					
Citrullus colocynthis, *C. lanatus*; Cucurbitaceae; colocynth, watermelon	A As	FR	cucurbitacins	TEM TCM	purgative; analgesic; anti-tumor activities; insecticide
Citrus aurantium subsp. *aurantium*; Rutaceae; bitter orange, Seville orange; *zhi shi*	As EAs	FR	essential oil (mainly limonene, linalool, terpineol); flavanone glycosides; triterpenes	TCM TEM	appetite stimulant, aromatic, stomachic (against flatulence, bloating); essential oil used in perfumes; peels for marmalade
Citrus limon; Rutaceae; lemon	As EAs	FR	essential oil (limonene, citral); flavonoids	TCM TEM	aromatic, stomachic; treatment of scurvy; oil used in flavouring, perfumes and aromatherapy
Citrus reticulata; Rutaceae; clementine, *chen pi* (ripe fruits), *qing pi* (green fruits)	EAs	FR	methylanthranylic acid methylester, limonene, terpineol	TCM	appetite stimulant, aromatic, stomachic
Claviceps purpurea; Clavicipitaceae; ergot (a fungus on rye)	Eu As		ergot alkaloids: ergometrine, ergotamine	TEM MM	migraine; uterus contraction
Clematis recta; *C. vitalba*; *C. armandii*; Ranunculaceae; clematis	Eu EAs	H	ranunculin, protoanemonin, saponins	TEM TCM	skin disorders; arthritis; rheumatism
Clerodendron trichotomum; Verbenaceae; harlequin glorybower	EAs	H	clerodendrin, acacetin	TCM TIM	hypotonic, analgesic; digestive disorders
Cnicus benedictus (see *Centaurea benedicta*)					
Cnidium (*Selinum*) *monnieri*; Apiaceae; snowparsley	EAs	S, O	pinene and other monoterpenes	TCM	skin disorders; antifungal (e.g. for vaginitis)
Cochlearia officinalis; Brassicaceae; scurvy grass	Eu	H	glucosinolates; vitamin C	TEM	against scurvy; liver disorders; diuretic, stomachic, antiseptic (mouthwash)
Cochlospermum gossypium; Bixaceae/Cochlospermaceae; silk-cotton tree	As EA	gum	mucilage	TEM	laxative; dietetic
Cocos nucifera; Arecaceae; cocos palm	As	O	triglycerides	MM	important for ointments
Codonopsis pilosula; *C.tangshen*; Campanulaceae; *dang-shen*	EAs	R	triterpene saponins; alkaloids	TCM	general tonic; expectorant
Coffea arabica; Rubiaceae; coffee tree, Arabian coffee	NA	S	purine alkaloids (mainly caffeine)	TAM TEM	stimulant, diuretic; important commercial product
Cola acuminata, *C. nitida*; Sterculiaceae; cola, Abata cola	WA	S	purine alkaloids (caffeine, theobromine)	TAM TEM	stimulant; various traditional uses; formerly in cola drinks
Colchicum autumnale; Colchicaceae; autumn crocus, meadow saffron	Eu NA	S, corm FL	phenethylisoquinoline alkaloids (mainly colchicine)	MM	colchicine is used to treat acute gout attacks (and familial Mediterranean fever); very toxic!
Coleus forskohlii; (=*Plectranthus barbatus*); Lamiaceae	As	H, R	forskolin (activator of adenylcyclase)	TIM ExM	treatment of heart failure, glaucoma, bronchial asthma; hypertension

Collinsonia canadensis; Lamiaceae; horse balm, stone root	NAm	R, F	essential oil; tannins, saponins	TNAM	diuretic, dyspepsia, wounds, kidney stones
Combretum caffrum; Combretaceae; bushwillow	SA	C	combretastatins	TAM MM	pure compounds used in cancer treatment (selective disruption of blood supply to tumour)
Commiphora abyssinica; Burseraceae; Arabian or Fadhli myrrh tree	NA	E	oleo-resin (terpenoids, polysaccharides)	TAM	antiseptic; aromatherapy
Commiphora gileadensis; Burseraceae; Mecca myrrh tree	NA	E	oleo-resin (terpenoids, polysaccharides)	TAM	antiseptic, aromatherapy; known as "balm of Gilead" or "Mecca myrrh"
Commiphora guidottii; Burseraceae; scented myrrh tree	NA	E	oleo-resin (terpenoids, polysaccharides)	TAM	antiseptic, aromatherapy; the myrrh of the Bible, now known as "scented myrrh"
Commiphora mukul; Burseraceae; gugulon, *guggul*	As	E	oleo-resin, guggulsterones, (terpenoids, poly-saccharides)	TIM TCM	used to reduce blood cholesterol; anti-inflammatory; wound-healing; numerous traditional uses
Commiphora myrrha; Burseraceae; myrrh tree	NA	E	oleo-resin (terpenoids, polysaccharides)	TAM TEM TCM	astringent, antiseptic, anti-inflammatory; aromatherapy
Commiphora wrightii; Burseraceae; *gum guggul*	As	E	oleo-resin (terpenoids, polysaccharides)	TIM	arthritis
Conium maculatum; Apiaceae; poison hemlock	Eu	H, S	coniine and other piperidine alkaloids	TEM	sedative; antispasmodic; analgesic; very toxic
Consolida regalis; Ranunculaceae; larkspur;	Eu As	FL, S	FL: anthocyanins; S: delphinine and other ester alkaloids	TEM	FL: diuretic; S: narcotic, antispasmodic, anthelmintic; against parasites
Convallaria majalis; Convallariaceae; lily-of-the-valley	Eu	H	convallatoxin and other cardiac glycosides	TEM	heart stimulant (treatment of mild cardiac insufficiency)
Convolvulus arvensis; Convolvulaceae; common bindweed	Eu	H	glycoretin (esterglycoside)	TEM	laxative
Convolvulus scammonia; Convolvulaceae; scammony	Eu As	R	glycoretin and derivatives	TEM	laxative ("Resina Scammoniae")
Conyza canadensis (=*Erigeron*); Asteraceae; Canadian fleabane	NAm	H	limonene, linalool, other monoterpenes; tannins	TNAM	astringent; diarrhoea; diuretic; colds, insect repellent,
Copaifera langsdorffii and related species; Fabaceae; copaiba balsam tree	SAm	L, O	oleo-resin with caryophyllene and other terpenoids	TSAM	antiseptic, diuretic, expectorant, for diarrhoea, skin disorders
Coptis chinensis and other species; Ranunculaceae; Chinese goldthread, *huang lian*	EAs	RH	berberine (protoberberine alkaloid) and isoquinoline alkaloids	TCM	antidysenteric, antimicrobial; used against ulcers, inflammations, conjunctivitis
Coriandrum sativum; Apiaceae; coriander	Eu As	FR	essential oil with linalool; triterpenes, coumarins	TIM TEM	stomachic, spasmolytic, carminative; an important spice
Cornus officinalis and related species; Cornaceae; dogwood	EAs	F	verbenalin and other iridoid glycosides; saponins, tannins	TCM	menstrual disorders; inhibits secretion glands
Corydalis cava; C. solida, C. yanhusuo; Fumariaceae	Eu As	FL	bulbocapnine, corydaline and other aporphine alkaloids	TCM TEM MM	analgesic; sedative, narcotic; bulbocapnine in neurology
Crataegus monogyna, C. laevigata and other species; Rosaceae; hawthorn	Eu As	F & FL	oligomeric procyanidins, flavonoids, organic acids	TEM TCM MM	cardiotonic: NYHA I, II, possibly III
Crateva (Crataeva) nurvula; Capparaceae; garlic pear	As	F, C	glucosinolates; saponins, flavonoids	TIM	infections of urinary tract; kidney stones; expectorant; skin disorders
Crithmum maritimum; Apiaceae; sea samphire	Eu As	H	volatile oil, mucilage, vitamin C	TEM	scurvy; diuretic, carminative
Crocus sativus; Iridaceae; saffron, saffron crocus	Eu As	stig-mas	crocetin (diterpene); picrocrocin (a glycoside); safranal (in essential oil)	TEM	sedative; antispasmodic; stomachic; an important spice (flavour, colour)

Plant; Family; common name	Distr.	Part	Constituents	Cat.	Uses
Croton tiglium; Euphorbiaceae; purging croton	A As	S, O	phorbol esters	TEM	strong purgative; application obsolete, co-carcinogen!
Cucurbita pepo; Cucurbitaceae; pumpkin	CAm SAm	S	sterols, sterol glycosides, tocopherols; cucurbitine	TEM	prostrate hyperplasia; diuretic; tapeworm remedy
Cuminum cyminum; Apiaceae; cumin; *jeeraka*	Eu A As	S	up to 5% essential oil with pinene, terpineol and aldehydes; flavonoids	TEM TIM TAM	dyspepsia; carminative; colds, weak analgesic
Cupressus sempervirens; Cupressaceae; cypress	Eu As	O	pinene, camphene and other monoterpenes	TEM	cough; pertussis, antispasmodic; skin disorders
Curcuma longa; Zingiberaceae; tumeric, *haridra*	As	RH	curcumin and other yellow pigments (curcuminoids); essential oil (bisabolane)	TIM TEM	cholagogue; anti-inflammatory; carminative; an important spice and vegetable dye
Curcuma zedoaria; Zingiberaceae; zedoary	As	RH, ess. oil	curcuminoids, essential oil with monoterpenoids and sesquiterpenoids	TIM	stomachic, choleretic, aromatic
Cuscuta epithymum and related species; Convolvulaceae; dodder	Eu As	H	flavonoids; acquires phytochemicals from host plants	TEM TIM	cholagogue, laxative
Cyanopsis tetragonoloba (see *Psophocarpus tetragonolobus*)					
Cyclamen purpurascens (= *C. europaeum*); Primulaceae; cyclamen	Eu	RH	triterpene saponins	TEM	gout, rheumatism, menstrual disorders, toothache
Cyclopia intermedia, C. genistoides, C. subternata, *C. sessilifolia*; Fabaceae; honeybush tea	SA	H	phenolic compounds (mangiferin, flavones, organic acids); pinitol	TAM	anti-oxidant, health drink
Cydonia oblonga; Rosaceae; quince tree	As	S	mucilage; tannins; amygdalin in seeds	TEM	diarrhoea; bronchitis; skin disorders (lips; nipples)
Cymbopogon citratus and several other species; Poaceae; lemon grass	As	H	essential oil with citral (geranial and neral)	TIM	weak sedative, stomachic; aromatherapy; oriental cooking
Cynara scolymus; Asteraceae; globe artichoke	Eu	F	cynaropicrin (sesquiterpene lactone); phenolic acids; flavonoids	TEM	choleretic, liver protectant, lipid lowering
Cynoglossum officinale Boraginaceae; hound's tongue	Eu	R	allantoin; pyrrolizidine alkaloids; (carcinogenic !)	TEM	antineuralgic; haemostyptic; skin disorders; wounds
Cyperus esculentus; Cyperaceae; tiger nut, *chufa*	As Eu	T	fixed oil ("tiger nut oil")	TIM	tonic; dyspepsia, carminative
Cyperus rotundus; Cyperaceae; coco grass, nutgrass, *mustha*	As	RH	tubers contain cyperene, cyperinol	TIM	cyperene is antifebrile, said to inhibit prostaglandin synthesis; antipyretic; galactogogue
Cypripedium calceolus var. *pubescens*; Orchidaceae; lady's slipper orchid	NAm	R	essential oil; tannins	TNAM	sedative, ("phyto-tranquillizer")
Cytisus scoparius; Fabaceae; common broom, Scotch broom	Eu	H	sparteine (quinolizidine alkaloid); flavonoids	TEM MM	heart and circulatory disorders; diuretic
Daemonorops draco; Arecaceae; dragon's blood palm	EAs	resin	benzoylesters of dracoresinotannol	TEM	plasters
Daphne mezereum; Thymelaeaceae; mezereon	Eu As	C	mezerein and other phorbol esters, mucilage, tannins	TEM	skin disorders; skin irritant; co-carcinogen!
Datura stramonium and other species; *Brugmansia* species; Solanaceae; thorn-apple, Jimson weed	NAm	F, S	hyoscyamine and scopolamine (tropane alkaloids)	TSAM TNAM TEM MM	anti-asthmatic, sedative, analgesic; an intoxicant; pure alkaloids: parasympatholytic; toxic!
Daucus carota; Apiaceae; wild carrot	Eu As	H, R, FR	F: flavonoids, furanocoumarins; FR: essential oil, flavonoids	TEM	diuretic, carminative
Delphinium staphisagria; Ranunculaceae; stavesacre	Eu As	FL, S	FL: anthocyanins; S: delphinine and other ester alkaloids	TEM	FL: diuretic; S: narcotic, antispasmodic, anthelmintic; against parasites

Derris elliptica; Fabaceae; derris root	As	R	rotenone		insecticide
Desmodium gangeticum; Fabaceae; desmodium	As A	R	volatile oil; alkaloids	TIM	bitter tonic; dyspepsia; colds; liver protection
Dianthus superbus; Caryophyllaceae; wild carnation	As Eu	H	eugenol, benzyl benzoate, methylsalicylate	TCM	diuretic; inflammation of urinary tract
Dictamnus albus; Rutaceae; burning bush, dittany	Eu As	R	dictamine and other furoquinoline alkaloids; trigonelline, anethole	TEM	diuretic; spasmolytic; anthelmintic
Digitalis lanata, D. purpurea, D. lutea; Scrophulariaceae; foxglove	Eu	F	cardiac glycosides	TEM MM	cardiac stimulant
Dionaea muscipula; Droseraceae; venus fly trap	NAm	H	proteases and other enzymes	TNAM	formerly against cancer
Dioscorea batatas; Dioscoreaceae; wild yam, *shan yao*	As	RH	steroidal glycosides	TCM	general tonic
Dioscorea dregeana and other species; wild yam, *isidakwa*	A	RH	alkaloids, steroidal saponins	TAM	traditional sedative and tranquilliser
Dioscorea villosa and many other species; Dioscoreaceae; wild yam	CAm As	RH	dioscin and other steroidal saponins; alkaloids	TSAM TAM	anti-inflammatory, antispas- modic, cholagogue; starting material for steroidal hormone synthesis (contraceptives)
Diospyros kaki; Ebenaceae; persimmon tree	Eu As	FR	tannins, iodine	TEM	thyroidal disorders
Dipsacus fullonum; Dipsacaceae; teasel	Eu As	R	inulin; scabioside	TEM	diuretic, astringent; antidiarrhoeal
Dipteryx odorata; Fabaceae; Tonka bean	SAm	S	coumarins; sitosterol	TSAM	aromatic
Dorema ammoniacum; Apiaceae; dorema	As	E	gum (*ammoniacum*) with resin, polysaccharides, volatile oil, coumarins	TIM TEM	expectorant, antispasmodic, counter-irritant; used in perfumery
Dorstenia contrajerva; Moraceae; contrayerva	CAm SAm	RH	volatiles, tannins	TSAM	febrifuge
Drimia maritima (see *Urginea maritima*)					
Drimys winteri; Winteraceae; Winter's bark	SAm	C	eugenol, pinene	TEM	stomachic
Drosera rotundifolia and other species; Droseraceae; sundew	Eu	H	naphthoquinones (mainly ramentaceone, plumbagin)	TEM	antispasmodic, antitussive; other sources are *D. ramentacea* (Africa, Madagascar) and *D. peltata* (China)
Dryopteris filix-mas; Polypodiaceae; male fern	Eu As	RH	phloroglucinol, triterpenes	TEM	against tape worms; skin disorders ; abortifacient
Duboisia myoporoides; Solanaceae; corkwood	Aus	F	scopolamine and other tropane alkaloids	MM	sedative, spasmolytic, hypnotic; source for scopolamine
Ecballium elaterium; Cucurbi- taceae; squirting cucumber	Eu	FR	cucurbitacins	TEM	purgative
Echinacea pallida; E. angusti- folia; Asteraceae; pale purple coneflower; narrow-leaved coneflower	NAm	R	polysaccharides, alkami- des, polyacetylenes, caffeic acid derivates	TNAM TEM	immune stimulant
Echinacea purpurea; Asteraceae; purple coneflower	NAm	H, R, juice	polysaccharides, caffeic acid derivatives (cichoric acid); polyacetylenes	TNAM TEM	immune stimulant
Echium vulgare; Boraginaceae; viper's bugloss	Eu As	R	allantoin; cynoglossine and other pyrrolizidine alkaloids	TEM	wound healing; epilepsy; carcinogenic!
Eclipta alba (=*E. prostrata*); Asteraceae; *bhringiraj*	A As Aus	H	ecliptine and other steroidal alkaloids	TIM TCM	haemostyptic; skin disorders, inflammations; tonic; asthma, antifungal

Elettaria cardamomum; Zingiberaceae; cardamom; *ela*	As	S, RH	essential oil (mainly 1,8-cineol)	TIM TEM	cholagogue, antimicrobial; important spice and flavourant
Eleutherococcus senticosus; Araliaceae; Siberian ginseng, eleuthero	As	R, RH	coumarins, lignans, phenylpropanoids, triterpene saponins	TCM TEM	adaptogenic tonic
Elymus repens (=*Agropyron repens*); Poaceae; couchgrass	Eu As NAm	Rh	polysaccharides (triticin), mucilage; saponins, silica	TEM	diuretic, laxative, urinary tract disorders
Embelia ribes; Myrsinaceae; false pepper	As	F	embelin and other naphthoquinones	TIM	diuretic; dyspepsia; contraceptive, anthelmintic
Emblica officinalis (see *Phyllanthus emblica*)					
Entada phaseoloides; Fabaceae; Queensland bean	Aus	S	saponins	TAUM	indigestion; analgesic, treatment of female sterility; hair wash
Ephedra distachya and other species; Ephedraceae; ephedra	Eu	H, R	phenylethylamine alkaloids, mainly ephedrine	TEM	bronchodilatory; analeptic, central stimulant
Ephedra sinica and other species; Ephedraceae; *mu huang*	As EAs	H, R	phenylethylamine alkaloids, mainly ephedrine	TCM	bronchodilatory; analeptic, central stimulant
Epilobium parviflorum, E. hirsutum, E. angustifolium; Onagraceae; willow-herb	Eu As NAm	H	flavonoids, phytosterols, gallic acid derivatives	TEM TNAM TCM	benign prostate hyperplasia; wound healing; respiratory problems; menstrual disorders
Equisetum arvense; Equisetaceae; horsetail	Eu As NAm	H	silicic acid, potassium and aluminum salts; flavonoids	TEM	diuretic, haemostyptic
Eriodictyon californicum; Hydrophyllaceae; *yerba santa*	NAm	F	eriodictyol, volatile oil	TNAM	diuretic, expectorant; inflammation of respiratory tract; taste improvement (sweet)
Eryngium campestre, E. planum; E. maritimum; Apiaceae; eryngo	Eu As	H, R	tannins, saponins,	TEM	diuretic, expectorant; pertussis; inflammation of urinary tract
Erysimum cheiri (=*Cheiranthus cheiri*); Brassicaceae; wallflower	Eu	FL	cheiranthin and other cardenolides; glucosinolates	TEM	heart and liver disorder; diuretic, laxative
Erysimum crepidifolium; Brassicaceae; hedge mustard	Eu	H	cardenolides; glucosinolates	TEM	source of helveticoside
Erythrina variegata; Fabaceae; Indian coral tree	As	F, C	*Erythrina* alkaloids	TIM	anti-inflammatory; menstrual disorders; dyspepsia; skin disorders
Erythrophleum suaveolens; Fabaceae; ordeal tree	A	C	diterpenes alkaloids	TAM TEM	heart disorders; arrow poison
Erythroxylum coca; Erythroxylaceae; coca plant	SAm	F	cocaine and other tropane alkaloids	TSAM MM	anaesthetic, intoxicant
Eschscholzia californica; Papaveraceae; Californian poppy	NAm	H	isoquinoline alkaloids	TNAM	sedative
Eucalyptus globulus; Myrtaceae; eucalyptus, bluegum	Aus	F	essential oil (mainly 1,8-cineol); sesquiterpenes	TAUM TEM	antiseptic, expectorant
Eucommia ulmoides; Eucommiaceae; *duzhong*	EAs	C	gutta-percha, alkaloids, iridoids	TCM	reduces blood pressure; tonic
Euodia (Evodia) rutaecarpa; Rutaceae	EAs	F	evodiamine, rutecarpine and other indole alkaloids	TCM	analgesic; hypotonic; dyspepsia
Euonymus europaeus; E. atro-purpureus; Celastraceae; spindle-tree; Indian arrow wood	Eu NAm	C, R	cardenolides, alkaloids, tannins	TEM TNAM	liver and gallbladder disorders; skin conditions; toxic!
Eupatorium perfoliatum; Asteraceae; boneset	NAm	H	sesquiterpene lactones; diterpenes, triterpenes	TNAM	immune stimulant; treatment of colds

Eupatorium purpureum, *E. cannabinum*; Asteraceae; gravel root	NAm	H	sesquiterpene lactones; diterpenes, triterpenes; pyrrolizidine alkaloids!	TNAM TEM	diuretic, used against cystitis, prostatitis, urethritis, kidney stones and urinary stones (gravel)
Euphorbia cyparissias; Euphorbiaceae; cypress spurge	Eu	H	phorbol esters (co-carcinogens!)	TEM	diuretic, purgative; skin irritant
Euphorbia pekinensis; Euphorbiaceae	EAs	R	phorbol esters	TCM	purgative; kidney disorders
Euphorbia resinifera; Euphorbiaceae	A	resin	triterpenes (euphorbols), polyterpenes	TEM	skin irritant
Euphrasia officinalis and related species; Scrophulariaceae; eyebright	Eu	H	iridoid glycosides (aucubin, catalpol); lignans, tannins	TEM	traditional eye lotion; anti-inflammatory
Fabiana imbricata; Solanaceae; *pichi*, Chilean heath	SAm	H	essential oil; fabianine and other alkaloids	TSAM	cystitis; gonorrhoea
Fagopyrum esculentum; Polygonaceae; buckwheat	As	H	flavonoids (so-called bioflavonoids), mainly rutin; fagopyrine	TEM	venotonic; a natural source of rutin, used to treat capillary and venous disorders
Ferula assa-foetida; Apiaceae; asafoetida, devil's dung	As	E	oleo-resin, with sesquiter-penes, disulphides, polysulphanes	TIM TEM	carminative, antispasmodic, expectorant; externally as counter-irritant
Ficus benghalensis, *F. religiosa*; Moraceae; banyan, peepul, bo-tree	As	FR,F C, R	ficin (a proteinase), flavonoids, tannins	TIM	astringent; laxative; warts; skin inflammations
Ficus carica; Moraceae; fig tree	Eu	FR	proteases and other enzymes; sugars	TEM	laxative
Filipendula ulmaria; Rosaceae; meadowsweet, queen-of-the-meadow	Eu As	FL, H	flavonoids, tannins, rich in methylsalicylate	TEM	anti-inflammatory, analgesic, febrifuge
Foeniculum vulgare; Apiaceae; fennel	Eu	FR	essential oil (anethole); flavonoids, coumarins	TEM	carminative, expectorant, aromatic; ingredient of gripe water
Forsythia x intermedia (=*F. suspensa*); Oleaceae;	EAs	F	forsythin, triterpenoids	TCM	antimicrobial; reduces nausea and vomiting
Fragaria vesca; Rosaceae; wild strawberry	Eu As	F	tannins	TEM	astringent, anti-diarrhoeal
Frangula alnus (see *Rhamnus frangula*)					
Frasera carolinensis; Gentianaceae	NAm	R	gentiopicrine; tannins	TNAM	astringent; amarum
Fraxinus excelsior; Oleaceae; common ash	Eu As	C, F	tannins, flavonoids, glucosides, secoiridoids	TEM	anti-inflammatory
Fraxinus ornus; Oleaceae; manna ash	As	E	sugary exudates (manna) contains mainly mannitol	TEM	osmotic laxative
Fritillaria imperialis, *F. thunbergii*; Liliaceae; crown imperial	As	B	steroidal alkaloids	TCM	analgesic; fever; expectorant; treatment of tumours
Fucus vesiculosus; Fucaceae; bladderwrack	At-lantic	algae	iodine; mucilage, tannins	TEM	iodine deficiency; source for alginate
Galanthus nivalis, *G. woronowii*; Amaryllidaceae; snowdrop	As	B	galanthamine	MM	cholinesterase inhibitor; *Myasthenia gravis*, poliomyelitis; Alzheimer's disease
Galega officinalis; Fabaceae; goat's rue	Eu	H	galegine (a guanidine derivative); quinoline alkaloids; flavonoids	TEM	diuretic; traditional antidiabetic
Galeopsis segetum; Scrophulariaceae; hemp-nettle	Eu	H	tannins, silicic acid, flavonoids, iridoids	TEM	expectorant, astringent
Galipea officinalis; Rutaceae; angostura tree	CAm SAm	C	cusparine and other quinoline alkaloids; essential oil with sesquiterpenes	TSAM	stomachic, bitter tonic; antispasmodic; febrifuge

410

Galium aparine; Rubiaceae; clivers	Eu As	H	tannins, phenolic acids, iridoid glycosides	TEM	diuretic, astringent; externally for slow healing wounds
Galium odoratum; Rubiaceae; sweet woodruff	Eu As	H	tannins, phenolic acids, iridoid glycosides, coumarins	TEM	respiratory tract ailments; sedative; gastrointestinal disorders; wounds
Galium verum; Rubiaceae; lady's bedstraw	Eu As	H	tannins, phenolic acids, iridoid glycosides	TEM	diuretic; externally for slow healing wounds and psoriasis
Galphimia glauca (= *Thryallis*); Malpighiaceae; rain of gold	CAm	F	triterpenes (galphimin B)	TCAM	treatment of wounds, urinary disorders; sedative
Garcinia hanburyi; Clusiaceae; gamboge	As	resin	resin with gambogic acid	TEM	purgative
Gardenia augusta (=*G. jasminoides*); Rubiaceae; gardenia, *zhi zi*	EAs	F	gardenin and other flavonoids, crocin (red colour), volatile oil	TCM	haemostyptic; anti-inflammatory; colds, flu
Gastrodia elata; Orchidaceae *tian ma*	As	RH	vanillyl alcohol, vanillin, mucilage	TCM	against headache, hypertension, arthritis
Gaultheria procumbens; Ericaceae; wintergreen, checkerberry	NAm	F, ess. oil	essential oil (almost pure methylsalicylate); leaves with arbutin, tannins	TNAM TEM	anti-inflammatory; analgesic; counter-irritant; ingredient of cosmetics, oral hygiene products
Gelidium species; Rhodophyceae	As	algae	acidic polygalactans; agarose, agaropectin (agar)	TEM	laxative, used in galenics and microbiology (agar plates)
Gelsemium sempervirens; Gelsemiaceae; false jasmine, yellow jasmine	NAm	R, RH	monoterpene indole alkaloids (e.g. gelsemine); iridoids, coumarins	TNAM	antispasmodic, analgesic, sedative; toxic!
Genista tinctoria; Fabaceae; dyer's greenweed	Eu	H	cytisine and other quinolizidine alkaloids; luteolin (flavonoid)	TEM	diuretic, laxative; yellow colour
Gentiana lutea; Gentianaceae; yellow gentian	Eu	R, RH	bitter secoiridoids (mainly gentiopicroside)	TEM	digestive bitter; cholagogue; stomachic
Geranium maculatum; Geraniaceae; American cranesbill	NAm	R,H	up to 30% tannins	TNAM	inflammations of the respiratory tract; dyspepsia: wounds; menstrual disorders
Geranium robertianum; Geraniaceae; herb Robert	Eu As	H	essential oil, phenolic acids, flavonoids, tannins (mainly geraniin)	TEM	anti-inflammatory; anti-diarrhoeal; externally for wound treatment, eczema
Geum urbanum; Rosaceae; wood avens	Eu As NAm	R, RH	tannins, volatile oil with eugenol	TEM	astringent, tonic, anti-diarrhoeal
Ginkgo biloba; Ginkgoaceae; Ginkgo, maidenhair tree	EAs	F, S	flavonoids, oligomeric proanthocyanidins, diterpene lactones	TCM TEM MM	leaf extracts: central and peripheral circulatory disturbances; seeds: expectorant
Gladiolus communis; Iridaceae; whistling jacks	Eu	B	essential oil; vitamin C	TEM	scurvy
Glechoma hederacea; Lamiaceae; ground ivy, alehoof	Eu As	H	essential oil with sesquiterpenes; tannins, saponins	TEM	antidiarrhoeal; diuretic; colds, expectorant; wounds,
Globularia alypum; Globulariaceae	Eu	F	globularin, picrogloburalin	TEM	purgative; diuretic
Gloriosa superba; Colchicaceae; flame lily, *langali*	A As	T	colchicine	MM	source for colchicine
Glycine max; Fabaceae; soybean	As EAs	S	soybean phospholipids; isoflavonoids; saponins	TCM TEM	blood lipid reduction; phytoestrogenic
Glycyrrhiza glabra; Fabaceae; liquorice, licorice, *mulethi*; *yashti*	Eu As	R, RH	flavonoids, saponins, glycyrrhizinic acid	TEM TIM	expectorant, anti-inflammatory, antispasmodic
Glycyrrhiza uralensis; Fabaceae; Chinese liquorice, *gan cao*	As EAs	R, RH	flavonoids, saponins, glycyrrhizinic acid	TCM	tonic, expectorant, anti-inflammatory
Gnaphalium uliginosum; Asteraceae; cudweed	Eu As	H	volatile oil; tannins	TEM	astringent, antiseptic, against catarrh

411

Gossypium hirsutum; *G. herbaceum*; Malvaceae; cotton	As	C, S	gossypol and other polyphenols	TIM TSAM	haemostyptic; causes infertility in men
Gratiola officinalis; Scrophulariaceae; hedge hyssop	Eu As	H	gratioside and other cucurbitacin-like triterpenes	TEM	purgative; diuretic
Grindelia squarrosa, **G. robusta**; Asteraceae; gumweed	NAm CAm	H	grindelic acid and other diterpenes	TNAM	antitussive, spasmolytic
Guaiacum officinale; Sapindaceae; guaiac, lignum vitae tree	CAm SAm	L, LE	lignans, volatile oil with guajol, saponins	TSAM TEM	anti-inflammatory, antimicrobial, antioxidant
Guarea rusbyi; *G. guara*; Meliaceae; cocillana tree	SAm	C	sitosterol; tannins, alkaloids	TSAM	emetic; expectorant; haemostyptic
Gymnema sylvestre; Asclepiadaceae / Apocynaceae; *gurmar*	Aus A	F	gymnemic acid (a triterpene saponin)	TIM	inhibits taste perception, hypoglycemic
Gymnocladus dioicus; Fabaceae; chicot, Kentucky coffee	NAm	S	polysaccharides, saponins	TNAM	seeds are used as a coffee substitute
Gypsophila paniculata; Caryophyllaceae; white soapwort, baby's breath	Eu As	R, RH	triterpene saponins	TEM	expectorant; externally against skin disorders
Haematoxylum campechianum; Fabaceae; logwood, *campeche*	CAm	L	haematoxylin, tannins	TSAM	astringent; colour
Hagenia abyssinica; Rosaceae; hagenia	A	FL	kosin and other acylphloroglucond derivatives, tannins	TAM	female flowers (*koso*) used against tapeworms
Hamamelis virginiana; Hamamelidaceae; witch hazel	NAm	F, C	hamamelitannins and catechols; proanthocyanidins; essential oil	TNAM TEM	astringent, antihaemorrhagic; anti-inflammatory
Haplopappus baylahuen; Asteraceae	SAm	H	essential oil; tannins	TSAM TEM	astringent; liver and gall disorders
Harpagophytum procumbens; Pedaliaceae; devil's claw, harpago	SA	R	iridoid glycosides	TAM TEM	bitter tonic; anti-inflammatory; antirheumatic; weakly analgesic
Harungana madagascariensis; Clusiaceae; haronga	A	F, C	anthracene derivatives; flavonoids, tannins	TAM TEM	secretolytic; choleretic; cholekinetic; externally for skin disorders
Hedeoma pulegioides; Lamiaceae; American pennyroyal	NAm	H	menthone, pulegone and other monoterpenes	TNAM	diaphoretic, aromatic, stomachic, insecticide
Hedera helix; Araliaceae; ivy	Eu As	L, F	saponins, polyacetylenes	TEM	expectorant; spasmolytic; secretolytic
Helianthus tuberosus; Asteraceae; Jerusalem artichoke	SAm	T	inulin, oligosaccharides	TEM	diet for patients with diabetes; source for inulin
Helichrysum arenarium; Asteraceae; sandy everlasting	Eu	FL	flavonoids: glycosides of naringenin	TEM	bitter; choleretic; diuretic
Helleborus viridis; *H. niger*; Ranunculaceae; green hellebore; black hellebore	Eu	RH	helleborin and other bufadienolides	TEM	cardiac disorders; emetic, laxative, anthelmintic
Hepatica nobilis; Ranunculaceae; liverwort	Eu NAm	H	ranunculin, protoanemonin, tannins	TEM	skin irritant; tonic; liver disorders
Heracleum sphondylium; Apiaceae; hogweed	Eu As	H	furanocoumarins	TEM	dyspepsia; skin ulcers
Herniaria glabra; *H. hirsuta*; Caryophyllaceae; rupturewort; hairy rupturewort	Eu As	H	mainly saponins, flavonoids; also tannins, coumarins	TEM	traditional diuretic, disinfectant of urinary tract
Hibiscus sabdariffa; Malvaceae; hibiscus	A	FL calyx	polysaccharides, pectins, organic acids, sugars, anthocyanins	TAM TEM	health tea; colourful tea additive; externally against skin conditions
Hieracium pilosella; Asteraceae; hawkweed	Eu As	H	umbelliferon and other coumarins; flavonoids, caffeic acid	TEM	disorders of respiratory tract; haemostyptic; wound healing

412

Hippophae rhamnoides; Eleagnaceae; sea buckthorn, sallow thorn	Eu	FR	vitamin C; flavonoids and other phenolics	TEM	food and drink additive
Hoodia pilifera; H. gordonii; Asclepiadaceae/Apocynaceae hoodia, ghaap	A	stem	pregnane glycosides	TAM ExM	appetite and thirst suppressant
Hordeum vulgare; Poaceae; barley	Eu	S	mucilage	TEM TCM	inflammation of the digestive tract
Humulus lupulus; Cannabaceae; hop plant	Eu As NAm	FL hops	lupulone, humulone (phloroglucinol derivatives)	TEM	sedative, bitter tonic; hops is used in beer brewing
Huperzia selago; Lycopodiaceae; fir club-moss	Eu	H	lycopodine and other alkaloids	TEM	purgative; emetic; anthelmintic; skin parasites
Hydnocarpus kurzii; Flacourtiaceae; chaulmoogra oil tree	As	O	chaulmoogric acid and other cyclopentene fatty acids	TEM	leprosy and other skin diseases
Hydrangea arborescens; Hydrangaceae; tree hydrangea	NAm	R	flavonoids; hydrangein (a cyanogen), saponins	TNAM	diuretic (kidney and bladder stones and other disorders of the urinary tract)
Hydrastis canadensis; Ranunculaceae; goldenseal	NAm	RH, R	isoquinoline alkaloids	TNAM TEM	haemostatic; stomachic; laxative
Hygrophila spinosa; Acanthaceae	As	H, R	mucilage; alkaloids, volatile oil	TIM	diuretic; liver disorders; inflammation of urinary tract
Hyoscyamus niger; H. albus; Solanaceae; henbane; white henbane	Eu As	F, S, R	tropane alkaloids (hyoscyamine, scopolamine)	TEM MM	antispasmodic, narcotic
Hypericum perforatum; Hypericaceae St. John's wort	Eu As	H	hyperforin (phloroglucinol derivative); hypericin (dianthrone)	TEM	anti-depressant; wound-healing
Hypoxis hemerocallidea (=H. rooperi); Hypoxidaceae; hypoxis, "African potato"	A	RH T	phytosterols; rooperol	TAM TEM	traditional tonic; prostate hyperplasia
Hyssopus officinalis; Lamiaceae; hyssop	Eu	H	flavonoids; phenolic acids; diterpene lactones; essential oil	TEM	expectorant; antiseptic; stimulant
Iberis amara; Brassicaceae; white candytuft, bitter candytuft, clown's mustard plant	Eu	H	ibamarin (bitter cucurbitacins); glucoiberin and other glucosinolates	TEM	amarum; choleretic
Ilex aquifolium; Aquifoliaceae; holly	Eu	F	flavonoids, tannins, ilicin	TEM	tonic in case of fever and spasms
Ilex paraguariensis; Aquifoliaceae; maté	SAm	F	caffeine	TSAM TEM	stimulant, diuretic; popular herbal tea in South America
Illicium verum; Illiciaceae; star anise	As EAs	FR	essential oil (mainly anethole)	TCM TEM	expectorant; antispasmodic; stomachic
Indigofera tinctoria; Fabaceae; indigo plant	A	F	indican	TEM	neuralgia; production of indigo (blue dye)
Inula helenium; Asteraceae elecampane	Eu As	RH, R	sesquiterpene lactones	TEM	expectorant
Ipomoea purga; I. orizabensis; Convolvulaceae; jalap	CAm	T, R	resin with convolvuline and other glycoretins	TSAM	purgative
Ipomoea violacaea; Convolvulaceae; morning glory	CAm	S	ergine and other lysergic acid derivatives	TSAM	central stimulant (hallucinogen)
Iris germanica; Iridaceae orris, garden iris	Eu	RH	triterpenes; essential oil with irones (irone and isomers)	TEM	traditional expectorant and demulcent; orris root is used in potpourris
Iris versicolor; Iridaceae; iris	NAm	RH	essential oil, tannins, salicylic acid	TNAM	laxtive; for liver and kidney conditions, migraine
Jacaranda procera; Bignoniaceae; caroba	SAm	F	carobine, resin	TSAM	diuretic

Jasminum grandiflorum; J. sambac; Oleaceae; Catalonian/Spanish jasmine; Arabian jasmine, *sambac*	As	FL,O	benzyl acetate; linalool and other monoterpenes	TEM TIM	sedative, antidepressant; perfume
Jateorhiza palmata; Menispermaceae; *calumba, colomba, columba*	A	R	jatrorrhizine and other protoberberine alkaloids	TEM	amarum, stomachic, astringent; anthelmintic
Jatropha curcas; Euphorbiaceae; physic nut, purging nut	CAm	S	phorbol esters, curcin (a lectin)	TSAM TEM	purgative, toxic!
Juglans nigra; Juglandaceae; American walnut	NAm	F, FR husk	F: tannins, juglone; FR: juglone	TNAM	astringent, anti-diarrhoeal; wound-healing
Juglans regia; Juglandaceae; English walnut, Black Sea walnut	Eu	F, FR husk	F: tannins, juglone; FR: juglone	TEM	astringent, anti-diarrhoeal; wound-healing
Juniperus communis; Cyperaceae; common juniper	Eu As NAm	FR	essential oil; phenolics	TEM	diuretic; antiseptic; antirheumatic
Juniperus sabina; Cupressaceae; savin	Eu As	H	savinin, podophyllotoxin, other lignans, sabinene	TEM	abortifacient; against warts (condylomata)
Justicia adhatoda (Adhatoda vasica); Acanthaceae; Malabar nut, *vasaka, vasa*	As	FL	vasicine and other quinazoline alkaloids	TEM TIM	bronchodilatory, expectorant and antitussive; anthelmintic, antimicrobial
Kigelia africana; Bignoniaceae; sausage tree	A	FR	lapachol (a naphtho-quinone); kigelin (a dihydroisocoumarin); iridoids, phytosterols	TAM	wound-healing; skin care
Krameria lappacea (= *K. triandra*); Krameriaceae; rhatany	SAm	R	tannins, proanthocyani-dins; »ratanhia phenols«	TSAM TEM	astringent; anti-diarrhoeal
Laburnum anagyroides; Faba-ceae; golden chain	Eu	S,F	cytisine and other quinolizidine alkaloids	TEM	emetic
Lachnanthes tinctoria; Haemodoraceae; spirit-weed	NAm	T, H	red colour	TNAM	colourant, for neuralgia
Lactuca virosa; Asteraceae; opium lettuce	Eu	H	lactucerin, lactucopicrin and other sesquiterpene lactones	TEM	narcotic, hypnotic, sedative, analgesic
Lamium album and other species; Lamiaceae; white dead nettle	Eu As	H	iridoid glycosides, saponins, mucilage	TEM	traditional expectorant; menstrual disorders
Larix decidua; Pinaceae; larch	Eu	C, resin	pinene, limonane and other monoterpenes; lignans	TEM	astringent, diuretic, antiseptic; urinary tract disorders; skin conditions
Larrea tridentata (=*L. divaricata* subsp. *tridentata*); Zygophyllaceae; creosote bush	NAm	H	resin; nordihydroguaiaretic acid	TNAM	dyspepsia; skin disorders; rheumatism; urinary infections; liver toxic!
Laurus nobilis; Lauraceae; bay laurel, true laurel	Eu	F	essential oil; isoquinoline alkaloids	TEM	digestive tonic; numerous traditional uses; a popular spice
Lavandula angustifolia and other species; Lamiaceae; lavender	Eu	H, FL	essential oil (mainly linaloyl acetate, linalool);	TEM	sedative, spasmolytic, anti-microbial; oil used in aromatherapy, cosmetics
Lawsonia inermis; Lythraceae; henna	As	F	lawsone (a naphthoqui-none)	TIM	astringent, antimicrobial; natural dye (henna)
Ledebouriella divaricata; Apiaceae, *fang feng*	As	R	no information	TCM	diaphoretic, antispasmodic, analgesic, antirheumatic, antimicrobial
Ledum palustre (see *Rhododendron tomentosum*)					
Leonurus cardiaca; Lamiaceae; motherwort	Eu	H	iridoid glycosides, alkaloids, diterpenes	TEM	cardiotonic

Lepidium sativum, L. virginicum; Brassicaceae; pepperwort, peppercress	Eu As NAm	H,R	glucotropaeolin and other glucosinolates; vitamin C	TEM TNAM	diuretic; scurvy; anthelmintic;
Leptadenia reticulata; Asclepiadaceae; *jivanti*	A As	R	leptadenol and other triterpenoids	TIM	nourishing and rejuvenating tonic; aphrodisiac; against tuberculosis; chicken pox; respiratory disorders
Lespedeza capitata; Fabaceae; lespedeza, bush clover	NAm	H	orientin and other C-glucosides	TNAM	diuretic
Levisticum officinale; Apiaceae; lovage	Eu	RH, R	essential oil with alkylphthalides	TEM	carminative; diuretic
Ligusticum sinense, L. chuan-xiang, L. jeholense and other species; Apiaceae; *gao ben*	As	R	phenylpropanoids, tetra-methylpyrazines, perlo-lyrine and other alkaloids	TCM	headache, after stroke
Lilium candidum; L. lancifolium; Liliaceae; Madonna lily, Bourbon lily; tiger lily	As	FL; B	steroidal alkaloids, saponins	TEM	expectorant; epilepsy
Linaria vulgaris; Scrophulariaceae; common toadflax	Eu	H	linarin and other flavonoids; peganine and other alkaloids; mucilage	TEM	diuretic, laxative; liver disorders; wounds and haemorrhoids
Linum catharticum; Linaceae; purging flax, fairy flax	Eu	H	lignans, podophyllotoxin, tannins	TEM	purgative
Linum usitatissimum; Linaceae; common flax, linseed	Eu	S	mucilage, linamarin (cyanogenic glucoside)	TEM	bulk laxative
Lippia javanica and other species; Verbenaceae; fever tea	A	H	essential oil	TAM	Herbal teas used against fever; insect repellent properties
Liquidambar orientalis; Hamamelidaceae; storax	As	resin	cinnamic acid and its esters	TEM	skin disorders; source of Levant storax ("balm of Gilead")
Liriodendron tulipifera; Magnoliaceae; tulip tree, tulip poplar	NAm	L, C	glaucine and other aporphine alkaloids, lignans, monoterpenes, sesquiterpene lactones	TNAM	against fever (malaria), tonic
Litchi chinensis; Sapindaceae; lichi tree	EAs	S	non-protein amino acids	TCM	against tumours; antidiabetic
Lithospermum officinale; Boraginaceae; gromwell	Eu As	S	lithospermic acid, pyrrolizidine alkaloids (carcinogenic!)	TEM	antigonadotropic; antithyreotropic
Lobaria pulmonaria; Stictaceae (lichen)	Eu	li-chen	stictic acid; mucilage; tannins	TEM	expectorant; catarrhs; astringent; skin disorders
Lobelia chinensis; Campanulaceae; Chinese lobelia	EAs	H	piperidine alkaloids, (lobeline)	TCM	diuretic
Lobelia inflata; Campanulaceae; Indian tobacco	NAm	H	piperidine alkaloids lobeline	TNAM TEM	respiratory stimulant; cough treatment
Lobelia siphilitica; Campanulaceae; blue cardinal flower	NAm	H	piperidine alkaloids, lobeline	TNAM TEM	reputedly a cure for syphilis
Lobelia tupa; Campanulaceae; Chilean cardinal flower	SAm	H	piperidine alkaloids, lobeline	TSAM	toothache remedy; narcotic
Lolium temulentum; Poaceae; darnel	Eu	S	loline and other pyrrolizidine alkaloids	TEM	narcotic
Lonicera caprifolium; Caprifoliaceae; honeysuckle	Eu	FL	salicylic acid and other phenolics; tannins; volatiles	TEM	diuretic, diaphoretic; inflammation of bronchial tract; antimicrobial
Lonicera japonica; Caprifo-liaceae; *jin yin hua*	As	FL	secologanin, tannins	TCM	prostatitis, hypertension; against cancer

Lophophora williamsii; Cactaceae; peyote cactus	CAm	H	mescaline and other alkaloids	TSAM	central stimulant (hallucinogen)
Lophophytum leandri; Balanophoraceae	Am	T	naringin and other flavonoids; tannins	TNAM	dyspepsia; liver disorders
Luffa operculata; L. aegyptiaca; Cucurbitaceae; loofah	SAm A,As	FR	cucurbitacins, saponins	TEM TCM	diuretic, laxative; expectorant
Lupinus albus; L. angustifolius, L. mutabilis; Fabaceae; lupin	Eu SAm	S	lupanine and other quinolizidine alkaloids	TEM TSAM	antidiabetic; skin disorders; diuretic
Lycium chinense; L. barbarum Solanaceae; Chinese wolfberry; Duke of Argyll's tea-tree; *gou qi zi*	EAs	FR	amino acids, polysaccharides, carotenoids,	TCM	traditional tonic, functional food (the berries of both species are known as *gou qi zi* in China)
Lycopersicon esculentum; Solanaceae; tomato	SAm	FR	lycopin and other carotenoids	TSAM MM	antioxidant (ripe fruit)
Lycopodium clavatum; Lycopodiaceae; club moss	Eu As	H, spo-res	lycopodine and other alkaloids; triterpenes	TEM	diuretic (inflammations of urinary tract), sedative, antispasmodic
Lycopus europaeus; *L. virginicus*; Lamiaceae; bugleweed, gypsywort; American bugleweed	Eu NAm	H	phenolic acids; flavonoids; terpenes; essential oil	TEM TNAM	antithyreotropic; mastodynia
Lysimachia nummularia; L. vulgaris; Primulaceae; moneywort; yellow loosestrife	Eu	H	tannins, salicylic acid derivatives, saponins	TEM	astringent, cough; antidiarrhoeal; haemostyptic; wounds
Lythrum salicaria; Lythraceae; purple loosestrife	Eu NAm	H	tannins, mucilage; flavonoids	TEM	astringent; antidiarrhoeal; wounds and other skin conditions; antiseptic
Macleaya cordata; Papaveraceae; plume poppy	EAs	H	sanguinarine (isoquinoline alkaloids)	TCM	a source of sanguinarine (see *Sanguinaria*)
Magnolia grandiflora; M. officinalis; Magnoliaceae; loblolly magnolia; Chinese magnolia	NAm EAs	FL, C	FL: cineol, sesquiterpenes, rutin; C: magnoflorine and other aporphine alkaloids	TNAM TCM	aromatic, rheumatism; C: antimicrobial and active against malaria and amoeba parasites
Mahonia aquifolium; Berberidaceae; Oregon grape	NAm	C	berberine and other isoquinoline alkaloids	TNAM TEM	infections; psoriasis
Mallotus philippinensis; Euphorbiaceae; *kamala*	As Aus	FR	rottlerin and other chromenes, tannins	TIM	purgative, anthelmintic; skin disorders
Malpighia glabra (= *M. punicifolia*); Malpighiaceae; Barbados cherry, *acerola*	CAm	FR	up to 25% vitamin C	TSAM	fruit with highest vitamin C
Malus domestica; Rosaceae; apple	Eu	FR	skins with pectin, sugars, tannins	TEM	antidiarrhoeal; dyspepsia
Malva sylvestris; *M. neglecta*; Malvaceae; mallow	Eu As	F, FL	mucilage; anthocyanins; tannins, proanthocyanins	TEM	demulcent; cough medicine; flowers used a colourant
Mandragora officinarum; *M. autumnalis*; Solanaceae; mandrake	Eu	R	hyoscyamine and other tropane alkaloids	TEM	narcotic, analgesic, hypnotic, spasmodic, aphrodisiac
Manihot esculenta; Euphorbiaceae; cassava	CAm SAm	R	starch and cyanogenic glycosides	TSAM	HCN released from roots used to treat scabies; toxic!
Manilkara zapota; Sapotaceae; sapodilla, chicle	CAm	C	latex with resin, polyterpenes and rubber, gutta-percha	TSAM	source for chewing gum and for surgery and instruments
Maranta arundinacea; Marantaceae; arrowroot	SAm	RH	starch	TSAM	skin disorders; dyspepsia
Marrubium vulgare; Lamiaceae; white horehound	Eu As	H	diterpene lactones (marrubiin); flavonoids	TEM	choleretic; expectorant
Marsdenia cundurango; Asclepiadaceae/Apocyna-ceae; condurango	SAm	C	steroidal saponins; pregnane glycosides	TSAM TEM	digestive, bitter tonic

416

Matricaria recutita; Asteraceae; chamomile, German chamomile	Eu As	FL	essential oil, with chamazulene, bisabolol; polyacetylenes	TEM	anti-inflammatory; antispasmodic; carminative; antiseptic
Medicago sativa; Fabaceae; alfalfa, lucerne	As	H, S	canavanine (seeds), amino acids, coumarins, isoflavonoids, saponins, steroids	TEM	general tonic; possibly cholesterol-lowering; sprouts used as health food (avoid excessive amounts!)
Melaleuca alternifolia; Myrtaceae; tea tree	Aus	Ess. oil	terpenoids, mainly 1-terpenen-4-ol, terpinene	TAUM TEM	antimicrobial; expectorant; topically used in ointments and creams
Melilotus officinalis; *M. alba*; Fabaceae; sweet clover	Eu As NA	H	coumarins (mainly coumarin); phenolic acids; saponins	TEM	anti-oedemic; venotonic
Melissa officinalis; Lamiaceae; lemon balm	Eu As	F	essential oil with citranellal, geranial, neral; also rosmarinic acid	TEM	sedative, carminative, spasmolytic, antiviral; included in creams and lotions
Mentha arvensis; Lamiaceae; field mint	Eu As	ess. oil	essential oil is used for the production of pure menthol	TEM TIM TCM	antibacterial; cooling; carminative; cholagogue; dementholated oil used in toothpaste, chewing gum
Mentha x piperita; Lamiaceae; peppermint	Eu	F	essential oil with menthol, menthone	TEM TNAM	choleretic; carminative; cooling, antibacterial; cholagogue; spasmolytic; oil used industrially
Mentha spicata and other species; Lamiaceae; spearmint	Eu	F	essential oil with carvone, limonene	TEM TNAM	stomachic, carminative; antibiotic, decongestant; oil used industrially
Mentzelia cordifolia; Loasaceae	SAm	H	flavonoids, coumarins, mucilage, sitosterol	TSAM	spasmolytic; anti-inflammatory; disorders of digestive tract
Menyanthes trifoliata; Menyanthaceae; bogbean	NAm Eu As	F, RH	bitter-tasting secoiridoid glycosides, mainly dehydromenthiafoline	TEM	bitter tonic (*amarum*); improvement of appetite; topical products for skin disorders; used in liqueurs
Mercurialis annua; *M. perennis*; Euphorbiaceae; annual mercury; dog mercury	Eu	H	saponins, cyanogenic glycosides	TEM	laxative, diuretic, expectorant; anthelmintic
Millettia reticulata; Fabaceae; *ji xue teng*	EAs	R	rotenoids	TCM	anti-inflammatory; hypotonic; menstrual disorders
Mimusops globosa; Sapotaceae	CAm		polyterpenes, similar to gutta-percha	TSAM TEM	dentistry; plasters
Mitchella repens; Rubiaceae; partridge berry	NAm	H,FR	tannins, saponins	TNAM	menstrual disorders and childbirth; astringent
Momordica balsamina; Cucurbitaceae; balsam apple	EAs	FR,	cucurbitacins,	TCM	purgative, emetic, antispasmodic, stomachic
Momordica charantia; Cucurbitaceae; balsam pear, bitter cucumber	SAs	FR, F, S	an insulin-like peptide; momordicine (alkaloid)	TCM	hypoglycaemic; menstrual disorders; anthelmintic, wound healing
Monarda didyma; *M. punctata*; Lamiaceae; Oswego tea, bee balm, bergamot	NAm	H	thymol and other monoterpenes	TNAM	aromatic, stomachic; colds; digestive problems; diaphoretic; counter-irritant
Monsonia ovata; Geraniaceae	SA	H	tannins	TAM	astringent; digestive disorders
Montia perfoliata; Portulacaceae; blinks	NAm	H	vitamin C	TNAM	tonic; vegetable
Morinda officinalis; Rubiaceae; Indian mulberry, noni fruit	EAs	R, FR	morindin and other anthraquinones; vitamin C	TCM	sexual tonic; urinary tract problems; fermented fruits also used medicinally
Moringa oleifera; Moringaceae; horse-radish tree	As	R	antibiotic substances	TEM	purgative, emetic
Morus alba, *M. nigra*; Moraceae; mulberry, white mulberry	EAs	F, FR, C	flavonoids, anthocyanins, pectins, sugars, artocarpin	TCM	food for silkworms; expectorant; colds,
Mucuna pruriens; Fabaceae; *vanari*	As Am	FR	dihydroxyphenylalanine, alkaloids, serotonin	TIM	skin irritant; anthelmintic; used as aphrodisiac

Murraya koenigii; Rutaceae; curry leaf	SAs	F,FR	koenigin, volatile oil; tannins	TSAM	flavour; digestion disorders; wounds and burns
Musa acuminata; *M. x paradisiaca*; Musaceae; bananas	EAs	FR, F	unripe fruits: tannins, eugenol, tyramine	TSAM TAM TIM	astringent, for diarrhoea; leaves: bronchitis and colds
Myrica cerifera; Myricaceae; wax myrtle, candleberry; waxberry	NAm	R	flavonoids (myricetrin); tannins, triterpenoids	TNAM	emetic; astringent; anti-catarrhal; wax from berries traditionally for soap, candles
Myrica gale; Myricaceae; *Gale belgica*, sweet gale, bog myrtle	Eu NAm	F	flavonoids (myricetrin); essential oil	TEM	ectoparasites; skin disorders
Myristica fragrans; Myristicaceae; nutmeg	EAs	S	essential oil with sabinene, pinene, myristicine, eugenol	TEM	antispasmodic; digestive; seeds (nutmeg) and seed arils (mace) are spices used in food
Myroxylon balsamum; Fabaceae; Tolu balsam, Peruvian balsam	CAm SAm	E	oleoresin with benzoic acid, cinnamic acid, phenylpropanoids	TSAM TEM	antiseptic; expectorant; wound-healing (used in skin preparations)
Myrrhis odorata; Apiaceae; sweet cicely	Eu	H	anethol	TEM	expectorant, diuretic
Myrtillocactus geometrizans; Cactaceae	CAm	H	saponins, triterpenes	TSAM	cardiac disorders; fruit edible
Myrtus communis; Myrtaceae; myrtle	Eu As	F, FR	essential oil with cineol, limonene, pinene (myrtol); tannins	TEM	expectorant; astringent; urinary tract antiseptic; oil used in perfumery
Nabalus (*Prenanthes*) *serpenta-rius, P. albus*; Asteraceae	NAm	H	tannins	TNAM	against snake bites
Nardostachys grandiflora (=*N. jatamansi*); Valerianaceae; nard, spikenard	As	R	valeranon and other sesquiterpenes	TEM	sedative
Nasturtium officinale (see *Rorippa nasturtium-aquaticum*)					
Nelumbo nucifera; Nymphae-aceae; lotus, sacred lotus; *lian, padma, kamala, kanwal*	As EAs	F, RH, S, FL	alkaloids (nuciferine, neferine and others); flavonoids (quercetin)	TCM TIM	F, FL: astringent, haemostatic; RH, S: demulcent; general tonic; rhizomes used as food in China
Nepeta cataria; Lamiaceae; catnip, catnep	Eu As	H	essential oil rich in nepetalactone (iridoids)	TEM	mild sedative; mild soporific; digestive; once a popular tea; causes playful behaviour in cats
Nerium oleander; Apocynaceae; oleander	Eu	F	numerous cardiac glycosides, also flavonoids, saponins	TEM	heart stimulant; skin treatment; very toxic!
Nicotiana tabacum; Solanaceae; tobacco plant	SAm	H	nicotine and other alkaloids	TSAM	constipation, anthelmintic, insecticidal
Nigella sativa; Ranunculaceae; black cumin	As Eu NA	S	phytosterols; essential oil rich in thymoquinone; saponins, alkaloids	TIM	immune stimulation; tonic; antispasmodic; diuretic; seeds are an important culinary spice
Notopterygium incisium; Apiaceae; *qiang huo*	EAs	R	angelic acid and deriva-tives; furanocoumarins	TCM	colds and chills; diaphoretic
Nuphar luteum; Nymphaeaceae; yellow waterlily	Eu As	R	nupharin and other quinolizidine alkaloids	TEM	aphrodisiac
Nymphaea alba; Nymphaeaceae; white waterlily	Eu As	R	nupharin and other quinolizidine alkaloids; tannins	TEM	insomnia, anaphrodisiac; hypotonic
Ocimum basilicum; Lamiaceae; sweet basil	A As	H	essential oil with ocimene, estragole, linalool; also tannins, flavonoids	TEM	tonic; carminative; diuretic; anthelmintic
Ocimum tenuiflorum (=*O. sanctum*); Lamiaceae; holy basil, sacred basil, *tulsi*	As	H	essential oil; tannins, flavonoids	TIM	general medicine; tonic; wound-healing
Oenanthe crocata; Apiaceae; water dropwort	Eu	H	oenanthotoxin (a poly-acetylene), myristin, apiol	TEM	spasmolytic; very toxic!

Oenothera biennis; Onagraceae; evening primrose	NAm	S	seed oil with gamma-linolenic acid (essential fatty acid)	TNAM, TEM	nutritional supplement (treatment of atopic eczema)
Okoubaka aubrevillei; Santalaceae	A	C	catechol tannins	TAM	against intoxications; skin infections
Olea europaea; Oleaceae; olive tree	Eu As NA	F, oil	F: secoiridoids (oleuropein); cold-pressed oil: oleic acid, linoleic acid	TEM TAM	F: antihypertensive, diuretic; oil: cholagogue, mild laxative, also demulcent, emollient
Ononis spinosa; Fabaceae; spiny restharrow	Eu As NA	R	onocol (a triterpene); sterols, phenolic acids, isoflavonoids	TEM	diuretic
Operculina turpethum; Convolvulaceae; turpeth root	As	R	glycoretins (ester glycosides)	TIM	purgative, anthelmintic
Ophiopogon japonicus; Liliaceae; *mai men dong*	As	T	homoisoflavonoids, ophiopogonins, sitosterols	TCM	asthma, constipation
Opuntia ficus-indica; Cactaceae; prickly pear	CAm	FR, FL	mucilage, vitamin C; flavonoids	TSAM	astringent; haemostyptic; intestinal disorders
Orchis morio and other ground orchids; Orchidaceae	Eu	T	mucilage	TEM	antidiarrhoic, roborant
Origanum dictamnus; Lamiaceae; dittany	Eu	H	essential oil with carvacrol, *p*-cymene and terpinene	TEM	bronchitis, catarrh, cold, influenza, colic, dyspepsia; externally to treat wounds
Origanum majorana; Lamiaceae; marjoram	Eu	H	essential oil with terpinen-4-ol, terpineol, sabinene, linalool	TEM	bronchitis, catarrh, cold, influenza, colic, dyspepsia
Origanum vulgare; Lamiaceae; oregano	Eu	H	essential oil with carvacrol, *p*-cymene and terpinene	TEM	bronchitis, catarrh, cold, influenza, colic, dyspepsia; externally to treat wounds; important culinary herb
Orthosiphon aristatus; Lamiaceae; Java tea	EAs A US	H	potassium salts, essential oil, flavonoids, terpenes	TEM	urological uses; diuretic tea (Java tea) for treating inflammation of the bladder and kidneys
Oxalis acetosella; Oxalidaceae; wood sorrel	Eu NAm	H	calcium oxalate	TEM	dyspepsia
Pachycarpus rigidus and other species; Asclepiadaceae	SA	R	pregnanes	TAM	spasmolytic, sedative
Paeonia lactiflora; and other species; Paeoniaceae; white peony, *bai shao yao, chi shao*	As EAs	R	paeniflorin (a monoterpenoid glycoside)	TCM	antispasmodic; anti-inflammatory; analgesic; used mainly to treat menstrual disorders
Paeonia officinalis; Paeoniaceae; peony	Eu	S, R, FL	petals contain anthocyanins (such as paeonin) and flavonoids	TEM	roots, seeds of historic interest (epilepsy); petals added to herbal teas (colourant)
Panax ginseng; Araliaceae; ginseng, Asian ginseng, Korean ginseng	EAs	R	triterpenoids saponins (ginsenosides), polyacetylenes	TCM TEM	adaptogenic tonic (counteracting weakness, fatigue, declining stamina and concentration)
Panax quinquefolius; Araliaceae; American ginseng	NAm	R	ginsenosides, polyacetylenes	TNAM TCM	adaptogenic tonic (same uses as for *P. ginseng*)
Papaver rhoeas; Papaveraceae; corn poppy, field poppy	Eu As	FL	rhoeadine and other isoquinoline alkaloids, mucilage, anthocyanins	TEM	secretolytic, cough
Papaver somniferum; Papaveraceae; opium poppy	As	E (FR)	latex from unripe fruit: isoquinoline alkaloids (morphine, noscapine)	TIM TEM MM	analgesic; euphoric; morphine is chemically converted to codeine (antitussive, analgesic, less addictive)
Parietaria officinalis; *P. judaica*; Lamiaceae; pellitory-on-the-wall	Eu	H	organic acids, tannins, flavonoids	TEM	diuretic, anti-inflammatory; urinary tract disorders; wound healing
Paris quadrifolia; Trilliaceae / Liliaceae; herb Paris	Eu	RH	steroid saponins	TEM	wounds; infections; influenza

Passiflora incarnata; Passifloraceae; passion flower	NAm	H	flavonoids, pyrone derivatives, cyanogenic glycosides	TNAM TEM	sedative (hypnotic, antispasmodic)
Pastinaca sativa; Apiaceae; parsnip	Eu NAm	FR, R	imperatorin and other furanocoumarins	TEM	diuretic, spasmolytic, carminative
Paullinia cupana; Sapindaceae; guaraná	SAm	S	caffeine; also catechin, proanthocyanins	TSAM MM	stimulant tonic; anti-diarrhoeal; diuretic; ingredient of soft drinks
Pausinystalia johimbe; Rubiaceae; yohimbe	A	C	yohimbine (monoterpene indole alkaloid)	TAM MM	aphrodisiac, urological
Peganum harmala; Zygophyllaceae; harmala, African rue	Eu As NA	S	harmine and other indole (β-carboline) alkaloids	TAM TIM	hallucinogen, intoxicant; formerly used to treat Parkinson's disease
Pelargonium graveolens and various hybrids and cultivars; Geraniaceae; rose geranium, "attar-of-roses"	SA	ess. oil	geraniol, isomenthone, citronellol, phenylethyl alcohol (rose smell!)	TAM TEM	Bourbon oil: used in perfumery and aromatherapy (as a substitute for rose oil)
Pelargonium sidoides; Geraniaceae; umckaloabo	SA	R	coumarins (umckalin)	TAM TEM	natural antibiotic; immune-stimulant; bronchitis in children
Perilla frutescens; Lamiaceae; perilla	As	O	perillaldehyde and other monoterpenes;	TCM	oxime used as sweetening agent in Japan
Persea americana; Lauraceae; avocado tree	CAm	FR, F	fruit oil contains oleic acid, palmitic acid, some gamma-linolenic acid	TSAM MM	fruit oil is used in aromatherapy and cosmetic products; non-glyceride fraction in stomatology
Persicaria bistorta; Polygonaceae; bistort	Eu As NAm	RH	tannins, silicic acid	TEM TNAM	astringent; anti-diarrhoeal; anti-catarrhal; anti-inflammatory
Petasites hybridus; Asteraceae; butterbur	Eu As	F, RH	sesquiterpenoids (petasin, isopetasin); some pyrrolizidine alkaloids!	TEM	antispasmodic; analgesic; treatment of spastic pain, wounds, skin disorders
Petroselinum crispum; Apiaceae; parsley	Eu As	F, FR	essential oil with phenyl-propanoids (apiol, myristicin); flavonoids	TEM	diuretic; itch-relieving (skin ailments); best known as a culinary herb
Peucedanum ostruthium; Apiaceae; masterwort	Eu As	RH	mono-, sesquiterpenes (limonene); coumarins	TEM	stomachic, diuretic, gout, rheumatism, fever
Peumus boldus; Monimiaceae; boldo	SAm	F	aporphine alkaloids (mainly boldine); essential oil, flavonoids	TSAM TEM	choleretic; mild diuretic; stomachic; mild sedative; treatment of dyspepsia
Phaseolus vulgaris; Fabaceae; common bean	CAm SAm	FR	bean pods (without seeds) are rich in amino acids; silicic acid	TEM TSAM	diuretic
Phellodendron amurense; Rutaceae; cork tree	EAs	C	berberine and other isoquinoline alkaloids; sesquiterpene lactones;	TCM	antimicrobial; inflammation of urinary tract; meningitis, conjunctivitis
Phyllanthus amarus; Euphorbiaceae; *bhumi amalaki*	As	F FR	alkaloids, gallotannins, triterpenes	TIM	antiviral (hepatitis B); hepatoprotective; anti-inflammatory
Phyllanthus emblica; Euphorbiaceae; emblic myrobalan, *emblic, amla, amalaki*	As	F	alkaloids (phyllantine), triterpenoids, volatile oil; tannins	TIM	tonic, dyspepsia (rejuvenating, balancing); anti-diabetic; coolant; hair tonic
Physalis alkekengi; Solanaceae; Chinese lantern, winter cherry	Eu As	FR	physalin and other steroids	TEM	diuretic; urinary tract disorders
Physostigma venenosum; Fabaceae; calabar bean	A	S	physostigmine and other pyrrolidine alkaloids	MM	choline esterase inhibitor; miotic; treatment of tetanus, chorea, epilepsy; antidote for atropine, tricyclic antidepressants
Phytolacca americana; Phytolaccaceae; pokeroot	NAm	R, FR	saponins; betacyanins	TNAM	anti-inflammatory; traditionally used for many ailments

Phytolacca dodecandra; Phytolaccaceae; soapberry	A	FR	molluscicidal saponins (glycosides of oleanolic-phytolaccagenic acids)	TAM	cost-effective treatment of bilharzia-infested water
Picea abies and related species; Pinaceae; spruce	Eu	O	bornylacetate, pinene, phellandrene and other terpenes	TEM MM	skin irritant; induction of hyperaemia; expectorant;
Picramnia antidesma; Simaroubaceae; macary bitter	SAm	C	bitter triterpenes	TSAM	amarum, tonic; against syphilis
Picrasma excelsa; Simaroubaceae; Jamaica quassia	CAm	L	quassin and other triterpenes	TEM	amarum; anthelmintic, insecticidal; cytotoxic
Picrorhiza kurrooa; Scrophulariaceae; *kutki*	As	H	picroside and other iridoid glycosides; cucurbitacins, apocynin	TIM	immune stimulant; liver disorders; digestion disorders
Pilocarpus jaborandi, P. pennatifolius and related species; Rutaceae; jaborandi	SAm	F	pilocarpine and other alkaloids	MM	parasympathomimetic; induction of saliva production and perspiration; miotic, glaucoma treatment
Pimenta dioica; P. racemosa; Myrtaceae; allspice, pimento; bay rum tree	CAm	FR	eugenol, methyleugenol	TSAM TEM	topically to treat cold; stomachic, antiseptic; used for perfumes and liqueur
Pimpinella anisum; Apiaceae; anise	Eu As NA	FR	essential oil with *trans*-anethole	TEM TIM TAM	expectorant; carminative; used in cough remedies, alcoholic beverages (taste enhancement)
Pimpinella major; P. saxifraga Apiaceae; burnet saxifrage	Eu As	RH, R	essential oil; sesquiterpenes; furanocoumarins	TEM	antitussive; mild expectorant; antiseptic; treatment of respiratory tract infections
Pinguicula vulgaris; Lentibulariaceae; butterwort, bog violet	Eu	F	mucilage, tannins, benzoic and cinnamic acid	TEM	purgative; coughs
Pinus mugo; Pinaceae; pumilio pine	Eu	O	pinene, bornylacetate, phellandrene and other monoterpenes	TEM MM	inhalant to treat inflammation of the respiratory tract
Pinus sylvestris; Pinaceae; Scots pine	Eu As	H, ess. oil	needle oils and turpentine oils (monoterpenoids)	TEM	expectorant; counter-irritant; chronic bronchial disease; topical: pain, neuralgia, rheumatism
Piper betle; Piperaceae; betel vine	As EAs	F	essential oil (unusual sesquiterpenes)	TIM	throat inflammation; stomach ailments; fresh leaf (with betle nut) a stimulant masticatory
Piper longum; Piperaceae, Indian pepper, long pepper, *pippali*	As	F	piperine, piperidine (pseudoalkaloids)	TIM	stimulant; diuretic; antiasthmatic; spleen disorders; anti-inflammatory; carminative
Piper methysticum; Piperaceae; kava kava	EAs Polynesia	RH, R	kawain and other styrylpyrones (so-called kavapyrones)	TAUM (Polynesia) TEM	sedative (anxiolytic); treatment of sleep disturbances, anxiety, stress; (contraindication: liver disorders)
Piper nigrum; Piperaceae; pepper; *marich*	As	FR	pungent acid-amides (pseudoalkaloids), mainly piperine; essential oil (sharp smell)	TIM TEM	digestive; an important item in Ayurvedic medicine; stimulant of the digestive system; common spice
Piptadenia peregrina; Fabaceae	SAm	F	N,N-dimethyltryptamine, bufotenine, other tryptamines	TSAM	central stimulant; hallucinogen taken as sniff
Piscidia piscipula (=*P. erythrina*); Fabaceae; Jamaica dogwood	CAm	C, R	piscidic acid; jamaicin, rotenone and other isoflavones, tannins, saponins	TSAM	sedative, analgesic; antispasmodic; hypnotic, treatment of asthma, pertussis; fish poison
Pistacia integerrima; Anacardiaceae; crab's claw, *karkat shringi*	As	R	terpenoids	TIM	cough, vomiting, fever, excessive belching
Pistacia lentiscus; Anacardiaceae; mastic tree	Eu	resin	triterpenes; monoterpenes	TEM	stomachic, plasters, mouth washes; dental material

Plantago afra (=*P. psyllium*); *P. arenaria* (=*P. indica*); Plantaginaceae; psyllium, fleawort	Eu	S	swelling mucilages in epidermis of seed husks	TEM	bulk laxative
Plantago asiatica; Plantaginaceae; Japanese psyllium, *shazen-shi, che-qian-zi*	EAs	S	swelling mucilages in epidermis of seed husks	TCM	bulk laxative
Plantago lanceolata; Plantaginaceae; ribwort plantain	Eu As	F, H	iridoid glycosides (aucubin, catalpol, asperuloside); mucilage	TEM	anti-inflammatory; expectorant
Plantago major; *P. media*; Plantaginaceae; greater plantain, hoary plantain	Eu As	F, H	iridoid glycosides (aucubin); mucilage; tannins; phenolic acids	TEM	anti-inflammatory; diuretic; haemostyptic
Plantago ovata; Plantaginaceae; blond psyllium, ispaghula	As	S	swelling mucilages in epidermis of seed husks	TIM	bulk laxative
Platycodon grandiflorus; Campanulaceae; Chinese bellflower; *chieh keng*	EAs	R	triterpene saponins	TCM	expectorant, anti-inflammatory; (numerous traditional uses)
Plectranthus barbatus (see *Coleus forskohlii*)					
Plumbago europaea; *P. zeylanica*; Plumbaginaceae; leadwort	Eu As	H,R	plumbagin and other quinones	TEM	counter-irritant; analgesic; digestive disorders
Plumbago indica (=*P. rosea*); Plumbaginaceae; *chithrakam*	As	R	plumbagin and other quinones	TIM	non-bleeding haemorrhoids, ascitis, spleen disorders
Podophyllum hexandrum; Berberidaceae; Himalayan may apple	As	RH	podophyllum resin (=podophyllin) with podophyllotoxin (a lignan)	TIM MM	traditional purgative; source of podophyllotoxin, used in the treatment of cancer and warts
Podophyllum peltatum; Berberidaceae; may apple, American mandrake	NAm	RH	podophyllotoxin (a lignan)	TNAM MM	homoeopathy: liver and gall ailments; pure podophyllotoxin: treatment of cancer and warts
Pogostemon cablin; Lamiaceae; patchouli	EAs	F, ess. oil	essential oil with a unique sesquiterpene, patchoulol	TIM TCM	fresh herb: traditional aphrodisiac; essential oil: aromatherapy; cosmetics; insect repellent
Polemonium caeruleum; Polemoniaceae; Jacob's ladder, Greek valerian	Eu	R	saponins	TEM	expectorant
Polygala senega; Polygalaceae; senega snakeroot	NAm	R	bidesmosidic saponins (senegasaponins A-D)	TNAM	expectorant; secretolytic; antitussive
Polygonatum multiflorum; Convallariaceae / Liliaceae; Solomon's seal	Eu As	RH	steroidal saponins, flavonoids	TEM	wound healing; antibacterial; expectorant
Polygonum aviculare; Polygonaceae; knotweed	Eu As	H	tannins, flavonoids, silicic acid, coumarins	TEM TIM TCM	diuretic; expectorant; treatment of skin ailments
Polygonum hydropiper; Polygonaceae; red knees	Eu NAm	H	ess. oil with pungent sesquiterpenes; (tadeonal); rutin, tannins	TNAM	counter-irritant, haemostyptic; antirheumatic
Polygonum multiflorum (=*Fallopia multiflora*); Polygonaceae; flowery knotweed, *he shou wu*	EAs	R	tannins, flavonoids	TCM	tonic herb; liver ailments, kidney problems, nervous conditions, premature ageing, infertility
Polypodium vulgare; Polypodiaceae;	Eu As	RH	ecdysterone (insect hormone); ostadin (sweet saponin)	TEM	expectorant; cholagogue; laxative; anthelmintic; ostadin is 3000 times as sweet as sucrose
Populus balsamifera; *P. candicans* (=*P. gileadensis*); Salicaceae; balsam poplar; balm of Gilead	NAm As	buds	benzoyl esters of salicin (populin), phenolic glycosides, essential oil, flavonoids	TNAM TEM	ingredient of ointments to treat wounds, external haemorrhoids, frostbite, sunburn, myalgia

Populus tremula; Salicaceae; European white poplar, quaking aspen	Eu As	C, F	benzoyl esters of salicin, mainly populin (salicin-5-benzoate)	TEM	anti-inflammatory; analgesic; traditional uses include rheumatic conditions, cystitis, diarrhoea, common cold
Populus tremuloides; Salicaceae; white poplar, Canadian poplar, quaking aspen	NAm	C, F	benzoyl esters of salicin, mainly populin (salicin-5-benzoate)	TNAM	anti-inflammatory; analgesic; traditional uses include rheumatic conditions, cystitis, diarrhoea, common cold
Portulaca oleracea; Portulacaceae; purslane	Eu As	H	mucilage; vitamin C	TEM	diuretic; digestive disorders; antimicrobial; anthelmintic
Potentilla anserina; Rosaceae; silverweed	As Eu NAm	F	ellagitannins; flavonoids, proanthocyanidins, phenolic acids	TEM	astringent; used to treat non-specific diarrhoea, inflammations of the mouth and throat
Potentilla erecta; Rosaceae; tormentil	Eu	RH	tannins (agrimoniin); proanthocyanidins; saponin (tormentoside)	TEM	astringent; used in diarrhoea, dysentery, gastroenteritis, enterocolitis; gargle; skin disorders
Primula veris; *P. elatior*; Primulaceae; cowslip; oxlip	Eu As	FL, R, RH	FL: triterpene saponins, flavonoids; R: triterpene saponins, phenolic glycosides	TEM	R: expectorant, secretolytic (bronchitis, cough); FL: traditionally for nervous conditions, headache
Prunella vulgaris; Lamiaceae; selfheal	Eu As	H	triterpenes, tannins, vitamin C	TEM TCM	astringent, haemostyptic, wound healing; vasodilatory
Prunus africana (=*Pygeum africanum*); Rosaceae; pygeum, red stinkwood	A	C	sitosterol and its glucosides; triterpenes, tannins	TAM TEM	benign prostate hyperplasia
Prunus armeniaca; Rosaceae; apricot	As	S	prunasin (cyanogenic glucoside), fatty acids	TCM	traditional expectorant
Prunus avium; Rosaceae; European wild cherry	Eu As	fruit stalk	tannins	TEM	diuretic, astringent
Prunus cerasus; Rosaceae; morello cherry; amarelle cherry	Eu As	F	tannins	TEM	astringent; traditional tea
Prunus dulcis var. *amara*; Rosaceae; bitter almond	Eu As	S	amygdalin (cyanogenic glycoside)	TEM	flavouring agent; HCN: very toxic!; "laetrile" as cancer treatment, efficacy doubtful
Prunus laurocerasus; Rosaceae; cherry laurel	As	F	prulaurasin (cyanogen)	TEM	used in "Cherry-laurel water", a respiratory stimulant; HCN!
Prunus mume; Rosaceae; Japanese apricot; *wu mei*	EAs	FR	tannins	TCM	styptic; treatment of cough, diarrhoea
Prunus serotina; Rosaceae; American wild cherry, black cherry	NAm	C	tannins, cyanogens	TNAM	used in "Wild Cherry Syrup", an expectorant medicine
Prunus spinosa; Rosaceae; blackthorn, sloe	Eu As NA	FL, FR	tannins, flavonoids, cyanogens (prunasin)	TEM	astringent, diuretic; treatment of mucosal infections
Pseudognaphalium obtusifolium (*Gnaphalium polycephalum*); Asteraceae	NAm	H	gnaphalin and other flavonoids	TNAM	diuretic
Psidium guajava; Myrtaceae; guava	CAm	F	phenolic compounds (tannins, flavonoids); essential oil; triterpenoids	TSAM TIM TAM	anti-diarrhoeal; traditional anti-diabetic; fruits are rich in vitamin C
Psilocybe mexicana and related fungi	CAm		psilocybin, psilocine and other indole alkaloids	TSAM	central stimulant (hallucinogen)
Psophocarpus (*Cyamopsis*) *tetragonolobus*; Fabaceae; winged bean	As CAm	S	polysaccharide (guar gum)	TIM TEM	laxative; dietetic; antidiabetic
Psoralea coryfolia; Fabaceae; *bu gu zhi*, scurf pea	EAs	S	psoralin and other furanocoumarins	TCM	skin disorders, vitiligo, psoriasis
Psychotria ipecacuanha and several other species; Rubiaceae; ipecac	SAm	RH	isoquinoline alkaloids (emetine, cephaeline)	TSAM TEM	expectorant (low dose); emetic (high dose); emetic syrups

Ptelea trifoliata; Rutaceae; hop tree	NAm	F	kokusaginine and other alkaloids	TNAM	anthelmintic; fruits used as a hop substitute
Pterocarpus marsupium; Fabaceae; *gamalu*, Malabar kino	As	C	catechol tannins; marsupin	TIM	astringent; digestion disorders
Pterocarpus santalinus; Fabaceae; red sandalwood	As	L	santalin, pterocarpin and other isoflavones; sesquiterpenes	TEM	dyspepsia
Ptychopetalum olacoides, P. unicinatum; Olacaceae; potency wood	SAm	L	lupeolester, sitosterols; tannins	TSAM	aphrodisiac, tonic
Pueraria montana var. lobata; Fabaceae; kudzu vine, *ge gen*	EAs	R	puerarin, daidzein and other isoflavones	TCM	cerebral circulation; neck pain; hangover treatment
Pulmonaria officinalis; Boraginaceae; lungwort	Eu	F	mucilage, flavonoids, tannins, silicic acid, allantoin	TEM	expectorant; external use to treat haemorrhoids and wounds (mainly of historic interest)
Pulsatilla chinensis; Ranunculaceae; Chinese pasque flower, *bai tou weng*	EAs	R	ranunculin (terpenoid lactone) broken down to protoanemonin	TCM	traditional treatment of dysentery
Pulsatilla vulgaris; *P. pratensis* and other species; Ranunculaceae; pasque flower	Eu	H	ranunculin (terpenoid lactone) broken down to protoanemonin	TEM	antispasmodic, antimicrobial; numerous traditional uses
Punica granatum; Punicaceae; pomegranate	Eu	FR, C, R	fruit rind: tannins (punicalin, punicalagin); roots /bark: piperidine alkaloids	TEM TAM TIM	root bark: traditional anthelmintic; fruit rind / fruit pulp: stomach upsets, diarrhoea
Pygeum africanum (see *Prunus africana*)					
Quassia amara; Simaroubaceae quassia	SAm	L	bitter secotriterpenoids (quassinoids)	TSAM TEM	bitter tonic (*amarum*); antimicrobial; wood extracts mostly used
Quercus robur; Fagaceae; common oak	Eu	B	tannins	TEM	anti-diarrhoeal; astringent; anti-microbial
Quillaja saponaria; Rosaceae; soapbark tree, *quillai*	SAm	C	triterpene saponins, calcium oxalates, tannins	TSAM TEM	expectorant; detergent in washing powder; source of soapbark
Ranunculus acris and related species; Ranunculaceae	Eu As	H	ranunculin (terpenoid lactone) broken down to protoanemonin	TEM	skin irritant; treatment of warts; gout, rheumatism, pleural inflammation
Ranunculus ficaria; Ranunculaceae; celandine, pilewort	Eu As	R	saponins (glycosides of hederagenin and oleanolic acid), vitamin C	TEM	traditional and effective anti-haemorrhoidal; against scurvy
Raphanus sativus; Brassicaceae; radish	As	R	glucoraphanin and other glucosinolates, vitamin C	TEM	digestive disorders; cholagogue, choleretic, expectorant, spasmolytic
Rauvolfia serpentina; Apocynaceae Indian snakeroot, *sarpagandha*	As EAs	R	reserpine and other monoterpene indole alkaloids	TIM TEM	antihypertensive; tranquiliser; numerous traditional uses
Rauvolfia vomitoria; *R. tetraphylla* Apocynaceae; African-, American snakeroot	NAm	R	reserpine and other monoterpene indole alkaloids	TAM: TNAM	antihypertensive; tranquiliser; numerous traditional uses
Rehmannia glutinosa; Gesneriaceae; Chinese foxglove	EAs	R	catalpol and other iridoid glycosides; verbascoside	TCM	haemostyptic; liver protecting; reduces blood pressure, against fever
Rhamnus catharticus; Rhamnaceae; buckthorn	Eu As NA	FR	anthranoids of the emodin type	TEM TAM	stimulant laxative
Rhamnus frangula; (= *Frangula alnus*); Rhamnaceae; alder buckthorn	Eu As NA	C	anthrone- and dianthrone glycosides	TEM TAM	stimulant laxative

Rhamnus purshianus; Rhamnaceae; cascada sagrada	NAm	C	hydroxyanthraquinone glycosides;	TNAM TEM	stimulant laxative
Rheum officinale; Polygonaceae; rhubarb	EAs	RH	anthraquinone glycosides	TCM TEM	stimulant laxative
Rheum palmatum; Polygonaceae; Chinese rhubarb, *dai hoàng, da huang*	EAs	RH	anthraquinone glycosides	TCM TEM	stimulant laxative
Rheum rhaponticum; Polygonaceae; rhapontic rhubarb	EAs	RH	anthraquinone glycosides; rhaponticin (a stilbene)	TCM, TEM	stimulant laxative
Rhodiola rosea; Crassulaceae; rose root	Eu	RH	Phenylpropanoids (so-called rosavins)	TEM	adaptogenic tonic
Rhododendron ferrugineum, R. campylocarpum, R. aureum, R. ponticum; Ericaceae	Eu As	F	acetylandromedol (diterpenes), tannins, arbutin and other phenolglucosides;	TEM	diuretic, rheumatism; neuralgia; hypotonic
Rhododendron tomentosum (=*Ledum palustre*); Ericaceae; marsh tea, marsh rosemary	Eu As NAm	H	essential oil: palustrol, ledol (sesquiterpenes); tetracyclic diterpenes	TEM TNAM	traditional expectorant; anti-inflammatory; bronchitis, rheumatism, skin ailments
Rhus aromatica, R. typhina, R. glabra; Anacardiaceae; sumach, sumac	NAm	C, R, FR	gallotannins	TNAM	astringent; digestive disorders; gargle; skin disorders; bladder disorders
Rhus toxicodendron (*Toxicodendron quercifolium*); Anacardiaceae; poison ivy	NAm	H	urushiol; gallotannins	TNAM	skin irritant; urushiol causes strong contact allergies!
Ribes nigrum; Grossulariaceae; blackcurrant	Eu	F, FR	flavonoids; essential oil; proanthocyanidins	TEM	traditional diuretic; fruit: vitamin C; seed oil: gamma-linolenic acid
Ricinus communis; Euphorbiaceae; castor oil plant	A As	seed oil	ricinoleic acid (fatty acid); highly toxic: alkaloid (ricinine), lectin (ricin)	TEM	laxative; castor oil is an important industrial product; cold-pressing to avoid toxins!
Robinia pseudacacia; Fabaceae; false acacia, black locust	NAm	C, F	lectins, flavonoids, monoterpenes	TNAM	migraine
Rorippa nasturtium-aquaticum (=*Nasturtium officinale*); Brassicaceae; watercress	Eu As NAm	H	phenylethyl glucosinolate (=gluconasturtiin)	TEM	fresh herb used as diuretic and "Spring tonic"; dried herb in commercial cholagogues
Rosa canina; Rosaceae; dog rose	Eu As	FR	vitamin C; carotenoids; flavonoids, tannins, acids	TEM	traditional diuretic; flavour enhancement of herbal teas
Rosa x centifolia; *R. x damascena*; *R. gallica*; Rosaceae; roses	Eu As	FL ess. oil	essential oil ("attar-of-roses"); petals: tannins	TEM	aromatherapy; dried petals are used in mouth rinses; rosewater is a traditional eye lotion
Rosmarinus officinalis; Lamiaceae; rosemary	Eu	H	essential oil; rosmarinic acid; flavonoids	TEM	general tonic; antimicrobial; spasmolytic; carminative; stomachic
Rubia tinctorum; Rubiaceae; madder	Eu	R	alizarin and other coloured anthraquinones, asperuloside (iridoid glucoside)	TEM	diuretic: against kidney and bladder stones (Ca^{++}-chelator); inflammation of urinary tract
Rubus fruticosus; Rosaceae; bramble	Eu	F	gallotannins, ellagi-tannins, flavonoids	TEM	astringent; non-specific acute diarrhoea; inflammation of mouth and throat
Rubus idaeus; Rosaceae; raspberry	Eu As NAm	F	gallotannins, ellagi-tannins, flavonoids	TEM	treatment of diarrhoea; gargle for mouth and throat infections; ingredient of tea mixtures
Rumex acetosa, R. acetosella; Polygonaceae; sorrel	Eu As	H	potassium hydrogen oxalate; oxalic acid; vitamin C	TEM	diuretic, laxative; skin disorders; anthelmintic
Rumex crispus; Polygonaceae; yellow dock	Eu As	RH	chrysophanol and related anthracene glycosides; oxalic acid	TEM	stimulant laxative; traditionally used against bleeding, worms and ulcers
Ruscus aculeatus; Ruscaceae or Asparagaceae; butcher's broom	Eu As	RH, R	steroidal saponins (ruscin, ruscoside)	TEM	venotonic; anti-inflammatory; diuretic; treatment of varicose veins and haemorrhoids

Ruta graveolens; Rutaceae; rue	Eu	H	coumarins, furanocoumarins, alkaloids, flavonoids (rutin), essential oil	TEM	traditional tonic; wide range of ailments
Salix alba, *S. purpurea* and other species; Salicaceae; white willow, purple willow	Eu As	C	phenolic glycosides (salicylates, e.g. silicin); phenolic acids	TEM	anti-inflammatory; analgesic; antipyretic, antirheumatic
Salvadora persica; Salvadoraceae; mustard tree, *arak*, *miswak*	A As	L, R	alkaloids, tannins, anthraquinones	TAM	wood and roots are used as tooth sticks; extracts in toothpaste
Salvia miltiorrhiza; Lamiaceae;	As	R	tanshinones, tanshinol,	TCM	circulatory tonic, vasodilatory, sedative
Salvia officinalis; *S. fruticosa*; Lamiaceae; sage; trilobed sage	Eu	F	essential oil (mainly thujone); rosmarinic acid; bitter diterpenoids	TEM	antiseptic; antispasmodic; carminative; digestive medicine; a popular culinary herb
Salvia sclarea and other species Lamiaceae; clary sage	Eu As	F	essential oil (linalool, linalyl acetate); flavonoids, rosmarinic acid	TEM	antiseptic; carminative; astringent; used in beverages, cosmetics, perfumery
Sambucus nigra; *S. canadensis*; Caprifoliaceae; elder, elderberry; American elderberry	Eu NAm	FL, R, F	FL, FR: flavonoids (rutin, isoquercitrin, hyperoside)	TEM; TNAM	traditional diaphoretic (flowers, fruit); diuretic, laxative (fruit)
Sanguinaria canadensis; Papaveraceae; bloodroot	NAm	RH	isoquinoline alkaloids (mainly sanguinarine)	TNAM	antibiotic; anti-inflammatory; ingredient of expectorants, mouth rinses and toothpastes
Sanguisorba officinalis; Rosaceae; burnet, greater burnet	Eu As	R, H	mainly tannins; also flavonoids, saponins, proanthocyanidins	TCM TEM	astringent; anti-haemorrhoidal; main traditional use is to stop bleeding
Sanicula europaea; Apiaceae; sanicle, wood sanicle	Eu As A	H, R	saponins, flavonoids, organic acids, tannins	TEM	astringent; expectorant
Santalum album; Santalaceae; sandalwood, white sandalwood, *safed chandan*	As	L, C	essential oil with sesquiterpene alcohols (α-santalol, β-santalol)	TIM TEM	urological; infections of the lower urinary tract; oil is used in aromatherapy
Saponaria officinalis; Caryophyllaceae; soapwort, red soapwort	Eu As	RH, R, H	triterpene saponins	TEM	expectorant; numerous traditional uses; formerly a soap substitute
Saraca asoca; *S. indica*; Fabaceae; *asoka*	As	C	ketosterols, tannins	TIM	uterine tonic; dysmenorrhoea, leucorrhoea
Sassafras albidum var. *molle*; Lauraceae; sassafras	NAm	C, R, O	safrol, other mono- and sesquiterpenes, eugenol; tannins	TNAM TEM	aromatic, diuretic, diaphoretic, for rheumatism, gout; safrol has carcinogenic properties!
Satureja montana; Lamiaceae; winter savoury	Eu A	H	essential oil with carvacrol, *p*-cymol, γ-terpinene	TEM TAM	stomachic; carminative; wound treatment
Saussurea lappa; = *S. costus*; Asteraceae; costus root, *kuth*, *kushtha*, *mu xiang*	As	R, O	mono-, sesquiterpenes, saussurine (an alkaloid)	TIM TCM	bronchitis, asthma, coughs; parasympatholytic
Sceletium tortuosum; Mesembryanthemaceae; sceletium, *kougoed*	SA	H, R	mesembrine and other alkaloids	TAM	hypnotic, sedative; euphoric at high doses (but not hallucinogenic)
Schinus terebinthifolius, *S. molle*; Anacardiaceae; pepper tree	SAm CAm	FR, O	phellandren, pinene, and other monoterpenes	TSAM	aromatic, spice
Schisandra chinensis; Schisandraceae; schisandra	EAs	FR	schizandrine and other lignans; sitosterol	TCM	general tonic; liver protectant; sedative; skin disorders
Schizonepeta tenuifolia; Lamiaceae; *jing jie*	EAs	H	menthone, limonene and other monoterpenes	TCM	diaphoretic, colds, hyperaemic
Schoenocaulon officinale; Melanthiaceae /Liliaceae; sabadilla, cevadilla	SAm	S	veratridine and other steroid alkaloids	TSAM ExM	insecticidal; against ectoparasites (alkaloids affect Na^+ channels)

Scopolia carniolica; Solanaceae; scopolia	Eu	RH	tropane alkaloids (mainly hyoscyamine)	TEM	antispasmodic
Scrophularia nodosa; Scrophulariaceae; figwort	Eu As NAm	H	iridoid glycosides (harpagoside, harpagide)	TEM	anti-inflammatory; mild diuretic; skin disorders
Scutellaria baicalensis; Lamiaceae Baical skullcap, *huang quin*	As EAs	R	flavonoid glycosides; iridoid glycosides	TCM	treatment of allergies, inflammation, arteriosclerosis, dermatitis, high blood lipids
Scutellaria lateriflora and other species; Lamiaceae; skullcap	NAm	H	flavonoid glycosides; catalpol (iridoid glycoside)	TNAM	anticonvulsant; sedative; epilepsy, hysteria, nervous conditions
Secale cereale; Poaceae; rye	Eu	pol-len	phytosterols	TEM	pollen extracts are used to treat prostate hyperplasia; see also *Claviceps purpureus* (ergot)
Securidaca longepedunculata; Polygalaceae; violet tree	A	R, C, F	methyl salicylate; saponins, indole alkaloids, ergot alkaloids	TAM TEM	traditional panacea; general tonic; antirheumatic; antitussive
Sedum acre; Crassulaceae; wall pepper, stonecrop	Eu As	H	sedamine and other piperidine alkaloids; rutin, tannins	TEM	pungent taste; emetic, purgative, abortifacient, skin irritant
Selenicereus grandiflorus; Cactaceae; night-flowering cactus	CAm	H	N,N-dimethyltyramine, and other tyramine derivatives	TEM	cardiac disorders
Semecarpus anacardium; Anacardiaceae; marking nut tree	As	FR	cardol and other phenolics, anacardic acid	TEM	skin irritant; against warts and clavus
Sempervivum tectorum; Crassulaceae; houseleek	Eu	H	tannins, mucilage, organic acids (malate)	TEM	skin conditions
Senecio ovatus, **S.** *jacobaea,* S. *aureus* and other species; Asteraceae; ragwort	Eu; NAm	H	macrocyclic pyrrolizidine alkaloids (liver toxins, carcinogenic!)	TEM; TNAM	internal and external haemostyptic; some used externally as poultice
Senna alexandrina (=*Cassia senna; C. angustifolia; C. acutifolia*); Fabaceae; senna, Alexandrian senna, Tinnevelly senna	NA As	F, FR	dianthrone glycosides, including sennosides A and B; flavonoids	TAM TEM TIM	laxative
Serenoa repens; Arecaceae; saw palmetto, sabal	NAm	FR	short chain fatty acids; various phytosterols	TNAM TEM	benign prostate hyperplasia
Sesamum orientale (=*S. indicum*); Pedaliaceae; sesame	NA As	S	triglycerides, sesamin (a lignan)	TIM	hypoglycaemic; food and flavouring agent; used in galenics
Sida cordifolia; S. retusa; S. rhombifolia; Malvaceae; wild mallow, *bala*	As	R	mucilage	TIM	rejuvenating nerve tonic; degenerative disorders
Silybum marianum; Asteraceae; milk-thistle	Eu As NA	FR, H	silymarin (mixture of flavonolignans)	TEM MM	digestive tonic; hepatoprotective (*Amanita*-poisoning)
Simarouba cedron (=*Quassia cedron*); Simaroubaceae; cedron	SAm	S,O	cedrin (a naphthofurane derivative)	TSAM	against fever and snake bites
Simmondsia chinensis; Simmondsiaceae; jojoba	NAm	S	seed oil (liquid wax)	TNAM	hair and skin care; lubrication of fine machinery
Sinapis alba; Brassicaceae; white mustard	Eu As	S	sinalbin (a glucosinolate)	TEM	topically to treat cold and rheumatism; skin irritant; internally: dyspepsia
Siphonochilus aethiopicus; Zingiberaceae; African ginger	SA	RH, R	sesquiterpenes of the furanoid type; curcumin-like compounds	TAM	anti-inflammatory; bronchodilatory; traditional anti-malarial
Smilax aristolochiaefolia, **S.** *regelii,* **S.** *china* and other species; Smilacaceae; sarsaparilla	SAm CAm EAs	R	steroidal saponins	TSAM; TCM	skin treatment (psoriasis, anti-pruritic, anti-rheumatic); extracts are used in root beer and herbal teas

Solanum dulcamara; Solanaceae; bittersweet	Eu As	stems	steroidal alkaloids; steroidal saponins	TEM	anti-eczema; anti-pruritic; taken orally and applied topically
Solanum nigrum and other species; Solanaceae; black nightshade	Eu As	H	solanine, other steroid alkaloids; tannins	TEM	eye inflammation; skin disorders (haemorrhoids, ulcers, eczema)
Solidago virgaurea, S. canadensis; Asteraceae; goldenrod	Eu As NAm	H	flavonoids, triterpene saponins, organic acids, polysaccharides	TEM TNAM	diuretic; used as urinary antiseptic; numerous traditional uses, including topical uses
Sophora pachycarpa; Fabaceae	As	F, S	sparteine and other quinolizidine alkaloids	TNAM	inflammation of veins, muscle pains
Sorbus aucuparia; Rosaceae; mountain ash	Eu As	FR	sorbitol, ascorbic acid	TEM	osmotic laxative; sweetener for diabetics
Spigelia anthelmia; S. marilandica; Loganiaceae; spigelia; Maryland pinkroot	NAm	H, R	tannins, spigeleine and other isoquinoline alkaloids	TNAM	strong anthelmintic, emetic,
Spilanthes acmella (=*S. oleracea*); Asteraceae; spilanthes, Brazilian cress	SAm	H, FL	spilanthol (an isobutylamide)	TSAM	local anaesthetic (dental care); antibiotic, antiphlogistic, sialagogue
Stachys officinalis; Lamiaceae; wood betony	Eu As	H	alkaloids (stachydrine, betonicine); tannins	TEM	sedative, bitter tonic
Stellaria media; Caryophyllaceae; chickweed	Eu	H	triterpene saponins; coumarins, flavonoids	TEM	treatment of skin disorders; itch relief
Stephania triandra; Menispermaceae; stephania	EAs	R	tetrandrine and other bisbenzoylisoquinoline alkaloids	TCM ExM	vasodilatory, hypotensive, anti-inflammatory, antipyretic
Sterculia urens; Sterculiaceae	As A	resin	mucilage; tannins ("karaya gum")	TEM	laxative; used to make tablets
Stevia rebaudiana; Asteraceae; stevia, *caa-ehe*	SAm	F	stevioside (diterpenoid glycoside)	TSAM	sweetener (300 times as sweet as sucrose)
Stillingia sylvatica; Euphorbiaceae; stillingia	NAm	R	stillingine (an alkaloid), phorbol esters; tannins; essential oil	TNAM	laxative; emetic; skin disorders (phorbol esters: co-carcinogenic!)
Strophanthus gratus; S. kombe; Apocynaceae; strophanthus	WA A	S	heart glycosides; *S. gratus*: ouabain; *S. kombe*: k-strophanthin	TAM MM	treatment of cardiac insufficiency; traditional arrow and spear poisons
Strychnos nux-vomica; Loganiaceae; nux vomica	As	S	monoterpene alkaloids (strychnine, brucine)	TEM MM	stimulant, bitter tonic; formerly an animal poison
Styphnolobium japonicum (=*Sophora japonica*); Fabaceae; Japanese pagoda tree	EAs	FL	up to 30% rutin and other flavonoids	MM	source for rutin
Styrax benzoin; Styracaceae; benzoin tree	EAs	Gum	esters of cinnamic, benzoic acid; benzaldehyde, vanilline	TEM	antiseptic, astringent; skin disorders; inflammations of respiratory tract
Sutherlandia frutescens and other species; Fabaceae; cancer bush, sutherlandia	SA	H	triterpenoid saponins; amino acids, L-canavanine; flavonoids; pinitol	TAM	adaptogenic tonic; traditional general tonic, cancer tonic; treatment of skin disorders
Swertia chirata; Gentianaceae; chiretta, *chirata*	As	H	chiratin, swertiamarin; amarogentin and other iridoids, alkaloids, phenolics	TIM	bitter tonic; dyspepsia; laxative; febrifuge; used in alcoholic beverages
Symphytum officinale; Boraginaceae; comfrey	Eu As	R, RH	allantoin; mucilage (fructans); pyrrolizidine alkaloids!; tannins	TEM	wound healing; numerous traditional uses (internal use now considered unsafe)
Symplocarpus foetidus; Araceae; skunk cabbage	NAm	H	hydroxytryptamine; essential oil	TNAM	spasmolytic; expectorant; counter-irritant
Symplocos racemosa; Symplocaceae; lodh bark, *lodhra*	As EAs	R, B	loturine and other alkaloids	TIM	conjunctivitis and other eye disorders; diarrhoea with fever; anti-diabetic; uterine disorders
Synsepalum dulciferum; Sapotaceae; miraculous berry	A CAm	S	miraculin (a glycoprotein)	TAM	conversion of sour into sweet taste

Species; Family; Common name	Origin	Part	Constituents	System	Uses
Syringa vulgaris; Oleaceae; common lilac	Eu	H, FL	syringin, syringopicrin	TEM	stomachic, against fever
Syzygium aromaticum; Myrtaceae; clove tree	EAs	FL	essential oil with eugenol; flavonoids, tannins	TEM TIM	local anaesthetic; carminative; important spice
Syzygium cumini; Myrtaceae; jamboloan	EAs	C, S	tannins, triterpenes, flavonoids	TIM	astringent; traditional anti-diabetic
Tabebuia impetiginosa; Bignoniaceae; *lapacho*	SAm CAm	C	anthraquinones, naphtho-quinones (lapachol)	TSAM	antimicrobial; anti-inflamma-tory; traditional cure-all
Tabernaemontana divaricata (= *T. coronaria*; *Ervatamia coronaria*); Apocynaceae; crepe jasmine, moon beam	As	R, F, L	indole alkaloids, resins	TIM	skin disorders; diarrhoea; relieves toothache; anthelmintic
Tamarindus indica; Fabaceae; tamarind	A	FR pulp	pectins; monosaccharides; organic acids; aromatic substances	TAM TIM	mild laxative; tonic to improve appetite and digestion; used in the food industry
Tanacetum balsamita (see *Chrysanthemum balsamita*)					
Tanacetum parthenium (see *Chrysanthemum parthenium*)					
Taraxacum officinale; Asteraceae; dandelion	Eu As NAm	F, R	sesquiterpene lactones; phenolic acid derivatives; triterpenoids; inulin	TEM	diuretic; mild choleretic; bitter tonic; externally used for skin ailments
Taxus baccata, *T. brevifolia* and other species; Taxaceae; yew tree	Eu NAm	F, (C)	diterpene pseudoalkaloids such as taxol (=paclitaxel); diterpenes from leaves now chemically modified	MM	cancer treatment; mainly ovarian and breast cancer
Tecoma lapacho (see *Tabebuia impetiginosa*)					
Terminalia arjuna; Combretaceae; arjuna	As	C	gallotannins, triterpene saponins	TIM	astringent; laxative; antiseptic; digestive disorders; cardiac tonic; urinary tract infections
Terminalia bellirica; Combretaceae belliric myrobalan	As	FR	gallotannins, triterpene saponins	TIM	astringent; laxative; antiseptic; wound healing; digestive disorders
Terminalia chebula; Combretaceae black myrobalan; chebulic myrobalan	As	FR rind	gallotannins, triterpene saponins; anthraquinones	TIM	memory tonic; astringent; laxative; antiseptic; wound healing; digestive disorders; inflammation of mucosa
Tetraclinis articulata; Cupressaceae; *arar, alerce*	WA	resin	pimaric acid, callitrolic acid, sandaricinic acid	TAM	tooth cement, pharmaceutical aid in ointments and plasters
Teucrium chamaedrys and other species; Lamiaceae; germander	Eu As	H	diterpene lactones; triterpenes; essential oil; phenolic acid glycosides	TEM TAM	bitter tonic; astringent; numerous traditional uses; cases of liver damage reported!
Thaumatococcus daniellii; Marantaceae; *katamfe*	WA	seed aril	thaumatin (a peptide)		sweet taste (as a sugar substitute)
Theobroma cacao; Sterculiaceae; cacao	CAm SAm	S	theobromine, caffeine, tannins; triglycerides	TEM TSAM	triglycerides for ointments and cosmetics; source of theobro-mine; chocolate production
Thevetia peruviana; (= *T. neriifolia*); Apocynaceae; yellow oleander	SAm	S	peruvoside and other cardenolides	TEM TNAM	source for cardenolides; insecticide
Thuja occidentalis; Cupressaceae; arbor vitae	NAm	H	volatile oil with thujone; sesquiterpenes, flavonoids	TNAM	traditional diuretic; expectorant; immune stimulant
Thymus vulgaris, *T. serpyllum* and other species; Lamiaceae; thyme	Eu	H	essential oil rich in thymol, carvacrol; rosmarinic acid; flavonoids; triterpenes	TEM TAM	expectorant; spasmolytic; antibiotic; taken against gastrointestinal disturbances
Tilia cordata; *T. platyphyllos*; Tiliaceae; lime, linden	Eu As	FL	mucilage; phenolic compounds; tannins	TEM	traditional diaphoretic; mild sedative
Tinospora cordifolia; Menispermaceae; *giloe, gaduchi, guduchi, amruth*	As	stem	isoquinoline alkaloids	TIM	rejuvenating tonic; rheumatism; liver disorders; fevers; skin problems

Trachyspermum ammi (= *T. copticum*); Apiaceae; *ajowan*	As	FR,O	up to 57% thymol, several other monoterpenes	MM	carminative; spice; source of thymol
Trachyspermum roxburghii (=*Carum roxburgianum*); Apiaceae; *ajamoda*	As	F	essential oil	TIM	digestive, carminative; cardiac tonic; anti-microbial; antiasthmatic
Tragopogon pratensis; Asteraceae; goat's-beard	Eu	R	inulin, mannitol, phytosterols	TEM	diet for diabetes; liver and gall disorders
Trifolium pratense; Fabaceae; red clover	Eu As	FL	flavonoids, salicylic acid; isoflavones	TEM	estrogenic; skin conditions
Trigonella foenum-graecum; Fabaceae; fenugreek	Eu A,As	S	mucilage; saponins; furostanol glycosides	TAM TEM	digestive tonic; demulcent; expectorant; food uses
Trillium erectum; Trilliaceae/ Liliaceae; birthroot	NAm	RH	saponins, tannins	TNAM	menstrual disorders; child birth
Tropaeolum majus; Tropaeolaceae; nasturtium	SAm	F	benzyl-glucosinolates (glucotropaeolin, benzyl-isothiocyanate)	TSAM TEM	antibiotic; diuretic; cholagogue
Tsuga canadensis; Pinaceae; Canadian /eastern hemlock	NAm	O, C	O: mainly bornylacetate; C: tannins	TNAM	catarrh; expectorant
Turnera diffusa; Turneraceae; damiana	CAm	F	cyanogenic glycoside (tetraphyllin B); arbutin; essential oil	TSAM TNAM	general tonic; traditional aphrodisiac
Tussilago farfara; Asteraceae; coltsfoot	Eu As A	F	mucilage; tussilagone (a sesquiterpene); pyrrolizidine alkaloids!	TEM	expectorant; antitussive
Tylophora asthmatica; Asclepiadaceae /Apocynaceae; *asmatica*, Indian lobelia	As	F	tylophorine and other indole alkaloids; flavonoids, tannins	TIM	asthma treatment; anti-inflammatory; cytotoxic!
Typha angustifolia; Typhaceae; bulrush	Eu As	pol-len	isorhamnetin and other flavonoids; phytosterols	TCM	skin conditions; haemostyptic, tonsillitis treatment
Typhonium giganteum; Araceae; *bai fu zi*	As	RH	cerebrosides	TCM	sedative, headache, post stroke syndroms
Ulmus rubra; Ulmaceae; slippery elm, red elm	NAm	C	mucilage; also tannins, phytosterols	TNAM	demulcent; emmolient; used to treat inflammation of mucosa
Uncaria gambir; Rubiaceae; pale catechu	As	F, H ex-tract	tannins, alkaloids (extract is known as pale catechu)	TIM	astringent, used to treat diarrhoea, dysentery and excessive mucous discharges
Uncaria tomentosa; Rubiaceae; cat's claw	CAm SAm	C	monoterpene indole alkaloids; saponins	TSAM	immune stimulant; used against numerous ailments
Urginea maritima; Hyacinthaceae; squill, sea onion	Eu	bulb	cardiac glycosides (bufa-dienolides); flavonoids	TEM MM	heart tonic; diuretic; expectorant
Urtica dioica, U. urens; Urticaceae; stinging nettle	Eu As	H, R	F: minerals, silicic acid; amines; R: phenolic compounds; sterols	TEM	F: anti-rheumatic; R: urologica, treatment of benign prostate hyperplasia
Usnea barbata; Parmeliaceae; beard moss, hanging lichen	Eu A NAm	li-chen	lichenic acid, usnic acid (lichenolic acids)	TEM	demulcent and expectorant (cough and throat irritation)
Vaccinium myrtillus; Ericaceae; bilberry, blueberry	Eu As NAm	FR, F	catechol tannins, proanthocyanidins; anthocyanins; flavonoids	TEM TNAM	anti-diarrhoeal
Vaccinium oxycoccos; Ericaceae; cranberry, small cranberry	Eu As NAm	FR	arbutin, organic acids; anthocyanins; vitamin C	TEM TNAM	urinary tract infections
Valeriana officinalis; Valerianaceae /Caprifoliaceae; valerian	Eu As	RH, R	valepotriates (valtrate, acevaltrate); sesquiterpenoids	TEM	sedative; tranquillizer; included in numerous herbal sedative preparations
Vanilla planifolia; Orchidaceae; vanilla orchid	CAm	FR	vanilline (derives from vanilloside after hydrolysis)	TSAM TEM	aromatic, spice
Veratrum album (*V. viride*); Melanthiaceae/ Liliaceae; white hellebore	Eu As NAm	RH	protoveratrine A, B, germerine and other steroid alkaloids	TNAM ExM	alkaloids affect Na^+ channels; some are mutagenic; hypotonic; emetic; analgesic, antirheumatic, insecticidal; very toxic!

Verbascum phlomoides, *V. densiflorum* and other species; Scrophulariaceae; mullein	Eu As NA	FL	triterpene saponins; mucilage; iridoid glycosides; flavonoids	TEM	respiratory catarrhs; diuretic; numerous traditional uses; wounds and skin disorders
Verbena hastata; Verbenaceae; American vervain	NAm	H	iridoid glycosides	TNAM	colds; catarrhs of the respiratory tract
Verbena officinalis; Verbenaceae; vervain	Eu	H	iridoid glycosides; caffeic acid derivatives	TEM	diuretic, expectorant; bitter tonic
Veronica officinalis; Scrophulariaceae; speedwell	Eu As NAm	H	iridoid glycosides, flavonoids, organic acids, tannins, triterpenoids	TEM TNAM	traditional expectorant; general tonic; wound healing
Veronicastrum virginicum; Scrophulariaceae; black root	NAm	R	essential oil; leptandrine; organic acids; iridoids?	TNAM	laxative, to treat chronic constipation; liver ailments; bladder inflammation
Vetiveria zizanioides; Poaceae; vetiver	As	R, O	vetivone and other sesquiterpenes	TIM	perfume; insecticidal
Viburnum opulus; Caprifoliaceae; guelder rose, crampbark	Eu	C	flavonoids; terpenoids; organic acids; sitosterols	TEM	menstrual disorders; numerous traditional uses, e.g. the prevention of miscarriage
Viburnum prunifolium; Caprifoliaceae; black haw	NAm	C	flavonoids; terpenoids; organic acids; sitosterols	TNAM	spasmolytic; menstrual disorders; symptoms of menopause
Vinca minor; *V. major*; Apocynaceae; periwinkle	Eu	H	monoterpene indole alkaloids (vincamine)	TEM MM	cerebral circulation; pure alkaloid (vincamine) mainly used; side-effects!
Vincetoxicum hirundinaria; Asclepiadaceae; white swallow wort	Eu As	R, RH	steroid saponins ("vincetoxin")	TEM	diuretic, emetic
Viola odorata; Violaceae sweet violet	Eu	FL	mucilage, flavonoids and saponins	TEM	used as expectorant and as ingredient of skin creams
Viola tricolor; Violaceae; pansy	Eu As	H	methylsalicylic acid; flavonoids; anthocyanins tannins; mucilage	TEM	supportive treatment of various skin conditions; numerous traditional uses
Virola calophylloidea, *V. sebifera*; Myristicaceae	SAm	C, S	myristin; *N,N*-dimethyl-tryptamine, and tryptamine derivatives	TSAM	central stimulant (hallucinogen); dyspepsia; wounds
Viscum album; Viscaceae; mistletoe	Eu	H	lectins; viscotoxins	TEM MM	cytostatic; non-specific immune stimulation (extracts, by injection only)
Viscum capense; Viscaceae; Cape mistletoe	A	H	flavonoids	TAM	tonic; health tea
Vitellaria paradoxa; Sapotaceae; shea butter tree	A	S	triglycerides; essential oil	TAM	source of "shea butter"; used for margarine and ointments; substitute for cacao butter
Vitex agnus-castus; Verbenaceae; chaste tree	Eu As	FR	iridoid glycosides; flavonoids; essential oil	TEM	gynaecological; menstrual disorders; traditional anaphrodisiac
Vitex negundo; Verbenaceae; *nirgundi*, *karinochi*, Chinese chaste tree	As EAs	F, R	iridoids, flavonoids	TIM	memory tonic; anti-inflammatory; anti-rheumatic; low back pain
Vitis vinifera; Vitaceae; grape vine	Eu	S	proanthocyanidins, often called pycnogenols	TEM MM	antioxidant (free-radical scavenger)
Voacanga africana; *V. thouarsii*; Apocynaceae	A	S	tabersonine (indole alkaloid)	MM	source of tabersonine; for semisynthesis of vincamine
Warburgia salutaris; Canellaceae; pepperbark tree	A	C, F	drimane sesquiterpenoids (warburganal, polygodial)	TAM	antibiotic; general tonic
Warburgia ugandensis; Canellaceae; east African pepperbark	A	C	drimane sesquiterpenoids	TAM	aromatic bitter; emetic
Wedelia calendulacea; Asteraceae	As	H	coumestans	TIM	liver protectant
Withania somnifera; Solanaceae; winter cherry, *ashwagandha*	A Eu As	R, F	numerous steroids (withanolides), alkaloids (withasomnine),	TIM TAM	roots: sedative, adaptogenic tonic; leaves: wound healing

Woodfordia fruticosa; Lythraceae; woodfordia, *dhathaki*	As EAs	FL, R	tragacanth-like gum and dye	TIM	natural fermenting agent; "balancing herb"
Xysmalobium undulatum; Asclepiadaceae/Apocynaceae; uzara	SA	R	cardiac glycosides (uzarin)	TAM	anti-diarrhoeal; spasmolytic; topically for wound treatment
Yucca filamentosa; Agavaceae; yucca	NAm CAm	H	steroid saponins	TNAM MM	laxative; fibre plant; source of steroids for production of steroid hormones
Zanthoxylum piperitum; Rutaceae	EAs	FR	ess. oil, citral, cineol, pungent acid amides	TCM	stomachic; against worms; spice
Zea mays; Poaceae; corn, maize (corn silk; *yu mi shu*)	CAm	FL pollen	corn silk / maize silk: essential oil, saponins, flavonoids; pollen: sterols	TSAM TCM TEM	diuretic, oedema treatment (corn silk); urological (pollen); appetite stimulant (raw pollen)
Zingiber officinale; Zingiberaceae; ginger, *sonth*	As	RH	diterpene lactones (galanolactone); sesquiterpenes (zingiberene, curcumene); pungent gingerols	TIM TEM	anti-emetic (post-operative nausea, travel sickness); carminative; cholagogue; antispasmodic; important spice
Ziziphus jujuba; Rhamnaceae; Chinese date	Eu As EAs	FR, S	peptide alkaloids; triterpenoid saponins; flavonoids, mucilage	TCM	fruit: anti-allergic, anti-catarrh, tonic; seed: sedative
Ziziphus mucronata; Rhamnaceae; buffalo thorn	A	F, R, C	peptide alkaloids	TAM	treatment of boils and wounds; allegedly sedative
Ziziphus spinosa; Rhamnaceae; *suan zau ren*	As EAs	S	peptide alkaloids	TCM	insomnia; nervous conditions

GLOSSARY OF CHEMICAL, MEDICAL AND PHARMACEUTICAL TERMS

For more detailed explanations see Introductory Chapters (pages 8-26), the section on Secondary Metabolites (pages 371-394) and the section on Health Disorders (pages 351-370)

Abortifacient – a substance that causes abortion

Absorption – uptake of a substance through the skin or a mucous membrane (see resorption)

ACE – angiotensin converting enzyme; important target for the treatment of cardiac insufficiency

Acetylcholine – a neurotransmitter that binds to nicotinic (nACh-R) or muscarinic (mACh-R) receptors

Acetylcholine esterase inhibitor – a substance that inhibits acetylcholine esterase (AChE) and thus the breakdown of acetylcholine to acetate and choline

Acne – chronic skin condition resulting from the inflammation of sebaceous glands and hair follicles

Acute – a symptom or condition that appears suddenly (and lasts for a short period)

Adaptogen – a substance with a non-specific action that causes improved resistance to physical and mental stress

Adaptogenic tonic – see adaptogen

Addiction – physical or psychological dependence on a substance

Additive – a substance that is added to a mixture (typically for taste, colour or texture)

Adenoma – an abnormal growth of glandular epithelial tissue

Adenylylcyclase – enzyme of signal transduction; catalyses the formation of the second messenger cAMP from ATP

Adjuvant – a substance added to a mixture to modify the activity of the active ingredient in a predictable way

Adrenalin – the hormone, that binds to adrenergic receptors; causes the "fight or flight" response

Adrenergic (sympathomimetic) – a substance that binds to adrenergic neuroreceptors and produces an effect similar to the normal impulses (caused by adrenaline, noradrenaline) of the sympathetic nervous system; antagonists are sympatholytics

Aesthenia – diminishing strength and energy

Aetheroleum – essential (volatile) oil

Aglycone – the non-sugar part of a glycoside (after removal of the sugar part)

Agonist – substance that binds and activates a membrane receptor

AIDS – acquired immunodeficiency syndrome, a condition (weakened immune system) caused by HIV (a retrovirus)

Alcoholic extract – soluble fraction of plant material obtained after extraction with ethanol

Alkaloid – a chemical substance containing nitrogen as part of a heterocyclic ring structure; often highly active

Alkylation – reactive secondary metabolites can form covalent bonds with DNA and proteins

Allergen – a substance that triggers an allergic reaction

Allergy – a hypersensitivity to some substance (often pollen) that causes itching and swelling

Allopathy – a medicine system using substances that cause an effect different to those caused by the condition under treatment

Alopecia – loss of hair

Alzheimer's disease – see dementia

Amarum – a bitter substance that stimulates the secretion of digestive juices

Amino acid – chemical substances that form the building blocks of proteins ("proteinogenic amino acids")

Amoebiasis – a (sub-)tropical protozoan infection with *Entamoeba histolytica*

Amoebicidal – a substance that kills amoeba

Anaemia – reduced number of red blood cells in the blood

Anaesthetic – a substance that causes localised or general loss of sensation

Analeptic – a substance that stimulates the central nervous system

Analgesic – a substance that relieves pain

Anaphrodisiac – a substance that reduces sexual desire

Anaphylactic shock – a severe, life-threatening form of a general allergic reaction

Anemia (see anaemia)

Angina pectoris – severe pain in the chest

Antagonist – inhibitor at membrane receptors; blocks the activity of an endogenous ligand

Anthelmintic – a substance that kills or expels intestinal worms

Anthraquinones – secondary metabolites with an anthracene skeleton; anthrones show strong laxative effects

Anthroposophic – a philosophy that links health to internal life force and energy

Antiarrhythmic – a substance that counteracts irregular heart beat

Antiasthmatic – a substance that alleviates the spasms of asthma

Antibacterial – a substance that kills or inhibits the growth of bacteria

Antibiotic – a substance that kills or inhibits the growth of micro-organisms

Anticholinergic – a substance that blocks the parasympathetic nerves

Anticoagulant – a substance that prevents blood from clotting

Anticonvulsant – a substance that prevents or relieves convulsions

Antidepressant – a substance that alleviates depression

Antidiabetic – a substance that prevents or alleviates diabetes

Antidiuretic – a substance that prevent or slows urine formation

Antidote – a substance that counteracts poisoning

Antiemetic – a substance that prevents vomiting

Antifungal – a substance that kills or inhibits the growth of fungi

Antihistamine – a substance that improves allergic symptoms by blocking the action of histamine

Antihydrotic – a substance that reduces perspiration

Antihypertensive – a substance that reduces high blood pressure

Anti-inflammatory – a substance that causes symptomatic relief of inflammation

Antimicrobial – a substance that kills or inhibits the growth of micro-organisms

Antimitotic – a substance that prevents or inhibits cell division (mitosis)

Antimycotic – see antifungal

Antioedema – a substance that prevents swelling

Antioxidant – a substance that is able to protect cells or counteract the damage caused by oxidation and oxygen free radicals

Antiparasitic – a substance that kills parasites

Antiphlogistic – a substance that prevents inflammation

Antipruritic – a substance that alleviates or prevents itching

Antipyretic – a substance that alleviates fever

Antirheumatic – a substance that relieves the symptoms of rheumatism

Antiseptic – a substance that stops or inhibits infection

Antispasmodic – a substance that reduces muscular spasms and tension

Antitumour – a substance that counteracts tumour formation or tumour growth

Antitussive – a substance that reduces the urge to cough

Anuria – the inability to urinate

Anxiety – symptoms of fear not caused by any danger or threat

Aperitif – a drink that stimulates the appetite

Aphrodisiac – a substance that increases sexual desire

Apnea – cessation of breathing

Aqueous extract – soluble fraction of plant material obtained after extraction with water

Aromatherapy – the medicinal use of aroma substances by inhalation, bath, massage etc.

Aromatic bitter – a partly volatile substance that promotes appetite and digestion by stimulating the secretion of digestive juices

Arrhythmia – abnormal heart rhythm

Arteriosclerosis – accumulation of fatty deposits in the blood vessels causing them to narrow and harden, resulting in heart disease or strokes

Arthritis – inflammation of joints

Asthenia – see aesthenia

Astringent – a substance (often tannins) that reacts with proteins in wounds, on the surface of cells or membranes, resulting in a protective layer and causing contraction

Ataxia – loss of muscle coordination

Atherosclerosis – changes of arterial walls that lead to arteriosclerosis

Autonomic nervous system – that part of the nervous system that regulates the heart muscle, smooth muscles and gland; it comprises the sympathetic nervous system and the parasympathetic nervous system

Ayurvedic medicine – traditional Indian medicine

Bacteriostatic – a substance that prevents the multiplication of bacteria

Bacterium – all bacteria consist of a single cell surrounded by a cell wall; DNA is circular; bacteria do not have internal membrane systems

Benign – not cancerous, not malignant

Benign prostatic hyperplasia – a non-cancerous enlargement of the prostate that may interfere with urination

Benzodiazepine receptor – binding site for benzodiazepines at the GABA receptor; target for several sedatives and tranquillisers

Beta-carotene – an orange plant pigment that is converted in the body to vitamin A

Bile – a bitter fluid excreted by the liver via the gall bladder that helps to digest fats

Biliary dyskinesia – inability to secrete bile

Biomembrane – permeation barrier around every cell or cellular compartments consisting of phospholipids, cholesterol and membrane proteins

Bitter – a substance that stimulates the secretion of digestive juices

Bitter tonic – a substance that promotes appetite and digestion by stimulating the secretion of digestive juices

Bitterness value – that concentration at which a bitter substance can still be tasted (bitterness value of 100 000: when one part of the substance in 100 000 parts of water still tastes bitter)

Blood brain barrier – blood vessels of the brain are covered with especially tight endothelial tissues, so that only few substances can enter the brain

Blood purifier – a substance that causes the removal of impurities from the bloodstream (outdated term)

Bradycardia – pulse under 60 beats per minute

Bronchitis – inflammation of the mucous membranes of the bronchial tubes

Bronchodilatory – a substance that reduces bronchial spasm

Bruise – a non-bleeding injury to the skin

Bulbus – dried bulbs

Cachexia – weight loss due to chronic illness or prolonged emotional stress

Cancer – various types of malignant cells that multiply out of control

Candidiasis – infection with the fungus *Candida albicans*

Carcinogen – a substance that causes cancer

Carcinoma – malignant growth of epithelial cells

Cardiac glycosides – a steroidal glycoside that increases the strength or rhythm of the heart beat

Cardiotonic – a substance that has a strengthening or regulating effect on the heart

Carminative – a substance that reduces flatulence

Catarrh – inflammation of mucous membranes

Catechol-O-methyltransferase (COMT) – enzyme which inactivates neurotransmitters with a phenolics OH group (dopamine, nordrenaline, serotonin) through methylation

Cathartic – laxative, purgative

Chemotherapy – treatment of cancer with chemical substances

Cholagogue – a substance that stimulates the flow of bile from the gall bladder; distinction between cholekinetics and choleretics

Cholekinetic – a substance that stimulates the release of bile by contraction of the gall bladder and bile ducts

Choleretic – a substance that stimulates the liver to produce bile

Cholesterol – the most common steroid (fat-like material) found in the human body; important for membrane fluidity and as a precursor for steroid hormones; high cholesterol levels are associated with an increased risk of coronary diseases

Chronic ailment – a condition that extends over a long period

Clinical trials – the development of new drugs consists of 4 phases: 1. preclinical studies, 2. clinical studies phase I, 3. clinical studies phase II and 4. clinical studies phase III

CNS – central nervous system

Colic – abdominal pains, caused by muscle contraction of an abdominal organ, accompanied by nausea, vomiting and perspiration

Commission E – recommendations of a group of German experts regarding the usefulness and efficacy of plant drugs

Condyloma – warts of the genital-anal region (caused by viruses of the Papilloma group)

Conjunctiva – the mucous membranes of the eyes and eyelids

Constipation – lack of bowel movement leading to prolonged passage times of faeces

Corpus luteum – endocrine body in the ovary that secretes oestrogen and progesteron

Cortex – dried bark

Crohn's disease – chronic inflammation of the intestinal tract

Cyanogenic glycosides – secondary metabolites that are activated upon wounding, releasing the toxic HCN

Cyclooxygenase – key enzyme of prostaglandin biosynthesis

Cystitis – inflammation of the bladder

Cytostatic – a substance that slows down cell growth and multiplication

Cytotoxic – a substance that is toxic to cells

Decoction – watery extract obtained by boiling

Decongestant – a substance that removes mucus from the respiratory system and opens the air passages so that breathing becomes easier

Dementia – loss of individually acquired mental skills; Alzheimer is a severe form of dementia

Demulcent – a substance that soothes the mucous membranes (sometimes the term is restricted to internal membranes; see emollient)

Depression – psychic disturbance, often associated with low concentrations of dopamine and noradrenaline

Dermatitis – inflammation of skin

Detergent – a substance capable of dissolving lipids

Diabetes mellitus – abnormally high blood sugar levels caused by lack of insulin

Diaphoretic – a substance that increases sweating

Diarrhoea – abnormally frequent discharge of watery stool (more than 3 times per day)

Dietary supplement – a substance that is marketed and sold as a food item but not as a therapeutic agent

Diuresis – discharge of urine

Diuretic – a substance that increases the volume of urine

DNA – desoxyribonucleic acid, the biomolecules in cells that store genetic information

Doctrine of signatures – old concept of traditional medicine assuming that the form or colour of a plant could indicate its medicinal application

Dropsy – outdated term for oedema

Drug-resistance – having a (often acquired) resistance against a drug, by developing modified targets, increasing the degradation of an active compound or by exporting it out of a cell

Dysentery – inflammation of the colon; often caused by bacteria (shigellosis) or viruses, accompanied by pain and severe diarrhoea

Dysmenorrhoea – abnormal or painful menstruation

Dyspepsia – indigestion

Dysuria – painful urination

Eczema – inflammation of the skin with redness, itching and oozing vesicular lesions

Elixir – a nonspecific term generally applied to a liquid alcoholic preparation, emulsion or suspension

Emesis – vomiting

Emetic – a substance causing vomiting

Emollient – a substance that soothes and softens the skin

Endoplasmic reticulum – endomembrane system, in which many proteins are modified posttranslationally

Endorphins – peptides made by the body with similar actions as morphine

Enteritis – inflammation of the intestines

Enzyme – protein that catalyses a chemical reaction, e.g. the hydrolysis of acetylcholine

Epilepsy – chronic brain condition characterised by seizures and loss of consciousness

Ergot – a fungus (*Claviceps purpurea*) that infects grasses (especially rye) and produces pharmacologically active alkaloids

Ergotism – poisoning by eating ergot-infected grain

Essential oil (= volatile oil) – mixture of volatile terpenoids responsible for the taste and smell of many plants, especially spices

Estrogen (oestrogen) – a female sex hormone

Expectorant – a substance that increases mucous secretion or its expulsion from the lungs; distinction between secretolytics and secretomotorics

Extract – a concentrated preparation (semiliquid, solid or dry powder) of the soluble fraction of plant material

Familial Mediterranean fever – a condition with recurrent attacks of fever and pain

Febrifuge – a substance that reduces fever

Febrile – relating to fever

Flatulence – accumulation of excessive gas in the intestines

Flos – dried flowers

Flu – see influenza

Fluidextract – an alcohol-water extract concentrated to the point where 1 ml equals 1 g of the original herb

Fluor albus (= leukorrhoea) – white or yellow vaginal discharge

Folium – dried leaves

Free radical – an unstable form of oxygen molecule that can damage cells

Fructus – dried fruits

Galactogogue – a substance that stimulates milk secretion

Galenical preparations – preparations of herbal drugs, such as tinctures, lotions, extracts etc. (often interpreted as referring to non-surgical medicine)

Gallstone – a solid or semi-solid body in the gall bladder or bile duct

Gargle – a fluid used as throat wash

Gastritis – inflammation of the stomach

Gastroenteritis – inflammation of the gastrointestinal tract, associated with nausea, pain and vomiting

Gingivitis – inflammation of the gums

Glaucoma – an eye disease characterised by increased intraocular pressure

Glucosinolates – secondary metabolites that are activated upon wounding, releasing active isothiocyanates

Glycoside – a chemical substance that yields at least one simple sugar upon hydrolysis

GMP – good manufacturing practice; a manufacturing system that complies with the highest standards of hygiene, safety and quality

Gout – increased uric acid level in blood and sporadic episodes of acute arthritis

Granulation – new cell layers (in the form of small granular prominences) over capillaries and collagen in a wound

GRAS – abbreviation for "generally regarded as safe", the status given to foods and herbal medicines by the American Food and Drug Administration (FDA)

Gravel – small concretions in the bladder or kidney

Haematuria – blood in the urine

Haemolysis – the disruption of red blood cells in blood

Haemorrhage – profuse bleeding

Haemorrhagic nephritis – blood in the urine

Haemorrhoids (= piles) – painful and swollen anal veins

Haemostatic – a substance that reduces or stops bleeding

Haemostyptic – a substance that reduces or stops bleeding

Hallucinogen – a substance that induces the perception of objects that are not actually present

Heartburn – uncomfortable burning sensation in the chest, rising towards the throat (due to the return of stomach acid into the oesophagus)

Hepatitis – inflammation of the liver

Hepatotoxic – toxic to the liver

Herbalist – a person with experience in herbal medicine and / or herbal therapy

Herpes simplex – localised infection on the lips or genitalia caused by the herpes virus

HIV – human immunodeficiency virus that causes AIDS

Hodgkin's disease – a cancer of lymph cells that originates in one lymph node and later spreads to other organs

Homoeopathy – a medicine system using minute amounts of substances that cause in a healthy person the same effect (symptoms) to those caused by the condition under treatment

Hormone – a substance released into the bloodstream that affects organs systems elsewhere in the body

HPLC – high performance liquid chromatography (a technique used to analyse chemical compounds and extracts)

Hydrophilic – a substance soluble in water

Hyperaemia (hyperemia) – abnormal blood accumulation in a localised part of the body

Hyperlipidemia – characterised by enhanced lipid values in the blood; triglycerides (>160 mg/100 ml) and cholesterol (>260 mg/100 ml)

Hypertension – high blood pressure (>140/90 mm Hg)

Hypertonic solution – abnormally high salt levels having a higher osmotic pressure than blood or another body fluid

Hypertrophy – abnormal increase in size of an organ (cell numbers remain constant)

Hypnotic – a substance that induces sleep

Hypoglycaemic – abnormally low level of blood sugar

Hypothermia – low body temperature

Hypotonia, hypotension – low blood pressure with values under 105/60 mm Hg

Icterus – jaundice

Immune stimulant – a substance capable of improving the immune system

In vitro – in the laboratory or test tube

In vivo – in a living animal or human

Inflammation – localised swelling, redness and pain as a result of an infection or injury

Influenza (flu) – an acute and highly contagious disease caused by viruses that infect mucous membranes of the respiratory tract

Inotropic – a substance that affects the contraction of muscles

Insomnia – inability to sleep

Insulin – a hormone made in the pancreas that controls the level of glucose in the blood

Intercalation – planar and lipophilic compounds can intercalate between base stacks of DNA; this leads to frame shift mutations

Ion channel – membrane protein that can form water-containing pores so that mineral ions can enter or leave cells

Iridoids – a subgroup of monoterpenoids, with iridoid glycosides, secoiridoids and secologanin

Irrigation therapy – rinsing the urinary tract by means of a diuretic substance

Itch (= pruritis) – skin irritation

Jaundice – yellow coloration of skins and mucosa; caused by abnormally high level of bile pigments in the blood

Kampo-medicine – traditional Japanese medicine

Lactation – production and secretion of milk by female mammary glands

Laxative – a substance that loosens the bowels

Leukopenia – low white blood cell count

Leukorrhea – vaginal discharge of white or yellowish fluid

Ligand – substance that binds to a receptor

Lignum – dried wood

Liniment – ointment for topical application

Lipid – a substance soluble in non-polar solvents; insoluble in water

Lipid-lowering – a substance that lowers triglyceride or cholesterol levels in blood

Lipophilic – a substance soluble in oil or a non-polar solvent

Maceration – preparation made by soaking plant material

Malaria – a parasitic disease caused by *Plasmodium* parasites; it is transmitted by mosquitoes

Malignant – cancerous

MAO inhibitor – inhibitor of monoamine oxidase that degrades the neurotransmitters adrenaline, noradrenaline, dopamine and serotonin

Mastitis – inflammation of the breast

Mastodynia – pain in the swollen female breasts

Materia medica – the various materials (from plants, animals or minerals) that are used in medicine (healing)

Melanoma – a tumour of skin and mucosa arising from the pigment producing cells

Menopause – permanent cessation of menstruation caused by decreased production of female sex hormones

Menorrhagia – abnormally severe menstruation

Microtubules – linear tubular structures of higher cells, formed from tubulin dimers; essential for cell division and vesicular transport processes

Micturition – urination

Migraine – recurrent condition of severe pain in the head accompanied by other symptoms (nausea, visual disturbance)

Mineralocorticoid – the steroid of the adrenal cortex (aldosteron) that regulates salt metabolism

Mitochondria – important compartment of eukaryotic cells; site of the Krebs cycle and respiration chain (production of ATP); mitochondria have their own DNA, replication, transcription and ribosomes

Mitosis – cell division

Monoamine oxidase (MAO) – the enzyme that catalyses the removal of amine groups (e.g. dopamine, noradrenaline)

Mucilage – solution of viscous (slimy) substances (usually polysaccharides) that form a protective layer over inflamed mucosal tissues

Mucolytic – a substance that dissolves mucous, e.g. in the bronchia

Mucosa – mucous tissue layer on the inside of the respiratory or gastrointestinal tract

Mucus – clear, viscose secretion formed by mucous membranes

Multiple sclerosis – disorder of the central nervous system caused by a destruction of the myelin around axons in the brain and spinal cord that lead to various neurological symptoms

Mutagenic – a substance that induces genetic mutations

Myalgia – non-localised muscle pain

Mydriasis – dilation of the pupil of the eye

Na^+, K^+-ATPase – important ion pump of animal cells; pumps Na^+ out of the cell and K^+ into the cell; is inhibited by cardiac glycosides

Narcotic – a substance that produces insensibility or stupor, combined with a sense of well-being

Naturopathy – a holistic system of healing that emphasises the body's inherent power of regaining balance and harmony

Necrosis – death of cells or tissue

Nephritis – kidney inflammation

Neuralgia – severe pain along nerve ends

Neuritis – inflammation of nerves

Neurotransmitter – signal compounds in synapses of neurones that help to convert an electric signal into a chemical response; important neurotransmitters are acetylcholine, noradrenaline, adrenaline, dopamine, serotonin, histamine, glycine, GABA, glutamate, endorphins and several other peptides

Neurovesicle – small vesicles in the presynapse, that are filled with neurotransmitters

Nonprotein amino acids – secondary metabolites, that are analogues of proteinogenic amino acids; if incorporated into proteins, the latter are usually inactivated

Nutritional supplement – a preparation that supplies additional nutrients or active compounds to the body that may not be obtained by the normal diet

Nutritive – nourishing, nutritious

Nycturia – nightly urge to urinate

Oedema (edema) – swelling of tissue due to an accumulation of fluids, often caused by kidney or heart failure

Ointment – semisolid medicinal preparation that is used topically

Oleum – non-volatile oil; fat

Ophthalmic – relating to the eye

Oral – by mouth

Organic (bio-organic) – terms used for products that are grown and processed without the use of artificial chemicals (wild-harvested materials usually qualify as organic).

Osteoporosis – a reduction in bone mass, resulting in fractures

OTC – over the counter, a drug that is sold without prescription

Otitis – inflammation of the ear

Oxytocic – speeding up of parturition

Oxytocin – a hormone of the pituitary gland that stimulates lactation and induces labour

Parasympathetic nervous system – that part of the nervous system that slows the heart rate, increases intestinal (smooth muscle) and gland activity, and relaxes sphincter muscles

Parenteral administration – administration of medicinal substances by injection (i.v.= intravenous; i.m. = intramuscular; s.c. = subcutaneous) or intravenous drip

Parkinson's disease – a progressive neurological disease (caused by a degeneration of the *Substantia nigra* and a reduction of dopamine concentrations) marked by lack of muscular coordination and mental deterioration

Parkinsonism – one of several neurological disorders manifesting in unnaturally slow or rigid movements

Pathogen – a micro-organism that may cause disease

Periodontitis – inflammation of the area around a tooth

Peristalsis – waves of involuntary contraction in the digestive system

Pharmacodynamics – the study of how medicinal substances work in the body; e.g. whether they bind to a receptor

Pharmacognosy – the study of herbal drugs, their identification, properties and uses.

Pharmacokinetics – the study of how medicinal substances are absorbed, moved, distributed, metabolised and excreted

Pharmacology – the study of the nature, properties and uses of drugs (see pharmacodynamics, pharmacokinetics); includes the study of endogenous active compounds

Pharmacopoeia (Pharmacopeia) – an official and authoritative book or publication listing all the various drugs that may be used

Phlegm – catarrhal secretion or sputum

Phorbolester – diterpenes from Euphorbiaceae and Thymelaeaceae, resembling diacylglycerol in structure and therefore activate protein kinase C

Phosphodiesterase – enzyme of signal transduction; inactivates cAMP or cGMP

Phospholipase C – enzyme of signal transduction; splits inositol phosphates to IP3 and diacylglycerol (DAG)

Phospholipids –phosphorylated lipids, that are building blocks of cell membranes

Photosensitisation – increasing sensitivity to sunlight

Phytotherapy – application of plant drugs or products derived from them to cure diseases or to relieve their symptoms

Placebo – drug preparation without active ingredients, that cannot be distinguished from the original drug; used in placebo-controlled clinical trials

Placebo effect – an improvement of a health condition that cannot be ascribed to the treatment used

PMS – premenstrual syndrome; can occur a few days before menstruation with symptoms of fear, irritability, changing mood, insomnia, headache, swollen breasts, abdominal pain and oedema

Poultice – a semisolid mass of plant materials in oil or water applied to the skin

Prescription drug – a drug that requires a prescription from a physician

Prodrug – a substance that is converted to its active form within the body

Prophylactic – a substance that prevents disease

Prostaglandins – a group of physiologically active substances within tissues that cause stimulation of muscles and numerous other metabolic effects; important for inflammation processes

Prostate – a gland at the base of the male bladder that secretes a fluid that forms part of semen (stimulating sperm motility)

Prostatitis – bacterial infection of the prostate (also see benign prostate hyperplasia)

Protein kinases – enzymes that phosphorylate other proteins; important are protein kinase A and protein kinase C

Pruritis – itching

Psoriasis – inherited skin condition caused by an enhanced growth of dermal cells resulting in the production of dandruffs

Psychotropic – a substance that affects the mind or mood

Pyretic – a substance that induces fever

Radix – dried roots

Receptor – protein (often a membrane protein) that has a binding site for another molecule ("ligand"); important for signal transduction in cells

Relaxant – a substance that reduces tension

Replication – duplication of DNA prior to cell division

Resin – amorphous brittle substance resulting from a plant secretion

Resina – resin

Resorption – uptake of a substance through the skin or a mucous membrane (see absorption)

Re-uptake inhibitor – inhibitors of transporters for the neurotransmitters dopamine, noradrenaline and serotonine at presynaptic and vesicle membrane

Rheumatism – general term referring to painful joints

Rhinitis – inflammation of the mucosa of the nose

Rhizoma – dried rhizomes; underground stem

Ringworm – a fungal infection of skin

Roborant – tonic or strengthening mixture

Rubefacient – a substance (counter-irritant) that causes reddening of skin

Saluretic – a substance that increases the concentration of salts in urine

Saponins – glycosides of triterpenes and steroids; the aglycone is usually lipophilic, whereas the saponins are amphiphilic with detergent properties; distinguished are monodesmosidic saponins with one sugar chain and bidesmosidic saponins with two sugar chains

Saturated fats – fats with fatty acids without double bonds (animal fats, coconut oil etc.)

Scar tissue – new cell growth following injury

Secondary metabolite – chemical substances of plants (usually of low molecular weight) with a high structural diversity that are used as defence or signal compounds by the plants producing them. Several secondary metabolites have a restricted occurrence in the plant kingdom. In contrast, primary metabolites are essential and present in all plants.

Secretolytic – a substance that leads to a better solubilisation of mucus and favours its discharge

Sedative – a substance that calms down the nerves

Semen – seeds

Sesquiterpene lactones – secondary metabolites with an exocyclic methylene group that can bind to SH-groups of proteins

SH-group – functional group in proteins, which can form disulphide bonds with other proteins

Simple – term used for a herb that is used on its own

Sitz-bath – an immersion bath used for medicinal purposes

Soporific – a substance that induces or promotes sleep

Spasm – involuntary contraction of muscles

Special extract – extract that is enriched in the active principle whereas unwanted compounds have been discarded

Spondylitis – inflammation of vertebrae

Steam distillation – a method of selectively extracting volatile compounds oil from plant material by boiling or steaming in water, followed by condensation

Stomachic – a substance that promotes appetite and digestion

Styptic – a substance applied externally to stop bleeding by contracting the tissue and blood vessels

Sudorific – a substance that causes sweating

Sympathetic nervous system – that part of the nervous system that accelerates the heart rate, constricts blood vessels and raises blood pressure.

Synapse – neurons are connected with other neurons or target tissues via synapses where the action potential is converted into a chemical signal (neurotransmitter)

Synergistic – the phenomenon that the combined effect of two or more substances is greater than the sum of their individual effects

Syrup – a sugary solution intended for oral administration (such as cough syrups)

Tachycardia – pulse over 100 beats per minute

Tannins –secondary metabolites with several phenolic OH-groups, that can form hydrogen- and ionic bonds with proteins, thereby altering their conformation; distinguished are gallotannins and catechol tannins, which derive from catechin or epicatechin

Target – any component of the human body that can be affected by a drug

TCM – traditional Chinese medicine; oldest therapeutic system of mankind, which is still in use and esteemed

Tea – an infusion made by pouring boiling water over a measured quantity of dried plant material and leaving it for a while to steep

Teratogenic – a substance that causes abnormal growth in an embryo

Terpenoids – a very large group of secondary metabolites, including monoterpenes (with 10 carbons), sesquiterpenes (15 C), diterpenes (20 C), triterpenes (30 C), steroids (27 or less), tetraterpenes (40 C)

Testosterone – the male sex hormone

Thrush – a fungal infection of mucous membranes marked by white patches (see *Candida*)

Tincture – an extract of medicinal plant material made with alcohol (ethanol) or a mixture of alcohol and water

Tinnitus – noise in the ear

Tisane – a herbal tea (often made from flowers) that is not as strong as an infusion

Tonic – a substance that maintains or restores health and vigour (usually taken over a lengthy period)

Topical application – external application (on the skin)

Toxicology – science that studies toxins and their effects in humans or animals

Transcription – process of copying the base sequence of a gene into mRNA

Translation – process of copying the base sequence of mRNA into the amino acid sequence of proteins in the ribosome

Transporter – a membrane protein that catalyses the transport of a molecule from one side of a biomembrane to the other side

Tuber – dried tubers (fleshy roots)

Tuberculosis – a bacterial disease caused by *Mycobacterium tuberculosis* that affects the lungs and other organs (often chronic and fatal if not treated with antibiotics)

Tumour (tumor) – an abnormal growth of tissue (benign or malignant)

Ulcer – a lesion on the skin or on a mucous membrane

Unsaturated fats – fats with fatty acids with double bonds between the carbon atoms

Urinary calculi – concretions in the urethra

Varicose veins – abnormally distended veins

Vasoconstrictor – a substance that causes a narrowing of the blood vessels

Vasodilator – a substance that causes an increase in the internal diameter of blood vessels

Venous tone – the firmness of the walls of veins

Vermifuge – a substance that kills or expels intestinal worms

Vertigo – dizziness

Virus – infectious complex of macromolecules that contain their genetic information either as DNA or RNA; viruses need host cells for replication and the formation of new viral particles

Virustatic – a substance that inhibits the multiplication of viruses

Volatile oil – various terpenoids that evaporate easily (they add taste and smell to many plants)

Vomit – the expulsion of matter from the stomach via the mouth

Vulnerary – a substance that heals external wounds

Wild-crafting – the collection of medicinal material from natural plant populations in a sustainable way

Wild-harvesting – the collection of medicinal material from natural plant populations with or without considering their sustainable use

Yeast – simple eukaryotic cells (belonging to the fungal kingdom), containing a nucleus, organelles and compartments surrounded by membranes

FURTHER READING

Ayensu ES (1978) Medicinal Plants of West Africa. Reference Publications Inc., Algonac

Ayensu ES (1981) Medicinal Plants of the West Indies. Reference Publications Inc., Algonac

Balick MJ, Evans L (1993) Rainforest Remedies – 100 Healing Herbs of Belize. 2nd enlarged edn. Lotus Press, Twin Lakes

Balick MJ, Cox PA (1996) Plants, People and Culture. Scientific American Library, New York

Barnes J, Anderson LA, Phillipson JD (1996) Herbal Medicines – A Guide for Health Care Professionals. 2nd edn. Rittenhouse Book Distributors, King of Prussia

Bellamy D, Pfister A (1992) World Medicine – Plants, Patients and People. Blackwell Publishers, Oxford

Bindon P (1996) Useful Bush Plants. Western Australian Museum, Perth

Blaschek W, Hänsel R, Keller K, Reichling J, Rimpler G, Schneider G (eds) (1998) Hagers Handbuch der Pharmazeutischen Praxis. 5th edn. New vol 2 and 3. Springer Verlag, Berlin

Blumenthal M, et al. (eds) (1998) The Complete German Commission E Monographs. American Botanical Council, Austin

Boulos L (1983) Medicinal Plants of North Africa. Reference Publications Inc., Algonac

Bown D (1995) The RHS Encyclopedia of Herbs and Their Uses. Dorling Kindersley, London

Brown RG (2002) Dictionary of Medicinal Plants. Ivy Publishing House, Raleigh

Bruneton J (1999) Pharmacognosy, Phytochemistry, Medicinal Plants. 2nd edn. Lavoisier, Paris

Bruneton J (1999) Toxic Plants Dangerous to Humans and Animals. Intercept, Hampshire

Bruneton J (2002) Phytothérapie – les données de l'évaluation. Lavoisier, Paris

Burger A, Wachter H (eds) (1998) Hunnius Pharmazeutisches Wörterbuch. 8th edn. Walter de Gruyter, Berlin

Chen K (ed) (1996) Imperial Medicaments. Foreign Languages Press, Beijing

Chevallier A (2001) Encyclopedia of Medicinal Plants. New edn. Dorling Kindersley, London

D'Amelio FS (1998) Botanicals – A Phytocosmetic Desk Reference. CRC Press, Boca Raton

De Smet PAGM (1999) Herbs, Health & Healers – Africa as Ethnopharmacological Treasury.

Afrika Museum, Berg en Dal

Dingermann T, Loew D (2003) Phytopharmakologie. Wissenschaftliche Verlagsgesellschaft, Stuttgart

Duke JA, Foster S (1998) A Field Guide to Medicinal Plants and Herbs of Eastern and Central North America. Expanded edn. Houghton Mifflin Company, Boston

Duke JA (1992) Database of Phytochemical Constituents of GRAS Herbs and Other Economic Plants. CRC Press, Boca Raton

Duke JA (2002) Handbook of Medicinal Herbs. 2nd edn. CRC Press, Boca Raton

Duke JA, Ayensu ES (1984) Medicinal Plants of China. CRC Press, Boca Raton

Erhardt W, Götz E, Bödeker N, Seybold S (eds) (2002) Zander Dictionary of Plant Names. 17th edn. Ulmer Verlag, Stuttgart

ESCOP (ed) (1996-1999) Monographs on the Medicinal Uses of Plant Drugs. Fasc. 1–6. European Scientific Cooperative on Phytotherapy, Exeter

Foster S (1998) An Illustrated Guide – 101 Medicinal Herbs. Interweave Press, Loveland

Foster S, Hobbs C (2002) Western Medicinal Plants and Herbs. Houghton Mifflin, New York

Frohne D, Pfänder HJ (1986) Giftpflanzen. Wissenschaftliche Verlagsgesellschaft, Stuttgart

Frohne D (2002) Heilpflanzenlexikon. 7th edn. Wissenschaftliche Verlagsgesellschaft, Stuttgart

Ghazanfar SA (1994) Handbook of Arabian Medicinal Plants. CRC Press, Boca Raton

Goodman LS, Gilman AG, Limbird LE, Hardman JG, Goodman Gilman A (2001) The Pharmacological Basis of Therapeutics. 10th edn. The McGraw-Hill Co., London

Hänsel R (1991) Phytopharmaka. 2nd edn. Springer Verlag, Berlin

Hänsel R, Keller K, Rimpler H, Schneider G (eds) (1992–1994) Hagers Handbuch der Pharmazeutischen Praxis. 5th edn. Vol 4–6. Springer Verlag, Berlin

Hänsel R, Hölzl J (1996) Lehrbuch der pharmazeutischen Biologie. Springer Verlag, Berlin

Hänsel R, Sticher O, Steinegger E (1999) Pharmakognosie – Phytopharmazie. 6th edn. Springer Verlag, Berlin

Harborne JB, Baxter H (eds) (1993) Phytochemical Dictionary – A Handbook of Bioactive Compounds from Plants. Taylor & Francis, London

Hegnauer R (1962–2001) Chemotaxonomie der Pflanzen. Vol 1–11. Birkhäuser Verlag, Basel

Heinrich M (2001) Ethnopharmazie und Ethnobotanik. Wissenschaftliche Verlagsgesellschaft, Stuttgart

Hocking G M (1997) A Dictionary of Natural Products. Plexus Publishing, Medford

Isaacs J (1987) Bush Food. Lansdowne Publishing, Sydney

Iwu MM (1993) Handbook of African Medicinal Plants. CRC Press, Boca Raton

Kapoor LD (2000) CRC Handbook of Ayurvedic Medicinal Plants. CRC Press, Boca Raton

Kaul MK (1997) Medicinal Plants of Kashmir and Ladakh (Temperate and Cold Arid Himalaya). Indus Publishing Co., New Delhi

Kletter C, Kriechbaum M (2001) Tibetan Medicinal Plants. Medpharm, Stuttgart

Kokwaro JO (1976) Medicinal Plants of East Africa. East Africa Literature Bureau, Nairobi

Langenheim JH (2003) Plant Resins – Chemistry, Evolution, Ecology and Ethnobotany. Timber Press, Portland

Lassak EV, McCarthy T (2001) Australian Medicinal Plants. JB Books, Marleston

Lewis WH, Elvin-Lewis MPF (1977) Medical Botany – Plants Affecting Man's Health. John Wiley & Sons, New York

Leung AY, Foster S (1996) Encyclopedia of Common Natural Ingredients Used in Food, Drugs, and Cosmetics. 2nd edn. John Wiley & Sons, New York

Loew D (1995) Phytopharmaka in Forschung und klinischer Anwendung. Steinkopff Verlag, Darmstadt

Loew D (1996) Phytopharmaka – Forschung und klinische Anwendung. Steinkopff Verlag, Darmstadt

Loew D., Rietbrock N. (1997) Phytopharmaka – Forschung und klinische Anwendung. Steinkopff Verlag, Darmstadt

Mabberley DJ (1997) The Plant Book – A Portable Dictionary of the Vascular Plants. 2nd edn. Cambridge University Press, Cambridge

Mann J (1992) Murder, Magic and Medicine. Oxford University Press, Oxford

Manniche L (1989) An Ancient Egyptian Herbal. University of Texas Press, Austin

Martindale W (1993) Extra Pharmacopoeia. 30th revised edn. The Pharmaceutical Press, London

Martinetz D, Lohs K, Janzen J (1989) Weihrauch und Myrrhe. Wissenschaftliche Verlagsgesellschaft, Stuttgart

Moerman DE (1998) Native American Ethnobotany. Timber Press, Portland

Mors W, Rizzini CT, Pereira NA, DeFilipps R (2000) Medicinal Plants of Brazil. Latino Herbal Press, Spring Valley

Morton JF (1981) An Atlas of Medicinal Plants of Middle America. Charles C. Thomas, Springfield

Mutschler E, Geisslinger G, Kroemer HK, Schäfer-Korting M (2001) Arzneimittelwirkungen – Lehrbuch der Pharmakologie und Toxikologie. 8th edn. Wissenschaftliche Verlagsgesellschaft, Stuttgart

Neuwinger HD (1994) Afrikanische Arzneipflanzen und Jagdgifte. Wissenschaftliche Verlagsgesellschaft, Stuttgart

Neuwinger HD (1996) African Ethnobotany, Poisons and Drugs. Chapman & Hall, London

Neuwinger HD (2000) African Traditional Medicine – A Dictionary of Plant Use and Applications. Medpharm Scientific Publishers, Stuttgart

Newall CA, Anderson LA, Phillipson JD (1996) Herbal Medicine – A Guide for Health Care Professionals. The Pharmaceutical Press, London

Ody P (1993) The Complete Medicinal Herbal. Dorling Kindersley, London

Ody P (1996) Handbook of Over-The-Counter Herbal Medicines. Kyle Cathie Limited, London

Oliver-Bever B (ed) (1986) Medicinal Plants of Tropical West Africa. Cambridge University Press, Cambridge

Pahlow M (1993) Das große Buch der Heilpflanzen. Gräfe und Unzer Verlag, München

Rätsch C (1998) Enzyklopädie der psychoaktiven Pflanzen – Botanik, Ethnopharmakologie und Anwendung. Wissenschaftliche Verlagsgesellschaft, Stuttgart

Rietbrock N (2000) Phyto-Pharmaka. Vol 6. Steinkopff Verlag, Darmstadt

Rimpler H (1999) Biogene Arzneistoffe. Deutscher Apotheker Verlag, Stuttgart

Roberts MF, Wink M (1998) Alkaloids. Plenum Press, New York

Roth L, Daunderer M, Kormann K (1994) Giftpflanzen – Pflanzengifte. Ecomed Verlagsgesellschaft, Landsberg

Roth I, Lindorf H (2002) South American Medicinal Plants. Springer Verlag, Berlin

Saller R, Reichling J, Hellenbrecht D (1995) Phytotherapie – Klinische, pharmakologische und pharmazeutische Grundlagen. Karl F. Haug Verlag, Heidelberg

Samuelsson G (1992) Drugs of Natural Origin. Swedish Pharmaceutical Press, Stockholm

Schultes RE, Hofmann A (1987) Pflanzen der Götter. 2nd edn. Hallwag Verlag, Bern

Schulz V, Hänsel R, Tyler VE (2001) Rational Phytotherapy – A Physician's Guide to Herbal Medicine. 4th edn. Springer Verlag, Berlin

Seigler DS (1995) Plant Secondary Metabolism. Kluwer Academic Publishers, Boston

Small E, Catling PM (1999) Canadian Medicinal Crops. NRC Research Press, Ottawa

Steinegger E, Hänsel R (1992) Pharmakognosie. 5th edn. Springer Verlag, Berlin

Swerdlow JL (2000) Nature's Medicine – Plants that Heal. National Geographic, Washington

Tang W, Eisenbrand G (1992) Chinese Drugs of Plant Origin. Springer Verlag, Berlin

Teuscher E (1997) Biogene Arzneimittel. Wissenschaftliche Verlagsgesellschaft, Stuttgart

Teuscher E, Lindequist U (1994) Biogene Gifte – Biologie, Chemie, Pharmakologie. 2nd edn. Gustav Fischer Verlag, Stuttgart

Tyler VE (1993) The Honest Herbal. 3rd edn. Pharmaceutical Products Press, New York

Tyler VE (1994) Herb of Choice – The Therapeutic Use of Phytomedicinals. Pharmaceutical Products Press, New York

Van Wyk B-E, Van Oudtshoorn B, Gericke N (1997) Medicinal Plants of South Africa. Briza Publications, Pretoria

Van Wyk B-E, Gericke N (2000) People's Plants – A Guide to Useful Plants of Southern Africa. Briza Publications, Pretoria

Wagner H (1999) Arzneidrogen und ihre Inhaltsstoffe. Wissenschaftliche Verlagsgesellschaft, Stuttgart

Wagner H, Bladt S (1995) Plant Drug Analysis – A Thin Layer Chromatography Atlas. Springer Verlag, Berlin

Wagner H, Wiesenauer M (1995) Phytotherapie. Gustav Fischer Verlag, Stuttgart

Wagner H, Wiesenauer M (2003) Phytotherapie – Phytopharmaka und pflanzliche Homöopathika. 2nd edn. Wissenschaftliche Verlagsgesellschaft, Stuttgart

Watt JM, Breyer-Brandwijk MG (1962) The Medicinal and Poisonous Plants of Southern and Eastern Africa. 2nd edn. Livingstone, London

Weiß RF, Fintelmann V (2002) Lehrbuch der Phytotherapie. 10th edn. Hippokrates Verlag, Stuttgart

Wichtl M, Bisset NG (eds) (2000) Herbal Drugs and Phytopharmaceuticals. CRC Press, Boca Raton

Williamson EM, Okpako DT, Evans FJ (1996) Selection, Preparation and Pharmacological Evaluation of Plant Material. John Wiley & Sons, New York

Williamson, EM (ed) (2002) Major Herbs of Ayurveda. Churchill Livingstone, London

Wink M (1999) Biochemistry of Plant Secondary Metabolism. Annual Plant Reviews, Vol 2. Sheffield Academic Press, Sheffield

Wink M (1999) Functions of Plant Secondary Metabolites and their Exploitation in Biotechnology. Annual Plant Reviews, Vol 3. Sheffield Academic Press, Sheffield

Wolters B (1994) Drogen, Pfeilgift und Indianermedizin. Urs Freund Verlag, Greifenberg

Wolters B (1996) Agave bis Zaubernuß. Urs Freund Verlag, Greifenberg

INDEX

Names and page numbers in **bold print** indicate main entries and illustrations.

451

452

453

458

ACKNOWLEDGEMENTS

The authors wish to thank the following institutions and persons:

Briza Publications and the production team, especially Reneé Ferreira, David Pearson and Melinda Stark.

Dr Coralie Wink for translating the book into German and for her help in refining and editing the English text.

Rand Afrikaans University, Johannesburg, South Africa and the University of Heidelberg, Germany, for providing the authors with institutional support.

Persons and institutions who have contributed photographs (see below), or provided samples, support or encouragement: Siegmar Bauer (Medpharm Scientific Publishers, Stuttgart); Dr Albert Borchardt (Hirsch-Apotheke, Heidelberg); Dr Ute Engelhardt (University of Munich); Thinus Fourie (RAU University); Dr Klaus Kramer (Heidelberg University); Mei (Rebecca) Liu (RAU University, Johannesburg); Director and staff, Botanical Garden of Mainz; Dr Günter Schwarz (Harbin University, China); André Simard (www.bioclic.ca; Montreal, Quebec, Canada); Ellery Troyer (Andrews University, Michigan); Dr Patricia Tilney, (RAU University, Johannesburg); Prof Fanie R.van Heerden (RAU University, Johannesburg); Eben van Wyk (Sannieshof); Mariana, Teodor and Signe van Wyk (Johannesburg); Dr Doris Väth (Bornträger & Schlemmer, Offstein); Dr Alvaro Viljoen (Wits University, Johannesburg); Charlotte and Lucie Wink (Heidelberg).

PHOTOGRAPHIC CONTRIBUTIONS

All photographs were taken by **Prof. Ben-Erik van Wyk** except those listed below. These are arranged alphabetically from top to bottom and from left to right, according to photographer and page number. **Anna-Lena Anderberg** (Swedish Museum of Natural History, Stockholm, Sweden): 237 (*Petasites hybridus*); **Dr Arne Anderberg** (Swedish Museum of Natural History, Stockholm, Sweden): 271b (*Rhodiola rosea*); **Dr Shigenobu Aoki** (Gumma University, Japan): 113a (*Coptis japonica*); **Michael W. Bordelon** (courtesy of the Smithsonian Institution, Washington, USA): 43a (*Alpinia officinarum*); **Dr Chris Briand** (Associate Professor, Department of Biological Sciences, Salisbury University, USA): 238b (*Phytolacca americana*); **Leslie E. Brothers** (courtesy of the Smithsonian Institution, Washington, USA): 43b (*Alpinia officinarum*); **Will Cook** (Duke University, Durham, USA): 95a,b (*Chionanthus virginicus*); **Ermias Dagne** (Professor, Department of Chemistry, Addis Ababa University, Ethiopia): 69b, 111a,b (*Boswellia papyrifera; Commiphora* sp. *Commiphora abyssinica*); **Dr Thomas Fester** (Institute of Plant Biochemistry, Halle, Germany; www.scientiaevitae.de): 11a (*Santalum album*); **Dr Mark Fishbein** (Mississipi State University, USA): 199a,b (*Marsdenia astephanoides, M. coulteri*); **Steven Foster** (Steven Foster Group, Brixey, Missouri, USA): 327 (*Turnera diffusa*); **W. John Hayden** (Professor of Biology, Department of Biology, University of Richmond, Virgina, USA): 96b (*Fucus vesiculosus*); **Andreas Held** (Eberbach, Germany): 261b (*Pulmonaria officinalis*); **Sonja K. Keohane**, Wayne, Pennsylvania, USA (www.twofrog.com): 110b (*Colchicum autumnale*); **Dr Klaus Kramer** (University of Heidelberg, Germany): 223b, 227b, 262b (*Paeonia officinalis, Passiflora incarnata, Pulsatilla vulgaris*); **Glen Lee**, Regina, Saskatchewan, Canada): 250a,b; 252a,b (*Polygala senega, Populus tremuloides*); **Leidulf Lund** (Institute of Biology, University of Tromso, Norway): 271c (*Rhodiola rosea*); **IMMODAL Pharmaka GmbH**, Volders, Tirol, Austria: 330a,b,c (*Uncaria tomentosa*); **Prof. Dr Stefan M. Maul** (Assyriology, Heidelberg University, Germany): 9a (Assyrian clay tablet); **Mei (Rebecca) Liu** (RAU University, Johannesburg, South Africa): 61a, 134a, 295c (*Astragalus membranaceus, Ephedra sinica, Scutellaria baicalensis*); **Leo Michels** (Untereisesheim, Germany): 77b, 149a,b, 151a,b, 328b, 340a (*Bupleurum falcatum, Galanthus nivalis, Galeopsis segetum; Tussilago farfara, Vinca minor*); **Lytton John Musselman** (Professor of Botany, Department of Biological Sciences, Old Dominion University, Norfolk, Virginia, USA: 116a (*Crocus sativus*); **Mark E Olson** (Associate Professor, Institute of Biology, National University of Mexico): 69a (*Boswellia sacra*); **Prof. Dr Jürgen Reichling** (Heidelberg University, Germany): 202a,b (*Melaleuca alternifolia*); **Vera Rosenkranz** (Heidelberg University, Germany): 331a (*Urginea* *maritima*); **Anita Sabarese** (New York Botanical Garden, USA): 239 (Jaborandi – *Pilocarpus pennatifolius* – in flower at the Enid A. Haupt Conservatory of The New York Botanical Garden); **Suzanne Sanders** (West Virginia University, USA): 173a,b (*Hydrastis canadensis*); **Dr Thomas Schoepke** (University of Greifswald, Germany): 73a, 136b, 222b, 239a (*Bupleurum falcatum, Equisetum arvense, Ortosiphon grandiflorus, Scopolia carniola*); **Seaweed Ltd**, Galway, Ireland: 96a,b,c (*Chondrus crispus, Ascophyllum nodosum*); **Dr Michel Séret/Sylvain Cazalet** (Homéopathe International, Montpellier, France) 171 (*Euphrasia officinalis*); **James C. Solomon** (Missouri Botanical Garden, St. Louis, **Missouri, USA): 186 (*Krameria lappacea*).** **Heidi Staudter** (Heidelberg University, Germany): 331b (*Urginea maritima*); **Nicholas Tatar** (courtesy Washington and Lee University, Lexington, Virginia, USA): 196b (*Lycopus virginicus*); **Dr Jens Treutlein** (Heidelberg University, Germany): 331c (*Urginea maritima*); **Eben van Wyk** (Sannieshof, South Africa): 120b, 210a (*Cymbopogon citratus, Myristica frangrans*); **Dr Piet van Wyk** (Pretoria, South Africa): 29a,b, 166b, 282a,b, 310b (*Acacia senegal, Harungana madagascariensis, Salvadora persica, Strophanthus kombe*); **Dr Karan Vasisht** (Panjab University, Chandigarh, India): 64, 190b, 266a, 289a, 320a,b,c (*Azadirachta indica, Lawsonia inermis, Rauvolfia serpentina, Santalum album, Terminalia chebula, T. bellirica, Phyllanthus emblica*); **Tarmo Virtanen** (University of Helsinki, Finland): 271a (*Rhodiola rosea*); **Dr Anne Lise Schutte-Vlok** (Oudtshoorn, South Africa): 242c (*Picea abies*); **Prof. Dr Michael Wink** (Heidelberg University, Germany): 33, 109c, 155a,b, 194c, 228b, 236b,c, 255a,b (*Adonis vernalis; Gentiana lutea, Lobelia tupa; Paullinia cupana, Peumus boldus, Primula veris, Primula elatior*); **Pieter Winter** (University of the North, Polokwane, South Africa): 406b (*Aloe ferox*); **Teresa Wong** (University of Malaya, Kuala Lumpur, Malaysia): 71a (*Brucea javanica*); **Dennis W. Woodland** (Professor of Botany, Andrews University, Berrien Springs, Michigan, USA): 329 (*Ulmus rubra*); **Prof Kazuo Yamasaki** (Professor, Institute of Pharmaceutical Sciences, Hiroshima University, Japan): 113b, 190c (*Coptis japonica, Lawsonia inermis*); **Prof. Zu Yuangang** (Director: Laboratory for Forest Ecology, Harbin University, China): 76b,c (*Camptotheca acuminata*); **Liang De Zhang** (Wandashan Ginseng Farm, Hulin, Heilongjiang Province, China): 11c, 224a,b (*Panax ginseng*).